G000298202

STREE

Berkshire

Bracknell, Camberley, Maidenhead, Newbury, Reading, Slough, Windsor

www.philips-maps.co.uk

First published in 1990 by

Philip's, a division of
Octopus Publishing Group Ltd
www.octopusbooks.co.uk
2–4 Heron Quays, London E14 4JP
An Hachette Livre UK Company
www.hachettelivre.co.uk

Fourth colour edition 2008
First impression 2008
BERDA

ISBN 978-0-540-09295-6 (pocket)

© Philip's 2008

O|S Ordnance Survey®

This product includes mapping data licensed
from Ordnance Survey®, with the permission of
the Controller of Her Majesty's Stationery Office.

© Crown copyright 2008. All rights reserved.
Licence number 100011710

Data for the speed cameras provided by
PocketGPSWorld.com Ltd.

Ordnance Survey and the OS symbol are
registered trademarks of Ordnance Survey, the
national mapping agency of Great Britain

Printed and bound in China by Toppan

Contents

II **Mobile safety cameras**

III **Key to map symbols**

IV **Key to map pages**

VI **Route planning**

VIII **Administrative and Postcode boundaries**

1 **Street maps** at 2⅔ inches to 1 mile

154 **Index** of towns, villages, streets, hospitals, industrial estates, railway stations, schools, shopping centres universities and places of interest

Digital Data

The exceptionally high-quality mapping found in this atlas is available as digital data in TIFF format, which is easily convertible to other bitmapped (raster) image formats.

The index is also available in digital form as a standard database table. It contains all the details found in the printed index together with the National Grid reference for the map square in which each entry is named.

For further information and to discuss your requirements, please contact victoria.dawbarn@philips-maps.co.uk

On-line route planner

For detailed driving directions and estimated driving times visit our free route planner at www.philips-maps.co.uk

Mobile safety cameras

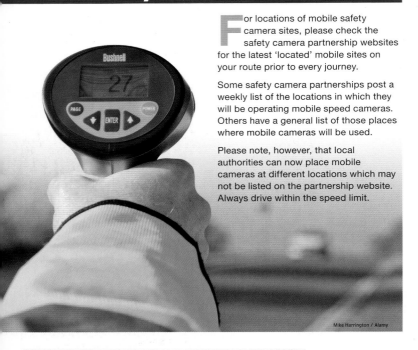

For locations of mobile safety camera sites, please check the safety camera partnership websites for the latest 'located' mobile sites on your route prior to every journey.

Some safety camera partnerships post a weekly list of the locations in which they will be operating mobile speed cameras. Others have a general list of those places where mobile cameras will be used.

Please note, however, that local authorities can now place mobile cameras at different locations which may not be listed on the partnership website. Always drive within the speed limit.

Mike Harrington / Alamy

Useful websites

Thames Valley Safety Camera Partnership
http://www.saferroads.org/

London Safety Camera Partnership
www.lscp.org.uk/

Surrey Safety Camera Partnership
www.surrey-safecam.org

Further information
www.dvla.gov.uk
www.thinkroadsafety.gov.uk
www.dft.gov.uk
www.road-safe.org

Symbol	Description	Symbol	Description
	Motorway with junction number	◆	**Ambulance station**
	Primary route – dual/single carriageway	◆	**Coastguard station**
	A road – dual/single carriageway	◆	**Fire station**
	B road – dual/single carriageway	◆	**Police station**
	Minor road – dual/single carriageway	✚	**Accident and Emergency entrance to hospital**
	Other minor road – dual/single carriageway		
	Road under construction	Ⓗ	**Hospital**
	Tunnel, covered road	✛	**Place of worship**
	Speed cameras - single, multiple	🅘	**Information Centre** (open all year)
	Rural track, private road or narrow road in urban area	🛒	**Shopping Centre**
		🅿	**Parking**
	Gate or obstruction to traffic (restrictions may not apply at all times or to all vehicles)	P&R	**Park and Ride**
		PO	**Post Office**
	Path, bridleway, byway open to all traffic, restricted byway	Å	**Camping site**
	Pedestrianised area	🚐	**Caravan site**
DY7	**Postcode boundaries**	⛳	**Golf course**
	County and unitary authority boundaries	✕	**Picnic site**
	Railway, tunnel, railway under construction		**Important buildings, schools, colleges, universities and hospitals**
	Tramway, tramway under construction	Prim Sch	
	Miniature railway		**Built up area**
Walsall	**Railway station**		**Woods**
	Private railway station	River Medway	**Water name**
	London Underground station		**River, weir, stream**
	Tram stop, tram stop under construction		**Canal, lock, tunnel**
	Bus, coach station		**Water**
			Tidal water

Acad	**Academy**	Inst	**Institute**	Recn Gd	**Recreation Ground**	Church	**Non-Roman antiquity**
Allot Gdns	**Allotments**	Ct	**Law Court**				
Cemy	**Cemetery**	L Ctr	**Leisure Centre**	Resr	**Reservoir**	ROMAN FORT	**Roman antiquity**
C Ctr	**Civic Centre**	LC	**Level Crossing**	Ret Pk	**Retail Park**		
CH	**Club House**	Liby	**Library**	Sch	**School**		
Coll	**College**	Mkt	**Market**	Sh Ctr	**Shopping Centre**		
Crem	**Crematorium**	Meml	**Memorial**	TH	**Town Hall/House**		
Ent	**Enterprise**	Mon	**Monument**	Trad Est	**Trading Estate**		
Ex H	**Exhibition Hall**	Mus	**Museum**	Univ	**University**		**Adjoining page indicators**
Ind Est	**Industrial Estate**	Obsy	**Observatory**	W Twr	**Water Tower**		
IRB Sta	**Inshore Rescue Boat Station**	Pal	**Royal Palace**	Wks	**Works**		
		PH	**Public House**	YH	**Youth Hostel**		

■ The small numbers around the edges of the maps identify the 1 kilometre National Grid lines

■ The dark grey border on the inside edge of some pages indicates that the mapping does not continue onto the adjacent page

The scale of the maps on the pages numbered in blue is 4.2 cm to 1 km • 2⅔ inches to 1 mile • 1: 23810

0	¼	½	¾	1 mile
0	250m	500m	750m	1 kilometre

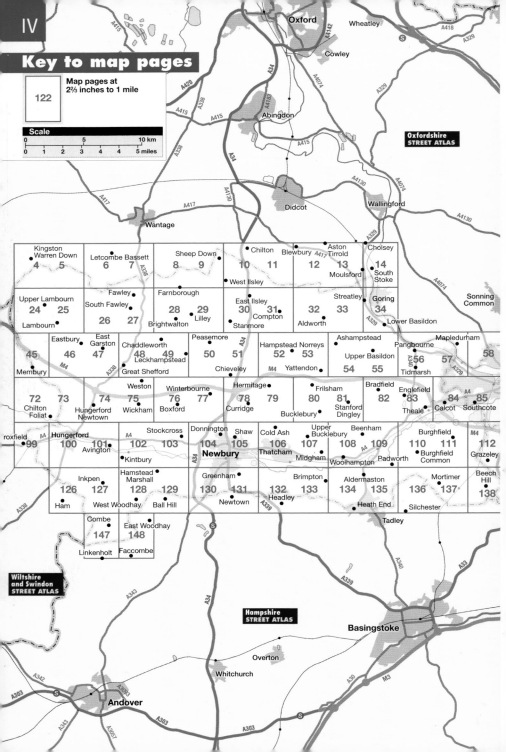

IV

Key to map pages

Map pages at
2⅔ inches to 1 mile

122

Scale
0 ___ 5 ___ 10 km
0 1 2 3 4 4 5 miles

Oxfordshire STREET ATLAS

Oxford
Wheatley
Cowley
Abingdon
Didcot
Wallingford
Wantage

| Kingston Warren Down 4 | 5 | Letcombe Bassett 6 | 7 | Sheep Down 8 | 9 | Chilton 10 | 11 | Blewbury 12 | Aston Tirrold 13 | Cholsey 14 |
West Ilsley
Moulsford
South Stoke

Sonning Common

| Upper Lambourn 24 | 25 | Fawley South Fawley 26 | 27 | Farnborough 28 | 29 | East Ilsley 30 | 31 | 32 | Streatley 33 | Goring 34 |
Lambourn
Brightwalton
Lilley
Stanmore
Compton
Aldworth
Lower Basildon

| Eastbury 45 | 46 | East Garston 47 | Chaddleworth 48 | 49 | Peasemore 50 | 51 | Hampstead Norreys 52 | 53 | Ashampstead 54 | 55 | Pangbourne 56 | 57 | Mapledurham 58 |
Membury
Leckhampstead
Great Shefford
Chieveley
Yattendon
Upper Basildon
Tidmarsh

| 72 | 73 | Weston 74 | 75 | Winterbourne 76 | 77 | Hermitage 78 | 79 | Frilsham 80 | 81 | Bradfield 82 | Englefield 83 | 84 | 85 |
Chilton Foliat
Hungerford Newtown
Wickham
Boxford
Curridge
Bucklebury
Stanford Dingley
Theale
Calcot
Southcote

| roxfield 99 | Hungerford 100 | 101 | Stockcross 102 | 103 | Donnington 104 | Shaw 105 | Cold Ash 106 | Upper Bucklebury 107 | Beenham 108 | 109 | Burghfield 110 | 111 | 112 |
Avington
Kintbury
Newbury
Thatcham
Midgham
Woolhampton
Padworth
Burghfield Common
Grazeley

| Inkpen 126 | 127 | Hamstead Marshall 128 | 129 | Greenham 130 | 131 | Brimpton 132 | 133 | Aldermaston 134 | 135 | Mortimer 136 | 137 | Beech Hill 138 |
Ham
West Woodhay
Ball Hill
Newtown
Headley
Heath End
Silchester
Tadley

| Combe 147 | East Woodhay 148 |
Linkenholt
Faccombe

Wiltshire and Swindon STREET ATLAS

Hampshire STREET ATLAS

Basingstoke

Overton
Whitchurch

Andover

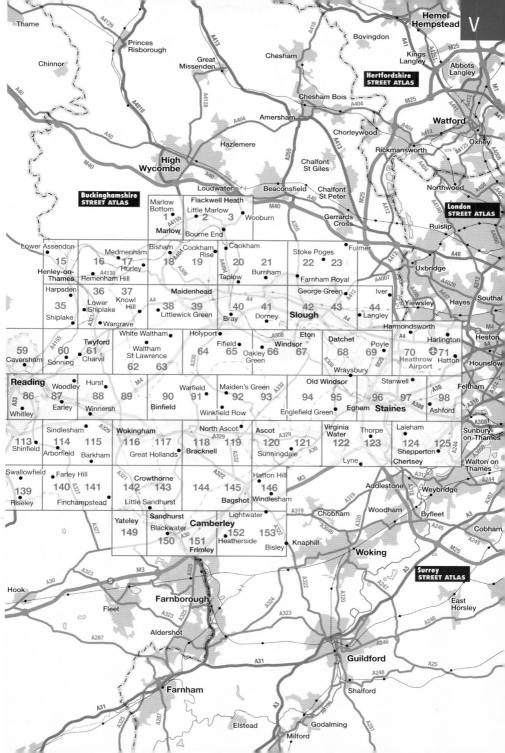

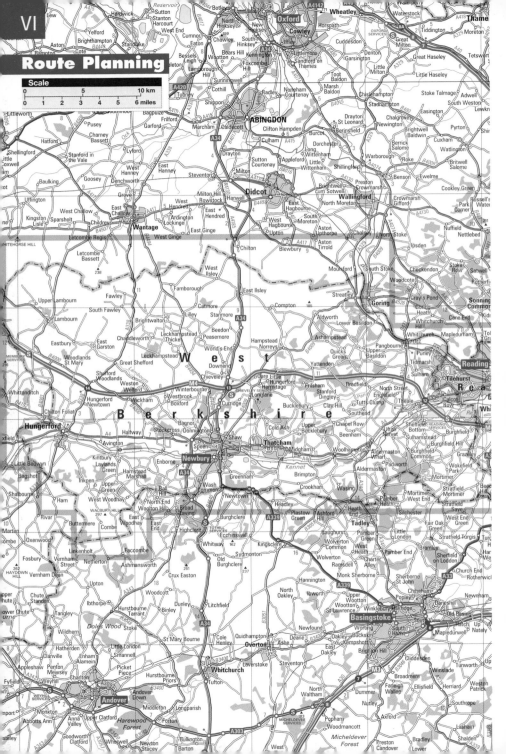

Route Planning

Scale

0			5			10 km
0	1	2	3	4	5	6 miles

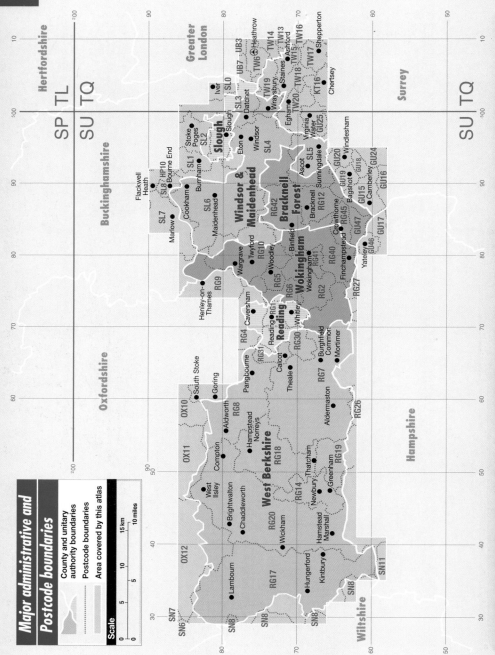

Major administrative and Postcode boundaries

County and unitary authority boundaries

Postcode boundaries

Area covered by this atlas

Scale

0   5   10   15 km

0   5   10 miles

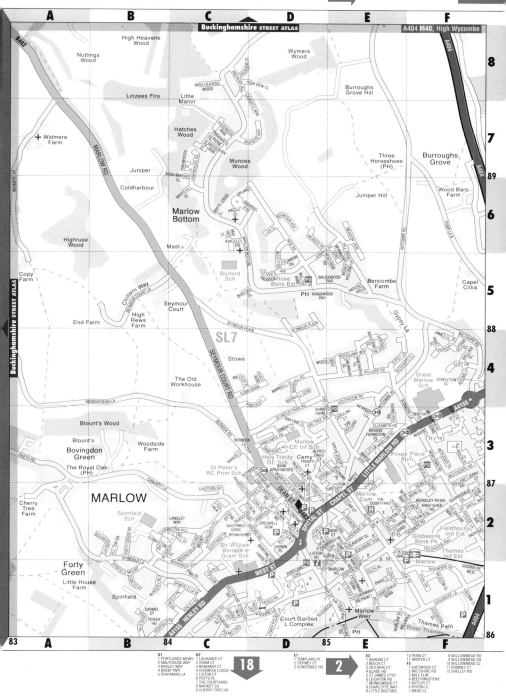

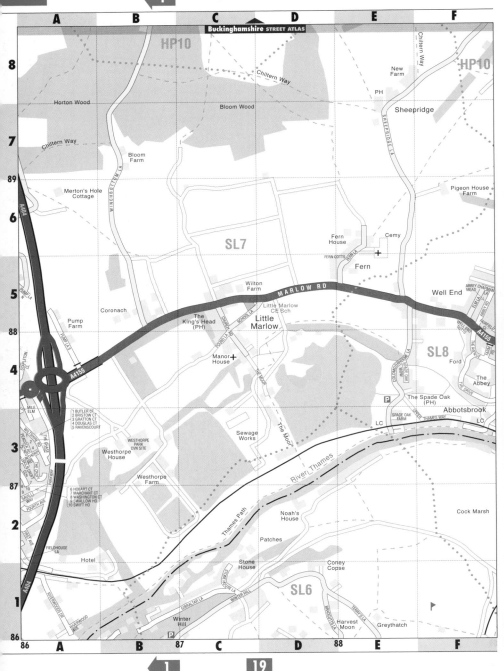

Buckinghamshire STREET ATLAS

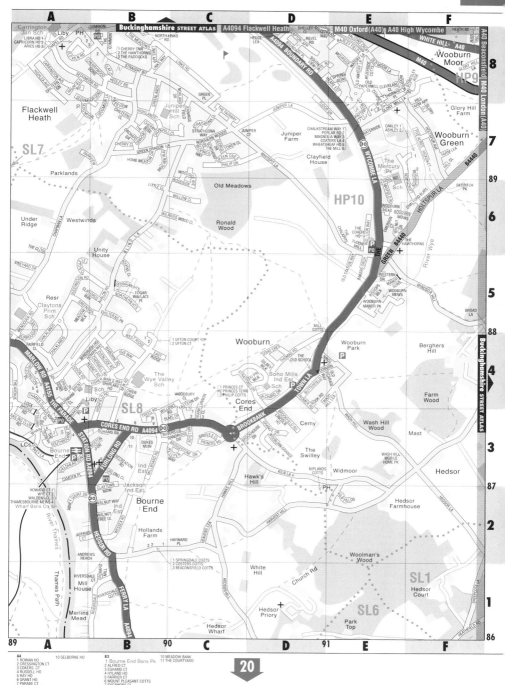

A4
1 ROWAN HO
2 CRESSINGTON CT
3 COKERS CT
4 RUSSELL HO
5 RAY HO
6 GRANT HO
7 PARADE CT
8 ORCHARD HO
9 BAILEY HO

10 SELBORNE HO

B3
1 Bourne End Bsns Pk
2 ALFRED CT
3 EGHAMS CT
4 HYLAND HO
5 FARRIER CT
6 MOUNT PLEASANT COTTS
7 SYCAMORE CL
8 THE WILLOWS
9 THE MAPLES

10 MEADOW BANK
11 THE COURTYARD

20

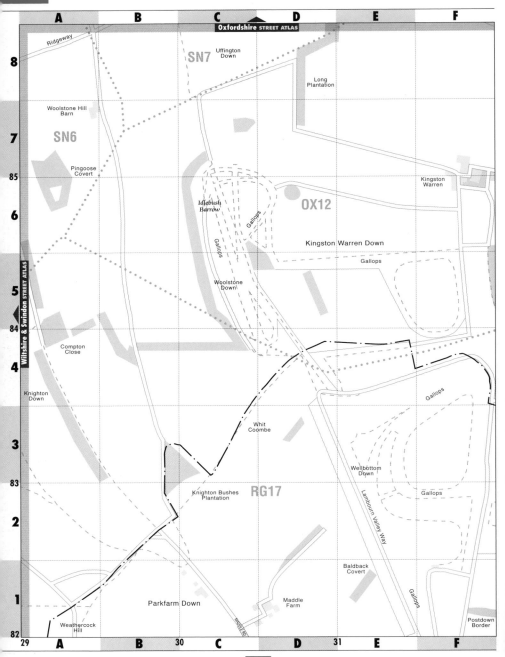

Ridgeway

SN7

Uffington
Down

Long
Plantation

Woolstone Hill
Barn

SN6

Pingoose
Covert

Kingston
Warren

Idlebush
Barrow

Gallops

OX12

Gallops

Kingston Warren Down

Gallops

Woolstone
Down

Compton
Close

Knighton
Down

Gallops

Whit
Coombe

Wellbottom
Down

Gallops

Knighton Bushes
Plantation

RG17

Gallops

Lambourn Valley Way

Baldback
Covert

Parkfarm Down

Maddle
Farm

Gallops

Postdown
Border

Weathercock
Hill

29   A   B   30   C   D   31   E   F

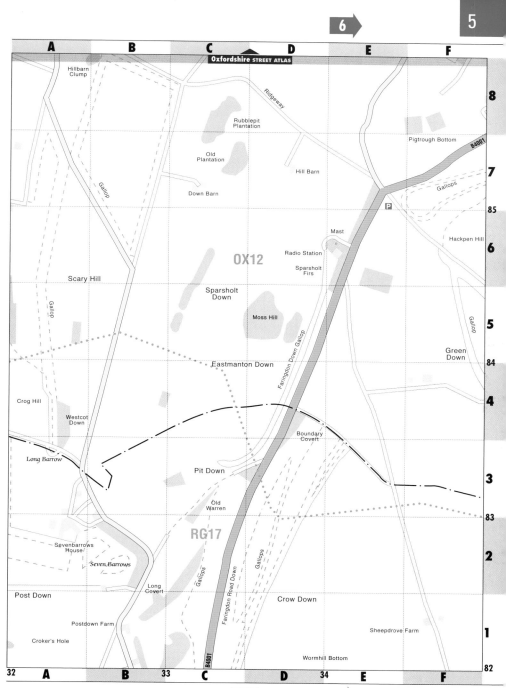

Oxfordshire STREET ATLAS

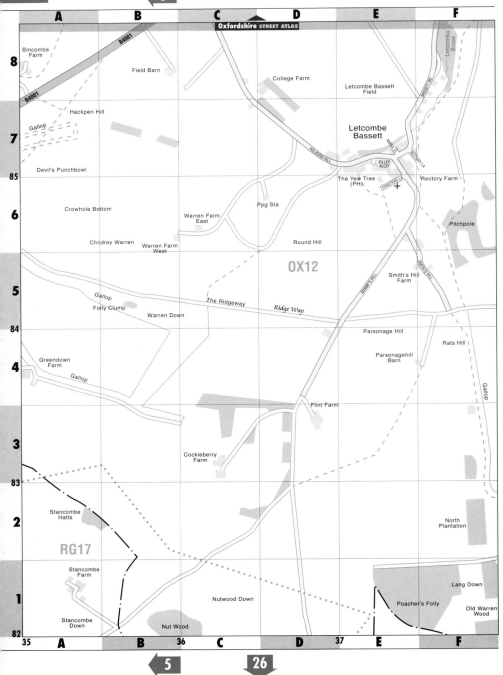

Oxfordshire STREET ATLAS

B4001

Sincombe Farm

Field Barn

College Farm

Letcombe Bassett Field

8

B4001

Hackpen Hill

Gallop

Letcombe Bassett

HOLBORN HILL

KNOWL CT

RECTORY LA

BASSETT RD

Letcombe Brook

7

Devil's Punchbowl

FILLEY ALLEY

85

The Yew Tree (PH)

FORSTERS LA

Rectory Farm

Crowhole Bottom

Ppg Sta

Warren Farm East

Pitchpole

6

Childrey Warren

Warren Farm West

Round Hill

OX12

Smith's Hill Farm

SMITH'S HILL

5

Gallop

The Ridgeway

Ridge Way

BRAMPS HILL

Folly Clump

Warren Down

84

Parsonage Hill

Rats Hill

Parsonagehill Barn

Greendown Farm

4

Gallop

Gallop

Flint Farm

3

Cockleberry Farm

83

Stancombe Hatts

North Plantation

2

RG17

Stancombe Farm

Lang Down

1

Nutwood Down

Poacher's Folly

Old Warren Wood

Stancombe Down

82

Nut Wood

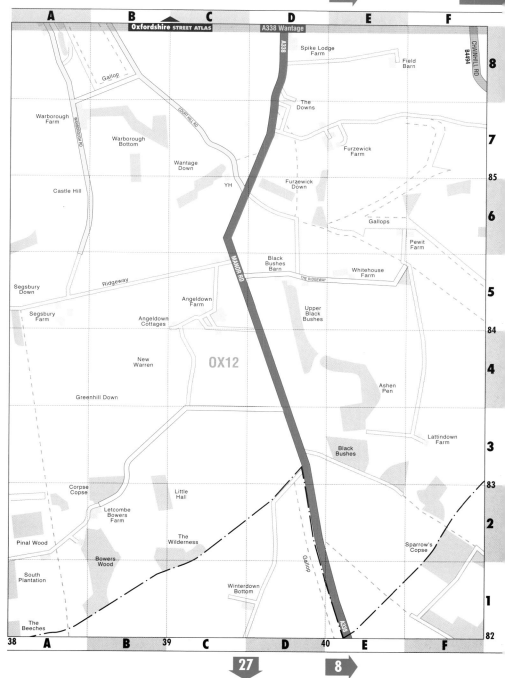

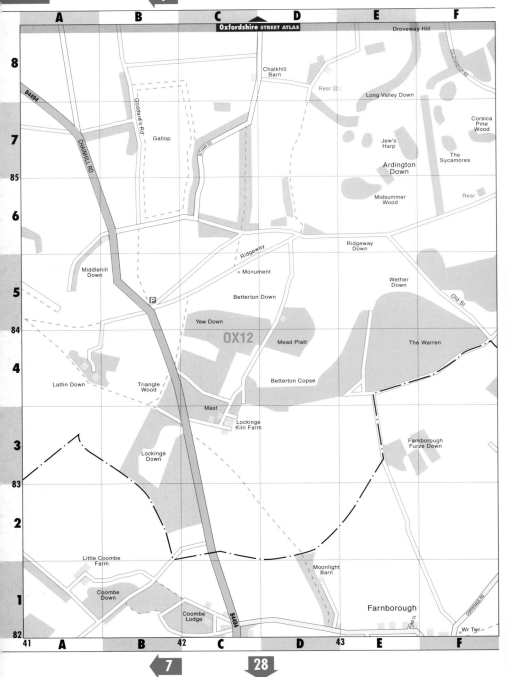

Oxfordshire STREET ATLAS

Droveway Hill

Chalkhill
Barn

Resr

Long Valley Down

Corsica
Pine
Wood

Gallop

Jew's
Harp

The
Sycamores

Ardington
Down

Midsummer
Wood

Resr

Ridgeway
Down

Ridgeway

Middlehill
Down

Monument

Wether
Down

Betterton Down

Old St

Yew Down

OX12

Mead Platt

The Warren

Lattin Down

Triangle
Wood

Betterton Copse

Mast

Lockinge
Kiln Farm

Farnborough
Furze Down

Lockinge
Down

Little Coombe
Farm

Moonlight
Barn

Coombe
Down

Coombe
Lodge

Farnborough

Wr Twr

B4494

CHAINHILL RD

Goddard's Rd

BITHAM RD

COLDHARBOUR RD

COPEHORNE RD

41   A   B   42   C   D   43   E   F

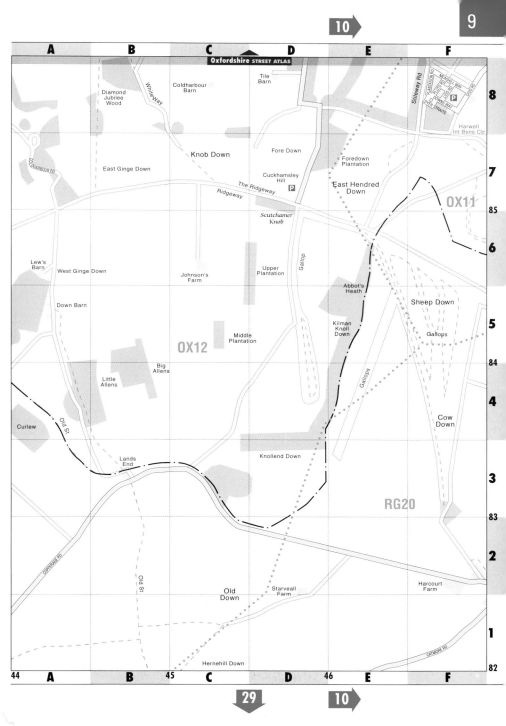

Oxfordshire STREET ATLAS

Tile Barn
Coldharbour Barn
Diamond Jubilee Wood
White Way
Knob Down
Fore Down
Foredown Plantation
East Ginge Down
Cuckhamsley Hill
East Hendred Down
The Ridgeway
Ridgeway
Scutchamer Knob
COLDHARBOUR RD
OX11
Lew's Barn
West Ginge Down
Johnson's Farm
Upper Plantation
Gallop
Abbot's Heath
Sheep Down
Down Barn
Kilman Knoll Down
Gallops
Middle Plantation
OX12
Gallops
Big Allens
Little Allens
Cow Down
Curlew
Old St
Lands End
Knollend Down
RG20
Silleway Rd
PLANTATION RD
MEADELL WAY
AUTO RD
USE RD
BOWING WAY
DYER STRAITS
Harwell Int Bsns Ctr
Old Down
Starveall Farm
Harcourt Farm
COPPERAGE RD
Old St
CATMORE RD
Hernehill Down

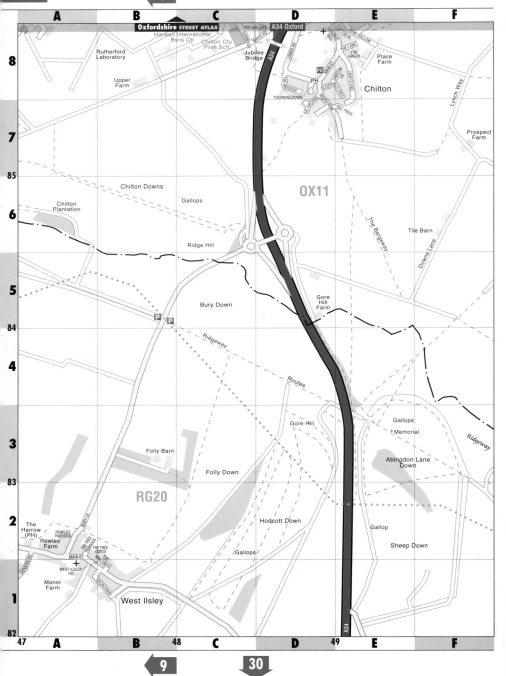

Oxfordshire STREET ATLAS

THE GALLOPS
A34 Oxford

Harwell International Bsns Ctr
Chilton Cty Prim Sch
Rutherford Laboratory
Jubilee Bridge
LOWER RD
DENE HOLLOW
CLAPTON CL
THE LANE
THE GREEN
Place Farm
Upper Farm
POUND
CLUMBERLY
CRAFTS END
Chilton
THE PADDOCK
ELDERS
HILL CRES
HILL PIECE
Lynch Way
THORNINGDOWN
THE ORCHARD
SOUTH VIEW

Prospect Farm

Chilton Downs
Gallops
OX11
Chilton Plantation
Tile Barn
The Bargeway
Ridge Hill
Downs Lane

Bury Down
Gore Hill Farm
P P
Ridgeway
Routes
Gore Hill
Gallops
Memorial
Ridgeway
Folly Barn
Abingdon Lane Down
Folly Down
RG20
Hodcott Down
Gallop
The Harrow (PH)
ROWLES PADDOCK
BIRD LA
Rowles' Farm
FIR TREE PADDOCK
FIR TREE COTTS
THE MALT HO(S)
Gallops
Sheep Down
MAIN ST
WEST ILSLEY HO
CATMORE RD
CHURCH LA
A34
Manor Farm
West Ilsley

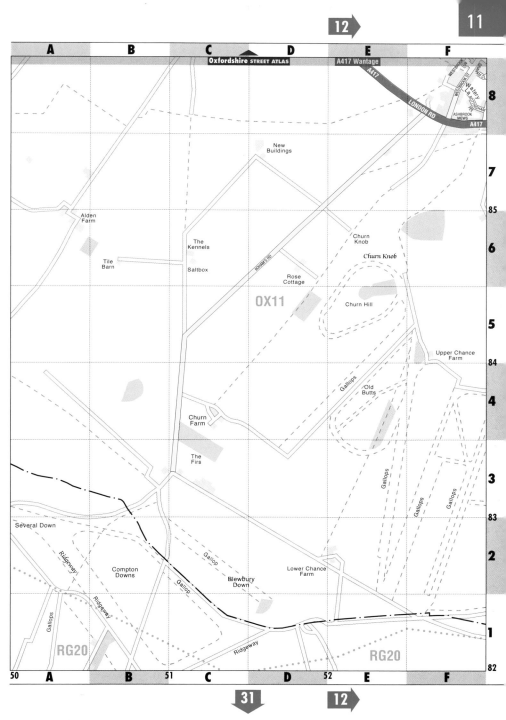

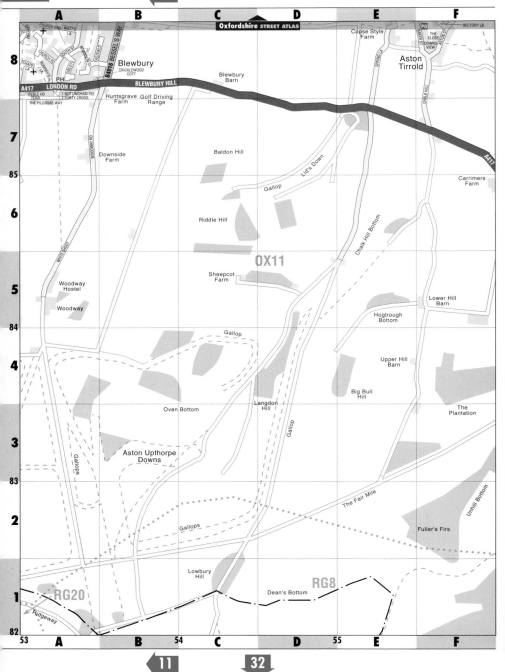

A **B** **C** **D** **E** **F**

8

Blewbury
CRICKLEWOOD
COTT

CHURCH END WATT'S LA

SOUTH ST
WORKING RD
EASTFIELD

B4016 BESSEL'S WAY

PH

A417 LONDON RD

TREBLE HO
TERR
THE PILGRIMS WAY

1 NOTTINGHAM FEE
2 FORTY CROSS

Blewbury
Barn

BLEWBURY HILL

Copse Style
Farm

Aston
Tirrold

PO
THE
CLOSE
DOWNS
VIEW

BAKER
CHALK HILL

RECTORY LA

7

Huntsgrave
Farm

Golf Driving
Range

WOODWAY RD

Downside
Farm

Baldon Hill

Lid's Down

A417

85

Gallop

Carrimers
Farm

6

WHITE SHOOT

Riddle Hill

Chalk Hill Bottom

OX11

5

Woodway
Hostel

Woodway

Sheepcot
Farm

Hogtrough
Bottom

Lower Hill
Barn

84

Gallop

Upper Hill
Barn

4

Oven Bottom

Langdon
Hill

Big Bull
Hill

Gallop

The
Plantation

3

Gallops

Aston Upthorpe
Downs

83

2

Gallops

The Fair Mile

Fuller's Firs

Unhill Bottom

Lowbury
Hill

RG8

1

RG20

Ridgeway

Dean's Bottom

82

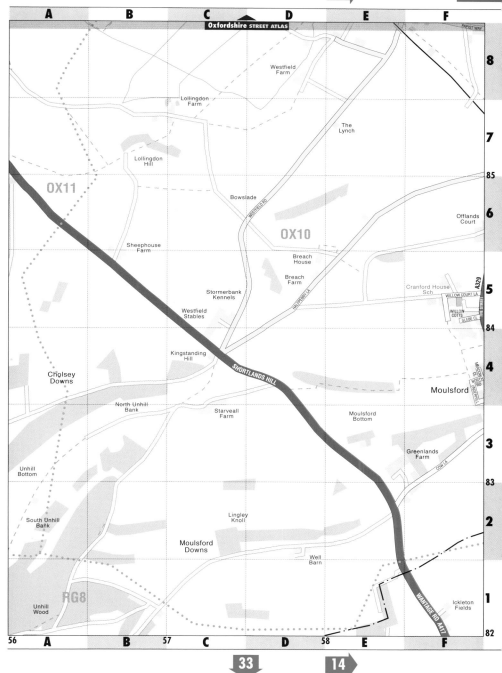

Oxfordshire STREET ATLAS

PAPIST WAY

Westfield Farm

8

Lollingdon Farm

The Lynch

7

Lollingdon Hill

85

OX11

Bowslade

WESTFIELD RD

6

OX10

Offlands Court

Sheephouse Farm

Breach House

Breach Farm

Cranford House Sch

A329

WILLOW COURT LA

THE STREET

5

Stormerbank Kennels

HALFPENNY LA

WILLOW COTTS

GLEBE CL

84

Westfield Stables

MEADOW RD

4

Kingstanding Hill

SHORTLANDS HILL

NORTH LADE HILL

Cholsey Downs

Moulsford

North Unhill Bank

Starveall Farm

Moulsford Bottom

3

Greenlands Farm

COW LA

83

Unhill Bottom

Lingley Knoll

2

South Unhill Bank

Moulsford Downs

Well Barn

RG8

WANTAGE RD A417

Ickleton Fields

1

Unhill Wood

82

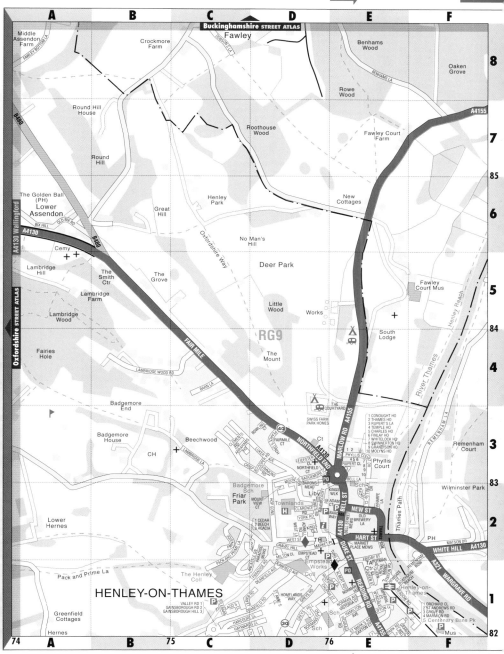

Buckinghamshire STREET ATLAS

Oxfordshire STREET ATLAS

HENLEY-ON-THAMES

RG9

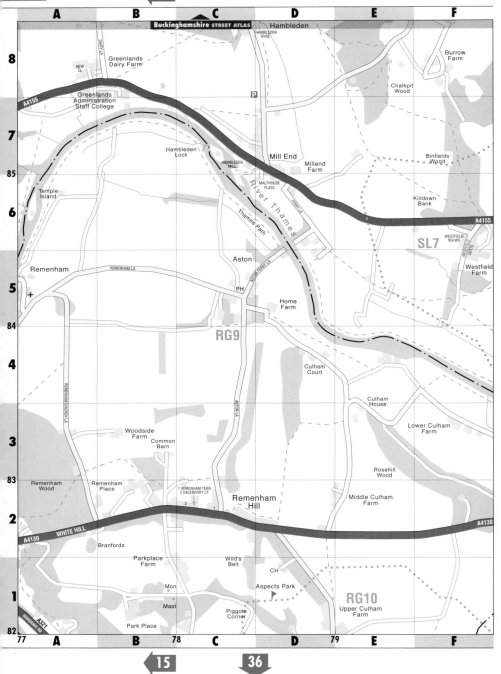

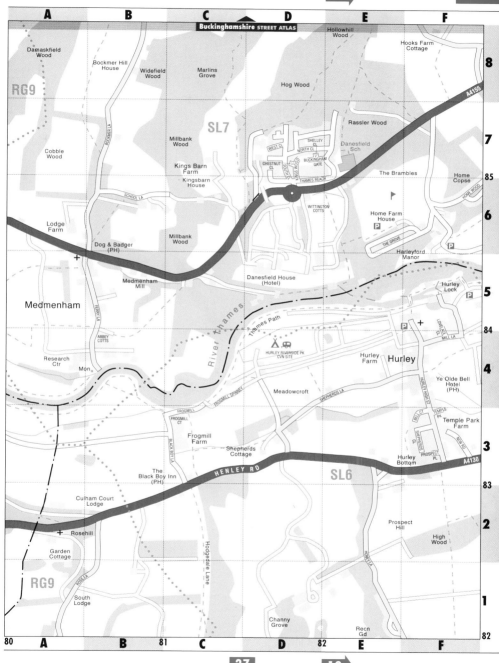

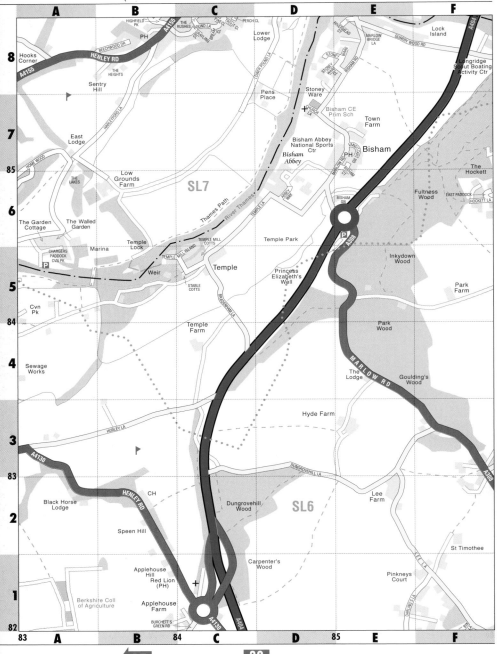

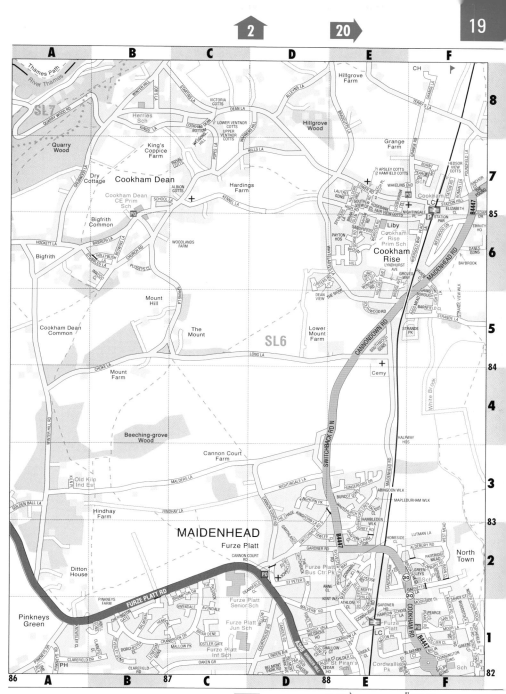

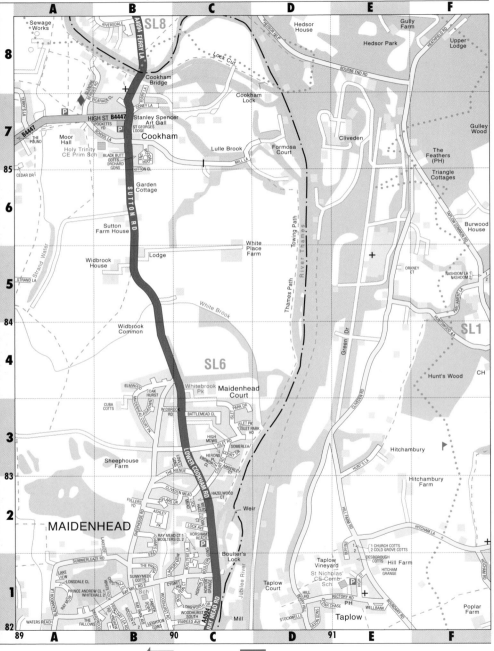

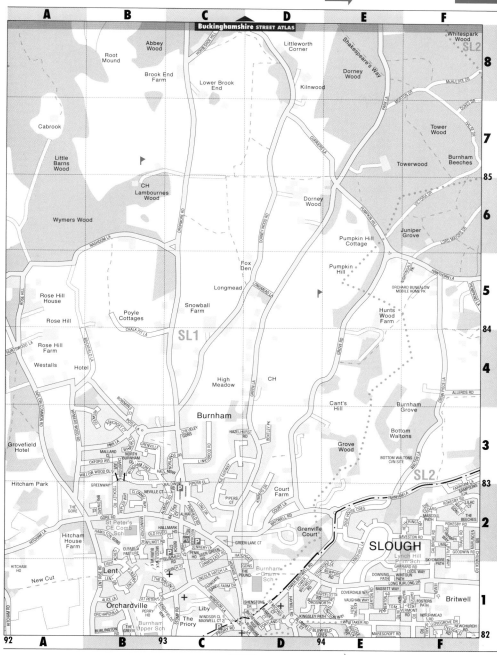

Buckinghamshire STREET ATLAS

Whitespark Wood
SL2

Abbey Wood
Root Mound
Littleworth Corner
Shakespeare's Way
Dorney Wood
McAULIFFE DR

Brook End Farm
Lower Brook End
Kilnwood
MORTON DR
DUKES DR
PARK LA

Cabrook
CURBERS LA
Tower Wood

Little Barns Wood
Towerwood
Burnham Beeches

CH Lambournes Wood
DROPMORE RD
VICTORIA DR

Wymers Wood
Dorney Wood
Juniper Grove
LORD MAYORS DR

NASHDOM LA
DORNEY WOOD RD
Pumpkin Hill Cottage
PUMPKIN HILL
HAWTHORN LA
TAPLOW COMMON RD

ROSE HILL
Fox Den
Pumpkin Hill
ORCHARD BUNGALOW MOBILE HOME PK

Rose Hill House
Longmead
LONGMEAD LA
Hunts Wood Farm

Poyle Cottages
Snowball Farm
GROVE RD

Rose Hill
CHALK PIT LA
SL1

BRACKEN LA
HUNTSWOOD LA
High Meadow
CH
ALLERDS RD

Rose Hill Farm
Westalls
Hotel
GREEN LA
BENTLEY PK
Cant's Hill
Burnham Grove
DRIVI PIECE LA
WALTON LA

HAW TOR COMMON RD
Grovefield Hotel
Bottom Waltons

Hitcham Park
WYMERS WOOD RD
Burnham
HAZELHURST RD
CHEVELEY GDNS
Grove Wood
BOTTOM WALTONS CVN SITE
SL2
FARNHAM LA
SAMPSONS LA

GREENWAY
MALLARD CL
OXFORD AVE
NORTH BURNHAM CL
WYNDHAM CRES
HALL MDW
PIPERS CL
Court Farm
DOVE HOUSE CRES
FARNHAM LA
THE CEDARS
ROKESBY RD
LILAC CT
THE BEECHES
GAVESTON RD
ROKESBY RD

HITCHAM HO
Hitcham House Farm
HAMILTON GDNS
BALDWIN
NEVILLE CT
PIPERS CT
Grenville Court
SLOUGH
MASCOLL PATH
SKYDMORE PATH
GOODWIN RD
CHURCH RD

New Cut
THE GORE
GORE RD
CLEARES PASTURE
HALLMARK
OLD FIVES
GREEN LANE CT
Lynch Hill Prim Sch
GARRARD RD
CECIL WAY
LONG FURLONG DR
GABLES RD

HITCHAM LA
Lent
St Peter's CE Comb Sch
WILMOT RD
MIDDLE CT
BEECH
CHURCH ST
Burnham Gram Sch
THE POUND
DOWNING PATH
WINTOUN PATH
BASSETT WAY
UMBERVILLE WAY
VAUGHAN WAY

Orchardville
ORCHARDVILLE
PERRY HO
ST PETERS
The Priory
WINDSOR CL
PRIORY RD
SHENSTONE
KINGSLEY PATH
COVERDALE WAY
WORDSWORTH
TOM
VERMONT
NORTHMEAD
Britwell

Burnham Upper Sch
THE GREEN
Liby
BLUNFIELD CRES
WHITTAKER RD
MARESCROFT RD

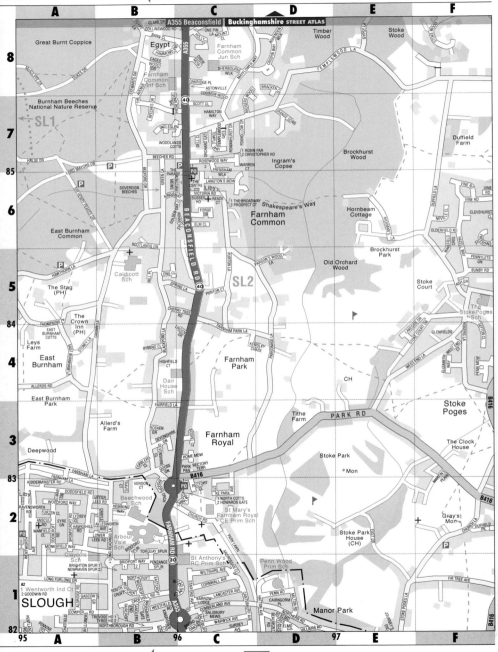

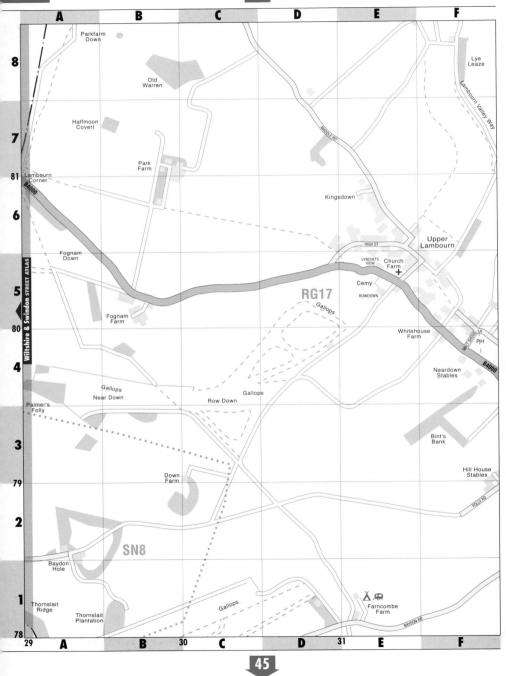

A **B** **C** **D** **E** **F**

Wiltshire & Swindon STREET ATLAS

Parkfarm Down

Old Warren

Halfmoon Covert

Park Farm

Lambourn Corner

B4000

Fognam Down

Fognam Farm

Gallops Near Down

Palmer's Folly

Down Farm

SN8

Baydon Hole

Thornslait Ridge

Thornslait Plantation

Gallops

Row Down

Gallops

Kingsdown

HIGH ST

LYNCHETS VIEW

Church Farm

Cemy

ROWDOWN

Gallops

RG17

Upper Lambourn

Lye Leaze

Lambourn Valley Way

SADDLE RD

Whitehouse Farm

MILE DROVE LA

PH

B4000

Neardown Stables

Bint's Bank

Hill House Stables

FOLLY RD

Farncombe Farm

BAYDON RD

8
7
81
6
5
80
4
3
79
2
1
78

29   30   31

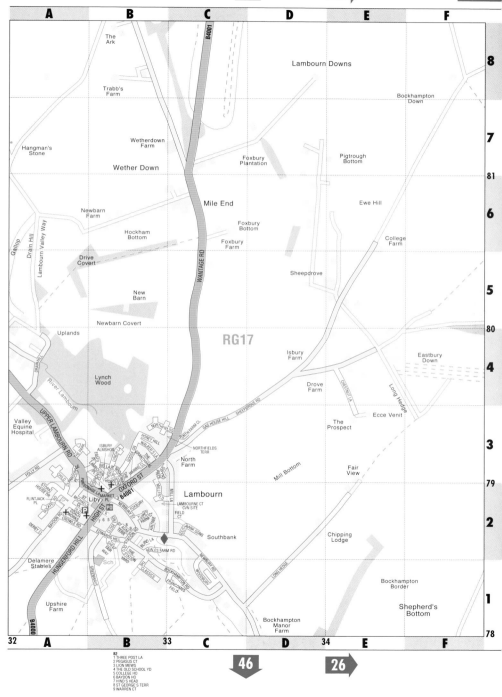

A B C D E F

The Ark

Lambourn Downs

Trabb's Farm

Bockhampton Down

Wetherdown Farm

Hangman's Stone

Foxbury Plantation

Pigtrough Bottom

Wether Down

Mile End

Ewe Hill

Newbarn Farm

Foxbury Bottom

Hockham Bottom

Foxbury Farm

College Farm

Drive Covert

Sheepdrove

New Barn

Newbarn Covert

RG17

Uplands

Isbury Farm

Eastbury Down

Lynch Wood

Drove Farm

Ecce Venit

Valley Equine Hospital

The Prospect

ISBURY ALMSHOS

NORTHFIELDS TERR

North Farm

Fair View

OXFORD ST

Mill Bottom

Lambourn

LAMBOURNE CT CVN SITE FIELD CT

Liby PL

HIGH ST

FLINTJACK PL

Southbank

Chipping Lodge

Delamere Stables

Bockhampton Border

Upshire Farm

Bockhampton Manor Farm

Shepherd's Bottom

32 A B 33 C D 34 E F

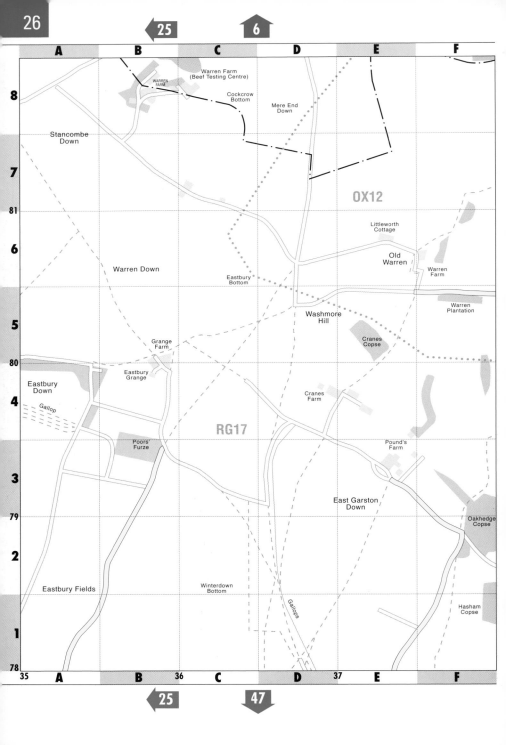

8

Warren Farm
(Beef Testing Centre)

WARREN
FARM

Cockcrow
Bottom

Mere End
Down

Stancombe
Down

7

81

OX12

Littleworth
Cottage

6

Old
Warren

Warren Down

Warren
Farm

Eastbury
Bottom

Warren
Plantation

5

Washmore
Hill

Cranes
Copse

Grange
Farm

80

Eastbury
Grange

Eastbury
Down

Cranes
Farm

4

Gallop

RG17

Pound's
Farm

Poors'
Furze

3

East Garston
Down

79

Oakhedge
Copse

2

Eastbury Fields

Winterdown
Bottom

Hasham
Copse

Gallops

1

78

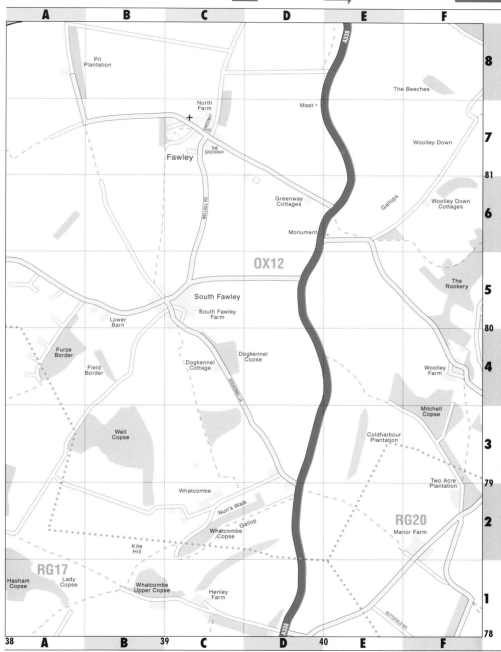

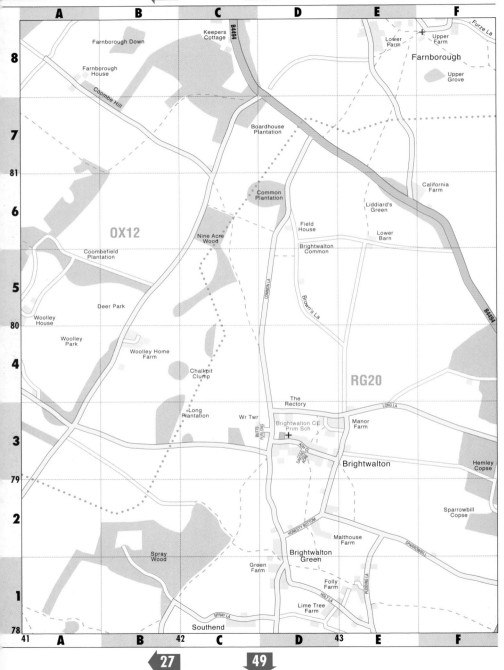

A B C D E F

8

Farnborough Down

Keepers Cottage

B4494

Lower Farm

Upper Farm

Furze La

Farnborough

Farnborough House

Coombe Hill

Upper Grove

7

Boardhouse Plantation

81

California Farm

Common Plantation

Liddiard's Green

6

OX12

Field House

Lower Barn

Nine Acre Wood

Brightwalton Common

Coombefield Plantation

5

Deer Park

COMMON LA

Brown's La

B4494

Woolley House

80

Woolley Park

Woolley Home Farm

4

Chalkpit Clump

RG20

The Rectory

LONG LA

Long Plantation

Wr Twr

Manor Farm

BUTTS

FURLONG

Brightwalton CE Prim Sch

3

SACKFIELD ACRE

ASH CL

Brightwalton

Hemley Copse

79

Sparrowbill Copse

2

HOMESTY BOTTOM

Malthouse Farm

SPARROWBILL

Spray Wood

Brightwalton Green

Green Farm

PUDDING LA

HOLT LA

Folly Farm

1

Lime Tree Farm

SPRAY LA

78

Southend

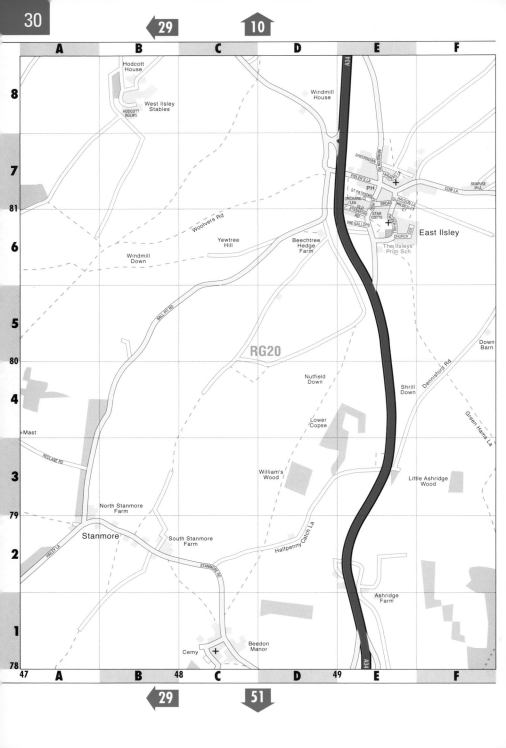

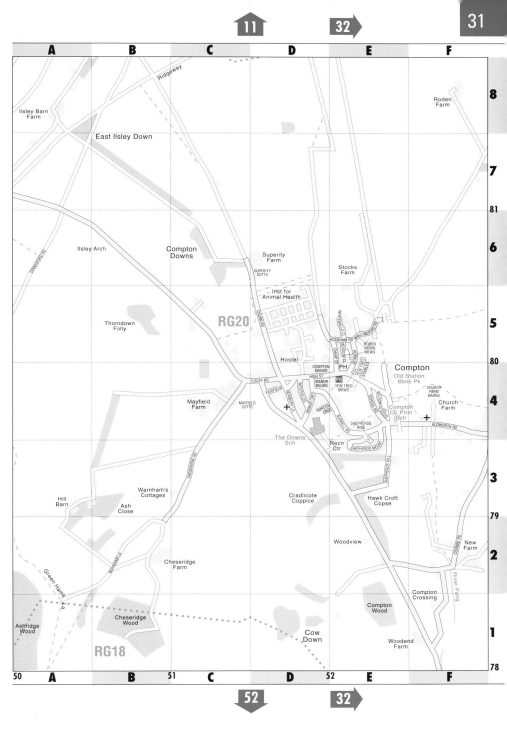

Ridgeway

Roden Farm

8

Ilsley Barn Farm

East Ilsley Down

7

81

DENNSFORD RD

Ilsley Arch

Compton Downs

Superity Farm

Stocks Farm

6

SUPERITY COTTS

Inst for Animal Health

RG20

5

Thorndown Folly

CHURN RD

Hostel

COMPTON MANOR

PH

WHITEHALLS CL

HOCKHAM RD

MEADOW PL

CHEAP ST

HORNS

WALLINGTON RD

RODEN DOWN MEWS

Compton

Old Station Bsns Pk

80

Mayfield Farm

MAYFIELD COTTS

ILSLEY RD

FAIRFIELD

HIGH ST

MANOR BGLWS

WESTFIELD

MANOR CRES

PO

YEW TREE MEWS

GORDON CRES

YEW TREES

STABLES

WILSON CL

SCHOOL RD

CHURCH FARM BARNS

Compton CE Prim Sch

Church Farm

4

+

BURNETT RD

SHEPHERDS RISE

+

ALDWORTH RD

The Downs Sch

Recn Ctr

SHEPHERDS MEAD

CHESERIDGE RD

Warnham's Cottages

Cradicote Coppice

Hawk Croft Copse

THE SHEPHERDS

3

79

Hill Barn

Ash Close

New Farm

POPE RD

Woodview

River Pang

2

WARNHAM LA

Cheseridge Farm

Compton Crossing

Green Hams La

Ashridge Wood

Cheseridge Wood

Compton Wood

Cow Down

Compton Wood

Woodend Farm

1

78

RG18

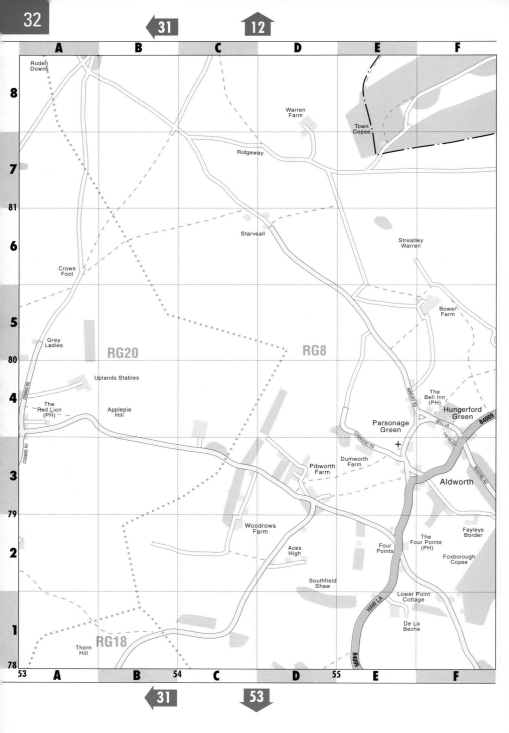

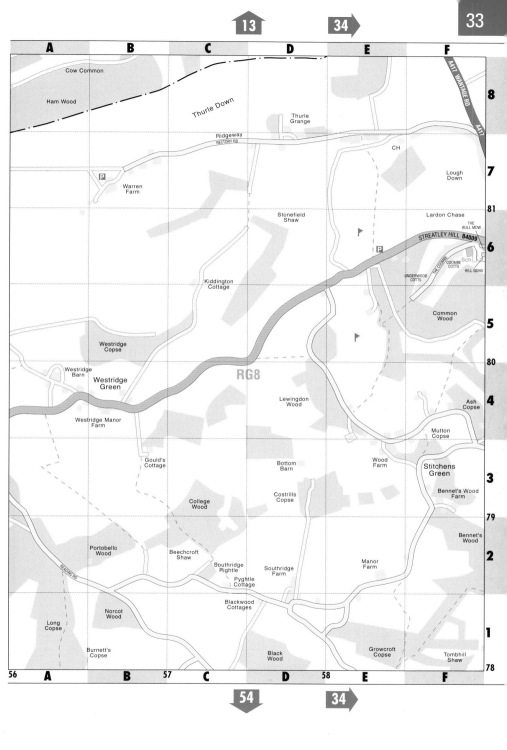

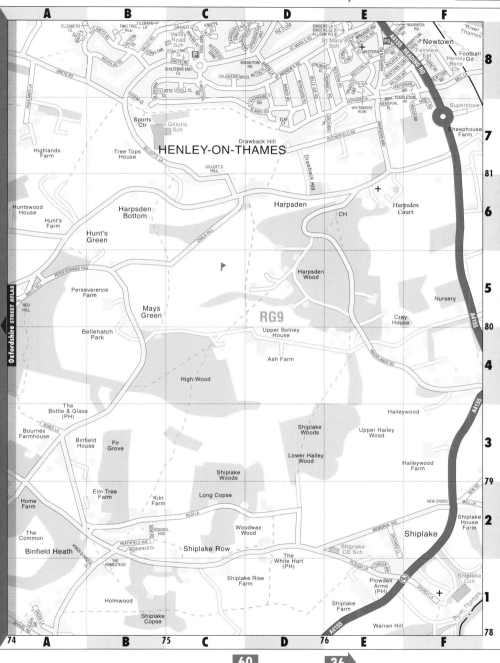

HENLEY-ON-THAMES

RG9

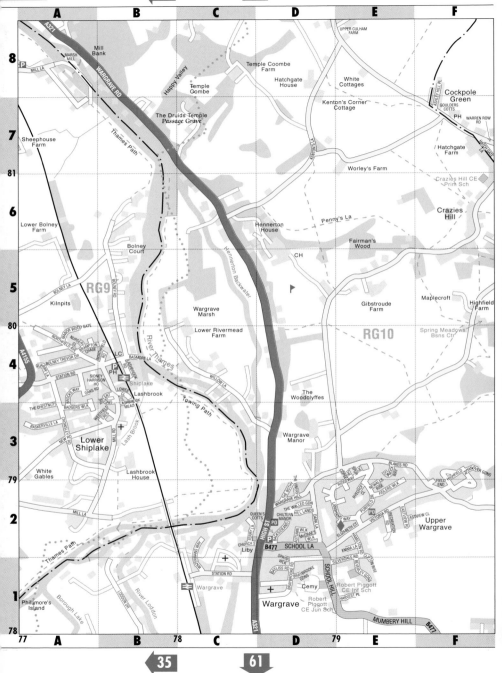

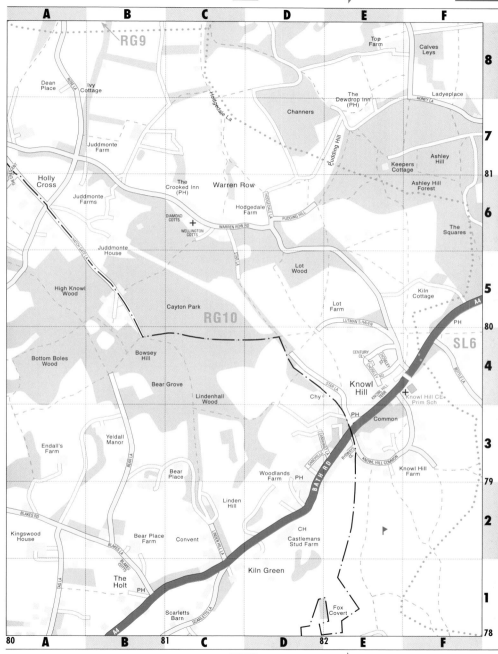

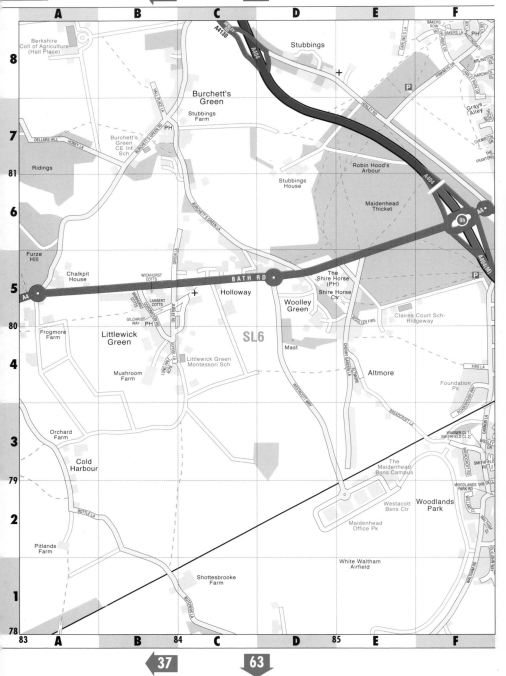

A   B   C   D   E   F

8

Berkshire
Coll of Agriculture
(Hall Place)

Stubbings

BAKERS
ROW

BAKERS LA

DARLINGTON DR

PINKNEYS DR

ARLINGTON CL

CARET PARK DR

HARDWICK CL

P

Grays
Alley

7

DELLARS HILL

HONEY LA

HALL PLACE LA

Burchett's
Green

Stubbings
Farm

PH

Burchett's
Green
CE Inf
Sch

BURCHETT'S GREEN RD

HENLEY RD

CHENISTON
DR

THE
FRANTONS

81

Ridings

Robin Hood's
Arbour

A404

6

Furze
Hill

BURCHETT'S GREEN LA

Stubbings
House

Maidenhead
Thicket

9b

A4

A404(M)

5

A4

Chalkpit
House

WICKHURST
COTTS

VALUE RD

BATH RD

The
Shire
Horse
(PH)

Shire Horse
Ctr

P

Holloway

Woolley
Green

LARBERT
COTTS

PINKNEYS
COTTS

COLDHARBOUR

JUBILEE RD

WOOLLEY FIRS

Claires Court Sch-
Ridgeway

80

Frogmore
Farm

GILCHRIST
WAY

PH

Littlewick
Green

SCHOOL LA

SL6

Mast

CHERRY GARDEN LA

TITHE

Altmore

FIRS LA

Foundation
Pk

4

Mushroom
Farm

LONG HALF ACRE

Littlewick Green
Montessori Sch

WESTACOTT WAY

BREADCROFT LA

RICHMOND WAY

LA HUNT DR

BISSLEY
DR

3

Orchard
Farm

WARNER CL 1
SMITHFIELD CL 2

SMITHFIELD
RD

BREADCROFT RD

Cold
Harbour

The
Maidenhead
Bsns Campus

WOODLANDS
PARK RD

THE DELL

79

BOTTLE LA

Westacott
Bsns Ctr

Woodlands
Park

WILLART CL

WALTHAM CL

2

Maidenhead
Office Pk

FOLLY JOHN WAY

1

Pitlands
Farm

Shottesbrooke
Farm

BUTCHERS LA

White Waltham
Airfield

OLD WALTHAM

78

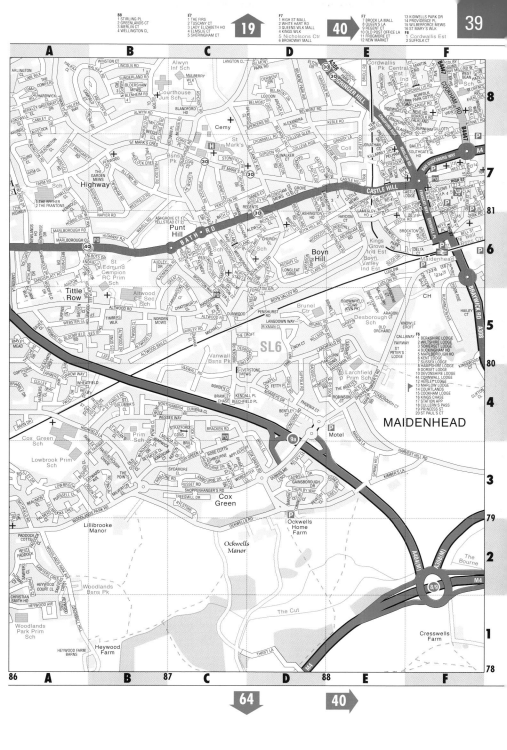

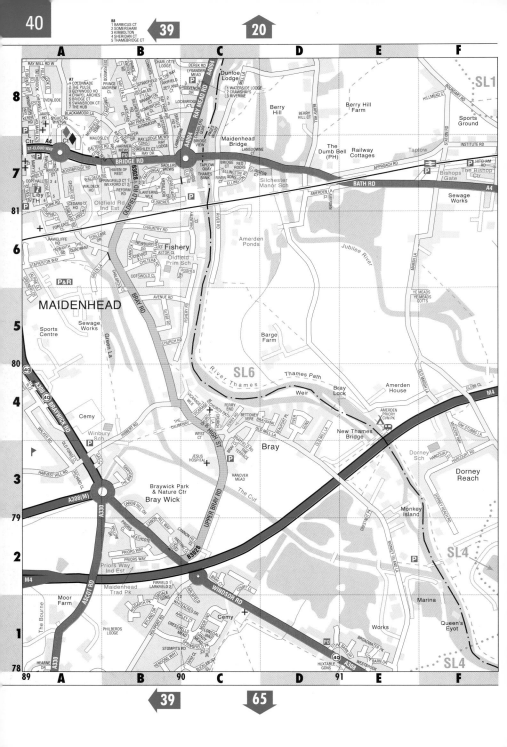

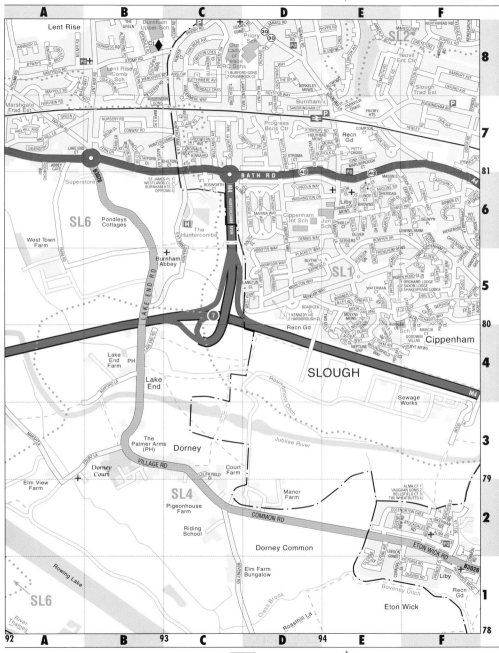

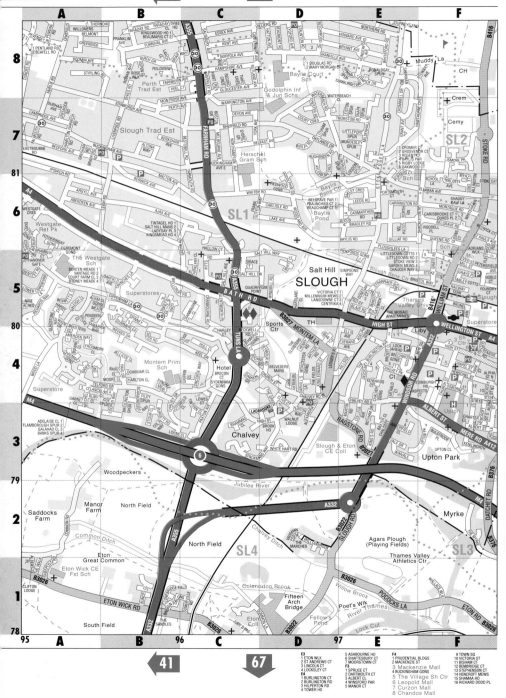

E3
1 ETON WLK
2 ST ANDREWS CT
3 LINCOLN CT
4 LOCKSLEY CT
E4
1 BURLINGTON CT
2 BURLINGTON RD
3 HILPERTON RD
4 TOWER HO

5 ASHBOURNE HO
6 SHAFTESBURY CT
7 MOORSTOWN CT
F3
1 SPRUCE CT
2 DARTMOUTH CT
3 ALBERT CL
4 WINSFORD PAR
5 MANOR CT

F4
1 PRUDENTIAL BLDGS
2 MACKENZIE ST
3 Mackenzie Gdns
4 BUCKINGHAM GDNS
5 The Village Sh Ctr
6 Leopold Mall
7 Curzon Mall
8 Chandos Mall

9 TOWN SQ
10 VICTORIA ST
11 BISHAM CT
12 BEMBRIDGE CT
13 STEPHENSON CT
14 HENCROFT MEWS
15 SHAMAA HO
16 RICHARD DODD PL

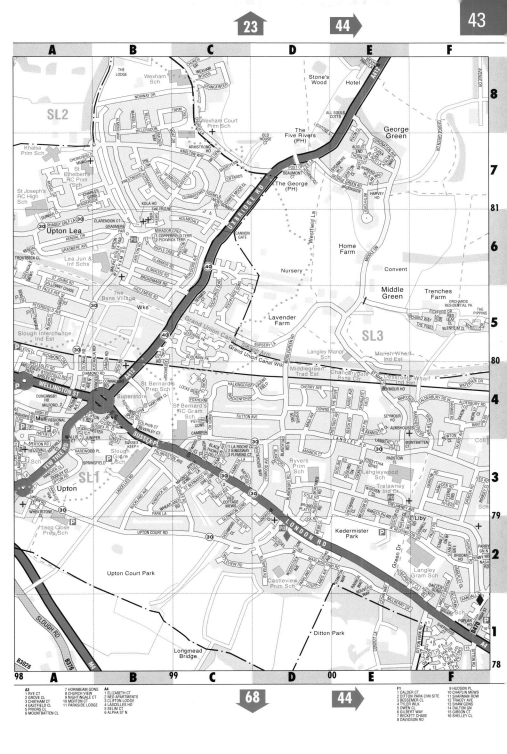

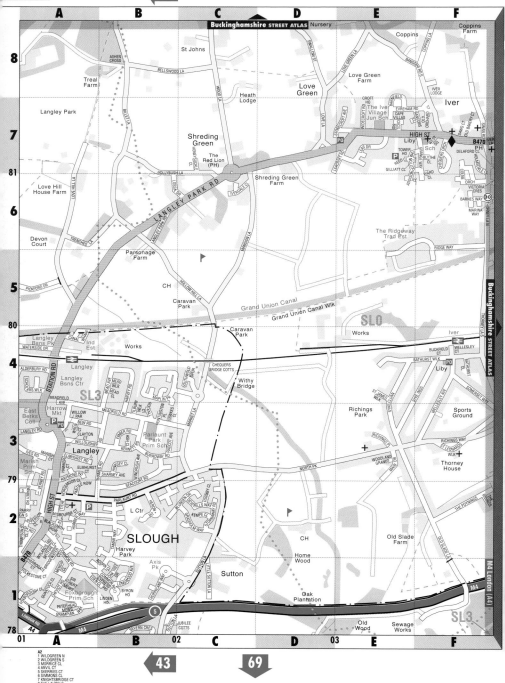

Buckinghamshire STREET ATLAS

A2
1 WILDGREEN N
2 WILDGREEN S
3 MORRICE CL
4 ANVIL CT
5 SKERRIES CT
6 SIMMONS CL
7 KNIGHTSBRIDGE CT
8 THE LAURELS

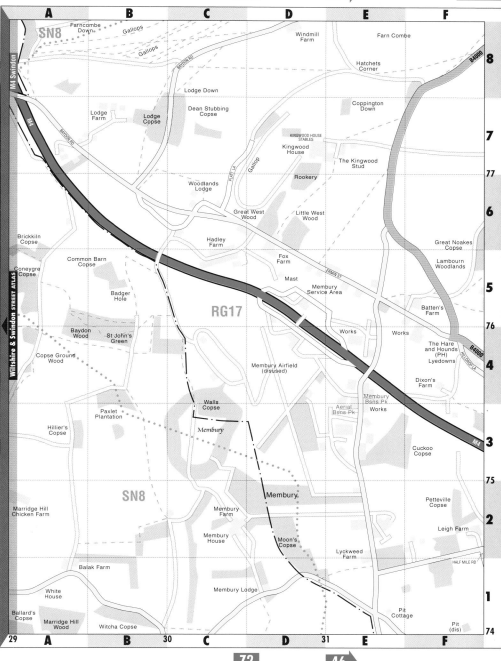

SN8

Farncombe Down
Gallops
Gallops

Windmill Farm
Farn Combe

8

Hatchets Corner

Lodge Down

Dean Stubbing Copse

Coppington Down

Lodge Farm
Lodge Copse

KINGWOOD HOUSE STABLES
Kingwood House

The Kingwood Stud

7

77

Woodlands Lodge

Gallop

Rookery

Great West Wood
Little West Wood

6

Brickkiln Copse

Hadley Farm

Fox Farm

Great Noakes Copse

Common Barn Copse

Mast

Lambourn Woodlands

Coneygre Copse

Badger Hole

Membury Service Area

ERMIN ST

5

RG17

Works
Works

Batten's Farm

76

Baydon Wood
St John's Green

The Hare and Hounds (PH)
Lyedowns

Copse Ground Wood

Membury Airfield (disused)

Dixon's Farm

4

Hillier's Copse

Paxlet Plantation

Walls Copse

Membury

Aerial Bsns Pk

Membury Bsns Pk
Works

Cuckoo Copse

3

SN8

Membury

Petteville Copse

75

Marridge Hill Chicken Farm

Membury Farm

Leigh Farm

2

Membury House

Moon's Copse

Lyckweed Farm

HALF MILE RD

Balak Farm

White House

Membury Lodge

Pit Cottage

1

Ballard's Copse

Marridge Hill Wood

Witcha Copse

Pit (dis)

74

Wiltshire & Swindon STREET ATLAS

M4 Swindon

B4000
B4000

FELDIOG LA

M4

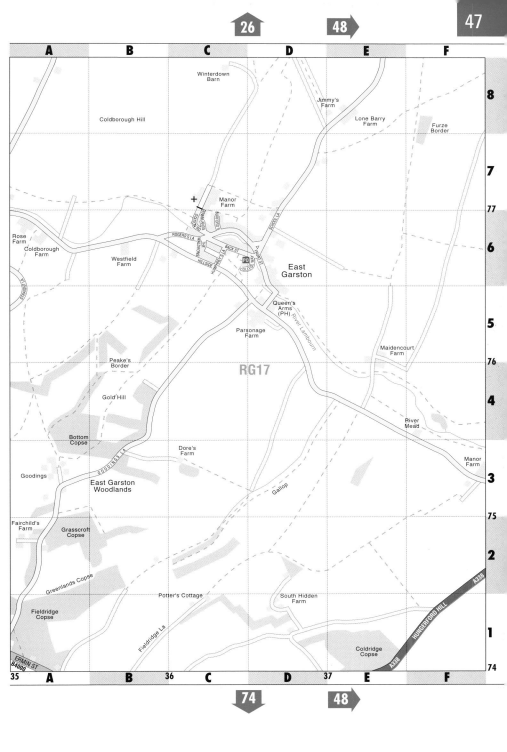

8

7

77

6

5

76

4

3

75

2

1

74

Winterdown
Barn

Coldborough Hill

Jimmy's
Farm

Lone Barry
Farm

Furze
Border

Manor
Farm

Rose
Farm

Coldborough
Farm

ROGERS'S LA

BACK ST

Westfield
Farm

HILLSIDE

PO

East
Garston

SCHOOL LA

Queen's
Arms
(PH)

Parsonage
Farm

River Lambourn

Maidencourt
Farm

RG17

Peake's
Border

Gold Hill

River
Mead

Bottom
Copse

Dore's
Farm

GOODINGS LA

Manor
Farm

Goodings

East Garston
Woodlands

Gallop

Fairchild's
Farm

Grasscroft
Copse

Greenlands Copse

Potter's Cottage

South Hidden
Farm

Fieldridge
Copse

Fieldridge La

A338

HUNGERFORD HILL

Coldridge
Copse

A338

ERMIN ST
B4000

35   A   B   36   C   D   37   E   F

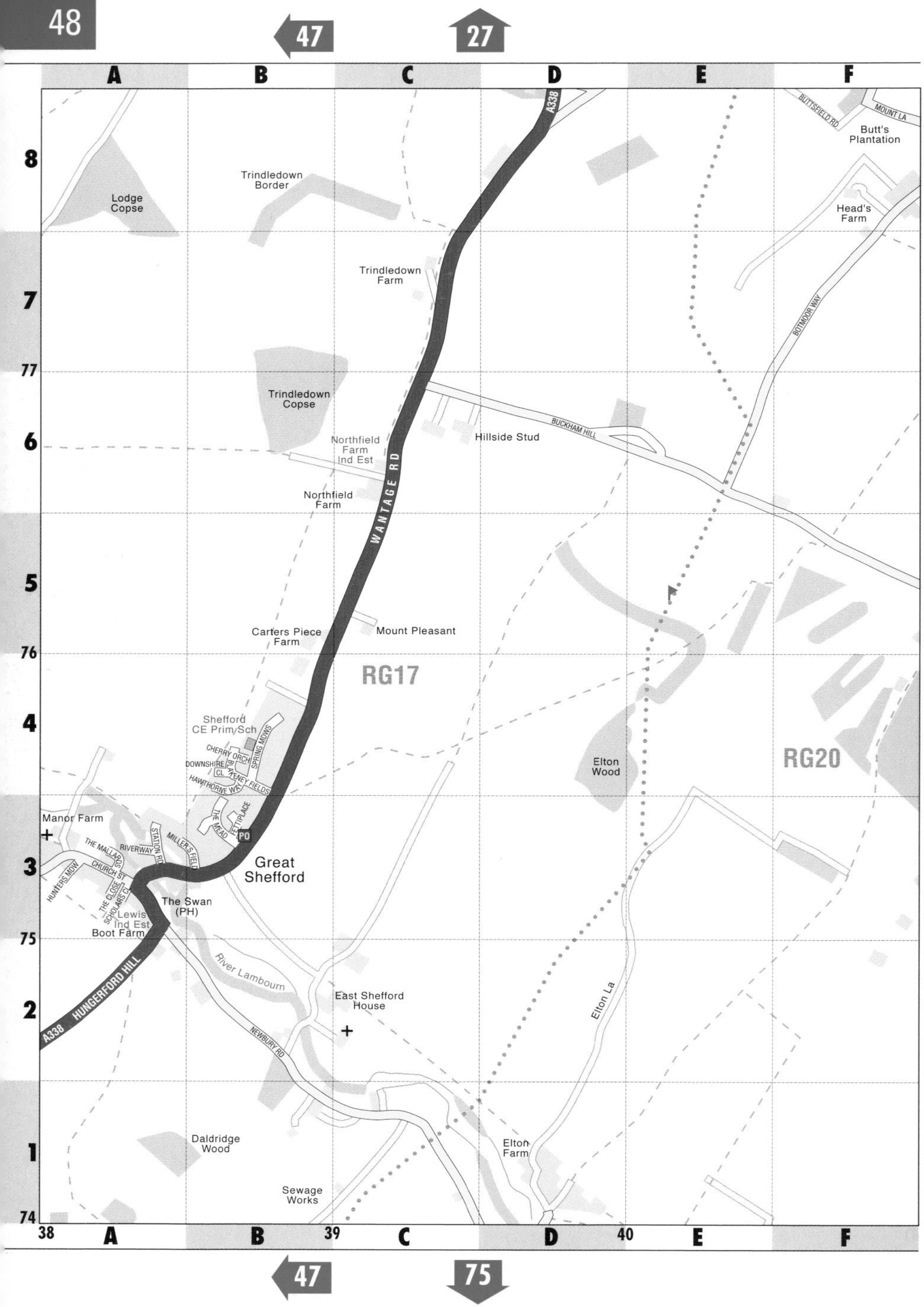

47 27

A B C D E F

8

BUTTSFIELD RD
MOUNT LA
Butt's
Plantation

Lodge
Copse

Trindledown
Border

Head's
Farm

7

Trindledown
Farm

A338

77

Trindledown
Copse

BUCKHAM HILL

BOTHADOR WAY

6

Northfield
Farm
Ind Est

Hillside Stud

WANTAGE RD

Northfield
Farm

5

Carters Piece
Farm

Mount Pleasant

76

RG17

4

Shefford
CE Prim Sch

CHERRY ORCH
DOWNSHIRE PL
PENNY FIELDS
HAWTHORNE WY
SPITAL MOUND

Elton
Wood

RG20

THE MEAD
PO

THE MALLARDS
RIVERWAY RD
MILLER'S FLD

Manor Farm

3

Great
Shefford

HUNTERS MEW
CHURCH ST
THE CLOSE
SCHOOL ST
STATION RD

Lewis
Ind Est

The Swan
(PH)

75

Boot Farm

A338 HUNGERFORD HILL

River Lambourn

East Shefford
House

2

NEWBURY RD

Elton La

Daldridge
Wood

1

Elton
Farm

Sewage
Works

74

38 A B 39 C D 40 E F

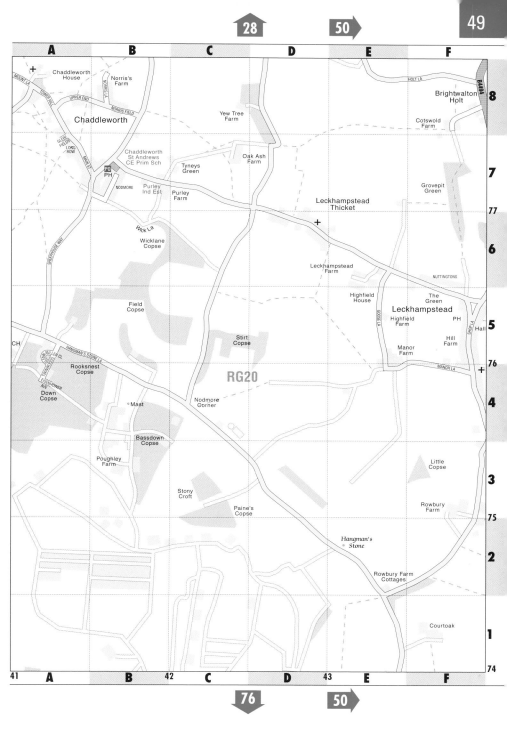

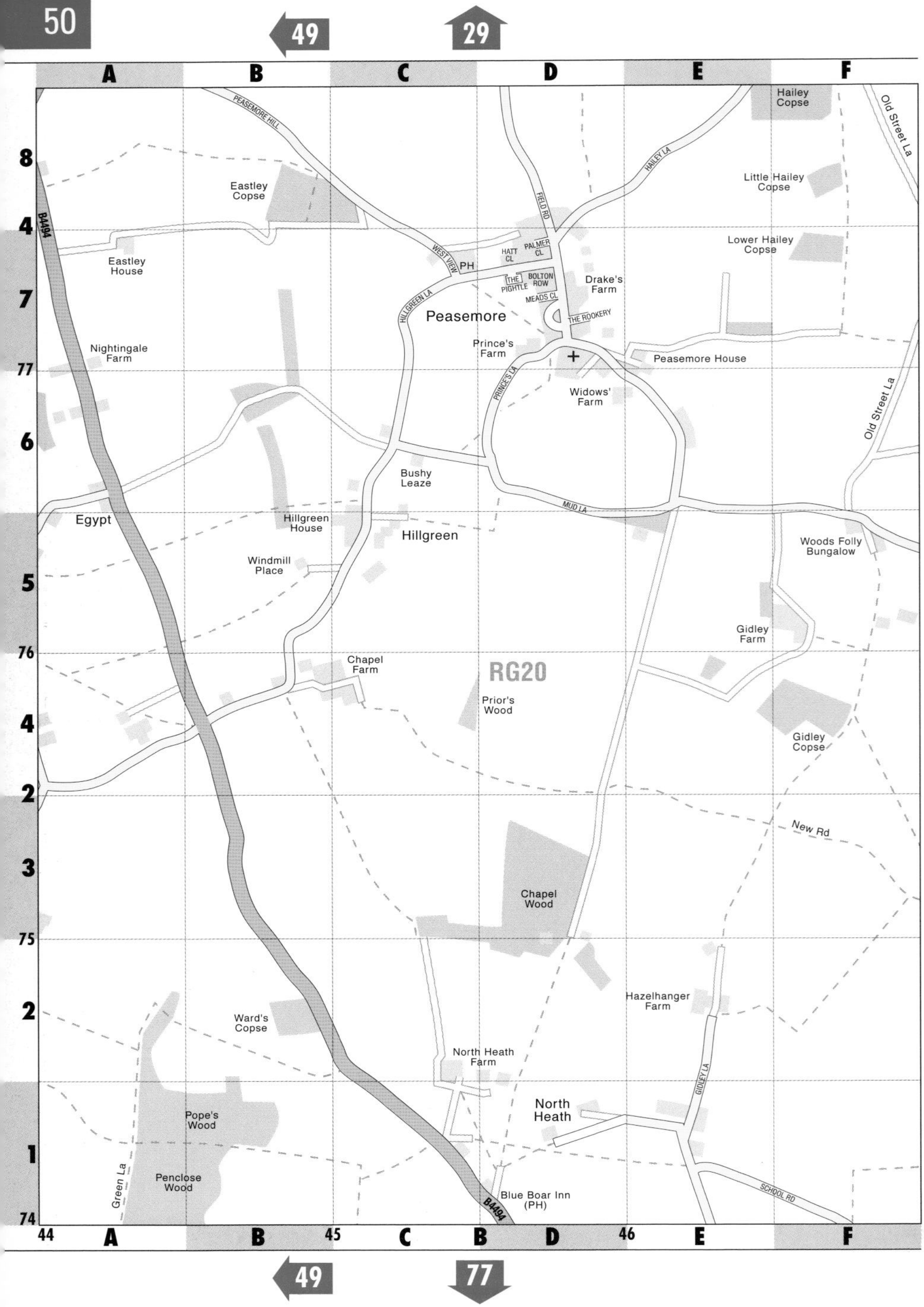

49
29

Hailey
Copse

Old Street La

8

Little Hailey
Copse

4

PEASEMORE HILL

Eastley
Copse

HAILEY LA

B4494

Lower Hailey
Copse

Eastley
House

WEST STREET

HATT
CL

PALMER
CL

PH

THE
PIGHTLE

BOLTON
ROW

Drake's
Farm

7

HILLGREEN LA

MEADS CL

THE ROOKERY

Peasemore

Nightingale
Farm

Prince's
Farm

Peasemore House

Old Street La

77

+

PRINCE'S LA

Widows'
Farm

6

Bushy
Leaze

MUD LA

Egypt

Hillgreen
House

Hillgreen

Woods Folly
Bungalow

Windmill
Place

5

Gidley
Farm

76

Chapel
Farm

RG20

Prior's
Wood

4

Gidley
Copse

2

New Rd

3

Chapel
Wood

75

Hazelhanger
Farm

2

Ward's
Copse

BIRKET LA

North Heath
Farm

North
Heath

Pope's
Wood

1

SCHOOL RD

Green La

Penclose
Wood

B4494

Blue Boar Inn
(PH)

74

44

A

45

B

C

B

D

46

E

F

49
77

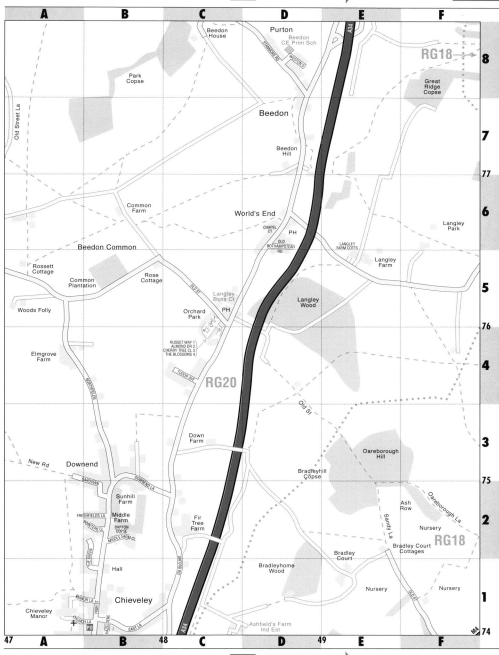

51
31

A B C D E F

Perborough Castle

RG20
Floodcross Cottage

8

Banterwick Farm

Northfield Row

Little Ridge Copse

Ramsworth Cottages

Milkhill Farm

7

Uplands

Green Hams La

77

RG20

Allen's Row

River Pang

6

New Copse

Middle Barn

FIVE WAYS

THE OLD SCHOOL

STATION HILL

WEST VIEW COTTS

HILLCREST

PENDALS CL

Oakhouse Farm

Laycroft Wood

Hampstead Norreys

SCOT VALLS LA

LILY CLOSE

B4009

5

Bothampstead Farm

Oakhouse Cottages

NEWBURY HILL CHURCH ST

Hollingsworth

Hampstead Norreys CE Prim Sch

76

RG18

4

Park Wood

Westbrook Copse

Bothampstead

Malthouse

Trumpletts Farm

Down Wood

New Cottages

Hatchgate Cottages

The Thatched Cottage

3

Elingpark Copse

Eling

75

Eling Farm

Four Elms

2

Pimbus Shaw

EVERINGTON LA

DAREBOROUGH LA

Sand Pit

Common Barn Cottages

Heather Piece

Spring Plantation

Everington Hill

1

M4

Newhouse Farm

B4009

Furze Hill

M4

74

50 A B 51 C D 52 E F

51
79

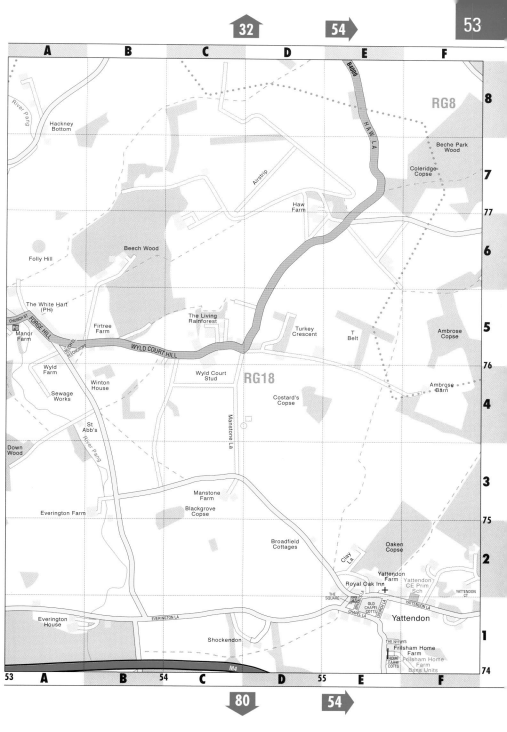

53
33
A
B
C
D
E
F
8
7
77
6
5
76
4
3
75
2
1
74
56
57
58
Hartridge Cottages
Hartridge Farm
Tombhill Row
Hare Green
The Row
Broom Wood
Bullard's Copse
HATTON HILL
Eastfield Wood
Bowler's Copse
Ashampstead Green
Dark Copse
Hartridge Lye Wood
CHAPEL LA
NOAKES HILL
Longcroft Shaw
Rushdown Farm
Drift Hill
DOG LA
WHITE HILL
Ashampstead
CHURCH LA
FLOWERS PIECE
HOLLY LA
Drift Farm
Rush Down
Hill Corner
Stubbles
Hanging Close Row
CAPTAINS GORSE
James's Copse
Westcroft Shaw
PALMER'S HILL
WHITEMOOR LA
TENAPLAS DR
OLD STOCKS CT
Clayhanger Farm
Factory
KILN RIDE
PINFOLD LA
Quick's Green
Greenaway's Copse
Flower's Copse
RG8
Captain's Gorse
Pyt House
Lay Fields
Young Plantation
Sodom La
PYKE'S HILL
Lye Wood
Calvesleys Farm
Pinfold La
Child's Court Farm
SUCK'S LA
Mumsgrove Copse
Home Copse
Ashampstead Common
Old Park
RG18
Bushy Copse
YATTENDON LA
Gravelpit Copse
Challengehook Plantation
Slade Gate
Clack's Copse
Yattendon Park
Mapletons
Burnthill Common
The Nut & Bolt (PH)
Burnt Hill
Strouds
Withy Copse
Burnthill House
Broomhill Copse
Upperlands Copse
53
81

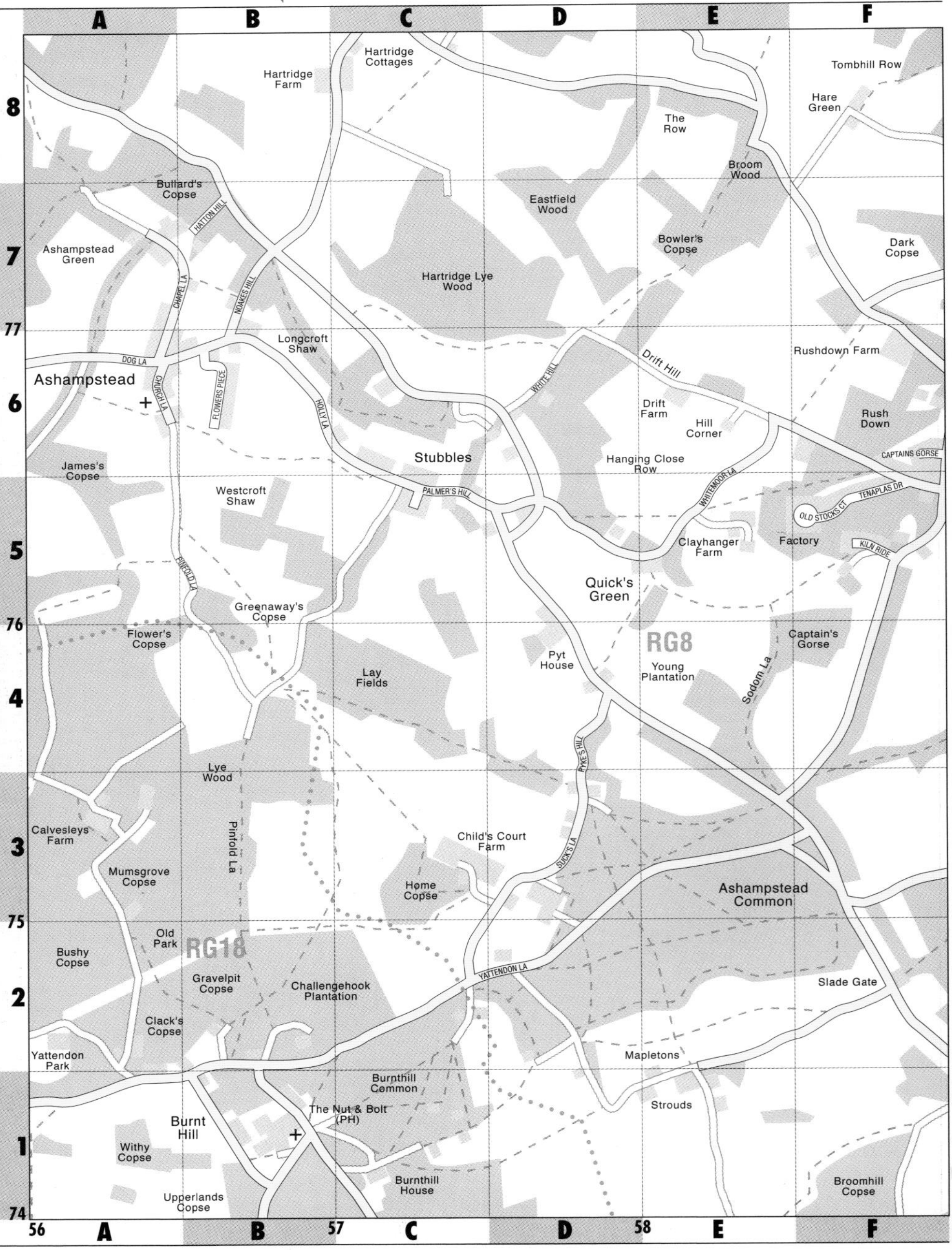

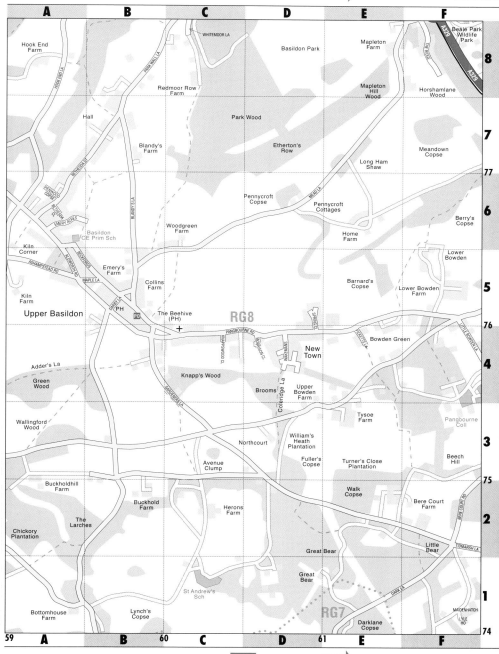

55

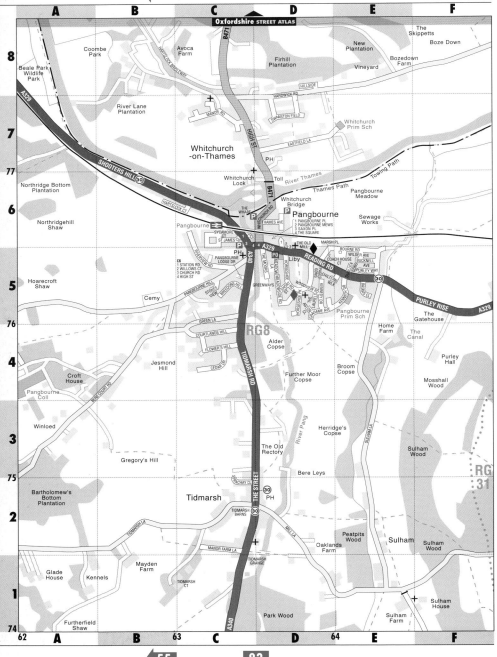

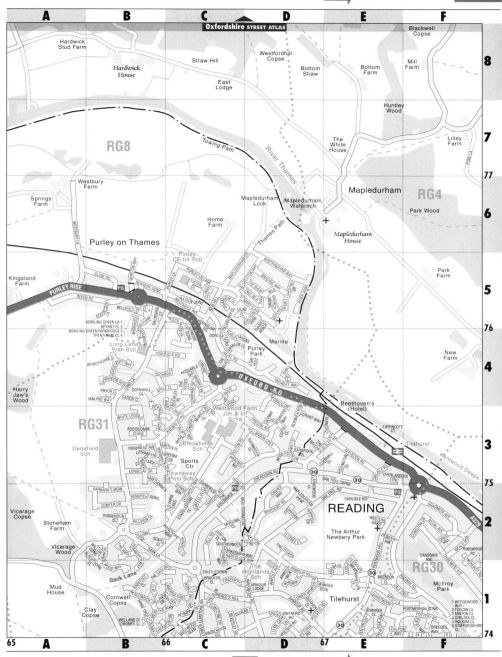

58

Oxfordshire STREET ATLAS

8

Blackwell Copse

Hardwick Stud Farm

Straw Hill

Westfordhill Copse

Bottom Shaw

Bottom Farm

Mill Farm

Hardwick House

East Lodge

Huntley Wood

7

RG8

Towing Path

River Thames

The White House

Lilley Farm

POND LA

77

Westbury Farm

Mapledurham

RG4

Springs Farm

Mapledurham Lock

Mapledurham Watermill

Park Wood

6

WESTBURY LA

Home Farm

Thames Path

Mapledurham House

Purley on Thames

Purley CE Inf Sch

Park Farm

5

Kingsland Farm

PURLEY RISE

GLEBE RD

BEECH RD

PO

New Farm

76

Long Lane Prim Sch

Marina

Purley Park

4

Harry Jaw's Wood

OXFORD RD

Beethoven's (Hotel)

LIPPINCOTE CT

Tilehurst

Kentwood Deeps

3

RG31

Denefield Sch

Westwood Farm Jun & Inf Schs

Sports Ctr

Downsway Prim Sch

75

PO

READING

PO

A329

2

Vicarage Copse

Stoneham Farm

The Arthur Newbery Park

Mcllroy Park

RG30

Vicarage Wood

Tilehurst

SANDGATE AVE

1

Mud House

Back Lane

The Highlands Sch

1 WEDGEWOOD WAY
2 TUSCAN CL
3 MINTON CL
4 CHELSEA CL
5 HOLKAM CL
6 STAFFORDSHIRE

Clay Copse

Cornwell Copse

WELLAND CL 1
CROMER CL 2

74

84   58

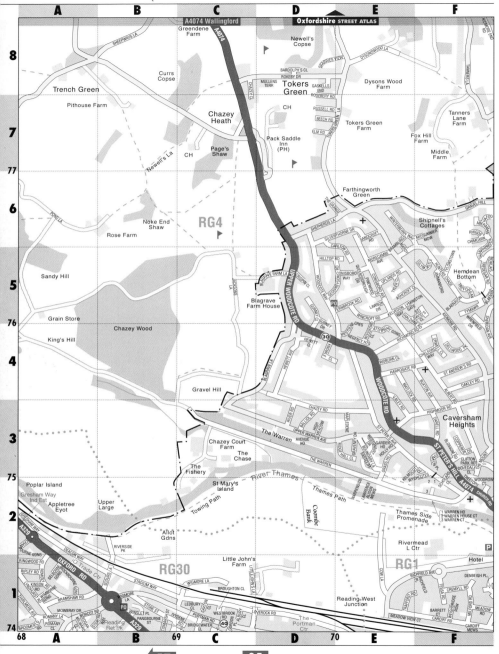

A4074 Wallingford

Oxfordshire STREET ATLAS

Greendene Farm

Newell's Copse

Currs Copse

Trench Green

Pithouse Farm

Dysons Wood Farm

Chazey Heath

Tokers Green

CH

Tanners Lane Farm

Tokers Green Farm

Page's Shaw

Pack Saddle Inn (PH)

Fox Hill Farm

Middle Farm

Newell's La

CH

Farthingworth Green

RG4

Shipnell's Cottages

Noke End Shaw

Rose Farm

Pond La

Hemdean Bottom

Sandy Hill

Blagrave Farm House

Grain Store

Chazey Wood

King's Hill

PO

Gravel Hill

Caversham Heights

WOODCOTE RD

Chazey Court Farm

The Chase

The Warren

The Fishery

St Mary's Island

River Thames

Poplar Island

Gresham Way Ind Est

Appletree Eyot

Upper Large

Towing Path

Thames Path

Coombe Bank

Thames Side Promenade

1 WARREN HO
2 WARREN HOUSE CT
3 WARREN CT

Allot Gdns

Riverside Pk

Rivermead L Ctr

RG30

Little John's Farm

RG1

Hotel

OXFORD RD

Wigmore La

Stadium Way

Reading West Junction

The Portman Ctr

Reading Ret Pk

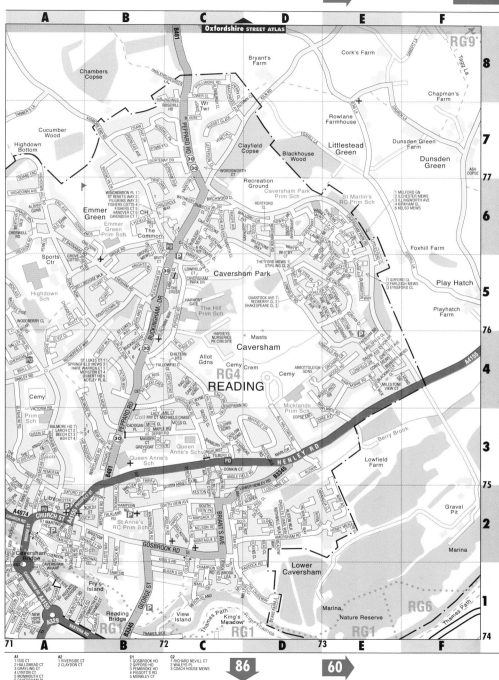

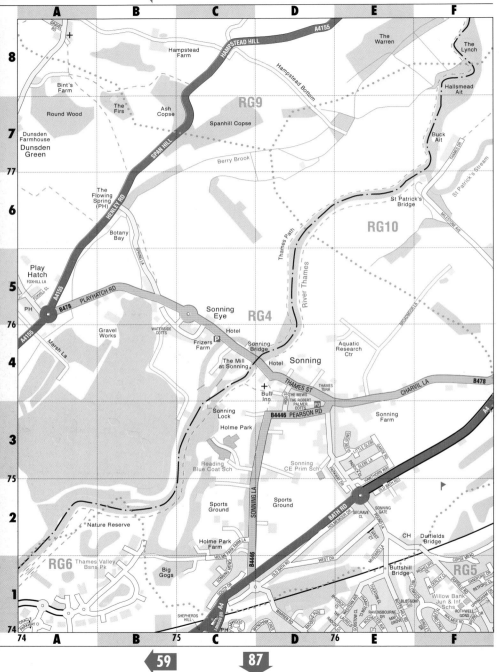

59
35
59
87

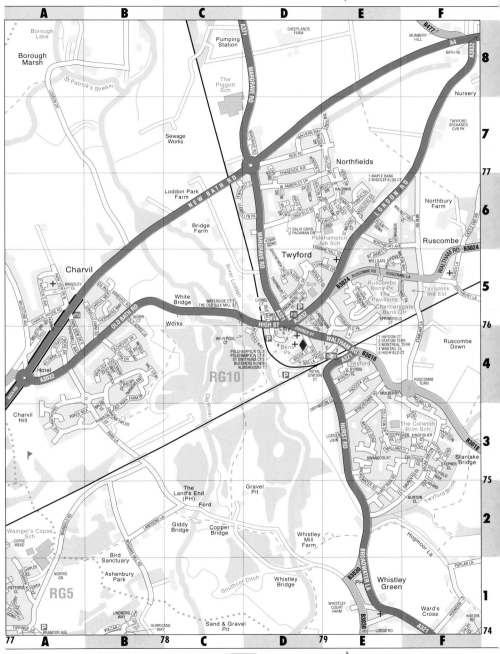

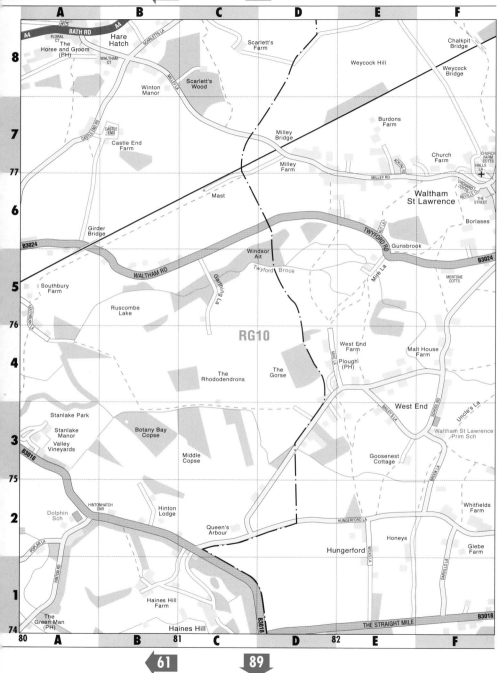

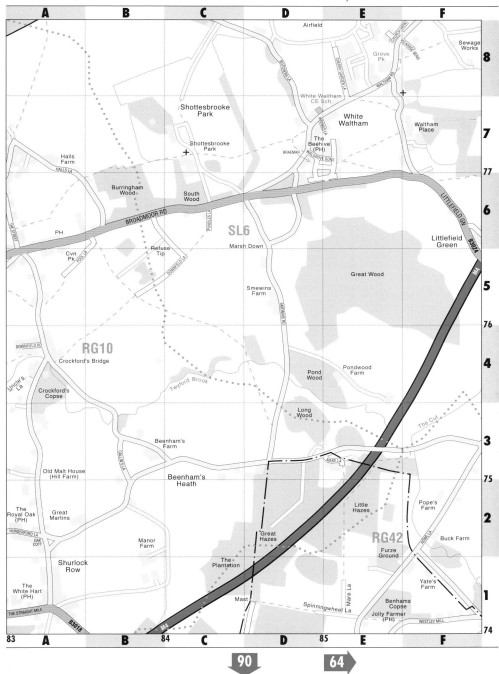

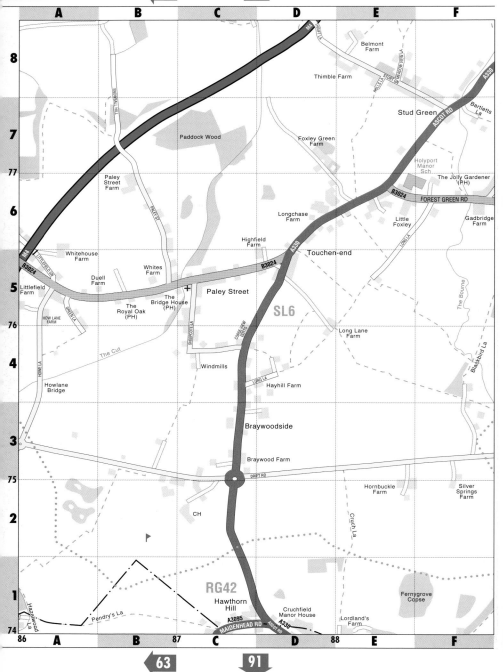

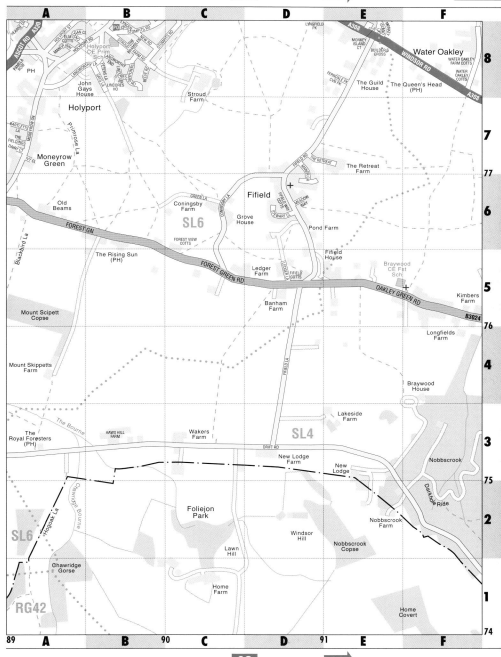

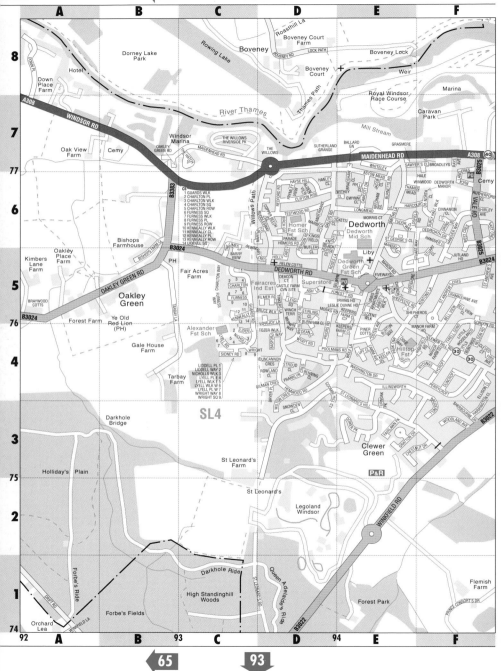

65
41

8

Roasthill La

Boveney Court Farm

Boveney Lock

Boveney

Rowing Lake

Dorney Lake Park

LOCK PATH

BOVENEY RD

Thames Path

Boveney Court

Weir

Royal Windsor Race Course

Marina

Hotel

Down Place Farm

A308

WINDSOR RD

Caravan Park

Mill Stream

GRASMERE

River Thames

7

Windsor Marina

THE WILLOWS RIVERSIDE PK

THE WILLOWS

SUTHERLAND GRANGE

BALLARD GN

77

Oak View Farm

Cemy

OAKLEY GREEN RD

MAIDENHEAD RD

THE MALTINGS

Willows Path

MAIDENHEAD RD

WHITELEY

SAWYER'S CL

BROADLEYS

A308

40

Cemy

B3383

HALE

WINWOOD

DEDWORTH MANOR

B3024

RUTHERFORD

ASTON MEAD

HAYSE HILL

HANLEY

HYLTT CL

WITHEY

FROME CL

CLIFTON RISE

GWYNNE CL

THAMES MEAD

HARCOURT

SHIRLEY AVE

EAST CRES

VALE RD

6

1 GUARDS WLK
2 CHARLTON PL
3 CHARLTON WLK
4 CHARLTON SQ
5 CHARLTON SQ
6 FURNESS SQ
7 FURNESS WLK
8 FURNESS PL
9 FURNESS ROW
10 KENNALLY WLK
11 KENNALLY CL
12 KENNALLY PL
13 KENNALLY ROW
14 LIDDELL SQ

TESTWOOD RD

COPPER BEECH

Homer Fst Sch

MARBECK CL

LOCKETTS CL

MORRIS CT

CINNAMON CL

Dedworth

Dedworth Mid Sch

DEDWORTH DR

JUTLAND HO

THE PARADE

HOMERS RD

KING'S FIELD

BUTLERS

KNIGHTS CL

BLACK

ST GEORGE'S CL

HANOVER CL

MANSEL

B3024

Bishops Farmhouse

BISHOPS TARRACE

LIMES LA

BARRY VIEW

HELEN COTTS

HOLLY

Liby

Dedworth Green Fst Sch

MANOR

FIVEWAYS

CASTLE HILL

Kimbers Lane Farm

Oakley Place Farm

PH

Fair Acres Farm

CHARLTON WAY

DEDWORTH RD

DEACON CT

CVN SITE

Superstore

ASH LA

FOREST CL

ST ANDREWS CRES

ST ANDREWS CL

5

BRAYWOOD COTTS

Oakley Green

OAKLEY GREEN RD

TARRAH LA

Fairacres Ind Est

FILMER RD

LEIGH SQ

WINCH CL

STIRLING CL

LESLIE DUNNE HO

MONKS RD

KEEPERS

SHEPHERDS

OAK VIEW

CRANBOURNE AVE

B3024

76

Forest Farm

Ye Old Red Lion (PH)

FURNESS WAY

Alexander Fst Sch

KENNEDDY LA

BRUCE WLK

LONGJOY LA

BURNHAM CL

KEEPERS FARM CL

PINER COTTS

MANOR HO

CLEWER HILL RD

GORDON RD

4

Gale House Farm

LIDDELL

TOZER WLK

WAY

DEAN

WYATT RD

POOLMANS RD

Hilltop Fst Sch

RYDINGS

PERRYCROFT

ELLISON CL

30

Tarbay Farm

SIDNEY RD

WRIGHT

LIDDELL PL 1
LIDDELL WAY 2
NICHOLLS WLK 3
LYELL PL E 4
LYELL WLK E 5
LYELL WLK W 6
LYELL PL W 7
WRIGHT WAY 8
WRIGHT SQ 9

DUNCANNON CRES

STROUD CL

ROWLAND CL

PRASKLYN

BENNING CL

WASHINGTON DR

FAIRLAWN

ILLINGWORTH

GILMAN CRES

FERNWOOD RD

ST LEONARD'S HILL

COMBERMERE

WOODLAND AVE

B3022

3

Darkhole Bridge

SL4

St Leonard's Farm

SNOWDEN CL

WILTON GDNS

Clewer Green

CHESTNUT DR

75

Holliday's Plain

P&R

St Leonard's

Legoland Windsor

2

Forbe's Ride

WINKFIELD RD

DRIFT RD

Darkhole Ride

Queen Adelaide's Ride

High Standinghill Woods

ST LEONARD'S RD

B3022

Forest Park

Flemish Farm

1

Orchard Lea

WINKFIELD LA

Forbe's Fields

PRINCE CONSORT'S DR

74

				67

C5
1 CAMPERDOWN HO
2 WARWICK CT
3 CHELMSFORD CT
4 HOUSTON CT
5 ELIZABETH CT
6 TRANSCEND

7 CROSSWAYS CT
8 KNIGHT'S PL
9 OSBORNE LODGE
10 ABERDEEN LODGE
C6
1 CAMBRIDGE HO
2 WARD ROYAL PAR

3 CHRISTIAN SQ
4 CRESCENT VILLAS
5 WARD ROYAL
6 BOWES-LYON CL
7 MOUNTBATTEN SQ
8 CHARLES HO
9 QUEEN ANNE'S CT

D6
1 CASTLEVIEW HO
2 HORSESHOE CLOISTERS
3 LODGINGS OF THE MILITARY KNIGHTS
4 HENRY III TWR
5 Windsor Royal Sta
6 KING EDWARD CT

42

7 AMBERLEY PL
8 MARKET ST
9 CHURCH ST
10 QUEEN CHARLOTTE ST
11 CHURCH LA
12 ST ALBANS CL
13 RED BRICK COTTS

68

14 BURFORD HO
15 COPPERFIELD HO
16 PEASCOD PL
17 MELLOR WLK
18 ROYAL FREE CT
19 SUN PAS
20 HIBBERT'S ALLEY

21 CHARLOTT'S PL
22 ELLISON HO
23 SHENSTON CT
24 WESSEX CT
25 RALSTON CT

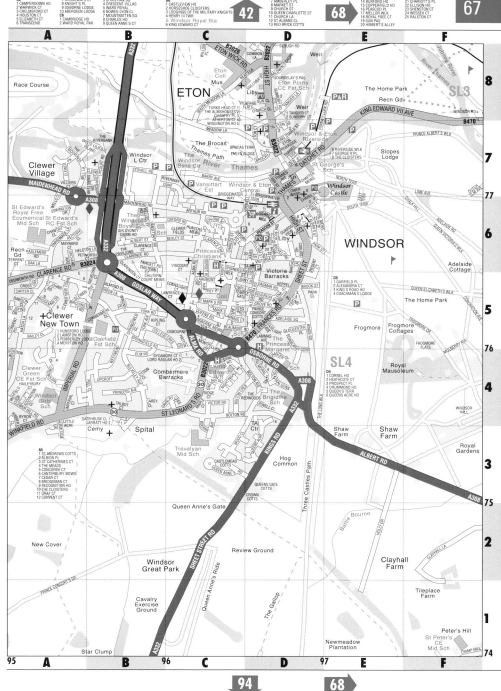

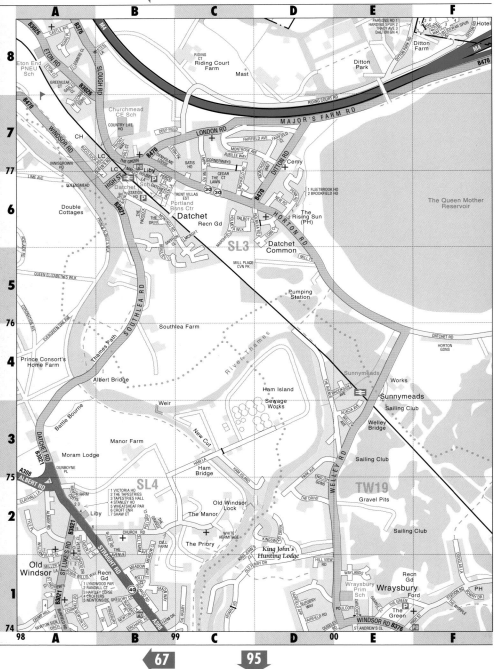

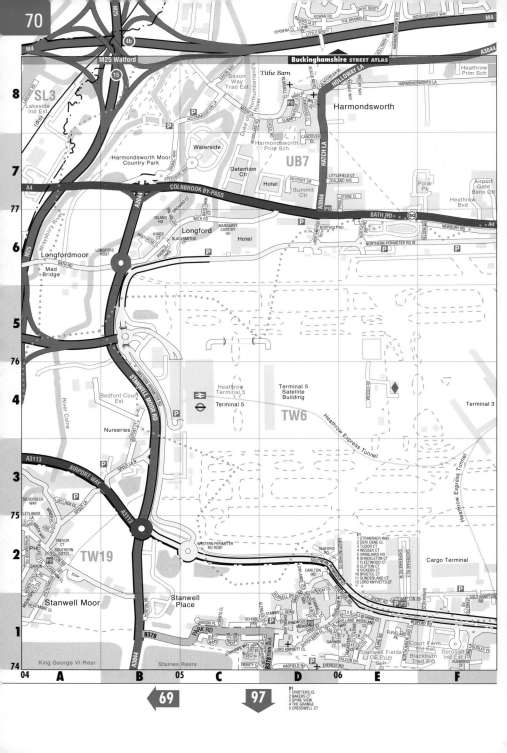

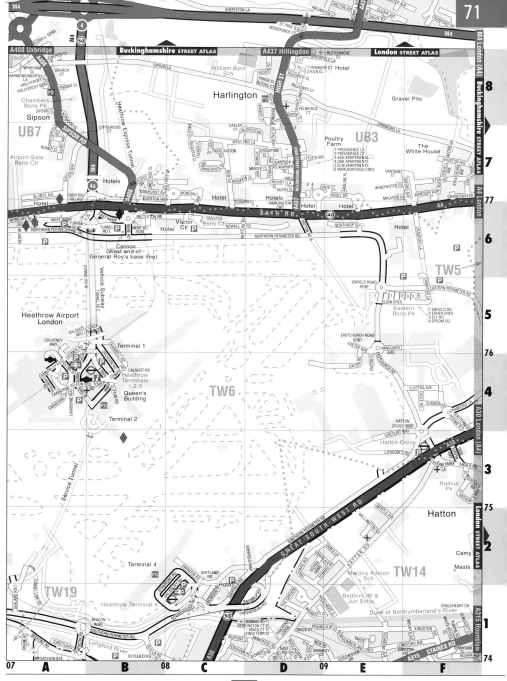

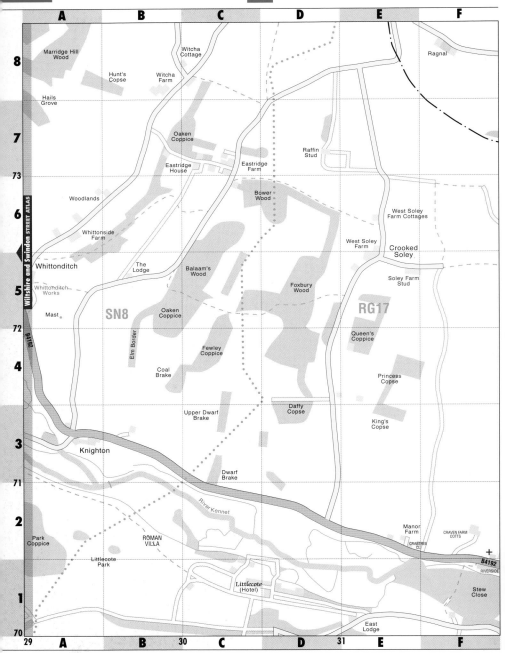

A **B** **C** **D** **E** **F**

8
Marridge Hill Wood
Witcha Cottage
Ragnal
Hunt's Copse
Witcha Farm

Hails Grove

7
Oaken Coppice
Raffin Stud

73
Eastridge House
Eastridge Farm

Woodlands
Bower Wood
West Soley Farm Cottages

6
Whittonside Farm
West Soley Farm
Crooked Soley

Whittonditch
The Lodge
Balaam's Wood
Soley Farm Stud

5
Whittonditch Works
Foxbury Wood

Mast
SN8
Oaken Coppice
RG17

72
Queen's Coppice

4
Fewley Coppice
Princess Copse

Coal Brake

Upper Dwarf Brake
Daffy Copse
King's Copse

3
Knighton

71
Dwarf Brake

River Kennet

2
Manor Farm
CRAVEN FARM COTTS

Park Coppice
ROMAN VILLA
CRABTREE CL

Littlecote Park
B4192
RIVERSIDE

1
Littlecote (Hotel)
Stew Close

70
East Lodge

29 **A** **B** 30 **C** **D** 31 **E** **F**

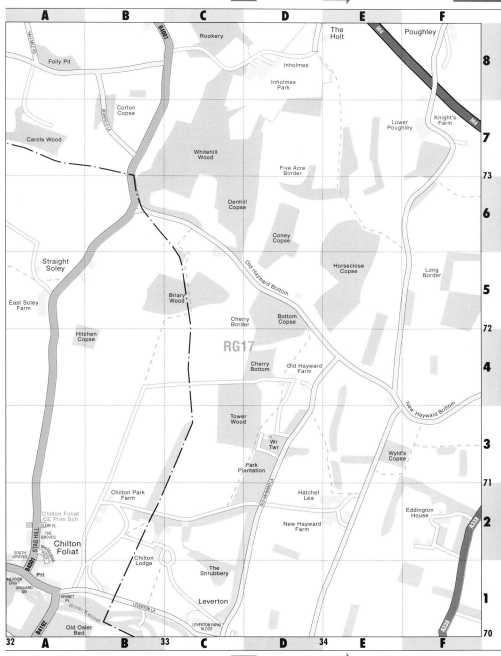

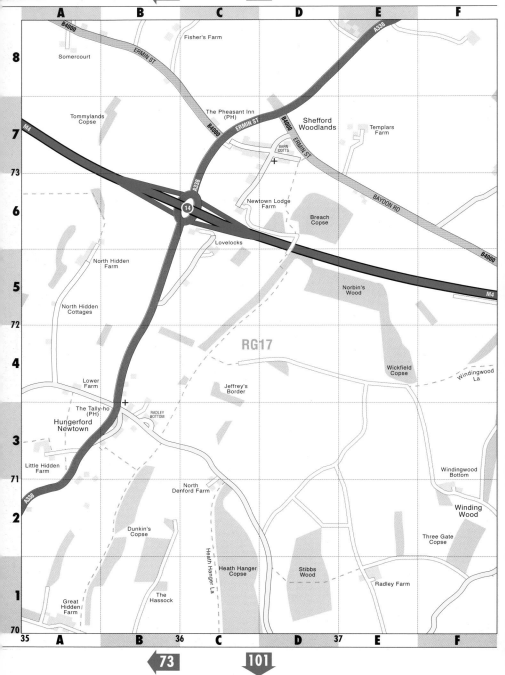

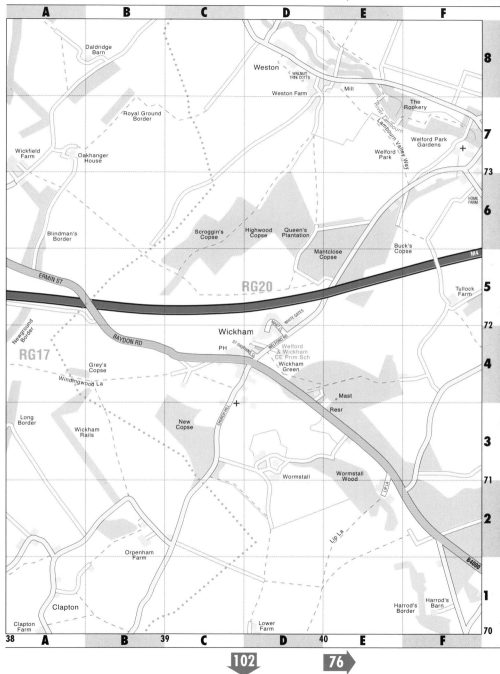

| | A | B | C | D | E | F |

8

Bradleywood Farm

Grove Corner

7

Welford Farm

Welford

73

M4

6

M4

Tullock Bottom

Westbrook Farm

Easton Farm

Borough Copse

5

SWEDISH HOS

Easton

River Lambourn

Knapps Farm

Showells

72

EASTON HILL

ROOD HILL

Westbrook

RG20

4

Boxford Farm

Sole Border

SHEPHERD'S HILL

SCHOOL LA

WINTERBOURNE RD

PH

SOUTHFIELDS

Boxford

3

Sole Farm

High Street Farm

Woodmansfield Cottages

Hoar Hill

71

HIGH ST

2

Sole Plantation

Ownham Old Farm

Moorbridge Farm

Upper Farm

Ownham

1

B4000

ERMIN ST

Ownham Plantation

B4000

Ownham Lower Farm

COOMBESBURY LA

Coombesbury Farm

William's Copse

Hunt's Green

Jannaways

70

| 41 | A | | B | 42 | C | | D | 43 | E | | F |

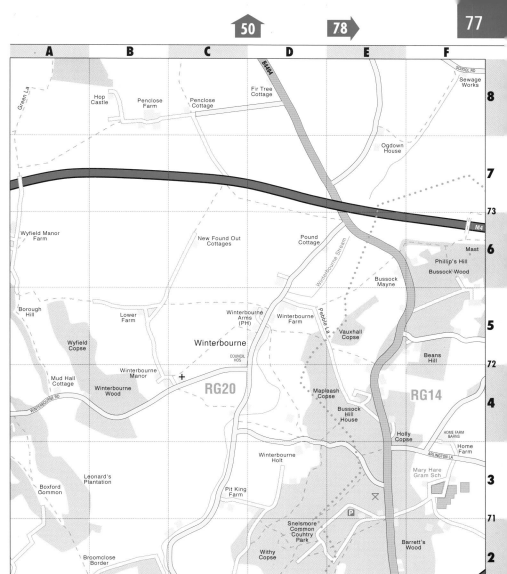

Green La

A B C D E F

SCHOOL RD
Sewage
Works

8

Fir Tree
Cottage

Hop
Castle

Penclose
Farm

Penclose
Cottage

Ogdown
House

Wyfield Manor
Farm

New Found Out
Cottages

Pound
Cottage

Winterbourne Stream

M4

73

7

Mast

Phillip's Hill

Bussock Wood

6

Bussock
Mayne

Borough
Hill

Lower
Farm

Winterbourne
Arms
(PH)

Winterbourne
Farm

Pebble La

Vauxhall
Copse

Beans
Hill

5

Wyfield
Copse

Winterbourne

COUNCIL
HOS

72

Mud Hall
Cottage

Winterbourne
Manor

+

RG20

Mapleash
Copse

RG14

4

Winterbourne
Wood

WINTERBOURNE RD

Bussock
Hill
House

Holly
Copse

HOME FARM
BARNS

Home
Farm

ARLINGTON LA

Leonard's
Plantation

Winterbourne
Holt

Mary Hare
Gram Sch

3

Boxford
Common

Pit King
Farm

P

71

Snelsmore
Common
Country
Park

Barrett's
Wood

Broomclose
Border

Withy
Copse

2

Sheppard's
Copse

A34

Honeybottom

Swilly
Copse

Copse
Barn

Mount
Hill

Bagnor
Marsh

Snelsmore
House

1

Bagnor
Wood

Ashpiece
Copse

Hill's
Pightle

A34

B4494

70

44 A 45 B C 46 D E F

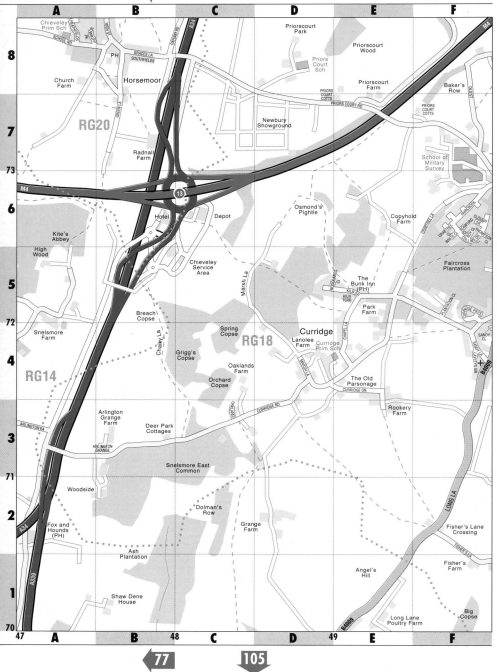

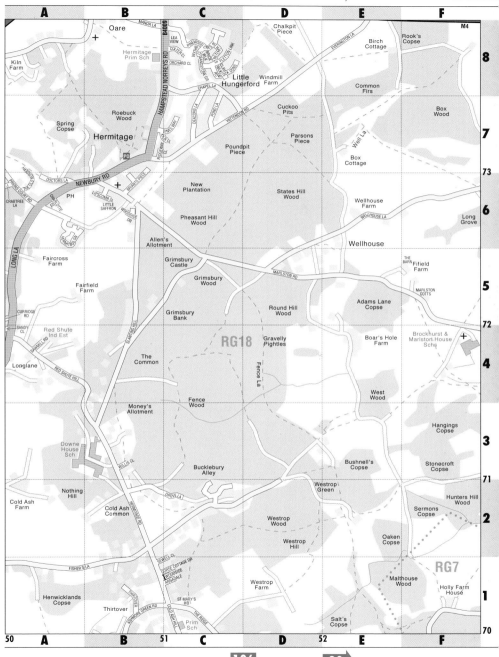

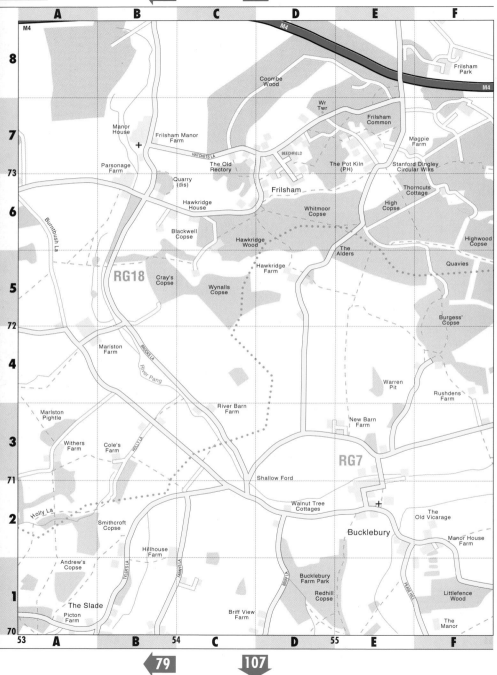

M4

8

7

73

6

5

72

4

3

71

2

1

70

A   B   C   D   E   F

Coombe Wood

Frilsham Park

M4

Wr Twr

Frilsham Common

Manor House

Frilsham Manor Farm

HATCHETS LA

BEECHFIELD

Magpie Farm

Parsonage Farm

The Old Rectory

The Pot Kiln (PH)

Stanford Dingley Circular Wlks

Quarry (dis)

Frilsham

Thorncuts Cottage

Hawkridge House

Whitmoor Copse

High Copse

Highwood Copse

Blackwell Copse

Hawkridge Wood

The Alders

Burntbush La

RG18

Cray's Copse

Hawkridge Farm

Quavies

Wynalls Copse

Burgess' Copse

Marlston Farm

BROOKS LA

River Pang

Warren Pit

Rushdens Farm

Marlston Pightle

River Barn Farm

New Barn Farm

Withers Farm

Cole's Farm

HOLLY LA

RG7

Shallow Ford

Walnut Tree Cottages

The Old Vicarage

Holly La

Smithcroft Copse

Bucklebury

Manor House Farm

Hillhouse Farm

TYLER'S LA

BUSHNELL LA

BRIFF LA

Bucklebury Farm Park

PEASE HILL

The Old Vicarage

Andrew's Copse

Redhill Copse

Littlefence Wood

The Slade

Picton Farm

Briff View Farm

The Manor

53   A   B   54   C   D   55   E   F

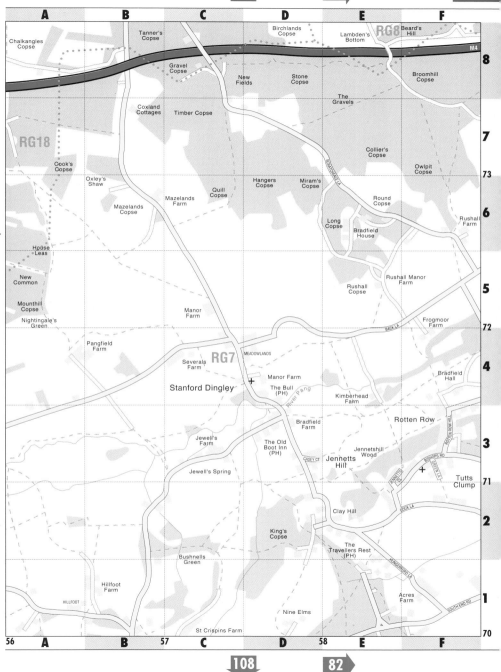

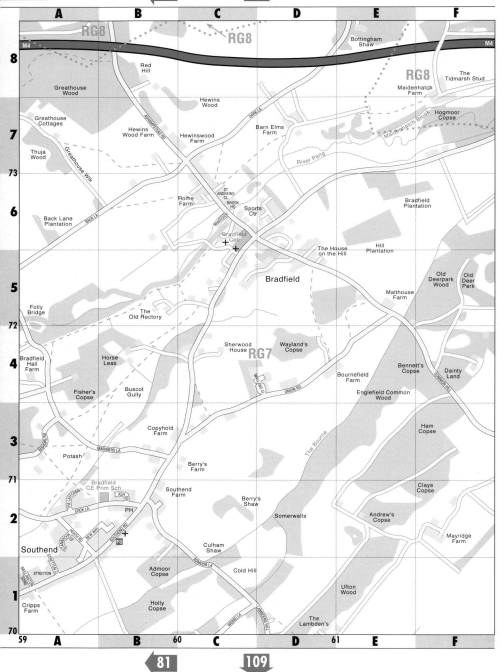

A
B
C
D
E
F
8
7
73
6
5
72
4
3
71
2
1
70
65
66
67
RG8
Little Heath
Hallplace Farm
Beal's Copse
Boxgrove Wood
Liby
Little Heath Sch
Springfield Prim Sch
Birch Copse Prim Sch
Park Lane Prim Sch
St Paul's RC Prim Sch
Sch Annexe
Moorlands Prim Sch
Upcroft Prim Sch
Churchend
Churchend Prim Sch
Churchend Copse
RG30
RG31
Hall
Hypermarket
Pincents Kiln Ind Pk
Calcot Row
Horncastle
CH
Schs
BATH RD
A4
M4
Low La
Underwood Sh Ctr
Kennet Valley Prim Sch
Beansheaf Community Centre
Calcot
Holy Brook
Calcot Mill House
Arlington Bsns Pk
LC
Arrow Head
River Kennet
Kennet and Avon Canal
Mill Dam
Burghfield Mill
DEWE LA
Burghfield Farm
MILL RD
RG7
Landing Stage
Moatlands Cottages
Reading Service Area
Motel
BURGHFIELD BRIDGE CL
BERRYS LA
GARSTON PARK HOME VILLAGE 1
FOURTH AVE 2
THIRD AVE 3
FIFTH AVE 4
SIXTH AVE 5
NINTH AVE 6
EIGHTH AVE 7
TENTH AVE 8
WILTSHIRE WLK 1
WOODBRIDGE RD 2
PENNINE CL 3
1 KEMERTON CL
2 KIRKSTALL CT
3 KEMBLE CT
4 KILBURN CL
SANDHILLS WAY 1
HARGREAVES WAY 2
BROOKSIDE 3
LADYMASK CL 4
LAMPLIGHTERS WLK 5
GREENCROFT GDNS 6
TUSCAN CL 1
MINTON CL 2
CHELSEA CL 3
HOLKAM CL 4
DARTINGTON CL 5
STAFFORDSHIRE CL 6
CORNERSTONES 7
HILL VIEW MEWS 8
MARY LYNE ALMSHOS 1
HORROCKS HO 2
BAMFORD PL 1
BANCROFT PL 2
SWISS COTTAGE CL 1
HOLFORD CL 2

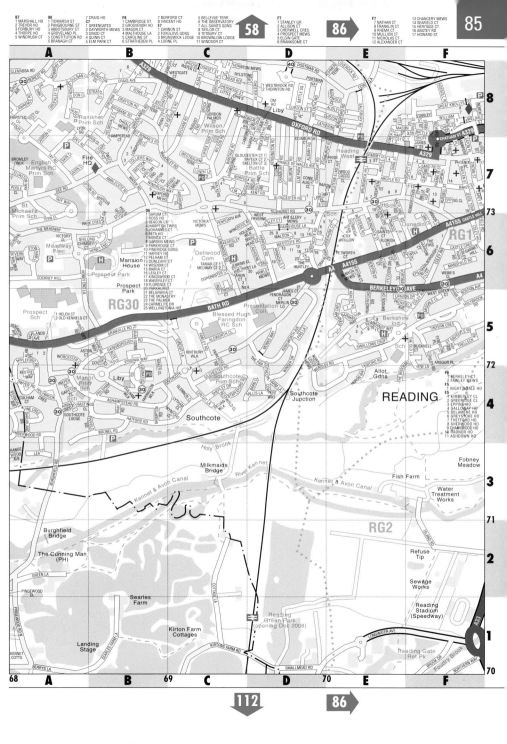

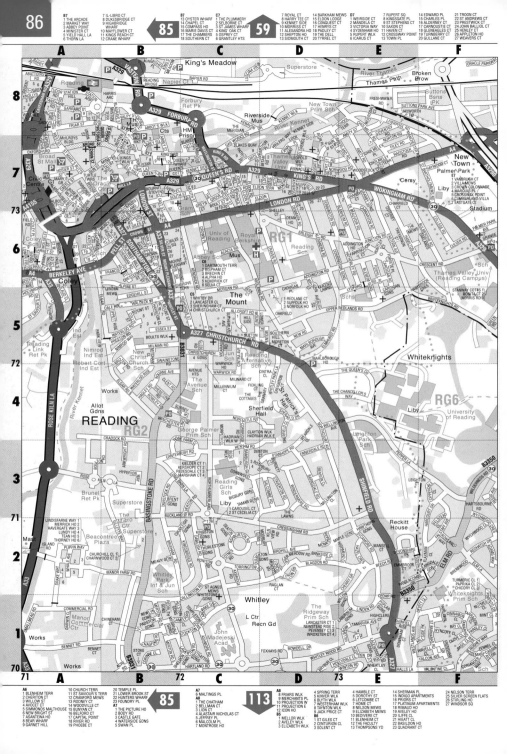

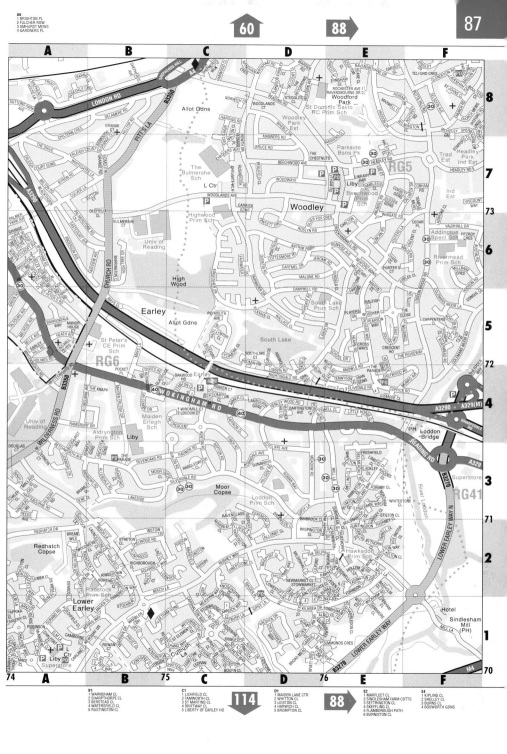

87 61

Grid columns: A B C D E F
Grid rows: 8 7 73 6 5 72 4 3 71 2 1 70

Woodley
Alder Moors
Sandford Farm
Whistley Park
Diamond Villas
Woodley CE Prim Sch
Sandford Park
Nursery Cl
Braybrooke Dr
Nicholas CE Prim Sch
Magnolia Ct
Hurst
Nursery
Woodley Green
RG5
Sandford Mill
Hurst House
The Castle Inn (PH)
Almshouses
Colemans Moor Rd
The Mus of Berkshire Aviation
Black Bridge
Lavell's Lake
Lea Farm
Sandfordmill Copse
1 Sopwith Cl
2 Vickers Cl
River Loddon
Sandford Lake
Hurst Grove
Heron's Water
Dinton Pastures Country Park
The Jolly Farmer (PH)
Hatch Gate Farm
Middle Marsh
White Swan Lake
Black Swan Lake
RG10
St Nicholas Farm
The Moor
Emm Brook
Dinton Pastures
Darvells Farm
Mungell's Pond
High Chimneys
Coronation Cotts
PH
Furze Covert
A329(M)
Eskdale Rd
Wharfedale Rd
Winnersh Triangle
Winnersh Triangle Ind Est
RG41
Windermere
Sylvester Rd
Merryhill
The Priory
Colts Bridge
Merryhill Green
Grovelands Avenue Workshops
A329
Arbor La
Winnersh
Forest Sch
Library
Winnersh Prim Sch
Grovelands Pk
1 Alderney Gdns
2 Fieldway
3 Birchmead
4 Donnington Pl
Bearwood Path
Reading Rd
Winnersh
Garth Cl
Eastbury Park
Winnersh Gate
RG40
Toutley Bridge
Beckford Cl
Jun Sch
River Loddon
Mill La
M4
Sandford Ct
Sandstone Cl
Longdon Rd
Laburnum Rd
Highgrove Ct
Forest Lodge
Inf Sch

87 115

A2
1 Lydiaville Mobile Home Pk
2 Bearwood Park Mobile Home Pk
A3
1 Cavendish Gdns
2 Belvedere Wlk
3 Fenchurch Mews
4 Riverdene Dr

B2
1 Westbrook Ct
2 Harman Ct
3 Hunters Ct

C2
1 English Ct
2 Stevens Ct
3 Bonham Ct

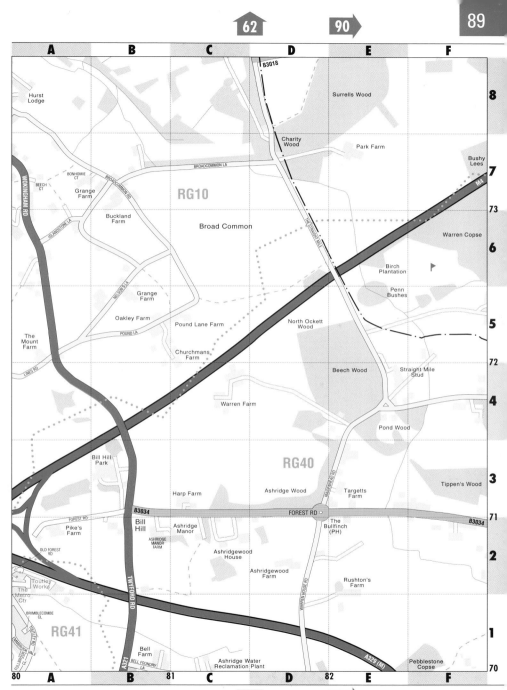

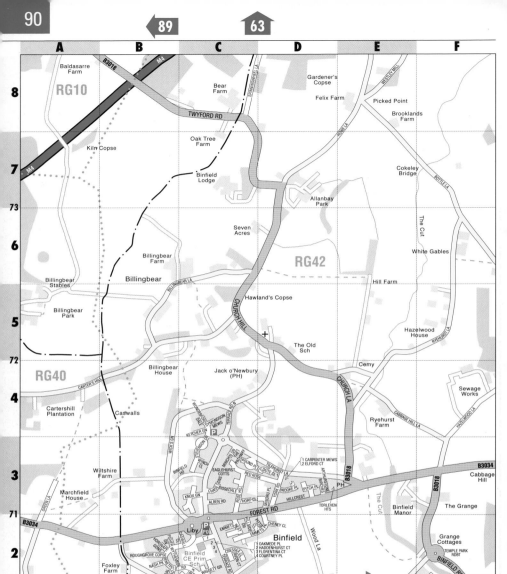

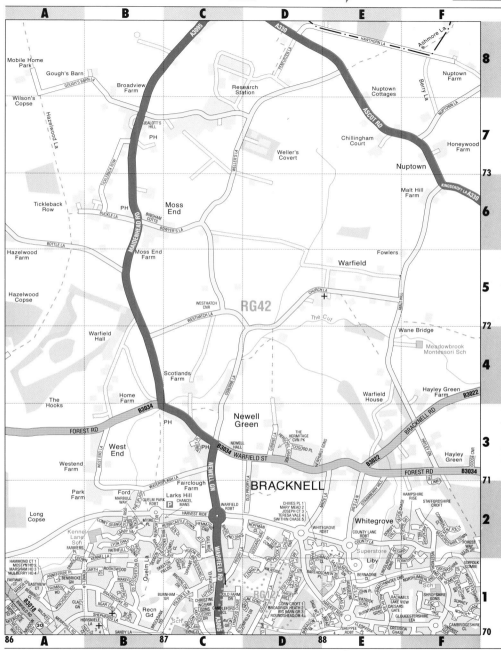

A B C D E F

8

7

73

6

5

72

4

3

71

2

1

70

SL4

Park Pale

Winkfield Plain Farm

Old Dairy Farm

Steven's Copse

Chawridge Manor Farm

Five Acres

Ash Farm

Tally Ho Farm

Hope Farm

WINKFIELD LA

Whitelock's Farm

BISHOP'S LA

CHAWRIDGE LA

FLORENCE COTTS

Stroud's Copse

A330

KINGSCROFT LA COCK'S LA

Abbey Farm

WINKFIELD ST

Handpost Farm

B3022

MAIDEN'S GN

Crown and Anchor (PH)

Maiden's Green

CHURCH RD

POPEL'S COTTS

ST MARY'S LA

Winkfield

Training Stables

Brock Hill

BRACKNELL RD

BROCK HILL COTTS

PARKER'S LA

THE HIGH PINES

The White Hart (PH)

RYMER'S LA

CHEVAL STUD FARM

Gallops

NORTH ST

Windmill Hill

HOPE COTTS

Planner's Farm

Sewage Works

PIGEONHOUSE LA

B3022

Brockhill Farm

B3017

RG42

Brockhill House

BRAITERS LA

The Belt

A330 LOVEL RD

Plaistow Green

Sch

B3022

CRICKETERS LA

GROVE LA

WINKFIELD ROW

Lambrook Haileybury Sch

Winkfield St Mary's CE Prim Sch

Round Copse

Ascot Place

P

B3034

Somerton Farm

71

CHAVEY DOWN RD

Winkfield Row

FOREST RD

B3034

2

FOREST WAY

THE ELMS

Recn Gd

New Covert

WINKFIELD MANOR

The Spinney

SL5

Brookside

BISHOPS CT

RANALD CT 1
RANALD COURT COTTS 2
GARDEN MEWS 3

The Rough

Warfield Park

Winkfield Row

MUSHROOM CASTLE

OSMAN'S CL

GORSE PL

LOCKS RIDE

B3017

1 KING EDWARDS RD
2 QUEEN'S CL
3 KING EDWARDS RISE
4 LAVENDER ROW
5 ADMIRAL KAPPLE CT
6 DRUMMOND CT

WELLINGTONIAS

Newell Green

Big Wood

1 LIME TREE COPSE
2 MACLAREN DR
3 CHESTNUT CHASE

THE LARCHES

MANOR CT

YEW CL

THE PLATEAU

Ascot Stud Farm

The Dell

Ascot Stud Farm

Ascot Heath Inf Sch

Ascot Heath CE Jun Sch

FERNBANK RD

BEECHWOOD AV

BRIDGE BRACKENBURY WALK

ST JOHN'S

KENNEL LA

OAKLANDS CT

89 A B 90 C D 91 E F

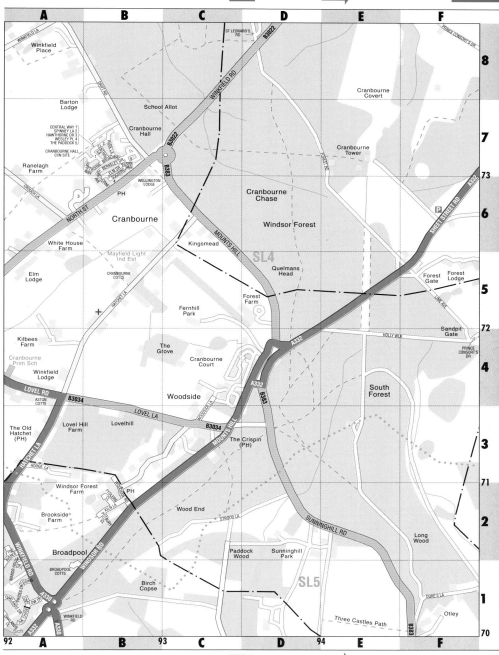

A **B** **C** **D** **E** **F**

8

A332

SHEET STREET RD

Bear's
Rails

Cemy

Rush
Pond

BEMPS CHELSEA

Prince of Wales
Pond

Bear's Rails
Pond

Battle Bourne

The Gallop

The Long Walk

Pickleherring
Pond

P

7

A332

Ranger's
Lodge

Beehive
Hill

Seymours
Plantation

73

Russel's
Pond

Fiddle
Covert

6

PRINCE CONSORT'S DR

Statue

Snow
Hill

Spring
Hill

Cookes Hill

Richardson's
Lawn

SL4

Three Castles Path

5

Isle of
Wight Pond

PO

RICHARDSON'S
LAWN COTTS

THE VILLAGE

QUEEN ANNE'S CL

The
Village

Deepstrood

Royal
Lodge

MAIN GATE
LODGES

BISHOPSGATE RD

The Fox &
Hounds
(PH)

Poets
Lawn

+

72

Queen Anne's Ride

Windsor Great Park

4

Dark
Wood

DUKE'S LA

Cow
Pond

Bishopsgate

Chapel
Wood

PARK CLOSE
COTTS

3

Hilton's
Covert

MEZEL HILL
COTTS

The Royal
Fst Sch

CUMBERLAND
LODGE

RHODODENDRON RIDE

PARK RD

The Sun
(PH)

Mezel
Hill

Square
Covert

Great
Meadow
Pond

Wilderness

Park
Close

71

Parkside
House

The Savill
Gardens

2

Leiper
Hill

Slans
Hill

Temple
Hill

TW20

P

Obelisk

SL5

Mill
Pond

Norfolk
Farm

Smith's
Lawn

Obelisk
Pond

1

Rosy
Bottom

Norfolk
Plantation

Statue

Polo Gds

70

A **C** **B** **E** **F**
D

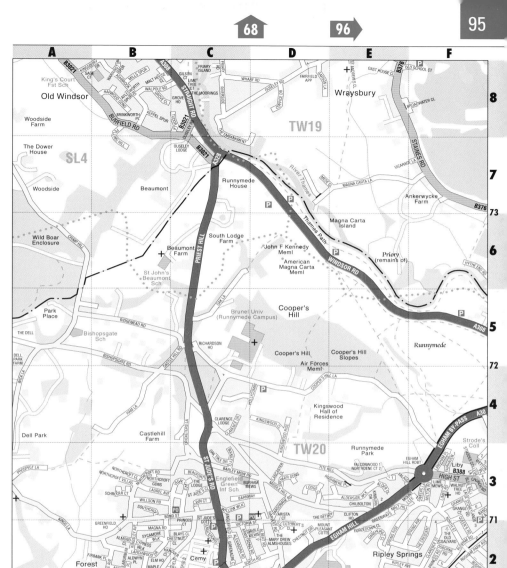

Old Windsor

Wraysbury

Woodside
Farm

The Dower
House

SL4

TW19

Woodside

Runnymede
House

Wild Boar
Enclosure

Beaumont

Beaumont
Farm

South Lodge
Farm

St John's
Beaumont
Sch

Magna Carta
Island

Magna Carta
Meml

John F Kennedy
Meml

American
Magna Carta
Meml

Ankerwycke
Farm

Priory
(remains of)

Park
Place

Bishopsgate
Sch

THE DELL

DELL
PARK
FARM

Brunel Univ
(Runnymede Campus)

Cooper's
Hill

Cooper's Hill
Air Forces
Meml

Cooper's Hill
Slopes

Runnymede

Dell Park

Castlehill
Farm

Clarence
Lodge

Kingswood
Hall of
Residence

Egham
Hill Rdbt

TW20

Runnymede
Park

Strode's
Coll

Liby
B388
HIGH ST

Englefield
Green Inf Sch

Forest
Estate

Cemy

St Jude's
CE Sch

Ripley Springs

1 WOODBINE COTTS
2 PEEL HO
3 HOLLOWAY CT
4 CLARENCE CT
5 WINDMILL SHOTT

Englefield
Green

1 HIGHFIELD CL
2 PENROSE CT
3 HIGHFIELD CT
4 VICTORIA MEWS

Liby

Royal Holloway
Univ of London

Egham
Wick

Bakeham
House

Prune
Hill

Rusham
Farm

Research
Laboratories

CROWN
COTTS

F3
1 FAIRHAVEN CT
2 LITTLECROFT RD
3 TAMARIND CT
4 HIGH ST
5 STATION RD N
6 STONEYLAND CT

Map

A | B | C | D | E | F

Wraysbury Resr

TW19

Bone Head

Works
RUNNYMEDE COTTS

River Colne

Sailing Club

Staines Moor

Colne Brook

B376
STAINES RD
Hythe End
B376
13
The Moor
PH
Church Lammas

STAINES

Staines Moor

Bonehead Ditch

Colne Valley Way

Wraysbury River

STAINES BY-PASS

River Ash

A30

WRAYSBURY RD

GLOUCESTER DR

A308
WINDSOR RD

Queensmead Lake (Resr)

Holm Island
Thames Path

Hotel

RUNNYMEDE RDBT

EGHAM

1 HAZEL LODGE
2 ROSE LODGE
3 RUNNYMEDE CT

A30
EGHAM BY-PASS
STRODE RD
MANDEVILLE
CEDAR CT
THE AVENUE
GREEN LA

River Thames

Works
Works

THE GLANTY A308
The Green Bsns Ctr

Watermans Bsns Pk

THE CAUSEWAY

CLARENCE ST
THAMES ST
SOUTH ST

Superstore

Mus
Liby

Ind Est

Causeway

WREN CT
HIGH
PO
Mus
B388
CHURCH RD

HIGH

MANOR CT
DAISY MEAD

LC

Hythe Prim Sch

RAILWAY TERR

Pine Trees Bsns Pk

BEECH LODGE FARM
MONSELL GDNS

Egham

Sports Ctr

VICARAGE RD

DUGDALE HO

CHAUCER CT

1 ST NAZAIRE CL
2 RHODES CT
3 FLANDERS CT
4 NORMANDY WLK

WENDOVER RD

OLD SCHOOL LA

WAPSHOTT RD

THE PADDOCKS

COLLEGE RD
VICARAGE CT

Mahorcroft Prim Sch

1 RUSHAM PARK AVE
2 BRAYWOOD AVE
3 RUSHAM TERR

Pooley Green
PO

MEAD CT
ARGENT CL
PRIORY CT

1 ROYDON CT
2 MILLER'S CT

The Magna Carta Sch

Egham Hythe

RIVERBANK
EDGECOMBE CT

TW18

TW20

Lodge

Milton Park

Nurseries

Thorpe Lea

B3376 THORPE LEA RD

Thorpe Lea Prim Sch

Egham Hythe

BARRINGTON CT
ARGOSY GDNS
DUNCOMBE CT
THAMES BANK
SWANDRIFT
ONSLOW LODGE
WYTHEGATE
NUTBOURNE CT
GLEN CT
WHEATSHEAF LA

GLOCKHOUSE LA W
GLOCKHOUSE LA E

Mead Lake Ditch

WARWICK AVE

FERRY AVE
A320

A B 02 C D 03 E F

A3
1 ST CATHERINES PL
2 NICHOLSON WLK
3 REGENTS HO
4 WINDSOR HO
5 SAVILLE HO
6 ETON HO
7 ASCOT HO
8 HERITAGE CT
9 CADDY CL

10 THE OLD BAKERY
11 WILLOWBROOK CT
12 HENLEY CT
13 RUNNYMEDE HO
14 TOWER CT
15 CHANCERY CT
16 GALLERY CT
17 CHAPTER CT
18 TUDOR CT
19 STEEPLE CT

20 MANOR FARM
21 TUDOR CT
B1
1 WINDERMERE CL
2 CONISTON WAY
3 BORROWDALE CL
4 BUTTERMERE WAY
5 GRASMERE CL

E4
1 ALDOUS HO
2 THAMES EDGE CT
3 COLNEBRIDGE CL

F3
1 FRIENDS WLK
2 WESTBROOK RD
3 BRACKLEY HO
4 MANSFIELD HO
5 CRESCENT CT
6 ABBEY LODGE
7 LAZARE CT
8 REGATTA HO
9 BOSSINGTON CT

10 TROSTON CT
11 IFFLEY CT
12 LAUDERDALE CT
13 AMBER CT
14 THE CYGNETS

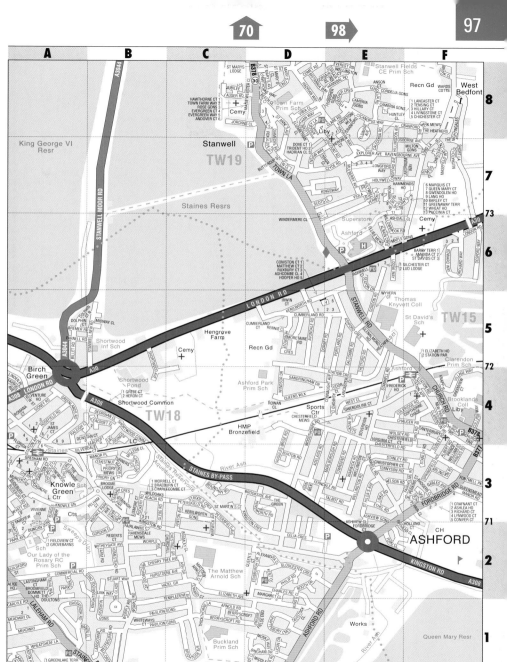

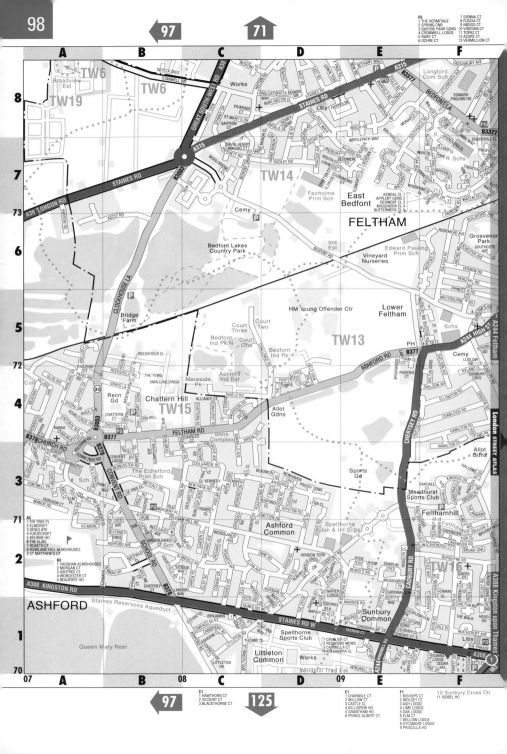

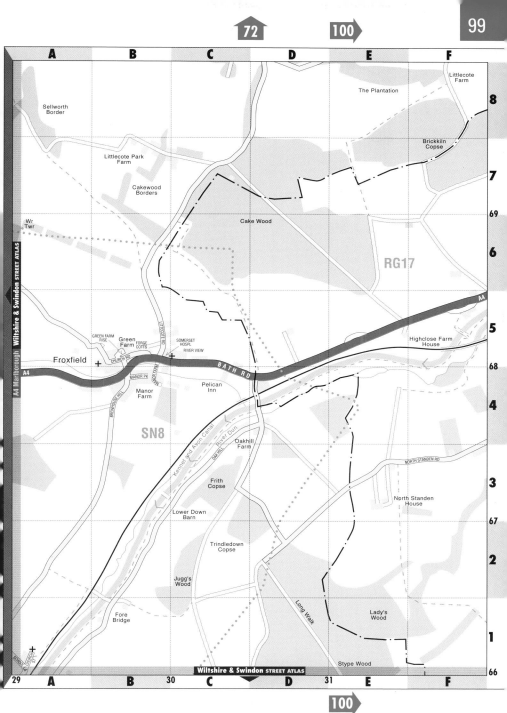

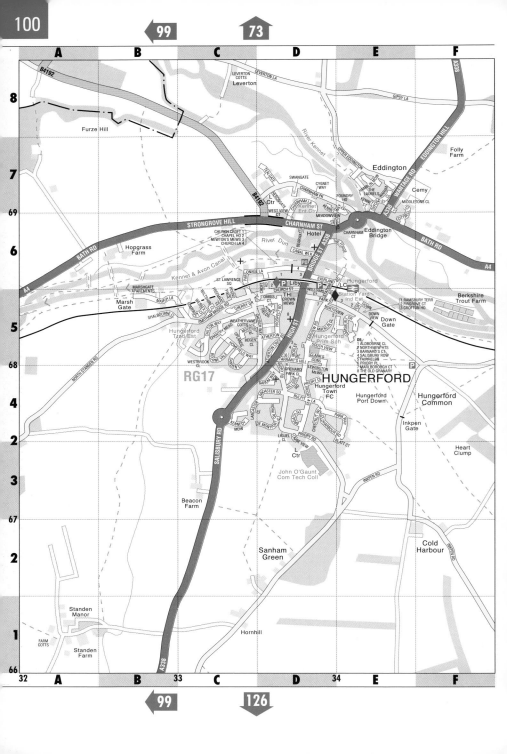

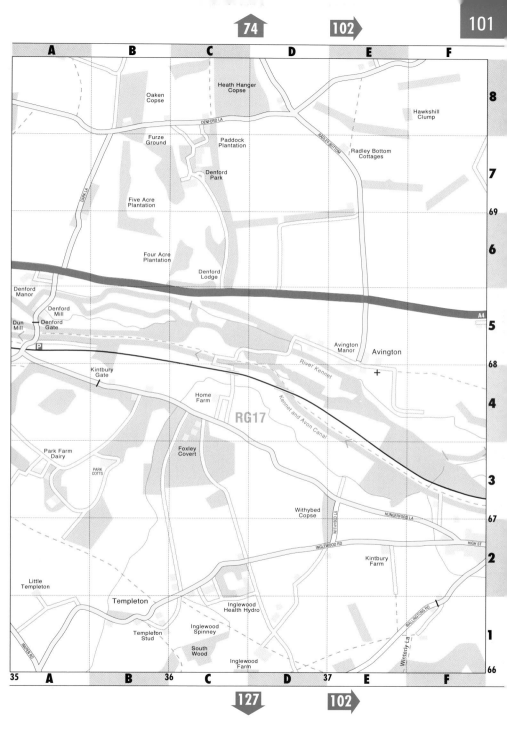

8

A B C D E F

Oaken
Copse

Heath Hanger
Copse

Hawkshill
Clump

DENFORD LA

Furze
Ground

Paddock
Plantation

RADLEY BOTTOM

Radley Bottom
Cottages

Denford
Park

DARK LA

7

Five Acre
Plantation

69

Four Acre
Plantation

6

Denford
Lodge

Denford
Manor

Denford
Mill

A4

Dun
Mill

Denford
Gate

5

P

Avington
Manor

Avington

Kintbury
Gate

River Kennet

68

Home
Farm

Kennet and Avon Canal

RG17

4

Park Farm
Dairy

Foxley
Covert

PARK
COTTS

3

Withybed
Copse

WITHYBED LA

HUNGERFORD LA

67

INGLEWOOD RD

HIGH ST

Little
Templeton

Kintbury
Farm

2

Templeton

Inglewood
Health Hydro

WALLINGTONS RD

Templeton
Stud

Inglewood
Spinney

South
Wood

Inglewood
Farm

Winterly La

1

35 A B 36 C D 37 E F 66

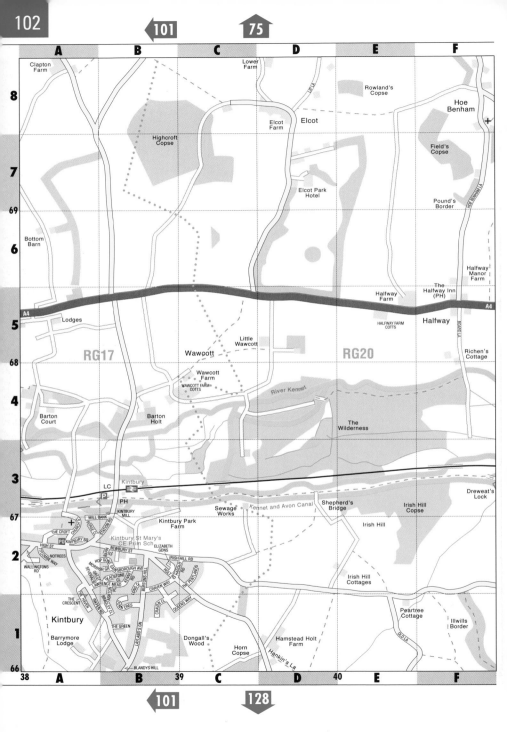

101
75

A B C D E F

8

Clapton
Farm

Lower
Farm

Rowland's
Copse

Hoe
Benham

Elcot
Farm

Elcot

Highcroft
Copse

Field's
Copse

7

Elcot Park
Hotel

Pound's
Border

69

Bottom
Barn

Halfway
Manor
Farm

6

The
Halfway Inn
(PH)

Halfway
Farm

A4

5

Lodges

HALFWAY FARM
COTTS

Halfway

Richen's
Cottage

RG17

Wawcott

Little
Wawcott

RG20

68

Wawcott
Farm

WAWCOTT FARM
COTTS

River Kennet

4

Barton
Court

Barton
Holt

The
Wilderness

3

Kintbury

Dreweat's
Lock

LC

P

PH

Sewage
Works

Kennet and Avon Canal

Shepherd's
Bridge

Irish Hill
Copse

67

MILL BANK

KINTBURY
MILL

Kintbury Park
Farm

Irish Hill

THE CROFT

CHURCH ST

STATION RD

Kintbury St Mary's
CE Prim Sch

PO

KINTBURY SQ

NEWBURY ST

ELIZABETH
GDNS

2

HIGH ST

NOTREES

IRISH HILL RD

Irish Hill
Cottages

WALLINGTONS
RD

GLADSTONE

CRAVEN WAY

THE PENTHAVES

THE CRESCENT

Peartree
Cottage

Illwills
Border

1

Kintbury

THE GREEN

Barrymore
Lodge

Dongall's
Wood

Horn
Copse

Hamstead Holt
Farm

Hankin's La

66

BLANDYS HILL

38

A

B

39

C

D

40

E

F

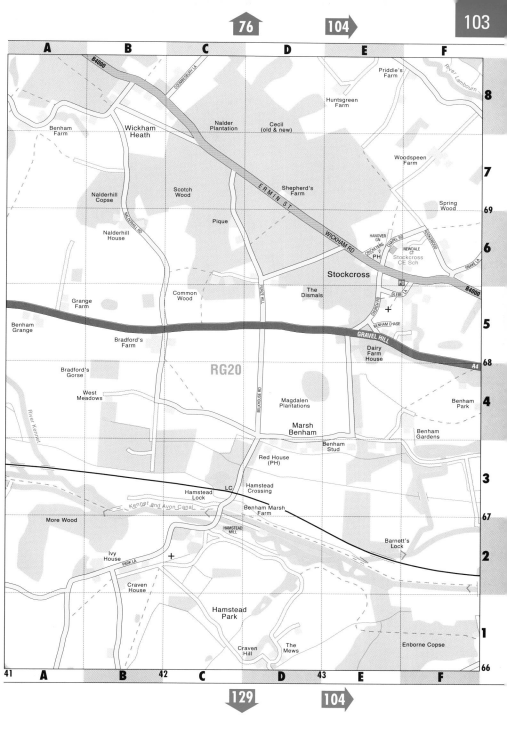

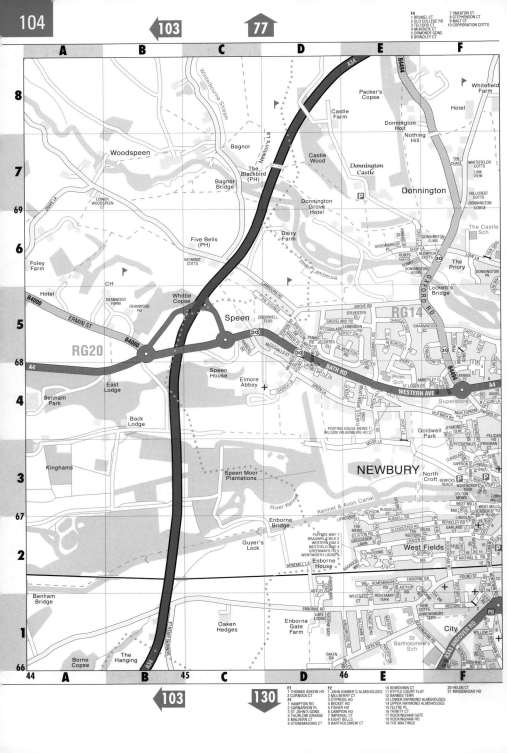

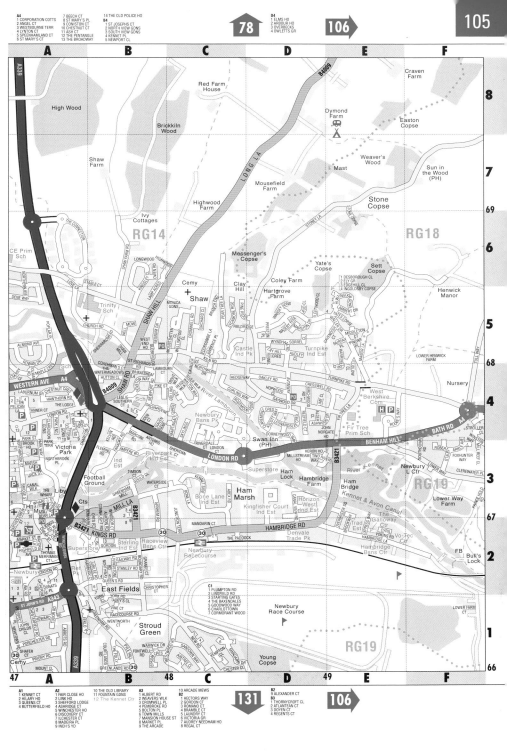

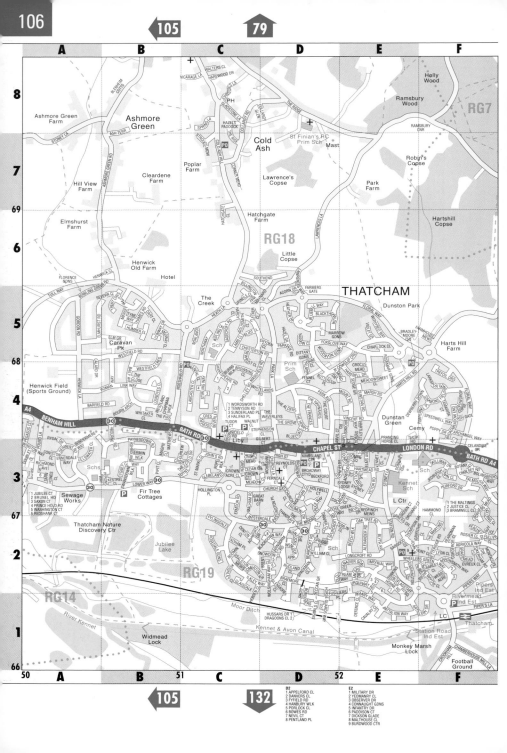

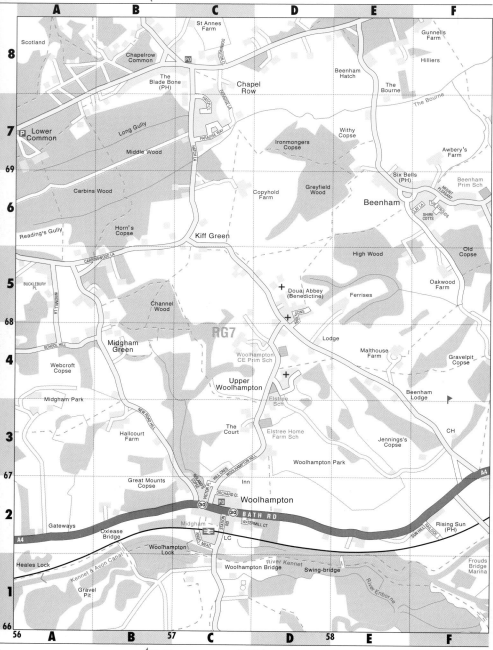

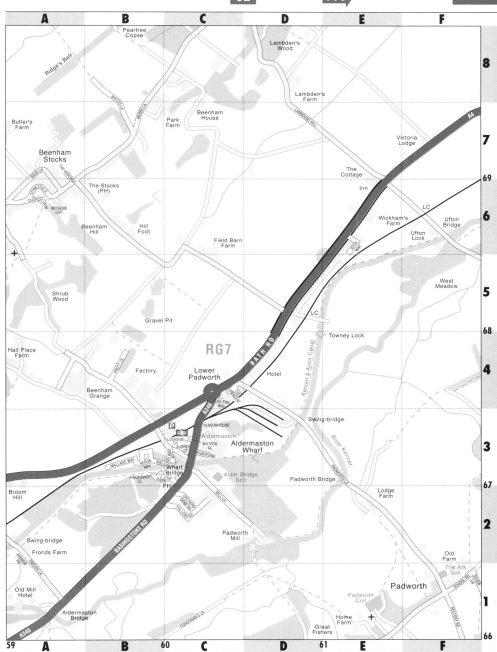

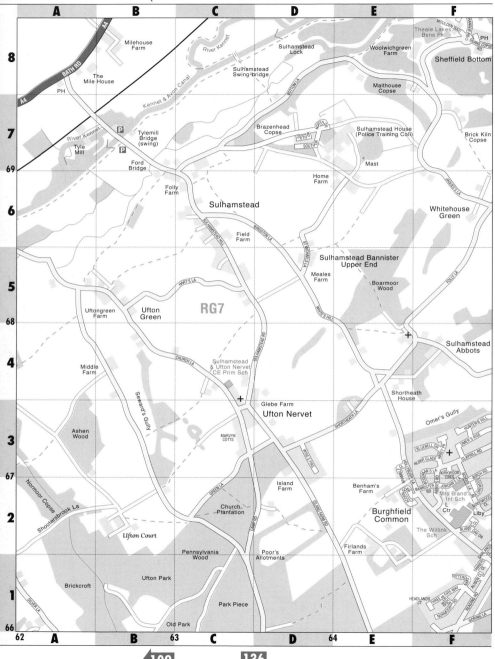

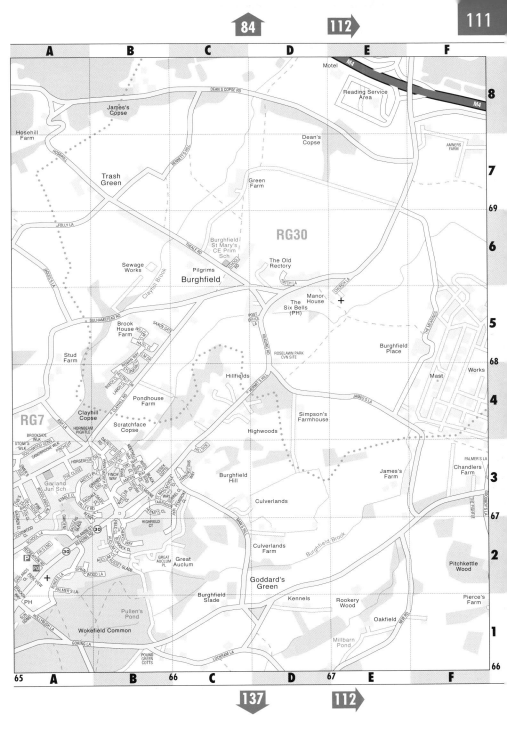

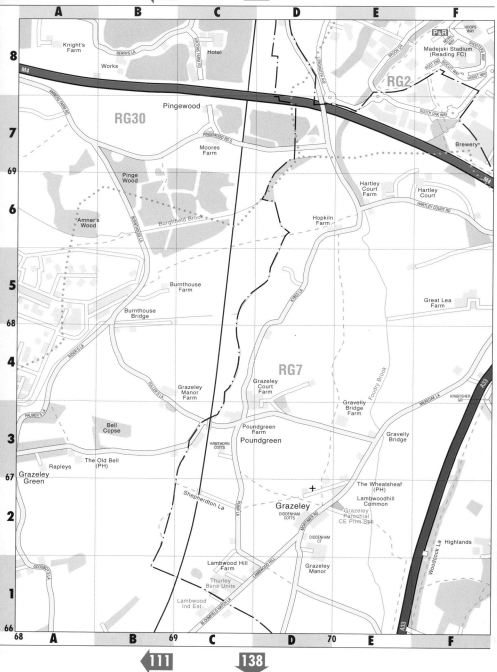

111
85

A   **B**   **C**   **D**   **E**   **F**

8

Knight's
Farm

BERRYS LA

KITTONS FARM RD

Hotel

P&R

HOOPS
WAY

REVEL WAY

BEVAL WAY

Madejski Stadium
(Reading FC)

BOOT END

BISCUIT WAY

SHOOTERS WAY

HURST WAY

Works

M4

RG2

RG30

Pingewood

SOUTH OAK WAY

7

PINGEWOOD RD S

Moores
Farm

Brewery

69

Pinge
Wood

Hartley
Court
Farm

Hartley
Court

BURNTHOUSE LA

Burghfield Brook

Hopkiln
Farm

HARTLEY COURT RD

M4

6

Amner's
Wood

KYBES LA

5

Burnthouse
Farm

Great Lea
Farm

68

Burnthouse
Bridge

RIDERS LA

Foudry Brook

4

RG7

FOLLIS LA

Grazeley
Manor
Farm

Grazeley
Court
Farm

Gravelly
Bridge
Farm

MEREOAK LA

KINGFISHER
GR

A33

PALMER S LA

Bell
Copse

Poundgreen
Farm

Gravelly
Bridge

3

HAWTHORN
COTTS

Poundgreen

The Old Bell
(PH)

Rapleys

67

Grazeley
Green

Shepherdton La

PUMP LA

The Wheatsheaf
(PH)

Lambwoodhill
Common

Woodcock La

Highlands

GOODBOYS LA

2

DIDDENHAM
COTTS

Grazeley

Grazeley
Parochial
CE Prim Sch

MORTIMER RD

DIDDENHAM
CT

Lambwood Hill
Farm

LAMBWOOD HILL

Grazeley
Manor

Thurley
Bsns Units

1

Lambwood
Ind Est

BLOOMFIELD HATCH LA

A33

66

68 **A**   **B**   69   **C**   **D**   70   **E**   **F**

111
138

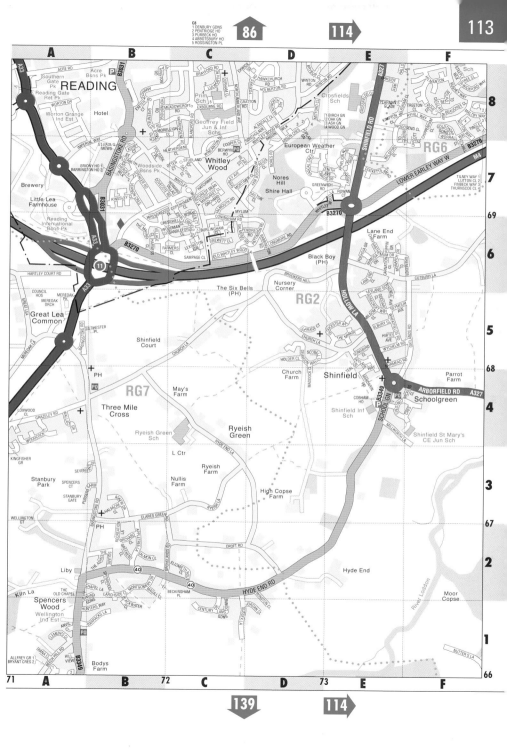

113 87

A **B** **C** **D** **E** **F**

M4

RG41

CHALFONT WAY
THE SQUARE
TILNEY WAY
RUSHEY WAY
CHATTEL
ODELL CL
BODMAN
PAVENHAM CL
CUTBUSH LA
RED HORSE LA
LEORAN CL
CHATTERS WAY
HARLTON
MERRIFIELD
MEADSTONE DR
PADDICK DR
B3270

FAKENHAM CL
MALTBY WAY
CRANSTON WAY
BRADMORE WAY
CARSTON WAY
CITY LIMITS
GRAFFHAM CL
OAKHILL
WIMBLINGTON
LITTLE
LOWER EARLEY WAY

8

LOWER EARLEY WAY W
B3270
M4
LOWER EARLEY WAY

1 FELTHORPE CL
2 UEACHAM CL
3 ANSTON CL
4 FINBECK WAY

5 RAINWORTH CL
6 FARNSFIELD CL

1 EBBORN SQ
2 IRVINE WAY
3 STONEA CL

Upperwood House

RG6

WHEATSHEAF CL
GIPSY LA
BETTY GROVE LA

7

Upperwood Farm

St John's Copse

Rushy Mead

Loader's La

Carter's Hill

NEWLANDS COTTS

The Holt

Carters Hill Farm

JULKES LA

PARKCORNER LA

B3030

69

OUTHGILL

River Loddon

Research Centre

Barrett's La

Copse Barnhill La

GARDEN COTTS

6

Shinfield Grange

Oldhouse Farm

The Grove

MOLE RD

Hall Farm

RG2

Newlands

Carter's La

5

68

ARBORFIELD RD
A327
Arborfield Bridge

Carter's La

BLISS'S HILL

Sewage Works

4

ARBORFIELD GRANGE

CHURCH LA

Arborfield

SINDLESHAM RD

Hazeltons Copse

Bridge Farm

Riding Sch

READING RD

WALTHAM RD

Cole La

RG41

3

Rounds Copse

Milkingbarn La

Pound Copse

Cross Lanes Farm

Pudding La

The Bull (PH)

B3030

Newland Farm

Coombes Inf Sch

Arborfield Newland & Barkham CE Jun Sch

WOODLA

67

GREENSWARD LA

B3349

BRANTS CL
PO

SCHOOL RD

B3349

2

Moor Copse

SINDLESHAM RD

Nursery

HARTS CL

DR CRES
EMBLEN CRES

Arborfield Cross

Langleypond Farm

LANGLEY COMMON RD

Arborfield Court

EVERSLEY RD

ROCKWELL

OAKLANDS CVN PK

School of Electronic Engineering

1

Kenney's Farm

White's Farm

Ducks Nest Farm

BAIRD RD

Aborfield Garrison

66

NUTTER'S

Bartlett's Farm

VALON RD

A327

A **B** **C** **D** **E** **F**

74 75 76

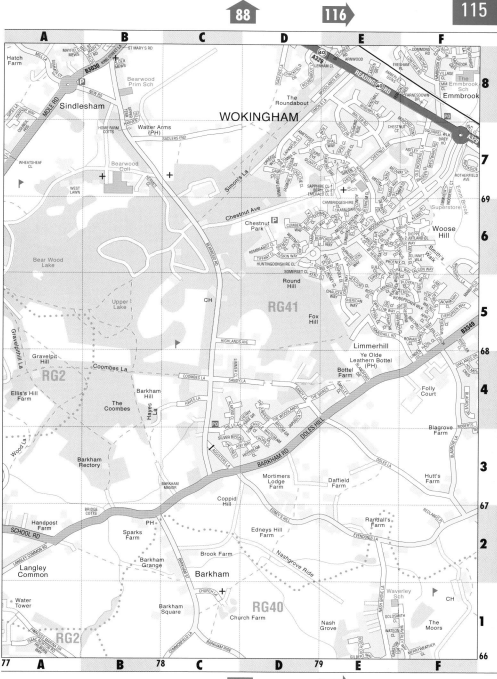

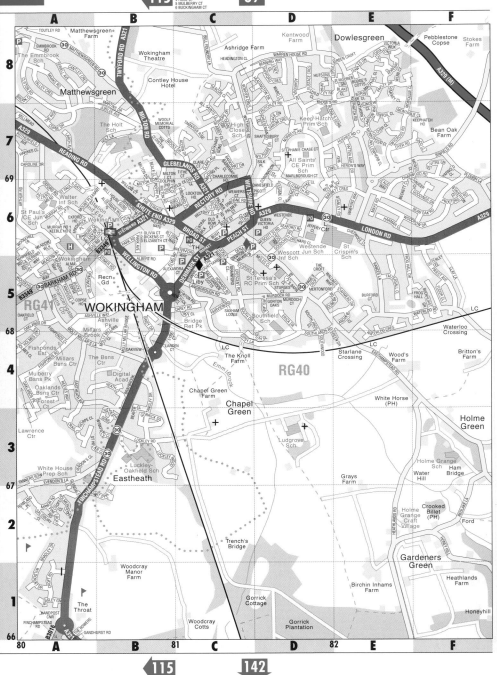

115

C6
1 WOODSTOCK
2 MEACHEN CT
3 WALNUT CT
4 ROSE CT
5 MULBERRY CT
6 BUCKINGHAM CT

7 BROAD ST WLK
8 ROSE GDNS

89

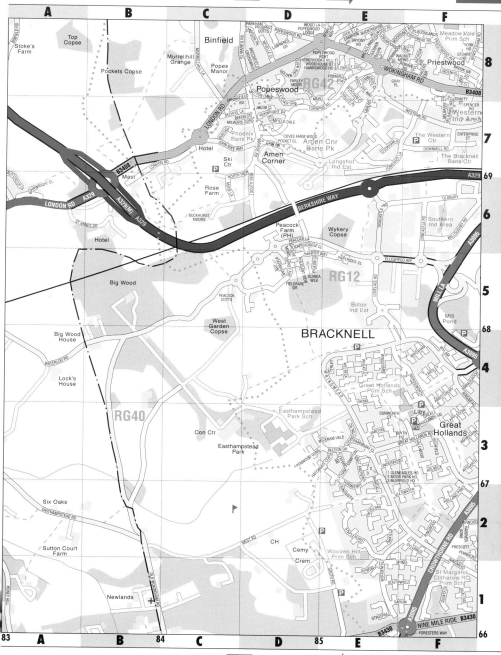

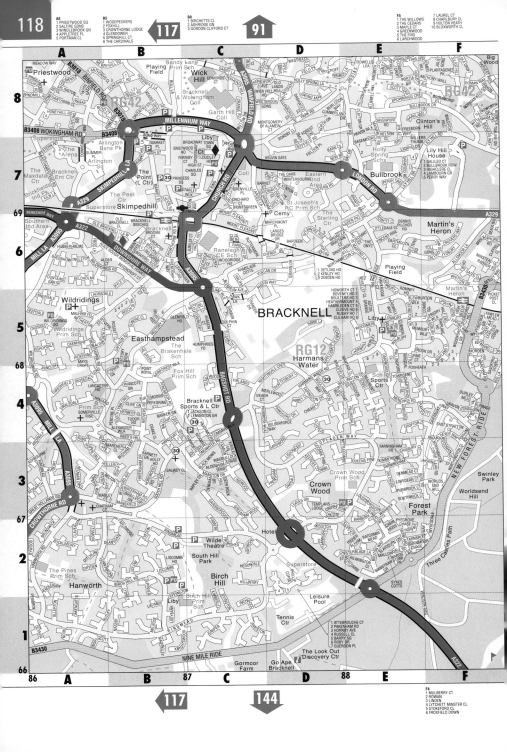

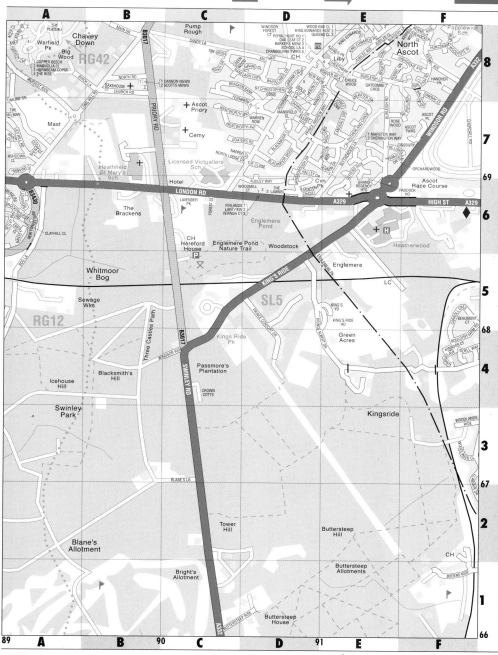

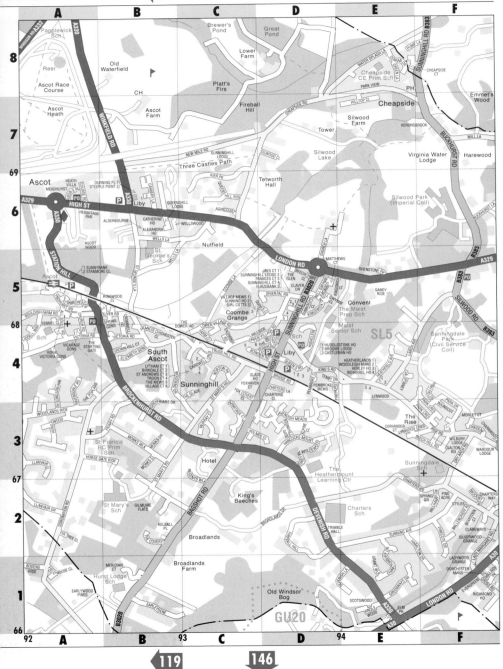

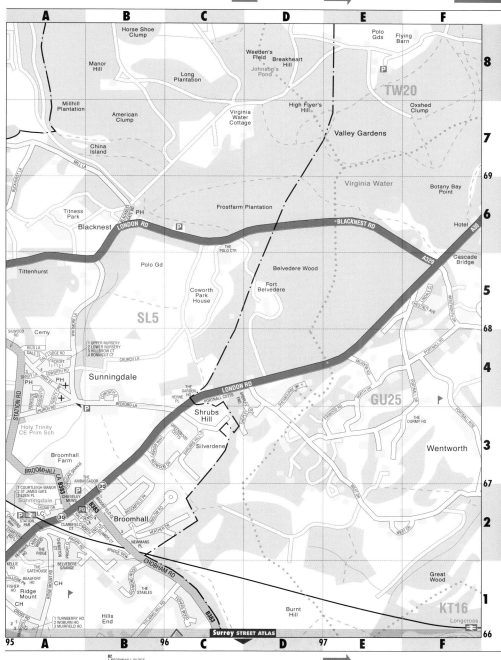

Surrey STREET ATLAS

B2
1 BROOMHALL BLDGS
2 HALFPENNY CT
3 FARTHING CT
4 SOVEREIGN CT
5 ROBINWOOD

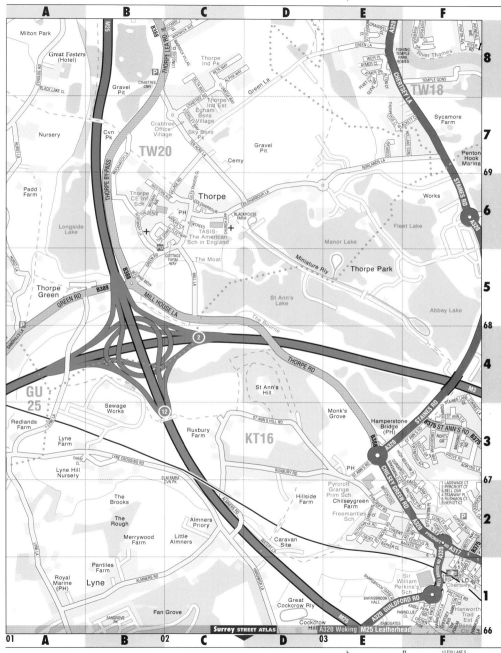

F1
1 EASTWORTH RD
2 LIBERTY HO
3 CHARLES HO
4 FOX HD
5 REGENCY HO
6 FOX CT
7 FOX LANE N
8 CHARLES ST
9 DOWNSIDE
10 FOX LANE S
11 FLORAL HO

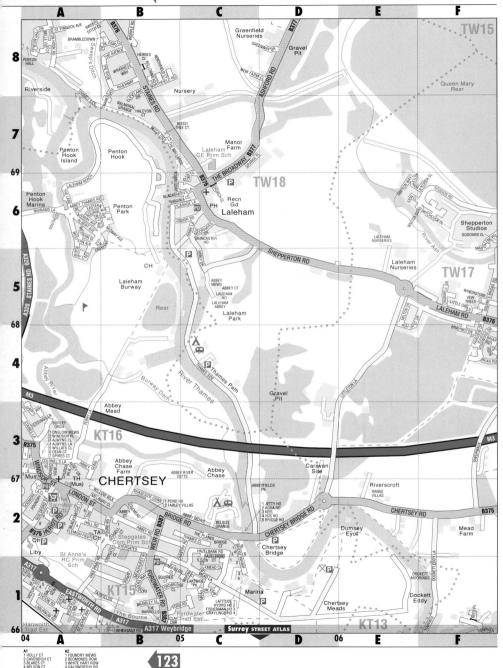

A1
1 HOLLY CT
2 CAVENDISH CT
3 BLAKES CT
4 NELSON CT
5 COLLINGWOOD CT
6 LABURNUM CT
7 REGENCY PL
8 PAINESFIELD DR

A2
1 FOUNDRY MEWS
2 BEOMONDS ROW
3 WHITE HART ROW
4 GALSWORTHY RD
5 BEOMONDS
6 CHERTSEY WLK
7 BURWOOD PAR
8 PRIORY MEWS

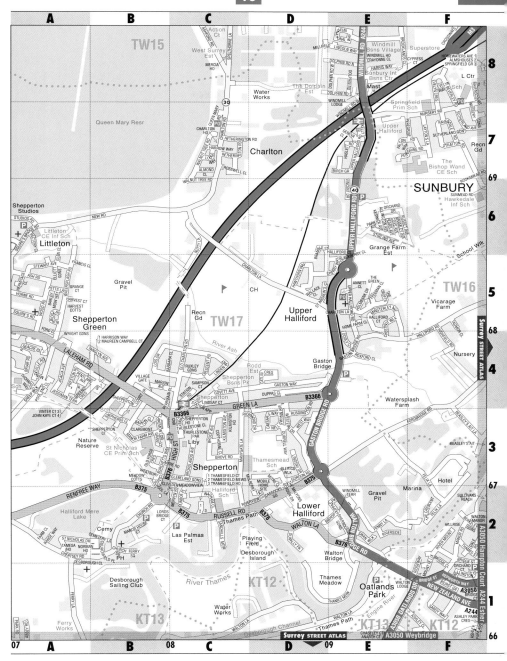

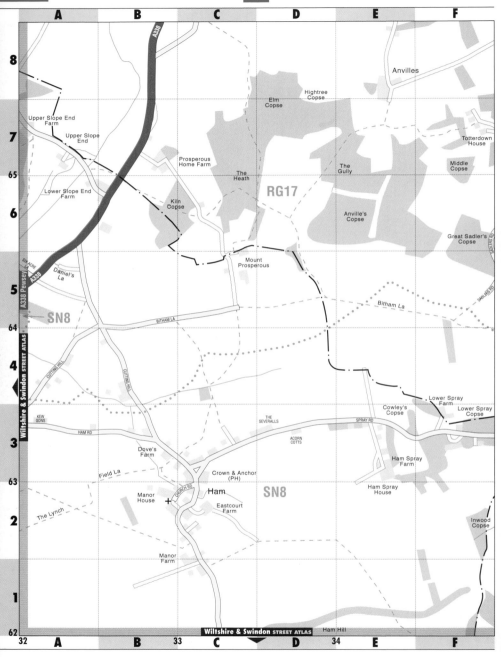

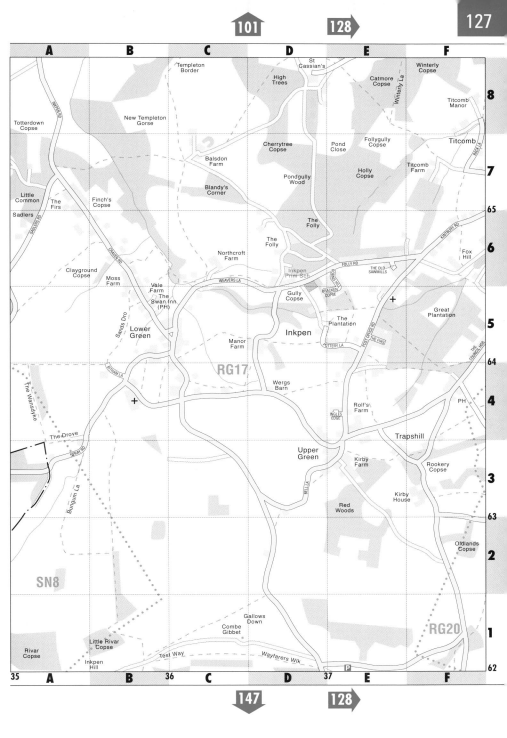

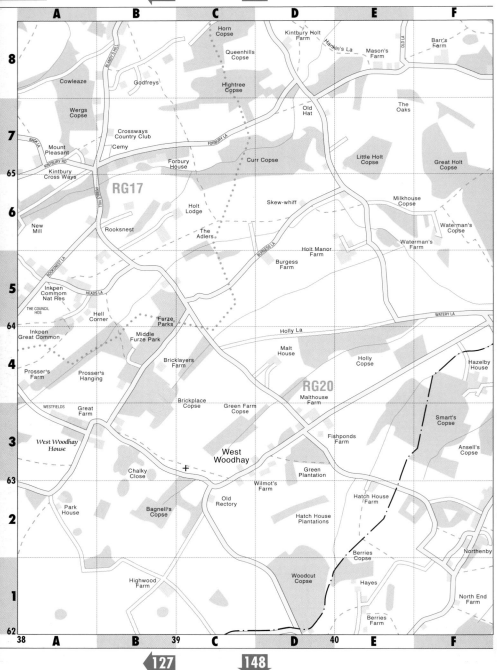

A B C D E F

8

Cowleaze

BLUNDELL'S HILL

Godfreys

Horn Copse

Queenhills Copse

Kintbury Holt Farm

Hankin's La

Mason's Farm

OLD LA

Barr's Farm

Hightree Copse

The Oaks

7

Wergs Copse

Crossways Country Club

Cemy

FORBURY LA

Old Hat

Mount Pleasant

KINTBURY RD

BAG LA

65

Kintbury Cross Ways

PEBBLE HILL

RG17

Forbury House

Curr Copse

Little Holt Copse

Great Holt Copse

6

New Mill

Rooksnest

Holt Lodge

The Adlers

Skew-whiff

Milkhouse Copse

Waterman's Copse

Waterman's Farm

BURGESS LA

Holt Manor Farm

Burgess Farm

5

Inkpen Common Nat Res

ROOKSNEST LA

HEADS LA

THE COUNCIL HOS

Hell Corner

Furze Parks

WATERY LA

64

Inkpen Great Common

Middle Furze Park

Holly La

Malt House

Holly Copse

Hazelby House

4

Prosser's Farm

Prosser's Hanging

Bricklayers Farm

RG20

Malthouse Farm

WESTFIELDS

Great Farm

Brickplace Copse

Green Farm Copse

Smart's Copse

3

West Woodhay House

West Woodhay

Fishponds Farm

Ansell's Copse

63

Chalky Close

+

Wilmot's Farm

Green Plantation

Hatch House Farm

2

Park House

Bagnell's Copse

Old Rectory

Hatch House Plantations

Northenby

Berries Copse

1

Highwood Farm

Woodcut Copse

Hayes

North End Farm

Berries Farm

62

38 A B 39 C D 40 E F

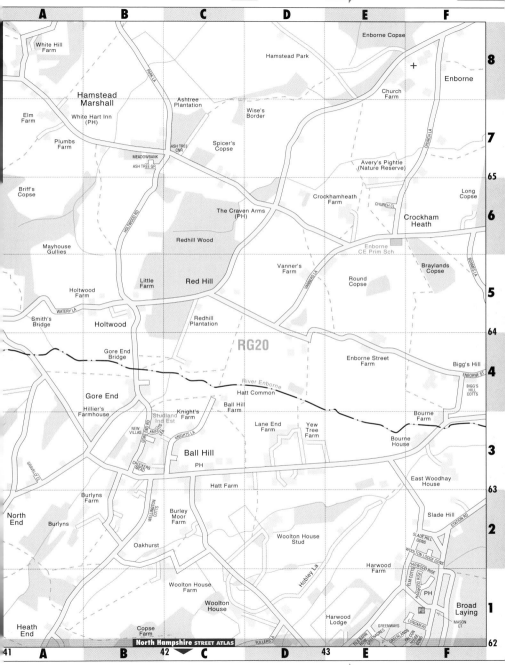

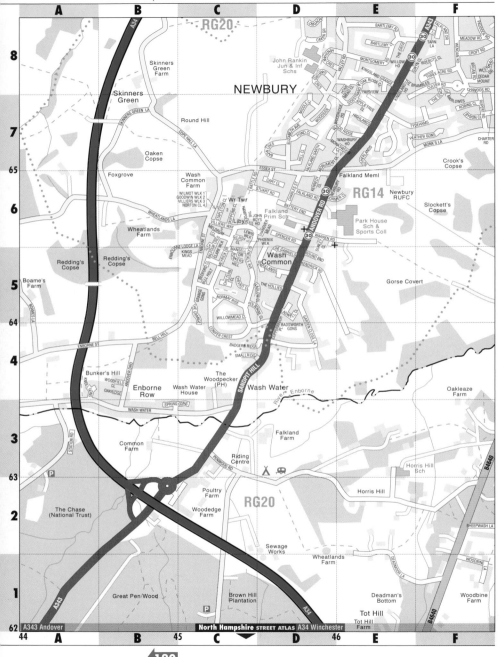

NEWBURY

RG20

Skinners Green Farm

Skinners Green

Round Hill

Oaken Copse

Foxgrove

Wash Common Farm

WILMOT WLK 1
GOODWIN WLK 2
VILLIERS WLK 3
NORTON CL 4

Wr Twr

Liby

Wheatlands Farm

Wheatlands Way

Redding's Copse

Redding's Copse

Boame's Farm

Kings Mead

Falkland Prim Sch

Wash Common

Gorse Covert

Bunker's Hill

Enborne Row

Wash Water House

The Woodpecker (PH)

Wash Water

SANDPIT HILL

River Enborne

Oakleaze Farm

Common Farm

Riding Centre

Falkland Farm

Poultry Farm

Woodedge Farm

RG20

Horris Hill Sch

Horris Hill

SHEEPWASH LA

WOODBINE LA

The Chase (National Trust)

Sewage Works

Wheatlands Farm

Great Pen Wood

Brown Hill Plantation

Deadman's Bottom

Woodbine Farm

Tot Hill

Tot Hill Farm

John Rankin Jun & Inf Schs

Falkland Meml

RG14

Newbury RUFC

Slockett's Copse

Crook's Copse

Park House Sch & Sports Coll

RG14

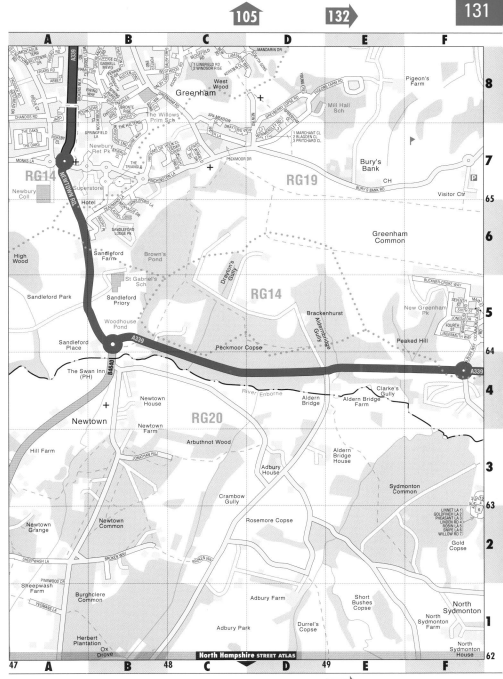

131

North Hampshire STREET ATLAS

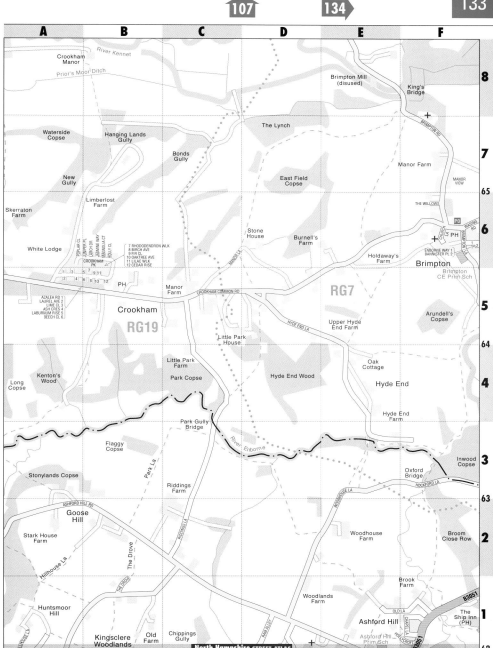

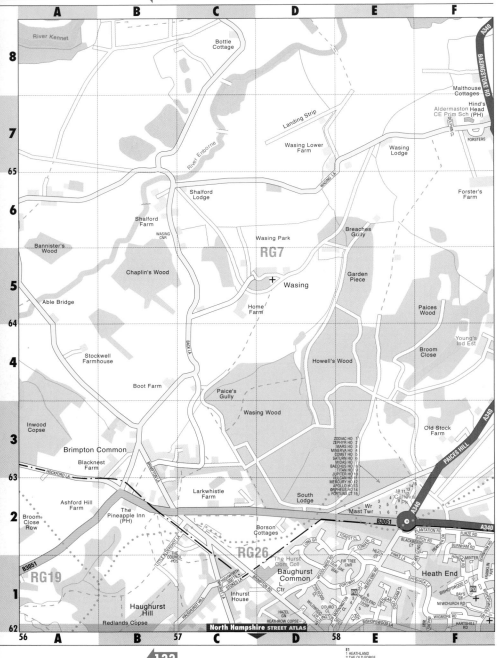

E1
1 HEATHLAND
2 THE OLD FORGE
3 BEECH COPSE
4 OAKLANDS
5 HEATH HO
6 LANDSEER CT
7 HEPPLEWHITE CL
8 CHIPPENDALE CL

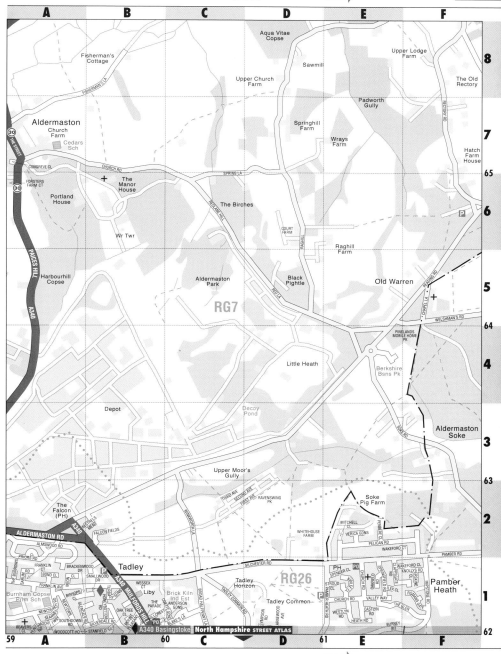

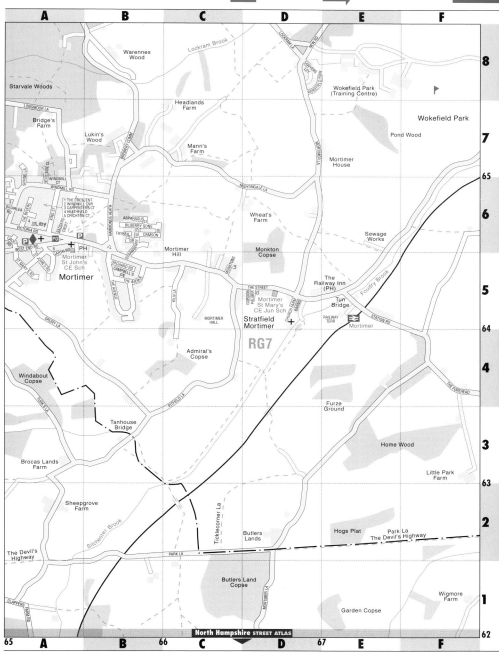

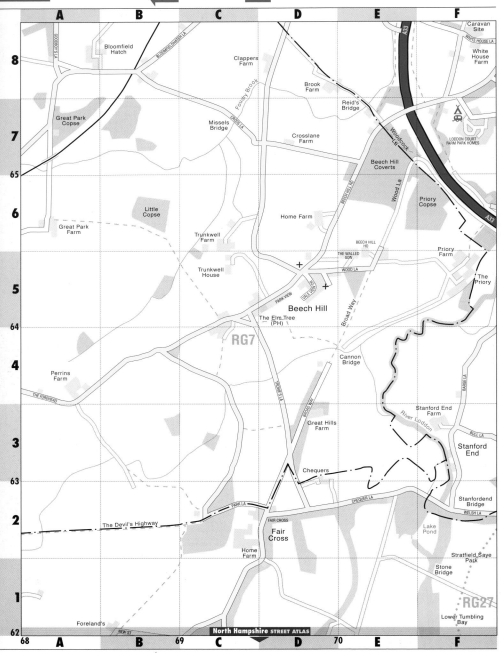

A B C D E F

8

Caravan Site
WHITE HOUSE LA
White House Farm

Bloomfield Hatch

BLOOMFIELDHAUGH LA

GODDARDS LA

Clappers Farm

Brook Farm

Reid's Bridge

A23

7

Great Park Copse

Foudry Brook

CROSS LA

Missels Bridge

Crosslane Farm

Woodcock La

LODDON COURT FARM PARK HOMES

65

6

Little Copse

Home Farm

Beech Hill Coverts

Wood La

Priory Copse

A33

Great Park Farm

Trunkwell Farm

BEECH HILL HO

Priory Farm

5

Trunkwell House

THE WALLED GDN

WOOD LA

The Priory

BEECH HILL RD

PARK VIEW

HALL VIEW

Broad Way

Beech Hill

64

RG7

The Elm Tree (PH)

4

Perrins Farm

Cannon Bridge

BARGE LA

THE FOREHEAD

THAME'S LA

BROAD WAY

Stanford End Farm

River Loddon

BULL LA

3

Great Hills Farm

Stanford End

63

Chequers

CHEQUER LA

Stanfordend Bridge

2

PARK LA

WELSH LA

The Devil's Highway

FAIR CROSS

Fair Cross

Lake Pond

Stratfield Saye Park

Home Farm

Stone Bridge

1

RG27

Foreland's

Lower Tumbling Bay

62

NEW ST

68 A B 69 C D 70 E F

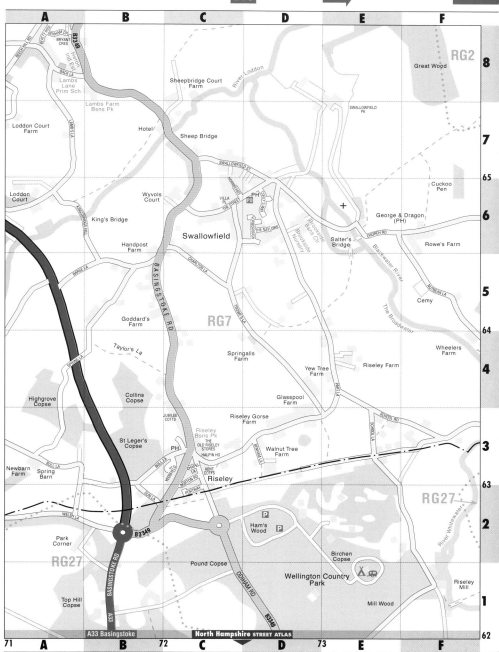

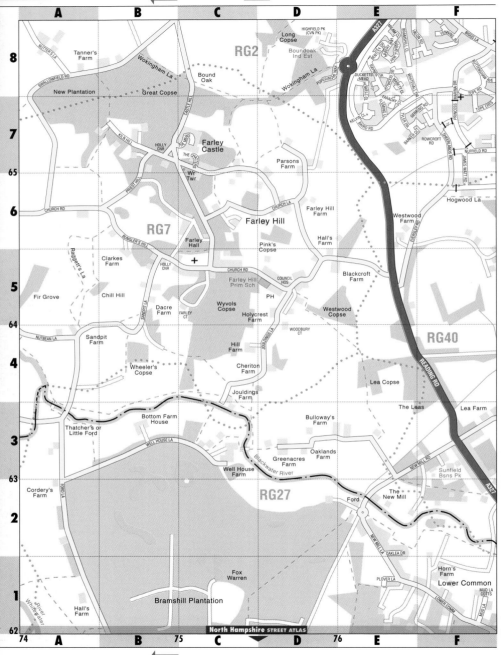

North Hampshire STREET ATLAS

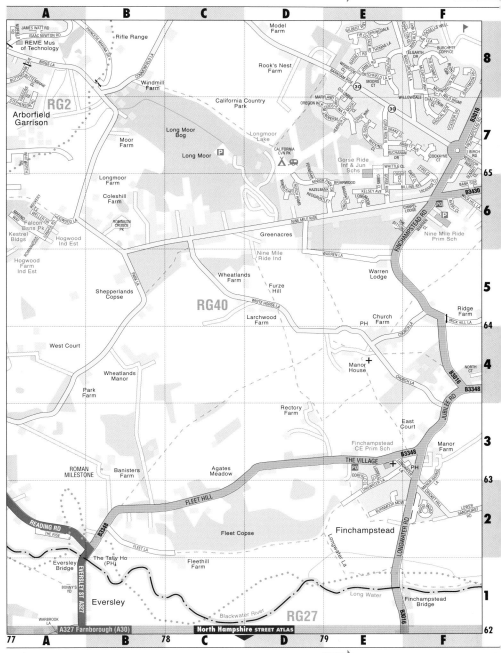

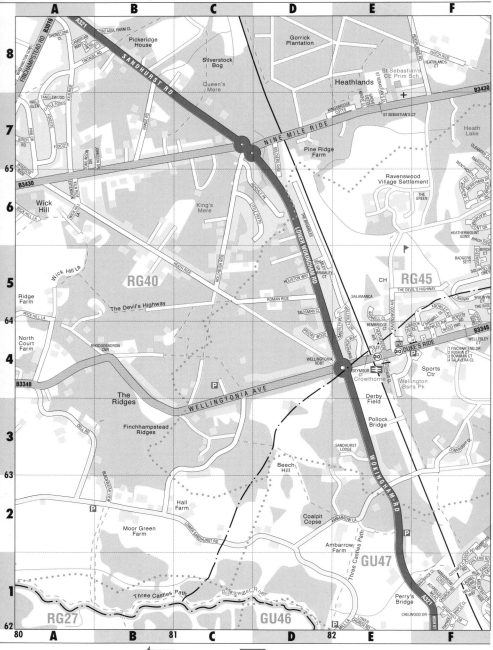

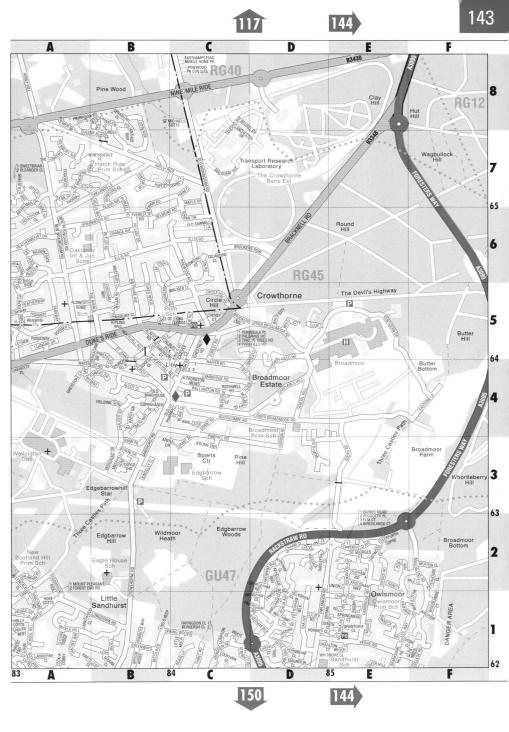

143
118

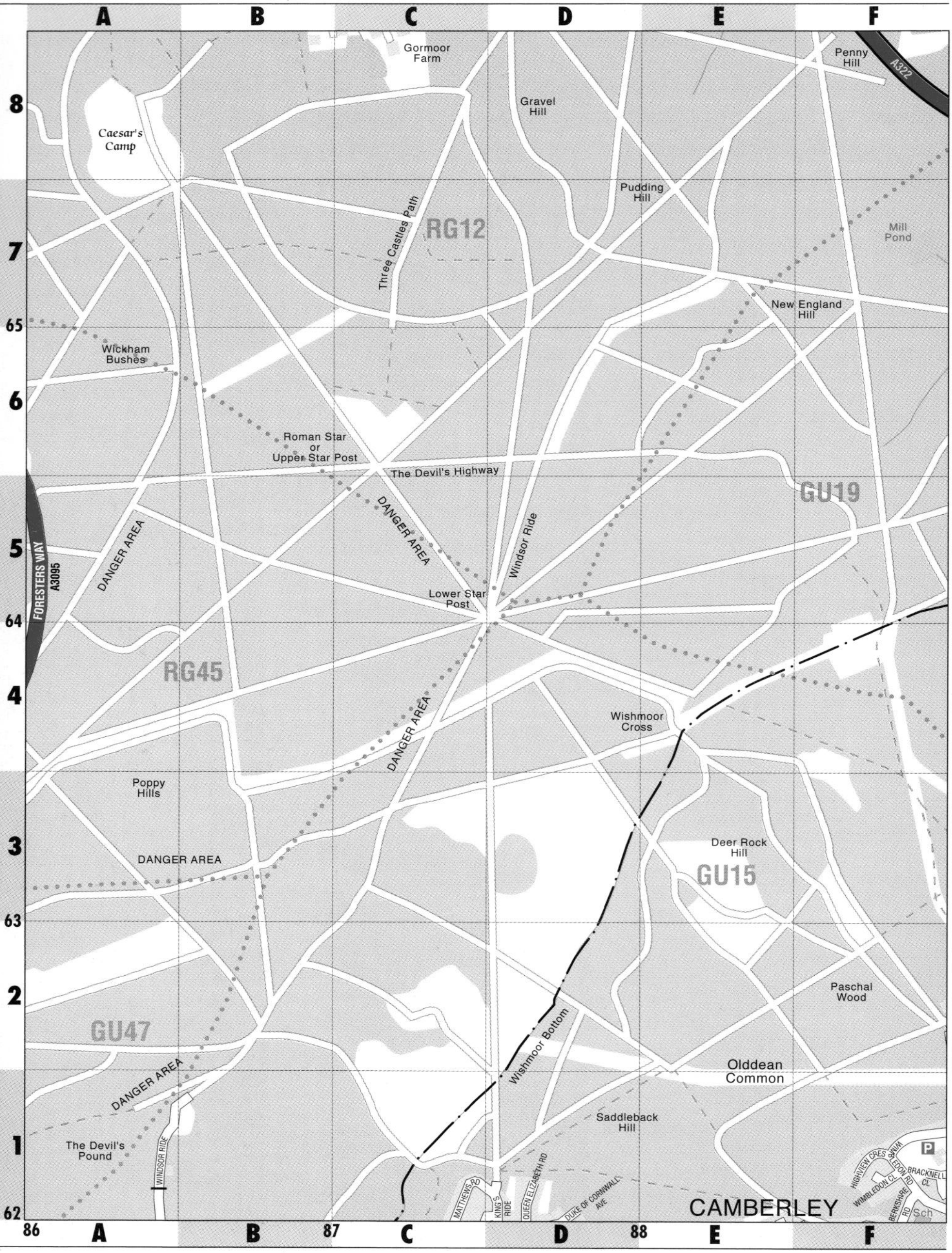

8

7

65

6

5

64

4

3

63

2

1

62

A B C D E F

Gormoor
Farm

Gravel
Hill

Penny
Hill

Caesar's
Camp

Pudding
Hill

Mill
Pond

RG12

Three Castles Path

New England
Hill

Wickham
Bushes

Roman Star
or
Upper Star Post

The Devil's Highway

GU19

FORESTERS WAY A3095

DANGER AREA

DANGER AREA

Windsor Ride

Lower Star
Post

RG45

Wishmoor
Cross

Poppy
Hills

Deer Rock
Hill

DANGER AREA

GU15

DANGER AREA

Paschal
Wood

GU47

Wishmoor Bottom

Olddean
Common

DANGER AREA

Saddleback
Hill

The Devil's
Pound

WINDSOR RIDE

CAMBERLEY

MATTHEWS RD
KING'S RIDE
QUEEN ELIZABETH RD
DUKE OF CORNWALL AVE

HIGHGATE LANES
WIMBLEDON RD
BRACKNELL
CL
BERKSHIRE RD
P
Sch

86 A B 87 C D 88 E F

A3322

143
151

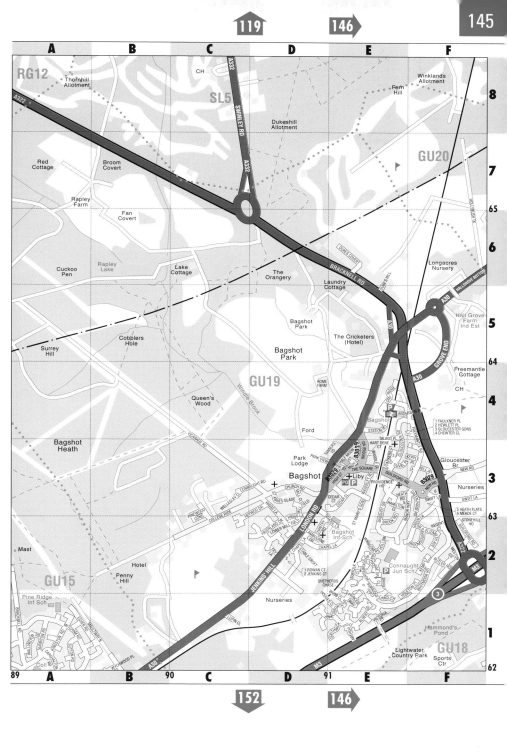

145
120

Earlywood

SL5

Windsor Manor

King's Hill

Windlesham Moor

SUNNING HO

SL5

Windlesham Hall Farm

Windlesham Hall

LAVERSHOT HALL

CHASEMOUNT

Windlemere

WOOD HALL

Lennoxwood

Windlesham Moor

The Windmill (PH)

TUDOR PADDOCK

Windlesham Court

HIGH CHIMNEYS

Ribs Down

Erl Wood Manor

Allerton Hill

Windlesham Village Inf Sch

Camus

Hatton Hill

Ribsden Hall

WAYSIDE COTTS

PH

B386

Woodcote House Sch

GU20

Mast

CHERTSEY RD

Hall Grove Sch

Recn Gd

Windlesham

UPDOWN HILL

Heathpark Wood

The Half Moon (PH)

CHURCH RD

Birch Hall

GRAHAM RD

PO

Oak Wood

Windlesham Park

1 OAKDALE
2 LONGBROOK CT
3 LEES CT

Ashleigh Farm

ORCHARD HILL

HUTTON CL

GU19

Twelve Oaks

SWIFT LA

Caravan Site

GU24

M3

South Farm

Windlesham Arboretum

Old House Farm

Windle Brook

Broadway Green Farm Ind Est

SCULLEY LA

Manor Farm Wood

Halebourne Copse

A322

KENWORTH GR

TUSCANY VILLAS 1
FLORENCE VILLAS 2
PASSFIELD LODGE 3

HAMMOND WAY

Lee Lane Farm

HOOK MILL LA

Cemy

Village Sch

Lightwater

GUILDFORD RD

PO

CHRISTIE CL

Rectory Farm

GU18

Sewage Works

Jun Sch

Liby

ALL SAINTS RD

THE SQUARE

BROOKFIELD CT

THE WILLOWS

Hale Bourne

A322

Surrey STREET ATLAS

M3 London (A316)

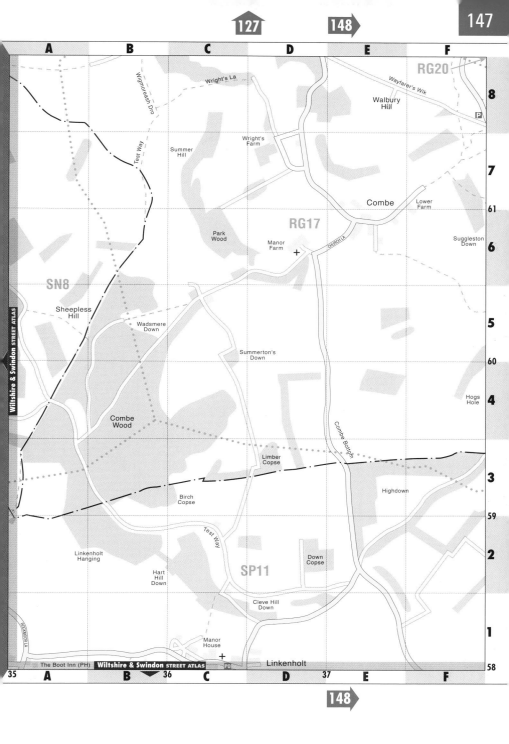

RG20

Waylarer's Wlk

Wright's La

Walbury
Hill

Wigmoreash Dro

Wright's
Farm

Summer
Hill

Test Way

Combe

Lower
Farm

RG17

Park
Wood

Manor
Farm

CHURCH LA

Suggleston
Down

SN8

Sheepless
Hill

Wadsmere
Down

Summerton's
Down

Hogs
Hole

Combe
Wood

Combe Botrgh

Limber
Copse

Highdown

Birch
Copse

Test Way

Linkenholt
Hanging

SP11

Down
Copse

Hart
Hill
Down

Cleve Hill
Down

BOXMOOR LA

Manor
House

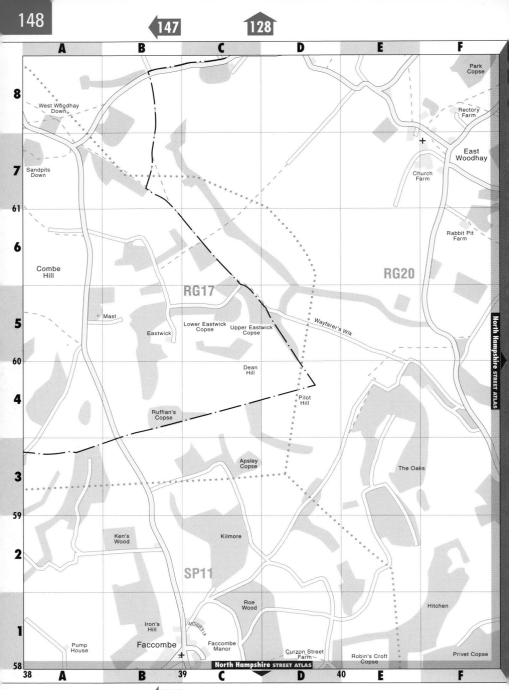

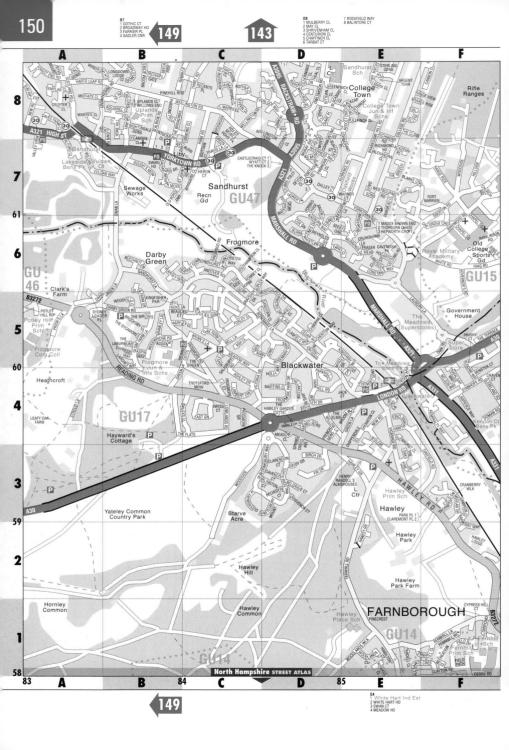

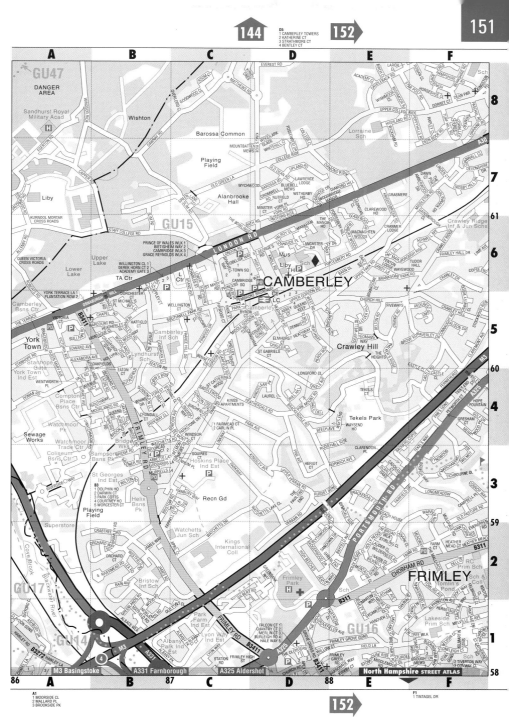

144
152

D5
1 CAMBERLEY TOWERS
2 KATHERINE CT
3 STRATHMORE CT
4 BENTLEY CT

A1
1 MOORSIDE CL
2 MALLARD PL
3 BROOKSIDE PK

F1
1 TINTAGEL DR

152

North Hampshire STREET ATLAS

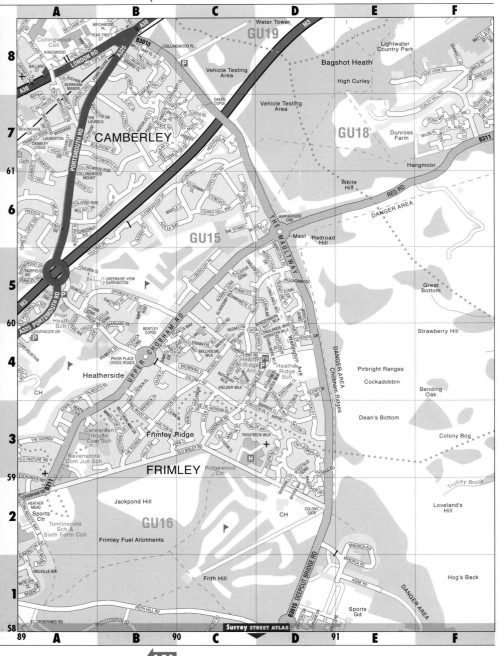

GU19

Water Tower

M3

Collingwood Coll
KINGSWOOD
WYCHWOOD PL
PEAR TREE CT
BALLARD CT

8

LONDON RD
LIME COPSE AVE
B3015
MAULTWAY CL

Collingwood Pl

Lightwater Country Park

COLLINGWOOD PL

Bagshot Heath

High Curley

Vehicle Testing Area

HIGH VIEW RD

A30

THE BUCHAN
BURNHAM MANOR

7

PORTSMOUTH RD

CAMBERLEY

THE LAURELS

BEAUFRONT CL

Vehicle Testing Area

GU18

Dunross Farm

OAKEN COPSE

CURLEY HILL RD

MILES PL

B311

61

OWTSWORTH DR

COLLINGWOOD RISE
COLLINGWOOD MOUNT
LODDON CL

Hangmoor

DEVONSHIRE DR
CRAWLEY RIDGE
LAURESTON DR
CRAWLEY LODGE
HIGHLEE DR

Sch

ELMWOOD CL
ELMWOOD CRES

COLARNE RISE
MULRO DR

White Hill

RED RD

DANGER AREA

6

PADDOCK CL
CONIFER DR
COPSE

BURNTHWAITE AVE
YORKTOWN RD

GU15

HEATHERSIDE CNR

Mast

THE SPINNEY
BEVERLEY

Redroad Hill

Great Bottom

FAIRFIELD HO
CRAWLEY LA

5

M3

YOULDEN CL
DUNCROFT CL

1 GREENSIDE VIEW
2 DARRINGTON

HILLSBROUGH PK

THE MAULTWAY

BRACKENWOOD

Strawberry Hill

PORTSMOUTH RD
A325

Prior Heath Sch
SOUTHCOTE DR

SPRINGFIELD RD
CHESTERS RD

SAMARKAND CL

BENTLEY COPSE

60

RIVER FOUNTAIN

KILMORIE DR

PRIOR PLACE
CROSS ROADS

Heatherside

CH

FRANCIS WAY
TREMAYNE CL
MILLHOLME WLK

BROWNING CL
GOLDNEY RD

HEATHER RIDGE
Heather Ridge Arc
KIELDER WLK

REDMAYNE

WINDERMERE

ESKDALE WAY
LONGLANDS WAY
HONISTER WLK
KENDAL GRI

WELLINGTON AVE

Heather Ridge Sch

DANGER AREA
Chobham Ridges

Pirbright Ranges
Cockadobbin

Bending Oak

4

UPPER CHOBHAM RD

ROTBURY WLK

REDWOOD DR

Dean's Bottom

Carwarden House Com Sch

SILVER

HERRICK CL

3

THE FAIRWAY

OLD PASTURE RD

Ravenscote Com Jun Sch

Frimley Ridge

FERN CL
OLD BISLEY RD

TROUTBECK WLK

CONISTON

RIPON CL

Colony Bog

59

EVERGREEN RD
B311

FRIMLEY

Ridgewood Ctr

H

Trulley Brook

CHOBHAM RD
HEATHER MEAD

Sports Ctr

Jackpond Hill

GU16

CH

COLONY GATE

Loveland's Hill

2

WOBURN
REGENT

MELVILLE AVE

Tomlinscote Sch & Sixth Form Coll

Frimley Fuel Allotments

MINORCA AVE

MINORCA RD

Hog's Back

1

DEEPCUT BRIDGE RD

Frith Hill

AISNE RD

DANGER AREA

58

ST CATHERINES RD

FRITH HILL RD

RHODODENDRON RD

B3015

Sports Gd

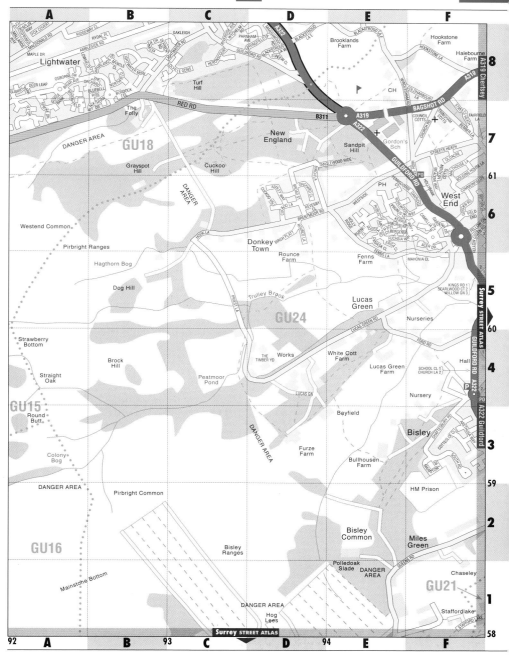

154

Index

Place name May be abbreviated on the map ○

Location number Present when a number indicates the
place's position in a crowded area of mapping ○

Locality, town or village Shown when more than one
place has the same name ○

Postcode district District for the indexed place ○

Page and grid square Page number and grid reference
for the standard mapping ○

Church Rd **6** Beckenham BR2..........**53** C6

Cities, towns and villages are listed in CAPITAL LETTERS   Public and commercial buildings are highlighted in magenta
Places of interest are highlighted in blue with a star★

Abbreviations used in the index

Acad	**Academy**	Comm	**Common**	Gd	**Ground**	L	**Leisure**	Prom	**Promenade**
App	**Approach**	Cott	**Cottage**	Gdn	**Garden**	La	**Lane**	Rd	**Road**
Arc	**Arcade**	Cres	**Crescent**	Gn	**Green**	Liby	**Library**	Recn	**Recreation**
Ave	**Avenue**	Cswy	**Causeway**	Gr	**Grove**	Mdw	**Meadow**	Ret	**Retail**
Bglw	**Bungalow**	Ct	**Court**	H	**Hall**	Meml	**Memorial**	Sh	**Shopping**
Bldg	**Building**	Ctr	**Centre**	Ho	**House**	Mkt	**Market**	Sq	**Square**
Bsns, Bus	**Business**	Ctry	**Country**	Hospl	**Hospital**	Mus	**Museum**	St	**Street**
Bvd	**Boulevard**	Cty	**County**	HQ	**Headquarters**	Orch	**Orchard**	Sta	**Station**
Cath	**Cathedral**	Dr	**Drive**	Hts	**Heights**	Pal	**Palace**	Terr	**Terrace**
Cir	**Circus**	Dro	**Drove**	Ind	**Industrial**	Par	**Parade**	TH	**Town Hall**
Cl	**Close**	Ed	**Education**	Inst	**Institute**	Pas	**Passage**	Univ	**University**
Cnr	**Corner**	Emb	**Embankment**	Int	**International**	Pk	**Park**	Wk, Wlk	**Walk**
Coll	**College**	Est	**Estate**	Intc	**Interchange**	Pl	**Place**	Wr	**Water**
Com	**Community**	Ex	**Exhibition**	Junc	**Junction**	Prec	**Precinct**	Yd	**Yard**

Index of towns, villages, streets, hospitals, industrial estates, railway stations, schools, shopping centres, universities and places of interest

Aba–ALD

A

Abattoirs Rd RG1 . . . . .86 A8
Abberbury Cl RG14 . . . . . .104 E6
Abbetts La GU15 . . . . .151 B3
Abbey Cl
  Bracknell RG12 . . . . 118 D4
  Newbury RG14 . . . . 131 A8
  Slough SL1 . . . . .41 E6
  Wokingham RG40 . . . . . .116 C7
Abbey Cotts SL7 . . . . .17 B4
Abbey Ct
  Camberley GU15 . . . . . . 151 D5
  Chertsey KT16 . . . . 124 B2
  Laleham TW18 . . . . 124 C5
Abbey Dr TW18 . . . . 124 C5
Abbeyfields Pk KT16 . . . . 124 C2
Abbey Gate SL6 . . . . .41 A7
Abbey Gdns
  Chertsey KT16 . . . . 124 A3
  Woolhampton RG7 . . . . . 108 D5
Abbey Gn KT16 . . . . 124 A3
Abbey Jun Sch The RG1 . .86 C5
Abbey Lodge ◻ TW18 . . . .96 F3
Abbey Mdws KT16 . . . . . . 124 C2
Abbey Mead GU8 . . . . .2 F5
Abbey Mews TW18 . . . . . 124 C5
Abbey Pk RG7 . . . . .110 F3
Abbey Pl
  Chertsey KT16 . . . . 124 A6
  Newell Green RG42 . . . . . .91 C3
Abbey Point ◻ RG1 . . . . . .86 B7
Abbey Rd
  Bourne End SL8 . . . . .2 F5
  Chertsey KT16 . . . . 124 B2
  Lower Halliford TW17 . . . 125 A1
  Virginia Water GU25 . . . . 122 D5
Abbey River Cotts KT16 . 124 C3
Abbey School The RG1 . . . .86 C6
Abbey Sq RG1 . . . . .86 B7
Abbey St RG1 . . . . .86 B7
Abbey Way SL7 . . . . .18 D6
Abbey Wood SL5 . . . . 121 A2
Abbot Cl TW18 . . . . .97 D1
ABBOTSBROOK 2 F3
Abbotsbury RG12 . . . . .117 F4
Abbotsbury Ct ◻ RG30 . . .85 B8
Abbotsbury Ho ◻ RG2 . . 113 C8

Abbots Dr GU25 . . . . 122 C5
Abbots Mead OX10 . . . . . . .14 A8
Abbotsmead Pl RG4 . . . . . .59 A2
Abbots Rd
  Burghfield Common RG7 . .110 F2
  Newbury RG14 . . . . 105 A1
Abbots Rd 123 F2
Abbot's Wlk
  Reading RG1 . . . . .86 B8
  Windsor SL4 . . . . .66 E5
Abbottsleigh Gdns RG4 . . .59 D4
Abbotts Way SL1 . . . . .41 D6
Abelia Cl GU24 . . . . .153 E6
Abell Gdns SL6 . . . . .19 B1
Aberaman RG4 . . . . .58 F6
Aberdeen Ave SL1 . . . . . . .42 A6
Aberdeen Lodge ◻ SL4 . .67 C5
Aberford Cl RG30 . . . . .85 C7
Abex Rd RG14 . . . . 105 C3
Abingdon Cl RG12 . . . . . . .118 E4
Abingdon Dr RG4 . . . . .59 C6
Abingdon Rd
  East Ilsley RG20 . . . . .30 E7
  Sandhurst GU47 . . . . 143 C1
Abingdon Wlk SL6 . . . . . . .19 E3
Abington SL3 . . . . .69 D6
Abney Court Dr SL8 . . . . . . .3 A2
Abrahams Rd RG9 . . . . .15 C3
Acacia Rd SL6 . . . . .15 D2
Acacia Ave
  Littleton TW17 . . . . 125 A4
  Sandhurst GU47 . . . . 143 D1
  Wraysbury TW19 . . . . .68 E3
Acacia Ct RG12 . . . . .118 B6
Acacia Mews UB7 . . . . .70 D8
Acacia Rd
  Reading RG1 . . . . .86 C6
  Staines TW18 . . . . .97 B3
Academy Cl GU15 . . . . . . 151 E8
Academy Gate GU15 . . . . 151 B6
Academy Pl GU47 . . . . . . 150 E7
Accommodation La UB7 . .70 C8
Acer Cl RG42 . . . . .119 A8
Acer Dr GU24 . . . . 153 F6
Ackrells Mead GU47 . . . . 142 F1
Acorn Cl SL3 . . . . .44 B1
Acorn Cotts SN8 . . . . 126 D3
Acorn Dr
  Thatcham RG18 . . . . 106 D5
  Wokingham RG40 . . . . . .116 C7
Acorn Gdns RG7 . . . . .110 C3
Acorn Gr UB3 . . . . .71 F7
Acorn Rd RG17 . . . . 150 B5

Acorn Wlk RG31 . . . . .84 C5
Acre Bsns Pk RG2 . . . . . . .113 B8
Acre Pas SL4 . . . . .67 D6
Acre Rd RG2 . . . . 113 A8
Acre The SL7 . . . . .1 F2
ACS Egham Int Sch
  TW20 . . . . 122 C7
Action Ct TW15 . . . . 125 C8
Adam Cl
  Slough SL1 . . . . .42 A5
  Tadley RG26 . . . . .134 E1
Adam Ct RG9 . . . . .15 E2
Adams Way RG6 . . . . .86 F2
Addington Cl SL4 . . . . .67 D5
Addington Ho RG1 . . . . . . .86 E6
Addington Rd RG1 . . . . . . .86 D6
Addington Specl Sch RG5 . 87 F6
Addiscombe Rd RG31 . . . .57 B3
Addiscombe Rd RG45 . . . 143 C4
Addison Cl SL0 . . . . .44 E6
Addison Ct SL6 . . . . .39 D8
Addison Rd RG1 . . . . .59 A1
Adelaide Cl SL1 . . . . .42 A4
Adelaide Rd
  Reading RG6 . . . . .87 A6
  Staines TW15 . . . . .97 D3
  Windsor SL4 . . . . .67 F6
Adelaide Sq SL4 . . . . .67 D5
Adelphi Gdns SL1 . . . . . . .42 E4
Adey's Cl RG14 . . . . 105 B1
Adkins Rd RG10 . . . . .62 E7
Admiral Kapple Ct SL5 . . .92 E1
Admirals Ct RG2 . . . . .86 A5
Admiralty Way GU15 . . . . 150 F4
Admoor La RG7 . . . . .82 C1
Adrians Wlk SL2 . . . . .42 F5
Adwell Dr RG6 . . . . .87 D1
Adwell Sq RG9 . . . . .15 D2
Adwood Ct RG19 . . . . 106 E3
Aerial Bsns Pk RG17 . . . . .45 E3
Agar Cres RG42 . . . . .91 B1
Agars Pl SL3 . . . . .43 A5
Agars Rd RG42 . . . . .115 E2
Aggisters La RG41 . . . . . . .115 C3
Agincourt Cl RG41 . . . . . . 115 C3
Agincourt Cl RG41 . . . . . . 115 E6
Agricola Way RG19 . . . . . 106 F2
Agua Ho KT16 . . . . 124 C2
Aintree Cl
  Newbury RG14 . . . . 105 C1
  Poyle SL3 . . . . .69 E6

Air Forces Meml★ TW20 . .95 D4
Airport Gate Bsns Ctr
  UB7 . . . . .71 A7
Airport Way TW19 . . . . . . .70 A3
Aisne Rd GU16 . . . . .152 E1
Ajax Ave SL1 . . . . .42 B6
Alandale Cl RG2 . . . . .113 D8
Alan Pl RG30 . . . . .85 A5
Alan Way SL3 . . . . .43 E7
Alastair Nicholas Ct ◻
  RG1 . . . . .86 A8
Albain Cres TW15 . . . . . . .97 E6
Albany Cl GU15 . . . . 151 C1
Albany Gdns RG4 . . . . .59 A6
Albany Park Dr RG41 . . . . .88 A3
Albany Park Ind Est
  GU15 . . . . 151 C1
Albany Pk
  Frimley GU15 . . . . 151 C1
  Poyle SL3 . . . . .69 D7
Albany Pl TW20 . . . . .96 B4
Albany Rd
  Old Windsor SL4 . . . . .68 A2
  Reading RG30 . . . . .85 D7
  Windsor SL4 . . . . .67 D5
Alben Rd RG42 . . . . .90 C3
Albert Ave KT16 . . . . .124 A6
Albert Cl SL1 . . . . .42 F5
Albert Dr TW18 . . . . .97 A3
Albert Illsley Cl RG31 . . . .84 D8
Albert Pl SL4 . . . . .42 A1
Albert Rd
  Ashford TW15 . . . . .97 F3
  Bagshot GU19 . . . . 145 E1
  Bracknell RG42 . . . . .118 B8
  Camberley GU15 . . . . . . 151 C5
  Caversham RG4 . . . . .58 F4
  Crowthorne RG45 . . . . . .143 B5
  Englefield Green TW20 . . . .95 D2
  Henley-on-T RG9 . . . . . . .15 E1
  ◻ Newbury RG14 . . . . . 105 A3
  Slough SL1 . . . . .43 B7
  Wokingham RG40 . . . . . .116 B5
Albert St
  Maidenhead SL6 . . . . .39 F7
  Slough SL1 . . . . .42 F3
  Windsor SL4 . . . . .67 B6
Albert Wlk RG45 . . . . 143 B5
Albion Cl SL2 . . . . .43 A5
Albion Cotts SL6 . . . . .19 C7
Albion Ct SL4 . . . . .67 A5
Albion Rd GU47 . . . . 150 B8
Albury Cl RG30 . . . . .58 C1

Albury Ct TW15 . . . . .98 D2
Albury Gdns RG31 . . . . . . .84 E3
Albury Way RG19 . . . . . . .131 F4
Alcot Cl RG45 . . . . .143 B4
Aldborough Spur SL1 . . . . .42 F7
Aldbourne Ave RG6 . . . . . .87 A4
Aldbourne Cl ◻ RG17 . . .100 D5
Aldbourne Rd SL1 . . . . .41 B8
Aldeburgh Cl RG4 . . . . .59 C8
Aldenham Cl RG4 . . . . .59 C6
Aldenham Terr RG12 . . . . 118 C3
Alden View SL4 . . . . .66 D6
Alderbourne SL5 . . . . 120 B6
Alderbourne La SL3 . . . . . .23 E8
Alder Bridge Sch RG7 . . . 109 C3
Alderbrook Cl RG45 . . . . .142 E4
Alderbury Rd SL3 . . . . .43 F4
Alderbury Rd W SL3 . . . . .43 F4
Alder Cl
  Englefield Green TW20 . . . .95 E3
  Lower Earley RG6 . . . . . . .87 D1
  Newbury RG14 . . . . 105 D4
  Slough SL1 . . . . .41 F5
Alder Ct RG12 . . . . .118 B6
Alder Dr RG31 . . . . .84 C6
Alderfield Cl RG7 . . . . .83 F4
Alder Glade RG7 . . . . .111 C5
Alder Gr GU46 . . . . 149 C5
Alderley Cl RG5 . . . . .60 F1
Alderman Willey Cl
  RG41 . . . . .116 B6
ALDERMASTON 135 A4
Aldermaston CE Prim Sch
  RG7 . . . . 134 F7
Aldermaston Rd RG26 . . . 135 A2
Aldermaston Sta RG7 . . . 109 C3
ALDERMASTON SOKE . . .135 F3
ALDERMASTON
  WHARF 109 D3
Alder Mews RG41 . . . . . . .115 B8
Alderney Gdns RG4 . . . . . .59 C6
Alderney Gdns RG41 . . . . .88 C2
Alderside Wlk TW20 . . . . . .95 E3
Alders The RG18 . . . . 106 D4
Aldin Ave N SL1 . . . . .43 A4
Aldin Ave S SL1 . . . . .43 A4
Aldous Ho ◻ TW18 . . . . . .96 E4
Aldridge Rd SL2 . . . . .22 C1
Aldridge Rd RG42 . . . . .92 B2
Aldrige Rd SL2 . . . . .22 C1
Aldryngton Prim Sch RG6 . 87 B4
Aldwick Dr SL6 . . . . .39 C6
ALDWORTH 30 B1

Aldworth Cl
Bracknell RG12 . . . . 118 A5
Reading RG30 . . . . .85 C5
Aldworth Gdns RG45 . . . . 143 A5
Aldworth Rd
Compton RG20. . . . . .31 F4
Upper Basildon RG18 . . . . .55 A5
Aldwych Cotts RG14 . . . . 104 F6
Aldwyn Pl TW20 . . . . .95 B2
Alexander Ct
9 Newbury RG14. . . . . . . 105 B2
12 Reading RG1 . . . . .85 F7
Alexander Fst Sch SL4 . . .66 C4
Alexander Rd
Egham TW20 . . . . .96 C3
Thatcham RG19 . . . . 106 E2
Alexander Wlk RG12 . . . . 118 B4
Alexandra Ave GU15 . . . . 151 A5
Alexandra Cl
Ashford TW15 . . . . .98 D1
Sandhurst GU47 . . . . 150 E7
Staines TW18. . . . . .97 D2
Alexandra Ct
Ashford TW15 . . . . .98 D2
2 Windsor SL4 . . . . .67 D5
Wokingham RG40 . . . . . . 116 C5
Alexandra Ho
Ascot SL5. . . . . 120 B6
11 Reading RG1 . . . . .86 C7
Alexandra Rd
Ashford TW15 . . . . .98 E2
Englefield Green TW20 . . . .95 C2
Maidenhead SL6 . . . . .39 D8
Reading RG1 . . . . .86 D6
Slough SL1. . . . . .42 D3
Windsor SL4 . . . . .67 D5
Alford Cl
Reading RG30 . . . . .84 D8
Sandhurst GU47 . . . . 150 A7
Alfred Ct **3** SL8 . . . . .3 B3
Alfred Davis Ct SL7 . . . . . .1 D3
Alfred Sutton Prim Sch
RG1 . . . . .86 F6
Alice Gough Memorial
Homes RG12 . . . . 118 B6
Alice Ho TW18. . . . . .97 A2
Alice La SL1. . . . . .21 B1
Alison Cl RG7. . . . . 110 F1
Alison Dr GU15 . . . . 151 F5
Allanson Rd SL7 . . . . .1 F3
Allcot Cl TW14. . . . . .98 F7
Allcroft Rd RG1. . . . . .86 C5
Allenby Rd
Maidenhead SL6 . . . . .39 B7
Sandhurst GU15 . . . . 151 A6
Allendale Cl GU47 . . . . . . 143 A2
Allendale Rd RG6. . . . . . . .87 B3
Allerds Rd SL2. . . . . .22 A4
Alleyns La SL6. . . . . .19 D8
Allfrey Gr RG7 . . . . 113 A1
All Hallows Rd RG4 . . . . . .59 D3
Allhusen Gdns SL3. . . . . . .23 E8
Alliance Ct TW11. . . . . . . .42 F6
Allington Ave TW17 . . . . . 125 E6
Allington Ct SL2 . . . . .42 F6
Allison Ct **2** RG1 . . . . . . .85 F7
Allison Gdns RG8 . . . . . . .57 C5
Allison Ho RG9 . . . . .35 E8
Allkins Ct SL4 . . . . .67 D5
Allnatt Ave RG41. . . . . . . 116 A5
Allonby Cl RG6 . . . . .87 D2
All Saints Ave SL6 . . . . . . .39 D7
All Saints CE Inf Sch RG1 .66 F6
All Saints' CE Prim Sch
RG40 . . . . 116 D7
All Saints Cl RG40 . . . . . . 116 C7
All Saints Cres GU14 . . . . 150 E1
All Saints Ct RG1 . . . . .85 E6
All Saints Rd GU18. . . . . . 146 C1
All Saints Rise **7** RG1. . . .85 E7
Allsmoor La RG12. . . . . . . 118 F6
All Souls Cotts SL3 . . . . . .43 E8
All Souls' Rd SL5 . . . . 120 A5
Allyn Cl TW18. . . . . .96 F2
Alma Ct
Burnham SL1 . . . . .21 C2
Eton SL4. . . . . .41 F2
Wokingham RG41 . . . . . . 116 A5
Alma Rd
Eton SL4. . . . . .41 F2
Windsor SL4 . . . . .67 C5
Alma St RG30. . . . . .85 C8
Almners Rd
Chertsey KT16. . . . . 123 C2
Lyne KT16 . . . . 123 B1
Almond Ave RG14. . . . . . . 105 A5
Almond Cl
Charlton TW17. . . . . 125 C7
Englefield Green TW20 . . . .95 B2
Windsor SL4 . . . . .67 B5
Wokingham RG41 . . . . . . 115 C4
Almond Dr
Caversham RG4 . . . . .59 F4
Chieveley RG20 . . . . .51 C5
Thatcham RG18 . . . . 106 D4
Almond Rd SL1. . . . . .21 C2
Almons Way SL2. . . . . .43 B8
Almshouses
Hurst RG10 . . . . .88 C6
Reading RG1 . . . . .86 A7
Slough SL3. . . . . .43 E4
Twyford RG10 . . . . .61 D5
Almshouses The SL4 . . . . .67 D7
Almswood Rd RG26 . . . . . 135 A2
Alpha Ho **4** RG1 . . . . .86 C6

Alpha St N **6** SL1 . . . . . . .43 A4
Alpha St S SL1. . . . . .42 F3
Alpha Way TW20. . . . . . . 123 C8
Alphington Ave GU16 . . . 151 F1
Alphington Gn GU16 . . . . 151 F1
Alphington Rd RG2 . . . . . 113 B8
Alpine Cl
Ascot SL5. . . . . 120 D3
Maidenhead SL6 . . . . .40 A6
Alpine St RG1 . . . . .86 B6
Alsace Wlk GU15 . . . . 151 B1
Alsford Cl GU18. . . . . 152 F7
Alston Gdns SL6. . . . . .39 E7
Alston Mews RG19 . . . . . . 106 C2
Alston Wlk RG4. . . . . .59 F2
ALTMORE. 38 E4
Altmore SL6. . . . . .38 E4
Altona Way SL1. . . . . .42 B7
Alton Ct TW18 . . . . 123 E8
Alton Ride GU17 . . . . 150 C6
Altwood Bailey SL6. . . . . . .39 B5
Altwood CE Sec Sch SL6 . .39 B5
Altwood Cl
Maidenhead SL6 . . . . .39 B5
Slough SL1. . . . . .41 E8
Altwood Dr SL6. . . . . .39 B5
Altwood Rd SL6. . . . . .39 B5
Alvista Ave SL6 . . . . .41 B7
Alwyn Inf Sch SL6 . . . . . . .39 C8
Alwyn Rd SL6. . . . . .39 B8
Alwyns Cl KT16 . . . . 124 A3
Alwyns La KT16. . . . . 124 A3
Alyson Ct **2** SL6. . . . . .19 F1
Amanda Ct
Ashford TW15 . . . . .97 F6
Slough SL3. . . . . .43 D3
Ambarrow Cres GU47 . . . 142 F1
Ambarrow La GU47 . . . . . 142 E2
Ambassador RG12 . . . . . . 117 F4
Ambassador The SL5. . . . . 121 B2
Amber Cl RG6 . . . . .87 C4
Amber Ct SL7 . . . . .1 D3
Amber Hill GU15. . . . . 152 B4
Amberley Cl RG14 . . . . . . 104 F4
Amberley Ct SL6. . . . . .20 C3
Amberley Dr RG10. . . . . . .61 D6
Amberley Gdns RG41. . . . 115 E8
Amberley Pl **7** SL4. . . . . . .67 D6
Amberley Rd SL2 . . . . .43 A6
Amblecote Rd RG30. . . . . .85 B7
Ambleside Rd RG45 . . . . . 143 C4
Ambleside Cl
Botley Dr TW14 . . . . .98 F7
Maidenhead Rd GU18. . . . 153 B8
Ambleside Way TW20 . . . . .96 B1
Ambleside Rd RG12. . . . . . 113 B8
Ambrose Pl RG1 . . . . .85 F7
Ambury Rd RG4 . . . . .32 E4
AMEN CORNER. 117 D7
Amen Corner Bsns Pk
RG12 . . . . 117 D7
Amerden Cl SL6 . . . . .40 D7
Amerden La SL6. . . . . .40 D7
Amerden Priory Cvn Pk
SL6. . . . . .40 E4
Amerden Way SL1 . . . . . . .42 A4
American Magna Carta
Meml* TW20. . . . . .95 D6
Amersham Rd RG4. . . . . . .59 D2
Amethyst Cl RG41. . . . . . . 115 D7
Amethyst La RG30 . . . . . . .85 C6
Amherst Rd RG6 . . . . .87 A6
Amhurst Mews **3** RG6. . .87 A6
Amity Rd RG1 . . . . .86 E7
Amity St RG1 . . . . .86 E8
Ammanford RG4 . . . . .58 F5
Amners Farm RG30. . . . . . 111 F7
Amners Farm Rd RG30. . . 112 A7
Ampere Rd RG14 . . . . 105 B3
Anarth Ct KT13 . . . . 125 E1
Ancaster Dr SL5. . . . . 119 E8
Ancastle Gn RG9. . . . . .15 D2
Anchor Ct SL6. . . . . .19 F7
Anchorite Cl RG10 . . . . . . .61 D5
Andermans SL4. . . . . .66 D6
Anders Cnr RG42 . . . . 117 F8
Anderson Ave RG6. . . . . . .87 A6
Anderson Cres RG22 . . . . 114 E2
Anderson Dr TW15 . . . . . . .98 C4
Anderson Pl GU19 . . . . . . 145 E4
Andover Cl
East Bedfont TW14 . . . . . . .98 F7
Reading RG31 . . . . .57 D1
Andover Ct TW19 . . . . .97 D8
Andover Dro RG20 . . . . . . 130 B4
Andover Rd
Blackwater GU17. . . . . . . 150 C6
Newbury RG14. . . . . 130 D6
Andrews Cl RG7 . . . . .83 E3
Andrews Rd RG6. . . . . .87 B3
Andrews Reach SL8. . . . . . . .3 A2
Andrews Way SL7. . . . . .1 D8
Angel Ct
Newbury RG14. . . . . 104 F4
Reading RG7 . . . . .83 E3
Angel Mead RG7 . . . . 108 C2
Angel Pl RG42 . . . . .90 C2
Angers Cl GU15 . . . . 152 C7
Angle Field Rd RG4 . . . . . .59 C3
Anglers Way RG1 . . . . .86 D7
Anglesey Ct TW15 . . . . . . .98 A5

Anne Cl SL6 . . . . .19 E2
Anneforde Pl RG42. . . . . . .91 A1
Anners Cl TW20. . . . . 123 C6
Annesley Gdns RG41 . . . . .88 C2
Annett Cl TW17 . . . . 125 E5
Annie Brookes Cl TW18 . . .96 D5
Anscull Rd SL2 . . . . .22 A2
Ansell Rd GU16. . . . . 151 C1
Anslow Pl SL1 . . . . .41 C8
Anson Cres RG2 . . . . 113 D8
Anson Ct TW19 . . . . .97 E8
Anson Wlk RG2. . . . . 113 D8
Anstey Pl RG7 . . . . 111 A3
Anstey Rd **8** RG1. . . . . . . .85 F7
Anston Cl RG6 . . . . .87 A3
Antares Ct RG41 . . . . 115 F6
Anthian Cl RG6. . . . . .55 B8
Anthony Wall RG42 . . . . . 118 F8
Anthony Way SL1 . . . . .41 D6
Antrim Rd RG5 . . . . .87 D6
Anvil Cl RG7. . . . . 113 A1
Anvil Ct
3 Slough SL3. . . . . .44 A2
Thatcham RG18 . . . . 106 D3
Wokingham RG40 . . . . . . 116 C5
ANVILLES. 126 E8
Apex Dr GU16 . . . . 151 D1
Aphelion Way RG2. . . . . . . 113 E7
Aplin Way GU18 . . . . 146 A1
Apollo Ho RG7. . . . . 134 E2
Appelford Cl RG19 . . . . . . 106 D2
Appley End RG30 . . . . .85 B7
Appley Gdns TW14. . . . . . .98 F7
Apple Cl
Purley on T RG31 . . . . .57 B4
Wokingham RG41 . . . . . . 115 F5
Applecroft SL6 . . . . .39 C3
Appledore RG12 . . . . 117 F3
Appleford Rd RG30 . . . . . . .85 A5
Appleshaw Cl **1** RG31 . . .84 D8
Appleton Ho **26** RG2. . . . .86 D7
Apple Tree Ct RG14 . . . . . 130 E7
Appletree La SL3 . . . . .43 C3
Appletree Pl **4** RG42. . . . 118 A8
Apple Tree Way GU47 . . . 143 D1
Appley Cl GU15 . . . . 151 B6
Appley Dr GU15. . . . . 151 B6
Approach Rd
Ashford TW15 . . . . .98 C2
Taplow SL6. . . . . .40 E7
April Cl GU15 . . . . 151 C2
Apsey Ct RG42. . . . . .90 E1
Apple Cotts SL6. . . . . .19 C7
Apsley Ho SL1. . . . . .43 A4
Aquila Cl RG41 . . . . 115 E6
Araby Cnr TW17 . . . . 125 C3
Aragon Cl TW16 . . . . .98 F1
Aragon Ct
Bracknell RG12 . . . . 118 C5
Maidenhead SL6 . . . . .39 E5
Aragon Rd GU46 . . . . 149 C4
Arbery Way RG42 . . . . 140 E8
ARBORFIELD 114 C4
Arborfield Cl SL1 . . . . .42 E3
ARBORFIELD CROSS. . . . 114 F7
ARBORFIELD
GARRISON. 114 F1
Arborfield Grange RG2 . . . 114 C4
Arborfield, Newland &
Barkham CE Jun Sch
RG2 . . . . 114 F2
Arborfield Rd RG2 . . . . . . 113 F4
Arbor La RG41 . . . . .88 B3
Arbor Mdws RG41 . . . . . . .88 B3
Arbrook Mews OX11. . . . . 11 B8
Arbrook Rd SL4 . . . . .95 B8
Arbour Vale Sch SL2 . . . . .22 B2
Arcade Mews **10** RG14 . . 105 A3
Arcade The
Goring RG8 . . . . .34 C6
9 Newbury RG14. . . . . . . 105 A3
1 Reading RG1 . . . . .86 B7
Archer Cl RG2. . . . . .59 A2
Archway Rd RG4 . . . . .59 A2
Arden Cl RG12 . . . . 119 A7
Ardingly RG12 . . . . 118 A4
Ardler Rd RG4 . . . . .59 C2
Ardrossan Ave GU15 . . . . 152 A5
Ardrossan Ct SL2 . . . . .22 C1
Ardwell Cl RG45 . . . . 142 E5
Arenal Dr RG45 . . . . 143 C3
Arena The RG12. . . . . 118 A7
Arethusa Way GU24. . . . . 153 F3
Argent Cl TW20. . . . . .96 C2
Argent Terr GU47. . . . . . . 150 D8
Argonaut Pk SL3 . . . . .44 B6
Argosy Gdns TW18 . . . . . . .96 F2
Argosy La TW19. . . . . .97 D8
Argyle Rd
Newbury RG14. . . . . 104 F2
Reading RG1 . . . . .85 E7
Argyle St RG1 . . . . .85 E7
Argyll Ave SL1 . . . . .42 A6
Arial Ho RG12 . . . . 118 A6
Arista Ct TW20. . . . . .95 D2
Arkle Ave RG19 . . . . 105 F3
Arkley Ct SL6. . . . . .40 C1
Ark Sch The RG42 . . . . . . 109 F1
Arkwright Dr RG42. . . . . . 117 D7
Arkwright Rd
Poyle SL3 . . . . .69 E5
Reading RG31 . . . . .84 E4
Arlington Bsns Pk
Theale RG7 . . . . .83 F3

Arlington Cl
Bracknell RG42 . . . . 118 A8
Maidenhead SL6 . . . . .39 A8
Arlington Grange RG18 . . .78 B3
Arlington La RG14 . . . . . . .77 F3
Arlington Sq RG12 . . . . . . 118 A7
Arlington Rd TW15. . . . . . .97 F3
Arlington Rd TW15. . . . . . .97 F3
Arlington Sq RG12 . . . . . . 118 A7
Armadale Ct RG30 . . . . . . .85 D6
Armitage Ct SL5 . . . . 120 D3
Armitage Dr GU16 . . . . . . 151 F1
Armour Hill RG31. . . . . . . .57 D1
Armour Lodge RG31 . . . . . .57 D1
Armour Rd RG31. . . . . .57 D1
Armour Wlk RG31. . . . . . . .57 D1
Armstrong Ho SL2 . . . . . . .43 D7
Armstrong Rd TW20. . . . . .95 C2
Armstrong Way RG5 . . . . . .88 A7
Arncliffe RG12 . . . . 118 A4
Arndale Way TW20 . . . . . . .96 A3
Arne Cl RG41 . . . . .88 A3
Arnett Ave RG40. . . . . 141 F7
Arnewood Ave RG26 . . . . 135 D1
Arnhem Rd RG14 . . . . 105 B3
Arnold Rd TW18 . . . . .97 C1
Arnside Cl RG10 . . . . .61 D7
Arnwood Rd RG41. . . . . . . 115 E8
Arrowhead Rd RG7 . . . . . .83 F2
Arrowsmith Way RG19 . . . 106 E1
Artemis Ho RG14 . . . . 105 B4
Arthur Cl GU19 . . . . 145 E1
Arthur Pl RG1 . . . . .86 D7
Arthur Rd
Newbury RG14. . . . . 104 E2
Slough SL1. . . . . .42 D4
Windsor SL4 . . . . .67 D6
Wokingham RG41 . . . . . . 116 A6
Arthur's La SP11. . . . . 148 C1
Arthurstone Birches
RG42 . . . . .90 D3
Artillery Dr RG19 . . . . 106 E1
Artillery Mews RG30 . . . . .85 D6
Arun Cl RG41 . . . . .88 B1
Arun Ct RG30. . . . . .85 C6
Arundel Cl SL3 . . . . .39 A8
Arundel Ct SL3 . . . . .43 D2
Arundel Rd
Frimley GU15. . . . . 152 C4
Woodley RG5 . . . . .87 F7
Asanteewa Ho **7** RG1 . . .86 A6
ASCOT. 120 A6
Ascot Cl RG14 . . . . 131 C8
Ascot Heath CE Jun Sch
SL5. . . . . .92 E1
Ascot Inf Sch SL5 . . . . . . .92 E1
Ascot Ho **7** TW20 . . . . . . .96 A3
Ascot Pl SL5 . . . . 119 F7
Ascot Race Course SL5 . . 119 F6
Ascot Rd
East Bedfont TW14 . . . . . . .98 B6
Holyport SL6 . . . . .65 A8
Newell Green RG42. . . . . . .91 E8
Ascot St SL5 . . . . 120 A5
Ascot Wood SL5. . . . . 120 A6
ASHAMPSTEAD 54 A6
Ashampstead Rd
Bradfield RG7 . . . . .82 B7
Reading RG30 . . . . .85 B4
Ash Apartments UB3 . . . . .71 D7
Ashbourne RG12. . . . . 117 F3
Ashbourne Cl SL6 . . . . .85 C7
Ashbourne Gr SL6 . . . . . . .39 C3
Ashbourne Ho **5** SL1. . . . .42 E4
Ashbourne Way RG19 . . . 106 B3
Ashbrook Mews OX11. . . . 11 B8
Ashbrook Rd SL4 . . . . .95 B8
Ashburton Rd RG2 . . . . . . .86 C2
Ashbury Dr
Farnborough GU17 . . . . . . 151 A1
Reading RG31 . . . . .84 C7
Ashby Ct RG22. . . . . 113 B7
Ashby Way UB7. . . . . .71 A7
Ash Cl
Blackwater GU17. . . . . . . 150 C5
Brightwalton RG20 . . . . . . .28 D3
Slough SL3. . . . . .44 B3
Ashcombe Cl TW15 . . . . . .97 E5
Ash Copse RG4 . . . . .59 F7
Ash Cres RG19 . . . . 132 A3
Ashcroft Cl RG4 . . . . .58 E5
Ashcroft Rd SL6 . . . . .21 B3
Ash Ct
Ashford TW15 . . . . .98 C3
Caversham RG4 . . . . .59 B3
1 Newbury RG14. . . . . . . 105 A3
Ashdale Cl TW15. . . . . .97 E6
Ashdale Pk RG40 . . . . 142 D6
Ashdene Cl TW15. . . . . . . .98 C1
Ashdene Gdns RG30 . . . . .85 D6
Ashdene Ho RG20 . . . . . . .95 C2
Ashdown Cl RG12 . . . . .20 D3
Ashdown Ct RG14 . . . . . . 131 A7
Ashdown Ho **11** RG1. . . . .86 A6
Ashen Cross SL0 . . . . .44 B8
Ashen Wlk SL2. . . . . .23 C8
Asher Dr SL5 . . . . 119 D7
Ashes The RG2 . . . . 113 B2
Ashfield Gn GU46 . . . . . . 149 F5
Ashfield's Farm Ind Est
RG20 . . . . .51 D1
Ashford Ave TW15 . . . . . . .98 B2
Ashford Bsns Complex
TW15 . . . . .98 C4

Ald–Ast **155**

Ashford CE Prim Sch
TW15 . . . . .98 B2
Ashford Cl TW15 . . . . .97 E4
ASHFORD COMMON. 98 D2
Ashford Cres TW15. . . . . . .97 E5
Ashford Ct RG14 . . . . 133 E1
ASHFORD HILL. 133 C1
Ashford Hill Prim Sch
RG19 . . . . 133 E1
Ashford Hill Rd RG19 . . . . 132 F2
Ashford Hospl TW15 . . . . .97 E6
Ashford Ind Est TW15 . . . .98 C4
Ashford La SL4 . . . . .41 B4
Ashford Park Prim Sch
TW15 . . . . .97 D4
Ashford Rd
Feltham TW13, TW15. . . . . .98 E4
Littleton TW15. . . . . .98 C1
Staines TW18. . . . . 124 D8
Ashford Sta TW15. . . . . . . .97 F4
Ash Gate RG18. . . . . 106 F4
Ash Gn RG21 . . . . 113 D8
Ash Gr
East Bedfont TW14 . . . . . . .98 E7
Southend RG7 . . . . .82 B2
Stoke Poges SL2. . . . . .22 F5
Ashgrove Ct SL6. . . . . .39 C6
Ashgrove Rd TW15 . . . . . . .98 D3
Ashington Ho SL6 . . . . .39 E6
Ash La
Burghfield Common RG7 . . 111 A4
Tadley RG26. . . . . 134 E1
Windsor SL4 . . . . .66 C5
Ashlea Ho TW15 . . . . .97 F3
Ashleigh Ave TW20. . . . . . .96 C1
Ashley Cl
Earley RG6. . . . . .87 B2
Oatlands Park KT12, KT13 . 125 F1
Ashley Ct SL6. . . . . .40 C4
Ashley Dr GU17 . . . . 150 C4
Ashley Hill RG10 . . . . .36 F7
Ashley Park Ave KT12. . . . 125 F1
Ashley Park Cres KT12 . . . 125 F1
Ashley Pk SL6 . . . . .20 B2
Ashley Rd RG1 . . . . .86 A6
Ashley Way GU24 . . . . 153 D6
Ash Lodge **3** TW16 . . . . . .98 F1
Ashman Rd RG19 . . . . 107 A3
Ashmere Cl RG31. . . . . . . .84 C4
Ashmere Terr RG30 . . . . . .85 E8
ASHMORE GREEN 106 B8
Ashmore Green Rd RG18 . 106 B7
Ashmore Rd RG2 . . . . .86 C1
Ash Rd
Littleton TW17 . . . . 125 A5
Reading RG4 . . . . .84 E7
Ashridge Ct **4** RG42 . . . . 105 A2
Ashridge Gn **2** RG42 . . . . 118 B8
Ashridge Manor Farm
RG40 . . . . .89 B2
Ashridge Rd RG40 . . . . . . 116 D8
Ash Terr RG18. . . . . 106 B8
Ashton Cl RG31 . . . . .84 C8
Ashton Pl
Kintbury RG17 . . . . 102 B2
Maidenhead RG8 . . . . .39 A6
Ashton Rd
Newbury RG14. . . . . 105 B2
Wokingham RG41 . . . . . . .88 F1
Ash Tree Cnr RG20 . . . . . . 129 C7
Ashtree Ct **3** TW15 . . . . . .98 B3
Ash Tree Gr RG20 . . . . .50 B8
Ashtrees Rd RG5. . . . . .87 F8
Ashurst Dr TW17. . . . . 124 E5
Ashview Cl TW15 . . . . .97 E3
Ashview Gdns TW15. . . . . .97 E3
Ashville Pk RG41 . . . . 116 B5
Ashville Way RG41 . . . . . . 116 A5
Ash Way RG41. . . . . 115 D3
Ashwell Cl RG15 . . . . .97 E6
Ashwell Ct TW15. . . . . .97 E6
Ashwood RG5 . . . . .87 D4
Ashwood Cl RG31 . . . . .84 B6
Ashwood Dr RG14 . . . . . . 105 D4
Ashwood Rd TW20 . . . . . . .95 B2
Ashworth Dr RG19 . . . . . . 106 C2
Askeys Ho **8** RG7. . . . . . . 113 B3
Asnapet La RG20 . . . . .22 E6
Aspasugas Cl RG7 . . . . . . 137 B6
Aspects Ct SL1. . . . . .42 E4
Aspen Cl
Slough SL2. . . . . .42 B8
Staines TW15. . . . . .96 F5
Aspen Ct GU25 . . . . 122 C5
Aspen Gdns TW15 . . . . . . .98 C3
Aspin Way GU17 . . . . 150 B5
Astleham Rd TW17. . . . . . 124 E6
Astley Cl
Newbury RG14. . . . . 104 D2
Wokingham RG41 . . . . . . 115 F7
ASTON. 16 C5
Aston Ave RG31 . . . . .84 B3
Aston Cl RG18 . . . . .56 D5
Aston Cotts SL4 . . . . .93 A4
Aston Dr RG30 . . . . .85 B5
Aston Ferry La RG9 . . . . . .16 D5
Aston La RG9. . . . . .16 C3
Aston Mead SL4 . . . . .66 F6
Aston St RG31 . . . . .12 F8
Astonville SL2 . . . . .22 C8
Astor Cl
Maidenhead SL6 . . . . .40 B6
Winnersh RG41 . . . . .88 D3

Astra Mead RG42 . . . . 92 B2
Atfield Gr GU20 . . . . 146 D4
Atherton Cl
Reading RG30 . . . . 84 F8
Stanwell TW19 . . . . 70 D1
Atherton Cres RG17 . . . . 100 D5
Atherton Ct SL4 . . . . 67 D7
Atherton Pl RG17 . . . . 25 B3
Atherton Rd RG17 . . . . 100 D5
Athlone Cl SL6 . . . . 19 E1
Athlone Sq SL4 . . . . 67 C6
Atlantean Ct 2 RG14 . . . . . 105 B3
Atrebatti Rd GU47 . . . . 143 C1
Attebrouche Ct RG12 . . . . 118 D2
Atte La RG42 . . . . 91 C2
Atterbury Gdns RG4 . . . . 58 E4
Attwood Dr RG2 . . . . 140 E8
Auburn Ct RG4 . . . . 59 A2
Auckland Cl SL6 . . . . 40 B8
Auckland Rd RG6 . . . . 87 A6
Auclum Cl RG7 . . . . 111 B2
Auclum La RG7 . . . . 111 B2
Audley Cl RG14 . . . . 105 D5
Audley Dr SL6 . . . . 39 B6
Audley St RG30 . . . . 85 E8
Audley Way SL5 . . . . 119 D6
Audrey Ct RG7 . . . . 109 C3
Audrey Needham Ho 7
RG14 . . . . 105 B2
Augur Cl TW18 . . . . 96 F3
August End
Reading RG30 . . . . 85 C8
Slough SL3 . . . . 43 E7
Augustine Cl SL3 . . . . 69 E4
Augustine Wlk RG42 . . . . . . 91 E1
Augustus Gdns GU15 . . . . 152 C5
Austen Gdns RG14 . . . . 131 B8
Austen Way SL3 . . . . 68 F8
Austin Rd RG5 . . . . 87 F6
Austinsgate SL6 . . . . 38 F8
Austin Way RG12 . . . . 118 D6
Australia Ave SL6 . . . . 39 F8
Australia Rd SL1 . . . . 43 B4
Auton Pl RG9 . . . . 35 D8
Autumn Cl
Caversham RG4 . . . . 59 C7
Slough SL1 . . . . 41 F5
Autumn Wlk
Maidenhead SL6 . . . . 39 A5
Wargrave RG10 . . . . 36 D2
Avalon Rd
Bourne End SL8 . . . . 3 B5
Earley RG6 . . . . 87 C3
Avebury
Bracknell RG12 . . . . 118 A3
Slough SL1 . . . . 42 A6
Avebury Sq RG1 . . . . 86 D5
Aveley Ho 19 RG1 . . . . 86 B6
Aveley Wlk 2 RG1 . . . . 86 B5
Avenue Dr SL3 . . . . 23 F1
Avenue Ho RG4 . . . . 58 D3
Avenue Hts RG2 . . . . 86 C4
Avenue Rd
Egham TW18 . . . . 96 D3
Feltham TW13 . . . . 98 F5
Maidenhead SL6 . . . . 40 B5
Avenue Sch The RG2 . . . . . . 86 C4
Avenue Sucy GU15 . . . . 151 B4
Avenue The
Bourne End SL8 . . . . 2 F4
Camberley GU15 . . . . 151 B5
Crowthorne RG45 . . . . 143 B5
Datchet SL3 . . . . 68 B6
Egham TW20 . . . . 96 B4
Farnham Common SL2 . . . . . 22 B8
Lightwater GU18 . . . . 146 A1
Maidenhead SL6 . . . . 20 C3
Mortimer RG7 . . . . 137 B5
North Ascot SL5 . . . . 92 F1
Old Windsor SL4 . . . . 68 B2
Staines TW18 . . . . 124 B8
Wraysbury TW19 . . . . 68 D4
Averil Ct SL6 . . . . 41 C7
Avery Cl RG40 . . . . 141 F6
AVINGTON 101 E5
Avington Cl RG31 . . . . 84 B8
Avocet Cres GU47 . . . . 150 E8
Avocet Ct 4 RG1 . . . . 86 A6
Avon Cl
Reading RG31 . . . . 84 F5
Slough SL1 . . . . 41 E6
Avon Ct RG42 . . . . 90 C2
Avondale SL6 . . . . 19 C1
Avondale Ave TW18 . . . . 96 F1
Avondale Rd TW15 . . . . 97 D5
Avon Gr RG12 . . . . 91 C1
Avonmoor SL6 . . . . 40 B8
Avon Pl RG1 . . . . 86 D8
Avon Rd TW16 . . . . 98 F1
Avonway RG14 . . . . 105 D4
Avon Way RG7 . . . . 109 E6
Axbridge RG12 . . . . 118 E4
Axbridge Rd RG2 . . . . 86 C2
Axis Pk SL3 . . . . 44 B1
Ayebridges Ave TW20 . . . . . 96 C1
Aylesbury Cres SL1 . . . . 42 D7
Aylesford Way RG19 . . . . . 107 A2
Aylesham Way GU46 . . . . . 149 B6
Aylesworth Ave SL2 . . . . 22 B2
Aylesworth Spur SL4 . . . . . . 95 B8
Aylsham Cl RG30 . . . . 84 E8
Aymer Cl TW18 . . . . 123 E8
Aymer Dr TW18 . . . . 123 E8
Ayrton Senna Rd RG31 . . . . 84 C7
Aysgarth RG12 . . . . 118 A3
Aysgarth Pk SL6 . . . . 40 B1
Azalea Cl RG41 . . . . 88 B2
Azalea Rd RG19 . . . . 133 A5
Azalea Way
Frimley GU15 . . . . 152 B6
Slough SL3 . . . . 43 E7
Azure Ct 12 TW13 . . . . 98 F5

B

Babbage Way RG12 . . . . . 118 A3
Babbington Rd RG2 . . . . . 113 D6
Bacchus Ho RG7 . . . . 134 E2
Bachelors Acre SL4 . . . . 67 D6
Back La
Beenham RG7 . . . . 109 A7
Brimpton RG7 . . . . 134 C4
Kintbury RG17 . . . . 127 F7
Shinfield RG7 . . . . 139 A8
Silchester RG7 . . . . 136 D4
Stanford Dingley RG7 . . . . . . 81 E4
Backsideans RG10 . . . . 36 D2
Back St RG17 . . . . 47 C6
Bacon Cl GU47 . . . . 150 D6
Baden Cl TW18 . . . . 97 B1
Bader Gdns SL1 . . . . 42 A4
Bader Way The RG5 . . . . 88 A5
Badgebury Rise SL7 . . . . 1 C7
Badgemore Com Sch
RG9 . . . . 15 D2
Badgemore La RG9 . . . . 15 D3
Badger Cl SL6 . . . . 39 D4
Badger Dr
Lightwater GU18 . . . . 146 A1
Twyford RG10 . . . . 61 D7
Badgers Cl TW15 . . . . 97 F3
Badgers Copse GU15 . . . . . 151 E4
Badgers Croft RG7 . . . . . . 137 A6
Badgers Glade RG7 . . . . . . 111 A2
Badgers Hill GU25 . . . . . . 122 C4
Badgers Holt GU46 . . . . . . 149 B5
Badgers Ridge RG20 . . . . . 130 C4
Badgers Rise
Caversham RG4 . . . . 59 A5
Woodley RG5 . . . . 60 D1
Badgers Sett RG45 . . . . 142 F5
Badgers Way
Bracknell RG12 . . . . 118 F7
Marlow Bottom SL7 . . . . 1 D7
Badgers Wlk RG9 . . . . 36 A3
Badgers Wood SL2 . . . . 22 C7
Badgerwood Dr GU16 . . . . 151 D2
Bad Godesberg Way SL6 . . 39 F7
Badminton Rd SL6 . . . . 39 B6
Badsworth Gdns RG14 . . . 130 D4
Bagnols Way RG14 . . . . 104 E2
BAGSHOT 145 D3
Bagshot Gn GU19 . . . . 145 E3
Bagshot Inf Sch GU19 . . . . . 145 E2
Bagshot Rd
Ascot SL5 . . . . 120 C2
Bracknell RG12 . . . . 118 C4
Englefield Green TW20 . . . . . 95 C2
Bagshot Sta GU19 . . . . 145 E4
Baigents La GU20 . . . . 146 D4
Bailey Cl
Maidenhead SL6 . . . . 39 F7
Windsor SL4 . . . . 67 A5
Bailey Ho 9 SL8 . . . . 3 A4
Baileys Cl GU17 . . . . 150 C4
Bailey's La RG10 . . . . 62 E3
Baily Ave RG18 . . . . 106 B4
Bain Ave GU15 . . . . 151 B2
Bainbridge Rd RG31 . . . . . . 84 B4
Bainhurst Cotts SL6 . . . . . . 38 B5
Baird Cl SL1 . . . . 42 B4
Baird Rd RG2 . . . . 140 E7
Bakeham La TW20 . . . . 95 D1
Bakehouse Ct SL5 . . . . 119 B8
Bakers Ct 2 TW19 . . . . 70 D1
Bakers La SL6 . . . . 38 F8
Bakers Orch HP10 . . . . 3 E5
Bakers Row SL6 . . . . 38 F8
Baker St
Aston Tirrold OX11 . . . . 12 F8
Reading RG1 . . . . 85 F7
Baldwin Ct RG10 . . . . 61 E6
Baldwin Pl SL6 . . . . 39 C7
Baldwin Rd SL1 . . . . 21 C2
Baldwin's Shore SL4 . . . . . . 67 D8
Balfour Cres
Bracknell RG12 . . . . 118 B4
Newbury RG14 . . . . 130 C6
Balfour Dr RG31 . . . . 84 B4
Balfour Pl SL7 . . . . 1 C4
Balintore Ct 8 GU47 . . . . . 150 D8
Ballamoor Cl RG31 . . . . 84 B3
Ballard Ct GU15 . . . . 152 A8
Ballard Gn SL4 . . . . 66 E7
Ballard Rd GU15 . . . . 152 A8
Ballencrieff Rd SL5 . . . . . . 120 F2
BALL HILL 129 C3
Balliol Rd RG4 . . . . 58 D3
Balliol Way GU47 . . . . 143 E1
Ball Pit Rd RG20 . . . . 30 B5
Balme Cl RG10 . . . . 61 B4
Balmoral SL6 . . . . 19 B1
Balmoral Cl SL1 . . . . 41 E7
Balmoral Gdns SL4 . . . . 67 D4
Balmoral Grange TW18 . . 124 B7
Balmore Dr RG4 . . . . 59 B4
Balmore Ho RG4 . . . . 59 B3
Balmore Pk RG4 . . . . 59 B3
Bamburgh Cl RG2 . . . . 86 C3
Bamford Pl RG31 . . . . 84 B4
Banbury RG12 . . . . 118 E2
Banbury Ave SL1 . . . . 41 F8
Banbury Cl RG41 . . . . 116 A6
Banbury Gdns RG4 . . . . 59 C3
Bancroft Cl TW15 . . . . 98 A3
Bancroft Pl RG31 . . . . 84 B3
Bangors Cl SL0 . . . . 44 F7
Bangors Rd S SL0 . . . . 44 E8
Bank Apartments SL7 . . . . . . 1 D3
Bank Side RG40 . . . . 141 F6
Bankside Cl RG2 . . . . 86 D2
Banks Spur SL1 . . . . 42 B4
Bannard Rd SL6 . . . . 39 A5
Bannister Cl SL3 . . . . 43 E4
Bannister Gdns GU46 . . . . 149 F5
Bannister Pl RG7 . . . . 133 F6
Bannister Rd RG7 . . . . 110 F2
Barbara Cl TW17 . . . . 125 B4
Barbara's Mdw RG31 . . . . . . 57 B2
Barbel Cl RG6 . . . . 87 B8
Barber Cl RG10 . . . . 88 E7
Barberry Way GU17 . . . . . . 150 F2
Barbicus Ct 1 SL6 . . . . 40 B8
Barbon Cl GU15 . . . . 152 D3
Barbrook Cl RG31 . . . . 57 D3
Barchester Rd SL3 . . . . 43 F4
Barclay Rd RG31 . . . . 84 D4
Barclose Ave RG4 . . . . 59 C3
Bardeen Pl RG12 . . . . 118 D6
Bardney Cl SL6 . . . . 39 D3
Bardolph's Cl RG4 . . . . 58 D8
Bardown RG20 . . . . 51 B2
Barefoot Cl RG31 . . . . 57 B1
Barfield Rd RG18 . . . . 106 A4
Barge La RG7 . . . . 139 A5
Bargeman Rd SL6 . . . . 39 E5
Barholm Cl RG6 . . . . 87 E2
Barkby RG6 . . . . 87 C2
Barker Cl
Arborfield Garrison RG2 . . . 140 E7
Chertsey KT16 . . . . 123 E2
Barker Ct RG10 . . . . 88 F8
Barker Gn RG12 . . . . 118 B4
Barker Rd KT16 . . . . 123 F2
Barkers Mdw SL5 . . . . 119 D8
BARKHAM 115 C2
Barkham Manor RG41 . . . . 115 C3
Barkham Mews 14 RG1 . . . 86 C7
Barkham Rd
Barkham RG41 . . . . 115 D3
Wokingham RG41 . . . . 116 A5
Barkham Ride RG40 . . . . . . 141 E8
Barkham St RG40 . . . . 115 C2
Barkhart Cl RG40 . . . . 116 C7
Barkhart Dr RG40 . . . . 116 C7
Barkhart Gdns RG40 . . . . . 116 C7
Barkis Mead GU47 . . . . 143 E2
Barkwith Cl RG6 . . . . 87 E2
Barley Cl RG19 . . . . 106 F2
Barley Ct TW19 . . . . 97 E7
Barley Fields HP10 . . . . 3 E8
Barley Gdns RG41 . . . . 88 B3
Barley Mead
Bracknell RG42 . . . . 91 E1
Maidenhead SL6 . . . . 39 A5
Barley Mow Rd TW20 . . . . . 95 C3
Barley Mow Way TW17 . . . 125 A5
Barley Way 3 SL7 . . . . 1 D1
Barley Wlk RG31 . . . . 84 A5
Barnard Cl RG4 . . . . 59 C6
Barnard's Ct 3 RG17 . . . . . 100 D5
Barnards Hill SL7 . . . . 1 C2
Barn Cl
Ashford TW15 . . . . 98 B3
Bracknell RG12 . . . . 118 D7
Camberley GU15 . . . . 151 E6
Farnham Common SL2 . . . . . 22 B8
Kintbury RG17 . . . . 102 B2
Maidenhead SL6 . . . . 19 F2
Reading RG30 . . . . 85 D4
Barn Cotts RG17 . . . . 74 D7
Barn Cres RG14 . . . . 130 D7
Barn Croft Dr RG6 . . . . 87 D1
Barn Dr SL6 . . . . 39 A4
Barnes Terr 8 RG14 . . . . . 104 F2
Barnes Way SL0 . . . . 44 F6
Barnet Ct RG12 . . . . 118 C7
Barnett Gn RG12 . . . . 118 B3
Barnett La GU18 . . . . 152 F7
Barn Farm SL7 . . . . 1 D3
Barnfield
Iver SL0 . . . . 44 E7
Slough SL1 . . . . 41 D5
3 Yateley GU46 . . . . 149 D5
Barnfield Cl SL6 . . . . 19 F5
Barnhill Cl SL7 . . . . 1 D4
Barnhill Gdns SL7 . . . . 1 D4
Barnhill Rd SL7 . . . . 1 D4
Barn La RG9 . . . . 15 C4
Barn Owl Way RG7 . . . . 111 B3
Barnsdale Rd RG2 . . . . 86 D3
Barn The RG18 . . . . 79 F5
Barnway TW20 . . . . 95 C3
Barnwood Cl RG30 . . . . 85 E8
Baroma Way RG9 . . . . 15 E2
Baron Ct RG30 . . . . 85 E7
Barons Ct 1 SL7 . . . . 1 E2
Baronsmead RG9 . . . . 15 D2
Barons Way TW20 . . . . 96 D2
Barossa Rd GU15 . . . . 151 D7
Barracane Dr RG45 . . . . . . 143 B5
Barrack La SL4 . . . . 67 D6
Barracks La RG7 . . . . 113 B1
Barrett Cres RG40 . . . . 116 E6
Barrett Ct RG1 . . . . 58 F1
Barrington Cl RG6 . . . . 87 B6
Barrington Ct TW18 . . . . 96 F2
Barrington Ho RG2 . . . . 113 B7
Barrington Way RG1 . . . . 85 E5
Barrow Lodge SL2 . . . . 22 C1
Barrsbrook Farm Rd
KT16 . . . . 123 E1
Barrsbrook Hall KT16 . . . . 123 E1
Barr's Rd SL6 . . . . 41 B7
Barry Ave SL4 . . . . 67 C7
Barry Pl RG1 . . . . 86 A8
Barry Sq RG12 . . . . 118 D2
Barry Terr TW15 . . . . 97 F6
Barry View SL4 . . . . 66 C5
Bartelotts Rd SL2 . . . . 21 E1
Bartholemew St RG14 . . . 105 A2
Bartholomew Ct 9
RG14 . . . . 104 F2
Bartholomew Pl RG42 . . . . . 91 E1
Bartlemy Cl RG14 . . . . 130 E8
Bartlemy Rd RG14 . . . . 130 E8
Bartletts La SL6 . . . . 65 A7
Barton Cl TW17 . . . . 125 B3
Barton Copse RG20 . . . . 51 B2
Barton Rd
Reading RG31 . . . . 84 B7
Slough SL3 . . . . 43 F4
Barton's Dr GU46 . . . . 149 D4
Barwell Cl RG45 . . . . 142 F4
Basemoors RG12 . . . . 118 E7
Basford Way SL4 . . . . 66 D4
Basil Cl RG6 . . . . 86 F1
Basildon CE Prim Sch
RG8 . . . . 55 A6
Basildon Ho 22 RG1 . . . . . . 86 B6
Basildon Pk★ RG8 . . . . 34 D1
Basingstoke Rd
Aldermaston RG7 . . . . 109 B2
Reading RG2 . . . . 86 B3
Riseley RG7 . . . . 139 B1
Shinfield RG7 . . . . 113 B3
Swallowfield RG7 . . . . 139 B5
Three Mile Cross RG7 . . . . 113 A5
Baskerville La RG9 . . . . 36 A3
Baslow Rd RG41 . . . . 88 B2
Basmore La RG9 . . . . 36 B4
Bassett Cl RG6 . . . . 114 C8
Bassett Rd OX12 . . . . 6 F8
Bassett Way SL2 . . . . 21 E1
Bass Mead SL6 . . . . 19 F5
Batcombe Mead RG12 . . . 118 E2
Bates Cl SL3 . . . . 43 E7
Bath Ct SL6 . . . . 39 C6
Bath Rd
Camberley GU15 . . . . 151 D6
Colthrop RG7, RG19 . . . . . . 107 D2
Froxfield SN8, RG17 . . . . 99 C4
Harlington TW6, UB7, TW5 . . 71 D6
Harmondsworth TW6, UB7 . . 70 E6
Hungerford RG17 . . . . 100 F6
Knowl Hill RG10, SL6 . . . . . . 37 D2
Littlewick Green SL6 . . . . . . 38 C5
Maidenhead SL6 . . . . 39 C6
Newbury RG18 . . . . 105 F4
Padworth RG7 . . . . 109 D4
Poyle SL3, UB7, TW6 . . . . 69 E6
Reading RG30, RG31, RG1 . . 85 C5
Slough, Cippenham SL1, SL6 41 D6
Slough SL1, SL6 . . . . 41 D6
Sonning RG4 . . . . 60 E2
Speen RG20 . . . . 104 D4
Thatcham RG18 . . . . 106 C4
Woolhampton RG7 . . . . 108 D2
Bath Road Cotts SL3 . . . . . . 69 E6
Bathurst Cl SL0 . . . . 44 F4
Bathurst Rd RG41 . . . . 88 B2
Bathurst Wlk SL0 . . . . 44 F4
Battalion Way RG19 . . . . . . 106 E1
Battery End RG14 . . . . 130 D6
Battle Cl RG14 . . . . 104 D4
Battlemead Cl SL6 . . . . 20 C3
Battle Pl RG30 . . . . 85 D8
Battle Prim Sch RG30 . . . . . 85 D7
Battle Rd
Goring RG8 . . . . 34 F7
Newbury RG14 . . . . 130 C6
Battle Sq RG30 . . . . 85 D8
Battle St RG1 . . . . 85 F8
Batty's Barn Cl RG40 . . . . . 116 D5
BAUGHURST COMMON . 134 D1
Baughurst Rd RG7 . . . . 136 A6
Baxendales The 4 RG14 105 C1
Baxter Cl SL1 . . . . 42 E3
Baybrook SL6 . . . . 19 F6
Bay Cl RG6 . . . . 86 F1
Baydon Dr RG1 . . . . 85 E5
Baydon Ho 6 RG17 . . . . 25 B2
Baydon Rd
Lambourn RG17 . . . . 24 E1
Lambourn RG17 . . . . 45 A7
Shefford Woodlands RG17 . . 74 E7
Wickham RG20 . . . . 75 B4
Bay Dr RG12 . . . . 118 E7
Bayeux Ct RG30 . . . . 85 D7
Bayfield Ave GU16 . . . . 151 E2
Bayford Cl GU17 . . . . 151 A1
Bayford Dr RG31 . . . . 84 F4
Bayley Cres SL1 . . . . 41 A8
Bayley Ct RG41 . . . . 88 B1
Baylis Bsns Ctr SL1 . . . . 42 D6
Baylis Court Sch SL1, SL2 . . 42 D8
Baylis Par SL1 . . . . 42 E7
Baylis Rd SL1 . . . . 42 E6
Bayliss Rd RG10 . . . . 36 D1
Bay Rd RG12 . . . . 118 E8
Bays Ct RG26 . . . . 134 F1
Bays Farm Ct UB7 . . . . 70 C6
Bay Tree Ct SL1 . . . . 21 C2
Bay Tree Rise RG31 . . . . 84 C5
Beach's Ho 2 TW18 . . . . . . 97 A3
Beacon Ct
Colnbrook SL3 . . . . 69 C7
3 Reading RG30 . . . . 85 D6
Beacon Rd TW6 . . . . 71 A1
Beacon Rdbt TW6 . . . . 71 B1
Beaconsfield Cotts SL8 . . . . 3 B2
Beaconsfield Rd SL2 . . . . . . 22 C6
Beaconsfield Way RG6 . . . . 87 A2
Beacontree Plaza RG2 . . . . 86 B2
Beale Cl RG40 . . . . 116 B7
Beale Park Wildlife Pk★
Lower Basildon RG8 . . . . . . 34 F1
Pangbourne RG8 . . . . 55 F8
Beales Farm Rd RG17 . . . . . 25 B2
Beal's La RG31 . . . . 84 A7
Beancroft Rd RG19 . . . . . . 106 D2
Bean Oak Rd RG40 . . . . . . 116 F6
Beard's Rd TW15 . . . . 98 E2
Bearfield La RG17 . . . . 73 B7
Bear La
Newbury RG14 . . . . 105 A3
Wargrave RG10 . . . . 37 B3
Bearsden Ct SL5 . . . . 120 F2
Bears Rail Pk SL4 . . . . 94 F8
Bears Rails Pk SL4 . . . . 94 F8
Bearwater RG17 . . . . 100 D6
Bear Wharf 8 RG1 . . . . 86 A6
Bearwood Coll RG41 . . . . . 115 B7
**Bearwood Park Mobile Home
Pk** 2 RG41 . . . . 88 A2
Bearwood Path RG41 . . . . . 88 A2
Bearwood Prim Sch
RG41 . . . . 115 B8
Bearwood Rd RG41 . . . . . . 115 C6
Beasley's Ait TW16 . . . . . . 125 F3
Beasley's Ait La TW16 . . . . 125 F3
Beattie Cl TW14 . . . . 98 F7
Beatty Dr RG30 . . . . 84 E8
Beatty Rise RG7 . . . . 139 A8
Beauchamp Ct SL1 . . . . 42 E6
Beauchief Cl RG6 . . . . 113 F8
Beaufield Cl RG5 . . . . 87 D7
Beaufort Cl SL7 . . . . 1 E2
Beaufort Gdns
Marlow SL7 . . . . 1 E2
North Ascot SL5 . . . . 119 E8
Beaufort Ho
5 Ashford TW15 . . . . 98 B3
Sunningdale SL5 . . . . 121 A1
Beaufort Pl SL6 . . . . 40 D4
Beauforts TW20 . . . . 95 C3
Beaufront Cl GU15 . . . . 152 A7
Beaufront Rd GU15 . . . . . . 152 B7
Beaulieu Cl
Bracknell RG12 . . . . 119 A6
Datchet SL3 . . . . 68 B5
Beaulieu Ct GU17 . . . . 150 B5
Beaulieu Gdns GU17 . . . . . 150 C5
Beaumaris Ct SL1 . . . . 42 C8
Beaumont Cl SL6 . . . . 39 A3
Beaumont Ct
Ascot SL5 . . . . 119 F5
Slough SL3 . . . . 43 D7
Beaumont Dr TW15 . . . . 98 D3
Beaumont Gdns RG12 . . . . 118 E4
Beaumont Rd
Slough SL2 . . . . 42 D8
Windsor SL4 . . . . 67 C5
Beaumont Rise SL7 . . . . 1 E2
Beaver Cl RG41 . . . . 116 B3
Beaver La GU46 . . . . 149 E5
Beavers Cl RG26 . . . . 135 A1
Beaver Way RG5 . . . . 88 B7
Beck Ct RG1 . . . . 86 C6
Becket Ho 4 RG14 . . . . 104 F2
Beckett Chase 7 SL3 . . . . . 43 F1
Beckett Cl RG40 . . . . 116 E6
Beckford Ave RG12 . . . . . . 118 B3
Beckford Cl RG41 . . . . 88 F1
Beckford Ct RG19 . . . . 106 D3
Beckfords RG8 . . . . 55 A5
Beckingham Pl RG7 . . . . . . 113 B2
Beckings Way HP10 . . . . 3 C7
Beckwell Rd SL1 . . . . 42 C4
Bede Wlk RG2 . . . . 86 C3
Bedfont Cl TW14 . . . . 71 C1
Bedfont Court Est TW19 . . . 70 B4
Bedfont Ct TW19 . . . . 70 B4
Bedfont Green Cl TW14 . . . 98 C7
Bedfont Ind Pk TW15 . . . . . 98 D5
Bedfont Ind Pk N TW15 . . . 98 C5
Bedfont Inf Sch TW14 . . . . . 71 E1
Bedfont Jun Sch TW14 . . . . 71 E1
Bedfont La TW14 . . . . 98 F8
Bedfont Lakes Ctry Pk★
TW14 . . . . 98 C6
Bedfont Rd
Feltham TW14, TW13 . . . . . . 98 D6
Stanwell TW19 . . . . 70 F1
Bedford Ave SL1 . . . . 42 A7
Bedford Cl
Maidenhead SL6 . . . . 39 A3
Newbury RG14 . . . . 130 C5
Bedford Dr SL2 . . . . 22 B6
Bedford Gdns RG41 . . . . . . 115 F7
Bedford La SL5 . . . . 121 B4
Bedford Rd RG1 . . . . 85 F8
Bedfordshire Down RG42 . . 91 F2
Bedfordshire Way RG41 . . 115 E6
Bedivere Ct 10 RG1 . . . . 86 B6
Bedwins La SL6 . . . . 19 B6
Beech RG9 . . . . 15 D2
Beecham Rd RG30 . . . . 85 C8
Beech Ave GU15 . . . . 151 D4
Beechbrook Ave GU46 . . . 149 D5
Beech Cl
Ashford TW15 . . . . 98 D3
Brimpton RG19 . . . . 133 B5
Burghfield RG30 . . . . 111 B4
Hampstead Norreys RG18 . . . 53 A5
Maidenhead SL6 . . . . 39 B8

Beech Cl *continued*
Stanwell TW19 . . . . **97** D8
Beech Copse 3 RG26 . . . . **134** E1
Beechcroft RG18 . . . . **53** A5
Beechcroft Cl SL5 . . . . . . **120** D5
Beechcroft Ct RG12 . . . . . . **118** B6
Beech Ct
Bracknell RG42 . . . . **117** D7
Burnham SL1 . . . . **21** C2
Caversham RG4 . . . . **59** B3
Hurst RG10 . . . . **89** A7
2 Marlow SL7 . . . . **1** E2
7 Newbury RG14 . . . . **105** A4
Beech Dr GU17 . . . . **150** D4
Beeches Dr SL2 . . . . **22** B7
Beeches Rd SL2 . . . . **22** B7
Beeches The
Goring RG8 . . . . **34** B5
Reading RG31 . . . . **57** D3
Slough SL2 . . . . **21** F2
8 Staines TW18 . . . . **97** A3
Beechfield RG18 . . . . **80** D7
Beechfield Pl SL6 . . . . **39** C4
Beech Glen RG12 . . . . **118** B5
BEECH HILL **138** D5
Beech Hill Ho RG7 . . . . **138** E6
Beech Hill Rd
Beech Hill RG7 . . . . **138** E6
Spencers Wood RG7 . . . . . . **113** A1
Sunningdale SL5 . . . . **120** F3
Beechingstoke 4 SL7 . . . . . . **1** F3
Beech La
Earley RG6 . . . . **87** B2
South Stoke RG8 . . . . **14** F1
Beech Lodge TW18 . . . . **96** E3
Beechmont Ave GU25 . . . **122** D4
Beechnut Cl RG41 . . . . **115** F5
Beechnut Dr GU17 . . . . . . **150** B6
Beech Rd
East Bedfont TW14 . . . . **98** E8
Newtown RG20 . . . . **132** A3
Purley on T RG8 . . . . **57** B5
Reading RG2 . . . . **86** E2
Slough SL3 . . . . **43** E4
Tokers Green RG4 . . . . **58** D7
Beech Ride GU47 . . . . **143** B1
Beechtree Ave
Englefield Green TW20 . . . . . **95** B2
Marlow Bottom SL7 . . . . **1** D5
Beech Tree Ct TW18 . . . . . . **124** B7
Beech Tree La TW18 . . . . . . **124** B7
Beech Wlk RG19 . . . . **106** E2
Beechwood Ave
Reading RG31 . . . . **84** D8
Staines TW18 . . . . **97** B2
Woodley RG5 . . . . **87** D7
Beechwood Cl SL5 . . . . **92** F1
Beechwood Dr
Maidenhead SL6 . . . . **39** A6
Marlow SL7 . . . . **18** B8
Beechwood Gdns SL1 . . . . . **42** E4
Beechwood Prim Sch
RG5 . . . . **87** E7
Beechwood Rd
Slough SL2 . . . . **42** D8
Wentworth GU25 . . . . **122** B1
Beechwood Sch SL2 . . . . **22** B2
BEEDON **51** D7
Beedon CE Prim Sch
RG20 . . . . **51** D8
Beedon Dr RG12 . . . . **117** E3
Beehive La RG12 . . . . **117** C7
Beehive Rd
Bracknell RG12, RG42 . . . . **117** D7
Staines TW18 . . . . **96** F3
BEENHAM **108** E6
Beenhamplace Rd RG19 . **132** D1
Beenham Prim Sch RG7 . . **108** F6
BEENHAM'S HEATH **63** C3
BEENHAM STOCKS **109** A7
Beeston Way RG6 . . . . **114** A8
Beggars Hill Rd RG10 . . . . . **61** B1
Beharrel Ho SL5 . . . . **120** E4
Beighton Cl RG6 . . . . **113** F8
Belfast Ave SL1 . . . . **42** D7
Belford Ct 16 RG1 . . . . **86** A6
Belfry Mews GU47 . . . . **149** F8
Belgrave Ct GU17 . . . . **150** D3
Belgrave Par SL1 . . . . **42** E6
Belgrave Rd SL1 . . . . **42** F6
Belgravia Ct 21 RG30 . . . . . **85** D6
Bel Bridge Rd KT16 . . . . . . **123** F1
Bell Bsns Ctr SL6 . . . . **39** F6
Bell Cl SL2 . . . . **43** B8
Bell Cnr KT16 . . . . **123** F2
Bell Ct
Caversham RG4 . . . . **59** B6
Hurley SL6 . . . . **17** F3
Twyford RG10 . . . . **61** D5
Belle Ave RG6 . . . . **87** A5
Belleisle RG8 . . . . **57** B5
Belleme Mews RG8 . . . . **34** B6
Bellever Hill GU15 . . . . . . **151** E5
Belle Vue Cl TW18 . . . . **124** A8
Belle Vue Rd
Henley-on-T RG9 . . . . **35** D8
Reading RG1 . . . . **85** F7
Bellevue Terr 5 RG1 . . . . . . **85** E7
Bell Foundry La RG40 . . . . **116** C8
Bell Hill RG14, RG20 . . . . . **130** B4
Bell Holt RG14 . . . . **130** C5
Bell House Gdns RG41 . . . **116** B6
Bellingham Cl GU15 . . . . . **152** C4
Bellingham Wlk RG4 . . . . . . **59** A5
Bell La
Aldworth RG8 . . . . **32** F4
Blackwater GU17 . . . . **150** C5
Eton SL4 . . . . **41** F2
Bell La *continued*
Henley-on-T RG9 . . . . **15** E3
Inkpen RG17 . . . . **127** D3
Bellman Ct 2 RG1 . . . . **86** A8
Bell Pl GU19 . . . . **145** F3
Bellsfield Ct SL4 . . . . **41** F2
Bells Hill SL2 . . . . **23** A4
Bells Hill Gn SL2 . . . . **23** A5
Bells La SL3 . . . . **69** B4
Bell St
Henley-on-T RG9 . . . . **15** E2
Maidenhead SL6 . . . . **39** F6
Bell Street Mews RG9 . . . . . **15** E2
Bellswood La SL0 . . . . **44** B8
Bell View SL4 . . . . **66** F5
Bell View Cl SL4 . . . . **66** F5
Bell Weir Cl TW19 . . . . **96** B6
Belmont SL2 . . . . **42** A8
Belmont Cotts
Colnbrook SL3 . . . . **69** C7
Speen RG20 . . . . **104** C6
Belmont Cres SL6 . . . . **39** D8
Belmont Dr SL6 . . . . **39** D8
Belmont Mews GU15 . . . . . **151** C3
Belmont Park Ave SL6 . . . . **39** D8
Belmont Park Rd SL6 . . . . . **39** D8
Belmont Rd
Camberley GU15 . . . . **151** C4
Crowthorne RG45 . . . . **143** B6
Maidenhead SL6 . . . . **39** D8
Reading RG30 . . . . **85** D7
Belmont Vale SL6 . . . . **39** D8
Belsize Grange KT16 . . . . . **124** C2
Belton Rd GU15 . . . . **151** E5
Belvedere Ct GU17 . . . . . . **150** D3
Belvedere Dr RG14 . . . . . . **131** A8
Belvedere Grange SL5 . . . **121** A1
Belvedere Mans SL1 . . . . . . **42** D4
Belvedere Wlk 2 RG41 . . . **88** A3
Belvoir Cl GU16 . . . . **151** F1
Bembridge Ct
Crowthorne RG45 . . . . **142** E4
12 Slough SL1 . . . . **42** F4
Bembridge Pl RG1 . . . . **86** C7
Benbricke Gn RG42 . . . . **91** A1
Bence The TW20 . . . . **123** B6
Bencombe Rd SL7 . . . . **1** E5
Benedict Dr TW14 . . . . **98** D8
Benedict Gn RG42 . . . . **91** E1
Benen-Stock Rd TW19 . . . . **70** A2
Benetfeld Rd RG42 . . . . **90** B2
Benett Cl RG14 . . . . **104** F5
Benett Gdns RG14 . . . . **104** F5
Benham Chase RG20 . . . . . **103** E5
Benham Dr RG7 . . . . **139** A8
Benham Hill
Newbury RG18 . . . . **105** F4
Thatcham RG18 . . . . **106** A4
Benham La RG7 . . . . **139** D3
Benhams La RG9 . . . . **15** E8
Benjamin Ct TW15 . . . . **98** C1
Bennet Ct RG2 . . . . **86** A1
Bennet Rd RG2 . . . . **86** A1
Bennett Ct GU15 . . . . **151** C5
Bennetts Cl SL1 . . . . **42** A5
Bennett's Hill RG7, RG30 . **111** C7
Benning Cl SL4 . . . . **66** D4
Bennings Cl RG42 . . . . **91** A1
Benning Way RG40 . . . . . . **116** D8
Bensington Ct TW14 . . . . . . **71** D1
Benson Cl
Reading RG2 . . . . **86** D3
Slough SL2 . . . . **43** A5
Bensonholme RG7 . . . . **109** C3
Benson Rd RG45 . . . . **142** F5
Bentley Copse GU15 . . . . . **152** B4
Bentley Ct
4 Camberley GU15 . . . . . . **151** D5
Maidenhead SL6 . . . . **39** D4
Bentley Dr RG2 . . . . **140** E8
Bentley Pk SL2 . . . . **21** D3
Bentley Rd SL1 . . . . **42** A5
Benyon Ct RG1 . . . . **85** E6
Benyon Mews RG1 . . . . **85** E6
Beomonds 5 KT16 . . . . **124** A2
Beomonds Row 2 KT16 . . **124** A2
Bere Court Rd RG8 . . . . **56** B4
Bere Rd RG12 . . . . **118** E3
Beresford Ave SL2 . . . . **43** C6
Beresford Rd RG30 . . . . **85** E8
Bergenia Ct GU24 . . . . **153** E6
Berkeley Ave RG1 . . . . **85** E6
Berkeley Cl TW19 . . . . **96** D6
Berkeley Ct 1 RG1 . . . . **85** F6
Berkeley Dr SL4 . . . . **93** B7
Berkeley Gdns KT12 . . . . . **125** F2
Berkeley Mews
Marlow SL7 . . . . **1** F2
Slough SL1 . . . . **41** E7
Berkeley Rd RG14 . . . . **104** F2
Berkley Cl SL6 . . . . **39** A8
Berkshire Ave SL1 . . . . **42** B7
Berkshire Bsns Ctr RG19 **107** A2
Berkshire Bsns Pk RG7 . . **135** E4
Berkshire Coll of Agriculture
SL6 . . . . **18** A1
Berkshire Coll of Agriculture
(Hall Place) SL6 . . . . **38** A8
Berkshire Dr
Reading RG31 . . . . **84** C7
Thatcham RG19 . . . . **107** A2
Berkshire Ind Hospl RG1 . . **85** E5
Berkshire Lodge 1 SL6 . . . **39** F6
Berkshire Rd
Camberley GU15 . . . . **151** F8
Henley-on-T RG9 . . . . **35** D8
Berkshire Way RG12 . . . . . **117** D6
Bernadine Cl RG42 . . . . **91** E1
Bernard Ct GU15 . . . . **151** B4
Berners Cl SL1 . . . . **41** E6
Bernersh Cl GU47 . . . . **143** C1
Berries Rd SL6 . . . . **20** A8
Berrybank GU47 . . . . **150** E6
Berrycroft RG12 . . . . **118** D8
Berryfield SL2 . . . . **43** C7
Berry Hill SL6 . . . . **40** D7
Berry Hill Ct SL6 . . . . **40** D8
Berrylands Rd RG4 . . . . **59** B3
Berryscroft Ct TW18 . . . . . . **97** C1
Berryscroft Rd TW18 . . . . . . **97** C1
Berrys La RG30 . . . . **85** A1
Berrys Rd RG7 . . . . **107** C5
Berstead Cl 3 RG6 . . . . **87** B1
Berwick Ave SL1 . . . . **42** B6
Berwick Cl SL7 . . . . **1** D3
Berwick La SL7 . . . . **1** C3
Berwick Rd SL7 . . . . **1** C3
Berwyn Ho RG2 . . . . **113** C7
Beryl Cl RG41 . . . . **115** E7
Bessel's Way OX11 . . . . **12** B8
Bessemer Cl 3 SL3 . . . . **43** F1
Bestobell Rd SL1 . . . . **42** C7
Beswick Gdns RG12 . . . . . . **118** F8
Beta Ho 6 RG30 . . . . **85** D6
Betam Rd RG1 . . . . **86** D7
Beta Way TW20 . . . . **123** C8
Betchworth Ave RG6 . . . . . . **87** A3
Bethany Waye TW14 . . . . . . **98** E8
Bethesda Cl RG8 . . . . **55** A6
Bethesda St RG8 . . . . **55** A7
Betjeman Wlk GU46 . . . . . . **149** B4
Betteridge Rd RG19 . . . . . . **106** F2
Bettoney Vere SL6 . . . . **40** C4
Betty Grove La RG41 . . . . . **114** F7
Bevan Gate RG42 . . . . **118** A8
Beverley Cl
Frimley GU15 . . . . **152** D6
Marlow SL7 . . . . **1** B2
Thatcham RG18 . . . . **106** C4
Beverley Ct SL1 . . . . **43** B4
Beverley Gdns
Maidenhead SL6 . . . . **19** B1
Wargrave RG10 . . . . **36** E1
Beverley Rd
Reading RG31 . . . . **57** C1
Sunbury TW16 . . . . **125** F8
Bevers The RG7 . . . . **137** A6
Bewicks Reach RG14 . . . . . **104** F3
Bexley Ct RG30 . . . . **85** D6
Bexley St SL4 . . . . **67** C6
Bibury Cl RG5 . . . . **87** D4
Bicknell Rd GU16 . . . . **151** E2
Biddles Cl SL1 . . . . **41** E5
Bideford Cl RG5 . . . . **87** C5
Bideford Spur SL2 . . . . **22** B2
Bietigheim Way GU15 . . . . **151** C6
Big Barn Gr RG42 . . . . **91** D1
Bigbury Gdns RG2 . . . . **86** C3
Bigfrith La SL6 . . . . **19** B6
Bigg's Hill Cotts RG20 . . . . **129** F4
Biggs La RG2, RG40 . . . . . . **141** A8
Big La RG17 . . . . **25** B3
Bilberry Gdns RG7 . . . . **137** B6
Billet La SL0, SL3 . . . . **44** B7
Billet Rd TW18, TW19 . . . . . **97** A5
BILL HILL **89** B2
Billing Ave RG40 . . . . **141** F6
BILLINGBEAR **90** B6
Billingbear La RG42 . . . . **90** B5
Billington Way RG18 . . . . . **106** C5
Bilton Ind Est RG12 . . . . **117** E5
Binbrook Cl RG6 . . . . **87** D2
Binbury Row TW18 . . . . **96** E4
BINFIELD **90** D2
Binfield CE Prim Sch
RG42 . . . . **90** C2
BINFIELD HEATH **35** A2
Binfield Ho RG42 . . . . **90** C3
Binfield Rd
Bracknell, Priestwood
RG42 . . . . **118** A8
Wokingham RG40 . . . . **116** F7
Bingham Cotts RG42 . . . . . . **91** B6
Bingham Dr TW18 . . . . **97** D1
Bingham Rd SL1 . . . . **41** A8
Binghams The SL6 . . . . **40** B3
Bingley Gr RG5 . . . . **60** F1
Binsted Dr GU17 . . . . **150** D5
Birch Ave
Brimpton RG19 . . . . **133** B5
Reading RG30 . . . . **85** A8
Birch Cl GU15 . . . . **151** E8
Birch Copse Prim Sch
RG31 . . . . **84** C8
Birch Ct RG45 . . . . **142** F6
Birch Dr GU17 . . . . **150** D3
Birches The
Blackwater GU17 . . . . **150** B5
Goring RG8 . . . . **34** B6
Birchetts Cl 1 RG42 . . . . . . **118** B8
Birchfields GU15 . . . . **151** C4
Birch Gn RG2 . . . . **113** D8
Birch Gr
Slough SL2 . . . . **42** B8
Upper Halliford TW17 . . . . . **125** E7
Windsor SL4 . . . . **66** D6
BIRCH GREEN **97** A4
BIRCH HILL **118** C2
Birch Hill Prim Sch
RG12 . . . . **118** B1
Birch Hill Rd RG12 . . . . **118** B2
Birchington Rd SL4 . . . . **67** A5
Birch La
Mortimer RG7 . . . . **136** E5
West End GU24 . . . . **153** D7
Winkfield RG12, SL5 . . . . . . **119** B8
Birchland Cl RG7 . . . . **136** E6
Birchlands Ct GU47 . . . . . . **143** E2
Birchmead RG41 . . . . **88** D2
Birch Platt GU24 . . . . **153** D6
Birch Rd
Burghfield Common RG7 . . **111** A3
Tadley RG26 . . . . **134** F2
Windlesham GU20 . . . . **146** E4
Wokingham RG40 . . . . **142** A7
Birch Side RG45 . . . . **143** A6
Birch Tree View GU18 . . . . **146** A1
Birchview Cl GU46 . . . . **149** D4
Birchwood Cl RG4 . . . . **59** C6
Birchwood Dr GU18 . . . . . . **146** C1
Birchwood Rd RG14 . . . . . . **105** D4
Birchwoods The RG31 . . . . . **84** B8
Birdhill Ave RG2 . . . . **86** D2
Bird Mews RG40 . . . . **116** B6
Birds La RG7 . . . . **107** E4
Birdwood Rd
Maidenhead SL6 . . . . **39** B7
Sandhurst GU15 . . . . **150** F6
Birkbeck Pl GU47 . . . . **143** E1
Birkdale RG12 . . . . **117** E2
Birkdale Ct SL5 . . . . **120** C4
Birkhall Cl RG31 . . . . **84** C5
Birley Rd SL1 . . . . **42** D7
Biscuit Way RG2 . . . . **112** F8
BISHAM **18** E7
Bisham Abbey National
Sports Ctr SL7 . . . . **18** D7
Bisham CE Prim Sch SL7 . . **18** D7
Bisham Ct
Bisham SL7 . . . . **18** E6
11 Slough SL1 . . . . **42** F4
Bisham Gn SL7 . . . . **18** E6
Bisham Rd SL7 . . . . **18** E8
Bishop Ct SL6 . . . . **39** D6
Bishop Ctr The SL6 . . . . **40** F7
Bishopdale RG12 . . . . **118** A5
Bishop Duppas Pk TW17 . **125** E2
Bishops Cl RG26 . . . . **135** A1
Bishops Ct
1 Ashford TW16 . . . . **98** F1
North Ascot SL5 . . . . **92** F2
Bishops Dr
East Bedfont TW14 . . . . **71** D1
Wokingham RG40 . . . . **116** C7
Bishops Farm Cl SL4 . . . . . . **66** B6
BISHOPSGATE **94** F4
Bishops Gate SL6 . . . . **40** F7
Bishopsgate Rd TW20 . . . . . **95** B5
Bishopsgate Sch TW20 . . . . **95** A5
Bishops Gr GU20 . . . . **146** C4
BISHOPS GREEN **132** A3
BISHOP'S GREEN **132** A3
Bishop's La SL4 . . . . **92** B7
Bishops Orch SL2 . . . . **22** B2
Bishops Rd
Slough SL1 . . . . **43** A4
Stanford Dingley RG7 . . . . . . **81** F3
Bishop's Rd RG6 . . . . **87** A6
Bishops Way TW20 . . . . **96** D2
Bishops Wlk HP10 . . . . **3** E5
Bishopswood Ct RG26 . . . . **134** F1
Bishopswood La RG26 . . . **134** E1
Bishopswood Rd RG26 . . . **134** F1
Bishop Wand CE Sch The
TW16 . . . . **125** F7
BISLEY **153** F3
Bispham Ct 2 RG1 . . . . **86** C6
Bissley Dr SL6 . . . . **39** A3
Bitham La
Ham RG17 . . . . **126** B5
Inkpen RG17 . . . . **127** B4
Bitham Rd OX12 . . . . **8** C7
Bittern Cl GU47 . . . . **150** D8
Bitterne Ave RG31 . . . . **84** B6
Bix Hill RG9 . . . . **15** A6
Bix La SL6 . . . . **38** F8
Blackamoor La SL6 . . . . **40** A8
Blackberry Cl TW17 . . . . . . **125** E5
Blackberry Ct RG26 . . . . . . **134** E2
Blackbird Cl
Burghfield Common RG7 . . . **111** B3
Sandhurst GU47 . . . . **150** D8
Blackbird La RG20 . . . . **132** A3
Black Boy La SL6 . . . . **17** C3
Blackburn Trad Est TW19 . . **70** F1
Blackbush Bsns Ctr
GU46 . . . . **149** C4
Blackbush Park Cvn Site
GU46 . . . . **149** C5
Black Butt Cotts SL6 . . . . . . **20** B7
Blackcap Pl GU47 . . . . **150** E8
Blackdown Way RG19 . . . . **106** D2
Blackett Cl TW18 . . . . **123** F7
Black Horse Cl SL4 . . . . **66** D5
Blackhouse Farm TW20 . . **123** C6
Black Lake Cl TW20 . . . . . . **123** A8
Blacklands Rd RG7 . . . . **107** C5
Blackley Cl RG6 . . . . **87** E3
Black Mdws RG12 . . . . **118** C3
Blackmoor Cl SL5 . . . . **119** D7
Blackmoor Wood SL5 . . . . **119** D7
BLACKNEST **121** B6
Blacknest Gate Rd SL5 . . . **121** B6
Blacknest Rd GU25, SL5 . . **121** E6
Black Park Ctry Pk & Visitor
Ctr* SL3 . . . . **23** F3
Black Park Rd SL3 . . . . **23** E4
Blackpond La SL2 . . . . **22** B4
Blacksmith Row SL3 . . . . **44** A2
Blacksmiths Ct UB7 . . . . **70** B6
Blacksmiths La KT16 . . . . . **124** A2
Blacksmith's La TW18 . . . . **124** C6
Blackstroud La E GU18,
GU24 . . . . **153** E8
Blackstroud La W GU18 . **153** D8
Blackthorn Cl
Earley RG6 . . . . **87** A7
Purley on T RG31 . . . . **57** B1
Blackthorn Dell SL3 . . . . **43** C3
Blackthorn Dr
Lightwater GU18 . . . . **153** B7
Thatcham RG18 . . . . **106** D5
Blackthorne Cres SL3 . . . . . **69** E5
Blackthorne Ct 3 TW15 . . . **98** C1
Blackthorne Rd SL3 . . . . **69** E4
BLACKWATER **150** D5
Blackwater Cl
Caversham RG4 . . . . **59** E4
Shinfield RG7 . . . . **113** B1
Blackwater Rise RG31 . . . . . **84** B4
Blackwater Sta GU17 . . . . . **150** E4
Blackwater View RG40 . . . **142** B2
Blaenant RG4 . . . . **58** F5
Blaenavon RG4 . . . . **58** F5
Blagden Cl RG19 . . . . **131** D7
Blagdon Rd RG2 . . . . **86** D2
Blagrave Farm La RG4 . . . . **58** D5
Blagrave La RG4 . . . . **58** D4
Blagrave Rise RG31 . . . . **84** C6
Blagrave St RG1 . . . . **86** B8
Blagrove Dr RG41 . . . . **115** F4
Blagrove La RG41 . . . . **115** F3
Blaire Pk GU46 . . . . **149** B8
Blair Rd SL1 . . . . **42** E5
Blake Cl
Crowthorne RG45 . . . . **143** C4
Wokingham RG40 . . . . **116** E8
Blakeney Ct SL6 . . . . **19** F1
Blakeney Fields RG17 . . . . . **48** B4
Blakes Cotts
Reading RG1 . . . . **86** C7
Wargrave RG10 . . . . **37** B1
Blakes Ct 3 KT16 . . . . **124** A1
Blakes La RG10 . . . . **37** B2
Blake's La RG26 . . . . **135** C1
Blakes Rd RG10 . . . . **36** F3
Blakes Ride GU46 . . . . **149** B6
Blamire Dr RG42 . . . . **90** F2
Blanchard Cl RG5 . . . . **88** B8
Blandford Cl SL3 . . . . **43** D3
Blandford Dr RG41 . . . . . . **115** E4
Blandford Ho SL6 . . . . **39** C8
Blandford Rd RG2 . . . . **113** C8
Blandford Rd N SL3 . . . . **43** D3
Blandford Rd S SL3 . . . . **43** D3
Bland's Cl RG7 . . . . **110** F2
Blands Ct RG7 . . . . **111** A2
Blandy Rd RG9 . . . . **35** D7
Blandys Hill RG17 . . . . **128** B8
Blandy's La RG8 . . . . **55** B6
Blane's La SL5 . . . . **119** C3
Blatchley Ho RG42 . . . . **90** C2
Blatch's Cl RG7 . . . . **83** D3
Blays Cl TW20 . . . . **95** C2
Blay's La TW20 . . . . **95** B2
Bledlow Cl RG14 . . . . **130** D5
Blenheim Ave RG12 . . . . . . **118** C5
Blenheim Cl
Slough SL3 . . . . **43** F5
Wokingham RG41 . . . . **115** E6
Blenheim Cotts RG18 . . . . **106** B8
Blenheim Ct
Egham TW18 . . . . **96** D4
11 Reading RG1 . . . . **86** B6
Blenheim Gdns RG1 . . . . **86** E6
Blenheim Pl GU15 . . . . **151** C3
Blenheim Rd
Caversham RG4 . . . . **59** A3
Maidenhead SL6 . . . . **39** B8
Newbury RG14 . . . . **104** F2
Reading RG1 . . . . **86** E6
Slough SL3 . . . . **43** D2
Blenheim Terr 1 RG1 . . . . . **86** A6
Blessed Hugh Faringdon RC
Sch RG30 . . . . **85** C5
Bletchmore Cl UB3 . . . . **71** D8
Blewburton Wlk RG12 . . . . **118** E5
BLEWBURY **12** B8
Blewbury Dr RG31 . . . . **84** B7
Blewbury Hill OX11 . . . . **12** B8
Blinco La SL3 . . . . **43** E7
Blind La
Bourne End HP10, SL8 . . . . **3** B6
Lambourn RG17 . . . . **25** B2
Block A SL2 . . . . **23** B1
Block B SL2 . . . . **23** B1
Block C SL2 . . . . **23** B1
Block Cotts RG7 . . . . **136** B6
Block D SL2 . . . . **23** B1
Block F SL2 . . . . **23** C1
Blomfield Dale RG42 . . . . . **117** D7
Blondell Cl UB7 . . . . **70** D8
Bloomfield Dr RG12 . . . . **91** C1
Bloomfieldhatch La RG7 . **138** B8
Bloomfield Rd SL6 . . . . **39** A5
Bloomsbury Way GU17 . . . **150** D3
Blossom Ave RG7 . . . . **83** E4
Blossom Gr RG5 . . . . **60** E1
Blossom La RG7 . . . . **83** E4
Blossom Rd RG4 . . . . **58** F3
Blossoms The RG20 . . . . **51** C4
Blount Cres RG42 . . . . **90** E1
Bloxworth Cl 10 RG12 . . . . **118** F5
Blue Ball La TW20 . . . . **95** F3
Bluebell Dr RG7 . . . . **110** F3
Bluebell Gdns RG4 . . . . **59** C7
Bluebell Hill RG12 . . . . **118** E8
Bluebell Mdw RG41 . . . . **88** C3
Bluebell Mews GU15 . . . . . **151** D7

Bluebell Rise GU18 ......153 B8
Bluebell Way RG18...... 106 D5
Bluecoats RG18......... 106 D4
Bluecoat Wlk RG12 ..... 118 D4
Bluethroat Cl GU47 ......150 E8
Blumfield Cres SL1 ....41 E8
Blumfield Ct SL1..........21 D1
Blundell's Rd RG30 ....84 E8
Blunden Dr SL3............44 C2
Blunts Ave UB7 ....71 A7
Blyth Ave RG19 ....106 E2
Blythe Cl SL0 ....44 F7
Blythe Ho SL1 ....41 D5
Blythewood La SL5 ......119 E7
Blyth Ho RG12 ....117 F3
Blyth Wlk 6 RG1 ....86 B5
Blythwood Dr GU16 ..... 151 D2
Boadicea Cl SL1 ....41 E5
Boames La RG20..........129 F5
Board La RG20...........102 F5
Boarlands Cl SL1 ....41 F6
Boathouse Reach RG9 ....15 E1
Bobgreen Ct RG2 .... 113 C6
Bobmore La SL7 ....1 F3
Bockhampton Rd RG17....25 C1
Bockmer La SL7 ....17 B7
Bodens Ride SL5 ....119 F1
Bodin Gdns RG14 ....131 B8
Bodmin Ave SL2 ....42 A8
Bodmin Cl RG19 .... 106 C2
Bodmin Rd RG5............87 C5
Body Rd 2 RG1 ....86 A7
Bog La RG12............. 119 A5
Boham's Rd OX11..........11 D6
Bolding House La GU24 ..153 F7
Boldrewood RG7..........110 F2
Bold's Ct SL2 ....23 A5
Boleyn Cl TW18............96 E3
Bolingbroke Way RG19...106 F3
Bolney La RG9.............36 A5
Bolney Rd RG9 ....36 B5
Bolney Trevor Dr RG9 .....36 A4
Bolton Ave SL4 ....67 D4
Bolton Cres SL4 ....67 C4
Bolton Pl 5 RG14 ...... 105 A3
Bolton Rd SL4 ....67 C4
Bolton Row RG20 ....50 D7
Boltons La RG42...........90 F1
Bolton's La TW6, UB7......71 B7
Bolwell Cl RG10 ....61 F4
Bomer Cl UB7 ....71 A7
Bomford Cl RG18 ....78 F6
Bond Cl RG26............ 135 A1
Bond St TW20 ....95 C3
Bond Way RG12..........118 B8
Bone La RG14 .... 105 C3
Bone Lane Ind Est RG14. 105 C3
Bonemill La RG20....... 104 D2
Bones La RG9 ....35 A3
Bonham Ct 3 RG41........88 C2
Bonhomie Ct RG10.........89 A7
Bonnicut Ct SL5 .... 121 A4
Bonny's Yd RG27........ 141 A1
Boole Hts RG12......... 118 A4
Boot End RG2 ....112 F8
Booth Dr
Finchampstead RG40......115 E1
Staines TW18.............97 D2
Borderers Gdns RG19 ... 106 D1
Borderside
Slough SL2...............43 A7
Yateley GU46........... 149 A6
Borrowdale Cl 3 TW20 ....96 B1
Borrowdale Gdns GU15 . 152 D4
Borrowdale Rd RG41......88 B4
Boscawen Way RG19.... 107 A3
Boscombe Cl TW20 ..... 123 C8
Bosham Cl RG6..........114 B8
Boshers Gdns TW20.......95 F2
Bosman Dr GU20 ....146 B6
Bossington Ct 9 TW18....96 F3
Bostock La RG7...........83 A2
Boston Ave RG1 ....85 F6
Boston Dr SL8..............3 B3
Boston Gr SL1.............42 C7
Boston Rd RG9 ....35 E8
Bosworth Ct SL1...........41 C6
Bosworth Gdns
Earley RG5...............87 E4
4 Woodley RG5...........87 E4
Botany Cl RG19 ....106 F3
Botham Dr SL1 ....42 E3
BOTHAMPSTEAD 52 B4
Bothy The RG10............36 D2
Botmoor Way RG20 ....48 F7
Bottisham Cl RG6....... 114 C8
Bottle La
Knowl Hill SL6 ....38 A2
Newell Green RG42.........91 A6
Bottom La RG7 .... 110 D8
Bottom Waltons Cvn Site
SL2.......................21 F3
Boughton Ho RG9 ....35 D8
Bouldish Farm Rd SL5 .. 120 A5
Boulters Cl
Maidenhead SL6 ....20 C1
Slough SL1...............42 A4
Woodley RG5..............87 F8
Boulters Ct SL6............20 C1
Boulters Gdns SL6.........20 C1
Boulters Ho RG12.........118 E5
Boulters La SL6............20 C1
Boulton Rd RG2 ....86 A3
Boult St RG1 ....86 C7
Boults Wlk RG2............86 B5
Boundary Cl RG31 ....84 C6
Boundary La RG4 ....58 E3
Boundary Pl HP10 ....3 D8
Boundary Rd
Newbury RG14...........105 B2
Staines TW15.............97 C3
Taplow SL1, SL6...........40 F8
Wooburn Green HP10 ....3 D8
Boundoak Ind Est RG2 .. 140 D8
Bourn Arch RG18 ....106 B4
Bourn Cl RG6.............87 C1
Bourne Ave
Chertsey KT16.......... 124 A6
Reading RG2 ....86 B4
Windsor SL4 ....67 C3
Bourne Cl
Bourne End SL8............3 B5
Reading RG31 ....84 B4
BOURNE END 3 B2
Bourne End Bsns Pk 1
SL8.........................3 B3
Bourne End Rd SL6, SL8 ...20 E8
Bourne End Sta SL8 ....3 A3
Bourne Ho 5 TW15.........98 A3
Bourne Mdw TW20.......123 B5
Bourne Rd
Pangbourne RG8 ....56 E5
Slough SL1...............42 D4
Thatcham RG18, RG19.....106 B4
Wentworth GU25........ 122 D4
Bourneside GU25 .... 122 A2
Bourne-Stevens Cl RG1...86 B7
Bourne Vale RG17....... 100 C5
Bourton Cl RG30..........84 F7
Bouverie Way SL3 ....43 E2
BOVENEY 66 C8
Boveney Cl SL1...........42 A4
Boveney Ho RG12........118 E5
Boveney New Rd SL4 .....41 E2
Boveney Rd SL4 ....41 C1
BOVINGDON GREEN 1 A3
Bovingdon Hts SL7 ....1 B2
Bowden Cl TW14..........98 E7
Bowden Rd SL5......... 120 D4
Bowdown Ct 10 RG14 ....104 F2
Bower Ct SL1..............41 F6
Bowers The RG40 ...... 116 A1
Bower Way SL1............41 E6
Bowes-Lyon Cl 6 SL4 ....67 C6
Bowes Rd
Egham TW18.............96 E2
6 Thatcham RG19 ...... 106 D2
Bowfell Cl RG31 ....57 C2
Bowland Dr RG12........118 E2
Bowling Ct RG9............15 D3
Bowling Green Farmhouse
RG8 ....57 B5
Bowling Green La RG8 ....57 B5
Bowling Green Rd RG18..106 B6
Bowlings The GU15 ..... 151 C6
Bowman Ct RG45 ....142 F4
Bowmans Cl SL1...........21 B3
Bowry Dr TW19............68 F1
Bowyer Cres RG40 ...... 116 C8
Bowyer Dr SL1 ....41 E6
Bowyer's La RG42.........91 C6
Bowyer Wlk SL5 ....119 E8
BOXFORD..................76 D3
Boxford Ridge RG12 .....118 B6
Boyd Ct RG42........... 118 A8
Boyndon Rd SL6...........39 D7
Boyne Hill CE Inf Sch SL6 39 D6
BOYN HILL 39 D6
Boyn Hill Ave SL6..........39 D6
Boyn Hill Cl SL6 ....39 D6
Boyn Hill Rd SL6...........39 D6
Boyn Valley Ind Est SL6 ..39 E6
Boyn Valley Rd SL6........39 D5
Bracebridge GU15 ...... 151 A5
Bracken Bank SL5 ...... 119 C8
Bracken Cl
Ashford TW16 ....98 F2
Farnham Common SL2......22 D8
Purley on T RG31..........57 C1
Bracken Copse RG17.....127 E5
Brackendale Cl GU15 ....151 E3
Brackendale Rd GU15 ... 151 D4
Brackendale Way RG6.....87 A5
Brackenforde SL3..........43 C4
Bracken La GU46 ....149 B6
Bracken Rd SL6............39 C4
Brackens The RG45 ..... 143 A7
Bracken Way
Burghfield Common RG7 .. 111 A2
Flackwell Heath HP10 ......3 B7
Brackenwood GU15 ..... 152 D5
Brackenwood Dr RG26 .. 135 A1
Brackley Ho 3 TW18.......96 F3
BRACKNELL..............118 D5
Bracknell Beeches RG12 .118 B6
Bracknell Bsns Ctr The
RG12 ....117 F7
Bracknell Cl GU15 ......144 F1
Bracknell Enterprise Ctr
RG12 .... 118 A7
Bracknell Rd
Bagshot GU19 ....145 E6
Camberley GU15 .... 145 A1
Crowthorne RG45 ...... 143 D6
Winkfield RG42 ....92 A5
Bracknell Sta RG12 ......118 B6
Bracknell & Wokingham Coll
Bracknell RG12 .... 118 C7
Bracknell, Wick Hill RG12 . 118 C8
Brackstone Cl RG4........59 C2
Bradbury Gdns SL3 ....23 D8
Bradcutts La SL6 ....19 E8
Bradenham La SL7.........18 C5
BRADFIELD 82 D5
Bradfield CE Prim Sch
RG7 ....82 B2
Bradfield Coll RG7........82 C6
Bradfields RG12 .... 118 D4
Bradford Rd SL1...........42 A7
Brading Way RG8 ....57 D5
Bradley Cl RG17 ....102 B1
Bradley Dr RG40........ 116 A2
Bradley-Moore Sq RG18 .106 E5
Bradley Rd SL1 ....42 E6
Bradmore Way RG6..... 114 A8
Bradshaw Cl SL4 ....66 E6
Bradwell Rd RG31 ....57 C3
Braeburn Ct TW18 ....97 B3
Braemar SL6 ....63 D7
Braemar Ct 3 SL7..........1 D2
Braemar Gdns SL1.........42 A4
Braemore Cl RG19 ...... 106 D2
Braeside RG12.......... 117 C7
Brakenhale Sch The
RG12 ....118 B5
Brakes Rise GU47........150 E8
Bramber Ct SL1 ....42 A5
Bramber Mews RG4.......59 E4
Bramble Cl
Burghfield Common RG7...110 E3
Upper Halliford TW17 .... 125 D6
Bramble Cres RG30 ....84 E8
Bramble Ct 4 RG14 .....105 B2
Brambledown TW18......124 B8
Bramble Dr SL6 ....39 A4
Bramblegate RG45 ...... 143 A6
Brambles The
Crowthorne RG45 .... 142 D6
Holyport SL6 ....65 B8
Newbury RG14...........130 E8
Bramblings RG4 ....58 E6
Bramcote GU15......... 152 C5
Bramley Ave TW17 ....125 E6
Bramley Chase SL6 ....39 C4
Bramley Cl
Chertsey KT16...........124 B1
Earley RG6...............87 B3
Maidenhead SL6 ....39 C3
Staines TW18.............97 C2
Bramley Ct
Crowthorne RG45 .... 142 D5
East Bedfont TW14 ....71 D1
Bramley Gr RG45 .... 142 D5
Bramley La GU17 ....150 B5
Bramley Rd
Camberley GU15 ....151 B2
Silchester RG7...........136 B1
Bramling Ave GU46 ......149 B6
Brammas Cl SL1...........42 C3
Brampton Chase RG9 .....36 A4
Brampton Ct SL6 ....40 B8
Bramshaw Rd RG30.......58 A1
Bramshill Cl RG2 ....140 E8
Bramwell Cl RG19 ....106 F2
Branagh Ct 6 RG30 ......85 B8
Branch End RG14 ...... 105 C5
Bran Cl RG30 ....84 E8
Brandon Ave RG5..........88 A8
Brandon Cl GU15 ...... 152 D4
BRANDS HILL 69 A8
Brands Rd SL3.............69 B8
Brandy Bottom GU46.....149 E3
Branksome Cl GU15......151 E6
Branksome Ct 6 RG1......85 F7
Branksome Hill Rd GU47 .150 E8
Branksome Park Rd
GU15 ....151 E6
Brants Bridge RG12......118 E7
Brants Cl RG2 ....114 E2
Brattain Ct RG12........ 118 D6
Braunfels Wlk RG14......104 E2
Bravington Cl TW17......124 F4
BRAY 40 D3
Braybank SL6..............40 D4
Braybrook RG41 ....116 B4
Braybrooke Dr RG10 .....88 F8
Braybrooke Gdns RG10....36 D1
Braybrooke Rd
Bracknell RG42 ....91 B1
Wargrave RG10............36 D1
Bray Cl SL6................40 C3
Bray Ct SL6................40 C2
Braye Cl GU47 .... 143 C1
Brayfield Rd SL6...........40 C4
Brayford Rd RG2........ 113 C8
Bray Rd
Maidenhead SL6 ....40 B5
Reading RG30 ....85 B4
BRAY WICK 40 B3
Braywick Park & Nature Ctr*
SL6........................40 B3
Braywick Rd SL6...........40 A4
Braywood Ave TW20 ......96 A2
Braywood CE Fst Sch SL4 65 E5
Braywood Cotts SL4 ....66 A5
BRAYWOODSIDE 64 D3
Braziers La RG42, SL4 .....92 D4
Breach Sq RG17 .... 100 D4
Breadcroft La SL6 ....38 E3
Breadcroft Rd SL6 ....38 F3
Bream Cl SL7..............18 C8
Brean Wlk RG6............87 A2
Brechin Ct 3 RG1 ....86 C6
Brecon Ct SL1 ....42 C4
Brecon Rd RG5 ....87 F8
Bredon Rd RG41...........88 F1
Bredward Cl SL1...........21 B2
Breech The GU47 ....150 E7
Breedons Hill RG8 ....56 C5
Breezes The SL6 ....39 E4
Bremer Rd TW18...........97 A5
Brendon Cl
Harlington UB7 ....71 C7
Reading RG30 ....57 E1
Brent Cl RG19 .... 106 D2
Brent Gdns RG2 ....86 B3
Brentmoor Rd GU24 .... 153 D6
Brent Rd SL8 ....3 A4
Brerewood RG6...........86 F2
Bret Harte Rd GU16.......151 E1
Brewery Comm RG7 .....137 B7
Brewery Ct RG7 ....83 E3
Brewhouse Hill SN8.......99 B4
Brew Twr 4 SL7 ....1 D1
Briant's Ave RG4..........59 C2
Briants Piece RG18 ......79 B6
Briar Ave GU18 .... 153 A8
Briar Cl
Burnham SL6.............41 B7
Caversham RG4...........59 A5
Briar Dene SL6 ....19 C1
Briar Glen SL6.............19 E6
Briarlea Rd RG7 ....136 F6
Briar Rd TW17 .... 125 A4
Briars Cl RG8..............56 E5
Briars The SL3.............43 F1
Briar Way SL2 ....42 B8
Briarwood RG40 ....141 E6
Briarwood Cl TW13 ....98 E5
Brickfield La
Burnham SL1..............21 B4
Harlington UB3 ....71 D8
Brickfields Ind Pk RG12 . 118 A7
Brick Kiln Ind Est RG26 . 135 C1
Brick Wlk RG18...........79 C8
Bridge Ave
Cookham Rise SL6.........19 E6
Maidenhead SL6 ....40 A7
Bridge Cl
Lower Halliford KT12......125 F1
Slough SL1................41 F6
Staines TW18.............96 E4
Bridge Cotts RG41 ....115 B2
Bridge Ct
Chertsey KT16.......... 124 C2
5 Maidenhead SL6.........40 A7
Oatlands Park KT12.......125 F1
Taplow SL6 ....40 C7
Bridge End GU15 ....151 B4
Bridge Gdns TW15 ....98 C1
Bridge Ho KT16......... 124 C2
Bridge La GU25..........122 F3
Bridgeman Ct 8 SL4 .....67 A5
Bridgeman Dr SL4 ....67 A5
Bridge Rd
Ascot SL5.............. 120 D4
Bagshot GU19 ....145 E3
Camberley GU15 ....151 B3
Chertsey KT16...........124 B2
Maidenhead SL6 ....40 B7
Bridge Ret Pk RG40......116 B5
Bridges Cl RG41 ....115 F7
Bridge St
Caversham RG4...........59 A2
Colnbrook SL3 ....69 D7
Hungerford RG17 .... 100 D6
Maidenhead SL6 ....40 A7
Newbury RG14.......... 105 A3
Oatlands Park KT12.......125 F2
Reading RG1 ....86 A7
Staines TW18.............96 E4
Bridges The RG7........ 136 C5
Bridgestone Dr SL8 ....3 C3
Bridge View
Maidenhead SL6 ....40 C7
Sunningdale SL5 ....121 B2
Bridgewater Cl RG30......58 C1
Bridgewater Ct SL3 ....44 A2
Bridgewater Terr SL4 .....67 D6
Bridgewater Way SL4 .....67 D6
Bridge Wharf KT16 ..... 124 C2
Bridge Wlk GU46 .... 149 D7
Bridge Works GU15 ......151 B3
Bridle Cl SL6 ....19 E1
Bridlepath Way TW14 .....98 E7
Bridle Rd SL6..............19 E1
Bridlington Spur SL1 .....42 B4
Bridport Cl RG6 ....87 D2
Bridport Way SL2 ....22 B1
Brierley Pl RG31 ....57 C4
Briff La RG7 .... 107 C7
Brigham Rd RG1...........59 A1
Brighton Pl 1 RG6 ....87 A6
Brighton Rd RG6...........87 A6
Brighton Spur SL2.........22 B1
Brightside Ave TW18......97 C1
BRIGHTWALTON............28 E3
Brightwalton CE Prim Sch
RG20 ....28 D3
Brightwalton Gn RG20 ....28 D2
BRIGHTWALTON GREEN....28 D2
BRIGHTWALTON HOLT 49 F8
Brigidine Sch The SL4 ....67 D4
Brill Cl
Caversham RG4...........59 A4
Maidenhead SL6 ....39 D3
Marlow SL7 ....1 C2
Brill Ho SL6 ....39 C3
Brimblecombe Cl RG41 ...89 A1
BRIMPTON................133 F6
Brimpton CE Prim Sch
RG7 ....133 F6
BRIMPTON COMMON ... 134 A3
Brimpton La
Brimpton Common RG7....134 B3
Brimpton RG7 ....133 F6
Brimpton Rd
Brimpton RG7 ....133 F7
Reading RG30 ....85 B4
Brimpton Rd *continued*
Tadley RG26........... 134 D1
Brindley Ct 6 RG14......104 F4
Brinkhurst SL7 ....1 D2
Brinkworth Pl SL4 ....95 B8
Brinns Cotts GU17 ...... 150 C5
Brinn's La GU17 .... 150 C5
Briony Ho RG2...........113 B7
Brisbane Rd RG30 ....85 B8
Bristol Cl TW19...........70 E1
Bristol Ct 10 TW19........70 E1
Bristol Way SL1...........42 F5
Bristow Ct
Caversham RG4...........59 B2
Marlow SL7 ....2 A3
Bristow Inf Sch GU15 ....151 B2
Bristow Rd GU15..........151 B3
Britannia Ind Est SL3 .....69 E5
Britannia Way TW19 ......97 D8
Brittain Ct GU47 .... 150 C7
Britten Rd RG2 ....86 B5
BRITWELL 21 F1
Britwell Rd SL1............21 D2
Brixham Rd RG2 ....86 B2
Broadacre TW18 ....97 A3
Broadcommon La RG10 ...89 C7
Broadcommon Rd RG10...89 B7
Broad Halfpenny La
RG26 .... 135 C1
Broad Hinton RG10 ....61 F3
Broad La
Bracknell RG12 .... 118 D6
Upper Bucklebury RG7 ... 107 C6
Wooburn Green HP10 ....3 F5
Broadlands Ave TW17 ... 125 C3
Broadlands Cl RG31.......84 D5
Broadlands Ct RG42.......117 E8
Broadlands Dr SL5...... 120 D2
BROAD LAYING..........129 F1
Broadley Gn GU20 ...... 146 D4
Broadleys SL4 ....66 F7
Broadmark Rd SL2.........43 B6
Broad Mead RG6 ....87 D1
Broadmeadow End RG18 .106 F4
BROADMOOR ESTATE... 143 D4
Broadmoor Hospl RG45 .. 143 E5
Broadmoor La RG4, RG10 . 60 E5
Broadmoor Prim Sch
RG45 .... 143 D4
Broadmoor Rd RG10, SL6 .. 63 B6
Broad Oak
Ashford TW16 ....98 F2
Slough SL2................22 C1
Broad Oak Ct SL2..........22 C1
Broad Platts SL3...........43 D3
BROADPOOL 93 A2
Broadpool Cotts SL5......93 A1
Broadrick Heath RG42 ....91 E1
Broad St Wlk 7 RG40.... 116 C6
Broad St
East Ilsley RG20 ....30 E7
Reading RG1 ....86 A7
West End GU24 .... 153 D6
Wokingham RG40 .... 116 C6
Broad Street Mall RG1 ....86 A7
Broadview Est TW19 ......98 A8
Broadwater Cl TW19 ......95 E8
Broadwater La RG10 ......61 E1
Broadwater Pk SL6 ....40 E1
Broadwater Rd RG10.......61 E2
Broadway
Bracknell RG12 .... 118 C7
Maidenhead SL6 ....39 F7
Staines TW18..............97 B3
Thatcham RG19 .... 106 D3
Winkfield SL4.............93 B7
Broad Way RG7 .... 138 D3
Broadway Ctyd RG19.... 106 D3
Broadway Green Farm Ind
Est GU18.............. 146 D2
Broadway Ho 2 GU47 ...150 B7
Broadway Mall 6 SL6 ....39 F7
Broadway Rd GU18, GU20 146 C2
Broadway The
Farnham Common SL2......22 C6
Laleham TW18.......... 124 C7
Lambourn RG17............25 B3
13 Newbury RG14........ 105 A4
Sandhurst GU47 ....150 B8
Broad Wlk GU16 ....151 E2
Brocas Rd RG7 ....110 F1
Brocas St SL4 ....67 D7
Brocas Terr SL4...........67 D7
Brockbank Ho RG42.......91 B1
Brockenhurst Dr 5
GU46 .... 149 D5
Brockenhurst Rd
Ascot SL5................120 B3
Bracknell RG12 .... 119 A6
Brock Gdns RG30 ....85 C8
BROCK HILL 92 A5
Brock Hill Cotts RG42 ....92 A5
Brockhurst & Marlston
House Schs RG18.........79 F4
Brock La SL6 ....39 F7
Brocklands GU46 ....149 B4
Brock Lane Mall 7 SL6 ...39 F7
Brockley Cl RG30 ....85 A8
Brocksett Cl RG30 ....85 D7
Brocks La RG7, RG18 ......80 B4
Brocks Way RG9 ....36 A4
Brockton Ct SL6 ....39 F6
Brock Way GU25 .... 122 C5
Broken Furlong SL4.......42 B1
Broken Way RG20........131 B2
Bromley Wlk RG30........84 F7
Brompton Cl 5 RG6 ....87 D1
Brompton Dr SL6..........19 C2

Bromycroft Rd SL2 22 A2
Bronte Cl SL1 42 E4
Bronte Rise RG14 131 B8
Brookbank HP10 3 D3
Brook Cl
Sandhurst GU47 143 E1
Stanwell TW19 97 F8
Wokingham RG41 116 A8
Brook Cotts GU46 149 C6
Brook Cres SL1 41 E7
Brookdene Cl SL6 19 F2
Brook Dr
Bracknell RG12 118 E5
Reading RG30 112 E8
Brooke Furmston Pl SL7 1 E3
Brooke Pl RG42 90 D3
Brookers Cnr RG45 143 C5
Brooker's Hill RG2 113 D6
Brookers Row RG45 143 C6
Brookfield Ct GU18 146 C1
Brookfield Ho SL3 68 D6
Brookfield Rd HP10 3 D3
Brookfields Sch RG31 57 C3
Brook Gn RG42 117 F8
Brook Ho
Bradfield RG7 82 C7
Newbury RG14 105 A3
Slough SL1 42 D3
Brookhouse Dr SL8 3 C3
Brook La RG10 63 B5
Brooklands Cl TW16 125 E8
Brooklands Coll Ashford Campus TW15 97 F4
Brook Lea RG4 59 C1
Brooklyn Dr RG4 59 B6
Brookmill The RG1 85 F5
Brook Path SL1 41 F6
Brook Rd
Bagshot GU19 145 E2
Camberley GU15 151 B4
Brook St W RG1 86 A6
Brooksby Cl GU17 150 B5
Brooksby Rd RG31 57 D2
BROOKSIDE 92 F2
Brookside
Chertsey KT16 123 E2
Colnbrook SL3 69 C7
Reading RG31 84 F4
Sandhurst GU47 150 C8
Slough SL3 43 E7
Wokingham RG41 115 F7
Brookside Ave
Staines TW15 97 D3
Wraysbury TW19 68 E4
Brookside Bsns Ctr RG7 139 D6
Brookside Cl RG6 87 D2
Brookside Nursery RG7 139 D6
Brookside Pk 3 GU14 151 A1
Brookside Wlk RG7 111 A4
Brooks Rd RG18 106 E4
Brook St
Twyford RG10 61 E3
Windsor SL4 67 D5
Brookway RG14 105 E2
Brookway Trad Est RG14 105 E2
Broom Acres GU47 143 B1
Broom Cl RG31 84 C5
Broome Cl GU46 149 C7
Broome Ct RG12 118 B6
Broome Lodge
Ascot SL5 120 D4
Staines TW18 97 B3
Broomfield
Bracknell RG42 117 D8
Staines TW18 97 A2
Broom Field GU18 153 A7
Broomfield Cl SL5 121 B2
Broomfield Gate SL2 22 B1
Broomfield Pk SL5 121 B2
Broomfield Rd RG30 84 F8
Broom Gr RG41 115 D4
BROOMHALL 121 B2
Broomhall Bldgs 1 SL5 121 B2
Broomhall La SL5 121 A3
Broom Hill
Cookham Rise SL6 19 E6
Stoke Poges SL2 23 A5
Broom Ho SL3 43 F2
Broomsquires Rd GU19 145 F2
Broom Way GU17 150 E4
Broughton Cl RG30 58 C1
Broughton Mews GU16 151 F1
Brownfield Gdns (Cvn Pk) SL6 39 E5
Browngraves Rd UB7 71 C7
Browning Cl
Frimley GU15 152 C4
Thatcham RG18 106 C4
Brownlow Dr RG42 91 C1
Brownlow Lodge 10 RG1 85 E7
Brownlow Rd RG1 85 E7
Brownrigg Cres RG12 118 E8
Brownrigg Rd TW15 98 A4
Browns Ct SL1 41 E6
Brownsfield Rd RG18 106 C4
Bruan Rd RG14 130 F8
Bruce Ave TW17 125 C3
Bruce Cl SL1 42 A5
Bruce Rd RG5 87 D7
Bruce Wlk SL4 66 D5
Brucewood Par SL7 1 E5
Brudenell SL4 66 F3
Brummell Rd RG14 104 E5
Brunel Cl SL6 39 E5
Brunel Ct 1 RG14 104 F4
Brunel Ctr SL6 39 D5
Brunel Dr
Crowthorne RG45 143 C8
Brunel Dr *continued*
Woodley RG5 60 F1
Brunel Ho RG19 106 A3
Brunel Rd
Maidenhead SL6 39 D5
Reading RG30 85 B4
Theale RG7 83 F2
Brunel Ret Pk RG2 86 A3
Brunel Univ (Runnymede Campus) TW20 95 C5
Brunel Way SL1 42 F5
Brunswick RG12 118 A2
Brunswick Hill RG1 85 E7
Brunswick Lodge 3 RG1 85 E7
Brunswick St RG1 85 E6
Bruton Way RG12 118 E2
Bryant Ave SL2 42 E8
Bryant Cres RG7 113 A1
Bryant Pl RG8 57 B5
Bryants La RG18 53 E1
Brybur Cl RG2 113 D8
Bryer Pl SL4 66 D4
Bryher The SL6 39 A7
Bryony Ho RG42 117 E8
Bryony Way TW16 98 F2
Buccaneer Cl RG5 88 B8
Buccleuch Rd SL3 68 A7
Buchanan Dr RG40 141 E7
Buchan The GU15 152 A8
Buckden Cl RG5 88 A6
Buckfield Ct SL0 44 F4
Buckham Hill RG17, RG20 48 D6
Buckhurst Gr RG40 116 F5
Buckhurst Hill RG12 118 F5
Buckhurst La SL5 121 A6
Buckhurst Moors RG12 117 C6
Buckhurst Rd SL5 120 F7
Buckhurst Way RG6 87 A3
Buckingham Ave SL1 42 B7
Buckingham Ave E SL1 42 C7
Buckingham Ct
Camberley GU15 151 C5
1 Staines TW18 97 A4
6 Wokingham RG40 116 C6
Buckingham Dr RG4 59 B5
Buckingham Gate
Caversham RG4 59 B4
Medmenham SL7 17 D7
Buckingham Gdns 4 SL1 42 F4
Buckingham Ho 4 SL6 39 F6
Buckingham Rd RG14 104 F1
Buckingham Way GU16 151 F1
Buckland Ave SL2 43 B3
Buckland Cres SL4 66 F6
Buckland Gate SL3 23 B2
Buckland Prim Sch TW18 97 C1
Buckland Rd RG2 86 B3
BUCKLEBURY 80 E2
Bucklebury RG12 118 A2
Bucklebury CE Prim Sch RG7 107 C5
Bucklebury Cl SL6 40 C1
Bucklebury Farm Pk★ RG7 80 D1
Bucklebury Pl RG7 108 A5
Buckle La RG42 91 B6
Bucknell Ave RG8 56 E5
Bucknell Cl RG31 84 F4
Bucknell Ct RG1 85 F5
Buckner-Croke Way RG19 131 F5
Bucks Copse RG41 116 A5
Buckside RG4 59 A2
Buckthorn Cl RG40 116 E7
Buckthorns RG42 117 E8
Budebury Ct TW18 97 A3
Budebury Rd TW18 97 A3
Budge's Cotts RG40 116 E8
Budge's Gdns RG40 116 E7
Budge's Rd RG40 116 D7
Budham Way RG12 118 B3
Buffins SL6 20 E2
Builder's Cross SL6 65 E8
Bulkeley Ave SL4 67 B4
Bulkeley Cl TW20 95 C3
BULLBROOK 118 E7
Bullbrook Dr RG12 118 F8
Bullbrook Row RG12 118 E7
Bullfinch Cl GU47 150 E8
Bull La
Bracknell RG42 118 B8
Riseley RG7 139 A3
Bull Mdw The RG8 33 F6
Bulmershe Ct RG6 87 B6
Bulmershe Rd RG1 86 F6
Bulmershe Sch The RG5 87 C7
Bulpit La RG17 100 D4
Bulstrode Pl SL1 42 F3
Bunby Rd SL2 22 F5
Bunces Cl SL4 42 B1
Bunces La RG7 111 A2
Bundy's Way TW18 96 F2
Bungalow Dr RG31 84 D8
Bungler's Hill RG7 140 B6
Bunkers Hill RG14 130 C5
Bunten Meade SL1 42 B5
Bunyan Ct 15 RG1 86 A6
Burbage Gn RG12 118 F4
Burbidge Cl RG31 84 F3
Burbidge Rd TW17 125 A5
Burbury Woods GU15 151 E6
Burchell Rd RG14 104 E5
Burchett Coppice RG40 141 F8
BURCHETT'S GREEN 38 C8
Burchett's Green CE Inf Sch SL6 38 B7
Burchetts Green La SL6 38 C6
Burchett's Green Rd SL6 38 B7
Burchetts Way TW17 125 B3
Burcombe Way RG4 59 B4
Burcot Gdns SL6 19 E3
Burdens Heath RG7 107 A6
Burdett Ct RG2 86 D3
Burdock Cl
Burghfield Common RG7 111 B2
Lightwater GU18 153 B8
Burdwood Ctr 9 RG19 106 E2
Burfield Rd SL4 95 B8
Burford Cl SL7 1 C5
Burford Ct
7 Reading RG1 85 F8
Wokingham RG40 116 E5
Burford Gdns SL1 41 C8
Burford Ho 14 SL4 67 D6
Burford Rd GU15 151 B4
Burford's RG17 47 C6
Burford Sch SL7 1 C5
Burgess Cl RG5 87 D4
Burgess La RG17, RG20 128 D6
Burges Way TW18 97 A3
Burgett Rd SL1 42 B3
Burghead Cl GU47 150 D7
BURGHFIELD 111 C6
Burghfield Bridge Cl RG30 84 F1
BURGHFIELD COMMON 110 E2
Burghfield Mill RG30 84 D2
Burghfield Rd RG30 85 A3
Burghfield St Mary's CE Prim Sch RG30 111 C6
Burgoyne Rd
Ashford TW16 98 F2
Camberley GU15 152 A6
Burham Mews TW20 95 D3
Burleigh Gdns TW15 98 C3
Burleigh La SL5 119 E8
Burleigh Mews RG4 59 C6
Burleigh Rd
Frimley GU16 151 D1
North Ascot SL5 119 E7
Burley Orch KT16 124 A3
Burley Way GU17 150 C6
Burlingham Cl RG2 113 C6
Burlings The SL5 119 F7
Burlington Ave SL1 42 E4
Burlington Cl TW14 98 D8
Burlington Ct
Blackwater GU17 150 D3
1 Slough SL1 42 E4
Burlington Rd
Burnham SL1 21 B1
Reading RG30 84 D7
2 Slough SL1 42 E4
Burlsdon Way RG12 118 E8
Burne-Jones Dr GU47 150 D6
Burnet Cl GU24 153 E6
Burnetts Rd SL4 66 E6
Burney Bit RG26 135 E1
BURNHAM 21 C3
Burnham Beeches National Nature Reserve★ SL2 22 A7
Burnham Cl
Bourne End SL8 3 A4
Windsor SL4 66 D5
Burnham Copse Prim Sch RG26 135 A1
Burnham Ct SL6 39 F8
Burnham Gr RG42 91 C1
Burnham Gram Sch SL1 21 D1
Burnham Hts SL1 41 C7
Burnham La SL1 41 E7
Burnham Manor GU15 152 A8
Burnham Rd RG26 134 F2
Burnham Rise RG4 59 C7
Burnham Sta SL1 41 D7
Burnham Upper Sch SL1 41 B8
Burniston Cl 6 RG6 87 E2
Burnmoor Chase RG12 118 E2
Burnmoor Mdw RG27 141 E2
Burns Cl 3 RG5 87 E4
Burns Wlk RG18 106 C4
BURNT HILL 54 B1
Burnthouse Gdns RG42 91 E1
Burnthouse La RG7, RG30 112 B6
Burnt Oak
Cookham Rise SL6 19 F7
Finchampstead RG40 141 F8
Burnt Pollard La GU24 146 E1
Burn Wlk SL1 21 B2
Burrcroft Rd RG30 85 A5
Burrell Rd RG20 31 E4
Burrells The KT16 124 B1
Burroughs Cres SL8 3 A4
BURROUGHS GROVE 1 F7
Burroway Rd SL3 44 B3
Burrows The RG26 135 A1
Burton Cl
Twyford RG10 61 E2
Windlesham GU20 146 D4
Burtons Hill RG17 102 B2
Burton Way SL4 66 E4
Burway Cres KT16 124 A5
Burwell Cl RG6 87 C1
Burwood Par 7 KT16 124 A2
Bury La RG20 10 A2
BURY'S BANK 131 E7
Bury's Bank Rd RG19 132 C6
Bushell Way RG2 140 E8
Bush Rd TW17 124 F4
Bush Wlk RG40 116 C6
Business Ctr The RG41 116 B4
Business Village The SL2 43 B5
Butchers La SL6 63 D8
Butchers Row RG10 61 D4
Bute St RG30 85 B5
Butler Ct 5 SL7 1 F3
Butler Rd
Bagshot GU19 145 F2
Crowthorne RG45 143 B6
Butlers Cl SL4 66 D6
Butson Cl RG14 104 E3
Buttenshaw Ave RG2 141 A8
Buttenshaw Cl RG2 141 A8
Buttercup Cl RG40 117 A6
Buttercup Pl RG18 106 D4
Buttercup Sq TW19 97 D7
Butterfield
Camberley GU15 151 B4
Wooburn HP10 3 D4
Butterfield Ho 4 RG14 105 A1
Butter Market RG1 86 B7
Buttermere Ave SL1 41 C8
Buttermere Cl TW14 98 F7
Buttermere Dr GU15 152 D4
Buttermere Gdns RG12 118 C6
Buttermere Way 4 TW20 96 B1
Buttersteep Rise GU20, SL5 119 C1
Buttsfield Rd RG20 48 F8
Butts Furlong RG20 28 D3
Butts Hill Rd RG5 87 F8
Buxton Ave RG4 58 F4
Buxton Rd TW15 97 D3
Bybend Cl SL2 22 B4
Byefield Rd RG30 85 B4
Byeways Cl RG10 37 E3
Byland Dr SL6 40 B1
Byreton Cl RG6 87 B2
Byron Ave GU15 152 B3
Byron Cl
6 Marlow SL7 1 F3
Newbury RG14 130 F7
Twyford RG10 61 E4
Yateley GU46 149 B4
Byron Ct
Camberley GU15 151 C5
Windsor SL4 67 A4
Byron Dr RG45 143 B3
Byron Ho SL3 44 B1
Byron Rd
Earley RG6 87 A7
Twyford RG10 61 E4
Bythorn Cl RG6 87 E2
Byways
Burnham SL1 41 A8
Yateley GU46 149 B5
Bywood RG12 118 A2
Byworth Cl RG2 113 B7

C

Cabbage Hill La RG42 90 E4
Cabin Moss RG12 118 E2
Cabrera Ave GU25 122 D3
Cabrera Cl GU25 122 D3
Cadbury Cl TW16 98 E1
Cadbury Rd TW16 98 E2
Caddy Cl 9 TW20 96 A3
Cadogan Cl
Holyport SL6 65 A8
Reading RG30 84 E7
Cadogan Ct GU15 151 E3
Cadogan Pl RG4 59 B3
Cadugan Pl RG1 86 D6
Cadwell Dr SL6 39 D3
Caesar's Camp Rd GU15 152 A8
Caesar's Cl 3 GU15 152 A8
Caesars Ct 2 GU15 152 A8
Caesars Gate RG42 91 E1
Caesar's Way TW17 125 D3
Cages Wood Dr SL2 22 B8
Cain Rd RG12 117 D7
Cain's La TW14 71 E2
Cairn Cl GU15 152 B3
Cairngorm Pl SL2 22 D1
Cairngorm Rd RG19 106 D2
Caistor Cl RG31 84 B4
Calard Dr RG18 106 A5
Calbourne Dr RG31 84 D4
Calbroke Rd SL2 21 F2
CALCOT 84 B3
Calcot Ct RG31 84 E5
Calcot Inf Sch RG31 84 C4
Calcot Jun Sch RG31 84 C4
Calcot Place Dr RG31 84 F4
Calcot Priory RG31 84 C4
CALCOT ROW 84 D5
Calcott Pk GU46 149 C6
Caldbeck Dr RG5 87 F7
Calder Cl
Maidenhead SL6 19 E1
Reading RG30 84 F8
Calder Ct
Maidenhead SL6 19 D1
1 Slough SL3 43 F1
Calder Way SL3 69 E4
Caldicott Sch SL2 22 B5
Caldwell Rd GU20 146 D5
Caledonia Rd TW19 97 E7
Caleta Cl RG4 59 D2
Calfridus Way RG12 118 F6
California Ctry Pk★ RG2 141 C7
California Cvn Pk RG40 141 D7
Callaway SL6 39 E5
Calleva Atrebatum Roman Town★ RG7 136 D1
Calleva Mus★ RG7 136 B1
Calleva Pk RG7 134 E2
Callington Rd RG2 86 C1
Callin's La RG10 63 B3
Callis Farm Cl TW19 70 E1
Callow Hill GU25 122 C7
Calshot Pl RG31 84 D4
Calshot Rd
Harlington TW6 71 B4
Harlington TW6 71 B5
Calshot Way TW6 71 A5
Calvin Cl GU15 152 B4
CAMBERLEY 151 D6
Camberley Bsns Ctr GU15 151 A5
Camberley Inf Sch GU15 151 C5
Camberley Rd TW6 71 A4
Camberley Sta GU15 151 D5
Camberley Towers 1 GU15 151 D5
Camborne Cl
Earley RG6 87 A1
Harmondsworth TW6 71 A4
Camborne Rd TW6 71 A4
Camborne Way TW6 71 A4
Cambria Ct
Slough SL3 43 C4
Staines TW18 96 E4
Cambria Gdns TW19 97 E8
Cambrian Cl GU15 151 B5
Cambrian Way
Reading RG31 84 D4
Wokingham RG40 142 A8
Cambridge Ave
Burnham SL1 21 B3
Slough SL1 42 A7
Cambridge Cl UB7 70 D8
Cambridge Ho 1 SL4 67 C6
Cambridge Rd
Crowthorne RG45 143 C4
Littleton TW15 98 C1
Marlow SL7 1 D2
Sandhurst GU47 143 E1
Cambridgeshire Cl
Bracknell RG42 91 F1
Wokingham RG41 115 E6
Cambridge Sq GU15 151 C6
Cambridge St 1 RG1 85 F8
Cambridge Wlk GU15 151 C6
Camden Pl
Bourne End SL8 3 A3
Reading RG31 84 B4
Camden Rd SL6 19 D1
Camelford Cl RG2 86 B1
Camellia Ct GU24 153 F6
Camellia Way RG41 115 D7
Camfield Ct SL6 39 A8
Camilla Cl TW16 98 F2
Camley Gdns SL6 39 A8
Camley Park Dr SL6 38 F8
Camm Ave SL4 66 E4
Campbell Cl GU46 149 F6
Campbell Pl GU16 151 F3
Campbell Rd RG5 87 D6
Campbell's Gn RG7 137 B5
Camperdown SL6 20 B1
Camperdown Ho 1 SL4 67 C5
Campion Cl GU17 150 F3
Campion Ho
Bracknell RG42 117 E8
6 Newbury RG14 104 F2
Campion Way RG40 116 E7
Camp Rd RG7 110 D2
Canada Rd SL1 43 B4
Canal View Rd RG14 105 D3
Canal Way RG1 86 D7
Canal Wharf SL3 44 A4
Canal Wlk
Hungerford RG17 100 D6
Newbury RG14 105 A3
Canberra Cl GU46 149 A7
Canberra Rd TW6 71 A4
Candleford Cl RG12 91 C1
Candover Cl UB7 70 D7
Canford Ct RG30 85 D8
Canhurst La RG10 37 D3
Cannock Cl SL6 40 B6
Cannock Way RG6 87 C1
Cannon Cl GU47 150 F8
Cannon Court Rd SL6 19 D3
Cannondown Rd SL6 19 E5
Cannon Gate SL2 43 C6
Cannon Hill RG12 118 C3
Cannon Hill Cl SL6 40 C2
Cannon La SL6 38 F3
Cannon Mews SL5 119 B8
Cannon St 1 RG1 85 E7
Cannon (West end of General Roy's base line)★ TW6 71 B6
Canon Hill Dr SL6 40 B3
Canon Hill Way SL6 40 B3
Canopus Way TW19 97 E8
Cansfield End RG14 104 F3
Canterbury Ave SL2 22 C1
Canterbury Ct TW15 97 F4
Canterbury Mews 6 SL4 67 A5
Canterbury Rd RG2 86 C3
Cantley Cres RG41 116 A8
Capercaillie Cl RG12 117 D6
Cape Villas SL0 44 E7
Capital Point 17 RG1 86 A6
Capper Rd GU15 151 A7
Capricorn Ho HP10 3 A8
Captains Gorse RG8 54 F6
Caraway Rd RG6 87 A1
Carbery La SL5 120 B6
Carbinswood La RG7 108 B5
Cardiff Mews RG4 58 F1
Cardiff Rd RG1 58 F1
Cardigan Cl SL1 41 F6
Cardigan Gdns RG1 86 E5

Cardigan Rd RG1 . . . . .86 E6
Cardinal Cl RG4 . . . . .59 B2
Cardinals The **6** RG12 . . .118 B5
Cardinals Wlk SL6 . . . . . . .41 C7
Cardinal's Wlk TW16 . . . . .98 E2
Cardwell Cres SL5 . . . . . .120 C4
Carew Cl RG3 . . . . .57 B4
Carew Rd TW15 . . . . .98 C2
Carey Cl SL4 . . . . .67 B4
Carey Rd RG40 . . . . .116 C5
Carey St RG1 . . . . .85 F7
Cariad Ct RG8 . . . . .34 B7
Caribou Cl RG5 . . . . .87 E8
Carisbrooke Cl
  Caversham RG4 . . . . .59 C6
  Maidenhead SL6 . . . . . . .39 C6
Carisbrooke Ct SL1 . . . . . .42 F6
Carland Cl RG6 . . . . .87 A1
Carlesgill Pl RG9 . . . . .35 E7
Carlile Gdns RG10 . . . . . . .61 D6
Carlin Pl GU15 . . . . .151 C4
Carlinwark Dr GU15. . . . .151 F7
Carlisle Rd
  Reading RG31 . . . . .57 E3
  Slough SL1 . . . . .42 D6
Carlton Cl
  Frimley GU15 . . . . .152 B3
  Woodley RG5 . . . . .87 E6
Carlton Ct TW18 . . . . .97 A3
Carlton Ho
  Feltham TW14 . . . . .71 F1
  Stanwell TW19 . . . . .70 D2
Carlton Rd
  Ashford TW16 . . . . .98 F1
  Caversham RG4 . . . . .58 E5
  Slough SL2 . . . . .43 B6
Carlyle Ct RG45 . . . . .143 C5
Carlyle Rd TW18 . . . . .97 A1
Carmarthen Rd SL1 . . . . . .42 E6
Carmel Ct SL7 . . . . .1 B1
Carmelite Dr **21** RG30 . . .85 D6
Carmella Ct TW15 . . . . . . .98 D1
Carnarvon P **2** RG14 . . .104 F1
Carnarvon Rd RG1 . . . . . . .86 E6
Carnation Cl
  Crowthorne RG45 . . . . . .143 B8
  Shinfield RG2 . . . . .113 C6
Carnation Dr RG42 . . . . . . .92 B2
Carnegie Rd RG14 . . . . . .105 A2
Carnoustie RG12 . . . . . . .117 E2
Carnoustie Ct **17** RG1 . . .86 D7
Carolina Pl RG40 . . . . . . .141 E7
Caroline Ct
  Ashford TW15 . . . . .98 B2
  Marlow SL7 . . . . .1 E3
  Reading RG1 . . . . .85 E6
Caroline Dr RG41 . . . . . . .116 A7
Caroline Pl UB3 . . . . .71 E7
Caroline St **3** RG1 . . . . . .85 F8
Caroline Way GU16 . . . . .151 F1
Carousel Ct RG2 . . . . .86 C2
Carpenter Mews RG42 . . . .90 D3
Carpenters Cl RG5 . . . . . . .87 F5
Carpenters Ct RG7 . . . . . .137 A6
Carrick Gdns RG5 . . . . . . .87 D7
Carrick La GU46 . . . . .149 E6
Carrington Ave HP10 . . . . . .3 A8
Carrington Jun Sch HP10 . .3 A8
Carrington Rd SL1 . . . . . . .42 E6
Carroll Cres SL5 . . . . .119 F5
Carron Cl RG30 . . . . .85 A7
Carsdale Cl RG1 . . . . .85 F5
Carshalton Rd GU15 . . . . .145 A1
Carshalton Way RG6 . . . . .87 C1
Carston Gr RG31 . . . . .84 F4
Carter Cl SL4 . . . . .67 A5
Carter's Hill RG40, RG42 . .90 A4
Carters Rise RG31 . . . . . . .84 F3
Cartmel Dr RG5 . . . . .88 C8
Carwarden House Com Sch
  GU15 . . . . .152 A3
Cary Cl RG14 . . . . .130 D6
Casey Ct RG7 . . . . .81 D3
Cassia Dr RG6 . . . . .86 F1
Cassiobury Ave TW14 . . . .98 F8
Cassocks Sq TW17 . . . . . .125 D2
Castle Ave SL3 . . . . .68 A8
Castle Cl
  Camberley GU15 . . . . . .151 F4
  3 Charlton TW16 . . . . . .98 E1
Castlecraig Ct GU47 . . . . .150 F8
Castle Cres RG1 . . . . .85 F6
Castle Ct SL6 . . . . .39 D7
Castle Dr SL6 . . . . .39 D7
Castle End RG10 . . . . .62 B7
Castle End Rd RG10 . . . . . .62 B7
Castle Farm Cvn Site SL4 .66 D5
Castle Gr **3** RG1 . . . . . . .86 A7
Castle Gr RG14 . . . . .104 F5
Castle Hill
  Farley Hill RG2, RG7 . . . .140 C7
  Maidenhead SL6 . . . . . . .39 E7
  Reading RG1 . . . . .85 E7
  Windsor SL4 . . . . .67 D6
Castle Hill Rd TW20 . . . . . .95 C5
Castle Hill Terr SL6 . . . . . .39 E7
Castle Ho P **4** RG14 . . . . .105 C5
Castle La RG14 . . . . .104 E6
Castle Lodge SL6 . . . . .39 F7
Castleman Ho SL5 . . . . . .120 D4
Castlemead Cotts SL4 . . . . .67 C3
Castle Mews SL6 . . . . .39 E7
Castle Rd GU15 . . . . .151 F4
Castle Sch The RG14 . . . .104 F6

Castle St
  Reading RG1 . . . . .86 A7
  Slough SL1 . . . . .42 F3
Castleton Ct SL7 . . . . .1 E2
Castleview Ho **1** SL4 . . . .67 D6
Castleview Prim Sch SL3 . .43 D2
Castleview Rd SL3 . . . . . . .43 C2
Castor Ct GU46 . . . . .149 B7
Caswall Cl RG42 . . . . .90 C2
Caswall Ride GU46 . . . . . .149 F5
Catalina Cl RG5 . . . . .88 B7
Catalina Rd TW6 . . . . .71 A4
Catcliffe Way RG6 . . . . . .113 F8
Catena Rise GU18 . . . . . . .146 B1
Catesby Gdns GU46 . . . . .149 A5
Catherine Dr TW16 . . . . . . .98 F2
Catherine Ho SL5 . . . . . . .120 B6
Catherine Rd RG14. . . . . .105 A2
Catherine St RG30 . . . . . . .85 E8
Catlin Cres TW17 . . . . . . .125 D4
CATMORE 29 C5
Catmore Rd RG20 . . . . . . .29 C7
Caunter Rd RG14 . . . . . . .104 D4
Causeway End TW20 . . . . .96 C4
Causeway The
  Bray SL6 . . . . .40 C4
  Caversham RG4 . . . . .59 D1
  Egham TW18 . . . . .96 D4
  Marlow SL7 . . . . .1 E1
Causmans Way RG31 . . . . .57 C2
Cavalier Cl
  Newbury RG14. . . . . . . .105 C5
  Theale RG7 . . . . .83 D2
Cavalier Ct TW15 . . . . .98 D1
Cavalry Cl RG19 . . . . .106 E1
Cavalry Cres SL4 . . . . .67 C4
Cavendish Cl
  Ashford TW16 . . . . .98 F2
  Burnham SL6 . . . . .41 A7
Cavendish Ct
  Ashford TW16 . . . . .98 F2
  Blackwater GU17 . . . . . .150 D3
  Caversham RG4 . . . . .59 A3
  2 Chertsey KT16 . . . . .124 A1
  Newbury RG14. . . . . . . .105 E5
  Poyle SL3 . . . . .69 E6
Cavendish Gdns **1** RG41 .88 A3
Cavendish Meads SL5 . . .120 D3
Cavendish Pk GU47 . . . . .150 E6
Cavendish Rd
  Ashford TW16 . . . . .98 F2
  Caversham RG4 . . . . .59 C6
CAVERSHAM 59 B4
CAVERSHAM HEIGHTS . . .58 F3
Caversham Park RG4 . . . . .59 C5
Caversham Park Dr RG4 . .59 C5
Caversham Park Prim Sch
  RG4 . . . . .59 D6
Caversham Park Rd RG4 . .59 E6
Caversham Prim Sch **2** RG1 .59 B1
Caversham Prim Sch RG4 . .59 A3
Caversham Rd RG1 . . . . . . .59 A1
Caversham Wharf RG1 . . . .59 A1
Caves Farm Cl GU47 . . . . .150 A8
Cawcott Dr SL4 . . . . .66 E6
Cawsam Gdns RG4 . . . . . . .59 C4
Caxton Cl RG30 . . . . .58 C1
Caxton Cl RG9 . . . . .15 E1
Cecil Aldin Dr RG31 . . . . . .57 C5
Cecil Cl TW15. . . . . .98 C1
Cecil Rd
  Ashford TW15 . . . . .98 C2
  Iver SL0 . . . . .44 E7
Cecil Way SL2 . . . . .22 F1
Cedar Ave RG18 . . . . .79 A6
Cedar Ct
  Bagshot GU19 . . . . .145 E3
  Laleham TW18 . . . . .124 C6
  Wokingham RG40 . . . . . .116 C6
  Cedar Court Pk RG19 . . .131 C7
Cedar Ct
  Bagshot GU19 . . . . .145 E3
  Datchet SL3 . . . . .68 C6
  Egham TW20 . . . . .96 A4
  Maidenhead SL6 . . . . . . .39 D7
  Marlow SL7 . . . . .1 E2
  Sunningdale SL5 . . . . . . .67 A5
Cedar Dr
  Bracknell RG42 . . . . .91 C1
  Cookham SL6 . . . . .20 A7
  Marlow Bottom SL7 . . . . .1 C7
  Pangbourne RG8 . . . . . . .56 C4
  Sunningdale SL5 . . . . . .121 A2
Cedar Dr CF RG19. . . . . . .106 C3
Cedar Ho
  Ashford TW16 . . . . .98 F1
  Maidenhead SL6 . . . . . . .39 E7
Cedar Mount RG14. . . . . .130 F8
Cedar Pl RG5 . . . . .87 F6
Cedars The
  East Bedfont TW14 . . . . .98 D7
  Reading RG2 . . . . .86 D4
Cedar Rise RG19. . . . . . . .133 B5
Cedars Cl GU47 . . . . .149 E4
Cedars Ho RG14 . . . . .40 A7
Cedars Rd SL6 . . . . .40 A7
Cedars Sch RG7 . . . . .135 A4
Cedar Way
  Charlton TW16 . . . . .98 E1
  Slough SL3 . . . . .43 E2
Cedar Wood Cres RG4 . . . .59 B4

Celandine Cl RG45 . . . . . .143 C6
Celandine Ct GU46 . . . . . .149 B7
Celandine Gr RG18 . . . . . .106 F3
Celia Cres TW15 . . . . .97 D2
Cell Farm Ave SL4 . . . . . . .68 B2
Cell Farm Ave SL4 . . . . . . .68 B2
Celsea Pl RG10 . . . . .14 A8
Cemetery La TW17 . . . . . .125 B2
Centenary Bsns Pk RG9 . . .15 E1
Central Dr SL1 . . . . .41 D6
Central Est SL6 . . . . .39 E8
Central La SL4 . . . . .93 B7
Central Way SL4 . . . . .93 B7
Central Wlk RG40 . . . . . . .116 C6
Centre The SL2 . . . . .22 C6
Centrika SL1 . . . . .42 E5
Centurion Cl
  2 Reading RG1 . . . . .86 B6
  4 Sandhurst GU47 . . . .150 D8
Century Cl RG10 . . . . .37 E4
Century Dr RG7 . . . . .113 C1
Century Rd TW18, TW20 . .96 C3
Cerotus Pl KT16 . . . . .123 F2
Chackfield Dr RG41 . . . . . .115 D8
CHADDLEWORTH 49 B8
Chaddleworth St Andrews CE
  Prim Sch RG20 . . . . .49 B7
Chaffinch Cl
  Reading RG31 . . . . .84 B7
  5 Sandhurst GU47 . . . .150 D8
  Wokingham RG41 . . . . . .115 E5
Chagford Rd RG2 . . . . .86 B1
Chainhill Rd Ox12 . . . . .8 A7
Chain St RG1 . . . . .86 A7
Chalcott SL1 . . . . .42 E3
Chalcraft Cl RG9 . . . . .35 C8
Chalfont Cl RG6 . . . . .87 A1
Chalfont Ct RG6 . . . . .87 A1
Chalfont Way RG6 . . . . . . .87 A1
Chalford Flats HP10 . . . . . . .3 F6
Chalford Rd RG14 . . . . . . .104 E2
Chalgrove Cl SL6 . . . . .40 B6
Chalgrove Way RG4 . . . . . .59 B6
Chalk Hill
  Aston Tirrold OX11 . . . . .12 F8
  Shiplake RG9 . . . . .35 C6
  Wargrave RG9 . . . . .36 C5
Chalkhousegreen La RG4 . .59 C8
Chalklands SL8 . . . . .3 A4
Chalkpit Cotts RG7 . . . . . . .83 C6
Chalkpit La SL7. . . . . .1 B2
Chalk Pit La SL1 . . . . .21 B4
Chalkpits The HP10 . . . . . . .3 E6
Chalkstream Way HP10 . . . .3 E7
Challenge Rd TW15 . . . . . .98 C3
Challenor Cl RG40 . . . . . .141 F7
Challis Pl RG42 . . . . .117 E8
Challow Ct SL6 . . . . .19 D1
Chalmers Rd TW15 . . . . . .98 B3
Chalmers Rd E TW15 . . . . .98 C3
CHALVEY 42 C3
Chalvey Gdns SL1 . . . . . . .42 E4
Chalvey Gr SL1 . . . . .42 B4
Chalvey Pk SL1 . . . . .42 E4
Chalvey Rd E SL1 . . . . .42 E4
Chalvey Rd W SL1 . . . . . . .42 D4
Chamberhouse Mill La
  RG19 . . . . .106 F1
Chamberlain's Gdns RG2 .114 E2
Chambers Bsns Pk UB7 . . .71 A8
Chambers The **17** RG1. . . .86 B7
Champion Rd RG14 . . . . . .59 C1
Champney Cl SL3 . . . . .69 A4
Chancellor's Way The RG2,
  RG6 . . . . .86 E4
Chancel Mans RG42. . . . . .91 C2
Chancery Ct **15** TW20 . . . .96 A3
Chancerygate Bsns Ctr
  Slough SL3 . . . . .43 E4
  Twyford RG10 . . . . .61 E5
  Wokingham RG41 . . . . . .116 A5
Chancery Mews **16** RG1 . .85 F7
Chanctonbury Dr SL5. . . .120 E1
Chandlers Cl TW14. . . . . . .98 F8
Chandlers La GU46 . . . . . .149 D8
Chandlers Quay SL6 . . . . . .40 C8
Chandos Mall **8** SL1. . . . .42 F4
Chandos Rd
  Egham TW18 . . . . .96 D3
  Newbury RG14 . . . . .131 A8
Chantry Cl SL4 . . . . .67 A6
Chantry Ct GU16 . . . . .151 D1
Chantry Mead RG17 . . . . .100 C5
Chantry Pl SL4 . . . . .67 D7
Chantry Rd
  Bagshot GU19 . . . . .145 D2
  Chertsey KT16 . . . . .124 C2
Chapel Arches **4** SL6. . . .40 A7
Chapel Cl RG8 . . . . .14 C3
Chapel Cotts SL2 . . . . .23 B5
Chapel Ct
  Chieveley RG20 . . . . .51 D6
  Hungerford RG17 . . . . . .100 C6
  Maidenhead SL6 . . . . . . .39 D4
  14 Reading RG1 . . . . .86 B7
  Thatcham RG18 . . . . . . .106 C3
CHAPEL GREEN 116 C3
Chapel Hill
  Reading RG31 . . . . .84 C8
  Windsor SL4 . . . . .67 D7
Chapel Ho RG17 . . . . .100 D6
Chapel La

Chapel La continued
  Headley RG19 . . . . .133 F1
  Hermitage RG18 . . . . . . .79 C8
  Lambourn RG17. . . . . . . .25 B3
  Riseley RG7 . . . . .139 C3
  Shinfield RG7. . . . . .113 B2
  Silchester RG7 . . . . .135 F5
  Stoke Poges SL2 . . . . . . .23 B5
  Yattendon RG18. . . . . . . .53 E1
Chapel Lodge RG40 . . . . .141 F6
Chapel Rd
  Camberley GU15 . . . . . .151 B5
  Flackwell Heath HP10 . . . .3 A8
  Silchester RG7 . . . . .136 C5
  Stockcross RG20 . . . . . .103 E6
CHAPEL ROW 108 C8
Chapels Cl SL1 . . . . .41 E5
Chapel Sq
  Sandhurst GU15 . . . . . . .150 F6
  Virginia Water GU25 . . . .122 C5
Chapel St
  Marlow SL7 . . . . .1 E2
  Slough SL1 . . . . .42 F4
  Thatcham RG18, RG19. . .106 D3
Chapel Terr RG42 . . . . .90 C1
Chaplain's Hill RG45 . . . . .143 D4
Chaplin Cl SL3 . . . . .43 F1
Chaplin Mews **10** SL3 . . . .43 F1
Chapman La HP10, SL8 . . . .3 A6
Chapman Wlk RG18 . . . . .106 B4
Chapter Ct **17** TW20 . . . . .96 A2
Chapter Mews SL4 . . . . . . .67 D7
Charbridge La RG5 . . . . . . .87 E6
Charfield Ct RG1. . . . . .86 E7
Chargers Paddock Cvn Pk
  SL7 . . . . .18 A5
Chariott's Pl **21** SL4 . . . . .67 D6
Charlbury Cl **8** RG12 . . . .118 F5
Charlcot Mews SL1 . . . . . . .41 E6
Charlecombe Ct TW40 . . .116 C6
Charlecombe Rd TW40 . . .116 C6
Charles Cl TW15 . . . . .98 C4
Charles Evans Way RG4 . . .59 D2
Charles Gdns SL2 . . . . .43 A7
Charles Ho
  3 Chertsey KT16 . . . . .123 F1
  Englefield Green TW20 . . .95 C1
  Henley-on-T RG9 . . . . . . .15 E3
  8 Windsor SL4 . . . . .67 C6
Charles Pl **15** RG1 . . . . . . .86 D7
Charles Rd
  Cholsey OX10 . . . . .14 A8
  Staines TW18. . . . . .97 D2
  Wokingham RG12 . . . . . .118 C7
Charles St
  8 Chertsey KT16 . . . . .123 F1
  Newbury RG14. . . . . . . .130 D6
  Reading RG1 . . . . .85 F8
  Windsor SL4 . . . . .67 C6
Charlock Cl RG18 . . . . . . .106 C5
Charlotte Ave RG12 . . . . . .118 E5
Charlotte Cl RG18 . . . . . . .79 A6
Charlotte Lodge SL6 . . . . .40 B8
Charlotte Way **1** SL7 . . . . .1 E2
Charlottown **6** RG14 . . . . .105 C1
CHARLTON 66 C5
Charlton Cl
  Finchampstead RG40. . . .141 F8
  Slough SL1 . . . . .42 B4
Charlton Ct GU47 . . . . . . .143 D1
Charlton Ho TW17 . . . . . .125 D4
Charlton La
  Swallowfield RG7 . . . . . .139 C5
  Upper Halliford TW17 . . .125 D5
Charlton Pl
  Newbury RG14. . . . . . . .105 A4
  2 Windsor SL4 . . . . .66 C5
Charlton Rd TW17 . . . . . . .66 C5
Charlton Row **5** SL4 . . . . .66 C5
Charlton Sq **4** SL4 . . . . . .66 C5
Charlton Wlk **3** SL4. . . . . .66 C5
Charnham Cl RG31 . . . . . . .84 B4
Charmile Ct **1** SL4 . . . . . .66 C5
Charnwood Cl RG14 . . . . .104 F5
Chandon Cl RG2 . . . . .86 B5
Charnham Ct RG17. . . . . .100 D6
Charnham Pk RG17 . . . . . .100 D6
Charnham St RG17 . . . . . .100 D6
Charnwood SL5 . . . . .120 E2
Charnwood Cl RG2 . . . . . . .86 B2
Charnwood Ho **9** RG1 . . . .85 E5
Charrington Rd RG31 . . . . .84 F5
Charter Cl SL1 . . . . .42 F3
Charter Ct SL6 . . . . .19 E6
Charterhouse Cl RG12 . . .118 E4
Charter Pl TW18 . . . . .97 A2
Charter Rd
  Newbury RG14. . . . . . . .130 F7
  Slough SL1 . . . . .41 E6
Charters Cl SL5 . . . . .120 E3
Charters La SL5 . . . . .120 E2
Charters Rd SL5 . . . . .120 F2
Charters Way SL5 . . . . . . .120 F2
CHARVIL 61 A5
Charvil House Rd RG10 . . .61 A5
Charvil Meadow Rd RG10 .61 B6
Charwood Rd RG40 . . . . . .116 F7
Chase Gdns RG42 . . . . .90 D1
Chaseley Ct KT13 . . . . . . .125 E1
Chasemount GU20 . . . . . . .146 C7
Chaseside Ave RG10 . . . . .61 D7
Chaseside Gdns KT16 . . .124 B2

Chase The
  Ascot SL5 . . . . .93 A1
  Crowthorne RG45 . . . . . .143 A6
  Maidenhead SL6 . . . . . . .19 C3
  Marlow SL7 . . . . .2 A3
  Newbury RG14. . . . . . . .104 F7
  Reading RG31 . . . . .84 D4
Chatfield SL2 . . . . .42 A8
Chatham Ct
  Bracknell RG12 . . . . .118 B3
  3 Slough SL1 . . . . .43 A3
Chatham St RG1 . . . . .85 F8
Chatham The **1** RG1. . . . . .86 A8
Chatsworth Ave RG41 . . . .88 B2
Chatsworth Cl
  Caversham RG4 . . . . .59 C6
  Maidenhead SL6 . . . . . . .39 C5
Chatsworth Hts GU15 . . . .152 B7
Chatteris Way RG6. . . . . . .114 C8
Chattern Ct TW15 . . . . .98 B4
CHATTERN HILL 98 B4
Chattern Hill TW15. . . . . . .98 B4
Chatters The RG7 . . . . .140 C7
Chatton Cl RG6 . . . . .114 A8
Chaucer Cl
  Caversham RG4. . . . . . . .59 A5
  Windsor SL4 . . . . .67 D4
  Wokingham RG40 . . . . . .116 F6
Chaucer Cres RG14 . . . . . .104 E5
Chaucer Ct TW20 . . . . .96 C2
Chaucer Gr GU15 . . . . . . .151 D5
Chaucer Rd
  Ashford TW15 . . . . .97 F4
  Crowthorne RG45 . . . . . .143 B4
Chaucer Way
  Slough SL1 . . . . .42 F5
  Wokingham RG41 . . . . . .115 E5
Chauntry Cl SL6 . . . . .40 C6
Chauntry Rd SL6. . . . . .40 C6
CHAVEY DOWN 119 A8
Chavey Down Rd RG42 . . . .92 B2
Chawridge La SL4 . . . . .92 C7
Chazey Cl RG4 . . . . .58 C8
CHAZEY HEATH 58 D3
Chazey Rd RG4 . . . . .58 D3
Cheam Cl RG12 . . . . .118 D4
CHEAPSIDE 120 E7
Cheapside SL5 . . . . .86 A7
Cheapside CE Prim Sch
  SL5 . . . . .120 E8
Cheapside Ct SL5 . . . . . . .120 E8
Cheapside Rd SL5 . . . . . . .120 D7
Cheap St
  Compton RG20. . . . . .31 E5
  Newbury RG14. . . . . . . .105 A2
Cheddington Cl RG30 . . . . .84 F6
Cheeseman Cl RG40 . . . . .116 D7
Cheffrey Ct TW15 . . . . .98 B2
Chelford Way RG4 . . . . . . .58 F4
Chelmsford Cl **8** SL4 . . . . .67 C5
Chelsea Cl RG30 . . . . .84 F8
Chelwood Dr GU47. . . . . .142 F1
Chelwood Rd RG6 . . . . .87 B2
Cheney Cl RG42. . . . . .90 D2
Cheney Ct RG45 . . . . .143 C5
Cheniston Ct SL5 . . . . .121 A2
Cheniston Gr SL6 . . . . .38 F7
Chepstow Rd RG31 . . . . . . .57 D2
Chequer La RG7 . . . . .138 C2
Chequers Bridge Cotts
  SL0 . . . . .44 C4
Chequers Orch SL0 . . . . . .44 F7
Chequers Way RG5 . . . . . . .87 C2
Cherbury Cl RG12 . . . . . . .118 E5
Cherington Gate SL6 . . . . .19 B1
Cherington Way SL5 . . . . .119 E7
Cheriton Ave RG10. . . . . . .61 D6
Cheriton Cl RG14 . . . . .131 B8
Cheriton Ct SL5 . . . . .121 A2
Cheriton Pl RG2 . . . . .86 A1
Cheriton Way GU17 . . . . . .150 D5
Cherries The SL2 . . . . .43 D4
Cherry Ave SL3 . . . . .43 D4
Cherry Cl
  Caversham RG4 . . . . .59 C8
  3 Newbury RG14 . . . . .104 F4
Cherry Cnr HP10. . . . . .3 B8
Cherry Garden La
  Littlewick Green SL6 . . . .38 E4
  White Waltham SL6 . . . . .63 E4
Cherry Gr
  Hungerford RG17 . . . . . .100 C5
  Reading RG2 . . . . .86 E2
Cherry Orch
  Great Shefford RG17. . . . .48 B4
  Staines TW18. . . . . .97 A3
  Stoke Poges SL2 . . . . . . .23 A5
Cherry Rise HP10 . . . . .3 E7
Cherry Tree Ave TW18. . . .97 A2
Cherry Tree Cl
  Chieveley RG20 . . . . .51 C4
  Sandhurst GU47 . . . . . . .143 D1
Cherry Tree Dr RG12 . . . . .118 D6
Cherry Tree Gr RG41 . . . . .115 D4
Cherry Tree Ho **9** SL7 . . . .1 D2
Cherry Tree La SL3 . . . . . . .23 F6
Cherry Tree Rd SL2 . . . . . . .22 C5
Cherry Way
  Horton SL3 . . . . .69 C4
  Upper Halliford TW17 . . .125 E5
Cherrywood Ave TW20 . . . .95 B1
Cherrywood Gdns HP10 . . . .3 B8
CHERTSEY 124 B2
Chertsey Bridge Rd
  KT16. . . . . .124 D2
Chertsey Bvd KT16. . . . . .123 F1

Chertsey La TW18. . . . . . . .96 F2
Chertsey Mus* KT15. . . . 124 A3
Chertsey Rd
  Ashford TW15 , TW16. . . . . .98 D2
  Feltham TW13, TW16. . . . . .98 E4
  Lower Halliford TW17 . . . 125 A2
  Shepperton TW17 . . . . . . .124 F2
  Windlesham GU20. . . . . . .146 E5
Chertsey Sta KT16 . . . . . . 123 F1
Chertsey Wlk **6** KT16. . . 124 A2
Chervil Way RG7. . . . . . . .111 B2
Cherwell Cl
  Brands Hill SL3 . . . . .69 B8
  Maidenhead SL6. . . . . .40 A8
Cherwell Cres **3** RG1. . . .85 F7
Cherwell Rd
  Bourne End SL8. . . . . .3 B4
  Caversham RG4. . . . . .59 A6
Cheseridge Rd RG20 . . . .31 C4
Cheshire Ct SL1 . . . . .43 B4
Cheshire Pk RG42. . . . . . . .91 E2
Chessholme Ct TW16. . . . .98 E1
Chessholme Rd TW15 . . . .98 C2
Chesterblade La RG12 . . .118 E2
Chester Cl
  Ashford TW15 . . . . .98 D3
  Newbury RG14. . . . . 105 C1
Chesterfield Ct TW15 . . . .97 E4
Chesterfield Mews TW15. .97 E4
Cherwell Rd
  Ashford TW15 . . . . .97 E3
  Newbury RG14. . . . . 105 A1
Chesterman St RG1 . . . . . .86 B6
Chesterment Way RG6 . . .87 D1
Chester Rd
  Harlington TW6 . . . . .71 A4
  Slough SL1 . . . . .42 D7
Chesters Rd GU15 . . . . . .152 B5
Chester St
  Caversham RG4. . . . . .59 A2
  Reading RG30 . . . . .85 D8
Chesterton Dr TW19 . . . . .97 F7
Chesterton Rd RG18 . . . 106 C5
Chestnut Ave
  Camberley GU15 . . . . .152 A6
  Caversham RG4. . . . . .59 E4
  Slough SL3. . . . . .43 E4
  Wentworth GU25. . . . . . . .121 F5
  Wokingham RG41 . . . . . . .115 E2
Chestnut Chase RG42 . . . .92 A1
Chestnut Cl
  Ashford, Chattern Hill
    TW15 . . . . .98 B4
  Ashford, Felthamhill TW16 . .98 F2
  Blackwater GU17. . . . . . . .150 E4
  Englefield Green TW20 . . . .95 C2
  Fawley OX12 . . . . .27 C7
  Harlington UB7 . . . . .71 B7
  Maidenhead SL6. . . . . .20 B1
  Medmenham SL7 . . . . .17 D7
  Theale RG7 . . . . .83 E4
Chestnut Cotts RG8 . . . . . .34 A6
Chestnut Cres
  Newbury RG14. . . . . 105 A4
  Shinfield RG2 . . . . .113 F4
Chestnut Ct
  10 Newbury RG14. . . . . . 105 A4
  Wokingham RG41 . . . . . . .115 E7
Chestnut Dr
  Burghfield RG30 . . . . .111 B4
  Englefield Green TW20 . . . .95 D2
  Windsor SL4 . . . . .66 F3
Chestnut Gr
  Purley on T RG8. . . . . .57 D5
  Staines TW18. . . . . .97 C2
Chestnut Ho RG45 . . . . . .143 C5
Chestnut La RG17. . . . . . . .25 E4
Chestnut Manor Cl TW18. .97 B3
Chestnut Pk SL6. . . . . .40 E3
Chestnut Rd TW15 . . . . . . .98 B4
Chestnuts The
  Lower Shiplake RG9 . . . . . .36 A3
  Woodley RG5. . . . . .87 D7
Chestnut Wlk
  Hungerford RG17 . . . . . . .100 D4
  Upper Halliford TW17 . . . .125 E5
Chetwode Cl RG40 . . . . . .116 E6
Cheval Stud Farm SL4 . . . .92 D5
Cheveley Gdns SL1 . . . . . . .21 C3
Cheviot Cl
  Frimley GU15. . . . . .152 C4
  Harlington UB3 . . . . .71 D7
  Maidenhead SL6. . . . . .40 B6
  Newbury RG14. . . . . 130 C5
Cheviot Dr RG10 . . . . .61 B4
Cheviot Rd
  Sandhurst GU47 . . . . .142 F2
  Slough SL3. . . . . .44 A1
Chewter Cl GU19 . . . . .145 F3
Chewter La GU20 . . . . . . .146 B6
Cheylesmore Dr GU16. . . .152 D3
Cheyne Rd TW15. . . . . .98 D2
Chichester Ct
  Slough SL1. . . . . .43 B4
  Stanwell TW19. . . . . .97 E7
Chichester Rd RG30. . . . . .84 E8
Chicory Cl RG6 . . . . .86 F1
CHIEVELEY 51 B1
Chieveley Cl RG31 . . . . . . .84 C8
Chieveley Mews SL5 . . . . 121 A2
Chieveley Prim Sch RG20 . .78 A8
Chilbolton TW20 . . . . .95 E8
Chilcombe Way RG6 . . . . . .87 D2
Child Cl RG40. . . . . .116 D8
Chillingham Way RG31. . . .84 B8
Child St RG17. . . . . .25 A3
Chillingham Way GU15. . .151 C4
Chilsey Green Rd KT16. . .123 E2

Chiltern Cl
  Henley-on-T RG9 . . . . .35 B8
  Newbury RG14. . . . . 130 C5
  Staines TW18. . . . . .97 A3
Chiltern Coll The RG4. . . . .59 B3
Chiltern Court Mews SL4. .67 B6
Chiltern Cres RG6 . . . . .87 A8
Chiltern Ct
  Caversham RG4. . . . . .59 B6
  Slough SL4. . . . . .67 B6
Chiltern Dr RG10 . . . . .61 B4
Chiltern Gn RG10 . . . . .3 A8
Chiltern Hts RG4. . . . . .59 C4
Chiltern Manor RG10. . . . .36 D2
Chiltern Rd
  Burnham SL1. . . . . .41 B8
  Caversham RG4. . . . . .59 C4
  Maidenhead SL6. . . . . .40 B6
  Marlow SL7 . . . . .1 C2
  Sandhurst GU47 . . . . .142 F1
Chilterns Cl RG10. . . . . .3 B7
Chilterns End Cl RG9 . . . . .35 C8
Chilterns Pk SL8. . . . . .3 B5
Chiltern View RG8 . . . . .57 D5
Chiltern Wlk RG8 . . . . .56 D5
CHILTON. 10 E8
Chilton Ct SL6. . . . . .41 C7
Chilton Cty Prim Sch
  OX11. . . . . .10 C8
Chilton Ent Ctr RG7. . . . . .83 E3
CHILTON FOLIAT. 73 A2
Chilton Foliat CE Prim Sch
  RG17. . . . . .73 A2
Chilton Way RG17. . . . . . .100 C5
Chilwick Rd SL2 . . . . .21 F1
Chimney Ct RG30 . . . . .86 A6
Chimney La HP10 . . . . .3 E8
Chineham Ct RG2. . . . . .86 B1
Chippendale Cl
  Blackwater GU17. . . . . . . .150 E4
  8 Tadley RG26. . . . . .134 E1
Chippenham Cl RG6 . . . . .113 F8
Chisbury Cl RG12 . . . . . . .118 E3
Chislett Gdns GU47 . . . . .149 F8
Chiswick Lodge **4** SL7. . . .1 D2
Chitterfield Gate UB7 . . . . .71 A7
Chittering Cl RG6. . . . . .87 C1
Chive Rd RG6. . . . . .87 A1
Chivers Dr RG40 . . . . .141 E7
Chives Pl RG42. . . . . .91 D1
Chobham La GU25 . . . . . . 122 B1
Chobham Rd GU16. . . . . . .152 A2
Choke La SL6. . . . . .19 B4
Cholmeley Pl RG1. . . . . . . .86 E7
Cholmeley Rd RG1. . . . . . . .86 E8
Cholmeley Terr RG1. . . . . .86 E7
CHOLSEY. 14 A8
Cholsey Rd RG19 . . . . . . .106 E3
Choseley Cl RG10 . . . . .37 E4
Choseley Rd RG10 . . . . . . .37 E4
Chrislaine Cl TW19. . . . . . .70 D1
Christ Church CE Inf Sch
  GU25. . . . . 122 B6
Christchurch Cotts GU25 .122 B6
Christchurch Ct **4** RG1. . . .86 C5
Christchurch Dr GU47. . . .150 D6
Christchurch Gdns RG2 . . .86 C5
Christchurch Rd
  Reading RG2. . . . . .86 C5
  Virginia Water GU25 . . . . 122 C5
Christian Smith Ho SL6. . .39 A1
Christian Sq **3** SL4. . . . . .67 C6
Christie Cl GU18. . . . . . . .146 C1
Christie Hts RG14. . . . . . .131 B8
Christie Wlk GU46 . . . . . .149 C4
Christine Ingram Gdns
  RG42. . . . . .91 C1
Christopher Ct
  Ashford TW15 . . . . .97 E3
  Newbury RG14. . . . . 105 B2
Christopher Ho SL2. . . . . . .22 C7
Christ the King RC Prim Sch
  RG2 . . . . .113 C8
Chrysanthemum Dr RG2 .113 E6
Chudleigh Gdns RG2. . . . . .86 C2
Chuff Cnr RG42 . . . . .57 E7
Church App TW20. . . . . . . 123 C6
Church Cl
  Eton SL4. . . . . .67 D8
  Hamstead Marshall RG20. .129 E6
  Laleham TW18. . . . . .124 C6
  Lambourn RG17. . . . . .25 B2
  Maidenhead SL6. . . . . .39 C3
  Thatcham RG19. . . . . .106 D3
  Winnersh RG41 . . . . .88 C2
Church Cotts SL6 . . . . .20 D2
Church Croft RG17. . . . . . .100 D6
Church Ct UB7. . . . . .71 A8
CHURCH END 50 C6
CHURCHEND. 84 F6
Church End La RG30 . . . . . .84 F7
Churchend Prim Sch
  RG30 . . . . .84 F6
Church Farm Barns
  Compton RG20. . . . . .31 F4
  Mortimer RG7 . . . . .137 D5
Church Farm Cotts RG10. .62 F7
Churchfield Mews SL2. . . .43 B7
Churchfield Pl TW17 . . . . .125 B2
Church Gate RG19 . . . . . .106 D3
Church Gr SL3. . . . . .43 C8
Church Hams RG40 . . . . . .141 D6
Church Hill
  Bradfield RG42. . . . . .90 C5
  Camberley GU15 . . . . .151 E5
  Chilton OX11 . . . . .10 D8
  East Ilsley RG20. . . . . .30 E6
  Hurst RG10 . . . . .88 E6

Church Hill *continued*
  Midgham RG7 . . . . .107 E3
  Wickham RG20 . . . . .75 C3
Churchill Cl
  East Bedfont TW14 . . . . . . .98 F7
  Flackwell Heath HP10 . . . . . .3 B7
  Reading RG2 . . . . .86 B2
Churchill Cres GU46 . . . . .149 D5
Churchill Ct **4** TW18 . . . . .97 C2
Churchill Dr
  Marlow SL7 . . . . .1 F4
  Winnersh RG41 . . . . .88 B1
Churchill Rd
  North Ascot SL5. . . . . .119 F7
  Slough SL3. . . . . .43 F2
Church La
  Arborfield RG2. . . . . .114 D4
  Ascot SL5. . . . . .120 D5
  Ashampstead RG8. . . . . . . .54 A6
  Barkham RG40. . . . . .115 C1
  Binfield RG42. . . . . .90 E4
  Bisham SL7 . . . . .18 D7
  Bisley GU24 . . . . .153 F4
  Bray SL6 . . . . .40 C4
  Brimpton RG7 . . . . .133 F6
  Burghfield Common RG30 . .111 E6
  Caversham RG4. . . . . .59 E2
  Chieveley RG20. . . . . .51 B1
  Combe RG17 . . . . .147 E6
  Farley Hill RG7. . . . . .140 B1
  Finchampstead RG40. . . . .141 E4
  Hamstead Marshall RG20 . .129 F7
  Hungerford RG17 . . . . . . .100 D6
  Newbury RG14. . . . . 104 D4
  Newell Green RG42. . . . . . .91 D5
  Shinfield RG2 . . . . .89 C5
  Shiplake RG9 . . . . .35 F1
  Silchester RG7. . . . . .136 E1
  Slough SL2, SL3. . . . . .43 C8
  Stoke Poges SL2 . . . . .22 F2
  Sunningdale SL5 . . . . .121 B4
  Wargrave RG10 . . . . .106 D3
  Twyford RG10 . . . . .61 F5
  Ufton Nervet RG7 . . . . . . .110 C4
  11 Windsor SL4 . . . . .67 D6
  Yattendon RG18. . . . . .53 E1
Churchmead CE Sch SL3 . .68 B7
Church Mews
  Purley on T RG8. . . . . .57 D5
  Woodley RG5 . . . . .87 F8
  Yateley GU46. . . . . .149 D7
Church Par TW15 . . . . .97 F4
Church Path SL6. . . . . .40 C4
Church Rd
  Aldermaston RG7 . . . . . . .135 B7
  Ascot SL5. . . . . .120 A5
  Ashford TW15 . . . . .97 F4
  Bagshot GU19 . . . . .145 D3
  Blewbury OX11 . . . . .12 A8
  Bracknell RG12 . . . . .118 C7
  Caversham RG4. . . . . .59 A2
  Cookham Dean SL6 . . . . . . .19 B6
  Egham TW20. . . . . .96 A3
  Farley Hill RG7. . . . . .140 C5
  Farnham Royal SL2 . . . . . . .22 C2
  Frimley GU16. . . . . .151 D1
  Froxfield SN8. . . . . .99 B5
  Ham SN8 . . . . .126 C2
  Little Marlow SL7 . . . . .2 C5
  Lower Halliford TW17 . . . .125 B2
  Maidenhead SL6. . . . . .39 E8
  Newbury RG14. . . . . 105 B5
  Old Windsor SL4 . . . . .68 B2
  Pamber Heath RG26 . . . . .135 E1
  3 Pangbourne RG8 . . . . .56 C6
  Sandhurst GU15 . . . . .150 F7
  Sandhurst, Little Sandhurst
    GU47. . . . . .142 F1
  Sandhurst, Owlsmoor
    GU47. . . . . .143 C1
  Silchester RG7. . . . . .136 C5
  Stockcross RG20 . . . . .103 E5
  Sunningdale SL5 . . . . .121 A3
  Swallowfield RG7 . . . . . . .115 E6
  West End GU24 . . . . .153 F7
  Windlesham GU20. . . . . . .146 D3
  Winkfield, Chavey Down
    SL5 . . . . .119 B8
  Winkfield SL4. . . . . .92 C5
Church Rd E RG45 . . . . . .143 B5
Church Rd W RG45 . . . . . .143 B4
Church Row SL3. . . . . .23 D8
Church Side RG20 . . . . .50 B6
Church Sq TW17 . . . . .125 B2
Church St
  Burnham SL1. . . . . .21 C1
  Caversham RG4. . . . . .59 A2
  Crowthorne RG45 . . . . . . .143 A4
  Froxfield SN8. . . . . .99 A1
  Hamstead Norreys RG18. . .52 F5
  Henley-on-T RG9 . . . . .15 D1
  Hungerford RG17 . . . . . . .100 D6
  Kintbury RG17 . . . . .102 A2
  Reading RG1 . . . . .86 A6
  Slough, Upton Park SL1. . . .42 D4
  Slough SL1. . . . . .42 D4
  Staines TW18. . . . . .96 E4
  Theale RG7 . . . . .83 D3
  Twyford RG10 . . . . .61 E5
  Warg rave RG10 . . . . .36 C2
  9 Windsor SL4. . . . . .67 D6
Church Terr
  Reading RG1 . . . . .86 A6
  8 Windsor SL4. . . . . .66 E5
Church View
  Beenham RG7 . . . . .109 A6
  8 Slough SL1. . . . . .43 A3

Church View *continued*
  White Waltham SL6 . . . . . . .63 E8
  Yateley GU46. . . . . .149 D7
Church Views SL6. . . . . . . .39 F8
Churchward Wlk RG31 . . . .84 F4
Churchway RG20. . . . . .10 B1
Church Way RG17. . . . . . . .100 D5
Church Wlk KT16 . . . . .124 A3
Churn Rd RG20. . . . . .31 D5
Cinnamon Cl
  Earley RG6. . . . . .86 F1
  Wokingham RG40 . . . . . . .116 F5
Cintra Ave RG2 . . . . .86 C5
Cintra Cl RG1. . . . . .86 D5
CIPPENHAM 41 F4
Cippenham Cl SL1 . . . . . . .41 F6
Cippenham Inf Sch SL1. . . .41 D6
Cippenham Jun Sch SL1. . .41 E6
Cippenham La SL1 . . . . . . .42 B5
Circle Hill Rd RG45 . . . . . .143 C5
Circuit La RG30 . . . . .85 C5
Cirrus Dr RG2 . . . . .113 D7
Cissbury SL5 . . . . .119 F7
CITY. 141 C1
City Gate RG1 . . . . .86 B6
City Limits RG6 . . . . .114 B8
City Rd RG31. . . . . .84 B7
Clacy Gn RG42 . . . . .91 A1
Claires Court Sch
  (Ridgeway Boys) SL6 . . . . .20 B1
Claires Court Sch (Senior
  College & Sixth Form
    SL6. . . . . .39 E7
Claires Court Schs-The
  Junior SL6 . . . . .39 F7
Clairmore Gdns RG31. . . . .57 C4
Clandon Ave TW20 . . . . . . .96 C1
Clanfield Cres RG31. . . . . . .57 C4
Clanfield Ride GU17 . . . . .150 D5
Clappers Farm Rd RG7. . . .136 F1
Clappers Mdw SL6 . . . . . . .20 C1
Clappsgate Rd RG26 . . . . .135 C1
CLAPTON 75 A1
Clapton App HP10 . . . . .3 D8
Clare Ave RG40 . . . . .116 C7
Clare Cl RG40 . . . . .116 C7
Clare Dr SL2. . . . . .22 B8
Clarefield Cl SL6. . . . . .19 B1
Clarefield Ct SL5 . . . . .121 A2
Clarefield Dr SL6. . . . . .19 A1
Clarefield Rd SL6. . . . . .19 A1
Clare Gdns TW20 . . . . .96 A3
Claremont
  Poyle SL3. . . . . .69 D6
  Shepperton TW17 . . . . . . .125 B3
Claremont Ave GU15 . . . .151 F5
Claremont Cres RG14 . . . .105 D4
Claremont Dr TW17 . . . . . .125 B3
Claremont Gdns SL7 . . . . . .1 E2
Claremont Pl GU17 . . . . . .150 F3
Claremont Rd
  Egham TW18. . . . . .96 D3
  Marlow SL7 . . . . .1 E2
  Windsor SL4 . . . . .67 C5
Clarence Cres SL4 . . . . . . .67 C6
Clarence Ct
  Brands Hill SL3 . . . . .69 B8
  Egham TW20. . . . . .96 A3
  Maidenhead SL6. . . . . .39 E8
  Windsor SL4 . . . . .67 C6
Clarence Dr
  Camberley GU15 . . . . .152 B7
  Englefield Green TW20 . . . .95 C4
Clarence Lodge **3** SL7 . . . .1 E2
Clarence Rd
  Henley-on-T RG9 . . . . .15 D2
  Windsor SL4 . . . . .67 B6
Clarence St
  Egham TW20. . . . . .95 F2
  Staines TW18. . . . . .96 E4
Clarence Way RG42 . . . . . .91 B4
Clarendon Cl RG41. . . . . . .88 D2
Clarendon Copse SL6 . . . .39 D6
Clarendon Ct
  Blackwater GU17. . . . . . . .150 D3
  Slough SL2. . . . . .43 B6
  Windsor SL4 . . . . .66 D2
Clarendon Gdns RG14. . . .105 A4
Clarendon Pl GU15. . . . . . .151 E3
Clarendon Prim Sch
  TW15 . . . . .97 F4
Clarendon Rd
  Ashford TW15 . . . . .97 F4
  Reading RG6 . . . . .87 A6
Clarendon Row RG31 . . . . .57 B4
Clare Rd
  Maidenhead SL6. . . . . .39 D6
  Stanwell TW19. . . . . .97 E8
Clareways SL6 . . . . .20 D2
Clare Wlk RG14. . . . . .130 C5
Clarewood Dr GU15. . . . . .151 E7
Clarewood Ho GU15. . . . . .151 E7
Clarke Cres GU15. . . . . . . .151 F5
Clark's Gdns RG17 . . . . . . .100 D5
Classics The RG7 . . . . .135 B7
Claverdon RG12 . . . . .118 A2
Claver Dr SL5. . . . . .120 D5
Clay Cl
  Flackwell Heath HP10 . . . . . .3 B8
  Purley on T RG31. . . . . .57 C4
Clay Cnr KT15. . . . . .124 B1
Claycots Sch SL2 . . . . .42 F5
Claydon Ct
  3 Caversham RG4. . . . . . .59 A2
  8 Staines TW18. . . . . . . .97 A4
Claydon Gdns GU17. . . . . .151 A1

CLAYHALL FARM 67 E2
Clayhall La SL4 . . . . .67 E2
Clayhill Cl RG12 . . . . .119 A6
Clay Hill Cres RG14 . . . . . .105 D5
Clayhill Rd RG7, RG30 . . . .111 B4
Clay La
  Beenham RG7 . . . . .108 F6
  Wokingham RG40 . . . . . . .116 F5
Clayton Ct SL3. . . . . .44 A3
Clayton Gr RG12 . . . . .118 E8
Clayton Rd GU14. . . . . . . .150 F1
Claytons Mdw SL8 . . . . .3 B3
Claytons Prim Sch SL8. . . . .3 A5
Clayton Wlk RG2. . . . . .96 C4
Clay Wlk RG18. . . . . .79 C6
Cleares Pasture SL1 . . . . . .21 B2
Clearsprings GU18. . . . . . .153 A8
CLEEVE. 34 D7
Cleeve Ct
  East Bedfont TW14 . . . . . . .98 E7
  Streatley SL8 . . . . .34 D7
Cleeve Down RG8. . . . . . . .34 D7
Cleeve Ho RG12 . . . . .118 E5
Cleeve Park Cotts RG8 . . . .34 D8
Cleeve Rd RG8 . . . . .34 B7
Clements Cl
  Slough SL1. . . . . .43 B4
  Spencers Wood RG7 . . . . .113 A1
Clements Mead RG31 . . . . .57 B1
Clements Rd RG9 . . . . .15 C3
Clent Rd RG2 . . . . .86 B4
Cleopatra Pl RG42 . . . . . . .91 E1
Clerewater Pl RG19. . . . . .105 F3
Clerics Wlk TW17. . . . . . . .125 D3
Clevedon Dr RG6 . . . . .87 A2
Clevedon Rd RG31. . . . . . . .57 E3
Clevehurst Cl SL2. . . . . .23 A6
Cleveland Cl
  Maidenhead SL6. . . . . .40 B6
  Wooburn Green HP10 . . . . . .3 E8
Cleveland Dr TW18. . . . . . .124 B8
Cleveland Gr RG14. . . . . . .104 F3
Cleveland Pk TW19 . . . . . . .70 E1
Clevemede RG8. . . . . .34 C7
Clevemede Ho RG8 . . . . . . .34 C7
Cleves Ct SL6. . . . . .66 F4
Cleves Way TW16 . . . . .98 F2
Clewborough Dr GU15 . . .152 B6
Clewborough House Sch
  GU16. . . . . .151 F1
Clewer Ave SL4 . . . . .67 A5
Clewer Court Rd SL4 . . . . .67 B7
Clewer Fields SL4 . . . . .67 C6
Clewer Hill Rd SL4 . . . . . . .66 E3
CLEWER GREEN 66 E3
Clewer Green CE Fst Sch
  SL4. . . . . .67 A4
Clewer Hill Rd SL4. . . . . . . .66 F4
Clewer Ho **5** SL4. . . . . . . .67 A7
CLEWER NEW TOWN 67 A6
Clewer New Town SL4 . . . .67 A7
Clewer Park SL4 . . . . .67 A7
CLEWER VILLAGE 67 A7
Clifford Gr TW15 . . . . .98 A4
Cliffords Way SL8 . . . . .3 B5
Clifton Cl SL6. . . . . .40 A4
Clifton Ho TW20 . . . . .79 E1
Clifton Lodge
  Slough SL4. . . . . .42 A1
  3 Slough SL3. . . . . .43 A4
Clifton Park Rd RG4 . . . . . .59 A2
Clifton Rd
  Harlington TW6 . . . . .71 B4
  Newbury RG14. . . . . 104 E2
  Slough SL1. . . . . .43 B4
  Wokingham RG41 . . . . . . .116 A8
Clifton Rise
  Wargrave RG10. . . . . .36 E1
  Windsor SL4 . . . . .66 D6
Clifton St RG1. . . . . .85 F7
Clintons Gn RG42 . . . . .91 A1
Clitheroe Rd GU17 . . . . . . .149 E1
Clive Cl RG42 . . . . .91 A1
Clivedale Rd RG5 . . . . .87 E4
Cliveden* SL6. . . . . .20 E7
Cliveden Mead SL6 . . . . . . .20 B3
Cliveden PI TW17 . . . . . . .125 C3
Cliveden Rd SL6 . . . . .20 A4
Clive Gn RG12 . . . . .118 B4
Clivemont Rd SL6 . . . . .39 E8
Clockhouse La
  Ashford TW14, TW15. . . . . .98 B5
  East Bedfont TW14, TW15. . .98 B5
Clockhouse La E TW20 . . . .96 B1
Clockhouse La W TW20 . . .96 A1
Cloister Mews RG7 . . . . . . .83 E3
Cloisters The
  Caversham RG4. . . . . .59 A3
  Eton SL4. . . . . .67 D7
  Frimley GU16. . . . . .151 D1
  Slough SL1. . . . . .42 D4
  10 Windsor SL4. . . . . . . .67 B6
Cloister Way RG40 . . . . . . .116 B7
Clonmel Cl RG6. . . . . .86 D5
Clonmel Way SL1 . . . . .21 B2
Close End RG17. . . . . .25 D2
Close The
  Aston Tirrold OX11. . . . . . . .12 F8
  Bourne End SL8. . . . . .3 A4
  Burghfield Common RG7. . .111 A3
  Burnham SL1. . . . . .41 C6
  Great Shefford RG17. . . . . .48 A3
  Hamstead Norreys RG18. . .52 F5
  Henley-on-T RG9 . . . . .35 D8
  Lightwater GU18 . . . . .146 A1

Close The continued
North Ascot SL5 . . . . 119 D7
Sandhurst GU47 . . . . 150 E8
Thatcham RG18 . . . . 106 B4
Virginia Water GU25 . . . . . 122 D4
Woodley RG5 . . . . 87 E5
Clough Dr RG18 . . . . 78 F6
Clove Cl RG6 . . . . 86 F1
Clover Cl RG40 . . . . 116 E7
Clover La GU46 . . . . 149 A6
Club La RG45 . . . . 143 D5
Clumps The TW15 . . . . . . 98 D4
Clyde Rd TW19 . . . . 97 E7
Clyve Way TW18 . . . . 123 E8
Coach Ho The HP10 . . . . . . 3 E6
Coach House Cl GU16 . . . 151 E3
Coach House Ct RG8 . . . . 56 E5
Coach House Mews 3
  RG4 . . . . 59 C2
Coachman's Ct RG14 . . . . 105 A3
Coachmans Gr GU47 . . . . 150 B7
Coachman's Lodge 4
  SL4 . . . . 67 D5
Coach Rd SL5 . . . . 92 E1
Coach Ride SL7 . . . . 1 D4
Coalmans Way SL1, SL6 . . 41 A8
Coargour Way RG30 . . . . . 57 E2
Coaters La HP10 . . . . 3 E7
Cobb Cl SL3 . . . . 68 D6
Cobbett's La GU46 . . . . . 149 F5
Cobblers Cl SL2 . . . . 22 B3
Cobham Cl SL1 . . . . 41 F5
Cobham Rd RG2 . . . . 87 F7
Cobham Rd RG5 . . . . 87 F7
Coburg Ho SL4 . . . . 67 D6
Cochrane Cl RG19 . . . . . . 106 E3
Cochrane Pl GU20 . . . . . . 146 D5
Cock-A-Dobby GU47 . . . . 143 A1
Cockayne Ct RG40 . . . . . . 141 F7
Cock Rd SL3 . . . . 43 E3
Cock La RG7 . . . . 82 A2
Cockney Hill RG30 . . . . . . 84 F6
COCKPOLE GREEN 36 F8
Cock's La RG42 . . . . 92 A6
Cody Cl RG5 . . . . 88 B8
Coe Spur SL1 . . . . 42 B3
Coftards SL2 . . . . 43 C7
Cokers Cl 3 SL8 . . . . 3 A4
Colby Gdns SL6 . . . . 39 E8
COLD ASH 106 C2
Cold Ash Hill SL6 . . . . . . 79 C1
Cold Grove Cotts SL6 . . . 20 E2
COLD HARBOUR
  Hungerford 100 F2
  Maidenhead 38 A3
Coldharbour Cl
  Henley-on-T RG9 . . . . 35 C8
  Thorpe TW20 . . . . . . 123 C6
Coldharbour La
  Thorpe TW20 . . . . . . 123 D6
  West End GU24 . . . . . 153 F8
Coldharbour Rd
  Chilton OX12 . . . . 9 A7
  Hungerford RG17 . . . . 100 D4
Coldicutt St RG4 . . . . 59 C1
Coldmoorholme La SL8 . . . 2 E4
Coldstream Way RG19 . . . 106 E2
Colemans Moor La RG5 . . . 87 A5
Colemans Moor Rd RG5 . . . 88 A6
Colenorton Cres SL4 . . . . 41 E2
Coleridge Ave GU46 . . . . 149 E5
Coleridge Cl
  Crowthorne RG45 . . . . 143 C4
  Twyford RG10 . . . . . . 61 F3
Coleridge Cres SL3 . . . . . 69 E6
Coleridge Rd TW15 . . . . . 97 F4
COLEY 86 A6
Coley Ave RG1 . . . . 85 F6
Coley Hill RG1 . . . . 85 F6
Coley Park Rd RG1 . . . . . 85 F6
Coley Pl RG1 . . . . 86 A6
Coley Prim Sch RG1 . . . . 86 A6
Colin Way SL1 . . . . 42 B3
Coliseum Bsns Ctr GU15 . 151 A3
Collaroy Glen RG18 . . . . . 106 C2
Collaroy Rd RG18 . . . . . . 106 C8
College Ave
  Egham TW20 . . . . 96 B2
  Maidenhead SL6 . . . . . 39 E7
  Slough SL1 . . . . 42 E3
College Cl GU15 . . . . . . 151 D7
College Cres
  Sandhurst GU47 . . . . . 150 D7
  Windsor SL4 . . . . 67 B5
College Glen SL6 . . . . 39 D7
College Ho 3 RG17 . . . . . 25 B2
College Piece RG7 . . . . . 136 F6
College Rd
  Maidenhead SL6 . . . . . 39 E7
  Reading RG6 . . . . 86 F6
  Sandhurst GU47 . . . . . 150 E8
  Slough SL1 . . . . 41 F5
College Ride
  Bagshot GU19 . . . . . . 145 C2
  Camberley GU15 . . . . . 151 D7
College Rise 39 D7
COLLEGE TOWN 150 E8
College Town Inf Sch
  GU47 . . . . 150 E8
College Town Jun Sch
  GU47 . . . . 150 E8
College Way
  Ashford TW15 . . . . . . 97 F4

College Way continued
  East Garston RG17 . . . . 47 D6
Colleton Dr RG10 . . . . . . 61 E3
Colleton Prim Sch The
  RG10 . . . . 61 E3
Collier Cl SL6 . . . . 19 F1
Colliers Way RG30 . . . . . 85 B7
Collingwood Coll GU15 . . 152 A8
Collingwood Ct 5 KT16 . . 124 A1
Collingwood Grange Cl
  GU15 . . . . 152 B8
Collingwood Mount
  GU15 . . . . 152 A7
Collingwood Pl GU15 . . . 152 B8
Collingwood Rise GU15 . . 152 A7
Collingwood Wlk RG31 . . . 84 B7
Collins Cl RG14 . . . . 105 C4
Collins Dr RG18 . . . . 78 F6
Collinswood Rd SL2 . . . . . 22 C8
Collis St RG2 . . . . 86 B5
Colliston Wlk RG31 . . . . . 84 F3
Collum Green Rd SL2 . . . . 23 A8
Colmworth Cl RG6 . . . . . 114 A8
COLNBROOK 69 D7
Colnbrook By-Pass
  Colnbrook SL3, SL8 . . . 69 D7
  Harmondsworth UB7 . . 70 C7
Colnbrook CE Prim Sch
  SL3 . . . . 69 D7
Colnbrook Ct SL3 . . . . . . 69 F6
Coln Cl SL6 . . . . 39 F8
Colndale Rd SL3 . . . . 69 E5
Colne Bank SL3, TW19 . . . 69 C4
Colne Orch SL0 . . . . 44 F6
Colne Reach TW19 . . . . . 69 F2
Colne Way TW19 . . . . . . 96 B6
Coln Trad Est SL3 . . . . . . 69 F6
Colonel's La KT16 . . . . . 124 A3
Colonial Rd
  East Bedfont TW14 . . . 98 E8
  Slough SL3 . . . . 43 A4
Colonnade 1 SL6 . . . . . . 40 A7
Colonnade The RG31 . . . . 57 C2
Colony Gate GU16 . . . . . 152 D2
Colston Ct RG31 . . . . 84 D4
COLTHROP 107 B2
Colthrop Bsns Pk RG19 . . 107 A1
Colthrop Cotts RG19 . . . . 107 B2
Colthrop La RG19 . . . . . . 107 B2
Colthrop Way RG19 . . . . . 107 B2
Coltsfoot Cl RG27 . . . . . 111 B3
Columbia Ct RG40 . . . . . 141 E8
Colville Gdns GU18 . . . . . 153 C8
Colwyn Cl GU46 . . . . 149 B6
Colyer Cl SL4 . . . . 67 B5
Colyton Way RG8 . . . . . . 57 D5
COMBE 147 E7
Combe Rd RG30 . . . . 84 F7
Combermere Cl SL4 . . . . . 67 B5
Combe View RG17 . . . . . 100 D4
Comet Ho RG7 . . . . 134 E2
Comet Rd TW19 . . . . 97 D8
Comet Way RG5 . . . . 88 B7
Comfrey Cl RG40 . . . . . . 116 E8
Commerce Pk RG7 . . . . . 83 C3
Commercial Rd
  Reading RG2 . . . . 86 A1
  Staines TW18 . . . . . . 97 A2
Commonfield La RG40 . . . 141 B8
Commonfields GU24 . . . . 153 F6
Common Hill RG7 . . . . . . 82 F4
Common La
  Brightwalton RG20 . . . . 28 D5
  Eton SL4 . . . . 42 D1
Common Rd
  Dorney SL4 . . . . 41 D2
  Eton SL4 . . . . 42 A2
  Flackwell Heath HP10 . . . 3 B8
  Headley RG19 . . . . . . 132 F1
  Slough SL3 . . . . 44 A1
Commons Rd RG41 . . . . . 88 F1
Common The HP10 . . . . . . 3 B8
Common Wood SL2 . . . . . 22 C8
Communications Rd
  RG19 . . . . 131 F5
Compass Cl TW15 . . . . . . 98 C1
Compass Ho 16 RG1 . . . . 86 B7
COMPTON 31 E4
Compton Ave RG31 . . . . . 84 B7
Compton CE Prim Sch
  RG20 . . . . 31 E4
Compton Cl
  Bracknell RG12 . . . . . 117 E3
  Earley RG6 . . . . 87 C4
  Sandhurst GU47 . . . . . 143 C1
Compton Ct SL1 . . . . 41 E7
Compton Dr SL6 . . . . 39 A8
Compton Manor RG20 . . . 31 D4
Compton Place Bsns Ctr
  GU15 . . . . 151 A4
Comsaye Wlk RG12 . . . . . 118 C4
Concorde Ct 5 SL4 . . . . . 67 A5
Concorde Rd SL6 . . . . . . 39 D4
Concorde Way
  Slough SL1 . . . . 42 C4
  Woodley RG5 . . . . 88 A7
Condor Ct SL5 . . . . 57 C3
Condor Rd TW18 . . . . . . 124 C6
Conduit La SL3 . . . . 43 E1
Conegar Ct SL1 . . . . 42 E5
Coney Grange RG42 . . . . . 91 B2
Congreve Cl RG7 . . . . . . 135 A2
Conifer Cl RG26 . . . . 134 E2
Conifer Crest RG45 . . . . . 130 C4
Conifer Ct TW15 . . . . 97 F3
Conifer Dr
  Camberley GU15 . . . . . 152 A6

Conifer Dr continued
  Purley on T RG31 . . . . 57 B2
Conifer La TW20 . . . . 96 C3
Conifers The
  Crowthorne RG45 . . . . 143 A7
  Maidenhead SL6 . . . . . 39 A8
Coningham Rd RG2 . . . . . 113 C6
Coningsby RG12 . . . . 118 C5
Coningsby Cl SL6 . . . . . . 39 D3
Coningsby La SL6 . . . . . . 65 C6
Conisboro Ave RG4 . . . . . 58 E5
Conisboro Way RG4 . . . . . 58 E5
Coniston Cl
  Frimley GU16 . . . . . . 152 C3
  Thatcham RG19 . . . . . 106 A3
  Woodley RG5 . . . . 87 F5
Coniston Cres SL1 . . . . . 41 C8
Coniston Ct
  Ashford TW15 . . . . . . 97 D5
  Lightwater GU18 . . . . 146 B1
  9 Newbury RG14 . . . . 105 A4
Coniston Dr RG30 . . . . . . 84 C7
Coniston Way 2 TW20 . . . 96 B1
Conkers SL6 . . . . 40 B8
Connaught Ave TW15 . . . . 97 E4
Connaught Cl
  Crowthorne RG45 . . . . 142 F3
  Maidenhead SL6 . . . . . 39 A8
  Reading RG30 . . . . . . 85 D7
  Yateley GU46 . . . . . . 149 B6
Connaught Ct SL4 . . . . . . 67 C5
Connaught Gdns 4
  RG19 . . . . 106 E2
Connaught Jun Sch
  GU19 . . . . 145 E2
Connaught Rd
  Bagshot GU19 . . . . . . 145 C3
  Camberley GU15 . . . . . 151 F5
  Newbury RG14 . . . . . . 105 B3
  Reading RG30 . . . . . . 85 D7
  Slough SL1 . . . . 43 B4
Connection The RG14 . . . 105 A6
Conniston Cl SL7 . . . . 1 B2
Connolly Ct GU25 . . . . . . 122 E5
Connop Way GU16 . . . . . 151 F3
Conought Ho RG9 . . . . . . 15 E3
Conquest Ct 6 RG1 . . . . . 86 C7
Consort Dr GU15 . . . . . . 118 E8
Constable Cl GU46 . . . . . 149 C7
Constable Way SL4, GU47 . 150 E6
Constitution Rd 5 RG30 . . 85 B8
Consul Ct RG5 . . . . 88 A6
Control Tower Rd TW6 . . . 71 B4
Convent Ct 3 SL4 . . . . . . 67 A5
Convent Lodge TW15 . . . . 98 B3
Convent Rd
  Ashford TW15 . . . . . . 98 B3
  Windsor SL4 . . . . 67 A5
Conway Cl GU16 . . . . . . 151 F1
Conway Dr
  Ashford TW15 . . . . . . 98 C2
  Thatcham RG18 . . . . . 106 B5
Conway Rd
  Burnham SL6 . . . . 41 B7
  Harlington TW6 . . . . . 71 B4
  Reading RG31 . . . . . . 84 C5
Congree Cl RG6 . . . . 87 B1
Cooke Rise RG42 . . . . . . 91 B2
COOKHAM 20 D7
Cookham Ct SL4 . . . . . . 143 C1
COOKHAM DEAN 19 B7
Cookham Dean Bottom
  SL6 . . . . 19 B7
Cookham Dean CE Prim Sch
  SL6 . . . . 19 F6
Cookham Lodge 15 SL6 . . 39 F6
Cookham Montessori Sch
  SL6 . . . . 19 F7
Cookham Rd
  Bracknell RG12 . . . . . 117 E2
  Maidenhead SL6 . . . . . 39 F1
COOKHAM RISE 19 E6
Cookham Rise Prim Sch
  SL6 . . . . 19 E6
Cookham Sta SL6 . . . . . . 19 F7
Coolarne Rise GU15 . . . . 152 A6
Coolgardie Rd TW15 . . . . 98 C3
Coombe Cotts RG8 . . . . . 33 F6
Coombe Hill Ct SL4 . . . . . 66 D4
Coombe La SL5 . . . . 120 C5
Coombe Pine RG12 . . . . . 118 D3
Coombe Rd
  Compton RG20 . . . . . . 31 F2
  Yateley GU46 . . . . . . 149 B7
Coombesbury La RG20 . . . 76 D1
Coombes End Sch RG2 . . . 114 E3
Coombes La RG40 . . . . . . 114 B5
Coombe Sq RG19 . . . . . . 106 B3
Coombe The RG8 . . . . . . 33 F6
Cooper Cl RG2 . . . . 113 C7
Cooper Rd
  Henley-on-T RG9 . . . . 15 D3
  Windlesham GU20 . . . 146 D4
Coopers Cl TW18 . . . . . . 98 A3
Coopers Cres RG18 . . . . . 106 E5
COOPER'S HILL 95 D5
Cooper's Hill La TW20 . . . 95 D4
Cooper Way SL1 . . . . 42 B3
Coote Ct RG42 . . . . 90 D3
Cope Ct SL6 . . . . 39 C7
Copenhagen Cl RG1 . . . . 113 B6
Copenhagen Wlk RG12 . . . 118 B4
Copped Hall Dr GU15 . . . 152 C6
Copped Hall Way GU15 . . 152 C6
Copperage Rd OX12 . . . . . 9 A2

Copper Beech RG42 . . . . 119 A8
Copper Beech Cl SL4 . . . . 66 D6
Copperbeech Pl RG14 . . . 130 D4
Copperdale Cl RG6 . . . . . 86 F3
Copperfield Ave GU47 . . . 143 E2
Copperfield Way
  RG7 . . . . 123 C6
Copperfields RG4 . . . . . . 58 F3
Copperfield Terr SL2 . . . . 43 B6
Coppermill Rd TW19 . . . . 69 B2
Coppice Cl RG14 . . . . . . 131 B8
Coppice Dr TW19 . . . . . . 95 D8
Coppice Gdns
  Crowthorne RG45 . . . . 142 F5
  Yateley GU46 . . . . . . 149 C5
Coppice Gn RG42 . . . . . . 90 F1
Coppice Rd RG5 . . . . 87 E4
Coppice The TW15 . . . . . 98 B2
Coppins La SL0 . . . . 44 F8
Copse Ave RG4 . . . . 59 E3
Copse Cl
  Camberley GU15 . . . . . 152 A6
  Marlow SL7 . . . . 1 C2
  Purley on T RG31 . . . . 57 D3
  Slough SL1 . . . . 42 E6
Copse Dr RG41 . . . . 116 A7
Copse End
  Camberley GU15 . . . . . 152 A6
  Newbury RG14 . . . . . . 59 D3
Copse Mdw RG41 . . . . . . 116 A5
Copse Mead RG5 . . . . . . 60 F2
Copse The RG10 . . . . 36 E3
Copse View Cotts SL6 . . . 64 C4
Copse Way RG40 . . . . . . 141 E7
Copsewood Ct GU47 . . . . 71 A7
Copthall Ho SL6 . . . . 40 A7
Copthorn Cl SL6 . . . . 39 A4
Copthorne Chase TW15 . . . 97 F4
Copthorne Cl TW17 . . . . . 125 D3
Copthorne Dr GU18 . . . . 146 B1
Corbett Dr GU18 . . . . . . 152 F7
Corbett Gdns RG5 . . . . . . 87 F7
Corbridge Rd RG2 . . . . . . 86 C4
Corby Cl
  Englefield Green TW20 . 95 C2
  Woodley RG5 . . . . 61 A1
Corby Dr TW20 . . . . 95 C2
Cordelia Croft RG42 . . . . 118 E8
Cordelia Gdns TW19 . . . . 97 E8
Cordelia Rd TW19 . . . . . . 97 E8
Corderoy Pl KT16 . . . . . . 123 F3
Cordwalles Jun Sch
  GU15 . . . . 151 F8
Cordwallis Est 1 SL6 . . . . 39 F8
Cordwallis Pk SL6 . . . . . . 39 E8
Cordwallis Rd SL6 . . . . . . 39 F8
Cordwallis St SL6 . . . . . . 39 E8
CORES END 3 D4
Cores End Rd SL8 . . . . . . 3 B3
Corfe Gdns
  Frimley GU16 . . . . . . 151 F1
  Slough SL1 . . . . 42 A6
Corfe Mews RG4 . . . . 59 E4
Corfe Pl SL6 . . . . 39 C7
Corfield Cl RG40 . . . . . . 141 E3
Corfield Gn RG41 . . . . . . 115 F8
Coriander Ct SL5 . . . . . . 120 E3
Coriander Way RG6 . . . . . 86 E1
Corinne Ct RG2 . . . . 86 C4
Cormorant Pl GU47 . . . . 150 E7
Cormorant Wood 7
  RG14 . . . . 105 C1
Cornbunting Cl GU47 . . . 150 D8
Corn Croft RG42 . . . . 91 E1
Cornel Ho 3 SL4 . . . . . . 67 A6
Corner Mead RG18 . . . . . 106 C7
Cornerside TW15 . . . . . . 98 C1
Cornerstones RG30 . . . . . 84 E8
Cornerways SL3 . . . . 68 C7
Cornfield Rd RG5 . . . . . . 88 A8
Cornfields GU46 . . . . . . 149 B4
Cornflower Cl RG41 . . . . 115 D7
Cornwall Ave SL2 . . . . . . 22 C1
Cornwall Cl
  Bracknell RG42 . . . . . 91 F2
  Camberley GU15 . . . . . 151 F7
  Eton SL4 . . . . 41 E1
  Maidenhead SL6 . . . . . 19 E2
  Purley on T RG31 . . . . 57 B4
  Wokingham RG41 . . . . 115 F8
Cornwall Lodge 11 SL6 . . . 39 F6
Cornwall Way TW18 . . . . . 96 E2
Cornwell Rd SL4 . . . . 68 A1
Cornwood Gdns RG2 . . . . 86 C3
Coronation Ave
  Slough SL3 . . . . 43 E7
  Windsor SL4 . . . . 67 F5
Coronation Cotts RG10 . . . 88 D4
Coronation Rd
  Ascot SL5 . . . . 120 A2
  Littlewick Green SL6 . . 38 B5
  Yateley GU46 . . . . . . 149 E7
Coronation Sq
  Reading RG30 . . . . . . 85 B4
  Wokingham RG40 . . . . 116 D7
Corporation Cotts 1
  RG14 . . . . 105 A4
Corrie Gdns GU25 . . . . . . 122 C2
Corsair Cl TW19 . . . . 97 E8
Corsair Rd TW19 . . . . 97 F8
Corsham Rd RG2 . . . . 86 A4
Corsham Way RG45 . . . . 143 B5
Corwen Rd RG30 . . . . . . 84 E7
Coster Cl RG14 . . . . 104 D5
Costers Cotts SL3 . . . . 3 B2
Cotswold Cl
  Maidenhead SL6 . . . . . 40 B6

Cotswold continued
  Slough SL1 . . . . 42 B3
  Staines TW18 . . . . . . 97 A3
Cotswold Rd GU47 . . . . . 142 F1
Cotswold Way RG31 . . . . . 57 C2
Cotage Farm Way
  TW20 . . . . 123 C6
Cottage La RG30 . . . . 85 C2
Cottages The RG2 . . . . . . 86 C4
Cotterell Cl RG42 . . . . . . 91 B1
Cotterell Gdns RG10 . . . . 61 F3
Cottesbrooke Cl SL3 . . . . 69 B6
Cottesloe Cl GU24 . . . . . 153 F3
Cottesmore RG12 . . . . . . 118 A2
Cottesmore Rd RG5 . . . . . 87 D6
Cottrell Cl RG17 . . . . 100 E8
Coulson Way SL1 . . . . 41 B7
Council Cotts GU24 . . . . 153 F7
Council Hos
  Eastbury RG17 . . . . . . 46 F6
  Mortimer RG7 . . . . . . 140 D5
  Shiplake RG9 . . . . 35 B2
  Sindlesham RG41 . . . . 115 A7
  Three Mile Cross RG7 . . 113 A5
  Winterbourne RG20 . . . 77 C5
Council Hos The
  Inkpen RG17 . . . . . . 127 F5
  Tadley RG26 . . . . . . 134 B1
Country Life Ho SL3 . . . . 68 B7
County La RG42 . . . . 91 E1
County Lane Rdbt RG42 . . 91 E2
Courage Ct RG30 . . . . . . 85 B5
Courage Shire Horse Ctr★
  SL6 . . . . 38 A6
Course Rd SL5 . . . . 120 A6
Court Cl SL6 . . . . 40 C2
Court Cres SL1 . . . . 42 D7
Court Dr SL6 . . . . 39 C7
Courtenay Dr RG4 . . . . . . 59 B7
Court Farm Cl SL1 . . . . . . 42 D6
Court Farm Ind Est TW19 . . 70 F1
Courtfield Dr SL6 . . . . . . 39 C6
Courtfield Rd TW15 . . . . . 98 B2
Court Gdns
  Camberley GU15 . . . . . 151 D5
  Goring RG8 . . . . 34 C7
Court Hill Rd OX12 . . . . . . 7 C7
Courthouse Jun Sch SL6 . . 39 B8
Courthouse Rd SL6 . . . . . 39 B8
Court La
  Burnham SL1 . . . . 21 D2
  Dorney SL4 . . . . 41 B3
Courtlands 14 SL6 . . . . . . 39 F6
Courtlands Ave SL3 . . . . . 43 D2
Courtlands Hill RG8 . . . . . 56 C4
Courtlands Rd RG14 . . . . 105 B1
Courtleigh Manor SL1 . . . 121 A2
Courtney Hey 4 GU15 . . . 153 B2
Courtney Pl RG42 . . . . . . 90 C2
Courtney Rd TW15 . . . . . 71 A5
Court One TW15 . . . . 98 C5
Court Rd SL6 . . . . 20 C3
Courts Rd RG6 . . . . 87 B3
Court The RG18 . . . . 106 D4
Court Three TW15 . . . . . . 98 C5
Court Two TW15 . . . . 98 C5
Courtyard The
  12 Bourne End SL8 . . . . 3 B3
  Henley-on-T RG9 . . . . 15 E3
  7 Marlow SL7 . . . . 1 D2
  Marlow SL7 . . . . 1 E2
  Staines TW18 . . . . . . 96 E8
  Theale RG7 . . . . 83 E3
  Wokingham RG40 . . . . 116 C5
Coventry Rd RG1 . . . . 86 E8
Coverdale Way SL2 . . . . . 21 E1
Covert The SL5 . . . . 120 B2
Cow La
  East Ilsley RG20 . . . . . 30 F7
  Moulsford OX10 . . . . . 13 F3
  Reading RG1, RG30 . . . 85 E8
Cowley Ave KT16 . . . . . . 123 F2
Cowley La KT16 . . . . 123 E2
Coworth Cl SL5 . . . . 121 B4
Coworth Rd SL5 . . . . 121 B4
Cowper Ct KT16 . . . . 123 F3
Cowper Cl SL6 . . . . 22 A1
Cowper Way RG30 . . . . . 85 D4
Cowslade RG14 . . . . 104 D5
Cowslip Cl RG31 . . . . 84 C6
Cowslip Cres RG18 . . . . . 106 E5
Coxborrow Cl SL6 . . . . . . 19 E7
Coxeter Rd RG14 . . . . . . 104 E2
Cox Gn GU47 . . . . 150 D6
COX GREEN 39 C3
Cox Green La SL6 . . . . . . 39 C3
Cox Green Rd SL6 . . . . . . 39 D3
Cox Green Sch SL6 . . . . . 39 A4
Cox Hollow RG30 . . . . . . 85 E6
Coxs Ave TW17 . . . . 125 E6
Cox's La RG7 . . . . 107 D3
Crabtree Cl
  Chilton Foliat RG17 . . . 72 E2
  Hermitage RG18 . . . . . 78 E6
Crabtree Cnr TW20 . . . . . 123 B8
Crabtree La RG18 . . . . . . 78 F6
Crabtree Office Village
  RG7 . . . . 123 C7
Crabtree Rd
  Camberley GU15 . . . . . 151 B1
  Thorpe TW20 . . . . . . 123 C7
Cradock Rd RG2 . . . . 86 B4
Crafnant Ct TW11 . . . . . . 97 F3
Crafts End OX11 . . . . 10 F8

Craig Ave RG30 . . . . .85 B8
Craig Ho **7** RG30 . . . . .85 B8
Craigwell CI TW18 . . . .123 E8
Crail CI RG41 . . . . .116 A3
Crake PI GU47 . . . . .150 D8
Cramond Ct TW14 . . . . . . .98 E7
Cranberry Wlk GU17 . . . .150 F3
CRANBOURNE 93 B6
Cranbourne Ave
Reading RG31 . . . . .84 C4
Windsor SL4 . . . . .66 F5
Cranbourne CI SL1 . . . . . .42 C5
Cranbourne Cotts SL4 . . .93 B5
Cranbourne Gdns RG30 . .58 A2
Cranbourne Hall Cvn Site
SL4 . . . . .93 B7
Cranbourne Prim Sch
SL5 . . . . .93 A4
Cranbourne Rd SL1 . . . . . .42 C5
Cranbourne Twrs SL5 . . .119 D8
Cranbrook Dr SL6 . . . . . . .19 C1
Cranbury Rd RG30 . . . . . .85 D7
Crane Ct GU47 . . . . .150 D8
Crane Rd TW6, TW19. . . . .71 A1
Craneswater UB3 . . . . .71 F7
Crane Wharf **12** RG1 . . . .86 B7
Cranford Ave TW19 . . . . . .97 F8
Cranford CI TW19 . . . . .97 E8
Cranford Dr RG10. . . . . . . .88 F8
Cranford House Sch OX10 .13 F5
Cranford La
Harlington TW6 . . . . .71 F6
Harlington UB3 . . . . .71 E7
Hatton TW6 . . . . .71 F4
Hatton TW6 . . . . .71 F4
Cranford Mews **12** RG1. .86 A6
Cranford Park Dr GU46 .149 D6
Cranleigh Rd TW13 . . . . . .98 F4
Cranmer CI RG31 . . . . .57 B3
Cranmer Lodge GU15 . . .151 E6
Cranwell Gr
Lightwater GU18 . . . . . . .152 F8
Littleton TW17 . . . . .124 F5
Cranwell Rd TW6 . . . . .71 B5
Craufurd Ct SL6 . . . . .39 E8
Craufurd Rise SL6 . . . . . . .39 E8
Craven CI RG17 . . . . .102 B1
Craven Ct GU15. . . . . .150 F4
Craven Dene RG14 . . . . . .105 B4
Craven Farm Cotts RG17 . .72 F2
Craven Rd
Inkpen RG17 . . . . .127 B6
Newbury RG14 . . . . .104 F2
Reading RG1 . . . . .86 D6
Craven Way RG17 . . . . . .102 B2
Crawford CI RG6. . . . . .87 B3
Crawford Gdns GU15. . . .151 E5
Crawford PI SL1 . . . . .42 A4
Crawley Chase RG42 . . . . .92 B2
Crawley Dr GU15 . . . . . . .151 F6
CRAWLEY HILL 151 E5
Crawley Hill GU15 . . . . . .151 F5
Crawley Lodge GU15 . . . .152 A7
Crawley Ridge GU15 . . . .151 F6
Crawley Ridge Inf Sch
GU15 . . . . .151 F7
Crawley Rise GU15. . . . . .152 A7
Crawley Wood CI GU15. .151 F5
Crawshay Dr RG4 . . . . .59 B7
Crawshays SL6 . . . . .40 C8
Crayle St SL2. . . . . .22 B2
Crayonne CI TW16 . . . . . .125 E8
CRAZIES HILL 36 F6
Crazies Hill CE Prim Sch
RG10 . . . . .36 F6
Crecy CI RG41 . . . . .115 C6
Creden CI SL6 . . . . .19 D1
Crediton CI RG5 . . . . .88 A6
Cree's Mdw GU20. . . . . . .146 E4
Creighton Ct RG2. . . . . . . .86 D4
Cremyll Rd RG1. . . . . .58 F1
Crendon Ct RG4 . . . . .59 A2
Crescent Ct **5** TW18 . . . .96 F3
Crescent Dale SL6 . . . . . . .39 F6
Crescent Dr SL6 . . . . .39 E7
Crescent Rd GU15 . . . . . . .87 E5
Crescent Rd
Reading, Tilehurst RG31 . .57 D1
Reading, Whiteknights RG1 . .86 F6
Shepperton TW17 . . . . . .125 C4
Wokingham RG40 . . . . . .116 C5
Crescent The
Aldermaston Wharf RG7 . .109 C4
Ashford TW15 . . . . .97 F3
Chertsey KT16 . . . . .124 A6
Earley RG6 . . . . .87 C4
Egham TW20 . . . . .95 F2
Harlington UB7 . . . . .71 D7
Kintbury RG17 . . . . .102 A1
Knowl Hill RG10. . . . . .61 E4
Lower Halliford TW17 . . .125 F2
Lower Shiplake RG9 . . . . .36 B4
Maidenhead SL6 . . . . .39 E7
Mortimer RG7 . . . . .137 A6
Slough SL1. . . . . .42 E4
Theale RG7 . . . . .83 E4
Yateley GU46. . . . . .149 E6
Crescent Villas **4** SL4. .67 C6
Cressex CI RG42 . . . . .90 C2
Cressida Chase RG42 . . . . .91 E1
Cressingham Rd RG2 . . . . .86 D2
Cressington CI **3** SL4 . . . .3 A4
Cressington PI SL8 . . . . . . .3 A4
Cress Rd SL1 . . . . .42 B4
Cresswell Ct RG2 . . . . . . .113 C6
Cresswell Ct **5** TW19. . . .70 D1

Cresswell Rd RG14. . . . . . .105 D4
Cresswells Mead SL6 . . . . .40 C1
Crest CI RG10. . . . . .61 E6
Crest Ho TW15. . . . . .98 A3
Crest The RG4 . . . . .59 C5
Creswell Row SL7 . . . . .1 D2
Crichton Ct RG7 . . . . .137 A6
Cricketers RG20 . . . . .103 E6
Cricketers La
Englefield Green TW20 . . . .95 C4
Windlesham GU20. . . . . . .146 D4
Winkfield RG42 . . . . .92 A3
Cricket Field Gr RG45. . . .143 D4
CRICKET HILL 149 E5
Cricket Hill RG40 . . . . . . .141 F2
Cricket Hill La GU17,
GU46 . . . . .149 E4
Cricklewood Cott OX11 . .12 A8
Crimp Hill SL4, TW20 . . . . .95 A6
Crisp Gdns RG42. . . . . .90 E1
Crispin CI RG4 . . . . .58 D5
Crispin Way SL2 . . . . .22 D8
Crisp Rd RG9 . . . . .15 C3
Crocker CI SL5 . . . . .119 F8
Crockers Mead RG20. . . . .129 B3
Crockford PI RG42 . . . . . . .90 F1
CROCKHAM HEATH. 129 F6
Crockhamwell Rd RG5 . . . .87 E6
Crocus Mead RG18. . . . . .106 E4
Crocus Way RG41 . . . . . . .115 D7
Croft CI
Harlington UB7 . . . . .71 C7
Wokingham RG41 . . . . . .116 A2
Croft Cnr SL4. . . . . .68 A2
Crofters SL4 . . . . .68 A2
Crofters CI
Frimley GU16. . . . . .152 D1
1 Stanwell TW19 . . . . . . .70 D1
Crofter's CI GU47 . . . . . . .150 A8
Crofthill Rd SL2 . . . . .22 B1
Croft Ho SL0 . . . . .44 E7
Croft La
Newbury RG14. . . . . .104 E4
Yateley GU46 . . . . .149 D7
Crofton CI RG12 . . . . .118 E4
Crofton Ho RG12. . . . . . . .100 E5
Croft Rd
Goring RG8 . . . . .34 C5
Hungerford RG17 . . . . . .100 D6
Mortimer RG7 . . . . .136 F6
Newbury RG14. . . . . .130 F8
Shinfield RG2 . . . . .113 C2
Wokingham RG40 . . . . . .116 A1
Crofts The TW17 . . . . .125 E5
Croft The
Bracknell RG42 . . . . .91 B1
Kintbury RG17 . . . . .102 A2
Maidenhead SL6 . . . . .39 C5
Marlow SL7 . . . . .2 A3
Wokingham RG40 . . . . . .116 A1
Croft Way GU16 . . . . .151 F2
Cromer CI RG31 . . . . .57 C1
Cromer Rd TW6. . . . . .71 A5
Cromwell CI RG9 . . . . .35 E8
Cromwell Dr SL1 . . . . .42 E8
Cromwell Gdns SL7 . . . . . . .1 E2
Cromwell Lodge **4** TW13 . .98 F5
Cromwell PI **3** RG14. . . .105 A3
Cromwell Rd
Ascot SL5. . . . . .120 B4
Camberley GU15 . . . . . . .151 D7
Caversham RG4 . . . . .59 B2
Henley-on-T RG9 . . . . .15 E1
Maidenhead SL6 . . . . .39 D7
Marlow SL7 . . . . .1 E2
Newbury RG14. . . . . .105 C5
Cromwell Terr RG14. . . . .104 D5
Crondall Ct GU15 . . . . . . .151 B4
Crondall End GU46. . . . . .149 C7
CROOKED SOLEY. 72 E6
CROOKHAM. 133 B5
Crookham Common Rd RG7,
RG19 . . . . .133 C5
Crookham Hill
Crookham RG19. . . . . . . .132 E6
Thatcham RG19 . . . . .106 F1
Crookham Pk RG19 . . . . .133 B6
Crookham Rd SL3 . . . . .43 E6
Cropper CI RG19 . . . . .107 A3
Crosby Gdns GU46 . . . . . .149 A7
Crosby Hill Dr GU15. . . . .151 F7
Crosfields CI 113 E8
Crosfield Sch RG2 . . . . . . .113 E8
Crossfell RG12 . . . . .118 A5
Cross Gates CI GU47 . . . . .143 E4
Cross Keys Rd RG8. . . . . . .14 C4
Cross La RG7 . . . . .138 C7
Crossland Ho GU25 . . . . .122 E5
Crossland Rd RG1 . . . . .86 B7
Cross Oak SL4 . . . . .67 A5
Cross Rd SL3 . . . . .121 A1
Cross St
Reading RG1 . . . . .86 B8
Wokingham RG40 . . . . . .116 C6
Crossway RG12 . . . . .118 C7
Crossway Point
12 Reading RG1 . . . . .86 D7
5 Reading RG1 . . . . .86 E7
Crossways
Ashford TW16 . . . . .98 F1
Bracknell RG42 . . . . .117 D8
Egham TW20 . . . . .96 D2
Woodley RG5 . . . . .87 E5
Crossways Ct **7** SL4. . . . .67 C5
Crosswell Ct TW17 . . . . . .125 C7
Crosthwaite Way SL1 . . . . .41 D8
Crouch La SL4 . . . . .92 F7
Crowfield Dr RG19. . . . . . .106 C3

Crowle Rd RG17 . . . . .25 A2
Crown Acre CI RG19 . . . . .106 C3
Crown CI SL3. . . . . .69 C7
Crown Colonnade **3** RG1 .86 E7
Crown Cotts
Bracknell SL5. . . . . .119 C4
Englefield Green TW20 . . . .95 A1
Windsor SL4 . . . . .67 D3
Crown Ct RG19 . . . . .118 A4
Crown Hill Ct SL5. . . . . . . .120 B4
Crown La
Farnham Royal SL2 . . . . . .22 A4
Maidenhead SL6 . . . . .40 A7
Marlow SL7 . . . . .1 D2
Theale RG7 . . . . .83 E3
Wentworth GU25. . . . . . .122 D3
Crown Mdw SL6 . . . . .69 B7
Crown Mead RG18, RG19. .106 C3
Crown Mews RG17. . . . . .100 D5
Crown Pl
Marlow SL7 . . . . .1 D2
Reading RG1 . . . . .86 C6
Sandhurst GU47 . . . . .143 E1
Crown Rd
Marlow SL7 . . . . .1 D2
Wentworth GU25. . . . . . .122 C3
Crown Rise KT16 . . . . .123 F1
Crown Row RG12 . . . . . . .118 D3
Crown St
Egham TW20 . . . . .96 A4
Reading RG1 . . . . .86 B6
CROWN WOOD. 118 D3
Crown Wood Prim Sch
RG12 . . . . .118 E3
Crow Piece La SL2 . . . . . . .21 F4
Crowsley Rd RG9 . . . . .36 A3
CROWTHORNE 143 D5
Crowthorne Bsns Est The
RG45 . . . . .143 D7
Crowthorne CE Prim Sch
RG45. . . . . .143 C5
Crowthorne Lodge **3**
RG12 . . . . .118 B5
Crowthorne Rd
Bracknell, Easthampstead
RG12 . . . . .118 A5
Sandhurst GU47 . . . . .143 B2
Crowthorne Rd N RG12 . .118 B6
Crowthorne Sta RG45 . . .142 E4
Croxley Rise SL6 . . . . .39 D6
Croydon Rd TW6 . . . . .71 B4
Cruikshank Lea GU47 . . .150 E6
Crummock CI SL1 . . . . .41 C7
Crutchley Rd RG40. . . . . .116 D7
Cuba Cotts SL6 . . . . .40 E3
Cuckoo La GU24 . . . . .153 D6
Cuckoo Vale GU24 . . . . . .153 D6
Culford CI RG6 . . . . .87 D2
Culham Ct RG30 . . . . .85 A4
Culham Ho RG12. . . . . . . .118 E2
Cullen CI GU46 . . . . .149 C5
Cullen's Pass **18** SL6 . . . .39 F6
Culley Way SL6 . . . . .39 A4
Culloden Way RG41. . . . . .115 B6
Culver Croft RG42 . . . . . . .90 E1
Culver La RG6 . . . . .87 A7
Culver Rd
Newbury RG14. . . . . .130 F8
Reading RG6 . . . . .86 F6
Sandhurst GU47 . . . . .143 D1
Cumberland Ave SL2 . . . . .22 C1
Cumberland Ct TW15 . . . .97 D5
Cumberland Dr RG12 . . . .118 E8
Cumberland Lodge SL4 . . .94 D3
Cumberland Rd
Ashford TW15. . . . . .97 D5
Frimley GU15 . . . . .152 C4
Reading RG1 . . . . .86 D7
Cumberland St TW18. . . . .96 D3
Cumberland Villa **6** RG1 .86 E7
Cumberland Way RG41. . .115 D6
Cumbernauld Gdns TW16 .98 F3
Cumbrae SL2 . . . . .43 A5
Cumbria CI SL6 . . . . .39 C4
Cumnor Way RG12 . . . . . .118 E5
Cunworth Ct RG12 . . . . . .117 F3
Curfew Bell Rd KT16 . . . .123 F2
Curlew Dr RG19. . . . . .106 C3
Curlew Dr RG31 . . . . .84 C6
Curley Hill Rd GU18. . . . .152 F7
Curling Way RG14 . . . . . . .105 C4
Curls La SL6 . . . . .39 E4
Curl Way RG41 . . . . .116 A5
Curly's Way RG7 . . . . .139 D6
Curnock Ct **2** RG14. . . . .104 E1
CURRIDGE 78 D4
Curridge Gn RG18 . . . . . . .78 E4
Curridge Piece RG18 . . . . .78 F5
Curridge Prim Sch RG18 . .78 D4
Curridge Rd RG18 . . . . . . .78 D4
Curriers La SL1 . . . . .21 D7
Curtis CI GU15. . . . . .152 C7
Curtis Rd RG31 . . . . .84 C4
Curzon Mall **7** SL1 . . . . . .42 F4
Curzon St RG30 . . . . .85 E8
Cuthbush La 114 B8
Cutbush La
Earley RG6. . . . . .87 C1
Lower Earley RG6 . . . . . . .114 B8
Shinfield RG2 . . . . .113 F6
Cutting Hill SN8, RG17 . . .126 A4
Cuttings The RG18 . . . . . . .52 F5
Cwmcarn RG4 . . . . .58 F5
Cygnet CI RG19 . . . . .106 B3
Cygnet SL7 . . . . .1 E1
Davis Gdns GU47 . . . . . . .150 E7

Cygnets The **14** TW18 . . . .96 F3
Cygnet Way RG17 . . . . . . .100 D7
Cypress CI RG40 . . . . .142 A8
Cypress Ct
Charlton TW16. . . . . .125 E8
Virginia Water GU25 . . . .122 F5
Cypress Hill Ct GU14 . . . .150 F1
Cypress Ho
3 Newbury RG14. . . . . . .104 F2
Slough SL3. . . . . .44 B1
Cypress Rd RG5 . . . . .88 A6
Cypress Way GU17 . . . . . .150 B5
Cypress Wlk TW20. . . . . . .95 B2
Cyril Vokins Rd RG14. . . .105 E2

D

Daceberry Ct RG9 . . . . .16 C2
Dacre Ave RG4 . . . . .59 E4
Dagmar Rd SL4. . . . . .67 D5
Dair House Sch SL2. . . . . . .22 C4
Dairy Ct SL6. . . . . .65 A7
Dairy La RG9 . . . . .16 B8
Daisy Mdw RG30 . . . . .96 A3
Dalby CI RG10 . . . . .88 F8
Dalby Cres RG14 . . . . .131 B8
Dalby Gdns SL6 . . . . .19 F1
Dalcross RG12 . . . . .118 E3
Dale CI SL5 . . . . .121 A4
Dale Ct SL1 . . . . .42 C4
Dale Gdns GU47 . . . . .150 A8
Daleham Ave TW20 . . . . . .96 A2
Dale Lodge Rd SL5 . . . . . .121 A4
Dale Rd
Ashford TW16 . . . . .98 F1
Oatlands Park KT12. . . . .125 F2
Reading RG2 . . . . .86 B5
Daley Ct GU47 . . . . .150 C8
Dalston CI GU15 . . . . .152 D3
Dalton CI RG30 . . . . .84 E8
Dalton Gr
Datchet SL3 . . . . .68 F8
14 Newbury RG14. . . . . . .43 F1
Damask CI GU14 . . . . .153 E6
Damer Gdns RG9 . . . . .35 E8
Damson Dr RG2 . . . . .137 B6
Damson Gr SL1 . . . . .42 C4
Dandridge CI SL3 . . . . .43 D2
Dandridge Dr SL8 . . . . .3 C3
Danehill RG6 . . . . .114 B8
Danehurst Ct RG19 . . . . . . .95 E2
Dane Rd TW15 . . . . .98 D2
Danesfield RG40 . . . . .116 D6
Danesfield Sch SL7 . . . . . . .17 E7
Danes Gdns SL6 . . . . .19 F6
Danescourt **2** RG19 . . . .106 D2
Danywern Dr RG41. . . . . . .88 C2
DARBY GREEN 150 B6
Darby Green La GU17 . . . .150 B6
Darby Green Rd GU17. . . .150 B5
Darby La RG8. . . . . .55 B5
Darby Vale RG42 . . . . .91 B2
Darell Rd RG4 . . . . .59 C5
Dark La
Bradfield RG7 . . . . .82 C7
Purley on T RG31. . . . . . . .57 B2
Wargrave RG10. . . . . .36 D2
Wickham RG17 . . . . .101 A7
Darleydale CI GU47 . . . . .143 D2
Darling's La SL6 . . . . .18 E1
Darracott CI GU15 . . . . . . .152 B8
Darrell CI SL3 . . . . .43 F2
Darrington Ct GU15 . . . . .152 A5
Dart CI
Brands Hill SL3 . . . . .69 B8
Finchampstead RG40. . . .141 F6
Thatcham RG18 . . . . .106 B5
Dartington Ave RG5. . . . . .87 D4
Dartington CI RG12 . . . . . .118 E6
Dartmouth CI RG12 . . . . . .118 E6
Dartmouth Terr **1** RG1. . .86 C6
Darvills La SL1 . . . . .42 F1
Darvill's La SL1. . . . . .42 F1
Darwall Dr SL5 . . . . .119 D7
Darwin Ct **2** GU15. . . . . .151 A5
Darwin PI RG12 . . . . .118 C5
Darwin Rd SL3 . . . . .43 F4
Dashwood CI
Bracknell RG12 . . . . .118 D8
Slough SL3. . . . . .43 C2
DATCHET 68 C6
DATCHET COMMON 68 D6
Datchet Rd
Horton SL3. . . . . .68 F4
Old Windsor SL4 . . . . .68 A3
Slough SL3. . . . . .42 F2
Windsor SL4 . . . . .67 D7
Datchet St Mary's CE Prim
Sch SL3. . . . . .68 B6
Datchet Sta SL3 . . . . .68 B6
Dauntless Rd RG7 . . . . . . .111 B3
Davenport Rd RG12 . . . . .118 E8
Daventry Ct RG12 . . . . .69 F6
Daventry La TW6 . . . . .71 E5
David CI UB3 . . . . .71 F7
David Ct **3** TW18 . . . . .97 A4
David Henry Waring Ct
TW14 . . . . .98 C7
David Rd SL3 . . . . .69 E5
David Smith Ct RG31. . . . .84 F5
David Stirling Ct RG30. . . .85 A8
David St RG30 . . . . .85 C8
Davis CI SL7. . . . . .1 E1
Davis Ct RG1 . . . . .86 B6

Davis St RG10 . . . . .88 D5
Davis Way RG10 . . . . .88 D4
Davy CI RG40. . . . . .116 C5
Dawes East Rd SL1 . . . . . . .21 C2
Dawes Moor CI SL2. . . . . . .43 C7
Dawley Ride SL3. . . . . .69 E6
Dawlish Rd RG2 . . . . .86 C2
Dawnay CI SL5 . . . . .119 F8
Dawnay Rd GU15 . . . . . . .151 B7
Dawn Ct GU15 . . . . .151 F7
Dawn Redwood CI SL3. . . .69 A4
Daws Ct SL0. . . . . .44 F7
Dawsmere CI GU15 . . . . .152 C5
Dawson CI SL4 . . . . .67 A5
Daytona Dr RG19 . . . . . . .107 B2
Dayworth Mews **8** RG30 . .85 C7
Deacon CI RG40 . . . . .116 C8
Deacon Ct SL4 . . . . .66 D5
Deaconfield RG8. . . . . .14 C3
Deacons La RG18 . . . . .79 C7
Deacon Way RG30 . . . . . . .58 A2
Deadman's La RG4, RG19 .131 B6
Deadman's La RG7. . . . . . .83 D3
Deadmoor La RG20 . . . . .130 E1
Deal Ave SL1 . . . . .41 F7
Dean CI SL4 . . . . .66 D4
Dean Ct KT16. . . . . .124 A3
Deanfield Ave RG9. . . . . . .15 D1
Deanfield CI SL7. . . . . .1 D3
Deanfield Rd RG9 . . . . .15 D1
Dean Gr RG40 . . . . .116 C7
Dean Ho RG1. . . . . .86 D6
Dean La SL6. . . . . .19 C8
Dean Par GU15 . . . . .151 F8
Deans CI SL2 . . . . .23 B4
Deans Copse Rd RG7,
RG30 . . . . .111 C8
Deans Ct GU20 . . . . .146 D4
Deans Farm RG4 . . . . .59 D1
Deansfield CI SL6. . . . . . . .19 D2
Deansgate RG12 . . . . .118 B2
Deansgate Rd RG1. . . . . . .86 B6
Deanside SL1 . . . . .151 F8
Dean St SL7 . . . . .1 E2
Dean View SL6 . . . . .19 E6
Deanwood Farm RG20 . . .104 B5
Deanwood Ho RG20. . . . .104 B5
Dearden Way RG2 . . . . . . .113 D5
Debden Ho RG12 . . . . . . .118 D6
De Beauvoir Rd RG1 . . . . .86 E6
Deccan Gr RG9 . . . . .106 D2
Decies Way SL2 . . . . .23 A4
Dedmere Ct SL7 . . . . .1 F2
Dedmere Rd SL7. . . . . .1 F2
Dedmere Rise SL7. . . . . .1 E2
DEDWORTH 66 E6
Dedworth Dr SL4 . . . . .66 E6
Dedworth Green Fst Sch
SL4. . . . . .66 E5
Dedworth Manor SL4. . . . .66 E6
Dedworth Mid Sch SL4. . . .66 E5
Dedworth Rd SL4 . . . . .66 E5
Deena CI SL1 . . . . .41 A5
Deepdale RG12. . . . . .118 A5
Deepdene CI RG1 . . . . .85 E7
Deepfield Rd RG12. . . . . .118 D8
Deep Well Dr GU15 . . . . .151 E5
Dee Rd RG30. . . . . .85 A7
Deerhurst Ave RG41. . . . . .88 D2
Deerhurst CI TW13. . . . . . .98 E4
Deer Leap GU18 . . . . .153 A8
Deer Rock Hill RG12 . . . . .118 C3
Deer Rock Rd GU15. . . . . .151 F8
Deerswood SL6. . . . . .20 B1
Defence CI RG19. . . . . . . .106 E1
Defford CI RG41 . . . . .88 F1
De Havilland Way TW19 . .70 F1
Delafield Dr RG31. . . . . . . .84 C4
Delaford CI SL0 . . . . .44 F7
Delamere Ho **5** RG41. . . .85 E5
Delamere Rd RG6. . . . . . . .87 B8
Delane Dr RG41. . . . . .88 B1
Delaney CI RG30 . . . . .84 F8
Delft CI RG30 . . . . .84 E7
Dellars Hill SL6 . . . . .38 A7
Dell CI SL2 . . . . .22 C7
Deller St RG42 . . . . .90 F1
Dell Gr GU16 . . . . .151 F2
Dell Park Farm TW20 . . . . .95 A5
Dell Rd
Finchampstead RG40. . . .142 A3
Purley on T RG31. . . . . . . .57 C2
Dell The
Englefield Green TW20 . . . .95 A5
Maidenhead SL6 . . . . .38 A5
10 Reading RG1 . . . . .86 E7
Yateley GU46. . . . . .149 C5
Woodford Com Hospl
RG30 . . . . .85 C6
Dellwood Pk RG4 . . . . .58 F4
Delph The RG6 . . . . .87 D2
Delta Ct SL6. . . . . .39 F6
Delta Way TW20 . . . . .96 B1
De Montfort Gr RG17. . . .100 D4
De Montfort Rd
Newbury RG14. . . . . .104 E5
Reading RG1 . . . . .59 A1
Dempsey Ho RG30 . . . . . . .84 F7
Denbigh Gdns RG4 . . . . . . .59 C5
Denbury Gdns **1** RG2 . .113 C8
Denby Way RG30 . . . . .84 E7
Dene CI
Bracknell RG42 . . . . .91 C1
Denefield Sch **3** TW15 . .98 A3

Dene Cl continued
Camberley GU15 . . . . 152 A8
Earley RG6. . . . . .87 A3
Denefield Gdns RG31 . . . . 57 B2
Denefield Sch RG31. . . . . . 57 B3
Dene Ho SL4 . . . . .67 C4
Dene Hollow OX11. . . . . . . 10 E8
Dene Way RG14. . . . . 105 A5
Denford La RG17. . . . . . . 101 C8
Denham Cl SL6 . . . . .39 C6
Denham Dr 1 GU46 . . . . 149 D5
Denham Gr RG12 . . . . 118 C3
Denham Rd TW20. . . . . 96 A4
Denholme Lodge SL3 . . . . 68 B7
Denison Rd TW13. . . . . 98 F4
Denly Way GU18 . . . . 146 C1
Denman Dr TW15 . . . . .98 B2
Denmark Ave RG5 . . . . . . .61 A1
Denmark Rd
Newbury RG14. . . . . 105 A3
Reading RG1 . . . . .86 D6
Denmark St
Maidenhead SL6 . . . . .39 E8
Wokingham RG40 . . . . . . 116 C5
Denmead Ct RG12 . . . . . . 118 E3
Dennis Cl TW15. . . . . .98 D1
Dennisford Rd RG20 . . . . . 31 A6
Dennis Pilcher Ho RG12. 118 E6
Dennistoun Cl GU15 . . . . 151 D5
Dennis Way SL1 . . . . .41 D6
Dennose Cl RG6 . . . . .87 A1
Denny Rd SL3 . . . . .43 F2
Denton Cl RG19. . . . . 106 C2
Denton Ct
Marlow SL7 . . . . 1 F3
Reading RG2 . . . . .86 D3
Denton Mews RG40 . . . . . 116 C6
Denton Rd RG40. . . . . 116 C6
Denton Way GU16 . . . . . . 151 D2
Denvale Trade Pk RG14. . 105 D2
Derby Cl RG17 . . . . .25 A2
Derby Rd
Caversham RG4. . . . . 59 B3
Newbury RG14 . . . . 104 F1
Derbyshire Gn RG42 . . . . . 91 F1
Derby St RG1. . . . . .85 F8
Derek Horn Ct GU15 . . . . 151 B6
Derek Rd SL6 . . . . .40 C8
Deri Dene Cl 2 TW19 . . . . 70 E1
De Ros Pl TW20 . . . . .96 A2
Derrick Cl RG31 . . . . .84 C4
Derry Rd GU14 . . . . 150 F1
Derwent Ave RG30 . . . . . . .57 E2
Derwent Cl
East Bedfont TW14 . . . . . .98 F7
Wokingham RG41 . . . . . . 115 E6
Derwent Dr
Burnham SL1 . . . . .41 C8
Maidenhead SL6 . . . . .39 D8
Derwent Rd
Lightwater GU18 . . . . 153 B8
Thatcham RG19 . . . . 106 A3
Thorpe Lea TW20. . . . . . . .96 B1
Desborough Cl
Lower Halliford TW17 . . . 125 A2
Newbury RG14. . . . . 105 E5
Desborough Cotts SL6 . . . 20 E1
Desborough Cres SL6 . . . .39 C5
Desborough Sch SL6 . . . . .39 E5
Deseronto Wharf Ind Est
SL3. . . . . 43 E4
Desford Way TW15 . . . . . . 97 F6
Detling Ho RG12. . . . . 118 D6
Devenish La GU20, SL5 . . 120 D1
Devenish Rd GU20, SL5 . 120 D2
Devereux Rd SL4 . . . . .67 D5
Deverills Way SL3 . . . . . . .44 C2
Deveron Dr RG30 . . . . .85 A8
Devil's Highway The
RG45 . . . . 142 F5
Devils La TW20 . . . . .96 C2
De-Vitre Gn RG40. . . . . . . 116 F7
Devitt Cl RG2. . . . . .87 C3
Devon Ave SL1 . . . . .42 C7
Devon Chase RG42. . . . . . .91 E2
Devon Cl
Sandhurst GU47 . . . . 150 D7
Wokingham RG41 . . . . . . 115 E6
Devon Dr RG4 . . . . .59 E4
Devonshire Cl SL2 . . . . . . .22 B3
Devonshire Dr GU15 . . . . 151 F7
Devonshire Gdns RG31. . . 57 B3
Devonshire Gn SL2 . . . . . . 22 B3
Devonshire Lodge 10 SL6 .39 F6
Devonshire Pk RG2 . . . . . .86 E2
Dewar Spur SL3 . . . . .68 F8
Dewgrass Down RG18. . . 106 F4
Dewe La RG30. . . . . .84 E2
Dexter Way RG41 . . . . .88 B2
Dhoon Rise SL6 . . . . .39 F6
Diamedes Ave TW19 . . . . .97 D7
Diamond Cotts RG10 . . . . .37 C6
Diamond Hill GU15 . . . . . 151 E7
Diamond Rd RG30 . . . . . . .85 A8
Diamond Ridge GU15 . . . 151 E7
Diamond Villas RG10. . . . .88 F8
Diamond Way RG41 . . . . . 115 E7
Diana Cl
Slough SL3. . . . . .43 E7
Spencers Wood RG7 . . . . 113 A1
Dianthus Cl KT16 . . . . 123 E2
Dianthus Pl RG42 . . . . .92 B2
Dibleys OX11 . . . . .12 A8
Dickens Cl RG4 . . . . .59 D2
Dickens Ct RG41 . . . . 116 B6

Dickens Pl SL3 . . . . .69 E6
Dickens Way GU46 . . . . . 149 C5
Dickens Wlk RG14 . . . . . . 131 A8
Dickson Glade 7 RG19 . . 106 E2
Dick Turpin Way TW14 . . . 71 F3
Diddenham Cotts RG7 . . 112 D2
Diddenham Ct RG7 . . . . . 112 D2
Dido Rd OX11 . . . . .9 F8
Dieppe Cl RG41 . . . . 115 E6
Digby Rd RG14 . . . . 104 E4
Digital Acad RG41 . . . . . . 116 B4
Dines Way RG18 . . . . .79 C7
Dingle Rd TW15 . . . . .98 B3
Dinton Pastures Ctry Pk★
RG10. . . . . .88 C5
Discovery Ct 6 RG14 . . . 105 A2
Disraeli Ct SL3 . . . . .69 B8
Ditchfield La RG40 . . . . . . 141 E8
Ditchling RG12 . . . . 118 A2
Dittany Gdns RG18. . . . . . 106 D5
Ditton Park Cvn Site 2
SL3. . . . . 43 F1
Ditton Park Rd SL3 . . . . . . 68 E8
Ditton Rd
Datchet SL3 . . . . 68 D7
Slough SL3. . . . . .68 F8
Dittons The RG40 . . . . . . 141 F6
Dobson's La RG9 . . . . 15 C8
Dockett Eddy La TW17 . . 124 F1
Dockett Moorings KT16 . 124 F1
Doctors La RG18. . . . . .79 A6
Doddington Cl RG6 . . . . . . 87 C1
Doddsfield Rd SL2 . . . . . . .22 A2
Dodsells Well RG40 . . . . . 141 F8
Doghurst Ave UB7 . . . . . . .71 B7
Doghurst Dr UB7 . . . . .71 B7
Dogkennel La OX12 . . . . . .27 C4
Dog La RG8 . . . . .54 A6
Doles Hill RG41. . . . . 115 D4
Doles La RG41 . . . . 115 E3
Dolman Rd RG14. . . . . 105 A4
Dolphin Cl
Aldermaston RG7 . . . . . . 134 F7
Winnersh RG41 . . . . .88 C1
Dolphin Ct
Bracknell RG12 . . . . 118 C5
Slough SL1 . . . . .43 B4
Stanwell TW19. . . . . .97 A5
Dolphin Ct N TW19. . . . . . .97 A5
Dolphin Est The TW16 . . 125 D8
Dolphin Ho
Charlton TW16 . . . . 125 E8
Slough SL1 . . . . .43 B4
Dolphin Rd N TW16 . . . . . 125 E8
Dolphin Rd S TW16. . . . . . 125 E8
Dolphin Rd W TW16. . . . . 125 E8
Dolphin Sch RG10 . . . . . . .62 A2
Dolton Mews RG14 . . . . . 104 F3
Doman Rd GU15 . . . . 151 A4
Dommett Ho TW18. . . . . . .97 A2
Domoney Cl RG41 . . . . . . .88 B4
Donaldson Way RG5 . . . . .88 B8
Doncastle Rd RG12 . . . . . 117 E6
Don Cl RG30. . . . . 85 A8
Donegal Cl RG4 . . . . .59 C3
Donkey La SL8. . . . . 3 A3
DONKEY TOWN 153 D6
Donkin Cl SL6 . . . . .39 C5
Donkin Hill RG4 . . . . .59 C3
DONNINGTON 104 F7
Donnington Castle★
RG14 . . . . 104 E7
Donnington Cl
Bucklebury RG7 . . . . 108 C8
Camberley GU15 . . . . 151 B4
Donnington Elms RG14. . 104 F6
Donnington Gdns
Maidenhead SL6 . . . . 19 F1
Reading RG1 . . . . .86 E6
Donnington Hospl RG14. 104 F6
Donnington Lodge RG14 104 F7
Donnington Pk RG14. . . . 104 F6
Donnington Pl RG41 . . . . .88 D2
Donnington Rd RG1. . . . . .86 D6
Donnington Sq RG14 . . . . 104 F6
Donnybrook RG12 . . . . . . 118 A2
Dorcas Ct GU15. . . . . 151 B3
Dorchester Cl SL6 . . . . . . .19 E1
Dorchester Ct
Camberley GU15 . . . . 151 B5
Reading RG30 . . . . .85 C6
8 Staines TW18. . . . . . . .97 A4
Dorchester Dr TW14 . . . . .71 E1
Dorchester Mans SL5 . . . 120 F1
Dorian Dr SL5 . . . . 120 E8
Doris Rd TW15. . . . . .98 D2
Dorking Way RG31 . . . . . . .84 B4
Dorly Cl TW17 . . . . 125 E4
Dormer Cl
Crowthorne RG45 . . . . . . 143 A5
Newbury RG14. . . . . 130 E6
Dormy Ho The GU25 . . . . 121 F3
Dorndon Ho RG10 . . . . . . .88 F8
Dornels SL2 . . . . .41 C3
DORNEY. 41 C3
Dorney Court★ SL4 . . . . . .41 B3
DORNEY REACH. 40 F3
Dorney Reach Rd SL6. . . . .40 F3
Dorney Sch SL6 . . . . .40 F4
Dorney Wood Rd SL1. . . . .21 D6
Dorothy St RG1 . . . . .86 B6
Dorset Cl RG14 . . . . 151 F8
Dorset Lodge 9 SL6. . . . . .39 F6

Dorset Rd
Ashford TW15 . . . . .97 D5
Windsor SL4 . . . . .67 C6
Dorset St RG30 . . . . .85 C8
Dorset Vale RG42 . . . . .91 E2
Dorset Way RG41 . . . . 115 E5
Dorton Villas UB7 . . . . .71 A6
Doublet Cl RG19 . . . . 106 A3
Douglas Ct
Earley RG6. . . . . .87 A3
Marlow SL7 . . . . .2 A3
Douglas Grange RG10. . . . 88 D4
Douglas La TW19 . . . . .68 F1
Douglas Rd
Caversham RG4. . . . . .59 D2
Slough SL2. . . . . .42 D8
Stanwell TW19 . . . . .70 D1
Doultons The TW18 . . . . . .97 A2
Douro Cl RG26. . . . . 134 D1
Dove Cl RG6. . . . . 113 F8
Dovecote Rd RG2 . . . . 113 B7
Dove Ct TW19 . . . . .97 E8
Dovedale Cl
Caversham RG4. . . . . .58 F3
Sandhurst GU47 . . . . 143 D2
Dove House Cres SL2 . . . .21 E2
Dover Rd SL1. . . . . .41 F7
Dover St RG1 . . . . .86 A6
Doveton Way RG14. . . . . . 105 B4
Dowding Cl RG5 . . . . .88 A2
Dowding Ct RG45 . . . . . . 143 C6
Dower Ho The SL5 . . . . . . 120 C4
Dower Pk SL4 . . . . .66 E3
Dowles Gn RG40. . . . . 116 E8
DOWLESGREEN 116 E8
Downe House Sch RG18. .79 A3
DOWNEND 51 A3
Downend La RG20 . . . . . . .51 B2
Downfield La SL6. . . . . .63 C5
Downfield Rd RG10 . . . . . .63 A4
Downham Ct RG2. . . . . . . .86 E1
Downing Path SL2 . . . . . . .21 E1
Downing Rd RG31 . . . . . . .84 D8
Downlands RG17 . . . . .47 C6
Downmill Rd RG12 . . . . . . 117 F7
Down Pl SL4 . . . . .66 A8
Downs Cl RG17 . . . . .46 F7
Downshire Cl RG17 . . . . . .48 B4
Downshire Sq RG1. . . . . . . 85 E6
Downshire Way
Bracknell, Priestwood RG12,
RG42. . . . . 118 A7
Bracknell RG12 . . . . 118 B6
Downside
9 Chertsey KT16 . . . . . . 123 F1
Chilton OX11 . . . . 10 C8
Downs Rd
Aldworth RG20 . . . . 32 A4
Slough SL3. . . . . .43 D4
Downs Sch The RG20 . . . . 31 D4
Downs View OX11. . . . . 12 F8
Downs Way
Chilton OX11 . . . . 9 F8
Purley on Thames RG8 . . . .57 C2
Downsway Prim Sch
RG31 . . . . .57 C3
Down View RG17. . . . . 100 E5
Doyen Ct 3 RG14. . . . . . . 105 B3
Doyle Rd RG45 . . . . 143 B3
Dragons Cl RG19 . . . . 106 D1
Drain Hill RG17 . . . . .25 A4
Drake Ave
Slough SL3. . . . . .43 D2
Staines TW18 . . . . .96 F3
Drake Cl
Bracknell RG12 . . . . 118 A4
Finchampstead RG40. . . . 141 E7
Drake Way RG2 . . . . .86 A2
Draper Cl RG19 . . . . 106 D2
Draycott RG12 . . . . 118 E4
Drayhorse Dr RG19 . . . . . 145 E2
Draymans La 5 SL7. . . . . . . 1 D1
Drayton Cl RG12 . . . . 118 D7
Drayton Rd RG30 . . . . .85 B8
Dresden Way RG30 . . . . . . 57 F1
Drewett Cl RG2 . . . . 113 C6
Drew Mdw SL2 . . . . .22 C8
Drey Ho RG41 . . . . 115 F7
Drifters Dr GU16. . . . . 152 D1
Drift Rd SL4, SL6 . . . . 65 D3
Drift Way SL3. . . . . .69 C7
Driftway Ct 8 RG6. . . . . . . .87 C1
Driftways GU46 . . . . 149 D7
Drill Hall Rd KT16. . . . . . . 124 A2
Drive The
Ashford TW15 . . . . .98 D1
Bourne End SL8. . . . . 2 F4
Datchet SL3 . . . . 68 A6
Earley RG6. . . . . .87 A7
Newbury RG14. . . . . 130 E8
Slough SL3. . . . . .43 E4
Virginia Water GU25 . . . . 122 F4
Wraysbury TW19 . . . . .68 D2
Droitwich Cl RG12 . . . . . . 118 E6
Dropmore Rd SL1 . . . . .21 C5
Drove La RG18. . . . . .79 C2
Drovers Way
Bracknell RG12 . . . . 118 F6
Woodley RG5 . . . . .87 E5
Drove The RG19. . . . . 133 B1
Druce Way OX11 . . . . 10 E2
Druid's Wood SL5. . . . . . . 119 E8
Drummond Cl RG12 . . . . . 118 E4
Drummond Ho 4 SL4. . . . .67 D4

Drury La RG7 . . . . 137 A5
Dry Arch Rd SL5. . . . . 120 F3
Dryden RG12 . . . . 118 A2
Dryden Cl RG12 . . . . 106 D5
Dryden Ct RG18. . . . . 106 D5
Dryland Ho RG30 . . . . .84 F7
Duchess Cl RG45 . . . . 143 B7
Duchess St SL1. . . . . .41 C5
Ducketts Mead
Arborfield Garrison RG2 . 140 E8
Reading RG2 . . . . 113 E7
Dudley Cl RG31 . . . . .57 E1
Dudley Ct SL1 . . . . .43 A3
Dudley Ho RG12 . . . . 118 C7
Dudley Mews RG31 . . . . . .57 E1
Dudley Pl TW19. . . . . .70 F1
Dudley Rd
East Bedfont TW14 . . . . . .98 D7
Feltham TW14 . . . . .98 D7
Duffield La SL2 . . . . .22 F6
Duffield Pk SL2. . . . . .23 A2
Duffield Rd RG5 . . . . .88 A2
Dugdale Ho TW20. . . . . . . .96 C3
Duke of Cornwall Ave
GU15. . . . . 144 D1
Dukesbridge Ct 6 RG1. . .86 B7
Dukes Cl TW15. . . . . .98 C4
Dukes Covert GU19 . . . . . 145 E6
Dukes Dr SL1, SL2. . . . . . .22 A8
Duke's Hill GU19 . . . . 145 E5
Duke's Rd RG40 . . . . 118 B8
Duke's La
Old Windsor SL4, SL5 . . . .94 B3
Winkfield SL5. . . . . .93 F1
Dukes Mdw SL8 . . . . 3 B3
Dukes Pl
Marlow SL7 . . . . 1 D2
Slough SL1 . . . . .42 F6
Dukes Ride RG7 . . . . 136 B1
Duke's Ride RG45 . . . . 143 B5
Duke St
Eton SL4. . . . . .67 C7
Henley-on-T RG9 . . . . 15 E2
Reading RG1 . . . . .86 B7
Dukes Wood RG45 . . . . . . 143 B5
Dulnan Cl RG30. . . . . .85 A8
Dulverton Gdns RG2 . . . . .86 C2
Dumas Cl GU46 . . . . 149 C5
Dumbarton Way RG4. . . . . 59 E5
Dunally Pk TW17 . . . . 125 D2
Dunaways Cl RG6. . . . . . . .87 D3
Dunbar Cl SL2 . . . . .43 A6
Dunbar Dr RG5. . . . . .88 A6
Dunboe Pl TW17 . . . . 125 C2
Dunboyne Pl SL4 . . . . .68 A3
Duncan Dr RG40 . . . . 116 E6
Duncan Gdns
Purley on T RG8. . . . . .57 C4
Staines TW18. . . . . .97 A2
Duncannon Cres SL4. . . . .66 D4
Duncan Rd RG6 . . . . .87 E6
Duncansby Ho SL1. . . . . . .43 A4
Duncombe Ct TW18. . . . . .96 F1
Duncroft Manor TW18. . . .96 F1
Dundaff Cl GU15 . . . . 152 A5
Dundas Ct RG12 . . . . 118 B5
Dundee Rd SL1 . . . . .42 A8
Dundela Cl RG5. . . . . .87 E6
Dunedin Hospl RG1 . . . . . .85 F6
Dunford Pl RG42. . . . . .90 E1
Dungells Farm Cl GU46 . 149 D4
Dungells La GU46 . . . . 149 C4
Dungrovehill La SL6 . . . . . 18 D3
Dunholme Cl RG6. . . . . . . .87 C2
Dunholme End SL6 . . . . . . 39 D3
Dunkirk Cl RG41. . . . . 115 E6
Dunleary Ct 13 RG29. . . . .85 D6
Dunluce Gdns RG8. . . . . . .56 E5
Dunn Cres RG17 . . . . 102 B1
Dunnock Way RG10 . . . . . .36 E3
Dunoon Cl RG31 . . . . .84 E4
DUNSDEN GREEN 59 F7
Dunsfold Rd RG30. . . . . . . .84 F7
Dunsmore Gdns GU46 . . 149 A5
Dunstable Ho 3 SL7. . . . . . 1 E1
Dunstall Cl RG31 . . . . .57 E1
Dunstan Ct TW18 . . . . .97 A4
Dunstan Rd RG18 . . . . 106 E4
Dunstans Dr RG41 . . . . . . .88 A2
Dunster Cl RG42 . . . . .59 C6
Dunster Gdns SL1 . . . . . . .42 A6
Dunt Ave RG10 . . . . .88 E4
Dunt La RG10. . . . . .88 E4
Dunwood Ct SL6. . . . . .39 C5
Duppas Cl TW17 . . . . 125 D4
Dupre Cl SL1 . . . . .41 E4
Du Pre Wlk HP10 . . . . .3 D4
Durand Rd RG6 . . . . 114 A8
Durant Way RG17. . . . . . . .97 D3
Duran Cl SL1 . . . . .42 A7
Durham Cl
Reading RG2 . . . . 113 C8
Wokingham RG41 . . . . . . 115 E6
Durham Dr GU16 . . . . 152 D1
Durham Rd RG2 . . . . 113 C8
Durley Mead RG12 . . . . . . 118 E4
Durnford Ave RG41 . . . . . 143 E2
Durrell Way TW17 . . . . . . 125 D3
Dutch Barn Cl TW19 . . . . .70 D1
Dutton Way SL6 . . . . .44 E7
Duval Cl GU47 . . . . 143 D1
Duval Pl GU19 . . . . 145 E3
Dwyer Rd RG30. . . . . .85 A4
Dyelap Rd RG14 . . . . 130 E4
Dyer Straits Cl SL2 . . . . . . 23 A6
Dysart Gdns RG17 . . . . . . .67 B4
Dysons Cl RG14. . . . . 104 E3
Dysonswood La RG4 . . . . .58 E4

E

Eagle Cl
Crowthorne RG45 . . . . . . 143 A7
Wokingham RG41 . . . . . . 115 F5
Eagle House Sch GU47. . 143 B2
Eaglehurst Cotts RG42 . . .90 C3
Eagle Rd
Hatton TW6 . . . . .71 F4
Newtown RG20 . . . . 132 A2
Eagles Nest GU47 . . . . . . 143 A1
Earle Croft RG42. . . . . .91 C1
EARLEY. 87 B5
Earleydene SL5 . . . . 120 B1
Earley Hill Rd RG6 . . . . . . .87 A5
Earley Pl RG1 . . . . .86 B7
Earley Sta RG6 . . . . .87 C4
Earlsfield SL6 . . . . 40 C2
Earlsfield Cl RG4 . . . . .59 E4
Earls Gr GU15 . . . . 151 C6
Earls La SL1 . . . . .41 F5
Earls Rd RG14. . . . . 104 E2
Earlswood RG12 . . . . 118 B2
Easby Way RG6. . . . . .87 D1
Easington Dr RG6. . . . . . . .87 E2
EAST BEDFONT 98 E7
East Berkshire Coll
Slough SL3 . . . . 44 A3
Windsor SL4 . . . . .67 C5
Eastbourne Rd SL1 . . . . . .42 A7
Eastbridge SL2 . . . . .43 B5
EAST BURNHAM 22 A4
East Burnham Cotts SL2 .22 A4
East Burnham La SL2 . . . .22 A4
EASTBURY. 46 F7
Eastbury Ave RG31. . . . . . .84 B8
Eastbury Ct RG42. . . . . . . .90 F1
Eastbury Pk RG41. . . . . . . .88 D2
Eastbury Shute RG17. . . . .46 E2
Eastchurch Rd TW6 . . . . . .71 E4
Eastchurch Rd Rdbt TW6 . 71 E5
Eastcliff RG4 . . . . .58 E3
Eastcourt Ave RG6. . . . . . .87 A6
East Cres SL4. . . . . 66 F6
Eastcroft SL2 . . . . 22 B1
East Dr
Reading RG31 . . . . .84 E5
Stoke Poges SL2 . . . . .22 E2
Wentworth GU25. . . . . . . 122 B3
Eastern Ave
Chertsey KT16 . . . . 124 A6
Reading RG1 . . . . .86 C6
Eastern Bsns Pk TW6 . . . .71 E5
Eastern Dr SL8 . . . . .3 C4
Eastern Ind Area RG12 . . 118 D7
Eastern La RG45 . . . . 143 F4
Eastern Perimeter Rd
Hatton TW6 . . . . .71 F4
Hatton TW14, TW6. . . . . . .71 F5
Eastern Rd RG12 . . . . 118 D7
Eastfield OX11. . . . . .12 A8
Eastfield Cl 4 SL1 . . . . . . .43 A3
Eastfield La RG8 . . . . .54 A8
Eastfield Rd SL1 . . . . .41 A8
EAST FIELDS 105 B2
EAST GARSTON 47 D6
EAST GARSTON
WOODLANDS 47 B3
Eastgate Ct 7 RG1 . . . . . . .86 E7
East Gn GU17. . . . . 150 D4
EASTHAMPSTEAD 118 B5
Easthampstead Mobile Home
Pk RG40 . . . . 143 C8
Easthampstead Park Sch
RG12 . . . . 117 D3
Easthampstead Rd
Bracknell RG12 . . . . 118 A7
Wokingham RG40 . . . . . . 116 E4
EASTHEATH 116 B3
Eastheath Ave RG41 . . . . 116 A4
Eastheath Gdns RG41 . . . 116 B3
EAST ILSLEY 30 F6
East La SL1 . . . . .22 B1
Eastleigh Rd TW6. . . . . 71 F4
Eastlyn Rd RG26. . . . . 135 E1
EASTON 2 D6
Easton Hill RG20. . . . . .76 A4
East Paddock SL6. . . . . . . .18 F6
East Park Farm Dr RG10 . .61 B4
East Ramp TW6. . . . . .71 B6
East Rd
East Bedfont TW14 . . . . . .98 D8
East Ridge SL8 . . . . .3 B4
East St Mary's SL6 . . . . . .88 B7
East Stratton Cl RG12 . . . 118 F4
East Terr SL4 . . . . .67 E6
Eastview Cl RG10 . . . . .36 E2
Eastview Ct RG42 . . . . .91 A1
Eastwick Cl 3 SL6. . . . . . . .19 A1
Eastwood Ct 1 SL4. . . . . . .67 A7
EAST WOODHAY 148 F7
Eastwood Rd RG5 . . . . .88 B8
Eastworth Rd KT16. . . . . . 124 A1
Eaton Cl GU15 . . . . 151 B4
Eaton Pl RG1. . . . . .85 F7
Eaton Rd GU15 . . . . 151 B4
Ebborn Sq RG6 . . . . 114 C8
Ebbsworth Cl SL6. . . . . . . .20 C3
Eccles Cl RG4. . . . . .59 F5
Echelforde Dr TW15. . . . . .98 A4
Echelford Prim Sch The
TW15. . . . . .98 B3
EDDINGTON 78 B6
Eddington Hill RG17 . . . . 100 D7
Eddington Rd RG12 . . . . . 117 C3
Eddington Sch RG17 . . . . 100 D6
Eddystone Wlk TW19 . . . . .97 E8
Eden Cl SL3 . . . . .43 A1

Edenhall Cl RG31 . . . . . . 57 D3
Edenham Cl RG6 . . . . 87 E2
Edenham Cres RG1 . . . . . 85 E5
Eden Pl SL5 . . . . 121 A2
Eden Way RG41 . . . . 88 B1
Edgar Milward Cl RG30 . . 58 A1
Edgar Wallace Pl SL8 . . . . 3 B5
Edgbarrow Rise GU47 . . . 143 A2
Edgbarrow Sch RG45 . . . 143 C3
Edgcumbe Park Dr RG45 143 A5
Edgecombe La RG14 . . . . 105 C5
Edgecumbe Ct TW18 . . . . 96 F2
Edgedale Cl RG45 . . . . . . 143 B4
Edgehill Cl RG14 . . . . . . 105 E5
Edgehill St RG1 . . . . 86 B5
Edgell Cl GU25 . . . . 122 F6
Edgell Rd TW18 . . . . 96 F3
Edgemoor Rd GU16 . . . . 152 C3
Edgewood Cl RG45 . . . . . 143 A7
Edinburgh Ave SL1 . . . . . 42 B7
Edinburgh Ct RG30 . . . . . 85 D7
Edinburgh Dr TW18 . . . . . 97 D2
Edinburgh Gdns SL4 . . . . 67 D5
Edinburgh Ho SL1 . . . . . . 42 F4
Edinburgh Rd
  Maidenhead SL6 . . . . . . 19 E2
  Marlow SL7 . . . . 1 E3
  Reading RG30 . . . . 85 E7
Edith Ct TW14 . . . . 71 D1
Edith Rd SL6 . . . . 39 A7
Edmonds Ct RG12 . . . . . 118 C8
Edmunds Way SL2 . . . . . 43 B7
Edneys Hill RG41 . . . . . . 115 D2
Edward Ave SL5 . . . . 121 A5
Edward Ct TW18 . . . . 97 C2
Edward Pauling Ho TW14 98 F8
Edward Pauling Prim Sch
  TW13 . . . . 98 E6
Edward Pl **14** RG1 . . . . 86 D7
Edward Rd
  Hatton TW14 . . . . 71 E2
  Twyford RG10 . . . . 61 B5
  Windlesham GU20 . . . . . 146 D4
Edwards Ct SL1 . . . . 42 E4
Edwards Hill RG17 . . . . . 25 B2
Edward Way TW15 . . . . . 97 F6
Edwin Cl RG19 . . . . 106 F3
Eeklo Pl RG14 . . . . 105 A1
Egerton Rd
  Reading RG2 . . . . 86 E1
  Sandhurst GU15 . . . . . . 150 F7
  Sandhurst GU15 . . . . . . 151 A7
  Slough SL2 . . . . 21 E1
Egerton Way UB7 . . . . . . 71 B7
EGHAM 96 A4
Egham Bsns Village
  TW20 . . . . 123 C7
Egham By-Pass TW20 . . . 96 A4
Egham Hill TW20 . . . . . . 95 E2
Egham Hill Rdbt TW20 . . 95 F3
EGHAM HYTHE 96 E2
Egham Mus* TW20 . . . . . 96 A3
Eghams Ct **4** SL8 . . . . . 3 B3
Eghams Gn SL8 . . . . 3 B3
Egham Sta TW20 . . . . 96 A3
EGHAM WICK 95 A1
Egremont Dr RG6 . . . . . . 87 D3
Egremont Gdns SL1 . . . . . 42 A5
EGYPT
  Farnham Common 22 B8
  Leckhampstead 50 A5
Egypt La SL2 . . . . 22 B8
Eight Acres SL1 . . . . 21 E2
Eight Bells **8** RG14 . . . . 104 F2
Eighth Ave RG31 . . . . . . 84 B6
Eisenhower Ave RG20 . . . 49 A4
Elan Cl RG30 . . . . 84 F7
Elbow Mdw SL3 . . . . 69 F6
ELCOT 102 D8
Eldart Cl RG30 . . . . 85 B7
Elderberry Way RG6 . . . . 87 D1
Elder Cl RG41 . . . . 57 C1
Elderfield Cres OX11 . . . . 10 D8
Elderfield Rd SL2 . . . . 22 C5
Eldon Lodge **15** RG1 . . . 86 C7
Eldon Pl RG1 . . . . 86 C7
Eldon Rd RG1 . . . . 86 C7
Eldon Sq RG1 . . . . 86 D7
Eldon St RG1 . . . . 86 D7
Eldon Terr RG1 . . . . 86 D7
Eliot Cl TW14 . . . . 98 D7
Electra Ave TW6 . . . . 71 F4
Elford Cl RG6 . . . . 87 C1
Elford Ct RG42 . . . . 90 D3
Elgar Ave RG45 . . . . 143 B4
Elgar Rd RG2 . . . . 86 A5
Elgar Rd S RG2 . . . . 86 B4
Elgarth Dr RG40 . . . . . . 141 F8
Elgin Ave TW15 . . . . 98 C2
Elgin Cres TW6 . . . . 71 E5
Elgin Gate **5** RG1 . . . . . 85 F7
Elgin Ho SL3 . . . . 69 E6
Elgin Rd GU17 . . . . 149 E1
ELING 52 E3
Eliot Cl
  Camberley GU15 . . . . . . 152 B7
  Caversham RG4 . . . . 59 A4
  Thatcham RG18 . . . . . . 106 C5
Eliot Dr SL7 . . . . 1 F4
Elizabethan Cl TW19 . . . . 97 D8
Elizabethan Way TW19 . . 97 D8
Elizabeth Ave
  Bagshot GU19 . . . . 145 F2
  Newbury RG14 . . . . 130 D7
  Staines TW18 . . . . 97 C2
Elizabeth Cl
  Bracknell RG12 . . . . 118 C5
  Cookham Rise SL6 . . . . . 19 F7

Elizabeth Cl *continued*
  Henley-on-T RG9 . . . . . . 35 B8
Elizabeth Ct
  2 Reading RG31 . . . . . 84 D8
  1 Slough SL1 . . . . 43 A4
  Theale RG7 . . . . 83 F3
  Wargrave RG10 . . . . 36 E2
  3 Windsor SL4 . . . . . . 67 C5
  Wokingham RG41 . . . . . 116 B6
Elizabeth Gdns
  Ascot SL5 . . . . 120 B4
  Kintbury RG17 . . . . 102 B2
Elizabeth Ho TW15 . . . . . 97 F4
Elizabeth Mews **9** RG1 . 86 B6
Elizabeth Par GU46 . . . . 149 D4
Elizabeth Rd
  Henley-on-T RG9 . . . . . . 35 B8
  Marlow SL7 . . . . 1 E3
  Wokingham RG40 . . . . . 116 D6
Elizabeth Rout Cl RG7 . . 113 C2
Elizabeth Way SL2 . . . . . 22 F4
Elizabeth Wlk **3** RG1 . . . 86 B5
Ellenborough Cl RG12 . . 118 D8
Ellerton Cl RG7 . . . . 83 E4
Ellesfield Ave RG12 . . . . 117 E5
Ellesmere Cl
  Caversham RG4 . . . . 59 B3
  Datchet SL3 . . . . 68 A8
Ellies Mews TW15 . . . . . . 97 E6
Elliman Ave SL2 . . . . 42 F6
Ellington Ct SL6 . . . . 40 C7
Ellington Gdns SL6 . . . . . 40 C7
Ellington Pk SL6 . . . . 19 E1
Ellington Prim Sch SL6 . . 19 F1
Ellington Rd
  Feltham TW13 . . . . 98 F4
  Taplow SL6 . . . . 40 C7
Elliot Rise SL5 . . . . 119 D7
Elliots Way RG4 . . . . 59 B2
Elliott Ct RG42 . . . . 90 C1
Elliott Gdns TW17 . . . . . 125 A5
Ellis Ave SL1 . . . . 42 C4
Ellison Cl SL4 . . . . 66 F4
Ellison Ho **2** SL4 . . . . . . 67 D6
Ellison Way RG40 . . . . . . 116 B6
Ellis Rd RG45 . . . . 143 B6
Ellis's Hill RG2 . . . . 114 F4
Elm Apartments UB3 . . . . 71 D7
Elmar Gn SL2 . . . . 22 A2
Elm Bank GU46 . . . . 149 C7
Elmbank Ave TW20 . . . . . 95 B2
Elm Cl
  Farnham Common SL2 . . 22 C6
  Stanwell TW19 . . . . 97 D7
Elm Cotts
  Ball Hill RG20 . . . . 129 F1
  Holyport SL6 . . . . 65 A8
Elmcroft
  2 Ashford TW15 . . . . . 98 A3
  Goring RG8 . . . . 34 C5
Elm Croft SL3 . . . . 68 C6
Elmcroft Cl TW14 . . . . . . 71 F1
Elmcroft Dr TW15 . . . . . . 98 A3
Elm Ct
  3 Ashford TW16 . . . . . 98 F1
  Henley-on-T RG9 . . . . . . 35 D7
  Sandhurst GU47 . . . . . . 143 E2
Elmdon Rd TW6 . . . . 71 F4
Elm Dr
  Burghfield RG30 . . . . . . 111 B5
  Winkfield SL4 . . . . 93 B7
Elm Farm Cvn Pk KT16 . . 123 C3
Elmfield Gdns RG14 . . . . 104 E4
Elm Gr
  Maidenhead SL6 . . . . . . 39 E7
  Thatcham RG18 . . . . . . 106 B5
Elmhurst Ct
  Camberley GU15 . . . . . . 151 D5
  Slough SL3 . . . . 44 A3
Elmhurst Rd
  Goring RG8 . . . . 34 C7
  Reading RG1 . . . . 86 D5
  Slough SL3 . . . . 44 A3
  Thatcham RG18 . . . . . . 106 A5
Elm La
  Bourne End SL8 . . . . 2 F5
  Earley RG6 . . . . 86 F2
Elmleigh Ct RG4 . . . . 59 C3
Elmley Cl RG41 . . . . 88 F1
Elm Lodge Ave RG30 . . . 85 D8
Elm Park Cl **5** RG30 . . . 85 C7
Elm Pk
  Reading RG30 . . . . 85 C7
  Sunningdale SL5 . . . . . . 120 E1
Elm Pl TW15 . . . . 98 A3
Elm Rd
  Earley RG2 & RG6 . . . . . 86 F2
  East Bedfont TW14 . . . . . 98 D8
  Tokers Green RG4 . . . . . 58 D5
  Windsor SL4 . . . . 67 B4
Elms Ave RG19 . . . . 106 B3
Elms Dr SL8 . . . . 3 C3
Elms Ho **1** RG14 . . . . . . 105 E6
Elmshade La SL1 . . . . 41 E6
Elmsleigh Ctr The TW18 . 96 F4
Elmsleigh Rd TW18 . . . . . 96 F4
Elmslie Ct **4** SL6 . . . . . . 39 E7
Elms Rd RG40 . . . . 116 B5
Elms The
  6 Ashford TW15 . . . . . 98 A3
  Slough SL3 . . . . 44 A3
Elmstone Dr RG31 . . . . . . 57 C1
Elmsway TW15 . . . . 98 A3
Elm Tree Cl TW15 . . . . . . 98 B3
Elmwood SL6 . . . . 20 B4

Elmwood Cl RG5 . . . . 87 D8
Elmwood Rd SL2 . . . . 43 B6
Elsenwood Cres GU15 . . 152 A6
Elsenwood Dr GU15 . . . . 152 A7
Elsinore Ave TW19 . . . . . 97 E8
Elsley Rd RG31 . . . . 57 E3
Elstow Ave RG4 . . . . 59 C6
Elstree Cl RG31 . . . . 57 D2
Elstree Home Farm Sch
  RG7 . . . . 108 D3
Elstree Sch RG7 . . . . . . 108 D4
Elsworth Cl TW14 . . . . . . 98 E7
Eltham Ave
  Caversham RG4 . . . . 59 B5
  Slough SL1 . . . . 41 E4
Elton Dr SL6 . . . . 39 D8
Elvaston Way RG30 . . . . . 85 A7
Elveden Cl RG6 . . . . 87 E2
Elvedon Rd TW13 . . . . . . 98 F5
Elvendon Rd RG8 . . . . . . 34 D7
Elwell Cl TW20 . . . . 96 A2
Ely Ave SL1 . . . . 42 C8
Ely Cl RG14 . . . . 105 E5
Elyham RG8 . . . . 57 B5
Ely Rd
  Hatton TW6 . . . . 71 F5
  Theale RG7 . . . . 83 F3
Embankment The TW19 . . 95 C7
Embankment The RG30 . . 84 B3
Emblen Cres RG2 . . . . . . 114 E2
Embrook Way RG31 . . . . . 84 A4
Emerald Cl RG41 . . . . . . 115 E7
Emerald Ct SL1 . . . . 42 E4
Emerson Ct
  Crowthorne RG45 . . . . . 143 B5
  Wooburn Green HP10 . . . 3 E6
Emery Acres RG8 . . . . 55 A6
Emery Down Cl RG12 . . . 119 A6
Emilia Cl SL6 . . . . 19 F1
Emlyn Bldgs SL4 . . . . 67 C8
Emma La RG10 . . . . 36 E2
EMMBROOK 115 F8
Emmbrook Ct RG41 . . . . 115 F8
Emmbrook Gate RG41 . . 115 F8
Emmbrook Inf Sch RG41 . 88 F1
Emmbrook Jun Sch RG41 88 F1
Emmbrook Rd RG41 . . . . 115 F8
Emmbrook Sch The
  RG41 . . . . 116 A8
Emmbrook Vale RG41 . . . 89 A1
Emm Cl RG41 . . . . 115 F8
EMMER GREEN 59 B6
Emmer Green Prim Sch
  RG4 . . . . 59 B6
Emmets Nest RG42 . . . . . 90 C2
Emmets Pk RG42 . . . . 90 C2
Emmview Cl RG41 . . . . . 115 F7
Empress Rd RG31 . . . . . . 84 B1
Empstead Ct RG9 . . . . . . 15 D2
Enborne CE Prim Sch
  RG20 . . . . 129 E6
Enborne Cl RG31 . . . . . . 84 C8
Enborne Gate RG14 . . . . 104 E3
Enborne Gr RG14 . . . . . . 104 E2
Enborne Lodge La RG14 . 130 C6
Enborne Pl RG14 . . . . . . 104 E2
Enborne Rd RG14 . . . . . . 104 D1
Enborne Rd RG14 . . . . . . 130 C6
ENBORNE ROW 130 B4
Enborne St RG14 . . . . . . 130 C6
Enborne Way RG7 . . . . . 133 F6
Enfield Pl SL6 . . . . 39 A6
Enfield Rd TW6 . . . . 71 E5
Enfield Road Rdbt TW6 . . 71 E5
Enid Wood Ho RG12 . . . . 118 A5
Ennerdale RG12 . . . . 118 A5
Ennerdale Cl TW14 . . . . . 98 D8
Ennerdale Cres SL1 . . . . . 41 C8
Ennerdale Rd RG2 . . . . . . 86 D3
Ennerdale Way RG19 . . . 106 A3
Ensign Cl
  Harlington TW6 . . . . 71 D4
  Stanwell TW19 . . . . 97 D7
Enstone Rd RG5 . . . . 88 A8
Enterprise Ct RG12 . . . . . 117 F7
Enterprise Way RG19 . . . 106 C3
EP Collier Prim Sch RG1 . 59 A1
Epping Cl RG1 . . . . 85 E5
Epping Ho **2** RG1 . . . . . 85 E5
Epping Way RG14 . . . . . . 97 E4
Epsom Cl GU15 . . . . 151 C8
Epsom Cres RG14 . . . . . . 105 A1
Epsom Ct RG1 . . . . 86 B5
Epsom Sq TW6 . . . . 71 F5

Equine Way RG14 . . . . . . 131 B7
Erica Cl
  Slough SL1 . . . . 41 E6
  West End GU24 . . . . 153 E6
Erica Dr RG40 . . . . 116 D5
Eric Ave RG4 . . . . 59 A6
Eriswell Cl RG6 . . . . 87 E2
Erkenwald Cl KT16 . . . . . 123 E3
Erleigh Court Dr RG6 . . . 87 B7
Erleigh Court Gdns RG6 . 87 A7
Erleigh Dene RG14 . . . . . 104 F1
Erleigh Rd RG1 . . . . 86 D6
Ermin St
  Lambourn RG17 . . . . . . 45 E5
  Shefford Woodlands RG17 74 C7
  Stockcross RG20 . . . . . . 103 D7
  Wickham RG17 . . . . 75 A5
  Woodlands St N RG17 . . 46 D2
Ermin Wlk RG19 . . . . 106 B3
Errington Dr SL4 . . . . 67 A6
Erskine Cl RG26 . . . . 135 F1
Escot Rd TW16 . . . . 98 E1
Esher Cres
  Harlington TW6 . . . . 71 E5
  Hatton TW6 . . . . 71 F5
Esher Rd GU15 . . . . 145 A1
Eskdale Gdns SL6 . . . . . . 40 B3
Eskdale Rd RG41 . . . . 88 B4
Eskdale Way GU15 . . . . . 152 D4
Esplanade RG30 . . . . 85 A7
Essame Cl RG40 . . . . 116 D6
Essex Ave SL2 . . . . 42 C8
Essex Cotts RG7 . . . . 111 B3
Essex Pl RG17 . . . . 25 B3
Essex Rise RG42 . . . . 91 F1
Essex St
  Newbury RG14 . . . . 130 D7
  Reading RG2 . . . . 86 B5
Ethel Rd TW15 . . . . 97 E3
ETON 67 C8
Eton Cl SL3 . . . . 68 A8
Eton Coll Mus* SL4 . . . . . 67 C8
Eton Ct
  Eton SL4 . . . . 67 C8
  Staines TW18 . . . . 96 F3
Eton End PNEU Sch SL3 . 68 A8
Eton Pl SL7 . . . . 1 D2
Eton Porny CE Fst Sch
  SL4 . . . . 67 D8
Eton Rd
  Datchet SL3 . . . . 68 A8
  Harlington SL3 . . . . 71 F7
Eton Riverside SL4 . . . . . . 67 D7
Eton Sq SL4 . . . . 67 C8
Eton Wick CE Fst Sch SL4 42 A1
ETON WICK 41 E1
Eton Wick Rd SL4 . . . . . . 67 B8
Eton Wlk **1** SL1 . . . . 42 A1
European Weather Ctr
  RG2 . . . . 113 D7
Eustace Cres RG40 . . . . . 116 D8
Evedon RG12 . . . . 118 A2
Evelyn Cres TW16 . . . . . . 125 F8
Evelyn Ct RG5 . . . . 87 F3
Evelyn Way TW16 . . . . . . 125 F8
Evendon's Cl RG41 . . . . . 116 A3
Evendon's La RG41 . . . . . 115 E3
Evenlode RG12 . . . . 118 A3
Evenlode Way
  Reading RG30 . . . . 84 A5
  Sandhurst GU47 . . . . . . 150 A4
Everard Ave SL1 . . . . 42 E4
Everest Rd
  Camberley GU15 . . . . . . 151 D8
  Crowthorne RG45 . . . . . 143 B6
  Stanwell TW19 . . . . 97 E8
Everest Ct RG9 . . . . 35 E8
Evergreen Ct TW19 . . . . . 97 E8
Evergreen Dr RG31 . . . . . 84 F4
Evergreen Oak Ave SL4 . . 68 A4
Evergreen Rd GU16 . . . . 152 A3
Evergreen Way
  Stanwell TW19 . . . . 97 E8
  Wokingham RG41 . . . . . 115 F5
Evesham Cl RG30 . . . . . . 85 C1
Evesham Rd RG30 . . . . . . 85 B3
Evesham Wlk GU47 . . . . 150 A4
Evreham Rd SL0 . . . . 44 E7
Evreux Cl RG9 . . . . 15 D2
Ewing Way RG14 . . . . . . 104 B2
Exborne Rd RG2 . . . . 113 C8
Exchange Rd SL5 . . . . . . 120 D4
Exeforde Ave TW15 . . . . . 98 A4
Exeter Ct RG27 . . . . 150 F7
Exeter Gdns GU46 . . . . . 149 B7
Exeter Way TW6 . . . . 71 F5
Exmoor Rd RG19 . . . . . . 106 C3
Explorer Ave TW19 . . . . . 97 E8
Express Way RG14 . . . . . 105 E2
Exwick Sq RG2 . . . . 113 D8
Eynsford Cl RG4 . . . . 58 E6
Eynsham Cl RG5 . . . . 87 F4
Eyre Cl RG40 . . . . 116 A8
Eyre Gn SL2 . . . . 22 A2

FACCOMBE 148 B1
Faculty The **12** RG1 . . . . 86 B6
Fagg's Rd TW14 . . . . 71 F3
Fairacre SL6 . . . . 39 C6
Fairacres Ind Est SL4 . . . 66 D5
Fair Close Ho **1** RG14 . . 105 A2
Faircroft SL2 . . . . 22 B1
FAIR CROSS 138 D2
Faircross
  Bracknell RG12 . . . . 118 B6
  Hermitage RG18 . . . . . . 78 F6
Fair Cross RG7 . . . . 138 D2
Faircross Rd RG30 . . . . . . 85 C5
Fairfax RG42 . . . . 118 A8
Fairfax Cl RG4 . . . . 59 B3
Fairfax Dr RG14 . . . . 105 E5
Fairfield RG20 . . . . 31 D4
Fairfield App TW19 . . . . . 68 E5
Fairfield Ave
  Datchet SL3 . . . . 68 D7
  Staines TW18 . . . . 96 F4
Fairfield Cl
  Bourne End SL8 . . . . 3 A4
  Datchet SL3 . . . . 68 D7
Fairfield Dr GU16 . . . . . . 151 E3
Fairfield Ho GU15 . . . . . . 152 A5
Fairfield La
  Farnham Royal SL2 . . . . . 22 B3
  West End GU24 . . . . 153 F7
Fairfield Pk RG7 . . . . 136 F5
Fairfield Rd
  Burnham SL1 . . . . 21 C2
  Goring RG8 . . . . 34 D7
  Wraysbury TW19 . . . . . . 68 D1
Fairfields
  Chertsey KT15 . . . . 124 B1
  3 Hungerford RG17 . . 100 D5
Fairford Rd
  Maidenhead SL6 . . . . . . 39 F8
  Purley on T RG31 . . . . . . 57 C2
Fairhaven TW20 . . . . 95 F3
Fairhaven Ct **1** TW20 . . . 95 F3
Fairholme Rd TW15 . . . . . 97 F3
Fairlawn Rd TW13 . . . . . . 98 E8
Fairholme Prim Sch
  TW14 . . . . 98 D7
Fairlawn Green SL6 . . . . . 66 E1
Fairlawn Pk SL4 . . . . 66 E3
Fairlawns Cl TW18 . . . . . 97 B2
Fairlea SL6 . . . . 39 B3
Fairle Rd SL1 . . . . 42 A8
Fairlight Ave SL4 . . . . 67 C5
Fairlop Cl RG31 . . . . 84 D4
Fairmead Cl GU47 . . . . . 150 E7
Fairmead Ct GU15 . . . . . 151 C4
Fairmead Rd RG2 . . . . . . 113 E5
Fair Mead The SL3 . . . . . 69 D7
Fairmile RG9 . . . . 15 E3
Fair Oak Way RG26 . . . . 134 D1
Fairsted Cl RG30 . . . . 85 C5
Fairview RG14 . . . . 130 E8
Fairview Ave RG6 . . . . . . 87 B6
Fairview Cotts GU25 . . . . 122 D3
Fair View Cotts SL6 . . . . . 19 E7
Fairview Ct
  Ashford TW15 . . . . 98 A3
  Staines TW18 . . . . 97 A2
Fairview Dr TW17 . . . . . . 124 F4
Fairview Est RG9 . . . . 35 F8
Fairview Rd
  Ashford TW15 . . . . 98 A3
  Hungerford RG17 . . . . . 100 D5
  Slough SL2 . . . . 21 F1
  Wokingham RG40 . . . . . 116 C5
Fairwater Dr RG5 . . . . 87 D6
Fairway
  Chertsey KT16 . . . . 124 B1
  Virginia Water GU25 . . . . 39 C6
Fairway Ave RG30 . . . . . . 84 D6
Fairway Ct RG42 . . . . 91 A1
Fairway Dr RG10 . . . . 61 A5
Fairway Hts GU15 . . . . . . 152 B6
Fairways Ho SL5 . . . . 121 A2
Fairways The
  Burnham SL1 . . . . 21 C3
  Flackwell Heath HP10 . . . 3 C7
  Frimley GU15 . . . . 152 A3
  Maidenhead SL6 . . . . . . 39 B3
Fairthull Ct RG42 . . . . 91 B2
Fakenham Cl RG6 . . . . . . 114 A8
Fakenham Way GU47 . . . 150 A4
Falaise TW20 . . . . 95 F3
Falcon Ave RG2 . . . . 86 F1
Falcon Bsns Pk RG40 . . . 141 A6
Falcon Cl GU18 . . . . 152 F8
Falcon Ct GU16 . . . . 151 D1
Falcon Dr TW19 . . . . 70 E1
Falcon Fields RG26 . . . . 135 B2
Falcon House Gdns
  RG20 . . . . 129 F1
Falcons Croft HP10 . . . . . 3 E8
Falcon Way
  Sunbury TW16 . . . . 125 E7
  Wokingham RG41 . . . . . 115 E4
  Yateley GU46 . . . . 149 D6
Falconwood TW20 . . . . . 123 A8
Falkland Dr RG14 . . . . . . 130 F8
Falkland Garth RG14 . . . 130 D7
Falkland Ho SL6 . . . . 39 F8

FAWLEY
Hambleden 15 C8
Wantage 27 C7
Fawley Bottom La RG9 .....15 A8
Fawley CI SL6 ....19 D2
Fawley Court House & Mus*
RG9 ....15 F5
Fawley Mews 2 RG1 .....85 F6
Fawley Rd RG30 ....85 D5
Fawns Manor CI TW14 .....98 C7
Fawns Manor Rd TW14...98 D7
Fawsley CI SL3 ....69 E7
Faygate Way RG6 ....87 B1
Feathers La TW19...........96 A6
Felbridge CI GU16 ....151 F1
Felbridge Ct UB3 ....71 D8
Felix La TW17 ....125 F3
Felixstowe CI RG6 ....87 D2
Fellowes Ct UB3 ....71 D8
Fellow Gn GU24 ....153 F6
Fellow Green Rd GU24 ..153 F6
Fellstead Ct SL6 ....39 C6
Fells The RG31.............84 A6
Felstead CI RG6 ....86 F3
FELTHAM.....................98 E6
FELTHAMHILL 98 F4
Feltham Hill Inf Sch TW13 98 F5
Feltham Hill Jun Sch
TW13 ....98 F5
Feltham Hill Rd TW15......98 C2
Feltham Rd TW15 ....98 C4
Felthorpe CI RG6 ....114 A8
Felton Way RG31 ....84 C8
Feltre PI 16 RG14 ....104 F2
Fenchurch Mews 3 RG41 88 A3
Fencote RG12 ....118 D3
Fennel CI
Ascot SL5.................120 A5
Earley RG6.................86 F1
Newbury RG14...........105 D5
Fennel Ct RG18 ....106 D4
Fennscombe Ct GU24 ...153 F6
Fenns La GU24 ....153 F6
Fenton Ave TW18 ....97 C3
Fenton Lodge GU15......151 E6
FERN 2 E5
Fernbank RG40 ....141 D6
Fernbank Cres SL5.........119 D8
Fernbank PI SL5............119 D7
Fernbank Rd SL5...........119 D8
Fernbrook Rd RG4 ....58 E5
Fern CI
Crowthorne RG45 ....143 A2
Frimley GU16..............152 C3
Reading RG31 ....84 C5
Fern Cotts SL7 ....2 A2
Ferndale Ave RG30.........85 A4
Ferndale CI RG31 ....57 E3
Ferndale Cres RG41.......115 E8
Ferndale Ct RG19 ....106 D3
Ferndale Pk Cvn Pk SL6...65 E8
Ferndale Rd TW15 ....97 E3
Fern La SL7 ....2 A6
Fern Ct RG8 ....34 C7
Ferney The TW18............96 E3
Fern Glen RG31.............57 C1
Fernhill CI
Bracknell RG42 ....90 F1
Farnborough GU17 ....150 F1
Farnham La GU17.........150 E1
Fernhill Prim Sch GU17...150 F1
Fernhill Rd GU14, GU17...150 E2
Fernhill Sch GU14 ....150 F1
Fernhill Wlk GU17 ....150 F1
Fernhurst Rd
Ashford TW15...............98 C4
Reading RG31..............84 C4
Ferniehurst GU15.........151 F4
Fern La SL7 ....2 A6
Fernley Ct SL6...............19 D1
Fern Wlk
Ashford TW15 ....97 D3
Reading RG31..............84 C5
Ferrard CI SL5.............119 D8
Ferrers CI SL1..............41 E3
Ferriby Ct RG12 ....118 C7
Ferris Ave RG6 ....87 A4
Ferry Ave TW18 ....96 E1
Ferry End SL6 ....40 C4
Ferry La
Bourne End SL8 ....3 B1
Chertsey KT16 ....124 A3
Cookham SL6 ....20 B7
Goring RG8 ....34 B6
Hambleden RG9...........16 D6
Laleham TW18 ....124 C6
Lower Halliford TW17....125 A1
Medmenham SL7 ....17 B5
Moulsford OX10, RG8....14 B4
South Stoke RG8 ....14 A4
Wargrave RG10 ....36 C2
Wraysbury TW19.........96 B5
Ferry Rd
Bray SL6 ....40 C4
South Stoke RG8 ....14 C4
Ferry Sq TW17 ....125 C6
Ferry Way OX10 ....14 B8
Ferry Works TW17.........125 A1
Festival Cotts SL3 ....69 C7
Fettiplace RG17 ....48 B3
Fetty PI SL6 ....39 D4
Fickling Ct RG2 ....86 F1
Fidler's La RG20 ....30 E7
Fidler's Wlk RG10 ....36 E6
Field CI
Burghfield Common RG7...111 B2
Harlington UB7 ....71 C7
Field Ct RG17...............25 C2

Field End
Wargrave RG10 ....36 F2
West End GU24 ....153 F6
Fielden PI RG12 ....118 D7
Fieldfare Ave GU46 ......149 B6
Fieldfare Dr RG12.........117 D5
Fieldhead Gdns SL8........3 A3
Field House CI SL5 ......120 A1
Fieldhouse Ind Est SL7....1 F2
Fieldhouse La SL7 ....1 F2
Fieldhouse Way SL7 ....1 F2
Field Hurst SL3 ....43 F1
Fielding Gdns
Crowthorne RG45 ....143 B4
Slough SL3 ....43 C4
Fielding Rd
Maidenhead SL6 ....39 B8
Sandhurst GU47 ....150 E6
Fieldings The SL6 ....65 A7
Field La GU16 ....151 E1
Field Path GU14 ....150 F1
Field Pk RG12 ....118 D8
Field Rd
Farnborough GU14 ......150 F1
Peasemore RG20...........50 D8
Reading RG1 ....86 A6
Fieldridge RG14 ....105 D5
Fields The SL1..............42 D4
Field View
Caversham RG4.............59 B3
Egham TW20 ....96 C3
Feltham TW13 ....98 D4
Fieldview Ct
Slough SL1..................42 C8
Staines TW18...............97 A2
Fieldway RG41..............88 D2
Fifehead Ct TW15..........97 E2
FIFIELD....................65 D6
Fifield La SL6, SL6.........65 D5
Fifield Rd SL6 ....65 D7
Fifield Way Cotts SL6.....65 D6
Fifth Ave RG31.............84 B8
Fifth Rd RG14 ....104 E1
Filbert Dr RG31............84 C8
Filey Rd RG1 ....86 F2
Filey Spur SL1 ....42 B4
Filley Alley OX12............6 E7
Filmer Rd SL4 ....80 A6
Finbeck Way RG6.........113 F8
Fincham End Dr RG45....142 F4
FINCHAMPSTEAD 141 E2
Finchampstead CE Prim Sch
RG40 ....141 E3
Finchampstead Rd
Finchampstead RG40.....141 F6
Wokingham RG41, RG40...116 B3
Finch CI SL6 ....39 D5
Finchdale RG6 ....87 C4
Finch Way RG7 ....111 B3
Findhorn CI GU47 ....150 D7
Finlay Dr RG9 ....15 E3
Finlay Ho RG9 ....15 E2
Finmere RG12 ....118 C2
Finney Dr GU20 ....146 D4
Finstock CI RG6 ....87 D1
Finstock Gn RG12........118 F5
Firbank PI TW20 ....95 B2
Fir CI RG19 ....133 B5
Fir Cottage Rd RG40 .....141 E8
Fircroft CI
Reading RG31 ....57 C1
Stoke Poges SL2 ....23 A6
Fircroft Ct SL2 ....23 A6
Fircroft Rd TW20..........95 C1
Fir Dr GU17 ....150 D3
Fireball Hill SL5 ....120 B4
Firglen Dr GU46 ....149 D7
Firgrove Ct RG17 ....100 E5
Firgrove Rd RG27, GU46...149 C6
Firlands
Bracknell RG12 ....118 C4
Virginia Water GU25.....119 D6
Firlands Ave GU15 ....151 D5
Firmstone CI RG6..........87 C1
Firs Ave SL4 ....64 F4
Firs CI RG40 ....141 F7
Firs Dr SL3 ....43 F5
Firs End RG7 ....136 E6
Fir's End RG7 ....111 A2
Firs La
Maidenhead SL6 ....38 F4
Reading RG30 ....80 D5
Firs Rd RG31 ....84 C6
First Ave
Marlow SL7 ....2 A2
Reading RG31 ....84 B6
Firs Rd RG31 ....135 D2
First Cres SL1 ....42 C8
Firs The
5 Bracknell RG12 ....118 F5
Inkpen RG17 ....127 E5
1 Maidenhead SL6 ......39 E7
Reading RG1 ....85 F6
Thatcham RG18 ....84 B8
Fir Tree Ave SL3 ....43 F1
Fir Tree CI SL5 ....119 A5
Firtree CI GU47 ....142 F1
Fir Tree CI SL5 ....120 A2
Fir Tree Cnr RG26 ....134 E2
Fir Tree La RG14 ....105 E4
Fir Tree Paddock RG20...30 D8
Fir Tree Prim Sch RG14..105 E4
Firview CI SL7 ....1 F1
Firwood CI SL5 ....151 C5

Firwood Dr GU15 ....151 C5
Firwood Rd GU25 ....121 E3
Fisher Gn RG42............90 B2
Fisher Ho
Hounslow TW10 ....124 C1
5 Newbury RG14.........104 F2
Sunningdale SL5 ....121 A1
Fisherman Ho KT16 ......124 C1
Fisherman's La SL6......135 B8
Fishermans Retreat SL7...1 E1
Fisherman's Way SL8 ......3 B4
Fishers Cotts RG4 ....59 C6
Fishers Ct RG4 ....59 C6
Fisher's La RG18...........79 A1
Fishers Wood SL5 ....121 C1
FISHERY 40 B6
Fishery Rd SL6 ....40 C5
Fishguard Spur SL1.......43 B4
Fishing Temple Park Homes
TW18 ....123 D8
Fishponds CI RG41 ....116 A4
Fishponds Est RG41......116 A4
Fishponds Rd RG41 ......116 A4
Fisk CI TW16 ....98 F2
Fiske Ct GU46 ....149 E6
Fitzgerald Ct RG14 ......104 F3
Fitzrobert PI TW20 ....96 A2
Fitzroy CI RG12 ....118 A3
Fitzroy Cres RG5...........88 A6
Five Acre RG31 ....57 B1
Five Acres RG10 ....3 F7
Fiveways
Camberley GU15 ....151 E5
Windsor SL4 ....66 E5
Five Ways RG18............52 F6
FLACKWELL HEATH 3 A7
Flagstaff Sq RG12 ....106 E2
Flambards RG4 ....59 C2
Flamborough CI RG6......87 E2
Flamborough Path 5
RG6 ....87 E2
Flamborough Spur SL1...42 A4
Flamingo CI RG41........115 E5
Flanders Ct TW20 ....96 C3
Flats The GU17 ....150 C4
Flaxman CI RG6 ....86 F2
Flecker CI RG18 ....106 C5
Fleetbrook Ho SL3.........68 D6
Fleet CI RG41..............115 A6
Fleet Hill RG40 ....141 C2
Fleet La RG40 ....141 B2
Fleetway TW20 ....123 C6
Fleetwood CI RG14......105 D5
Fleetwood Ct 7 TW19...70 E1
Fleetwood Rd SL2 ....42 A3
Fleming CI RG2.............140 E7
Fleming La RG40...........43 C3
Fleming Rd RG14.........105 B3
Flemish Fields KT16 ......124 A2
Flemish PI RG42 ....91 D1
Fletcher Gdns RG42......117 D7
Fletton Link RG18..........79 C8
Flexford Gn RG12........117 E3
Flintgrove RG12 ....118 D8
Flintjack PI RG17 ....25 A2
Flintlock Ct TW19 ....70 A3
Flodden Dr RG31 ....84 D4
Floral Ct RG10 ....62 A8
Floral Ho 11 RG8 ....62 E5
Floral Way RG18...........106 E5
Floreat Gdns RG14.......104 E1
Florence Ave SL6 ....40 A8
Florence CI GU46 ....149 C6
Florence Cotts SL4 ....92 C7
Florence Ct 19 RG30 .....85 D6
Florence Gdns
Staines TW18...............97 B1
Thatcham RG18 ....106 A5
Florence Rd GU47 ....150 E7
Florence Villas GU18 ....146 B1
Florence Wlk RG1 ....86 D7
Florentina Ct RG42 ....90 C2
Florian Gdns RG30........85 B5
Florida Ct
Reading RG31 ....85 E6
Staines TW18...............97 A3
Flower's Hill RG8 ....56 C4
Flowers Piece RG8.........54 B6
Fobney St RG1 ....86 B6
Fokerham Rd RG19 ....106 F2
Folder's La RG42 ....90 E4
Folejohn Way SL4..........38 F1
Folkestone Ct SL3 ....44 A1
Follett CI SL4, SL4.........68 C7
Folly La SL7, RG30 ....110 F5
Folly Orch RG40 ....115 F5
Folly Rd
Inkpen RG17 ....127 E6
Lambourn RG17...........25 A3
Fontmell CI TW15..........98 A3
Fontmell Pk TW15 ....98 A3
Fontwell Dr RG30 ....84 F6
Fontwell Rd RG14 ....85 F6
Forbes Chase GU47 ......150 D7
Forbury Ho 10 RG30......85 B7
Forbury La RG17, RG20...128 C2
Forbury Rd RG1, RG30...86 C8
Forbury Ret Pk RG1........86 B8
Forbury The RG1............86 B8
Fordbridge Ct KT16 ......124 B1
Fordbridge Ct TW15 ....97 E2
Fordbridge Rd
Ashford TW15...............97 F3
Upper Halliford TW16,
TW17 ....125 F3

Ford CI
Ashford TW15 ....97 E2
Littleton TW17 ....125 A4
Fordham Way RG6..........87 C1
Ford Ho TW20 ....95 C1
Ford La RG7 ....140 A2
Ford Rd
Ashford TW15 ....97 F4
Bisley GU24 ....153 F4
Chertsey KT16............124 B1
Fordwater Rd KT16 ......124 B1
Fordwater Trad Est
KT16 ....124 C1
Fordwells Dr RG12 ......118 F5
Forehead The RG7 ....137 F4
Forest CI
Bracknell SL5...............119 C6
Tadley RG26................134 E2
Forest Ct RG41 ....116 A4
Forest Dean RG2 ....113 C7
Forest Dr TW16 ....95 E7
Forest End GU47 ....143 A1
Forest End Rd GU47 ....150 A8
Foresters Sq RG12 ......118 E6
Foresters Way RG45 ....143 F1
FOREST ESTATE 95 B2
Forest Gn
Bracknell RG12 ....118 D7
Holyport SL6.................65 A6
Forest Green Rd SL6......65 C5
Forest Hill RG30 ....57 F2
Forest Hills GU15 ....151 B4
Forest Lodge RG41.........88 E1
FOREST PARK 118 E3
Forest Rd
Binfield RG42...............90 D3
Crowthorne RG45 ....151 A8
Windsor, Dedworth SL4...66 E5
Windsor SL4................93 E7
Winkfield RG42, SL5.....92 D2
Wokingham, Bill Hill RG40...88 C2
Wokingham RG40..........88 C2
Forest View Cotts SL6...65 C6
Forest Way RG42 ....92 A2
Forge CI
Caversham RG4............59 C2
Harlington UB3 ....71 D8
Kintbury RG17 ....102 A2
Forge Cotts SN8 ....99 B5
Forge Ct GU46 ....149 D7
Forge Dr SL2 ....22 C6
Forge Hill RG8 ....53 A5
Forge The RG17...........100 D6
Forlease CI SL6..............40 A6
Forlease Dr SL6.............40 A6
Forlease Rd SL6 ....40 A6
Formby CI
Earley RG6..................87 E3
Slough SL3 ....44 C2
Forndon CI RG6 ....87 E2
Forsete PI RG1..............86 A6
Forster Rd RG14 ....104 F1
Forsters
Forsters Farm Ct RG7 ...135 A6
Coldharbour OX13........6 E6
Forsythia Gdns SL3 ......43 E3
Fort Narrien GU15 ....150 F7
Fortrose CI GU47 ....150 D7
Fortrose Wlk RG31 ....84 E4
Fortuna Ct RG7 ....125 F3
Forty Cross OX11 ....12 A8
FORTY GREEN 1 A1
Forty Green Dr SL7 ....1 B2
Forum The RG11 ....123 F1
Fosseway RG45 ....143 A5
Fossewood Dr GU15 ....151 D7
Foster Ave SL4 ....42 C8
Fosters Gr GU20 ....146 B6
Fosters La RG5 ....87 E6
Fosters Path GU21 ....21 F1
Fotherby Ct SL6............40 A6
Fotheringay Gdns SL1...42 A6
Foundation Pk SL6 ......38 F4
Foundry Ct
Chertsey KT16.............124 A2
Slough SL2..................42 F5
Foundry La SL3 ....69 B4
Foundry Ho RG17 ....100 E7
Foundry Mews 1 KT16..124 A2
Foundry PI 22 RG1........86 A6
Fountain Gdns
11 Newbury RG14 ....105 A2
Windsor SL4 ....67 D4
Fountains Garth RG12...118 A6
Four Houses Corner
RG7 ....136 E8
Fourth Ave
Marlow SL7 ....2 A2
Reading RG31 ....84 B6
Fourth St RG19 ....131 F5
Fowler CI RG6 ....87 A3
Fowler's Rd GU14.........118 B8
Foxborough RG7...........139 D6
Foxborough Ct SL3 ....44 A1
Foxborough Ct SL6 ....39 E4
Foxborough Prim Sch
SL3 ....44 A1
Foxbury RG17................25 B2
Fox CI RG27 ....111 A3
Foxcombe Dr RG31 ....84 C7
Foxcote RG40 ....142 A7
Fox Court Mobile Home Pk
GU47 ....142 F1
Foxdown CI GU15 ....153 A8
Fox Covert GU18 ....153 A8
Fox Covert CI SL5 ....120 C4
Fox Ct 6 KT16 ....123 F1
Foxdown CI RG15 ....151 C5
Fox Dr GU46 ....149 D7
Foxes Piece SL7 ....1 E2

Foxes Piece Sch SL7 . . . . . . 1 E3
Foxes Wlk RG10 . . . . 61 A3
Foxglove Cl
  Stanwell TW19 . . . . 97 D7
  Winkfield RG42 . . . . 92 A2
  Wokingham RG41 . . . . . . 115 D7
Foxglove Gdns 2 RG1 . . 85 E7
Foxglove Way RG18 . . . 106 D5
Foxhaven Ct SL5 . . . . . . 120 C4
Foxhays Rd RG2 . . . . 113 D8
Foxheath RG12 . . . . 118 E4
Foxherne SL3 . . . . 43 C4
Foxhill 2 RG12 . . . . 118 B5
Foxhill Cl RG4 . . . . 60 A5
Foxhill Cres GU15 . . . . . 152 B8
Foxhill La RG4 . . . . 59 D7
Fox Hill Prim Sch RG12 . 118 B4
Foxhill Rd RG1 . . . . 86 E6
Fox Ho 4 RG16 . . . . 123 F1
Foxhollow Dr SL2 . . . . . . 22 C7
Foxhunter Way RG19 . . . 105 F3
Foxhunt Gr RG31 . . . . . . 29 A4
Fox La RG27 . . . . 149 A7
Fox Lane N 7 KT16 . . . . 123 F1
Fox Lane S 10 KT16 . . . 123 F1
Foxleigh Ct TW18 . . . . . . 96 C3
Foxley Cl GU17 . . . . 150 C5
Foxley La RG42 . . . . 90 C1
Fox Rd SL3 . . . . 43 D2
Framewood Manor SL2 . . 23 C6
Framewood Rd SL2,SL3 . . 23 C6
Framlingham Dr RG4 . . . 59 E5
Frampton Bridge Rdbt
  RG42 . . . . 90 F2
Frampton Cl RG5 . . . . 60 E1
France Hill Dr GU15 . . . 151 C5
Frances Ave SL6 . . . . 20 C1
Frances Ct SL5 . . . . 120 D5
Frances The RG18 . . . . . 106 D4
Francis Baily Prim Sch
  RG19 . . . . 106 F3
Francis Chichester Cl
  SL5 . . . . 120 B4
Francis Cl TW17 . . . . 125 A5
Francis Gdns RG42 . . . . . 91 D1
Francis St RG1 . . . . 86 B6
Francis Way
  Burnham SL1 . . . . 41 D6
  Frimley GU15 . . . . 152 C4
Francomes Field RG17 . . 25 C1
Franklin Ave
  Slough SL2 . . . . 42 B8
  Tadley RG26 . . . . 135 A1
Franklin Ct
  8 Reading RG1 . . . . . . 85 F7
  Tadley RG26 . . . . 135 A2
Franklin St RG1 . . . . 85 F7
Frank Lunnon Cl SL8 . . . . 3 C3
Franklyn Cres SL4 . . . . . . 66 D4
Frank Sutton Way SL1 . . . 42 D6
Frantons The SL6 . . . . 39 A7
Frascati Way SL6 . . . . 39 F7
Fraser Ave RG4 . . . . 59 C6
Fraser Mead GU47 . . . . 150 E6
Fraser Rd RG42 . . . . 118 B8
Fraunchies Ct SL1 . . . . . . 42 E6
Frederick Ho TW15 . . . . . 97 E4
Frederick Pl RG41 . . . . . 116 A6
Freeborn Way RG12 . . . 118 E7
Freeman Cl TW17 . . . . . 125 E5
Freeman Ct RG14 . . . . . 104 F3
Freemans Cl
  Hungerford RG17 . . . 100 C5
  Stoke Poges SL2 . . . . . 23 A6
Freemantle Rd GU19 . . 145 F4
Freemantles Sch KT16 . 123 E2
Free Prae Rd KT16 . . . . 124 A1
Freesia Cl RG41 . . . . . . 115 D7
French Gdns GU17 . . . . 150 D4
Frenchum Gdns SL1 . . . . 41 E6
Frensham RG12 . . . . 118 D3
Frensham Cl GU46 . . . . 149 B6
Frensham Gn RG2 . . . . . . 86 F1
Frensham Rd RG45 . . . 118.3 F3
Frensham Wlk SL2 . . . . . . 22 C7
Freshfield Cl RG6 . . . . . . 87 E3
Freshfields La RG20 . . . . 51 B2
Freshwater Rd RG1 . . . . . 86 E8
Freshwood Dr GU46 . . . 149 D4
Fresian Way RG41 . . . . . . 88 A2
Friars Ct GU47 . . . . 149 F8
Friars Keep RG12 . . . . . 118 B5
Friars Rd
  Newbury RG14 . . . . . . 131 A8
  Virginia Water GU25 . . 122 D5
Friar St RG1 . . . . 86 A8
Friars Way KT16 . . . . . . 124 A3
Friars Wlk 8 RG1 . . . . . . 86 A8
Friary Island TW19 . . . . 95 C8
Friary Rd
  Ascot SL5 . . . . 120 B3
  Wraysbury TW19 . . . . . 68 C1
Friary The SL4 . . . . 68 C1
Friday St RG9 . . . . 15 E2
Friendship Ho 4 TW18 . . 97 A3
Friendship Way RG12 . . 118 B5
Friends Wlk 4 TW18 . . . . 96 F3
Frieth Cl RG6 . . . . 87 A1
Frieth Rd SL7 . . . . 1 A3
FRILSHAM 80 D6
Frilsham Home Farm Bsns
  Units RG18 . . . . 53 F1
Frilsham Rd RG30 . . . . . . 85 D8
FRIMLEY 151 F2
FRIMLEY 87 D8
Frimley Cl RG5 . . . . 87 D8
Frimley Green Rd GU16 . 151 D1

Frimley Grove Gdns
  GU16 . . . . 151 E1
Frimley Hall Dr GU15 . . 151 F6
Frimley High St GU16 . . 151 D1
Frimley Park Hospl
  GU16 . . . . 151 D2
Frimley Rd GU15, GU16 . 151 B3
Frimley Sq GU16 . . . . . . 151 E1
FRIMLEY RIDGE 152 B3
Frimley Way GU16 . . . . 151 F1
Fringford Cl RG6 . . . . 87 C1
Frithe The SL2 . . . . 43 B7
Frith Hill Rd GU16 . . . . 152 B1
Frithwald Rd KT16 . . . . 123 F2
Frobisher RG12 . . . . 118 C2
Frobisher Cres TW19 . . . 97 E8
Frobisher Gdns TW19 . . . 97 E8
Frodsham Way GU47 . . . 143 E2
Frog Hall RG40 . . . . 116 F5
Frog Hall Dr RG40 . . . . 116 E5
Frog La RG12 . . . . 118 A6
Frogmill SL6 . . . . 17 C3
Frogmill Cl SL6 . . . . 17 C3
Frogmill Spinney SL6 . . . 17 C4
FROGMORE 150 C6
Frogmore Com Coll
  GU46 . . . . 149 F5
Frogmore Ct
  Blackwater GU17 . . . . 150 C4
  1 Maidenhead SL6 . . . 39 F7
Frogmore Dr SL4 . . . . 67 F5
Frogmore Flats SL4 . . . . . 67 F5
Frogmore Gr GU17 . . . . 150 C4
Frogmore Inf Sch GU17 . 150 B5
Frogmore Jun Sch GU17 . 150 B5
Frogmore Park Dr GU17 . 150 D4
Frogmore Rd GU17 . . . . 150 C5
Frogmore Way RG30 . . . . 85 B5
Fromer Rd HP10 . . . . 3 D4
Fromont Dr RG19 . . . . . 106 D3
Fromow Gdns GU20 . . . 146 D4
Fronds Pk RG7 . . . . 109 A2
Fronds The RG17 . . . . 47 D6
Frouds Bridge Marina
  RG7 . . . . 108 F1
Frouds La RG7 . . . . 109 A1
FROXFIELD 99 A5
Froxfield Ave RG1 . . . . . . 85 F5
Froxfield Down 8 RG12 . 118 F4
Fruen Rd TW14 . . . . 98 F8
Fry Ct RG4 . . . . 59 B3
Fry La GU19 . . . . 145 D2
Frymley View SL4 . . . . . . 66 D6
Fry's La GU46 . . . . 149 E7
Fuchsia Cl RG31 . . . . 84 C4
Fuchsia Way GU24 . . . . 153 E6
Fulcher Row 2 RG6 . . . . 87 A6
Fullbrook Cl
  Maidenhead SL6 . . . . . 40 A8
  Wokingham RG41 . . . . 89 A1
Fullbrook Cres RG31 . . . 57 D3
Fuller Cl RG19 . . . . 106 F2
Fullers La RG20 . . . . . . 129 D1
Fuller's La RG7 . . . . 112 A8
Fullers Yd SL6 . . . . 20 B2
Fulmead Rd RG30 . . . . . . 85 C8
FULMER 23 C8
Fulmer Chase SL3 . . . . . . 23 C8
Fulmer Cl RG6 . . . . 87 A2
Fulmer Common Rd SL3 . 23 E6
Fulmer Inf Sch SL3 . . . . 23 E8
Fulmer Rd SL3 . . . . 23 E8
Fulmer Rise Est SL3 . . . 23 E6
Fulwood Ct TW19 . . . . . . 70 F1
Funky Footprints Nature
  Reserve* TW17 . . . . . 125 B3
Furlong Cl SL8 . . . . 3 B3
Furlong Rd SL8 . . . . 3 B3
Furness SL4 . . . . 66 C5
Furness Pl 8 SL4 . . . . . . 66 C5
Furness Row 9 SL4 . . . . . 66 C5
Furness Sq SL4 . . . . 66 C5
Furness Wlk 7 SL4 . . . . . 66 C5
Furnival Ave SL2 . . . . 42 B8
Furrow Way SL6 . . . . 39 A4
Furse Cl GU15 . . . . 152 C4
Furzebank SL5 . . . . 120 D5
Furzecroft 4 TW15 . . . . . 98 A3
Furzedown Ct TW20 . . . . 95 E2
Furze Hill RG20 . . . . . . 103 D5
Furze Hill Cres RG45 . . . 118 F4
Furzemoors RG12 . . . . . 118 B4
Furzen Cl SL2 . . . . 22 A2
FURZE PLATT 19 D2
Furze Platt Bus Ctr Pk
  SL6 . . . . 19 D2
Furze Platt Halt SL6 . . . 19 E1
Furze Platt Inf Sch SL6 . 19 C2
Furze Platt Jun Sch SL6 . 19 C1
Furze Platt Rd SL6 . . . . 19 B1
Furze Platt Senior Sch
  SL6 . . . . 19 C2
Furze Rd
  Maidenhead SL6 . . . . . 19 D1
  Tadley RG26 . . . . 134 F2
Fuscia Ct 8 TW13 . . . . . . 98 F5
Fushsia Gr RG2 . . . . 113 E6
Fusiliers Rd RG19 . . . . . 106 D2
Fuzzens Wlk SL4 . . . . 66 E5
Fydlers Cl SL4 . . . . 93 B2
Fyfield Cl GU17 . . . . 150 D5
Fyfield Rd RG19 . . . . . . 106 C2
Fylingdales RG19 . . . . . 106 C2

G

Gables Ave TW15 . . . . . . 97 F3
Gables Cl
  Datchet SL3 . . . . 68 A8
  Maidenhead SL6 . . . . . 40 B8
Gables Way RG19 . . . . . 107 C2
Gabriel Dr GU15 . . . . . . 152 B4
Gabriel's Sq RG6 . . . . 87 D1
Gabriels The RG14 . . . . 130 D5
Gadd Cl RG40 . . . . 116 F7
Gage Cl SL6 . . . . 39 E4
Gainsborough
  Bracknell RG12 . . . . . 118 C3
  Cookham Rise SL6 . . . . 19 F5
Gainsborough Ave RG17 . 102 B2
Gainsborough Cl
  Camberley GU15 . . . . 151 F7
  Woodley RG5 . . . . 88 A6
Gainsborough Cres RG9 . 35 C8
Gainsborough Dr
  Maidenhead SL6 . . . . . 39 D3
  North Ascot SL5 . . . . . 119 D7
Gainsborough Hill RG9 . 35 D8
Gainsborough Rd
  Henley-on-T RG9 . . . . . 35 D8
  Reading RG30 . . . . 85 B5
Gairn Cl RG30 . . . . 85 A7
Galahad Cl SL1 . . . . 42 A4
Galaxy Ho RG18 . . . . . . 132 A5
Gale Dr GU18 . . . . 146 A1
Galileo Ct RG12 . . . . . . 118 E7
Gallery Cl 18 TW20 . . . . 96 A3
Galley La RG19 . . . . 132 D1
Galleymead Rd SL3 . . . . . 69 F6
Gallops The
  Chilton OX11 . . . . 10 D8
  East Ilsley RG20 . . . . . 30 E6
Gallop The GU46 . . . . . 149 D7
Galloway Chase SL2 . . . . 43 A6
Galloway Ctr The RG14 . 105 C2
Galloway Ho 4 RG1 . . . . 85 D6
Gallys Rd SL4 . . . . 66 D6
Galsworthy Dr RG4 . . . . . 59 E5
Galsworthy Rd 4 KT16 . 124 A2
Galton Rd SL5 . . . . 120 F3
Galvin Rd SL1 . . . . 42 C6
Gabby Way GU46 . . . . . 149 C4
Garden Cl
  Ashford TW15 . . . . 98 C2
  Maidenhead SL6 . . . . . 39 A5
Garden Close La RG14 . 130 D4
Garden Cotts
  Arborfield RG41 . . . . . 114 F6
  Colnbrook SL3 . . . . 69 D7
GARDENERS GREEN . . . 116 F2
Gardeners La RG8 . . . . . . 55 C4
Garden Ho RG4 . . . . 58 E3
Garden Ho The SL5 . . . 121 C4
Gardenia Dr GU24 . . . . 153 F6
Garden Mews
  North Ascot SL5 . . . . . 92 F1
  8 Reading RG30 . . . . . 85 D6
Garden Mews The SL6 . . 39 B7
Gardens The
  Hatton TW14 . . . . 71 D1
  South Stoke RG8 . . . . . 14 C3
Garde Rd RG4 . . . . 60 E3
Gardner Ho SL6 . . . . 19 E3
Gardner Rd SL6 . . . . 19 D2
Gardners Pl 4 RG40 . . . . 87 A6
Gardners Rd RG42 . . . . . 92 A2
Garfield Pl 1 SL4 . . . . . . 67 D5
Garfield Rd GU15 . . . . . 151 D4
Garford Cres RG14 . . . . 130 D8
Garland Ct RG14 . . . . . 104 F2
Garland Jun Sch RG7 . . . 111 A2
Garlands Cl RG7 . . . . . . 111 A2
Garner Ct TW19 . . . . 70 D1
Garnet Cl SL1 . . . . 42 A4
Garnet Ct SL7 . . . . 1 C1
Garnet Field GU46 . . . . 149 A5
Garnet Hill 1 RG1 . . . . . . 86 A6
Garrard Rd SL2 . . . . 21 F1
Garrard St RG1 . . . . 86 A8
Garrett Rd RG40 . . . . . . 141 E8
Garretts La SL6 . . . . 19 F2
Garrick Cl TW18 . . . . 97 A1
Garson La TW19 . . . . 95 D8
Garson's La SL4 . . . . 94 B6
Garston Cl RG30 . . . . 85 A4
Garston Cres SL4 . . . . . . 84 B5
Garston Gr RG40 . . . . . 141 E7
Garston Park Home Village
  RG31 . . . . 84 B6
Garswood RG12 . . . . 118 D3
Garth Cl RG14 . . . . 104 F7
Garth Hill Coll RG12 . . 118 C8
Garthlands SL6 . . . . 19 D2
Garth Rd RG7 . . . . 137 A5
Garth Sq RG42 . . . . 91 B1
Gascon's Gr SL2 . . . . 22 A1
Gas House Hill RG17 . . . 25 C3
Gaskell Mews RG14 . . . 131 B8
Gaskells End RG4 . . . . . . 58 D8
Gas La
  Maidenhead SL6 . . . . . 40 B3
  Twyford RG10 . . . . 61 D4
Gaston Bridge Rd
  Shepperton TW17 . . . 125 D3
  Upper Halliford TW17 . 125 E4
Gaston Way TW17 . . . . 125 D4
Gas Works Rd RG1 . . . . . 86 C7
Gatcombe Cl RG31 . . . . . 84 C4
Gatcombe Cres SL5 . . . . 119 F8

Gatehampton Rd RG8 . . . . 34 C5
Gatehouse Cl SL4 . . . . . . 67 B4
Gatehouse The SL5 . . . . 121 A1
Gate Lodge RG14 . . . . . 104 D1
Gatewick Cl SL1 . . . . 42 E5
Gatward Ave SL6 . . . . 39 A3
Gaveston Rd SL2 . . . . 21 F2
Gayhurst Cl RG4 . . . . 59 D6
Gays La SL6 . . . . 65 B8
Gaywood Dr RG14 . . . . 105 D4
Gazelle Cl RG41 . . . . 88 A3
Geffers Ride SL5 . . . . . . 119 E7
Gelder Cl RG6 . . . . 87 D1
Genesis Cl TW19 . . . . 97 F7
Genesis Ho TW18 . . . . . . 96 F4
Geneva Cl TW17 . . . . . . 125 E7
Geoffrey Field Inf Sch
  RG2 . . . . 113 C8
Geoffrey Field Jun Sch
  RG2 . . . . 113 C8
Geoffreyson Rd RG4 . . . . 58 E5
George Cl
  Caversham RG4 . . . . . 59 C3
  Marlow SL7 . . . . 1 F4
GEORGE GREEN 43 E7
George Green Dr SL3 . . . 43 F8
George Green Rd SL3 . . . 43 E7
Georgeham Rd GU47 . . . 143 D2
George Palmer Prim Sch
  RG2 . . . . 86 C4
Georges Dr HP10 . . . . 3 C7
George St
  Caversham RG4 . . . . . . 59 B1
  Reading RG1 . . . . 85 F8
  Staines TW18 . . . . 96 F4
George V Pl SL4 . . . . 67 D7
Georgian Cl
  Camberley GU15 . . . . 151 E7
  Staines TW18 . . . . 97 B4
Georgian Hts SL8 . . . . 3 B5
Geranium Cl RG45 . . . . 143 B8
Gerrards Cross Rd SL2 . . 23 A7
Gerring Rd RG2 . . . . 114 D3
Gervaise Cl SL1 . . . . 41 F5
Gibbet La GU15 . . . . 152 A7
Gibbins La RG42 . . . . 91 D3
Gibbons Cl GU47 . . . . . 150 D8
Gibbs Cl RG40 . . . . 141 E6
Gibbs Way GU46 . . . . . 149 B4
Gibraltar La SL6 . . . . 22 C5
Gibson Cl 19 SL3 . . . . . . 43 F1
Gibson Dr RG12 . . . . 118 D6
Gibson Pl TW19 . . . . 70 C1
Gidley La RG20 . . . . 50 E2
Gifford Cl RG4 . . . . 59 E5
Gifford Ho 2 RG4 . . . . . . 59 C1
Gilbert Cl RG18 . . . . . . 106 D3
Gilbert Rd GU15 . . . . . . 151 C2
Gilbert Way
  Finchampstead RG40 . 115 E1
  6 Slough SL3 . . . . 43 F1
Gilbey Wlk HP10 . . . . 3 D4
Gilchrist Way SL6 . . . . . . 38 B5
Giles Cl RG4 . . . . 104 F2
Giles Travers Cl TW20 . 123 D5
Gillespie Ho GU25 . . . . 122 E5
Gillette Ho RG2 . . . . 86 B2
Gilliat Rd SL1 . . . . 42 E6
Gilliatt Cl SL4 . . . . 67 A6
Gillott Cl SL6 . . . . 39 E8
Gillott's La RG9 . . . . 35 C8
Gillott's Hill RG9 . . . . . . 35 C7
Gillott's Sch RG9 . . . . . . 35 B7
Gillotts Ct RG9 . . . . 35 B7
Gill Rise RG42 . . . . 91 C2
Gilman Cres SL4 . . . . 66 D4
Gilmore Cl SL3 . . . . 43 C4
Gilmore Flats SL5 . . . . . 120 B8
Gilpin Way LN3 . . . . 71 D7
Gilroy Cl RG14 . . . . 130 C6
Gilson Ct SL4 . . . . 95 C8
Gingells Farm Rd RG10 . 61 B5
Gipsy La
  Bracknell RG12 . . . . . 118 D7
  Reading RG6 . . . . 87 D1
  Hungerford RG17 . . . 100 E8
  Lower Earley RG6 . . . . 87 D3
  Reading RG30 . . . . 57 E1
  Sindlesham RG41 . . . . 114 F7
  Wokingham RG40 . . . . 116 C4
Girton Cl GU47 . . . . 143 E1
Glade Ho
  Ascot SL5 . . . . 120 C4
  2 Marlow SL7 . . . . 1 E2
Glade Rd SL7 . . . . 1 E2
Glade The
  Ascot SL5 . . . . 120 B8
  Newbury RG14 . . . . . . 130 F7
  Purley on T RG8 . . . . . 57 C8
  Staines TW18 . . . . 97 B2
Gladridge Cl RG6 . . . . . . 87 C4
Gladstone Cl RG17 . . . . 102 B2
Gladstone Ind Est SL6 . . 39 E8
Gladstone La SL6 . . . . . 106 C8
Gladstone Way SL1 . . . . . 42 A5
Glaisdale RG12 . . . . 118 C3
Glamis Way RG31 . . . . . . 84 B4
Glanmor Rd SL2 . . . . 43 A6
Glanty The TW20 . . . . 96 B4
Glassonby Wlk GU15 . . 152 C5
Glebe Cl
  Dorney SL6 . . . . 40 F4
  Maidenhead SL6 . . . . . 39 B3
Glebe Cotts SL5 . . . . 93 C5
Glebefields RG20 . . . . . . 49 A7
Glebe Fields RG20 . . . . . 49 A7

Glebe Gdns RG4 . . . . 60 E3
Glebe La
  Sonning RG4 . . . . 60 E3
  Stockcross RG20 . . . . 103 E5
Glebeland Gdns TW17 . . 125 C3
Glebeland Rd GU15 . . . . 150 F4
Glebelands RG19 . . . . . 106 C3
Glebelands Rd RG40 . . . 116 C7
Glebe Pl RG17 . . . . 73 A2
Glebe Rd
  Egham TW20 . . . . 96 C2
  Maidenhead SL6 . . . . . 40 B5
  Old Windsor SL4 . . . . . 68 B2
  Purley on T RG8 . . . . . 57 B5
  Reading RG2 . . . . 86 C5
  Staines TW18 . . . . 97 B3
Glebe Ride RG8 . . . . 34 B6
Glebe The
  Aldworth RG8 . . . . 32 F3
  Blackwater GU17 . . . . 150 E4
Glebewood RG12 . . . . . . 118 C4
Glenalmond Ho TW15 . . 97 E5
Glenapp Grange RG7 . . 136 F6
Glen Ave TW15 . . . . 98 A4
Glenavon Gdns
  Slough SL3 . . . . 43 C3
  Yateley GU46 . . . . 149 D4
Glenbigh Terr RG1 . . . . . 86 E6
Glen Cl TW17 . . . . 125 A5
Glen Ct TW18 . . . . 96 F1
Glendale Ave RG14 . . . 130 C5
Glendale Cl RG41 . . . . . 116 A3
Glendale Rd RG26 . . . . 135 A1
Glendevon Rd RG5 . . . . . 87 F8
Glendower Ct 4 RG12 . . 118 B5
Gleneagles Cl TW19 . . . . 70 D1
Gleneagles Ct 18 RG1 . . 86 D7
Gleneagles Ho RG12 . . . 117 E3
Glenfield Ho RG12 . . . . 118 C5
Glenfield Rd TW15 . . . . . 98 C2
Glenfields SL2 . . . . 22 F4
Glenhurst GU20 . . . . 146 D4
Glenhurst Cl GU17 . . . . 150 E4
Glen Innes GU47 . . . . . 143 E1
Glenmore Ct RG19 . . . . 106 D3
Glenn Miller Cl RG20 . . 49 A5
Glenmon Ct RG30 . . . . . . 85 C4
Glenmore Cl SL6 . . . . 20 A8
Glenrhondda RG4 . . . . . . 58 F6
Glenridge Farm Cvn Site
  GU25 . . . . 122 B6
Glenrosa Rd RG30 . . . . . . 85 A8
Glen The
  Ascot SL5 . . . . 120 D5
  Pamber Heath RG26 . . 135 E1
  Slough SL3 . . . . 43 C2
Glentworth Pl SL1 . . . . . . 42 C5
Glenwood
  Bracknell RG12 . . . . . 118 D5
  Virginia Water GU25 . . 122 C8
Glenwood Dr RG31 . . . . . 84 C7
Glentham La GU17 . . . . 150 B8
Globeside Bsns Pk SL7 . . . 1 F2
Glory Cl HP10 . . . . 3 F7
Glory Hill La HP9 . . . . 3 F8
Glory Mill La HP10 . . . . . 3 E7
Gloucester Ave
  Shinfield RG2 . . . . 113 C6
  Slough SL1 . . . . 42 C8
Gloucester Cres RG30 . . 85 D7
Gloucester Dr TW18 . . . . 96 D5
Gloucester Gdns GU19 . 145 E3
Gloucester Pl SL4 . . . . . . 67 D5
Gloucester Rd
  Bagshot GU19 . . . . . . 145 E3
  Maidenhead SL6 . . . . . 19 E2
  Newbury RG14 . . . . . . 104 E2
  Reading RG30 . . . . 85 D7
Gloucestershire Lea RG42 . 91 F1
Glyme Wlk RG31 . . . . 84 F3
Glyncastle RG4 . . . . 58 F5
Glynswood GU15 . . . . . 151 E3
Glynwood Ho 8 SL4 . . . . 40 A7
Go Ape Bracknell*
  RG12 . . . . 118 E8
Goaters Rd SL5 . . . . 119 C7
Goddard Cl
  Littleton TW17 . . . . . . 124 F6
  Shinfield RG2 . . . . 113 E5
Goddard Ct SL6 . . . . 88 B1
Goddard Dr RG7 . . . . . . 107 F3
GODDARD'S GREEN . . . 111 D7
Goddards La GU15 . . . . 151 B3
Goddard Way RG42 . . . . 91 D2
Goddington Rd SL8 . . . . . 3 A5
Godfrey Cl RG40 . . . . . . 115 F3
Godfrey Ct TW18 . . . . 97 A1
Godolphin Inf Sch SL1 . . 42 C7
Godolphin Jun Sch SL1 . 42 D7
Godolphin Rd SL1 . . . . . . 42 D6
Godstow Cl RG5 . . . . 87 D3
Goffs Rd TW15 . . . . 98 D2
Goldcrest Cl RG16 . . . . 116 A6
Gold Cup La SL5 . . . . . . 119 D8
Golden Ball La SL6 . . . . . 19 A3
Golden Oak Cl SL2 . . . . . 22 C6
Golden Orb Wood RG42 . 117 D8
Golden Orb Wood RG42 . 117 D8
Golding Cl RG19 . . . . . . 106 F3
Goldney Rd GU15 . . . . . 152 C4
Goldsmid Rd RG1 . . . . . . 85 F7

Goldsmith Cl
Finchampstead RG40 115 E1
Thatcham RG18 106 C5
Goldsmith Way RG45 143 B4
Goldsworthy Way SL1 41 C7
Goldthorpe Gdns RG6 113 F8
Goldwell Dr RG14 104 F4
Golf Dr GU15 151 F4
Gooch Cl RG10 61 F3
Goodall Cl RG9 15 D1
Goodboy's La RG7 112 A1
Goodchild Rd RG40 116 D6
Goodings Gn RG40 116 F6
Goodings La RG17 47 B3
Goodliffe Gdns RG31 57 C4
Goodman Pk SL2 43 C5
Goodman Pl TW18 96 F4
Goodrich Cl RG4 59 E5
Goodways Dr RG12 118 D7
Goodwin Cl RG31 84 E4
Goodwin Mdws HP10 3 E6
Goodwin Rd SL2 21 F2
Goodwin Villas SL1 41 F5
Goodwin Wlk RG14 130 C6
Goodwood Cl
Burghfield Common RG7 111 A2
Camberley GU15 151 C8
Goodwood Rise SL7 1 C7
Goodwood Way [5] RG14 105 C1
Goose Cnr RG42 91 F3
Goosecroft La RG8 57 B5
Goose Gn
Farnham Royal SL2 22 B3
Lambourn RG17 25 B3
Goose Green Way RG19 106 D3
GOOSE HILL 133 A2
Goose La RG20 49 E5
Gordon Ave GU15 151 C4
Gordon Cl TW18 97 B2
Gordon Clifford Ct [3]
RG42 118 B8
Gordon Cres
Camberley GU15 151 C4
Compton RG20 31 D4
Gordon Ct [2] RG14 105 B2
Gordon Dr TW17 125 D2
Gordon Palmer Cl RG7 137 D5
Gordon Palmer Ct RG30 85 C8
Gordon Pl RG30 85 C8
Gordon Rd
Ashford TW15 97 E5
Camberley GU15 151 C5
Crowthorne RG45 143 D3
Egham TW18 96 C4
Maidenhead SL6 39 D7
Newbury RG14 105 B2
Shepperton TW17 125 D3
Thatcham RG18 106 A5
Windsor SL4 66 F5
Gordon's Sch GU24 153 E7
Gordon Wlk GU46 149 F5
GORE END 129 B4
Gore End Rd RG20 129 B3
Gore Rd SL1 21 B2
Gore The SL1 21 A2
GORING 34 D6
Goring CE Prim Sch RG8 34 C7
Goring La RG7 111 A1
Goring Rd TW18 96 E3
Goring's Sq TW18 96 E4
Goring & Streatley Sta
RG8 34 C6
Gorrick Sq RG41 116 B3
Gorse Bank GU18 153 A8
Gorse Cottage Dr RG18 79 C1
Gorse Dr RG5 88 A8
Gorse Hill La GU25 122 D5
Gorse Hill Rd GU25 122 D5
Gorselands
Caversham RG4 59 B6
Newbury RG14 130 D5
Gorse Meade SL1 42 B5
Gorse Pl RG42 92 B1
Gorse Rd
Cookham Rise SL6 19 E6
Frimley GU16 151 E2
Gorse Ride Inf Sch RG40 141 E7
Gorse Ride Jun Sch
RG40 141 E7
Gorse Ride N RG40 141 E7
Gorse Ride S RG40 141 E6
Gorton Oaks RG40 116 D5
Gosbrook Ho [1] RG4 59 C1
Gosbrook Rd RG4 59 B2
Gosden Rd GU24 153 F6
Gosforth Cl RG6 87 D2
Goslar Way SL4 67 B5
Gosling Gn SL3 43 E3
Gosling Rd SL3 43 E3
Gosnell Cl GU16 152 D3
Gossmore Cl SL7 1 F1
Gossmore La SL7 1 F1
Gossmore Wlk SL7 1 F1
Goswell Hill SL4 67 D6
Goswell Rd SL4 67 D6
Gothic Ct
Harlington UB3 71 D8
[1] Sandhurst GU47 150 B7
Gough's Barn La RG42 91 A8
Gough's La RG12 91 D1
Gough's Mdw GU47 150 B7
Gould Cl RG14 105 B3
Goulders Cotts RG10 36 F7
Gould Rd TW14 98 E8
Governor's Rd GU15 150 F6
Govett Ave TW17 125 C4
Govett Gr GU20 146 D5
Gower Pk GU47 150 D7
Gower St RG1 85 E8
Gower The TW20 123 C6
Gowings Gn SL1 41 E4
Grace Ct SL1 42 C5
Grace Reynolds Wlk
GU15 151 C6
Graces La RG20 78 B8
Graffham Cl RG6 114 B8
Grafton Cl
Maidenhead SL6 19 E2
Slough SL3 43 F7
Grafton Ct TW14 98 D7
Grafton Rd RG30 84 D7
Graham Cl
Blewbury OX11 12 A8
Maidenhead SL6 39 C5
Reading RG31 84 E4
Grahame Ave RG8 56 D5
Graham Rd
Cookham Rise SL6 19 E6
Windlesham GU20 146 C4
Grainford Ct RG40 116 C5
Grampian Cl UB3 71 D7
Grampian Rd GU47 143 A2
Grampian Way SL3 44 A1
Gramp's Hill OX12 6 E5
Granary The RG2 86 D4
Granby Ct RG1 86 E7
Granby End RG7 111 B3
Granby Gdns RG1 86 E7
Grand Ave GU15 151 C6
Grandison Ho RG9 15 E3
Grand Regency Hts SL5 119 E6
Grange Ave
Crowthorne RG45 143 B6
Reading RG6 87 A6
Grange Cl
Goring RG8 34 B6
Wraysbury TW19 68 E1
Grange Ct
Earley RG6 87 B8
Egham TW20 95 F3
Littleton TW17 125 A5
Newbury RG14 105 B2
[7] Staines TW18 97 A3
Grange Dr HP10 3 D3
Grange Gdns
Farnham Common SL2 22 D7
Newbury RG14 130 C5
Grange La SL6 19 F8
Grangely Cl RG31 84 D4
Grange Pl TW18 124 C7
Grange Rd
Bracknell RG12 118 C8
Camberley GU15 151 E5
Cookham Rise SL6 19 F7
Egham TW20 95 F3
Henley-on-T RG9 15 E1
Grange The
Caversham RG4 58 D6
Newbury RG14 130 C5
Old Windsor SL4 68 B2
Staines TW18 97 A3
[4] Stanwell TW19 70 D1
Virginia Water GU25 122 E5
Grange Way SL0 44 F7
Grangewood SL3 43 C8
Grant Ave SL1 42 E7
Grant Cl TW17 125 B3
Grantham Cl GU47 143 E1
Grantham Ho [5] TW16 98 E1
Grantham Rd RG30 84 F4
Granthams The RG17 25 B3
Grant Ho [6] SL8 3 A4
Grantley Hts [6] RG1 86 C7
Grant Rd RG45 143 C3
Grant Wlk SL5 120 E1
Granville Ave SL2 42 D8
Granville Rd RG30 85 B5
Grasholm Way SL3 44 C2
Grasmere
Camberley GU15 151 E7
Windsor SL4 66 E7
Grasmere Ave
Reading RG30 57 F2
Slough SL2 43 A6
Grasmere Cl
East Bedfont TW14 98 F7
[5] Thorpe Lea TW20 96 B1
Winnersh RG41 88 B1
Grasmere Par SL2 43 B6
Grasmere Rd GU18 146 B1
Grass Hill RG4 58 E3
Grassington Pl RG19 106 D3
Grassmead RG19 106 F2
Grassy La SL6 39 E7
Grattan Ct SL7 2 A3
Gratton Dr SL4 66 E3
Gratton Rd RG2 113 C8
Gratwicke Rd RG30 84 E8
Gravel Hill
Caversham RG4 59 A6
Henley-on-T RG9 15 D2
Stockcross RG20 103 E5
Gravelly Cl RG20 129 A3
Gravel Rd RG9 35 A1
Graveney Dr RG4 58 E3
Gravett Cl RG9 35 C8
Gray Ct [11] SL4 67 A5
Grayling Cl SL7 18 C8
Grayling Ct [3] RG1 59 A1
Graylings Ho KT16 124 C1
Gray Pl RG42 117 E8
Grays Cres RG5 87 C7
Grayshot Dr GU17 150 C5
Grays La TW15 98 B4
Gray's Mon★ SL2 22 F2
Grays Park Rd SL2 23 A2
Grays Pl SL2 42 F5
Grays Rd SL1 42 F5
GRAZELEY 112 D2
GRAZELEY GREEN 112 A3
Grazeley Parochial CE Prim
Sch RG7 112 E2
Grazeley Rd RG7 113 A4
Great Auclum Pl RG7 111 B2
Great Barn Ct RG19 106 C3
Great Cockrow Rly★
KT16 123 D1
Great Hill Cres SL6 39 C6
GREAT HOLLANDS 117 F3
Great Hollands Prim Sch
RG12 117 F4
Great Hollands Rd RG12 117 F3
Great Hollands Sq RG12 117 F3
Great Knollys St RG1 85 F8
Great Lea RG7 113 A5
GREAT LEA COMMON 113 A5
Great Marlow Sch SL7 1 F4
Great Severals RG17 102 A2
GREAT SHEFFORD 48 B3
Great South-West Rd TW14,
TW6, TW4, TW5 71 D2
Grebe Ct TW18 97 B4
Greenacre SL4 66 E5
Greenacre Ct TW20 95 C2
Green Acre Mount RG30 84 D8
Greenacres RG20 129 E1
Greenacres Ave RG41 88 A3
Greenacres La RG41 88 A3
Greenaway Terr TW19 97 E7
Greenbank Way GU15 151 D2
Green Bsns Ctr The TW18 96 C4
Green Cl
Burnham SL6 41 A7
Maidenhead SL6 19 F1
Green Cres HP10 3 C7
Green Croft RG40 116 E8
Greencroft Gdns RG30 84 F4
Green Ct TW16 98 F2
Greendale Mews SL2 43 A6
Green Dr RG40 116 E4
Green Dragon La HP10 3 B7
Greene Fielde End TW18 97 D1
Green End GU46 149 D7
Greenend Cl RG7 113 B2
Green Farm Rd GU19 145 F3
Green Farm Rise SN8 99 B5
Greenfern Ave SL1 41 C7
Greenfield Ho TW20 95 B2
Greenfields SL6 40 A5
Greenfields Rd RG2 113 B8
Greenfield Way RG45 143 A7
Greenfinch Cl
Crowthorne RG45 142 F6
Reading RG31 84 B6
Sandhurst GU47 150 D8
Greenfinch Dr RG10 61 D5
Greengates [1] RG30 85 C7
GREENHAM 131 C8
Greenham Cl
Greenham RG19 131 D8
Woodley RG5 88 A6
GREENHAM COMMON 132 B6
Greenham Mill RG14 105 B3
Greenham Rd RG14 105 B1
Greenham Road Ret Pk
RG14 105 A2
Greenham Wood RG12 118 C3
Greenhaven GU46 149 B5
Green Hill Cl GU15 152 C6
Green Hill Rd GU15 152 C6
Greenholme GU15 152 D5
Greenhow RG12 118 A6
Greenidge Cl [2] RG1 85 E5
Green La
Ascot SL5 120 E8
Ashford TW16 98 F2
Bagshot GU19 145 F2
Binfield RG40 90 A3
Blackwater GU17 150 B4
Blackwater, Hawley GU17 150 E4
Burghfield Common RG30 85 A2
Burnham SL1 21 D4
Caversham RG9 35 A1
Chieveley RG20 78 B7
Datchet SL3 68 B6
Egham TW20 96 B3
Farnham Common SL2 22 B6
Fifield SL6 65 C6
Henley-on-T RG9 35 D8
Holyport SL6 64 A5
Hurst RG10 88 E3
Littlewick Green SL6 38 B5
Maidenhead SL6 40 A6
Newbury RG14 104 E2
Pangbourne RG8 56 C5
Sandhurst GU47 150 C7
Shepperton TW17 125 C4
Staines TW18 123 E8
Stanford Dingley RG7 81 F3
Thatcham RG19 106 C3
Ufton Nervet RG7 110 C2
Windsor SL4 67 B5
Wokingham RG41 88 D1
Yateley GU46 149 B7
Greenlake Terr TW18 97 A1
Greenlands
Ball Hill RG20 129 E1
Flackwell Heath HP10 3 B8
Greenlands Ct
[2] Maidenhead SL6 39 B8
[7] Staines TW18 97 A4
Greenlands Rd
Camberley GU15 151 B1
Newbury RG14 105 B1
Staines TW18 97 A4
Green Lane Cl GU15 151 C7
Green Lane Ct SL1 21 C2
Greenleaf Ct SL3 68 A8
Greenleas GU16 151 E2
Green Leas TW16 98 F2
Greenleas Ave RG4 59 B7
Greenleas Cl GU46 149 C7
Green Leas Cl TW16 98 F2
Green Leys SL6 19 F2
Greenock Rd SL1 42 A7
Greeno Cres TW17 125 A4
Green Pk TW18 96 E5
Green Pl HP10 3 C8
Green Rd
Reading RG6 87 A5
Virginia Water TW20 123 A5
Greenside
Bourne End SL8 3 A5
Crowthorne RG45 142 F5
Slough SL2 42 A8
Greenside View GU15 152 A5
Greensward La RG2 114 C2
Green The
Ashford TW18 97 D3
Blackwater GU17 150 C5
Bracknell RG12 118 B5
Burnham SL1 21 B1
Chieveley RG20 51 B2
Chilton OX11 10 E8
Crowthorne RG45 142 F6
Datchet SL3 68 B7
Kintbury RG17 102 B1
Slough SL1 42 D3
Theale RG7 83 C2
Theale RG7 83 D2
Upper Halliford TW17 125 E5
Wokingham RG41 115 E7
Wooburn Green HP10 3 E5
Wraysbury TW19 68 E1
Green Verges SL7 1 E3
Greenview Ct TW15 97 F4
Greenway SL1 21 B3
Greenway Dr TW18 124 D8
Greenways
Ball Hill RG20 129 E1
Egham TW20 95 E3
Lambourn RG17 25 B1
Pangbourne RG8 56 D5
Sandhurst GU47 143 B1
Greenways Dr
Maidenhead SL6 39 A8
Sunningdale SL5 120 E1
Greenways Ho RG14 104 E2
Greenway The
Fawley OX12 27 C7
Slough SL1 41 D5
Greenwich Rd RG2 113 E7
Greenwood
[4] Bracknell RG12 118 F5
North Ascot SL5 119 C8
Greenwood Cotts SL5 121 C3
Greenwood Gr RG41 88 D3
Greenwood Rd
Crowthorne RG45 143 B6
Reading RG30 84 F5
Gregory Cl RG6 114 C8
Gregory Dr SL4 68 B1
Grenadier Gdns RG19 106 E2
Grenedier Cl RG2 113 E6
Grenfell Ave SL6 39 F6
Grenfell Pl SL6 39 F6
Grenfell Rd SL6 39 E6
Grenville Cl SL1 21 B3
Grenville Pl RG12 118 C7
Gresham Ct
Frimley GU15 151 F4
[3] Staines TW18 97 A3
Gresham Rd
Slough SL1 42 A7
Staines TW18 97 A3
Gresham Way RG30 58 A2
Gresham Way Ind Est
RG30 58 A2
Greyberry Copse Rd
RG19 131 D8
Greycoat Ct RG4 59 B3
Greyfriars Dr SL5 120 B3
Greyfriars Rd RG1 86 A8
Greys Ct RG1 86 C7
Greys Hill RG9 15 D1
Greys Rd RG9 35 C8
Greystock Rd RG42 91 D2
Greystoke Ct RG45 143 A4
Greystoke Ho [6] RG1 85 E5
Greystoke Rd
Caversham RG4 59 C4
Slough SL2 41 F8
Griffin Cl
Maidenhead SL6 39 E5
Slough SL1 42 C4
Griffiths Cl RG19 106 F2
Grindle Cl RG18 106 C5
Gringer Hill SL6 39 E8
Groombridge Pl RG14 104 E6
Grosvenor Ct
Blackwater GU17 150 D3
Slough SL1 42 E7
Grosvenor Dr SL6 40 C8
Grosvenor Ho [2] RG1 85 F8
Grosvenor Lawn RG14 104 E2
Grosvenor Rd
Caversham RG4 59 C4
Staines TW18 97 A1
Grouse Mdws RG12 117 D6
Grovebarns TW18 97 A2
Grove Cl
Old Windsor SL4 95 B8
[2] Slough SL1 43 A3
Wokingham RG40 142 E7
Grove Cotts
Caversham RG4 59 A5
Wokingham RG40 142 E7
Grove Cross Rd GU16 151 D1
Grove Ct
Egham TW20 96 A3
Maidenhead SL6 39 D7
Newbury RG14 131 A8
Grove End GU19 145 F5
Grovefields Ave GU16 151 D1
Grove Hill RG4 59 A4
Grove House SL4 95 C8
Grove La RG42 92 B4
Groveland Pl [4] RG30 85 B8
Groveland Rd RG14 104 E5
Grovelands Ave RG41 88 D2
Grovelands Avenue
Workshops RG41 88 D3
Grovelands Cl RG41 88 D3
Grovelands Pk RG41 88 D2
Grovelands Rd
Reading RG30 85 B8
Shinfield RG7 113 C2
Groveley Rd TW16 98 F3
Grove Mews RG4 59 B5
Grove Pk SL6 63 E8
Grove Prim Sch The
GU16 151 E2
Grove Rd
Burnham SL1 21 E4
Camberley GU15 151 F5
Caversham RG4 59 B6
Chertsey KT16 123 F3
Henley-on-T RG9 15 E1
Maidenhead SL6 39 F7
Newbury RG14 104 E5
Shepperton TW17 125 C3
South Stoke RG8 14 E2
Windsor SL4 67 D5
Groves Cl SL8 3 C3
Groves Lea RG7 136 F6
Groves The RG17 73 A2
Grovestile Waye TW14 98 D8
Groves Way SL6 19 E6
Grove The
Egham TW20 96 A3
Frimley GU16 151 D1
Medmenham SL7 17 E6
North Ascot SL5 119 C8
Reading RG1 86 C7
Slough SL1 43 A4
Thatcham RG18 106 D4
Twyford RG10 61 D5
Grubwood La SL6 19 A7
Guards Club Rd SL6 40 C7
Guards Ct SL5 121 B2
Guards Rd SL4 66 C5
Guards View SL4 67 D6
Guards Wlk [1] SL4 66 C5
Guerdon Pl RG12 118 D2
Guernsey Way RG41 88 A2
Guildford Ave TW13 98 F6
Guildford Rd
Bagshot GU19 145 E3
Bagshot GU19 145 F2
Bisley GU24 153 F4
Chertsey KT16 123 F1
Lightwater GU18, GU19 146 B1
West End GU24 153 F7
Guildford St
Chertsey KT16 124 A2
Staines TW18 97 A2
Guinea Wlk RG12 117 D5
Gullane Ct [20] RG1 86 D7
Gull Cl RG41 115 E4
Gulliver's SL4 67 D8
Gun St RG1 86 A7
Gunthorpe Rd SL7 2 A3
Gurney Cl RG4 58 D5
Gurney Dr RG4 58 D5
Gwendale SL6 19 C1
Gwendolen Ho TW19 97 E7
Gwendoline Ct TW15 97 E4
Gweneth Ct SL7 1 D3
Gwent Cl SL6 39 B4
Gwyn Cl RG14 130 E8
Gwynne Cl
Purley on T RG31 57 D3
Windsor SL4 66 E6
Gwyns Piece RG17 25 B3
Gypsy La
Marlow SL7 1 E4
Stoke Poges SL2 22 E8

H

Habershon Dr GU16 152 D2
Hackney Bottom RG18 53 A8
Haddenhurst Ct RG42 90 C2
Haddon Dr RG5 87 E8
Haddon Rd SL6 39 C5
Hadfield Rd TW19 70 D1
Hadleigh Rise RG4 59 E5
Hadley Ct SL3 69 E6
Hadlow Ct SL1 42 C5
Hadrian Cl TW19 97 E8
Hadrian Way TW19 97 D8
Hadrian Wlk E RG2 86 C4
Hadrian Wlk W RG2 86 C4
Hafod RG4 58 F6
Hag Hill La SL6 41 A7
Hag Hill Rise SL6 41 A7

Hagley Rd RG2 . . . . .86 B4
Haig Dr SL1 . . . . .42 B4
Haig Rd GU15 . . . . .150 F6
Haileybury Ct SL4. . . . . . . .67 A4
Hailey Ct SL6 . . . . .39 F5
Hailey La RG20 . . . . .29 F1
Hailsham Cl GU47. . . . . . . .143 D1
HAINES HILL 62 C1
Halcyon Ct TW18 . . . . .124 B7
Halcyon Terr RG30 . . . . .84 E8
Haldane Rd RG4 . . . . .58 F5
Hale SL4 . . . . .66 F6
Hale End RG12 . . . . .118 F5
Hale St TW18 . . . . .96 E4
Hale Way GU16 . . . . .151 D1
Halewood RG12. . . . . .117 F3
Halfacre Cl RG7 . . . . .113 B3
Half Mile Rd RG17 . . . . .46 A1
Half Moon St GU19 . . . . . .145 E3
Halfpenny Ct ❷ SL5 . . . . .121 B2
Halfpenny La
  Cholsey OX10 . . . . .13 D5
  Sunningdale SL5 . . . . . . .121 A2
HALFWAY 102 F5
Halfway Farm Cotts
  RG20 . . . . .102 E5
Halfway Hos SL6 . . . . .19 E4
Halifax Cl SL6 . . . . .39 A8
Halifax Pl RG18 . . . . .106 C4
Halifax Rd
  Bracknell RG12 . . . . .118 C6
  Maidenhead SL6 . . . . .39 B8
Halifax Way SL6 . . . . .39 A8
Halkingcroft SL3 . . . . .43 C4
Hallbrooke Gdns RG42 . . . . .90 E1
Hall Cl GU15. . . . . .151 E6
Hall Ct SL3 . . . . .68 B7
Halldore Hill SL6 . . . . .19 E7
Halley Dr SL5. . . . . .119 B7
Hall Farm Cres GU46. . . . . .149 D5
Hallgrove Bottom GU19 . . .145 F5
Hall Grove Farm Ind Est
  GU19 . . . . .145 F5
Hall Grove Sch GU19. . . . . .146 A5
Halliford Cl TW17 . . . . .125 C6
Halliford Ct TW17. . . . . . . .125 E5
Halliford Rd TW16, TW17 . .125 E5
Halliford Sch TW17 . . . . . . .125 C2
Hall La
  Harlington UB3 . . . . .71 D7
  Yateley GU46 . . . . .149 C6
Hallmark Cl GU47. . . . . . . .150 E8
Hallmark Ho SL1 . . . . .21 C2
Hall Mdw SL1 . . . . .21 C3
Hallows Gr TW16 . . . . .98 F3
Hall Place La SL6 . . . . .38 B7
Halls La
  Earley RG2. . . . . .86 E1
  Waltham St L RG10 . . . . . .63 A7
Hallsmead Ct ❽ RG1 . . . . . .59 A1
Halls Rd RG30 . . . . .84 D6
Hall's Way RG27 . . . . .149 A8
Halpin Cl RG31 . . . . .84 C4
Halpin Ho RG1 . . . . .139 C3
Halse Dr SL1, SL2 . . . . .21 F7
Halstead Cl RG5 . . . . .87 E7
Halters The RG14 . . . . .131 B7
HAM 126 C2
Hamble Ave GU17 . . . . . . .150 D5
Hambleberry Ct RG31 . . . . .84 C8
Hamble Ct ❹ RG1 . . . . .86 B6
HAMBLEDEN 16 D8
Hambleden Ct RG12 . . . . . .118 E5
Hambleden Mill RG9 . . . . . .16 C7
Hambleden Rise RG9 . . . . . .16 D8
Hambleden Wlk SL6 . . . . . . .19 E2
Hambledon Cl RG6 . . . . .87 E1
Hambledon Cl GU16 . . . . . .152 B3
Hamblin Mdw RG17 . . . . . .100 F7
Hambridge Bsns Ctr
  RG14 . . . . .105 E2
Hambridge La RG14. . . . . . .105 E2
Hambridge Rd RG14 . . . . . .105 D2
Hamfield Cotts SL6 . . . . .19 E7
Hamilton Ave RG9 . . . . .15 E1
Hamilton Cl
  Ashford TW13 . . . . .98 F1
  Chertsey KT16. . . . . .123 F1
  Sandhurst GU19 . . . . . . .145 E3
Hamilton Ct
  Farnborough GU17 . . . . . .150 E1
  Newbury RG14. . . . . .131 B8
Hamilton Dr SL5. . . . . .120 E2
Hamilton Gdns SL1 . . . . . . .21 B2
Hamilton Pk SL6. . . . . .39 A6
Hamilton Rd
  Feltham TW13 . . . . .98 F4
  Reading RG1. . . . . .86 E6
  Slough SL1. . . . . .42 A7
  Wargrave RG10. . . . . .36 E2
Hamilton Way SL2 . . . . .22 C7
Ham Island SL4 . . . . .68 C3
Ham La
  Englefield Green TW20 . . . .95 B4
  Old Windsor SL4 . . . . .68 C3
Hamlet St RG42. . . . . .118 E8
HAM MARSH 105 C3
Hammond Cl RG19. . . . . . .106 F2
Hammond Com Jun Sch
  GU18 . . . . .146 A1
Hammond Ct RG42. . . . . . . .91 A1
Hammond End SL2 . . . . .22 B8
Hammonds Heath RG7. . . . .137 B6
Hammonds Ho TW19 . . . . . .97 F7
Hammond Way GU18. . . . . .146 B1
Hampden Cl SL2. . . . . .23 A2
Hampden Rd
  Caversham RG4. . . . . .59 B2

Hampden Rd continued
  Maidenhead SL6 . . . . .39 B8
  Slough SL3. . . . . .43 F3
Hampdens The RG14 . . . . . .130 C6
Hampshire Ave SL1 . . . . . . .42 C8
Hampshire Lodge ❽ SL6 . . .39 F6
Hampshire Rd GU15 . . . . . .151 F8
Hampshire Rise RG42 . . . . . .91 F2
Hampshire Way RG41 . . . . .115 D6
Hampshire Wlk RG31 . . . . . .84 A7
Hampstead Ct RG30. . . . . . . .85 B7
Hampstead Hill RG9 . . . . . . .60 C8
HAMPSTEAD NORREYS 52 F5
Hampstead Norreys CE Prim
  Sch RG18 . . . . .52 F5
Hampstead Norreys Rd
  RG18. . . . . .79 C8
Hampton Ho SL3 . . . . .69 D7
Hampton Rd ❶ RG41 . . . . . .88 A7
Hampton Twrs ❹ RG30. . . . .85 D6
Ham Rd SN8. . . . . .126 A3
HAMSTEAD MARSHALL 129 B7
Hamstead Mill RG20 . . . . . .103 C2
Hanbury Cl SL1. . . . . .41 A8
Hanbury Dr RG31. . . . . .84 D4
Hanbury Way GU15 . . . . . . .151 C3
Hanbury Wlk ❹ RG19. . . . . .106 D2
Hancocks Mount SL5 . . . . . .120 D3
Hancombe Rd GU47. . . . . . .143 A1
Handford La GU46 . . . . . . .149 D5
Handpost Cnr RG40 . . . . . . .116 A1
Hangar Rd RG26. . . . . .134 F1
Hangerfield Cl GU46 . . . . . .149 C5
Hanger Rd RG7 . . . . .83 F1
Hangman's Stone La
  RG20 . . . . .49 A5
Hanley Cl SL4 . . . . .66 D6
Hannibal Rd TW19 . . . . .97 E8
Hanningtons Way RG7 . . . . .111 C3
Hanover Cl
  Englefield Green TW20 . . . .95 B2
  Frimley GU16 . . . . .151 E1
  Slough SL1. . . . . .43 A3
  Windsor SL4 . . . . .66 F6
  Yateley GU46 . . . . .149 D7
Hanover Ct
  Caversham RG4. . . . . .59 C6
  Reading RG30 . . . . .84 F6
Hanover Gate SL1 . . . . .42 A5
Hanover Gdns
  Bracknell RG12 . . . . .117 F2
  Wargrave RG10. . . . . .36 F3
  Reading RG20. . . . . .103 E6
Hanover Mead
  Bray SL6 . . . . .40 C3
  Newbury RG14. . . . . .130 D6
Hanover Pk SL5 . . . . .119 F8
Hanover Way SL4 . . . . .66 F6
Hanson Cl GU15 . . . . .152 B7
Hanworth Cl RG5 . . . . .87 D8
HANWORTH. 118 A2
Hanworth Cl RG12 . . . . . . .118 C3
Hanworth La KT16 . . . . . . .123 F1
Hanworth Rd RG12 . . . . . . .118 A2
Hanworth Trad Est KT16. . . .123 F1
Harborough Cl SL1 . . . . .41 D5
Harbury Cl RG14. . . . . .105 B2
Harcourt TW19 . . . . .68 E1
Harcourt Cl
  Dorney SL6 . . . . .40 F3
  Egham TW20 . . . . .96 C2
  Henley-on-T RG9 . . . . . . .15 C1
Harcourt Dr RG6. . . . . .86 F8
Harcourt Rd
  Bracknell RG12 . . . . .118 B4
  Camberley GU15 . . . . . . .151 B5
  Dorney SL6 . . . . .40 F3
  Windsor SL4 . . . . .66 F6
Hardell Cl TW20 . . . . .96 A3
Harding Pl RG40. . . . . .116 C7
Harding Rd RG5 . . . . .87 C8
Harding Spur SL3. . . . . .43 E3
Hardwell Way RG12 . . . . . .118 E5
Hardwick Cl SL6 . . . . .39 A8
Hardwick La KT16 . . . . . . .123 D1
Hardwick Rd
  Reading RG30 . . . . .84 F7
  Whitchurch-on-T RG8 . . . . .56 D7
Hardy Cl
  Caversham RG4. . . . . .59 C2
  Slough SL1. . . . . .42 A5
  Thatcham RG18 . . . . .106 C5
Hardy Gn RG45 . . . . .143 B4
Harebell Dr RG18 . . . . .106 E4
Harefield Cl RG41. . . . . .88 B2
Harefield Rd SL6 . . . . .39 A7
HARE HATCH. 62 B8
Hare Shoots SL6 . . . . .39 E5
Hare Warren Ct RG4 . . . . . . .59 B4
Harewood Dr RG18 . . . . . . .106 C8
Harewood Pl SL1 . . . . .43 A3
Hargrave Rd SL6 . . . . .39 B6
Hargreaves Way RG31. . . . . .84 F4
Harkness Rd SL1 . . . . .41 B8
Harlech Ave RG4 . . . . .59 D6
Harlech Rd GU17 . . . . .150 D4
Harley Ct SL1. . . . . .42 C4
Harleyford La SL7. . . . . .18 B7
Harlington Cl UB7. . . . . .71 C7
HARLINGTON. 71 C8
Harlington Cl UB7. . . . . .71 C7
Harlington Cnr UB3. . . . . . . .71 B6
Harlton Cl RG6 . . . . .114 C8
Harman Ct ❷ RG41. . . . . . . .88 A2
HARMANS WATER 118 D5
Harmans Water Prim Sch
  RG12. . . . . .118 E4

Harmans Water Rd
  RG12 . . . . .118 D4
Harmar Cl RG40 . . . . .116 E6
Harmer Mews SL6 . . . . .40 B7
HARMONDSWORTH. 70 E8
Harmondsworth La UB7. . . . .70 E8
Harmondsworth Moor Ctry
  Pk UB7 . . . . .70 B7
Harmondsworth Prim Sch
  UB7. . . . . .70 D7
Harmont Gate RG4. . . . . . . .59 C5
Harness Cl RG2 . . . . .113 B6
Harold Rd RG17. . . . . .102 B2
Harpdon Par GU46. . . . . . . .149 D7
HARPESFORD 122 C3
Harpesford Ave GU25 . . . . .122 C4
HARPSDEN 35 D6
HARPSDEN BOTTOM. 35 B6
Harpsden Rd RG9. . . . . .35 E8
Harpsden Way RG9 . . . . .35 F7
Harpton Cl GU46 . . . . .149 D7
Harrier Cl RG5. . . . . .88 A6
Harrier Way RG12. . . . . . . .117 D5
Harrington Cl
  Earley RG6. . . . . .87 C2
  Newbury RG14. . . . . .105 E5
  Windsor SL4 . . . . .66 F3
Harris Arc RG1 . . . . .86 B8
Harris Cl
  Lambourn RG17 . . . . .25 B3
  Woodley RG5. . . . . .88 B8
Harris Gdns SL1 . . . . .42 C4
Harrison Cl RG10 . . . . .61 F8
Harrison Way
  Burnham SL1. . . . . .41 D5
  Shepperton TW17 . . . . . .125 B4
Harris Way TW16 . . . . .125 E8
Harrogate Ct SL3 . . . . .44 A1
Harrogate Rd RG4 . . . . .58 E4
Harrow Bottom Rd GU25 . .122 F3
Harrow Cl SL6 . . . . .19 E1
Harrow Ct RG1 . . . . .85 F6
Harrow La SL6. . . . . .19 E1
Harrow Mkt SL3 . . . . .44 A3
Harrow Rd
  Ashford TW15 . . . . .98 A6
  Slough SL3. . . . . .43 F3
Harrow Way
  Charlton TW17 . . . . .125 C7
  Sindlesham RG41. . . . . . .115 A8
Harry Tee Ct ❽ RG1 . . . . . . .86 C7
Hart Cl RG42 . . . . .91 B1
Hart Dene Ct GU19 . . . . . . .145 E3
Hart Dyke Cl RG41 . . . . . . .116 B2
Hartford Rise GU15 . . . . . . .151 D6
Hartigan Pl RG5 . . . . .88 A8
Hartland Cl SL1. . . . . .42 D5
Hartland Rd RG2. . . . . .86 C1
Hartley Cl
  Blackwater GU17. . . . . . .150 B5
  Stoke Poges SL3 . . . . .23 C4
Hartley Copse SL4. . . . . .68 A1
Hartley Court Rd RG7 . . . . .112 F6
Hartley Way RG18. . . . . . . .106 E4
Hartmead Rd RG19 . . . . . . .106 E3
Hart Mews GU46. . . . . .149 B6
Hartsbourne Rd RG6 . . . . . . .87 A3
Harts Cl RG2 . . . . .114 E2
HART'S HILL. 107 A5
Hartshill Rd RG26. . . . . .134 F1
Harts Hill Rd RG18 . . . . . . .106 F4
Hart's La RG7 . . . . .110 C5
Harts Leap Cl GU47 . . . . . .143 B1
Harts Leap Rd GU47. . . . . . .150 A8
Hartslock Bridleway RG8. . . .56 B8
Hartslock Ct RG8 . . . . .56 C6
Hartslock View RG8. . . . . . . .34 E2
Hartslock Way RG31 . . . . . . .57 C2
Hart St
  Henley-on-T RG9 . . . . . . .15 E2
  Reading RG1. . . . . .85 E8
Hartvale Ct ❶ GU15 . . . . . .152 A8
Harvard Cl RG5 . . . . .88 B8
Harvard Rd GU47 . . . . .143 E1
Harvaston Par RG30 . . . . . . .84 F7
Harvest Cl
  Reading RG31 . . . . .84 B6
  Yateley GU46 . . . . .149 B4
Harvest Cotts TW17 . . . . . . .125 A5
Harvest Ct TW17 . . . . .125 A5
Harvest Dr RG41 . . . . .115 B7
Harvest Gn RG14. . . . . .104 E1
Harvest Hill SL8 . . . . .3 D2
Harvest Hill Rd SL6 . . . . .39 F1
Harvest Lea RG42. . . . . .119 A8
Harvest Pl RG10 . . . . .36 E1
Harvest Rd TW20 . . . . .95 D2
Harvest Ride
  Bracknell RG42. . . . . .91 C2
  Winkfield RG12, RG42, SL5 .119 A8
Harvey Ho
  ❶ Reading RG30 . . . . .85 D6
Harvey Rd
  Oatlands Park KT12. . . . . .125 F2
  Slough SL3. . . . . .43 E7
Harveys Nurseries Pk Cvn
  Site RG4 . . . . .59 A7
Harwell International Bsns
  Ctr OX11 . . . . .10 C8
Harwich Cl ❹ RG42 . . . . . . .87 D1
Harwich Rd SL1. . . . . .42 A7
Harwood Gdns SL4 . . . . .95 B8
Harwood Rd SL7 . . . . .1 C1
Harwood Rise RG20. . . . . . .129 F2
Haslemere Cl GU16 . . . . . . .152 C3
Haslemere Rd SL4 . . . . .67 A6

Haslett Rd TW17 . . . . .125 E7
Hasting Cl SL6. . . . . .40 C2
Hastings Cl RG30 . . . . .85 A4
Hastings Mdw SL2 . . . . .23 A4
Hatch Cl RG7 . . . . .108 C7
Hatch End GU20 . . . . .146 C4
Hatchet La SL4, SL5 . . . . . . .93 B5
Hatchets La RG18 . . . . .80 C7
Hatchett Rd TW14 . . . . .98 C7
Hatchgate Cl RG18. . . . . . . .106 C7
Hatchgate Copse RG12. . . . .117 E3
Hatch Gate Gn RG10. . . . . . .88 E6
Hatchgate Gdns SL1 . . . . . . .21 D1
Hatch Gate La RG10. . . . . . . .37 A6
Hatch La
  Bucklebury RG7 . . . . .108 C7
  Burghfield RG30 . . . . . . .111 D6
  Harmondsworth UB7. . . . . .70 D7
  Windsor SL4 . . . . .67 A5
  Reading RG1. . . . . .19 E7
Hatch Ride
  Crowthorne RG45 . . . . . .143 B7
  Wokingham RG40 . . . . . .142 F8
Hatch Ride Prim Sch
  RG45 . . . . .143 B7
Hatch The SL4 . . . . .66 C7
Hatchway RG2 . . . . .113 C7
Hatfield Cl SL6 . . . . .39 C6
Hatfield Ct
  Camberley GU15 . . . . . . .151 B5
  Reading RG31 . . . . .84 B4
Hatfield Rd SL1. . . . . .43 A4
Hatford Rd RG30 . . . . .85 B4
Hatherley Rd RG1. . . . . .86 E6
Hatherwood GU46 . . . . . . .149 F5
Hatt Cl RG20 . . . . .50 D7
HATTON 71 F2
Hatton Ave SL2 . . . . .22 D1
Hatton Cross Rdbt TW6 . . . .71 F4
Hatton Cross Sta TW6. . . . . .71 F3
Hatton Ct SL4 . . . . .67 C5
HATTON HILL 142 B7
Hatton Hill
  Ashampstead RG8. . . . . . . .54 B7
  Windlesham GU20 . . . . . .146 C5
Hatton Rd
  East Bedfont TW14 . . . . . .98 D8
  Hatton TW14, TW6. . . . . . .71 E2
Hatton Rd N TW6 . . . . .71 D6
Haughurst Hill RG26 . . . . . .134 C1
Havelock Bsns Pk SL6 . . . . . .39 C7
Havelock Cres SL6. . . . . .39 B7
Havelock Rd
  Maidenhead SL6 . . . . .39 B7
  Wokingham RG41 . . . . . .116 A6
Havelock St RG41. . . . . .116 A6
Haven Cl ❶ RG1. . . . . .86 D7
Haven Of Rest SL6 . . . . .40 B7
Haven Rd TW15 . . . . .98 B5
Haven The RG17 . . . . .102 A1
Haversgate Way RG2 . . . . . .113 B6
Haversham Dr RG12 . . . . . .118 B3
Hawkchurch Rd RG2 . . . . . .113 D8
Hawkedale Inf Sch TW16 . . .125 B6
Hawkedon Prim Sch RG6. . . .87 E2
Hawkedon Way RG6 . . . . . . .87 E3
Hawker Ct SL3. . . . . .44 A3
Hawkes Leap GU20 . . . . . . .146 B6
Hawkesworth Dr GU19 . . . .145 E1
Hawkins Cl
  Bracknell RG12 . . . . .119 A7
  Yateley GU46 . . . . .149 B5
Hawk La
  Bracknell, Harmans Water
  RG12. . . . . .118 D5
  Bracknell RG12 . . . . .118 D5
Hawkridge Ct RG12 . . . . . .118 E6
Hawks Hill SL8 . . . . .3 C2
Hawksworth Rd RG7 . . . . . .111 B3
Haw La RG8, RG18 . . . . .53 E7
HAWLEY 150 C4
Hawley Cl RG31. . . . . .84 C4
Hawley Garden Cotts The
  GU17 . . . . .150 D4
Hawley Gn GU17 . . . . .150 E3
Hawley Gr GU17. . . . . .150 E2
Hawley Hill GU17. . . . . . . .150 D3
Hawley Lodge GU17. . . . . .150 E2
Hawley Mews SL6 . . . . .85 D6
Hawley Place Sch GU17. . . .150 E3
Hawley Prim Sch GU17. . . . .150 E3
Hawley Rd GU14, GU17. . . .150 D3
Hawley Way TW15 . . . . .98 B3
Hawthorn Cl
  Hampton TW15 . . . . .65 B3
  Reading RG31 . . . . .84 B5
Hawthorn Cotts RG7 . . . . . .112 C3
Hawthorn Ct ❶ TW15. . . . . .98 C1
Hawthorne Ave SL3 . . . . . . .43 B6
Hawthorne Cl
  Marlow SL7 . . . . .1 E4
  Wokingham RG41 . . . . . .116 B4
Hawthorne Cres
  Blackwater GU17. . . . . . .150 C4
  Slough SL1. . . . . .42 B5
Hawthorne Ct TW19. . . . . . .97 D8
Hawthorne Dr SL4 . . . . .93 B6

Hawthorne Rd
  Caversham RG4. . . . . .59 E4
  Egham TW18 . . . . .96 C4
Hawthornes RG31. . . . . .57 B3
Hawthorne Way
  Great Shefford RG17. . . . . .48 B4
  Stanwell TW19 . . . . .97 D8
  Winkfield SL4. . . . . .93 B7
Hawthorn Gdns
  Maidenhead SL6 . . . . .39 E5
  Reading RG2 . . . . .86 C1
HAWTHORN HILL 64 C1
Hawthorn La
  Farnham Royal SL2 . . . . . .22 A5
  Newell Green, Hawthorn Hill
  RG42. . . . . .91 E8
  Newell Green SL4 . . . . . . .92 A7
Hawthorn Rd
  Frimley GU16. . . . . .151 F2
  Newbury RG14. . . . . .105 A4
Hawthorns Prim Sch The
  RG41. . . . . .115 E7
Hawthorns The
  Charvil RG10 . . . . .61 A3
  Flackwell Heath HP10 . . . .3 B8
  Poyle SL3. . . . . .69 F6
  Wooburn Green HP10 . . . .3 E6
Hawthorn Way
  Sonning RG4 . . . . .60 E3
  Upper Halliford TW17 . . . .125 D5
Hawtrey Cl SL1 . . . . .43 B4
Hawtrey Rd SL4 . . . . .67 C5
Haydon Cl
  Maidenhead SL6 . . . . .39 E6
  Twyford RG10. . . . . .61 E4
Haydon La RG20 . . . . .30 E7
Haydon Pl GU46. . . . . .149 E6
Hayes La RG41 . . . . .115 C4
Hayes Pl SL7. . . . . .1 D1
Hayfield Cl RG31. . . . . .84 C8
Hayfield Ct RG17. . . . . .46 F6
Hay La SL3 . . . . .43 C6
Hayley Gn RG42. . . . . .91 F3
Haymill Rd SL1, SL2 . . . . . . .21 F3
Haynes Cl SL3 . . . . .43 F1
Hay Rd RG1 . . . . .85 F5
Hayse Hill SL4 . . . . .66 E6
Haysoms Dr RG19. . . . . . . .131 B7
Hayward Pl SL8. . . . . .3 C2
Haywards Cl RG9 . . . . .15 C1
Haywards The RG18 . . . . . .106 D4
Haywood RG12 . . . . .117 E3
Haywood Ct RG1. . . . . .86 F7
Haywood Way RG30 . . . . . . .84 F5
Hazelbank RG40 . . . . .141 E6
Hazelbank Ct KT16. . . . . . .124 C1
Hazelbank Rd KT16 . . . . . . .124 C2
Hazel Cl
  Burghfield RG30 . . . . . . .111 B5
  Englefield Green TW20 . . . .95 B2
  Marlow Bottom SL7 . . . . . .1 C6
  Wokingham RG41 . . . . . .115 F5
Hazel Cres RG2. . . . . .86 E2
Hazel Dr RG5 . . . . .87 C5
Hazel Gn RG20. . . . . .134 C1
Hazel Gr
  Staines TW18. . . . . .97 C2
  Thatcham RG18 . . . . .106 C5
Hazelhurst Rd SL1 . . . . .21 D3
Hazell Cl SL6 . . . . .39 F8
Hazell Hill RG12 . . . . .118 C6
Hazel Lodge TW20. . . . . . . .96 A4
Hazell Way SL2 . . . . .22 F6
Hazelmere Cl TW14 . . . . . . .71 E1
Hazel Rd RG8 . . . . .57 C8
Hazels Paddock RG18. . . . . .106 C8
Hazelwood Cl SL6. . . . . .20 C2
Hazelwood La SL6 . . . . .92 F4
Hazlemere Rd SL2 . . . . .43 A5
Heacham Cl RG6. . . . . .114 A8
Headington Cl
  Maidenhead SL6 . . . . .39 A7
  Wokingham RG40 . . . . . .116 D8
Headington Dr RG40 . . . . . .116 D8
Headington Rd SL6 . . . . .39 A7
Headlands Ct RG7 . . . . .110 F1
HEADLEY 132 D2
Headley Cl RG5. . . . . .88 A8
Headley Park Ind Est RG5 . . .87 F7
Headley Rd RG5 . . . . .87 A7
Headley Rd E RG5 . . . . .88 A7
HEAD'S HILL 132 A4
Heads La RG17 . . . . .128 A5
Headman Ct RG19. . . . . . . .106 F4
Hearmon Cl GU46. . . . . . . .149 E6
Hearne Dr SL6. . . . . .40 A1
Hearn Rd RG5. . . . . .87 F4
Hearn Wlk RG12 . . . . .118 E8
Hearsey Gdns GU17 . . . . . . .150 C6
Heathacre SL3 . . . . .69 E6
Heath Cl
  Harlington UB3 . . . . .71 D7
  Stanwell TW19 . . . . .97 D7
  Virginia Water GU25 . . . . .122 D5
Heath Cl ❷ RG30. . . . . .84 D6
Heath Cnr GU15 . . . . .152 A3
Heathcote SL6 . . . . .40 B2
Heathcote Cl RG31. . . . . . . .57 B3
Heathcote Ct ❷ SL4. . . . . . .67 D4
Heathcote Rd GU15. . . . . . .151 D5
Heathcroft Ave TW16. . . . . .98 F1
Heath Dr RG9 . . . . .35 A1

HEATH END
Ball Hill **129** A1
Tadley **134** F1
Heath End Farm RG26 . . **134** E1
Heath End Rd RG26 . . . . **134** E1
Heather Cl RG40 . . . . **141** E7
Heatherdale Rd GU15 . . . **151** D4
Heatherdene Ave RG45. . **142** E4
Heatherdene Cl RG2 . . . **113** C7
Heather Dr
Sunningdale SL5 . . . . **121** B2
Tadley RG26. . . . . **134** F2
Thatcham RG18 . . . . **106** D5
Heather Gdns RG14 . . . . **130** F7
Heatherlands SL5. . . . . . . **120** E4
Heatherley Cl GU15 . . . . **151** B5
Heatherley Rd GU15 . . . . **151** B5
Heather Mead GU16 . . . . **151** F2
Heather Mead Ct GU16. . **151** F2
Heathermount RG12 . . . . **118** E5
Heathermount Dr RG45 . **143** A6
Heathermount Gdns
RG45 . . . . **142** F6
Heathermount Learning Ctr
The SL5. . . . . **120** E3
Heather Ridge Arc GU15 **152** C4
Heather Ridge Inf Sch
GU15 . . . . **152** D4
HEATHERSIDE. **152** B4
Heatherside Cnr GU15 . **152** D6
Heatherside Dr GU25 . . . **122** A3
Heathers The TW19 . . . . . **97** F8
Heatherway RG45. . . . . . . **143** A5
Heatherwood Hospl SL5 **119** E6
Heathfield RG7 . . . . **137** A6
Heathfield Ave
Reading RG30 . . . . **84** D6
Shiplake RG9 . . . . **35** B2
Sunningdale SL5 . . . . **120** E4
Heathfield Cl RG9. . . . . . . **35** B2
Heathfield Ct TW15 . . . . . **97** E5
Heathfield Rd SL1 . . . . **3** F1
Heathfields RG20 . . . . **78** A8
Heathfield St Mary's Sch
SL5. . . . . **119** B7
Heath Flats GU19 . . . . . . **145** E3
Heath Gr TW16 . . . . **98** F1
Heath Hill Rd N RG45. . . **143** B5
Heath Hill Rd S RG45 . . . **143** B4
Heath Ho **8** RG26 . . . . . . **134** E1
Heath La RG18. . . . . **106** C5
Heathland **1** **134** E1
HEATHLANDS **142** E8
Heathlands Ct
Wokingham RG40 . . . . **142** F8
Yateley GU46. . . . . **149** E4
Heathlands Dr SL6. . . . . . . **39** A6
Heathlands Rd RG40 . . . . **116** E2
Heathlea Ho RG31 . . . . **84** B7
Heathmoors RG12 . . . . . . **118** C4
Heathpark Dr GU20 . . . . **146** E4
Heath Rd
Bagshot GU19 . . . . **145** E3
Pamber Heath RG26 . . . . **135** E1
Reading RG6. . . . . **87** A5
Southend RG7 . . . . **82** A2
Wooburn Moor HP9 . . . . . . **3** F8
Heath Ride RG40, RG45. . **142** C5
Heath Rise
Camberley GU15 . . . . **151** D5
Virginia Water GU25 . . . . **122** D5
Heathrow Airport London
TW6 . . . . **71** A5
Heathrow Airport Visitor
Ctr★ TW6 . . . . **71** C6
Heathrow Bvd UB7. . . . . . . **70** F7
Heathrow Cl TW6 . . . . **70** B6
Heathrow Copse RG26 . . **134** D1
Heathrow Int Trad Est. UB7 . **70** F8
Heathrow Terminal 4 Sta
TW6 . . . . **71** D4
Heathrow Terminal 5 Sta
TW6 . . . . **70** C4
Heathrow Terminals 1, 2, 3
Sta. **71** B4
Heathside Pk GU15 . . . . **152** C7
Heath Villa SL5 . . . . **120** A6
Heathway
Camberley GU15 . . . . **151** D5
North Ascot SL5. . . . . **119** E8
Reading RG31 . . . . **84** C8
Heathway Cl GU15 . . . . . **151** D5
Heathwood Cl GU46. . . . **149** D7
Heavens Lea SL3 . . . . **3** C2
Hebbecastle Down RG42 . **91** C2
Hebden Cl RG31 . . . . **106** C2
Hectors Way **1** RG14 . . . **105** B2
Hedge Croft GU46 . . . . . **149** B6
Hedge Lea HP10 . . . . **3** D8
Hedgerows The RG5 . . . . . **87** D8
Hedgeway RG14 . . . . **105** C4
Hedingham Mews SL6 . . . **39** D7
Hedley Rd HP10 . . . . **3** B8
HEDSOR. **3** F3
Hedsor Hill SL8. . . . . **3** C1
Hedsor La HP10, SL1. . . . . . **3** F2
Hedsor Rd SL8 . . . . **3** C1
Hedsor View Cotts SL6. . . **19** F7
Heelas Rd RG41 . . . . **116** A5
Heights The
Camberley GU15 . . . . **151** E5
Marlow SL7. . . . . **18** B8
Helena Rd SL4 . . . . **67** D5
Helen Cotts SL4. . . . . **66** D5

Helen Ct
20 Newbury RG14. . . . . . **104** F2
Reading RG30 . . . . **85** A5
Helgiford Gdns TW16 . . . . **98** E1
Helix Bsns Pk GU15 . . . . **151** B3
Helksham Cl GU47. . . . . . **143** D1
Hellyer Way SL8 . . . . **3** C3
Helmsdale RG12 . . . . **118** E4
Helmsdale Cl RG30 . . . . . . **85** B8
Helston Gdns RG2 . . . . **86** B1
Helston La SL4 . . . . **67** B6
Helvellyn Cl TW20 . . . . **96** C1
Hemdean Hill RG4 . . . . **59** A3
Hemdean House Sch RG4 **59** A3
Hemdean Rd RG4. . . . . **59** A3
Hemdean Rise RG4 . . . . . . **59** A3
Hemming Way SL2. . . . . . . **22** B2
Hemmyng Cnr RG42 . . . . . **91** C2
Hempson Ave SL3 . . . . **43** C3
Hemsdale SL6 . . . . **19** B1
Hemwood Rd SL4. . . . . **66** D4
Hencroft Mews **15** SL1 . . . **42** F4
Hencroft St N SL1. . . . . **42** F4
Hencroft St S SL1. . . . . **42** F3
Hendons Way SL6 . . . . **40** B1
Hendon Terr TW15 . . . . **98** D2
Hendon Way TW19 . . . . . . **70** D1
Hengrave Cl RG6 . . . . **87** E2
Hengrove Cres TW15. . . . . **97** D5
Henley Bsns Ctr RG9. . . . . **35** F8
Henley Coll The (Deanfield
Bldgs) RG9 . . . . **15** D1
Henley Coll The (Rotherfield
Bldgs) RG9 . . . . **15** C1
Henley Ct
12 Egham TW20 . . . . **96** A3
25 Reading RG1 . . . . **86** D7
Henley Gdns GU46 . . . . . **149** D5
Henley Ho SL5. . . . . **120** E4
Henley Lodge **12** SL6. . . . . **39** F6
HENLEY-ON-THAMES. . . **15** C1
Henley-on-Thames Sta
RG9 . . . . **15** E1
Henley Rd
Caversham RG9. . . . . **59** D3
Hurley SL6. . . . . **17** D3
Maidenhead SL6 . . . . **20** A7
Marlow SL7. . . . . **18** B8
Shiplake RG9 . . . . **60** B6
Slough SL1. . . . . **41** F7
Henley Wood Rd RG6 . . . . **87** D4
Henry Ct **17** RG1 . . . . **86** C7
Henry III Twr **4** SL4. . . . . . **67** D6
Henry Randell's Almshouses
GU17 . . . . **150** E3
Henry Rd SL1 . . . . **42** D4
Henry St RG1. . . . . **86** B6
Henrys The RG18 . . . . **106** D4
Henshaw Cres RG14 . . . . **130** D8
Hensworth Rd TW15 . . . . . **97** D3
Henwick Cl RG18 . . . . **106** B6
Henwick La RG18 . . . . **106** A4
Henwood Copse RG8. . . . . **55** A6
Hepplewhite Cl **7** RG26. . **134** E1
Hepworth Croft GU47 . . . **150** E6
Hepworth Way KT12 . . . . **125** F1
Herald Way RG5 . . . . **88** A6
Herbert Ct RG12 . . . . **118** B4
Hereford Cl TW18. . . . . . . **124** B8
Herewood Cl RG14. . . . . . **104** F4
Heriot Ct
Camberley GU15 . . . . **151** D3
Chertsey KT16. . . . . **123** F2
Heriot Rd KT16 . . . . **124** A2
Heritage Ct
18 Egham TW20 . . . . **96** A3
19 Reading RG1 . . . . **85** F7
Hermes Cl RG41 . . . . **115** B7
HERMITAGE. **79** B7
Hermitage Cl
Frimley GU16. . . . . **151** F1
Littleton TW17. . . . . **125** A5
Slough SL3. . . . . **43** C3
Hermitage Ct TW18. . . . . . **96** F3
Hermitage Cvn Pk The
RG42 . . . . **91** D3
Hermitage Dr
North Ascot SL5. . . . . **119** E7
Twyford RG10 . . . . **61** D5
Hermitage Gn RG18 . . . . . **79** A6
Hermitage La SL4. . . . . **67** A4
Hermitage Par SL6 . . . . . **120** A6
Hermitage Prim Sch
RG18 . . . . **79** B8
Hermitage Rd RG18. . . . . . **79** B2
Hermitage The
Eastbury RG17 . . . . **46** E7
1 Feltham TW13 . . . . **98** F5
Hermits Cl RG7 . . . . **111** B3
Hermit's Hill RG7, RG30. . **111** D4
Herndon Cl TW20 . . . . **96** A4
Herne Pl SL5 . . . . **121** C4
Hernes Cl TW18. . . . . **124** B8
Heroes Wlk RG2 . . . . **113** B7
Heron Cl SL5. . . . . **120** A6
Heron Ct
Sandhurst GU47. . . . . **150** C7
Staines TW18. . . . . **97** A4
Stanwell TW19. . . . . **97** E7
Herondale RG12 . . . . **118** C2
Heron Dr
Slough SL3. . . . . **44** B2
Twyford RG10 . . . . **61** E6
Heronfield TW20. . . . . **95** C2
Herongate RG17 . . . . **100** D7
Heron Ho RG14 . . . . **105** D3
Heron Ind Est RG7 . . . . . . **139** A8
Heron Island SL4. . . . . **59** D1

Heron Rd RG41 . . . . **115** E6
Heronsbrook SL5 . . . . **120** F7
Heronscourt GU18 . . . . . . **153** C8
Heron Shaw RG8 . . . . **34** C7
Herons Pl
Maidenhead SL6 . . . . **20** C3
Marlow SL7. . . . . **1** E3
Herons Way RG19. . . . . . **106** B3
Heron's Way RG40 . . . . . **116** E7
Heron Way
Aldermaston Wharf RG7 . **109** B3
Reading RG1. . . . . **85** E4
Herrick Cl GU16 . . . . **152** C3
Herries Sch SL6 . . . . **19** B8
Herrings La
Chertsey KT16. . . . . **124** A3
Windlesham GU20. . . . . . **146** D4
Herriot Ct GU46 . . . . **149** C4
Herschel Gram Sch SL1. . **42** C7
Herschel Grange RG42 . . . **91** D3
Herschel St SL1 . . . . **42** F4
Hertford Cl
Caversham RG4. . . . . **59** D6
Wokingham RG41 . . . . . . **115** E5
Hetherington Cl SL2 . . . . . **21** F2
Hetherington Rd TW17. . **125** C7
Hever Cl SL6 . . . . **39** C6
Hewett Ave RG4 . . . . **58** D4
Hewett Cl RG4. . . . . **58** D4
Hewgate Ct RG9 . . . . **15** E1
Hewlett Pl GU19 . . . . **145** E3
Hexham Cl GU47. . . . . . . **143** D2
Hexham Rd RG2 . . . . **86** C3
Heynes Gn SL6 . . . . **39** B3
Heythrop Dr RG4. . . . . . . **145** D3
Heywood Ave SL6. . . . . . . **39** A1
Heywood Court Cl SL6 . . . **39** A2
Heywood Farm Barns SL6 **39** B1
Heywood Gdns SL6 . . . . . . **39** A1
Hickox Ct HP10 . . . . **3** F7
Hibbert's Alley **12** SL4. . . . **67** D6
Hickox Ct HP10 . . . . **3** F7
Hicks La GU17 . . . . **150** B5
Hieatt Cl **21** RG1. . . . . **86** B6
Higgs La GU19 . . . . **145** D3
High Beech RG12 . . . . **118** F5
High Beeches Cl SL7. . . . . . **1** C6
Highbridge Cl RG4. . . . . . . **59** E5
Highbridge Wharf **9** RG1. **86** B7
Highbury Cres SL5 . . . . . **152** A8
Highbury Rd RG31 . . . . . . **84** B7
High Chimneys GU20. . . . **146** E7
Highclere SL5. . . . . **120** D4
Highclere Cl RG12 . . . . . . **118** E7
Highclere Ct RG22 . . . . **86** E1
Highclere Dr GU15. . . . . . **152** A7
Highcliffe Cl RG5 . . . . **60** F1
High Close Sch RG40 . . . . **116** C7
Highdown Ho RG4 . . . . **59** A6
Highdown Hill Rd RG4 . . . . **59** A6
Highdown Sch & Sixth Form
Ctr RG4. . . . . **59** A5
Higher Alham RG12 . . . . . **118** E2
Highfield
Bracknell RG12 . . . . **117** F3
Earley RG6. . . . . **87** B2
Highfield Ave RG14 . . . . . **105** A2
Highfield Cl
Englefield Green TW20 . . . **95** C2
Wokingham RG40 . . . . . . **116** B6
Highfield Ct
Burghfield Common RG7 . . **111** B3
Burnham SL2 . . . . **22** C7
Englefield Green TW20 . . . **95** D2
Twyford RG10 . . . . **61** E4
Highfield La SL6 . . . . **39** A4
Highfield Pk
Marlow SL7. . . . . **1** B1
Wargrave RG10. . . . . **36** F3
Highfield Pk (Cvn Pk)
RG2 . . . . **140** D8
Highfield Rd
Bourne End SL8. . . . . **3** B4
Chertsey KT16. . . . . **124** A1
Flackwell Heath HP10 . . . . . **3** A8
Maidenhead SL6 . . . . **39** B8
Newbury RG14. . . . . **104** F1
Purley on T RG8. . . . . **57** A5
Upper Halliford TW16 . . . **125** F4
Windsor SL4 . . . . **66** F4
High Fields SL5. . . . . **120** F4
Highfields Sch SL6. . . . . . . **39** E7
Highgate Rd RG5 . . . . **87** D5
Highgrove RG41 . . . . **88** C1
Highgrove Ave SL5. . . . . . **119** F6
Highgrove Rd SL5. . . . . **39** E8
Highgrove Pl RG1. . . . . **61** E5
Highgrove St RG1. . . . . **86** C5
Highgrove Terr RG1. . . . . . **86** B6
High Heavens Wood SL7 . . **1** C8
Highland Pk TW13 . . . . **98** F4
Highland Rd GU15 . . . . . . **151** E8
Highlands
Flackwell Heath HP10. . . . . **3** B7
Newbury RG14. . . . . **130** E7
Highlands Ave RG41 . . . . **115** C5
Highlands La SL7 . . . . **1** B1
Highlands Sch The RG31. . **57** D1
Highlea Cl RG41. . . . . **88** C1
High Mdw RG4 . . . . **58** D3
High Mdws SL6. . . . . **20** C1
Highmead Cl RG42. . . . . . . **86** E2
High Meadow Pl KT16 . . **123** F3
Highmoor Rd RG4 . . . . **58** F3
High Pines The RG42. . . . . **92** B5
High Rd SL6. . . . . **39** E5

High St Mall **1** SL6 . . . . . . **39** F7
High St
Ascot SL5. . . . . **120** A6
Ascot, Sunninghill SL5. . . **120** D4
Bagshot GU19 . . . . **145** E3
Boxford RG20 . . . . **76** B2
Bracknell RG12 . . . . **118** B7
Bray SL6 . . . . **40** E4
Burnham SL1. . . . . **21** C2
Camberley GU15 . . . . **151** D6
Chalvey SL1 . . . . **42** D3
Chieveley RG20 . . . . **51** B1
Colnbrook SL3 . . . . **69** C7
Compton RG20. . . . . **31** D4
Cookham SL6 . . . . **20** B7
Crowthorne RG45 . . . . . . **143** C4
Datchet SL3 . . . . **68** B6
East Ilsley RG20 . . . . **30** E7
Egham TW20 . . . . **96** A3
Eton SL4. . . . . **67** D8
Feltham, Lower Feltham
TW13 . . . . **98** F5
Goring RG8 . . . . **34** C6
Harlington UB3 . . . . **71** D8
Harmondsworth UB7. . . . . . **70** D8
Hungerford RG17 . . . . **100** D5
Iver SL0 . . . . **44** F7
Kintbury RG17 . . . . **102** A2
Lambourn RG17 . . . . **25** B2
Lambourn, Upper Lambourn
RG17. . . . . **24** E6
Maidenhead SL6 . . . . **39** F7
Marlow SL7 . . . . **1** E4
4 Pangbourne RG8 . . . . . **56** C6
Reading RG1 . . . . **86** B7
Sandhurst GU47 . . . . **149** F8
Sandhurst, Little Sandhurst
GU47. . . . . **143** A1
Shepperton TW17 . . . . . . **125** C3
Slough, Langley SL3. . . . . . **44** A2
Slough, Upton SL1. . . . . . . **42** F4
Sonning RG4 . . . . **60** D4
Stanwell TW19. . . . . **70** D1
Staines TW18. . . . . **96** F3
Stanwell TW19. . . . . **70** D1
Streatley RG8 . . . . **34** A6
Sunningdale SL5 . . . . **121** A4
Taplow SL6 . . . . **20** E1
Thatcham RG19 . . . . **106** D3
Theale RG7 . . . . **83** E3
Twyford RG10 . . . . **61** E4
Wargrave RG10. . . . . **36** D2
West End GU24 . . . . **153** F7
Whitchurch-on-T RG8 . . . . **56** C7
Wraysbury TW19 . . . . **68** F1
High Street Harlington
TW6 . . . . **71** D7
High Town Rd SL6 . . . . **39** F7
High Tree Dr RG6 . . . . **87** B6
Highview RG31 . . . . **84** B5
High View Cl SL7 . . . . **1** D8
Highview Cres GU15 . . . . **144** F1
High View Rd GU18 . . . . . **152** F8
HIGHWAY **143** A5
Highway RG45 . . . . **143** A5
Highway Ave SL6. . . . . **39** B3
Highwayman's Ridge
GU20. . . . . **146** B6
Highway Rd SL6 . . . . **39** B6
Highwood Cl
Newbury RG14. . . . . **105** A2
Yateley GU46. . . . . **149** D4
Highwood Prim Sch RG5 . **87** C6
Highwoods Dr SL7 . . . . **1** C7
Highworth Cotts RG26 . . **134** C1
Highworth Way RG31 . . . . **57** B2
Hilary Cl RG2 . . . . **113** D7
Hilary Ho **2** RG14. . . . . . . **105** A1
Hilborn Way RG2 . . . . **115** A1
Hilcot Rd RG30 . . . . **85** A3
Hildens Dr RG31. . . . . **84** C7
Hildesley Ct RG20. . . . . **30** E7
Hilfield GU46 . . . . **149** F5
Hilgrove Ho SL6 . . . . **39** A8
Hillary Ct TW19 . . . . **97** E7
Hillary Dr RG45 . . . . **143** B6
Hillary Rd SL3 . . . . **43** E3
Hillberry RG12 . . . . **118** C2
Hillbrow RG2 . . . . **86** E1
Hillbrow Cl SL5. . . . . **121** A4
Hill Cl
Newbury RG14. . . . . **130** D7
Wooburn Green HP10 . . . . . **3** E8
Hillcope View RG12 . . . . **118** C6
Hill Cres RG7. . . . . **138** C8
Hillcrest
Binfield RG42. . . . . **90** D3
Hampstead Norreys RG18. **52** F6
Tadley RG26. . . . . **135** B1
Hillcrest Ave SL6. . . . . **19** E6
Hillcrest Cotts RG14 . . . . **104** F5
Hillcrest Rd GU15 . . . . . . **152** B7
Hilldrop La RG17 . . . . **46** A3
Hillersdon SL2 . . . . **43** B8
Hill Farm Rd
Marlow Bottom SL7. . . . . . . **1** E6
Taplow SL6 . . . . **20** E2
Hillfoot Rd RG20 . . . . **81** A1
Hill Gdns RG8 . . . . **34** A6
HILLGREEN **50** C5
Hillgreen La RG20 . . . . **50** C5
Hillhampton SL5. . . . . **120** F2
Hill Ho SL5. . . . . **20** D1
Hillhouse La RG19 . . . . . . **133** A1
Hillingdon Ave TW19 . . . . **97** E7

Hill Lands RG10. . . . . **36** D2
Hillmead Ct SL6 . . . . **40** F8
Hill Piece OX11. . . . . **10** E7
Hill Pl SL2. . . . . **22** B5
Hill Prim Sch The RG4 . . . . **59** C5
Hill Rd
Arborfield Garrison RG2 . . **114** F1
Newbury RG14. . . . . **104** E4
Hillrise KT12. . . . . **125** F2
Hill Rise SL3. . . . . **69** A8
Hillside
Ascot SL5. . . . . **120** C4
Burghfield Common RG7. . **111** C3
East Garston RG17 . . . . . . **47** C6
Maidenhead SL6 . . . . **39** D5
Sandhurst GU15 . . . . **150** F7
Slough SL1. . . . . **42** E4
Windlesham GU20. . . . . . **122** C3
Whitchurch-on-T RG8 . . . . **56** D8
Hill Side RG1. . . . . **86** C5
Hillside Dr RG42 . . . . **90** C2
Hillside Pk
Earley RG6. . . . . **86** F1
Sunningdale SL5 . . . . **120** F1
Hillside Prim Sch RG6 . . . **113** F8
Hillside Rd
Earley RG6. . . . . **87** D3
Hungerford RG17 . . . . **100** D4
Marlow SL7. . . . . **1** E4
Hills La SL6 . . . . **19** B1
Hill St RG1 . . . . **86** B6
Hilltop Cl SL5. . . . . **120** E7
Hill Top Dr SL7 . . . . **1** B2
Hilltop Fst Sch SL4 . . . . **66** E4
Hilltop Rd
Caversham RG4. . . . . **58** D5
Earley RG6. . . . . **87** B8
Twyford RG10 . . . . **61** E7
Hilltop View GU46. . . . . . . **149** B5
Hill View RG7 . . . . **113** A1
Hillview Cl RG31. . . . . **57** B2
Hill View Mews RG30. . . . . **84** E8
Hill View Rd TW19 . . . . **68** D1
Hilmanton RG6 . . . . **113** F8
Hilperton Rd **3** SL1 . . . . . . **42** E4
Hindhay La SL6 . . . . **19** C3
Hindhead Rd RG6 . . . . **87** A3
Hind's Head **7** RG17. . . . . . **25** B2
Hinksey Cl SL3 . . . . **44** A2
Hinton Cl RG45 . . . . **143** B7
Hinton Dr RG45. . . . . **143** B7
Hintonhatch Cnr RG10 . . . **62** A2
Hinton Rd
Hurst RG10. . . . . **62** A1
Slough SL1. . . . . **41** E6
Hirstwood RG30 . . . . **57** F1
Hirtes Ave RG2 . . . . **113** E5
Hitcham Grange SL6. . . . . . **40** E8
Hitcham La SL1 . . . . **21** A1
Hitcham Rd SL1, SL6. . . . . . **41** A8
Hitchcock Cl TW17 . . . . . **124** E6
Hitherhooks Hill RG42 . . . . **90** E1
Hithermoor Rd TW19. . . . . **70** A2
Hobart Ct SL7. . . . . **2** A3
Hobbs Dr SL6. . . . . **39** B6
Hobbs End RG9 . . . . **35** B8
Hockett La SL6. . . . . **19** D4
Hockford La RG7 . . . . **134** A3
Hockham Rd RG20 . . . . **31** E5
Hockley La SL2 . . . . **23** B5
Hodcott Bglws RG20 . . . . . **30** B8
Hodgedale La RG10 . . . . . . **37** C6
Hodges La SL6 . . . . **93** A3
Hodges Cl GU19 . . . . **145** E1
Hodsoll Rd RG1 . . . . **85** F8
HOE BENHAM **102** F8
Hoe Benham La RG20. . . . **102** F7
Hogarth Ave
Ashford TW15 . . . . **98** C2
Reading RG30 . . . . **84** F5
Hogarth Cl
Sandhurst GU47 . . . . **150** E6
Slough SL1. . . . . **41** E6
Hogfair La SL1 . . . . **21** C1
Hogmoor La RG10 . . . . **61** F1
Hogoak La SL4 . . . . **122** E6
Hogwood Farm Ind Est.
RG40 . . . . **141** A5
Hogwood Ind Est RG40. . **141** A6
Hogwood La RG40 . . . . . . **141** A6
Holbeche Cl GU46 . . . . . . **149** A6
Holbeck RG12 . . . . **117** F3
Holberton Rd RG2 . . . . . . **113** C8
Holborne Cl RG14. . . . . . . **130** D5
Holborn Hill OX12 . . . . **6** D7
Holbrook Cl TW20 . . . . **96** C3
Holder Cl RG2 . . . . **113** D5
Holford Cl RG31 . . . . **84** C8
Holland Cl TW15 . . . . **97** F2
Holland La RG20 . . . . **123** F7
Holland Pines RG12 . . . . . **117** F2
Holland Rd
Marlow SL7. . . . . **1** F3
Reading RG30 . . . . **84** D7
Hollands The RG19 . . . . . **106** E3
Hollicombe Cl TW16 . . . . . **98** E1
Hollies The RG14. . . . . **130** D5
HOLLINGSWORTH **52** E5
Hollington Pl RG19 . . . . . **106** C3
Hollins Wlk RG30 . . . . **85** C6
HOLLOWAY. **122** E5
Holloway Ho TW20. . . . . . . **95** F2

Holloway La U87 . . . . .70 E8
Hollow Hill La SL0 . . . . . . .44 C5
Hollow La
Shinfield RG2. . . . . .113 E5
Virginia Water GU25 . . . . .122 C6
Holly Acre ◆ GU46 . . . . .149 D5
Holly Ave GU16 . . . . .152 B3
Hollybank GU24 . . . . .153 F6
Holly Bush RG19. . . . . . . .132 D2
Hollybush Hill SL2 . . . . . . .23 B5
Hollybush La
Burghfield Common RG7. . .110 E3
Cookham Dean SL6 . . . . . .19 B6
Iver SL0. . . . . .44 B7
Hollybush Ride RG40,
RG45. . . . . .142 C6
Hollybush Tk GU19, GU20 .145 F6
Holly Cl
Brimpton RG19 . . . . .133 B6
Englefield Green TW20 . . . .95 B2
Hollyman Common SL2. . . . .22 C8
Holly Cnr RG7 . . . . .140 B7
Hollycombe TW20. . . . . . . .95 D4
Holly Cotts GU47 . . . . . . .143 A1
Holly Cres SL4. . . . . .66 C5
Hollycroft RG19. . . . . .133 F1
Hollycroft Cl UB7 . . . . .71 A8
Hollycroft Gdns UB7 . . . . . .71 A8
HOLLY CROSS. 37 A6
Holly Ct
◆ Chertsey KT16 . . . . . . .124 A1
Crowthorne RG45 . . . . . . .142 E4
Slough SL1. . . . . .41 E6
Hollydale Cl RG2. . . . . .86 E1
Holly Dr
Maidenhead SL6 . . . . .39 F8
Windsor SL4 . . . . .67 E2
Hollyfields Cl GU15 . . . . . .151 B5
Holly Hedge Cl GU16. . . . .151 E2
Holly Hedge Rd GU16 . . . .151 E2
Holly Ho
Bracknell RG12 . . . . .118 B3
Caversham RG4. . . . . .58 E3
Hollyhook Cl RG45. . . . . . .143 A6
Holly La
Ashampstead RG8. . . . . . . .54 B6
Frilsham RG18. . . . . .80 B3
Hollyhill Cl RG6. . . . . .87 E2
Holly Rd RG5. . . . . .88 A6
Holly Ridge GU24. . . . . . .153 E6
Holly Spring Inf Sch
RG12. . . . . .118 E7
Holly Spring Jun Sch
RG12. . . . . .118 E7
Holly Spring La RG12 . . . .118 D8
Holly Way GU17. . . . . . . .150 D4
Holly Wlk SL4 . . . . .93 E4
Holmanleaze SL6 . . . . .40 A8
Holmbank Dr TW17 . . . . . .125 E5
Holmbury Ave RG45. . . . . .143 A7
Holme Cl
Brightwalton RG20 . . . . . . .49 F8
Wokingham RG41. . . . . . . .116 B7
Holton Heath ◆ RG12. . . .118 F5
Holt Rd RG17. . . . . .102 B2
Holt Sch The RG41. . . . . . .116 B7
Holtspur Ave HP10. . . . . . . .3 F7
Holtspur La HP10 . . . . .3 F6
HOLT THE 73 E8
Holt The RG6. . . . . .57 D4
HOLTWOOD. 129 B5
Holtwood Rd RG20. . . . . . .129 B6
Holybrook Cres RG30. . . . . .85 A4
Holybrook Rd RG1. . . . . . . .85 F5
Holy Brook Sch The RG30 .85 A4
Holy Family RC Prim Sch
SL3. . . . . .43 F1
Holyhead Mews SL1 . . . . . .41 D7
HOLYPORT 65 A7
Holyport CE Prim Sch
SL6. . . . . .65 B8
Holyport Manor Sch SL6. . .64 E6
Holyport Rd SL6 . . . . .40 B1
Holyport St SL6. . . . . .65 A8
Holyrood Cl RG4. . . . . .59 D6
Holy Trinity CE Prim Sch
Cookham SL6. . . . . .20 B7
Sunningdale SL5 . . . . .121 A3
Holy Trinity CE Sch SL7 . . . .1 D2
Holywell Cl RG19 . . . . .97 E7
Holywell Ct RG19 . . . . . . .106 D3
Holywell Way TW19 . . . . . .97 E7
Hombrook Dr RG42 . . . . . .117 E8
Hombrook Ho RG42. . . . . .117 E8
Home Cl GU25 . . . . .122 D3

Home Croft RG31. . . . . . . .57 B1
Home Ct ◆ RG1 . . . . .86 B6
Home Farm
Bagshot GU19 . . . . .145 D4
Welford RG20 . . . . .75 F6
Home Farm Barns RG14. . .77 F4
Home Farm Cl
Reading RG2 . . . . .86 C4
Upper Halliford TW17 . . . .125 E5
Home Farm Cotts
Sindlesham RG41. . . . . . . .115 B7
Yattendon RG18. . . . . .53 E1
Home Farm Way SL3. . . . . .23 C4
Homefield Way RG17. . . . .100 C5
Homelands Way RG9. . . . . .15 D1
Home Mdw SL2. . . . . .22 C3
Home Mead Cl RG4 . . . . . .130 E8
Home Meadow Dr HP10. . . .3 B7
Home Park Rd GU46 . . . . .149 D6
Homers Rd SL4. . . . . .66 D6
Homeside Cl SL6. . . . . .19 E2
Homestead Rd
Maidenhead SL6 . . . . .39 D4
Staines TW18. . . . . .97 B2
Homestead The RG9 . . . . . .35 B1
Homewaters Ave TW16. . .125 F8
Homewood SL3. . . . . .43 D7
Home Wood SL7. . . . . .17 F6
Hone Hill GU47 . . . . .150 B8
Honesty Bottom RG20. . . . .28 D2
Honeybottom Rd RG26. . . .135 B1
Honey End La RG30 . . . . . .85 A6
Honeyfields RG17 . . . . . . .100 D5
Honey Hill
Lambourn RG17. . . . . .25 B3
Wokingham RG40. . . . . . . .117 A1
Honeyhill Rd RG42. . . . . . .118 A8
Honey La SL6. . . . . .17 E2
Honey Meadow Cl RG4. . . .59 E2
Honeysuckle Cl
Crowthorne RG45 . . . . . . .143 A7
Iver SL0. . . . . .44 C7
Yateley GU46. . . . . .149 A6
Honeysuckle Ct SL3. . . . . . .69 C7
Honister Wlk GU15 . . . . . .152 D4
Honiton Rd RG2 . . . . .86 C2
Honnor Rd TW18. . . . . .97 D1
Hook Cl RG19. . . . . .131 B7
Hook End La RG8 . . . . .34 B2
Hook La GU24 . . . . .153 C6
Hook Mill La GU18 . . . . . .146 D2
Hookstone La GU24. . . . . .153 F8
Hooper Ho TW15. . . . . .97 E5
Hoops Way RG2 . . . . .112 F8
Hope Ave RG12 . . . . .118 E2
Hope Cotts RG42 . . . . .92 A5
Hope Fountain GU15. . . . .151 F4
Hopeman Cl GU47 . . . . . .150 D7
Hop Gdns
Henley-on-T RG9 . . . . .15 D2
Kintbury RG17 . . . . .102 B2
Hopper Vale RG12. . . . . . .118 A3
Hopwood Cl RG14 . . . . . . .105 D4
Horatio Ave RG42 . . . . . . .118 E8
Horewood Rd RG12. . . . . .118 B3
Horizon West Ind Est
RG14 . . . . .105 D3
Horner Cl GU47 . . . . .143 D1
Hornbeam Cl
Purley on T RG8. . . . . .57 C5
Sandhurst GU47 . . . . .143 D1
Wokingham RG41. . . . . . . .115 D3
Hornbeam Copse RG42. . . .119 A8
Hornbeam Dr RG40. . . . . . .87 D1
Hornbeam Gdns ◆ SL1. . . .43 A1
Hornbeam Pightle RG7. . . .111 B3
Hornbeams RG7 . . . . .139 C6
Hornby Ave RG12 . . . . . . .118 D2
HORNCASTLE. 84 E5
Horndean Rd RG12 . . . . . .118 F3
Horne Rd
Littleton TW17 . . . . .125 A5
Thatcham RG19 . . . . .106 E2
Hornsea Cl RG30. . . . . .57 E1
Horn St RG20. . . . . .31 E5
Horris Hill Sch RG20. . . . . .130 E3
Horrocks Ho RG30 . . . . . . .84 F5
Horsebrass Dr GU19 . . . . .145 E2
Horse Cl The RG4 . . . . .59 C4
Horsecroft Way RG31. . . . . .57 B4
Horse Gate Ride SL5. . . . . .120 A3
Horseguards Dr SL6 . . . . . .40 B7
Horse Guards Way RG19 . .106 D1
Horsell Ct KT16. . . . . .124 B2
HORSEMOOR. 78 B8
Horsemoor Cl SL3. . . . . . . .44 A2
Horseshoe Cl GU15 . . . . . .151 F8
Horseshoe Cloisters ◆
SL4. . . . . .67 D6
Horseshoe Cres
Burghfield Common RG7. . .111 B3
Camberley GU15 . . . . .151 F8
Horseshoe End RG14. . . . . .131 B7
Horseshoe Hill SL1 . . . . . . .22 D8
Horseshoe Pk RG8. . . . . . . .56 D5
Horseshoe Rd RG8 . . . . . . .56 D5
Horsham Rd
East Bedfont TW14 . . . . . . .71 C1
Sandhurst GU47 . . . . .143 D1
Horsham Reach SL6. . . . . . .20 C2
Horsnape Gdns RG42 . . . . .90 B2
Horsnele La RG42. . . . . . . .118 B8
HORTON. 69 A4
Horton Cl SL6. . . . . .20 C1
Horton Depot SL3 . . . . . . .69 C4
Horton Gdns SL3. . . . . .68 F4
Horton Grange SL6. . . . . . .20 C1

Horton Rd
Datchet SL3. . . . . .68 D6
Horton SL3. . . . . .69 A6
Poyle SL3, TW19 . . . . .69 E4
Stanwell TW19. . . . . .70 A2
Horton Trad Est SL3. . . . . .69 C4
Hose Hill RG7, RG30 . . . . .111 A7
Hosier St RG1. . . . . .86 A7
Hoskins Place Ind Est
GU15 . . . . .151 B3
Houlton Ct GU19. . . . . . . .145 F2
Houston Ct ◆ SL4. . . . . . .67 C5
Houston Way RG45 . . . . . .142 D5
Howard Ave SL2 . . . . .42 E8
Howard Cl
Ashford TW16 . . . . .98 F2
Bracknell RG12 . . . . .118 A4
Howard Ct SL8 . . . . .3 A3
Howard Mews SL3 . . . . . . .69 B8
Howard Rd
Newbury RG14. . . . . .105 A1
Wokingham RG40. . . . . . . .116 C5
Howards Gate SL2 . . . . . . .22 C2
Howard St ◆ RG1. . . . . . . .85 F7
Howard Villas RG2 . . . . . . .113 C7
Howarth Ct RG14 . . . . . . .131 B8
Howarth Rd SL6 . . . . .40 A6
Howe La RG42 . . . . .63 F2
Howell Cl
Arborfield Garrison RG2 . . .140 E8
Bracknell RG42 . . . . .91 C2
Howgate Dr RG8. . . . . .34 C7
How Lane Farm SL6 . . . . . .64 A5
Howorth Ave SL3 . . . . .43 A3
Howth Dr RG5. . . . . .87 D7
Hoylake Cl SL1. . . . . .41 E4
Hubbard Cl RG10. . . . . .61 F2
Hubberholme RG12 . . . . . .118 A6
Hubert Rd SL3. . . . . .43 D3
Hub The ◆ SL6. . . . . .40 A7
Huckleberry Cl SL6 . . . . . . .41 A6
Huddington Glade GU46. . .149 A5
Huddlestone Ho SL3 . . . . .120 D4
Hudson Pl ◆ SL3 . . . . .43 F1
Hudson Rd
Harlington UB7 . . . . .71 D8
Woodley RG5 . . . . .87 F6
Hughenden Cl SL6. . . . . . . .39 C6
Hughenden Rd SL1 . . . . . . .42 D7
Hughes Rd
Ashford TW15 . . . . .98 C2
Wokingham RG40. . . . . . . .116 F2
Hugh Fraser Dr RG31 . . . . .84 C6
Hulbert Gate RG40. . . . . . .116 B6
Hull Cl SL1. . . . . .42 C4
Humber Cl
Thatcham RG18 . . . . .106 B5
Wokingham RG41 . . . . . . .115 E7
Humber Way
Sandhurst GU47 . . . . .150 D8
Slough SL3. . . . . .44 A2
Hummer Rd RG20 . . . . .31 E6
Humphrey's La RG17. . . . . .47 C6
Humphries Yd RG12. . . . . .118 C5
HUNGERFORD
100 E4
Waltham St Lawrence 62 E2
Hungerford Ave SL2 . . . . . .22 E8
Hungerford Cl GU47 . . . . .150 C8
Hungerford Dr
Maidenhead SL6 . . . . .19 E3
Reading RG1 . . . . .85 E5
HUNGERFORD GREEN 32 F4
Hungerford Hill
East Garston RG17 . . . . . . .47 F1
Lambourn RG17 . . . . .25 A2
Hungerford La
Kintbury RG17 . . . . .101 E3
Stanford Dingley RG7 . . . . .81 F1
Waltham St L RG10 . . . . . . .62 E2
HUNGERFORD
NEWTOWN. 74 A3
Hungerford Prim Sch
RG17 . . . . .100 D5
Hungerford Sta RG17. . . . .100 E6
Hungerford Trad Est
RG17 . . . . .100 C5
Hunsford Lodge SL4 . . . . . .67 A4
Hunstanton Cl SL3. . . . . . . .69 C7
Huntercombe Cl SL6. . . . . .41 C7
Huntercombe Hosp The
SL6. . . . . .41 C6
Huntercombe La N SL6. . . .41 C7
Huntercombe La S SL6. . . .41 C6
Huntercombe Spur SL1. . . .41 C6
Hunter Cl SL1 . . . . .41 A6
Hunters Chase RG4. . . . . . .58 F5
Hunters Ct ◆ RG41. . . . . .88 E2
Hunter's Ct RG5 . . . . .87 E6
Hunter's Hill RG7. . . . . . . .110 F3
Hunters Mdw RG17 . . . . . .48 A3
Hunters Mews SL4. . . . . . . .67 C6
Hunters Way
Shinfield RG7. . . . . .113 B1
Slough SL1. . . . . .41 E4
Hunters Wharf ◆ RG1. . . .86 A6
Huntingdon Cl RG6. . . . . . .87 E2
Huntingdon Gdns RG1 . . . .105 C5
Huntingdonshire Cl
RG41. . . . . .115 D6
Huntingfield Way TW20. . . .96 D2
Huntley Cl TW19 . . . . .70 E1
Huntley Ct RG1. . . . . .86 E6
Huntley Rd SL3 . . . . .43 D8
Huntley The RG20. . . . . . . .85 D6
Hunts Cotts RG14. . . . . . . .104 E6
HUNT'S GREEN
Henley-on-Thames. 35 B6

HUNT'S GREEN *continued*
Newbury 76 E1
Huntsgreen Ct RG12 . . . . .118 C7
Hunt's La SL6 . . . . .20 E3
Huntsmans Mdw SL5. . . . . .119 F8
Huntsmoor Rd RG26 . . . . .135 A1
Huntswood La SL1, SL6. . . .20 F4
Hurford Dr RG19. . . . . . . .106 F3
HURLEY 17 F4
Hurley Ct RG12 . . . . .118 E5
Hurley High St SL6 . . . . . . .17 F4
Hurley La SL6 . . . . .18 B3
Hurley Riverside Pk Cvn Site
SL6. . . . . .17 D4
Hurricane Way
Slough SL3. . . . . .44 B1
Woodley RG5. . . . . .88 B8
Hursley Cl RG30 . . . . .84 E7
HURST 88 F7
Hurst Com Coll The
RG26 . . . . .134 D1
Hurstdene Ave TW18 . . . . .97 B2
Hurstfield Dr SL6. . . . . .41 B7
Hurst Gr KT12 . . . . .125 F1
Hurst La TW20. . . . . .123 A7
Hurst Lodge Sch SL5 . . . . .120 B1
Hurst Park Rd RG10. . . . . . .61 E2
Hurst Rd
Slough SL1. . . . . .41 D8
Twyford RG10 . . . . .61 E3
Hurst Way RG2 . . . . .112 F8
Hurstwood SL5 . . . . .120 A3
Hurworth Ave SL3 . . . . .43 C3
Huscarle Way RG31. . . . . . .57 C4
Huson Rd RG42 . . . . .91 C2
Hussars Dr RG19. . . . . . . .106 D1
Hutsons Cl RG40 . . . . .116 D8
Hutton Cl
Earley RG6. . . . . .87 A2
Newbury RG14. . . . . .105 B4
Windlesham GU20 . . . . . . .146 D2
Huxley Cl SL2. . . . . .23 B1
Hyde Cl TW15. . . . . .98 E2
HYDE END 133 E4
Hyde End La
Brimpton RG7 . . . . .133 D5
Shinfield RG7 . . . . .113 C3
Hyde End Rd RG7 . . . . . . .113 D2
Hyde Gn SL7 . . . . .1 F1
Hyde La RG20 . . . . .132 A1
Hydes The RG31 . . . . .57 C4
Hyde Terr TW15 . . . . .98 E2
Hydro Ho KT16 . . . . .124 C1
Hyland Ho ◆ SL8. . . . . .3 B3
Hylle Cl SL4 . . . . .66 C6
Hyperion Way RG2 . . . . . . .86 B3
Hythe Cl RG12 . . . . .118 E4
HYTHE END 96 B6
Hythe End Rd TW19 . . . . . .96 A5
Hythe Field Ave TW20 . . . . .96 D2
Hythe Park Rd TW20. . . . . .96 D2
Hythe Rd TW18 . . . . .96 D3
Hythe The TW18 . . . . .96 E3

I

Ian Mikardo Way RG4. . . . .59 D2
Iberian Way GU15. . . . . . . .152 B6
Ibotson Ct SL3. . . . . .69 E6
Ibstock Cl RG30. . . . . .85 B7
Ibstone Ave RG4 . . . . .59 E5
Icarus Ct ◆ RG1. . . . . .86 D7
Icknield Cotts RG8. . . . . . . .34 A6
Icknield Pl RG8. . . . . .34 A6
Icknield Rd RG8 . . . . .34 A6
Icon Ho ◆ RG1 . . . . .86 A8
Iden Ct RG14. . . . . .105 B4
Iffley Ct ◆ RG1 . . . . .86 A8
Ilbury Cl RG2 . . . . .113 E5
Ilchester Cl SL6. . . . . .39 C5
Ilchester Ct ◆ RG14 . . . . .105 A2
Ilchester Mews RG4 . . . . . .59 E6
Ilex Cl
Englefield Green TW20 . . . .95 B1
Pamber Heath RG26 . . . . .135 E1
Yateley GU46. . . . . .149 B6
Ilfracombe Way RG6 . . . . . .87 E3
Iliffe Cl ◆ RG1 . . . . .86 B6
Ilkley Rd RG4. . . . . .59 B4
Ilkley Way RG19 . . . . .106 C2
Il-libro Ct ◆ RG1 . . . . .86 B7
Illingworth SL4 . . . . .66 E4
Illingworth Ave RG4. . . . . . .59 E5
Illingworth Gr RG12. . . . . .118 E8
Ilsley Rd RG20 . . . . .31 D4
Imperial Ct
Henley-on-T RG9 . . . . .15 E1
◆ Newbury RG14 . . . . . . .104 F2
Windsor SL4 . . . . .67 A4
Imperial Ho GU25. . . . . . . .122 E4
Imperial Rd
East Bedfont TW14 . . . . . . .98 E8
Windsor SL4 . . . . .67 A4
Imperial Way
Reading RG2 . . . . .113 A7
Thatcham RG19 . . . . .106 E2
Impstone Rd RG26 . . . . . . .135 F1
Inch's Yd ◆ RG14. . . . . . .105 A2
Inchwood RG12. . . . . .118 C1
India Rd SL1. . . . . .42 E4
Indigo Apartments ◆
RG1. . . . . .86 B6
Indigo Ct ◆ TW13 . . . . . . .98 F5
Infantry Dr ◆ RG14. . . . . .106 E2

Ingle Dell GU15. . . . . .151 D4
Ingleglen SL2. . . . . .22 B7
Ingle Glen RG40 . . . . .142 A7
Ingles Edge RG17 . . . . . . .127 E4
Ingleside SL3. . . . . .69 F6
Ingleton RG12 . . . . .118 A6
Inglewood Ave GU15 . . . . .152 D5
Inglewood Ct RG30 . . . . . . .85 C6
Inglewood Rd RG17. . . . . .101 E2
Ingoldsby Copse RG14 . . . .105 E5
Inhurst La RG26 . . . . .134 C1
Inhurst Way RG26. . . . . . . .134 F1
Inkerman Rd SL4 . . . . .41 F2
INKPEN 127 D5
Inkpen Cl RG30. . . . . .85 A4
Inkpen Common Nature
Reserve* RG17 . . . . .128 A5
Inkpen Prim Sch RG17 . . . .127 D6
Inkpen Rd
Hungerford RG17 . . . . . . .100 F3
Kintbury RG17 . . . . .102 A1
Inner Ring E TW6. . . . . . . .71 B4
Inner Ring W TW6 . . . . . . .71 A4
Innings La
White Waltham SL6. . . . . . .63 D7
Winkfield RG12 . . . . .118 E8
Inniscrown Ho SL3. . . . . . . .68 B7
Institute Rd
Marlow SL7 . . . . .1 E1
Taplow SL6. . . . . .40 F7
Instow Rd RG6. . . . . .87 B2
International Way TW16. . . .125 E8
In The Ray SL6. . . . . .40 B8
Invergordon Cl RG31. . . . . .84 E4
Inverness Way GU47 . . . . .150 D7
Invicta Cl TW14 . . . . .98 F7
Inwood Cl SL6 . . . . .19 B6
Iona Cres SL1 . . . . .41 A6
IO Trade Ctr RG30. . . . . . . .58 A1
Ipswich Rd SL1 . . . . .42 A7
Iris Ct RG30 . . . . .84 E7
Irish Hill Rd RG17. . . . . . . .102 B2
Irvine Pl GU25 . . . . .122 E4
Irvine Way RG6 . . . . .114 C8
Irving Ho SL4 . . . . .66 E5
Irwin Ct TW15. . . . . .97 D5
Isaac Newton Rd RG2. . . . .115 A1
Isbury Almshouses RG17 . . .25 B3
Isis Cl RG41 . . . . .88 B1
Isis Ct ◆ SL3. . . . . .59 A1
Isis Ho KT16. . . . . .124 C2
Isis Way
Bourne End SL8. . . . . .3 B4
Sandhurst GU47 . . . . .150 D8
Island Cl TW18. . . . . .96 E4
Island Farm Rd RG7 . . . . . .110 D2
Island Rd RG2 . . . . .85 F2
Islandstone La RG10 . . . . . .89 B6
Island The TW19 . . . . .96 A5
Islet Park Dr SL6 . . . . .20 C3
Islet Park Ho SL6 . . . . .20 C3
Islet Pk SL6. . . . . .20 C3
Isobel Ho ◆ TW16 . . . . . . .98 F1
Ivanhoe Rd RG40 . . . . .141 A6
Iveagh Ct RG12. . . . . .118 C4
IVER 44 F7
Iverdale Cl SL0 . . . . .44 C6
IVER HEATH. 23 F3
Iver La SL0. . . . . .44 F7
Iver Lodge SL0 . . . . .44 F4
Iverna Gdns TW14 . . . . . . .71 D2
Iver Sta SL0. . . . . .44 F4
Iver Village Inf Sch
SL0. . . . . .44 F7
Iver Village Jun Sch The
SL0. . . . . .44 F7
Ives Cl GU46. . . . . .149 B7
Ives Rd SL3. . . . . .43 C6
Ivybank RG31. . . . . .57 C1
Ivy Cl SL6 . . . . .64 A7
Ivy Cres SL1. . . . . .41 F6
Ivydene Rd RG30. . . . . .58 C1
Ivy Dr GU18 . . . . .153 A7

J

Jack Ct GU17. . . . . .150 E4
Jack Price Ct ◆ RG1 . . . . . .86 B5
Jackson Cl RG12 . . . . .118 B4
Jackson Ind Est SL8 . . . . . . .3 B2
Jack St RG14 . . . . .105 A3
Jacob Cl
Bracknell RG42 . . . . .117 D7
Windsor SL4 . . . . .66 E6
Jacob Rd GU15 . . . . .151 A8
Jago Ct RG14. . . . . .131 A8
Jakes Ho SL6. . . . . .40 A8
James Butcher Dr RG7. . . . .83 F3
James Cl RG14 . . . . .131 A8
James Ct RG20. . . . . .85 D5
James Elliman Sch SL2 . . . .42 C6
James Mdw SL3. . . . . .43 E2
James St GU15. . . . . .151 B2
James's La RG7, RG30. . . . .111 B2
James St
Reading RG1 . . . . .85 F7
Windsor SL4 . . . . .67 C6
James Watt Rd
Arborfield Garrison RG2 . . .140 C7
Arborfield Garrison RG2 . . .141 A8
James Way GU15 . . . . .151 B2

Jamnagar Cl TW18 . . . .**96** F2
Janson Ct RG1 . . . .**85** F6
Japonica Cl RG41 . . . . **115** D4
Jaques's La RG7 . . . . **111** A6
Jardine Cotts SL2 . . . .**23** A8
Jarratt Ho SL4 . . . .**67** B4
Jarry Ct SL7 . . . .**1** F3
Jarvis Dr RG10 . . . .**61** D6
Jasmine Cl RG41 . . . . **115** D7
Jasmine Way RG19 . . . . . .**133** B6
Jay Cl RG6 . . . .**87** B1
Jays Cl SL5 . . . .**120** D5
Jays Nest Cl GU17 . . . .**150** D4
Jayworth Ho RG1 . . . .**86** E8
Jealott's Hill RG42 . . . .**91** B7
Jedburgh Cl RG19 . . . .**106** F3
Jefferson Cl
  Caversham RG4 . . . .**59** C7
  Slough SL3 . . . .**44** A2
Jeffery Cl RG40 . . . .**116** D6
Jeffrey Pl 5 RG1 . . . .**86** A8
Jeffries Ct SL8 . . . .**3** B2
Jellicoe Cl SL1 . . . .**42** B4
Jenkins Cl RG30 . . . .**85** C6
Jenkins Ct GU19 . . . .**145** D2
Jenkins' Hill London Rd
  GU19 . . . .**145** D2
Jenner Wlk RG31 . . . .**84** A7
Jennery La SL1 . . . .**21** C2
Jennetts Cl RG7 . . . .**81** E3
JENNETTS HILL **81** E3
Jennings Field HP10 . . . .**3** D7
Jenny's Wlk GU46 . . . .**149** E6
Jerome Cl SL7 . . . .**1** F4
Jerome Cnr RG45 . . . .**143** C3
Jerome Rd RG5 . . . .**87** E6
Jerrymoor Hill RG40 . . . . .**141** F8
Jersey Dr RG41 . . . .**88** A2
Jersey Pl SL5 . . . .**120** D3
Jesmond Dene RG14 . . . .**104** F4
Jesse Cl GU46 . . . .**149** F5
Jesse Terr RG1 . . . .**85** F7
Jessiman Terr TW17 . . . . .**125** A4
Jesus Hospital SL6 . . . .**40** C3
Jetty Ho KT16 . . . .**124** C2
Jevington RG12 . . . .**118** C1
Jig's La N RG42 . . . .**91** E2
Jig's La S
  Bracknell RG42 . . . .**91** E1
  Winkfield RG42 . . . .**118** E8
Job's La SL6 . . . .**19** B8
Jock's La RG42 . . . .**90** F1
Joel Cl RG6 . . . .**87** A3
Johannes Ct 5 RG30 . . . . .**85** D6
John Balliol Ct 24 RG1 . . . .**86** D7
John Boys Ho RG14 . . . . . .**130** C6
John Childs Cl RG14 . . . . .**105** A1
John F Kennedy Meml*
  TW20 . . . .**95** D6
John Hunt Cl RG14 . . . .**105** E2
John Kaye Ct TW17 . . . . . .**125** A4
John Kimber's Almshouses
  1 RG14 . . . .**104** F2
John Madejski Acad
  RG2 . . . .**86** C1
John Nike Way RG12 . . . . .**117** C7
John Norgate Ho RG14 . .**105** E3
John O'Gaunt Com Tech Coll
  RG17 . . . .**100** D3
John Pl RG42 . . . .**91** E1
John Rankin Inf Sch
  RG14 . . . .**130** D8
John Rankin Jun Sch
  RG14 . . . .**130** D8
Johns Cl TW15 . . . .**98** C4
Johnson Dr RG40 . . . .**142** B7
Johnsons La RG18 . . . .**106** C8
Jonathan Ct SL6 . . . .**39** E7
Jonathan Hill RG20 . . . . .**131** B3
Jones Cnr SL5 . . . .**119** E7
Jones Dr RG19 . . . .**131** F5
Jordan Cl
  Caversham RG4 . . . .**59** E5
  Shinfield RG7 . . . .**113** D1
Jordans Cl TW19 . . . .**97** C8
Jordan's La RG7 . . . .**110** F2
Joseph Ct RG42 . . . .**91** E2
Joseph Ho 4 RG30 . . . .**85** E6
Jouldings La RG7 . . . .**140** D4
Jourdelay's Pas SL4 . . . . . .**67** D8
Journeys End SL2 . . . .**42** E8
Joviel Ho TW18 . . . .**97** A1
Jubilee Ave
  North Ascot SL5 . . . .**119** E8
  Wokingham RG41 . . . .**116** B7
Jubilee Cl
  North Ascot SL5 . . . .**119** E8
  Pamber Heath RG26 . . . . . .**135** E1
  Stanwell TW19 . . . .**97** C8
  Woodley RG5 . . . .**87** A6
Jubilee Cotts
  Riseley RG7 . . . .**139** C3
  Slough SL3 . . . .**44** B1
Jubilee Ct
  Bracknell RG12 . . . .**118** C6
  9 Staines TW18 . . . .**97** A4
  Thatcham RG19 . . . .**106** A3
Jubilee Rd
  Finchampstead RG40 . . . . .**141** F3
  Littlewick Green SL6 . . . .**38** B5
  Newbury RG14 . . . .**105** B2
  Reading RG6 . . . .**87** A6
Jubilee Sq RG1 . . . .**86** B6
Jubilee Way
  Datchet SL3 . . . .**68** C7

Jubilee Way continued
  East Bedfont TW14 . . . .**98** F7
Juliet Gdns RG42 . . . .**118** F8
Julius Hill RG42 . . . .**118** F8
Julkes La RG2 . . . .**114** E7
Junction Rd
  Ashford TW15 . . . .**98** D3
  Lightwater GU18 . . . .**146** B1
  Reading RG1 . . . .**86** E6
Junction Terr RG14 . . . . . .**105** C2
Juniper RG12 . . . .**118** C1
Juniper Ct
  Flackwell Heath HP10 . . . .**3** C7
  Slough, Cippenham SL1 . . . .**41** E6
  Slough, Upton SL1 . . . .**43** A4
Juniper Dr SL6 . . . .**40** B8
Juniper Gdns TW16 . . . .**98** F2
Juniper Hill Sch HP10 . . . . . .**3** B7
Juniper La HP10 . . . .**3** D7
Juniper Pl RG19 . . . .**133** B6
Juniper Rd SL7 . . . .**1** D5
Junipers The RG41 . . . .**115** D4
Juniper Way RG31 . . . .**57** D2
Jupiter Ho RG7 . . . .**134** E2
Jupiter Way RG41 . . . .**115** F6
Justice Cl RG19 . . . .**106** F2
Jutland Cl RG41 . . . .**115** E6
Jutland Ho SL4 . . . .**66** F5
Jutland Pl TW20 . . . .**96** C3

K

Katesgrove La RG1 . . . .**86** A6
Katesgrove Prim Sch RG1 .**86** A6
Katherine Ct 2 GU15 . . . .**151** D5
Kathleen Sanders Ct RG7 .**83** E4
Kaynes Pk SL5 . . . .**119** E8
Kaywood Cl SL3 . . . .**43** C3
Keane Cl RG5 . . . .**87** E8
Kearsley Rd RG30 . . . .**85** C6
Keates Gn RG42 . . . .**118** B8
Keats Cl RG5 . . . .**87** E4
Keats La SL4 . . . .**67** C8
Keats Rd RG5 . . . .**87** E4
Keats Way
  Crowthorne RG45 . . . .**143** B6
  Yateley GU46 . . . .**149** B4
Keble Rd SL6 . . . .**39** E8
Keble Way GU47 . . . .**143** E2
Keeble Ho RG41 . . . .**116** A6
Keel KT16 . . . .**124** C2
Keel Dr SL1 . . . .**42** C4
Keeler Cl SL4 . . . .**66** E4
Keepers Coombe RG12 . . .**118** D3
Keepers Farm Cl SL4 . . . . . .**66** E5
Keepers Terr GU25 . . . .**122** A4
Keepers Wlk GU25 . . . .**122** D4
Keephatch Ho RG40 . . . . . .**116** F7
Keep Hatch Prim Sch
  RG40 . . . .**116** D7
Keephatch Rd RG40 . . . . . .**116** F7
Keighley Cl RG19 . . . .**106** C2
Kelburne Cl RG41 . . . .**88** C3
Keldholme RG12 . . . .**118** A6
Kellie Ho SL5 . . . .**121** A1
Kelly Cl TW17 . . . .**125** E7
Kelmscott Cl RG4 . . . .**58** F3
Kelpatrick Rd SL1 . . . .**41** E7
Kelsall Pl SL5 . . . .**120** B2
Kelsey Ave RG40 . . . .**141** E6
Kelsey Gr GU46 . . . .**149** E5
Kelso Mews RG4 . . . .**59** E6
Kelton Cl RG6 . . . .**87** E2
Kelvedon Way RG4 . . . .**58** A5
Kelvin Cl RG2 . . . .**140** E7
Kelvin Gate RG12 . . . .**118** D7
Kelvin Rd RG14 . . . .**105** B4
Kemble Ct RG31 . . . .**84** D4
Kemerton Cl RG31 . . . .**84** D4
Kemp Ct GU19 . . . .**145** F2
Kempe Cl SL3 . . . .**44** A2
Kempton Cl RG14 . . . .**105** C1
Kemsley Chase SL2 . . . .**22** C4
Kenavon Dr RG1 . . . .**86** C8
Kendal Ave
  Caversham RG4 . . . .**59** E5
  Shinfield RG2 . . . .**113** E6
Kendal Cl
  East Bedfont TW14 . . . .**98** F7
  Slough SL2 . . . .**43** A6
  Thatcham RG18 . . . .**106** C4
Kendal Dr SL2 . . . .**43** A6
Kendal Gr GU15 . . . .**152** D4
Kendall Ct Bsns Pk GU15 .**150** F4
Kendall Pl SL6 . . . .**39** C4
Kendrick Cl RG40 . . . .**116** C5
Kendrick Ct 5 RG1 . . . .**86** C6
Kendrick Girls' Gram Sch
  RG1 . . . .**86** C7
Kendrick Rd
  Newbury RG14 . . . .**130** D5
  Reading RG1 . . . .**86** D5
  Slough SL3 . . . .**43** B3
Kenilworth Ave
  Bracknell RG12 . . . .**118** D8
  Reading RG30 . . . .**85** D7
Kenilworth Cl SL1 . . . .**42** F3
Kenilworth Gdns TW18 . . .**97** C3
Kenilworth Rd TW15 . . . . . .**97** D5
Kenley Ho RG12 . . . .**118** D6
Kennedy Cl SL1 . . . .**41** E5
Kennealy Cl 11 SL4 . . . .**66** C5
Kennealy Pl 6 SL4 . . . .**66** C5
Kennealy Row 5 SL4 . . . . . .**66** C5
Kennealy Wlk 10 SL4 . . . . .**66** C5

Kennedy Cl
  Farnham Common SL2 . . . . . .**22** C6
  Maidenhead SL6 . . . .**39** C6
  Marlow SL7 . . . .**1** E3
  Newbury RG14 . . . .**130** D6
Kennedy Ct TW15 . . . .**98** C3
Kennedy Dr RG8 . . . .**56** E5
Kennedy Gdns RG6 . . . .**87** B3
Kennedy Ho SL1 . . . .**41** D5
Kennedy Mdw RG17 . . . . . .**100** C4
Kennel Ave SL5 . . . .**119** F8
Kennel Cl SL5 . . . .**119** E8
Kennel Gn SL5 . . . .**119** E8
Kennel La
  Bracknell RG42 . . . .**91** B1
  Cookham Dean SL6 . . . .**19** C7
  Windlesham GU20 . . . .**146** C5
Kennel Lane Sch RG42 . . . .**91** B2
Kennel Ride SL5 . . . .**92** F1
Kennel Wood SL5 . . . .**119** F8
Kennet Cl RG19 . . . .**106** E3
Kennet Cotts RG30 . . . .**85** A1
Kennet Ct
  Hungerford RG17 . . . .**100** E7
  1 Newbury RG14 . . . .**105** A1
  Wokingham RG41 . . . .**115** F6
  Kennet Ctr The **12** RG14 .**105** A2
  4 Newbury RG14 . . . .**105** A1
Kennet Pl
  Burghfield Common RG7 . . .**111** B3
  Chilton Foliat RG17 . . . .**73** A1
  4 Newbury RG14 . . . .**105** B4
Kennet Rd
  Bourne End SL8 . . . .**3** B4
  Kintbury RG17 . . . .**102** B2
  Maidenhead SL6 . . . .**39** F8
  Newbury RG14 . . . .**104** F2
  Kennet Sch RG19 . . . .**106** E3
Kennet Side
  Newbury RG14 . . . .**105** C3
  9 Reading RG1 . . . .**86** C7
Kennett Rd SL3 . . . .**44** B7
Kennet Rd SL3 . . . .**44** B7
Kennet Valley Prim Sch
  RG31 . . . .**84** F4
Kennet Way RG17 . . . .**100** D7
Kenner Weir Bsns Pk RG7 .**83** F2
Kennet Wlk RG1 . . . .**86** D8
Kensington Rd RG6 . . . .**87** B1
Kensington Rd RG30 . . . .**85** D7
Kent Ave SL1 . . . .**42** C8
Kent Cl
  Staines TW18 . . . .**97** D2
  Wokingham RG41 . . . .**115** D5
Kent Cotts RG7 . . . .**139** C3
Kent Folly RG42 . . . .**91** F2
Kentigern Dr RG45 . . . .**143** E5
Kent Lodge 6 SL6 . . . .**39** F6
Kenton Cl
  Bracknell RG12 . . . .**118** D7
  Frimley GU16 . . . .**151** F1
Kenton Rd RG6 . . . .**87** C4
Kentons La SL4 . . . .**66** F5
Kenton's La RG10 . . . .**36** D7
Kent Rd
  Reading RG30 . . . .**85** D7
  Windlesham GU20 . . . .**146** D5
Kent Way SL6 . . . .**39** C4
Kentwood Cl RG30 . . . .**57** E1
Kentwood Farm RG40 . . . .**116** D8
Kentwood Hill RG31 . . . .**57** E1
Kenwood Cl
  Harmondsworth UB7 . . . .**71** A8
  Maidenhead SL6 . . . .**39** B4
Kenworth Gr GU18 . . . .**146** A1
Keppel Spur SL4 . . . .**95** B8
Keppel St SL4 . . . .**67** D5
Kepple Pl GU19 . . . .**145** F3
Kernham Dr RG31 . . . .**57** C4
Kerria Way GU24 . . . .**153** F6
Kerris Way RG6 . . . .**87** B1
Kersey Cres RG14 . . . .**104** F5
Kershope Ct RG2 . . . .**86** C3
Kersten Cl RG14 . . . .**131** C8
Kesteven Way RG41 . . . . . .**115** E6
Keston Cl RG4 . . . .**59** C2
Kestrel Ave TW18 . . . .**96** F5
Kestrel Bldgs RG40 . . . . . .**141** A6
Kestrel Cl RG19 . . . .**106** B3
Kestrel Path SL2 . . . .**21** E1
Kestrels Mead RG26 . . . . . .**135** B2
Kestrel Way
  Burghfield Common RG7 . . .**111** B3
  Reading RG30 . . . .**85** A4
  Wokingham RG41 . . . .**115** F5
Keswick Cl
  Frimley GU15 . . . .**152** D4
  Reading RG30 . . . .**84** D7
Keswick Ct SL2 . . . .**42** F6
Keswick Dr GU18 . . . .**153** B8
Keswick Gdns RG5 . . . .**87** E5
Keswick Rd TW20 . . . .**96** B1
Ketcher Gn RG42 . . . .**90** D4
Kettering Cl RG31 . . . .**84** E4
Kevins Dr GU46 . . . .**149** E7
Kew Cotts RG14 . . . .**104** E1
Kew Gdns SN8 . . . .**126** A3
Keynsham Way GU47 . . . .**143** D2
Keys Pl SL6 . . . .**39** F6
Khalsa Prim Sch SL1 . . . . . .**42** B3
Kibble Gn RG12 . . . .**118** B3
Kibblewhite Cres RG10 . . . .**61** D6
Kidderminster Rd SL2 . . . . . .**22** B7
Kidmore End Rd RG4 . . . . . .**58** F7
Kidmore Rd RG4 . . . .**58** F5
Kidwells Cl SL6 . . . .**39** F8

Kidwells Park Dr 13 SL6 . .**39** F7
Kielder Ct RG2 . . . .**86** C3
Kielder Wlk GU15 . . . .**152** C4
Kier Pk SL5 . . . .**120** C6
KIFF GREEN **108** C6
Kilburn Cl RG31 . . . .**84** D4
Kildare Gdns RG4 . . . .**59** C3
Killarney Dr SL6 . . . .**39** E7
Killigrew Ho 4 TW16 . . . . . .**98** E1
Kilmartin Gdns GU16 . . . . .**151** F1
Kilmington Cl RG12 . . . . . .**118** E2
Kilmiston Ave TW17 . . . . . .**125** C3
Kilmiston House TW17 . . . .**125** C3
Kilmore Dr GU15 . . . .**152** B4
Kilmuir Cl GU47 . . . .**150** D7
Kiln Cl
  Harlington UB3 . . . .**71** D8
  Hermitage RG18 . . . .**79** C7
  Kiln Croft Cl** SL7 . . . .**2** A3
Kiln Dr RG18 . . . .**78** E5
Kiln Fields HP10 . . . .**3** E2
KILN GREEN **37** D1
Kiln Hill RG7 . . . .**140** B7
Kiln La
  Bracknell RG12 . . . .**118** A7
  Mortimer RG7 . . . .**137** C5
  Reading RG31 . . . .**84** B8
  Sunningdale SL5 . . . .**121** A4
  Winkfield SL4 . . . .**93** B2
  Wooburn SL8, HP10 . . . .**3** D3
Kiln Pl SL6 . . . .**19** A3
Kiln Rd
  Caversham RG4 . . . .**59** D8
  Newbury RG14 . . . .**105** C5
Kiln Ride
  Upper Basildon RG8 . . . .**54** F5
  Wokingham RG40 . . . .**142** A8
Kiln Ride Extension
  RG40 . . . .**142** A6
Kilnsea Dr RG6 . . . .**87** D1
Kilnside RG12 . . . .**91** D1
Kiln Terr RG18 . . . .**78** E5
Kiln View Rd RG2 . . . .**86** D2
Kilowna Cl RG10 . . . .**61** A4
Kilross Rd TW14 . . . .**98** E7
Kimber Cl SL4 . . . .**42** C4
Kimberley RG12 . . . .**118** C1
Kimberley Cl
  1 Reading RG1 . . . .**85** E5
  Slough SL3 . . . .**43** F2
Kimber's Cl RG14 . . . .**104** F3
Kimbers Dr
  Burnham SL1 . . . .**21** D2
  Newbury RG14 . . . .**104** C5
Kimber's La SL6 . . . .**39** E3
Kimbolton 3 SL6 . . . .**40** B8
Kimmeridge RG12 . . . .**118** B3
Kimpton Cl RG6 . . . .**113** E8
Kinburn Dr TW20 . . . .**95** E3
Kincraig 1 SL6 . . . .**19** A3
King Edward Ct 8 SL4 . . . . .**67** D6
King Edwards Cl SL5 . . . . .**119** E8
King Edwards Rd SL5 . . . . .**119** E8
King Edwards Rise SL5 . . .**119** F8
King Edward St SL1 . . . .**42** D4
King Edward VII Ave SL4,
  SL3 . . . .**67** E8
King Edward VII Hospl
  SL5 . . . .**67** C4
Kingfisher Cl RG7 . . . .**109** B3
Kingfisher Court Ind Est
  RG14 . . . .**105** D3
Kingfisher Ct
  Slough SL2 . . . .**22** B1
  Twyford RG10 . . . .**61** E3
Kingfisher Dr
  Staines TW18 . . . .**96** F4
  Woodley RG5 . . . .**87** C6
  Yateley GU46 . . . .**149** B4
Kingfisher Gr RG7 . . . .**113** A3
Kingfisher Ho SL7 . . . .**1** F2
Kingfisher Par GU17 . . . . . .**150** B5
Kingfisher Pl RG1 . . . .**86** B8
King George Cl TW16 . . . . .**98** E3
Kinghorn La SL6 . . . .**19** D3
Kinghorn Pk SL6 . . . .**19** D3
King James Way RG9 . . . . . .**35** C8
King John's Cl TW19 . . . .**68** C1
King John's Palace SL3 . . . .**69** D8
Kings Apartments GU15 . .**151** C4
King's Ave TW15 . . . .**98** F2
Kingsbridge Cotts RG40 . .**142** E7
Kingsbridge Ho RG7 . . . . .**139** A6
Kingsbridge Rd
  Newbury RG14 . . . .**104** E1
  Reading RG2 . . . .**86** C3
Kingsbury Cres TW18 . . . . .**96** D4
Kingsbury Dr SL4 . . . .**95** A8
Kings Chase 16 SL6 . . . .**39** F6
Kings Cl TW18 . . . .**97** D1
Kings Cl RG10 . . . .**61** D6
KINGSCLERE **152** A8
KINGSCLERE
  WOODLANDS **133** B1
Kingsclere Ct RG12 . . . .**118** A5
King's Court Fst Sch SL4 . . .**95** B8
Kings Cres GU15 . . . .**151** C8
Kingscroft Jun Sch TW18 .**97** A2
Kingscroft La RG42 . . . .**92** A6
Kings Ct UB7 . . . .**70** B6
Kings Ct SL4 . . . .**67** D6
Kingsdale Rd RG12 . . . .**118** D7
Kingsgate Pl 8 RG1 . . . .**86** D7
Kingsgate St RG1 . . . .**86** D7
Kings Gdns RG10 . . . .**61** D6
Kingsland Ct RG19 . . . .**106** D3
Kingsland Grange RG14 . .**130** E8
Kingsland Ho RG14 . . . .**130** E8
Kingsley Ave
  Camberley GU15 . . . .**151** D3
  Englefield Green TW20 . . . . . .**95** B2
Kingsley Cl
  Charvil RG10 . . . .**61** A5
  Crowthorne RG45 . . . .**143** B3
  Newbury RG14 . . . .**105** B5
  Reading RG2 . . . .**113** B7
Kingsley Dr SL7 . . . .**1** C6
Kingsley Path SL2 . . . .**21** D1
Kings Mead RG14 . . . .**130** C5
Kingsmead Ho SL1 . . . .**42** C5
KING'S MEADOW **86** C8
King's Meadow Rd RG1 . . .**86** B8
Kingsmere Rd RG42 . . . . . .**117** F8
King's Rd GU24 . . . .**153** F6
King's Oak Cl 4 RG1 . . . .**86** C7
Kings Rd
  Newbury RG14 . . . .**105** B2
  Silchester RG7 . . . .**136** B2
  West End GU24 . . . .**153** F5
  Windsor SL4 . . . .**67** D5
King's Rd
  Ascot SL5 . . . .**120** D4
  Caversham RG4 . . . .**59** C2
  Crowthorne RG45 . . . .**143** C5
  Egham TW20 . . . .**96** A4
  Henley-on-T RG9 . . . .**15** D2
  Reading RG1 . . . .**86** C7
  Slough SL1 . . . .**42** E3
Kings Rd W RG14 . . . .**105** A2
Kings Reach Ct 11 RG1 . . . .**86** B7
King's Ride
  Bracknell SL5 . . . .**119** D5
  Camberley GU15 . . . .**151** C5
King's Ride Ho SL5 . . . .**119** E5
Kings Ride Pk SL5 . . . .**119** C4
King's Road Ho 3 SL4 . . . . .**67** D5
King St
  Chertsey KT16 . . . .**124** A1
  Maidenhead SL6 . . . .**39** F6
  Mortimer RG7 . . . .**137** A6
  Reading RG1 . . . .**86** B7
King Stable St SL4 . . . .**67** D7
King's Terr SL3 . . . .**69** B8
King's Wlk GU15 . . . .**150** F6
King's Wlk SL7 . . . .**17** D7
Kingswood Cl
  Camberley GU15 . . . .**152** A8
  Englefield Green TW20 . . . . . .**95** D4
Kingswood Creek TW19 . . .**68** D2
Kingswood Ct
  Maidenhead SL6 . . . .**39** F5
  17 Reading RG30 . . . .**85** D6
Kingswood Hall of Residence
  TW20 . . . .**95** D4
Kingswood Ho SL1 . . . .**42** C5
Kingswood Par SL7 . . . .**1** D5
Kingswood Rise TW20 . . . . .**95** D4
King's Yd SL5 . . . .**119** C5
Kingwood House Stables
  RG7 . . . .**45** D7
Kinnaird Cl SL5 . . . .**45** D7
Kinross Ave SL5 . . . .**119** F4
Kinross Ct SL5 . . . .**119** F4
Kinross Ct TW16 . . . .**98** F3
Kinross Dr SL5 . . . .**119** F4
Kinson Rd RG30 . . . .**85** A1
KINTBURY **102** B2
Kintbury Mill RG17 . . . .**102** B3
Kintbury Rd RG17 . . . .**127** F6
Kintbury Sq RG17 . . . .**102** B3
Kintbury Sta RG17 . . . .**102** B3
Kinver Wlk 5 RG1 . . . .**85** C4
Kipling Cl
  Thatcham RG18 . . . .**106** C5
  1 Woodley RG5 . . . .**87** E4
  Yateley GU46 . . . .**149** C4
Kipling Ct SL4 . . . .**66** C5
Kirby Ct GU16 . . . .**151** E1

Kirkfell Cl RG31 . . . . .57 C2
Kirkham Cl
Caversham RG4. . . . . .59 E6
Sandhurst GU47 . . . . 143 D2
Kirkstall Ct RG31 . . . . .84 D4
Kirkstone Cl GU15 . . . . . .152 D4
Kirkwall Spur SL1 . . . . .42 E8
Kirkwood Cres RG7 . . . . . .110 F3
Kirton Cl RG30. . . . . .85 B7
Kirtons Farm Rd RG30 . . . .85 C1
Kitsmead La GU25, KT16 . 122 C1
Kittiwake Cl RG5. . . . . .88 B7
Kitwood Dr RG6 . . . . .87 E1
Klondyke SL7 . . . . .1 D2
Knappe Cl RG9 . . . . .35 C8
Knapp Rd TW15. . . . . .97 F4
Knappswood Cl RG8 . . . . .55 C4
Knapp The RG6 . . . . .87 B4
Knighton Cl RG4. . . . . .59 E3
Knightsbridge Cres TW18 .97 B2
Knightsbridge Ct 7 SL3 . .44 A2
Knightsbridge Dr RG19. .132 B3
Knightsbridge Rd GU15 .151 E7
Knights Cl
Egham TW20 . . . . .96 D2
Windsor SL4 . . . . .66 D6
Knights La RG20 . . . . .129 C3
Knights Lea RG20 . . . . . . .129 B3
Knight's Pl 8 SL4 . . . . . .67 C5
Knights Way
Caversham RG4 . . . . .59 B5
Frimley GU15 . . . . .152 C4
Knightswood RG12 . . . . .118 B1
Knock The GU47 . . . . . . .150 D7
Knole Wood SL5 . . . . . . .120 E1
Knoll Cl OX12. . . . . .6 E7
Knoll Gdns RG20 . . . . . . .130 A4
Knollmead RG31 . . . . .84 D4
Knoll Park Rd KT16 . . . . .123 F1
Knoll Rd GU15 . . . . .151 D6
Knoll The
Chertsey KT16 . . . . .123 F1
Purley on T RG31 . . . . . . .57 B2
Knollys Rd RG26 . . . . . . .135 F1
Knolton Way SL2 . . . . .43 C7
Knossington Cl RG6. . . . . .87 C2
Knott La RG7 . . . . .109 B4
Knowle Cl RG4 . . . . .58 D4
Knowle Croft SL5 . . . . .39 E5
Knowle Gn TW18. . . . . . . .97 A3
Knowle Gr GU25 . . . . . . .122 C2
KNOWLE GREEN 97 A3
Knowle Grove Cl GU25 . .122 C2
KNOWLE HILL 122 C2
Knowle Hill GU25 . . . . . .122 C2
Knowle Park Ave TW18. . .97 B3
Knowle Park Inf Sch
TW18. . . . . .97 A3
Knowle Rd RG5. . . . . .87 E4
Knowles Ave RG45 . . . . . .142 F5
KNOWL HILL. 37 E4
Knowl Hill CE Prim Sch
RG10 . . . . .37 F4
Knowl Hill Common RG10 37 E3
Knowl Hill Terr RG10 . . . . .37 E4
Knowsley Cl SL6. . . . . .19 A1
Knowsley Rd RG31 . . . . . .57 C3
Knox Gn RG42 . . . . .90 C2
Kola Ho SL2 . . . . .43 B6
Korda Cl TW17. . . . . .124 F6
Krooner Rd GU15 . . . . . . .151 B3
Kurnool Mortar Cross Roads
GU15 . . . . .151 A6
Kybes La RG7. . . . . .112 D5
Kyftle Court Flat 11
RG14 . . . . .104 F2
Kyle Cl RG12 . . . . .118 B6

L

Laburnham Rd SL6 . . . . . .39 E6
Laburnum Cl SL7 . . . . .1 E4
Laburnum Ct 2 KT16 . . .124 A1
Laburnum Gdns RG2 . . . . .86 E1
Laburnum Gr
Brands Hill SL3 . . . . .69 B8
Newbury RG14. . . . . . . .105 A4
Laburnum Pl TW20. . . . . . .95 B2
Laburnum Rd
Chertsey KT16 . . . . .124 A1
Winnersh RG41. . . . . .88 C1
Laburnum Rise RG19. . . . .133 B5
Laburnums The GU17 . . . .150 B5
Laburnum Way TW19. . . . .97 F7
Lacewood Gdns RG2 . . . . .86 E1
Lacey Cl TW20. . . . . .96 B1
Ladbroke Cl RG5. . . . . . . .87 F6
Ladbrooke Rd SL1 . . . . . .42 D3
Ladwell Cl RG14 . . . . . . .130 D5
Ladybank RG12 . . . . .118 B1
Ladyday Pl SL1 . . . . .42 C5
Lady Elizabeth Ho 3 SL3 44 A2
Lady Jane Ct RG4 . . . . . . .59 C3
Lady Margaret Rd SL5 . .120 F2
Ladymask Cl RG31 . . . . . .84 F4
Ladywood Grange SL5 . .120 F1
Laffords The RG7 . . . . . . .82 A2
Laggan Rd SL6 . . . . .19 F1
Laggan Sq SL6 . . . . .19 F1
Laird Ct GU19 . . . . .145 E1
Lake Ave SL1 . . . . .42 D6
LAKE END 41 B4
Lake End Cl SL6 . . . . .41 A7
Lake End Rd SL4, SL6. . . .41 B5
Lake End Way RG45. . . . .143 A4
Lakeland Dr GU16 . . . . . .151 E1
Lake Rd GU25 . . . . .122 B5

Lakeside
Bracknell RG42 . . . . .91 C1
Earley RG6. . . . . .87 B3
Maidenhead SL6 . . . . . . .20 B1
Lakeside Bsns Pk GU47 . 150 A7
Lakeside Dr SL2 . . . . .22 F4
Lakeside Ind Est SL3. . . . .70 A8
Lakeside Pk KT16. . . . . . .124 C1
Lakeside Prim Sch GU16 .151 F1
Lakeside Rd SL3 . . . . .69 F7
Lakeside The GU17. . . . . .150 D4
Lakes The SL7 . . . . .18 A6
Lakeview SL5. . . . . .119 D6
Lake View SL6 . . . . .20 A1
Lalande Cl RG41. . . . . . . .115 E6
LALEHAM 124 C6
Laleham Abbey TW18 . . .124 C5
Laleham CE Prim Sch
TW18. . . . . .124 C7
Laleham Ho TW18 . . . . . .124 C5
Laleham Nurseries
TW17 . . . . .124 E6
Laleham Rd
Littleton TW17. . . . . . . .125 A4
Staines TW18. . . . . .96 F2
Laleham Reach KT16 . . . .124 A6
Lamb Cl RG18 . . . . .106 C5
Lambdens Hill RG7 . . . . .109 D7
Lambert Ave SL3 . . . . .43 E3
Lambert Cres GU17 . . . . .150 C4
Lambert Dr RG14 . . . . . . .105 E5
Lambeth Ct RG30 . . . . . . .84 F7
Lambfields RG7. . . . . .83 D3
Lambly Hill GU25 . . . . . .122 E6
Lamborne Cl GU47 . . . . .143 A1
LAMBOURN 25 C2
Lambourn CE Prim Sch
RG17 . . . . .25 B1
Lambourne Ct RG14. . . . .105 B4
Lambourne Cl SL6 . . . . . . .84 D8
Lambourne Ct SL6 . . . . . .40 C7
Lambourne Ct Cvn Site
RG17 . . . . .25 B2
Lambourne Dr
Bagshot GU19 . . . . .145 D2
Maidenhead SL6 . . . . . . .39 C3
Lambourne Gdns RG6. . . .87 D4
Lambourn Pl RG17 . . . . . .25 B3
Lambourn Rd RG20 . . . . .104 C6
LAMBOURN
WOODLANDS 46 B4
Lambridge La RG9. . . . . . .15 C3
Lambridge Wood Rd RG9 .15 B4
Lambrook Haileybury Sch
RG42. . . . . .92 A3
Lambs Farm Bsns Pk
RG7 . . . . .139 B8
Lamb's La RG7 . . . . .139 A8
Lambs Lane Prim Sch
RG7 . . . . .139 A8
Lambton Ho SL4 . . . . .67 A4
Lambwood Hill RG7. . . . . .112 D1
Lambwood Ind Est RG7 . 112 C1
Lamden Way RG7. . . . . . .111 B3
Lamerton Rd RG2. . . . . . . .86 C1
Lamesley Ho SL6 . . . . . . .39 E6
Lammas Ave SL4. . . . . . . .67 D5
Lammas Cl TW18 . . . . . . .96 E5
Lammas Ct
Staines TW19. . . . . .96 D5
Windsor SL4 . . . . .67 C5
Lammas Dr TW18 . . . . . . .96 D5
Lammas Mead RG42 . . . . .90 E1
Lammas Rd SL1 . . . . .41 D8
Lamorna Cres RG31. . . . . .57 C2
Lamp Acres RG14. . . . . . .105 B5
Lamplighters Wlk RG31. . .84 F4
Lamtarra Way GU16 . . . . .131 C8
Lanark Cl
Frimley GU16. . . . . .151 E2
Woodley RG5. . . . . .88 A6
Lancashire Hill RG42. . . . .91 F2
Lancaster Ave SL2 . . . . . .22 C1
Lancaster Cl
Ashford TW15 . . . . .97 E4
Englefield Green TW20 . . .95 D3
Hungerford RG17 . . . . . .100 C4
2 Reading RG1 . . . . .86 C5
Stanwell TW19. . . . . .70 E1
Thatcham RG18. . . . . . .106 C4
Lancaster Ct
Reading RG2 . . . . .86 E1
Stanwell TW19. . . . . .70 E1
Lancaster Dr GU15 . . . . .151 D6
Lancaster Gdns RG6 . . . . .87 B3
Lancaster Ho RG12 . . . . .118 C4
Lancaster Rd SL6 . . . . . . .39 B8
Lancaster Sq RG17. . . . . .100 D4
Lancastria Mews SL6 . . . .39 D7
Lancelot Cl SL1 . . . . .42 A4
Lancers Dr RG19 . . . . . . .106 E2
Lanchester Dr RG45. . . . .143 C7
Lancing Cl RG30 . . . . .85 D7
Lancing Rd TW13 . . . . . . .98 F6
Landen Cl RG40 . . . . .116 B4
Landen Gr RG41 . . . . . . .115 E6
Landon Way TW15 . . . . . .98 B2
Landrake Cres RG6 . . . . . .86 C1
Landseer Cl 6 RG26. . . . .134 E1
Landsend La RG10 . . . . . .61 D5
Land End Cl RG2 . . . . .113 E6
Laneswood RG7 . . . . .136 E5
Lane The
Chertsey KT16 . . . . .124 A6
Chilton OX11 . . . . .10 E8
Virginia Water GU25 . . . .122 E6

Langborough Rd RG40 . . 116 C5
Langdale Cl SL6 . . . . .40 A6
Langdale Dr SL5 . . . . .119 E7
Langdale Gdns RG6. . . . . .86 F2
Langdon Cl GU15 . . . . . .152 C4
Langdown Way SL6 . . . . . .39 D5
Langford Cl RG4 . . . . .59 C5
Langham Pl TW20. . . . . . .95 F3
Langhams Way RG10. . . . .36 E2
Lang Ho TW15 . . . . .97 E7
LANGLEY 44 A3
Langley Broom SL3 . . . . . .43 F1
Langley Bsns Ct RG20. . . .51 C5
Langley Bsns Pk SL3. . . . .44 A4
Langley Bsns Pk SL3 . . . .44 A4
Langley Cnr SL3 . . . . .23 F6
LANGLEY COMMON 115 A2
Langley Common Rd RG2,
RG41 . . . . .114 F1
Langley Cres UB3. . . . . . . .71 F7
Langley Dr GU15 . . . . . . .151 D6
Langley Farm Cotts RG20 .51 E6
Langley Gram Sch SL3 . . .43 F2
Langley Hall Dr RG31 . . . .84 D4
Langley Hill RG31 . . . . . . .84 C5
Langley Hill Cl RG31 . . . . .84 C6
Langley Manor Sch SL3 . .43 E5
Langley Park Rd SL0 . . . . .44 C6
Langley Rd
Slough SL3 . . . . .43 E3
Staines TW18. . . . . .96 F2
Langley Sta SL3 . . . . .44 A4
Langley Way SL7. . . . . .1 C2
Langton Cl SL3 . . . . .43 E3
Langton Cl
Maidenhead SL6 . . . . . . .39 D8
Slough SL1 . . . . .41 D5
Langton's Mdw SL2 . . . . . .22 C6
Langton Way SL6 . . . . .40 C2
Langworthy End SL6 . . . . .65 B8
Langworthy La SL6 . . . . . .65 A8
Laniver Cl RG6 . . . . .87 B1
Lansdowne Ave SL1 . . . . .42 E5
Lansdowne Ct
Slough SL1. . . . . .42 E5
Taplow SL6 . . . . .40 C7
Lansdowne Gdns RG7 . . .113 C1
Lansdowne Rd
Reading RG30 . . . . .84 C7
Staines TW18. . . . . .97 B1
Lanterns Wlk SL6. . . . . . . .40 B7
Lapwing Cl RG31 . . . . . . .84 C6
Larbert Cotts SL6 . . . . . . .38 B5
Larch Ave
Sunningdale SL5 . . . . . . .120 E4
Wokingham RG41 . . . . . .116 A7
Larch Cl
Burghfield RG30 . . . . . . .111 B4
Camberley GU15 . . . . . .152 B5
Newbury RG14. . . . . . . .104 D5
Slough SL2. . . . . .42 E8
Larch Ct RG4 . . . . .59 B3
Larch Dr
Brimpton RG19 . . . . .133 B6
Woodley RG5 . . . . .87 E5
Larches The RG42. . . . . . .92 A1
Larches Way GU17 . . . . . .150 B5
Larchfield Prim Sch SL6 . .39 E4
Larchfield Rd SL6 . . . . . . .39 E4
Larchmoor Pk SL2 . . . . . . .23 A7
Larchside Cl RG7 . . . . . . .113 B2
Larchwood 6 RG12. . . . . .118 E5
Larchwood Dr TW20 . . . . .95 B2
Larchwood Glade GU15 . 152 A7
Lardon Cotts RG8. . . . . . . .34 A6
Larges Bridge Dr RG12 . .118 D6
Larges La RG12 . . . . .118 C7
Larissa Cl RG31. . . . . .57 E1
Lark Ave TW18 . . . . .96 F5
Larkes-Meade RG6 . . . . . .87 D3
Larkfield SL6 . . . . .40 B1
Larkham Cl TW13 . . . . . . .98 E5
Larkings La SL2 . . . . .23 B4
Larksfield TW20 . . . . .95 C6
Larkspur Cl RG41 . . . . . . .115 D7
Larkspur Gdns RG18 . . . .106 F4
Larkswood Cl
Reading RG31 . . . . .57 D3
Sandhurst GU47 . . . . . . .143 A1
Larkswood Dr RG45. . . . .143 B5
La Roche Cl SL3 . . . . .43 A3
Lascelles Ho 8 SL1. . . . . .43 A4
Lascelles Rd SL3 . . . . .43 B3
Lashbrook Mead RG8 . . . .36 B3
Lashbrook Rd RG8 . . . . . . .36 B4
Lassell Gdns SL6 . . . . .40 B8
Lasswade Ct KT16 . . . . . .123 F2
Lasswade Rd KT16 . . . . . .123 F2
Lastingham Ct TW18 . . . . .97 A2
Latham Ave GU16 . . . . . . .151 E2
Latimer RG12 . . . . .118 B1
Latimer Dr RG31 . . . . .84 C4
Latimer Rd RG41. . . . . . . .116 A6
Latitude KT16. . . . . .124 C1
Latton Cl OX11 . . . . .10 E8
Laud Cl
Newbury RG14. . . . . . . .105 D5
Reading RG2 . . . . .86 A6
Lauder Cl RG31 . . . . .151 A2
Lauderdale Ho 12 TW18 . .96 F3
Laud's Cl RG9 . . . . .15 C1
Laud Way RG40 . . . . .116 E6
Launceston Ave RG6. . . . .59 E6
Launceston Cl RG6 . . . . . .87 B2
Laundry Ct 5 RG41. . . . . .116 A5
Laundry La GU47 . . . . . . .150 E5
Lauradale RG12. . . . . . . .118 A5

Laurel Ave
Brimpton RG19 . . . . .133 A5
Englefield Green TW20 . . .95 B3
Slough SL3. . . . . .43 E4
Laurel Cl
Camberley GU15 . . . . . .151 D4
Poyle SL3. . . . . .69 E7
Wokingham RG41 . . . . . .115 F5
Laurel Ct 7 RG12 . . . . . .118 F5
Laurel Dr RG31 . . . . .84 B8
Laurel Gdns RG19. . . . . . .131 B6
Laurels The
Camberley GU15 . . . . . .152 A7
Hungerford RG17 . . . . . .100 E7
Pangbourne RG8 . . . . . . .56 D5
8 Slough SL3 . . . . .44 A2
Woodley RG5 . . . . .60 E1
Laurel Terr GU47. . . . . . . .142 F1
Laurence Ct 1 SL7 . . . . . . .1 D2
Laurence Ct GU15 . . . . . .152 A7
Lauser Rd TW19 . . . . .97 C8
Lautree Gdns SL6 . . . . . . .19 E7
Lavender Pk SL5. . . . . . . .119 C6
Lavender Row SL5 . . . . . . .92 C1
Lavenham Dr RG5 . . . . . . .87 F8
Lavershot Hall GU20 . . . .146 C8
Lawford Cres GU46 . . . . .149 D6
Lawkland SL2 . . . . .22 C2
Lawn Cl SL3 . . . . .68 C7
Lawns The
North Ascot SL5. . . . . . . .119 D6
Reading RG2 . . . . .86 D3
Lawn The SL3 . . . . .68 C6
Lawrence Alison Mews
RG42 . . . . .58 E2
Lawrence Cl RG40 . . . . . . .116 B8
Lawrence Cres GU20 . . . .146 D4
Lawrence Ct SL4 . . . . .67 B6
Lawrence Ct RG41 . . . . . .116 A4
Lawrence Gr RG42 . . . . . .117 D8
Lawrence Lodge GU15 . .151 D7
Lawrence Mead RG17 . . . .25 B2
Lawrence Pl RG14 . . . . . .105 C5
Lawrence Rd RG30. . . . . . .85 A8
Lawrences La RG18 . . . . .106 D5
Lawrences Way RG18 . . .106 D5
Lawrence Way
Camberley GU15 . . . . . .150 F4
Slough SL1. . . . . .41 D8
Lawson Dr RG4 . . . . .58 E5
Lawson La OX11 . . . . .10 E8
Lawson Rd RG9 . . . . .35 F7
Lawson Way SL5 . . . . . . .121 B3
Laxton Gn SL6 . . . . .39 C3
Layburn Cres SL3 . . . . . . .69 B8
Layham Gn RG17 . . . . . . .102 B1
Layland's Gn RG17 . . . . . .102 B1
Layleys Gn RG18 . . . . .78 F4
Laytom Rise SL6 . . . . .57 C3
Layton's La TW16 . . . . . . .125 F7
Lazare Ct 7 TW18 . . . . . . .96 F3
Lea Cl
Marlow Bottom SL7 . . . . . .1 D6
Reading RG30 . . . . .85 A3
Leacroft
Staines TW18. . . . . .97 B4
Sunningdale SL5 . . . . . . .121 A4
Lea Croft RG45 . . . . .143 B6
Leacroft Cl TW18 . . . . . . .97 B4
Leacroft Rd SL0 . . . . .44 C6
Leafield Copse RG12 . . . .118 E5
Leafy Oak Farm GU17 . . .150 A4
Lea Heath Way RG30 . . . . .85 D5
Leaholme Gdns SL1. . . . . .41 D8
Lea Inf Sch SL2 . . . . .43 B6
Lea Jun Sch SL2. . . . . . . .43 B6
Lea Pl RG31 . . . . .84 C4
Lea Rd GU15 . . . . .151 B2
Leas Dr SL0 . . . . .44 E7
Lea The
Finchampstead RG40. . . .141 F8
Thorpe Lea RG40 . . . . . . .96 B3
Leaver Rd RG9. . . . . .15 C1
Leaves Gn RG12 . . . . . . .118 D3
Lea View RG18 . . . . .79 C8
LECKHAMPSTEAD 49 E7
LECKHAMPSTEAD
THICKET 49 E7
Ledbury Cl RG30 . . . . .58 C1
Ledbury Dr RG31 . . . . .84 D4
Ledger's Rd SL1 . . . . .42 E5
Ledran Cl RG6 . . . . .87 C3
Ledger's Rd SL1. . . . . .42 D4
Lee Cl RG5 . . . . .87 E7
Leeds Rd SL1 . . . . .42 E6
Lee La SL6 . . . . .18 C2
Lees Cl SL6. . . . . .39 B8
Lee's Ct GU20 . . . . .146 D4
Lees Gdns SL6 . . . . .39 B8
Leeson Gdns SL4 . . . . . . .41 E2
Lees Wlk SL7 . . . . .1 C2
Legoland Windsor* SL4 . .66 D2
Leicester RG12 . . . . .118 E2
Leicester Cl RG9 . . . . .15 D3
Leigh Field RG7 . . . . .136 F6
Leigh Pk SL3 . . . . .68 C7
Leigh Rd SL1 . . . . .42 A6
Leigh Sq SL4 . . . . .66 D5
Leighton Ct RG2. . . . . .86 E3
Leighton Gdns RG42 . . . . .91 E1
Leighton Park Sch RG2 . . .86 D4
Leiston Cl 1 RG6. . . . . . . .87 D1
Leiston Spur SL1 . . . . .42 C6
Leith Cl
Crowthorne RG45 . . . . . .143 A7

Leith Cl continued
Slough SL1 . . . . .43 A5
Le Marchant Rd GU15,
GU16 . . . . .151 F3
Lemart Cl RG30. . . . . .84 E8
Lemington Gr RG12 . . . . .118 B3
Lemey Cl RG40 . . . . .116 D8
Lenham Cl RG41 . . . . .88 E1
Lennox Cl RG31. . . . . .84 B4
Lennox Rd RG6 . . . . .87 A5
LENT 21 B1
Lent Gn SL1 . . . . .21 B1
Lent Green La SL1 . . . . . . .21 B1
LENT RISE 41 A8
Lent Rise Comb Sch SL1 . .41 B8
Lent Rise Rd SL1 . . . . .21 B1
Leonard Ct RG7. . . . . .83 E3
Leonardslee Cres RG14 . .105 D4
Leopold Mall 8 SL1 . . . . .42 F4
Leopold Wlk RG1. . . . . . . .86 D7
Leppington RG12 . . . . . . .118 B2
Lerwick Dr SL1 . . . . .42 E8
Lesford Rd RG1. . . . . .85 E5
Lesley Cl RG16 RG30. . . . .85 D6
Leslie Dunne Ho SL4. . . . .66 E5
Leslie Southern Ct RG14 .109 B4
Lesters Rd SL6 . . . . .19 D6
Letchworth Ave TW14 . . . .98 F8
LETCOMBE BASSETT 6 E7
Letcombe Ct 6 RG1 . . . . .86 B6
Letcombe Sq RG12 . . . . .118 F5
Letcombe St RG1 . . . . . . .86 B7
Letts Gn RG5 . . . . .87 F5
Leverkusen Rd RG12 . . . .118 B6
LEVERTON 73 C1
Leverton Farm Bldgs
RG7 . . . . .73 C1
Leverton La RG17. . . . . . . .73 B1
Lewendon Rd RG14 . . . . .104 E5
Lewes Cl SL1 . . . . .42 C4
Lewington Mews RG17. . .100 D4
Lewins Farm Ct SL1 . . . . . .41 F6
Lewis Way SL1 . . . . .41 F6
Lewin Terr TW14 . . . . .98 D8
Lewisham Way GU47. . . . .143 D2
Lewis Ind Est RG17 . . . . . .48 A3
Lewis Wlk RG31 . . . . .130 C6
Lexington Ave SL6 . . . . . . .39 D5
Lexington Gr RG2 . . . . . . .113 A7
Leyburn Cl RG5. . . . . .88 A8
Leycester Cl GU20 . . . . . .146 B6
Leyland Gdns RG2 . . . . . .113 E6
Leylands La TW19 . . . . . . .97 A3
Leys Gdns RG14 . . . . . . .104 F4
Leyside RG45 . . . . .143 A5
Liberty Ho 2 RG42 . . . . . .90 B1
Liberty Ho RG19 . . . . .132 A5
Liberty Of Earley Ho 5
RG6 . . . . .87 C1
Library Par RG45 . . . . .88 E7
Licensed Victuallers Sch
SL5 . . . . .119 C7
Lichfield Cl 1 RG6 . . . . . .87 C1
Lichfields RG12 . . . . .118 E4
Liddell SL4 . . . . .66 C4
Liddell Cl RG40 . . . . .141 E3
Liddell Pl SL4 . . . . .66 C4
Liddell Sq 14 SL4 . . . . . . .66 C5
Liddell Way SL5 . . . . .119 F5
Lido Rd OX11. . . . . .9 F8
Lidstone Cl RG6 . . . . .114 D8
Liebenrood Rd RG30. . . . .85 C6
Highlands La SL6 . . . . .19 F5
LIGHTWATER 153 A8
Lightwater Ctry Pk*
GU18 . . . . .145 F1
Lightwater Mdw GU18 . .153 B8
Lightwater Rd GU18 . . . .153 C8
Lea View RG18 . . . . .79 C8
Lightwater Village Sch
GU18 . . . . .146 A1
Lightwood RG12 . . . . . . .118 D3
Liguel Cl RG17. . . . . .100 D4
Lilac Cl RG31 . . . . .84 C4
Lilac Cl SL2 . . . . .21 F2
Lilacs The RG41. . . . . . . .115 B4
Lilac Wlk
Brimpton RG19 . . . . .133 B5
Reading RG31 . . . . .84 B8
LILLEY 29 A4
Lilley Way SL1 . . . . .41 D6
Lillibrooke Cres RG6 . . . . .39 A3
Lilley La SL6 . . . . .18 C2
Lily Hill Dr RG12 . . . . . . .118 F7
Lily Hill Rd RG12 . . . . . . .118 F7
Lima Ct RG1 . . . . .85 F6
Lime Ave
Camberley GU15 . . . . . .152 A6
Windsor SL4 . . . . .67 F7
Windsor SL4 . . . . .93 F5
Lime Cl
Brimpton RG19 . . . . .133 A5
Newbury RG14. . . . . . . .105 D4
Wokingham RG41 . . . . . .115 F5
Limecroft GU46 . . . . .149 A4
Limefield Cl RG40 . . . . . . .87 E3
Lime Lodge 4 TW16 . . . . .98 F1
Lime Mews TW20 . . . . . . .95 B3
Limerick Cl RG42 . . . . . . .118 A8
Limes Cl TW15 . . . . .97 F3
Limes Rd SL0 . . . . .95 F3
Limes The
Windsor SL4 . . . . .66 C6

Limes The continued
Winkfield Row RG42 ...... 91 F3
Lime Tree Copse RG42 ...... 92 A1
Lime Tree Ct SL4 .... 95 C8
Lime Tree Rd RG8 .... 34 B6
Limetree Wlk GU25 ...... 122 E5
Lime Wlk
 Bracknell RG12 .... 118 C5
 Maidenhead SL6 .... 39 A8
Limmer Cl RG41 .... 115 C4
LIMMERHILL 115 E5
Limmerhill Rd RG41 ..... 115 E5
Linchfield Rd SL3 .... 68 C6
Lincoln Cl
 Frimley GU15 .... 152 B4
 Winnersh RG41 .... 88 A3
Lincoln Ct
 Newbury RG14 .... 104 F2
 3 Slough SL1 .... 42 E3
Lincoln Gdns RG10 ...... 61 D5
Lincoln Hatch La SL1 .... 21 C1
Lincoln Ho HP10 .... 3 D3
Lincoln Rd
 Maidenhead SL6 .... 39 B8
 Reading RG2 .... 86 C4
Lincolnshire Gdns RG42 . 91 E1
Lincoln Way
 Charlton TW16 .... 125 E8
 Slough SL1 .... 41 D6
Lindale Cl GU25 .... 121 F5
Lindberg Way RG5 .... 61 B1
Lind Cl RG6 .... 87 B2
Linden 3 RG12 .... 118 F4
Linden Ave SL6 .... 19 D1
Linden Cl
 Newbury RG14 .... 104 F4
 Wokingham RG41 ...... 115 F4
Linden Ct
 Camberley GU15 .... 151 F7
 Englefield Green TW20 . 95 B2
Linden Dr SL2 .... 22 C4
Linden Hill La RG10 ..... 37 C2
Lindenhill Rd RG42 ...... 117 F8
Linden Ho SL3 .... 44 B1
Lindenmuth Way RG19 .. 131 F5
Linden Pl TW18 .... 97 A4
Linden Rd
 Reading RG2 .... 86 C2
 Woodley RG5 .... 87 D4
Linden Way TW17 .... 125 C4
Lindisfarne Way RG2 .... 86 A2
Lindores Ho SL6 .... 65 B8
Lindores Rd SL6 .... 65 B8
Lindsay Cl TW19 .... 70 D2
Lindsay Ct TW17 .... 125 C4
Lindsay Dr TW17 .... 125 D3
Lindsey Cl RG41 .... 115 E6
Lindsey Gdns TW14 ..... 98 D8
Lines Rd RG10 .... 88 F5
Ling Dr GU18 .... 152 F7
Lingholm Cl
 Maidenhead SL6 .... 39 C6
 Reading RG30 .... 84 F5
Lingwood RG12 .... 118 C3
LINKENHOLT 147 D1
Link Ho 2 RG14 .... 105 A2
Link Rd
 Datchet SL3 .... 68 C6
 East Bedfont TW14 ..... 98 F8
 Newbury RG14 .... 105 A2
Links App HP10 .... 3 B8
Linkscroft Ave TW15 .... 98 B2
Links Dr RG30 .... 85 A8
Links Rd
 Ashford TW15 .... 97 E3
 Flackwell Heath HP10 .. 3 C8
Links The SL5 .... 119 E7
Links Way HP10 .... 3 B8
Linkswood Rd SL1 ...... 21 C3
Link The
 Slough SL3 .... 43 B7
 Yateley GU46 .... 149 C7
Link View RG14 .... 104 F7
Linkway
 Camberley GU15 .... 151 C4
 Crowthorne RG45 ...... 142 F5
Link Way
 Arborfield Cross RG2 .. 114 E2
 Staines TW18 .... 97 B2
 Thatcham RG18 .... 106 B4
Linnet Cl RG31 .... 84 B6
Linnet La RG20 .... 131 F3
Linnet Wlk RG41 ...... 115 F6
Lintott Ct TW19 .... 70 D1
Lion Cl TW17 .... 124 E6
Lion Ct 3 RG1 .... 86 A8
Lionel Ct RG10 .... 61 C5
Lion Mews 3 RG17 ..... 25 B2
Lip La
 Wickham, Elcot RG20 .. 102 D8
 Wickham RG20 .... 75 E2
Lippincote Ct RG31 ..... 57 E3
Lippscombe Cl RG18 .... 79 D6
Lipscombe Cl RG14 ..... 104 E2
Liscombe RG12 .... 118 B2
Liscombe Ho RG12 ..... 118 B2
Lisle Cl RG4 .... 104 F5
Lismore Cl RG5 .... 87 E4
Lismore Ct TW18 ...... 97 B3
Lismore Pk SL2 .... 22 F7
Lister Cl RG8 .... 57 C5
Liston Ct 5 SL7 .... 1 D2
Liston Ho SL7 .... 1 D2
Liston Rd SL7 .... 1 D2
Litcham Spur SL1 ...... 42 D7

Lithgow's Rd TW14, TW6 .. 71 F3
Littington Cl RG6 ...... 114 C8
Little Acre SL4 .... 67 A4
Little Acres SL3 .... 69 D7
Little Aldershot La RG26 134 B2
Little Boltons 9 SL7 .... 1 E2
Little Bowden La RG8 ... 55 F4
Littlebrook Ave SL2 ..... 41 E8
Little Buntings SL4 ..... 66 F4
Little Cl HP10 .... 3 B6
Little Copse GU46 ..... 149 D7
Littlecote Dr RG1 ...... 85 E6
Littlecote Rd SN8 ...... 99 B5
Little Croft GU46 ...... 149 D4
Littlecroft Rd 2 TW20 .. 95 F3
Little Croft Rd RG8 ..... 34 C5
Littledale Cl RG12 ..... 118 E6
Littledown Cotts SL1 ... 42 F5
Littledown Rd SL1 ...... 42 F5
Littledown Sch SL1 ...... 42 F6
Little Elms UB3 .... 71 D7
Littlefield Ct UB7 .... 70 D7
Littlefield Gn SL6 ...... 40 E8
LITTLEFIELD GREEN ... 63 F6
Little Foxes RG40 ...... 142 A7
Little Fryth RG40 ...... 142 D6
Little Glebe RG4 .... 60 E3
LITTLE HEATH 84 B8
Little Heath Rd RG31 ... 84 A7
Little Heath Sch RG31 .. 84 B7
Little Hill Rd RG10 ..... 88 D4
Little Horse Cl RG5 ..... 87 E4
LITTLE HUNGERFORD .. 79 C8
Littlejohn's La RG30 .... 58 C1
Little John's La RG30 ... 85 C8
Little La RG7 .... 107 C6
Little London Rd RG7 .. 136 B1
LITTLE MARLOW 2 D5
Little Marlow CE Sch SL7 2 C5
Little Marlow Rd SL7 .... 1 E3
Little Moor GU47 ...... 143 C1
Little Oak Cl TW17 .... 124 F5
Little Oaks Dr RG1 ..... 84 C8
Little Paddock GU15 ... 152 A8
Littleport Spur SL1 ..... 42 E7
Little Ringdale RG12 ... 118 E5
Little Saffron RG18 ..... 79 B6
Little St RG1 .... 85 E8
Littlestead Cl RG4 ..... 59 E5
LITTLESTEAD GREEN .. 59 E7
Little Sutton La SL3 .... 44 C1
LITTLETON 125 A6
Littleton CE Inf Sch
 TW17 .... 125 A6
LITTLETON COMMON .. 98 D1
Littleton Ho TW15 .... 98 C1
Littleton La TW17 ..... 124 E4
Littleton Rd TW15 ...... 98 C1
Little Vigo GU46 .... 149 B4
LITTLEWICK GREEN ... 38 B4
Littlewick Green Montessori
 Sch SL6 .... 38 C4
Little Woodlands SL4 ... 66 F4
Litton Rd RG2 .... 86 D2
Liverpool Rd
 Reading RG1 .... 86 E8
 Slough SL1 .... 42 B7
Livery Cl RG1 .... 86 B7
Living Rainforest The*
 RG18 .... 53 C5
Livingstone Ct TW19 ... 97 E7
Livingstone Gdns RG5 .. 87 E5
Livingstone Rd RG14 .. 105 B2
Llangar Gr RG45 ...... 143 A5
Llanvair Cl SL5 .... 120 A3
Llanvair Dr SL5 .... 119 F3
Llewellyn Pk RG10 ..... 61 D6
Lochinvar Cl SL1 ...... 42 B4
Lochnell Rd RG20 ..... 118 B2
Lock Ave SL6 .... 20 C2
Lockbridge Ct SL6 ..... 40 C8
Lock Bridge Rd SL8 .... 3 A3
Locke Gdns SL3 .... 43 C4
Lock Island SL6 .... 66 D6
Lock La SL6 .... 39 C4
Lock Mead SL6 .... 20 C2
Lock Path SL4 .... 66 D8
Lock Pl RG1 .... 86 D7
Lockram La RG7 ...... 111 C1
Lock Rd SL7 .... 1 E4
Lockside Ct RG7 ...... 109 C3
Locksley Ct 5 SL1 ..... 42 E3
Locksley Gdns RG41 ... 88 D3
Locks Ride SL5 .... 92 C2
Lockstile Mead RG8 ... 34 C7
Lockstile Way RG8 .... 34 C6
Lockton Chase SL5 ... 119 D6
Lockton Ho RG40 ..... 116 D6
Lockyer Cl RG41 ...... 88 A2
Loddon Bridge Rd RG5 . 87 F6
Loddon Cl GU15 ...... 152 A6
Loddon Court Farm Park
 Homes RG7 .... 138 F7
Loddon Dr
 Charvil RG10 .... 61 A8
 Maidenhead SL6 .... 39 D8
Loddon Hall Rd RG10 ... 61 E5
Loddon Prim Sch RG6 ... 87 D3
Loddon Rd SL8 .... 3 A4
Loddon Spur SL1 ..... 42 E7
Loddon Vale Ctr RG5 .. 88 A7
Lodge Cl
 Englefield Green TW20 . 95 D3
 Marlow SL7 .... 1 D1
 Slough SL1 .... 42 C4

Lodge Gr GU46 .... 149 F6
Lodge Rd RG10 .... 88 E7
Lodge The
 Englefield Green TW20 . 95 C3
 Newbury RG14 .... 105 A4
 Slough SL2 .... 43 B8
Lodge Way
 Charlton TW17 .... 125 C7
 Stanwell TW15 .... 97 E6
 Windsor SL4 .... 66 E4
Lodgings of the Military
 Knights 3 SL4 ...... 67 D6
Logan Cl RG30 .... 84 F7
Lois Dr TW17 .... 125 B4
Lomond Ave RG4 ..... 59 E5
London Ct RG14 ..... 105 C3
London Rd
 Ascot SL5 .... 120 D5
 Ashford TW15, TW18,
  TW19 .... 97 D5
 Bagshot GU15, GU19 . 145 D2
 Blackwater GU15, GU17 150 F4
 Blewbury OX11 .... 11 F8
 Bracknell RG12, SL5 .. 119 C6
 Brands Hill SL3 ...... 69 B8
 Camberley GU15 ..... 151 C6
 Datchet SL3 .... 68 C7
 Egham TW18 .... 96 F4
 Englefield Green TW20 . 95 E3
 Newbury RG14 .... 105 C3
 Reading RG1 .... 86 D7
 Slough SL3 .... 43 D2
 Sunningdale, Blacknest
  SL5 .... 121 B6
 Sunningdale, Shrubs Hill SL5,
  GU25 .... 121 C4
 Thatcham RG18, RG19 106 F3
 Twyford RG10 .... 61 E6
 Virginia Water GU25,
  TW20 .... 122 B7
 Windlesham GU19, GU20,
  SL5 .... 146 C7
 Wokingham RG40 .... 116 E6
Long Rd RG40 .... 87 B8
London St
 Chertsey KT16 .... 124 A2
 Reading RG1 .... 86 B7
Loneacre GU20 ...... 146 E4
Longacre RG14 ...... 130 D8
Long Barn La RG2 .... 86 C3
Longbourne Way KT16 123 F3
Longbridge Rd RG19 . 106 F2
Longbrook Ct GU20 .. 146 D4
Long Cl
 Farnham Common SL2 . 22 B5
 Kintbury RG17 .... 102 B2
Longcroft Rd RG19 ... 106 E2
Longcross Sta KT16 .. 121 F1
Longdon Rd RG41 .... 88 C1
Longdown Lodge GU47 150 B8
Longdown Rd GU47 .. 143 B1
Long Dr SL1 .... 21 C2
Longfield Rd RG10 ... 61 D6
LONGFORD 70 C6
Longford Ave
 Feltham TW14 .... 71 F1
 Stanwell TW19 ...... 97 E7
Longford Cl GU15 ... 151 D4
Longford Com Sch TW14 98 F8
Longford Rd TW19 ... 97 E7
Long Furlong Dr SL2 . 21 E1
Long Gr
 Tadley RG26 .... 134 D2
 Upper Bucklebury RG7 107 C5
Long Half Acre SL6 ... 38 B4
Long Hedge RG17 ... 25 D2
Long Hill Rd RG12, SL5 119 A7
Long La
 Brightwalton RG20 ... 28 E3
 Cookham Rise SL6 ... 19 D5
 Hermitage RG14, RG18 78 F2
 Holyport, Braywoodside SL6 64 B8
 Holyport, Touchen-end SL6 64 E6
 Newbury RG18 .... 78 F2
 Purley on T RG31 .... 57 B4
 Stanwell TW19 ...... 97 F7
Longlands Way GU15 . 152 D5
Long Lane Prim Sch RG31 57 B4
Longleat Dr RG31 .... 57 B3
Longleat Gdns SL6 ... 39 D6
Longmead TW14 ..... 98 D8
Long Mdw RG8 ...... 34 B5
Longmead
 Ball Hill RG20 .... 129 F1
 Windsor SL4 .... 66 E6
Longmead La SL1 .... 20 D5
Longmeadow RG15, GU16 151 F3
Long Mickle GU47 ... 143 C2
Longmoor La RG40 .. 141 E6
Longmoor La RG7 ... 137 A7
Longmoors RG42 .... 117 E8
Longmore Rd RG2 ... 113 D6
Longridge Cl RG30 .. 85 B7
Long Row RG45 ..... 35 E6
Longshot Ind Est RG12 117 E2
Longshot La RG12 ... 117 F2
Longview SL5 .... 119 C6

Longwater Ave RG2,
 RG30 .... 112 D8
Longwater La RG40 .. 141 E2
Longwater Rd
 Bracknell RG12 .... 118 C3
 Finchampstead RG40 . 141 E2
Long Wlk The SL4 .... 94 D7
Long Wlk The* SL4 .. 67 D4
Longwood Rd RG14 .. 105 B6
Longwood Ave SL3 ... 44 B1
Longworth Ave RG31 . 84 B7
Longworth Dr SL6 ... 20 C1
Lonsdale Cl SL6 ..... 20 A1
Lonsdale Way SL6 ... 40 F4
Look Ahead SL1 ..... 42 E4
Look Out Discovery Ctr The*
 RG12 .... 118 D1
Loosen Dr SL6 ...... 39 A3
Lord Knyvett Cl TW19 70 D1
Lord Knyvetts Ct 12 TW19 70 E1
Lord Mayors Dr SL2 . 22 A7
Lord Raglan Ho SL4 . 67 C4
Lords Bridge GU7 TW17 125 B2
Loring Rd SL4 .... 66 F6
Lorne Cl SL1 .... 42 B3
Lorne Pl 4 RG1 ..... 85 E7
Lorne St RG1 .... 85 E7
Lorraine Rd GU15 ... 151 F8
Lorraine Sch GU15 .... 151 E8
Lory Ridge GU19 .... 145 E4
Losfield Rd SL4 ..... 66 E6
Lossie Dr SL0 .... 44 B6
Loughborough RG12 118 E3
Loundyes Cl RG18 .. 106 B4
Lovatt Cl RG31 ..... 84 B7
Love Green Cl SL0 .. 44 C8
LOVE GREEN 44 D8
Love Lanes La SL0 .. 44 D8
Lovegrove Dr SL2 ... 21 F1
Love Hill La SL3 .... 44 C8
Lovejoy La SL4 ..... 66 D5
Love La
 Iver SL0 .... 44 D7
 Newbury RG14 ...... 105 A6
Lovelace Cl SL6 .... 17 F4
Lovelace Rd RG12 .. 118 E5
Lovel La SL4 .... 93 B3
Lovell Cl RG9 ...... 15 C8
Lovells Cl GU18 ... 146 B1
Lovel Rd SL4 ...... 93 A4
Loverock Rd RG30 . 58 D1
Love's Cl RG7 ..... 111 A3
Loves Wood RG7 .. 136 F5
Lovett Gdns SL6 ... 20 C3
Lovett Rd TW18 ... 96 C4
Lowbrook Dr SL6 .. 39 A3
Lowbrook Prim Sch SL6 39 A3
Lowbury RG12 ..... 118 E5
Lower Armour Rd RG31 57 D1
LOWER ASSENDON . 15 A6
Lower Boyndon Rd SL6 39 E6
Lower Britwell Rd SL2 21 D1
Lower Broadmoor Rd
 RG45 .... 143 D4
Lower Brook St 21 RG1 86 A6
Lower Canes GU46 . 149 A6
LOWER CAVERSHAM 59 D1
Lower Charles St GU15 151 C5
Lower Church Rd GU47 149 E8
Lower Cippenham La SL1 41 F6
Lower Comm RG27 . 140 F1
LOWER COMMON ... 140 E2
Lower Cookham Rd SL6 20 C2
LOWER EARLEY 87 A1
Lower Earley Way RG6 114 C8
Lower Earley Way N RG6 87 F2
Lower Earley Way W
 Earley RG6 .... 113 F7
 Lower Earley RG6 .... 114 A8
Lower Elmstone Dr RG31 57 C1
Lower Farm Ctr RG19 105 F1
LOWER FELTHAM ... 98 E5
Lower Gn GU46 .... 149 C7
LOWER GREEN 127 B5
Lower Henley Rd RG4 59 D3
Lower Henwick Farm
 RG18 .... 105 F5
Lower Lees Rd SL2 . 22 B2
Lower Mdw RG6 ... 87 B2
Lower Mill Field GU19 145 D2
Lower Moor 2 GU46 149 D5
Lower Nursery SL5 . 121 A4
LOWER PADWORTH 109 C4
Lower Pound La SL7 18 D8
Lower Raymond Almshouses
 3 RG14 .... 104 F2
Lower Rd
 Chilton OX11 .... 10 D8
 Cookham Rise SL6 ... 19 E7
Lower Sandhurst Rd RG40,
 GU47 .... 142 C2
Lower Ventnor Cotts SL6 19 C8
Lower Village Rd SL5 120 C4
Lower Wardle RG19 . 64 D7
Lower Way RG19 ... 106 B3
Lower Wokingham Rd RG40,
 RG45 .... 142 D5
Lower Woodsgreen Ct
 RG12 .... 104 A7

Loweswater Wlk GU15 152 D4
Lowfield Cl GU18 ... 153 A8
Lowfield Ct RG4 .... 59 C5
Lowfield Gn RG4 ... 59 E4
Lowfield Rd RG4 ... 59 D5
Lowlands Dr TW19 . 70 D2
Lowlands Rd GU17 . 150 C4
Lowry Cl GU47 ..... 150 D6
Lowther Cl RG41 ... 115 F8
Lowther Rd RG41 .. 115 F8
Loxwood RG6 ...... 87 C2
Loxwood Cl
 East Bedfont TW14 .. 98 D7
 Three Mile Cross RG7 113 A4
Lucan Dr TW18 .... 97 D1
Lucas Cl GU46 ..... 149 D5
Lucas Gn GU24 .... 153 E5
LUCAS GREEN 153 E5
Lucas Green Rd GU24 153 E5
Lucey Cl RG31 .... 57 B3
Luciano Way SL6 .. 98 B2
Luckley-Oakfield Sch
 RG40 .... 116 B3
Luckley Path RG40 116 C6
Luckley Rd RG41 .. 116 C6
Luckley Wood RG41 116 B3
Luckmore Dr RG6 .. 87 A3
Luddington Ave GU25 122 F7
Ludgrove Sch RG40 116 D3
Lud Lodge TW15 .. 97 E6
Ludlow RG12 ..... 118 B2
Ludlow Cl RG14 ... 105 E4
Ludlow Ho SL6 .... 39 E6
Ludlow Rd
 Feltham TW13 ..... 98 F5
 Maidenhead SL6 ... 39 E6
Luff Cl SL4 .... 66 E4
Luker Ave RG9 .... 15 D3
Lulworth Rd RG2 . 113 C8
Lunds Farm Rd RG5 88 A8
Lundy Cl SL1 ..... 41 E6
Lundy Ho RG2 .... 86 A2
Lundy La RG30 ... 85 C7
Lupin Cl GU19 ... 145 C1
Lupin Ride RG45 . 143 B7
Luscinia View RG1 86 C8
Luscombe Cl RG4 . 59 D2
Lutman La SL6 .... 2 F2
Lutman's Haven RG10 37 E5
Lutterworth Cl RG42 91 C1
Lutton Cl RG6 .... 113 F8
Lych Gate Cl GU47 149 F8
Lycroft Cl RG8 ... 34 C7
Lydbury RG12 .... 118 E5
Lydford Ave SL2 .. 42 D8
Lydford Rd RG1 .. 86 D6
Lydiaville Mobile Home Pk
 1 RG41 .... 88 A2
Lydney RG12 ..... 118 B2
Lydsey Cl SL2 .... 22 A2
Lyefield Ct RG4 .. 59 B6
Lyell Pl E SL4 .... 66 C4
Lyell Pl W SL4 ... 66 C4
Lyell Rd SL4 ..... 66 C4
Lyell Wlk E SL4 .. 66 C4
Lyell Wlk W SL4 . 66 C4
Lyle Ho RG8 ..... 55 F1
Lyme Gr RG31 ... 57 D1
Lymington Ave GU46 149 C5
Lymington Gate RG4 58 E5
Lynchets View RG17 24 E5
Lynch Hill La SL1 . 21 E2
Lynch Hill Prim Sch SL2 21 F2
Lynch La RG17 ... 25 B3
Lynden Cl SL6 ... 65 B8
Lynden Mews RG2 86 B5
Lyndhurst Ave
 Blackwater GU17 .. 150 C6
 Cookham Rise SL6 . 19 E6
Lyndhurst Ct RG12 119 A6
Lyndhurst Rd
 Ascot SL5 .... 120 A5
 Goring RG8 .... 34 C7
 Reading RG30 ..... 58 A1
Lyndhurst Sch GU15 151 B5
Lyndwood Dr SL4 . 68 A1
Lyndwood Par SL4 68 A1
LYNE 123 B1
Lyne Cl GU25 .... 122 F3
Lyne Crossing Rd KT16,
 GU25 .... 123 B3
Lyne Ct KT16 .... 122 F2
Lynegrove Ave TW15 98 C3
Lyneham Gdns SL6 19 B1
Lyneham Rd RG45 143 B5
Lyne La
 Lyne KT16, TW20 .. 123 A2
 Virginia Water KT16, TW20,
  GU25 .... 123 A3
Lyne Place Manor GU25 122 F2
Lyne Rd GU25 ... 122 E3
Lyngfield Pk SL6 . 65 D8
Lynmouth Ct RG1 59 B1
Lynmouth Rd RG1 59 A1
Lynton Cl RG3 ... 58 A3
Lynton Ct 4 RG14 105 A4
Lynton Ct 4 Reading RG1 59 B1
Lynton Gn SL6 .. 39 E7
Lynton Rd SL4 .. 120 E4
Lynwood Ave
 Egham TW20 ..... 95 E2
 Slough SL3 .... 43 D3
Lynwood Chase RG42 91 C1
Lynwood Cres SL5 120 E3
Lynwood Ct TW15 97 F3
Lyon Cl RG19 ... 106 F2

Lyon Oaks RG42 . . . . .91 B2
Lyon Rd RG45 . . . . 143 C6
Lyon Sq RG30. . . . . .85 A8
Lyon Way GU16. . . . . 151 C1
Lyon Way Ind Est GU16. . 151 C1
Lysander Cl RG5. . . . . .88 A8
Lysander Dr RG12. . . . . . . 118 C5
Lysander Mead SL6 . . . . . . .40 C8
Lytchett Minster Cl 4
RG12 . . . . 118 F4
Lytham RG12 . . . . 117 E3
Lytham Cl RG30. . . . . .85 C4
Lytham Ct SL5. . . . . 120 C4
Lytham End RG41. . . . . .57 B3
Lytham Rd RG5 . . . . .87 E7

M

Mabett Cl RG2. . . . . 140 E8
Mabley Ct RG12. . . . . 118 A3
MacAdam Ave RG45. . . . . 143 C7
Mc Ardle Way SL3 . . . . . . .69 D7
MacArthur Cl RG30 . . . . . . .84 F8
McAuliffe Dr SL1, SL2 . . . .21 F8
Macbeth Ct RG42 . . . . 118 E8
McCarthy Way RG40 . . . . . 141 F8
McCrae's Wlk RG10. . . . . . .36 D2
MacDonald Rd GU18 . . . . 153 A8
Mace Cl RG6 . . . . .87 A1
McIlroys Bldg RG1. . . . . . . .86 A7
Mackay Cl RG31. . . . . .84 E3
McKay Trad Est SL3 . . . . . .69 E5
McKenzie Ct 4 RG14 . . . . 104 F4
Mackenzie Mall 3 SL1. . . .42 F4
Mackenzie St 2 SL1 . . . . . .42 F4
McKernan Ct GU47. . . . . . 149 F8
Macklin Ct RG17. . . . . 100 D5
MacLarens Dr RG42. . . . . . 119 A8
Macnaghten Woods
GU15 . . . . 151 E6
McNair Cl RG6. . . . . .87 A1
MacPhail Cl RG40. . . . . . . 116 E8
Macrae Rd GU46. . . . . 149 C6
Maddle Rd RG17. . . . . .47 D7
Maddock Cl RG2. . . . . 113 D4
Madeira Pl 8 RG14 . . . . . 105 A2
Madejski Stad (Reading FC)
RG2 . . . . 112 F8
Madingley RG12 . . . . 118 B1
Madox Brown End GU47. 150 E6
Mafeking Rd TW19. . . . . . . .96 B6
Magdalene Rd
Littleton TW17 . . . . 124 F6
Sandhurst GU47 . . . . 143 F2
Magill Cl RG7. . . . . 113 B2
Magna Carta La TW19 . . . .95 E7
Magna Carta Sch The
TW18 . . . . .96 D2
Magna Rd TW20 . . . . .95 B2
Magnolia Cl
Sandhurst GU47 . . . . 143 D1
Winkfield RG42 . . . . 119 A8
Magnolia Ct
Brimpton RG19 . . . . 133 B6
Woodley RG5. . . . . .88 A7
Magnolia Gdns SL3 . . . . . .43 C3
Magnolia Way
Wokingham RG41 . . . . . . 115 F5
Wooburn Green HP10 . . . . .3 E7
Magpie Cl RG19 . . . . 106 B3
Magpie Way
Reading RG31 . . . . .84 B6
Slough SL2. . . . . .21 F1
Maguire Dr GU16 . . . . 152 C3
Mahonia Cl GU24 . . . . 153 F6
Maiden Erlegh Dr RG6 . . . .87 B4
Maiden Erlegh Sch RG6. . .87 B4
Maidenhatch RG8. . . . . .55 F1
MAIDENHEAD 39 F4
Maidenhead Bsns Campus
The SL6. . . . . .38 E3
MAIDENHEAD COURT 20 C4
Maidenhead Court Pk
SL6. . . . . .20 B3
Maidenhead Ho 21 RG14 .104 F2
Maidenhead Office Pk
SL6. . . . . .38 E2
Maidenhead Rd
Binfield RG40. . . . . .89 E3
Cookham Rise SL6. . . . . . .19 F6
Newell Green RG42. . . . . . .91 B6
Windsor SL4 . . . . .66 E7
Maidenhead Sta SL6 . . . . . .39 F6
Maidenhead Trad Pk SL6. .40 B2
Maiden Lane Ctr 1 RG6 . .87 D7
Maiden Pl RG6 . . . . .87 D2
Maidensfield RG41. . . . . . . .88 D2
Maiden's Gn SL4. . . . . .92 B6
MAIDEN'S GREEN 92 B5
Main Ave RG31 . . . . .84 B6
Main Dr
Bracknell RG42 . . . . .91 F2
Iver SL0. . . . . .44 E3
Winkfield, Newell Green
RG42. . . . . .92 A1
Winkfield RG42, SL5 . . . . 119 B8
Main Gate Lodges SL4 . . . .94 F5
Mainprize Rd RG12 . . . . . . 118 C7
Main St
Chaddleworth RG20. . . . . . .49 A7
Chilton OX11 . . . . .10 D8
Greenham RG19 . . . . 131 F5
Newtown RG19 . . . . 132 A5
West Ilsley RG20. . . . . .10 A2
Mainstone Rd GU24. . . . . . 153 F3
Maise Webster Cl TW19 . .97 D8
Maisonettes The RG8 . . . . .34 D8

Maist Prep Sch The SL5. . 120 D5
Maist Senior Sch SL5 . . . 120 D5
Maitland Rd RG1 . . . . .85 E7
Maiwand Gdns RG30 . . . . . .84 D7
Maize La RG42. . . . . .91 E2
Majendie Cl RG14. . . . . . . 104 D5
Major's Farm Rd SL3 . . . . .68 D7
Makepiece Rd RG42. . . . . . .91 B1
Maker Cl RG30. . . . . .85 B5
Makins Rd RG9 . . . . .35 B7
Malcolm Pl 6 RG1 . . . . . . .86 A8
Malders La SL6. . . . . .19 C3
Maldon Cl RG30 . . . . .85 D6
Malet Cl TW20. . . . . .96 D2
Malham Fell RG12 . . . . 118 A5
Malham Rd RG19 . . . . 106 C3
Mallard Cl
Burnham SL1 . . . . .21 B3
Earley RG6. . . . . .87 A3
Twyford RG10 . . . . .61 E3
Mallard Ct RG14 . . . . 104 F3
Mallard Dr SL1. . . . . .41 F6
Mallard Pl 2 GU14 . . . . . . 151 A1
Mallard Row RG1 . . . . .86 A7
Mallards The
Ashford TW15 . . . . .98 A3
Great Shefford RG17. . . . . .48 A3
Laleham TW18 . . . . 124 B7
Mallards Way GU18 . . . . . 153 A8
Mallard Way
Aldermaston Wharf RG7 . .109 B3
Yateley GU46. . . . . 149 B6
Mallory Ave RG4 . . . . .59 D6
Mallowdale Rd RG12. . . . . 118 E2
Mallow Gdns RG18 . . . . . . 106 D5
Mallow Pk SL6 . . . . .19 C1
Malone Rd RG5. . . . . .87 D6
MALPAS 83 E6
Malpas Rd SL2 . . . . .43 B6
Maltby Way RG6 . . . . .87 D3
Malt Ct 8 RG14 . . . . 104 F4
Malt Hill
Egham TW20 . . . . .95 E3
Newell Green RG42 . . . . . . .91 E5
Malthouse Cl 8 RG19. . . 106 E2
Malt House Cl SL4 . . . . .95 B8
Malthouse Flats RG9. . . . . .16 D6
Malthouse La
4 Reading RG1 . . . . .85 F8
West End GU24 . . . . 153 F7
Malthouse Way 2 SL7. . . . .1 D1
Maltings The 6 RG1 . . . . . .86 A7
Maltings The
8 Newbury RG14 . . . . . . .104 F2
Staines TW18. . . . . .96 E4
Thatcham RG19 . . . . 106 F2
West Ilsley RG20. . . . . .10 B1
Malton Ave SL1. . . . . .42 B6
Malt Shovel La RG17. . . . . .24 F4
Malton Way 7 SL7. . . . . . . .1 C3
Malvern Cl
Brands Hill SL3. . . . . .69 A8
5 Newbury RG14 . . . . . . .104 F1
Reading RG1. . . . . .86 D6
Malvern Rd
Harlington UB3 . . . . .71 E7
5 Maidenhead SL6 . . . . . . .19 D1
Yateley GU17 . . . . 149 F1
Malvern Way RG10. . . . . . . .61 D7
Malyns Way RG31. . . . . .57 B4
Managua Cl RG4. . . . . .59 E2
Manchester Rd RG1. . . . . . .86 E7
Mandarin Ct RG14 . . . . . . 105 C2
Mandarin Ct RG14 . . . . . . 105 C2
Mandarin Rd RG12. . . . . . . 117 F4
Mandela Ct 2 RG1. . . . . . . .86 D7
Mander Ct RG4 . . . . .59 B3
Mandeville Cl RG30 . . . . . . .84 F6
Mandeville Ct TW20. . . . . . .96 A4
Mandeville Rd TW17. . . . . 125 A4
Manea Cl RG6 . . . . 114 C8
Manfield Cl SL2 . . . . .22 A2
Manners Rd RG5. . . . . .87 D7
Mannock Way RG5. . . . . . . .88 A7
Manor Barns La RG40. . . . 141 F2
Manor Bglws RG20. . . . . . . .31 D4
Manor Cl RG42 . . . . .91 A1
Manor Commercial Ctr
RG2. . . . . .86 A1
Manor Cres RG20 . . . . .31 D4
Manorcroft Prim Sch
TW20. . . . . .96 A2
Manorcrofts Rd TW20 . . . . .96 A2
Manor Ct
Maidenhead SL6 . . . . .19 D3
Marlow SL7 . . . . .1 C3
Slough, Cippenham SL1 . . . .41 F5
Slough, Upton Park SL1 . . . .42 F3
Manor Farm
20 Egham TW20 . . . . .96 A3
Froxfield SN8. . . . . .99 B4
Poyle SL3 . . . . .69 E6
Manor Farm Ave TW17 . . . 125 B3
Manor Farm Cl SL4 . . . . . . .66 F4
Manor Farm Cotts SL4 . . . .68 A2
Manor Farm Ct TW20 . . . . .96 A3
Manor Farm Ho SL4 . . . . . .66 F4
Manor Farm La
Tidmarsh RG8 . . . . .56 C2
Manor Farm Rd RG2. . . . . . .86 B1
Manor Gdns HP10 . . . . .3 B8
Manor Gr SL6 . . . . .65 D6
Manor Ho The GU15 . . . . . 151 D6
Manor House Ct
Lower Halliford TW17 . . . . 125 B2
Reading RG1. . . . . .87 A5

Manor House Dr SL5. . . . . .93 A1
Manor House La SL3. . . . . . .68 B6
Manor La
Brimpton RG7 . . . . 133 C6
Chieveley RG20 . . . . .51 B1
Harlington UB3 . . . . .71 D8
Hermitage RG18 . . . . .79 B8
Leckhampstead RG20 . . . . .49 F4
Maidenhead SL6 . . . . .39 E4
Newbury RG14. . . . . 105 E5
Manor Leaze TW20. . . . . . . .96 B3
Manor Mead Sch TW17. . 125 B4
MANOR PARK. 22 D1
Manor Park Cl RG30 . . . . . .84 C6
Manor Park Dr
Finchampstead RG40. . . . 141 E6
Yateley GU46. . . . . 149 E6
Manor Pk
Froxfield SN8. . . . . .99 B4
Staines TW18. . . . . .96 D5
Manor Pl
Newbury RG14. . . . . 104 D5
Staines TW18. . . . . .97 B3
Manor Prim Sch RG30 . . . .85 A4
Manor Rd
Ashford TW15 . . . . .98 A3
Goring RG8 . . . . .34 B5
Henley-on-T RG9 . . . . .35 D8
Letcombe Bassett OX12 . . . .7 C5
Maidenhead SL6 . . . . .39 E4
Oatlands Park KT12. . . . . 125 F2
Whitchurch-on-T RG8 . . . . .56 C7
Windsor SL4 . . . . .66 E5
Wokingham RG40 . . . . . . 116 A2
Manor The RG42. . . . . 113 C5
Manor View RG7 . . . . 133 F7
Manor Way
Bagshot GU19 . . . . 145 F3
Egham TW20 . . . . .95 F2
Holyport SL6. . . . . .65 A8
Manor Wood Gate RG9. . . .36 A4
Manse Cl UB3 . . . . .71 D8
Mansel Cl SL2 . . . . .43 B8
Mansell Cl SL4 . . . . .66 E5
Mansell Ct RG2. . . . . .86 E2
Mansell Dr RG14. . . . . 130 C5
Mansfield Cl SL5. . . . . 119 D7
Mansfield Cres RG12. . . . . 118 B3
Mansfield Ho 4 TW18 . . . .96 F3
Mansfield Pl SL5. . . . . 119 D8
Mansfield Rd
Reading RG1. . . . . .86 B7
Wokingham RG41 . . . . . . 116 A5
Man's Hill RG7 . . . . 111 C2
Mansion House St 7
RG14 . . . . 105 A3
Mansion La SL0 . . . . .44 C6
Manston Dr RG12 . . . . 118 C3
Mant Cl RG20 . . . . .75 D5
Manuka Ct GU47 . . . . 149 F8
Manygate Mobile Home Site
TW17 . . . . 125 D3
Maple Bank RG10 . . . . .61 E6
Maple Cl
Blackwater GU17. . . . . . . 150 C5
Maidenhead SL6 . . . . .39 C5
Sandhurst GU47 . . . . 143 F1
Winnersh RG41. . . . . .88 D3
Maple Cres
Newbury RG14. . . . . 105 A2
Slough SL2. . . . . .43 B6
Maple Ct
Ashford TW15 . . . . .98 D1
8 Bracknell RG12. . . . . . . 118 F5
Englefield Green TW20 . . . .95 B2
Goring RG8 . . . . .34 B6
Marlow SL7 . . . . .1 C1
Windsor SL4 . . . . .67 C4
Mapledene RG4 . . . . .58 E3
Maple Dr
Crowthorne RG45 . . . . . . 143 C7
Lightwater GU18 . . . . 152 F8
Reading RG30 . . . . .84 D6
MAPLEDURHAM. 57 E6
Mapledurham Dr RG8. . . . . .57 C5
Mapledurham Ho * RG31. .84 D8
Mapledurham View RG31. . .57 D2
Mapledurham Watermill*
RG31. . . . . .57 D6
Mapledurham Wlk SL6. . . . .19 E3
Maple Gdns
Reading RG2. . . . . .86 E2
Stanwell TW19. . . . . .97 E8
Yateley GU46. . . . . 149 D5
Maple Ho
Maple Ho RG4 . . . . .59 C3
Maple La RG8 . . . . .55 B5
Maple Rise SL7 . . . . .1 E1
Maplespeen Ct RG14. . . . . 104 F4
Maples The 10 SL8 . . . . .3 B3
Maplin Pk SL3 . . . . .44 B4
Marathon Cl RG5 . . . . .88 B8
Marbeck Cl SL4. . . . . .66 D6
Marbull Way RG42 . . . . .91 B2
Marchant Cl RG19 . . . . 131 D7
Marchant Ct SL7 . . . . .2 A3
Marcheria Cl RG12 . . . . . . 118 A4
Marches The SL4 . . . . .42 D2
Marchment Pl RG12 . . . . . 118 C6
Marchwood Ave RG4. . . . . .59 C7
Marcia Ct SL1. . . . . .41 F5
Marconi Rd RG14 . . . . 104 F4
Marcus Cl RG30. . . . . .85 B7
Mardale GU15 . . . . 152 F4
Mardy RG4 . . . . .58 E5
Marefield RG6 . . . . .87 C2
Marefield Rd SL7 . . . . .1 D1

Mare La RG10 . . . . .63 E3
Marescroft Rd SL2. . . . . . . .21 E1
Mareshall Ave RG42. . . . . . .91 B2
Marfleet Cl 1 RG6 . . . . .87 E2
Margaret Cassidy Ho UB7 .70 C6
Margaret Cl
Reading RG2. . . . . .86 E2
Staines TW18. . . . . .97 D2
Maria Ct 15 RG30. . . . . .85 D6
Marie Davis Ct 16 RG1 . . . .86 B7
Marigold Cl RG45. . . . . 142 F6
Marina Cl KT16 . . . . 124 C1
Marina Way
Bourne End SL8. . . . . .3 A4
Iver SL0. . . . . .44 F6
Mariners La RG7. . . . . .82 B3
Marino Way RG40. . . . . 141 A6
Marion Ave TW17 . . . . 125 B4
Marish Ct SL3 . . . . .44 A3
Marish Prim Sch SL3 . . . . . .44 A3
Marish Wharf Ind Est SL3 .43 E4
Marjory Kinnon Sch
TW14 . . . . .71 E2
Markby Way RG6 . . . . .87 E2
Market La SL3 . . . . .44 C3
Market Pl
Bracknell RG12. . . . . 118 B7
Colnbrook SL3 . . . . .69 C7
Henley-on-T RG9 . . . . .15 D2
Lambourn RG17. . . . . .25 B2
8 Newbury RG14 . . . . 105 A3
Reading RG1. . . . . .86 B7
Wokingham RG40 . . . . . . 116 C6
Market Place Mews RG9 . .15 D2
Market Sq
6 Marlow SL7 . . . . .1 D2
Staines TW18. . . . . .96 E4
Market St
Bracknell RG12. . . . . 118 B7
Maidenhead SL6 . . . . .39 F7
Newbury RG14. . . . . 105 A2
8 Windsor SL4 . . . . .67 D6
Market Way 2 RG1. . . . . . . .86 B7
Markham Centre Trad Est
The RG7 . . . . .83 F2
Markham Ct GU15 . . . . 151 D6
Marks Rd RG41 . . . . 116 A8
Marlborough Ave RG6. . . . .86 D5
Marlborough Bsns Ctr
KT16. . . . . 123 F1
Marlborough Cl SL6 . . . . . . .39 A6
Marlborough Cres UB3. . . .71 D7
Marlborough Ct
7 Hungerford RG17. . . . . . 100 D5
Reading RG1. . . . . .85 F6
Slough SL1. . . . . .41 E7
Wokingham RG40 . . . . . . 116 D7
Marlborough Ho
5 Maidenhead SL6. . . . . . . .39 F6
Reading RG1. . . . . .86 D5
Marlborough Rd
Ashford TW15 . . . . .97 E3
Maidenhead SL6 . . . . .39 A6
Slough SL3. . . . . .43 A2
Marlborough Rise GU15. . 151 E6
Marlborough Way RG31 . . .84 A4
Marley Croft TW18. . . . . . . .96 E5
Marlin Cl SL7 . . . . .1 D1
Marling Cl RG31 . . . . .57 C2
Marlow Bottom 1 C6
Marlow Bridge La SL7 . . . . .18 E8
Marlow CE Inf Sch SL7. . . . .1 D3
Marlow Com Hospl SL7 . . . .1 E2
Marlow Ct RG4 . . . . .59 D3
Marlowes The RG14 . . . . . 130 F8
Marlow Ho SL7 . . . . .1 D1
Marlow Lodge 13 SL6 . . . . .39 F6
Marlow Mill SL7 . . . . .1 E1
Marlow Rd
Bisham SL6. . . . . .18 E4
Henley-on-T RG9 . . . . .15 E3
Little Marlow SL7, SL8 . . . . .2 D5
Maidenhead SL6 . . . . .39 F7
Marlow Bottom SL7. . . . . . . .1 B7
Marlow Sta SL7. . . . . .1 F2
Marlston Cotts RG18 . . . . . .79 F5
Marlston Rd RG18 . . . . .79 C6
Marmion Rd RG9 . . . . .35 E8
Marquis Ct TW19 . . . . .97 E7
Marquis Pl 4 RG1 . . . . .86 E7
Marriott Cl TW14 . . . . .71 D3
Marsack St RG4 . . . . .59 C2
Mars Cl RG41. . . . . 115 F6
Marshall Cl
Frimley GU16. . . . . 152 D2
Purley on T RG8. . . . . .57 C5
Marshall Ct
Marshall Ho 1 RG30. . . . . .85 B7
Marshalls Ct RG14 . . . . . . 104 D5
Marsham Ho RG42. . . . . . . .91 C1
Marsh Ct RG30. . . . . .85 B7
MARSH BENHAM 103 D4
Marshfield SL3 . . . . .68 C6
Marshgate Apartments
RG17. . . . . 100 B5
Marshgate Trad Est SL6 . . .41 A7
Marsh La
Curridge RG18 . . . . .78 D4
Hungerford RG17 . . . . 100 B5
Newbury RG17. . . . . 105 A3
Taplow SL6 . . . . .40 B8
Marshland Sq RG4 . . . . .59 B5
Marsh Mill RG9 . . . . .36 A8
Mars Ho RG7 . . . . 134 E2

Marsh Pl RG8. . . . . .56 D5
Marsh Rd RG18 . . . . 106 E4
Marshwood Rd GU18. . . . . 153 D8
Marston Dr RG14. . . . . 105 D5
Marston Way SL5 . . . . 119 E7
Martel Cl GU15 . . . . 152 C7
Marten Pl RG31. . . . . .57 B3
Martin Cl
Windsor SL4 . . . . .66 D6
Woodley RG5. . . . . .87 E6
Martindale Ave GU15 . . . . 152 C4
Martineau La RG10 . . . . . . .88 E7
Martingale Chase RG14. . . 105 C4
Martin Rd
Maidenhead SL6 . . . . .39 F8
Slough SL1. . . . . .42 E3
Martins Cl GU17 . . . . 150 D4
Martins Dr RG41. . . . . 116 D8
MARTIN'S HERON 118 F6
Martin's Heron Sta RG12. 118 F5
Martins La RG12 . . . . 118 E6
Martin's Plain SL2 . . . . .22 F3
Martins The RG19 . . . . 106 F2
Martin Way GU16 . . . . 151 E2
Marunden Gn SL2 . . . . .21 F2
Marwyn Cotts RG7 . . . . . . 110 C3
Mary Drew Almshouses The
TW20 . . . . .95 D2
Mary Hare Gram Sch
RG14 . . . . .77 F3
Maryland RG40 . . . . 141 E8
Mary Lyne Almshouses
RG30 . . . . .84 F5
Mary Mead RG42 . . . . .91 D2
Mary Morgan Ct SL2. . . . . . .42 D8
Maryside SL3 . . . . .43 E4
Mascoll Path SL2 . . . . .21 F2
Masdar Gdns RG40 . . . . . . 143 C6
Masefield Gdns RG45 . . . . 143 B3
Masefield Rd RG18. . . . . . . 106 D4
Masefield Way TW19 . . . . . .97 F7
Mason Cl GU46 . . . . 149 E5
Mason Ct
Ball Hill RG20 . . . . 129 F1
Reading RG1. . . . . .85 F8
Masonic Hall Rd KT16. . . . 123 F3
Mason Pl GU47 . . . . 149 F8
Mason's Ct SL1 . . . . .41 E6
Masons Rd SL1. . . . . .41 E6
Mason St RG1 . . . . .85 E8
Master Cl RG5. . . . . .88 B8
Mathisen Way SL3 . . . . .69 E6
Matlock Rd RG4 . . . . .58 E4
Matson Dr RG9 . . . . .15 F2
Matthew Arnold Cl TW18. .97 C2
Matthew Arnold Sch The
TW18 . . . . .97 C2
Matthews Cl RG19 . . . . . . 106 B4
Matthews Chase RG42 . . . .90 F1
Matthews Ct RG19 . . . . . . 106 B4
Matthews Cl RG19 . . . . . . 120 D5
MATTHEWSGREEN 116 A8
Matthewsgreen Rd RG41 116 A8
Matthews La TW18. . . . . . . .96 F4
Matthews Rd GU15 . . . . . . 151 C8
Maudsley Ho SL6. . . . . .40 B7
Maultway Cl GU15 . . . . 152 B8
Maultway Cres GU15. . . . . 152 B8
Maultway N GU15. . . . . 145 B1
Maultway The GU15,
GU16 . . . . 152 D6
Maureen Campbell Ct
SL6. . . . . 125 B4
Mawbray Cl RG6 . . . . .87 C2
Maxdata Ctr The RG12 . . . 118 A7
Maxine Cl GU47. . . . . 143 B1
Maxwell Cl RG5. . . . . .87 E8
Maxwell Cl SL1 . . . . .21 C1
Maxwell Rd TW15. . . . . .98 C2
Maybrick Cl GU47. . . . . 142 F1
Maybury Cl SL1 . . . . .41 D7
May Cl 2 GU47 . . . . 150 D8
Mayfair RG30. . . . . .84 D7
Mayfair Dr RG14 . . . . 104 E1
Mayfield Ave RG31. . . . . . . .84 B4
Mayfield Cl TW15 . . . . .98 B2
Mayfield Cotts RG20 . . . . . .31 C4
Mayfield Dr
Caversham RG4 . . . . .59 D3
Windsor SL4 . . . . .67 A4
Mayfield Gdns TW18 . . . . . .96 F2
Mayfield Light Ind Est
SL4. . . . . .93 B5
Mayfield Mews RG41. . . . . 115 A8
Mayfield Rd
Camberley GU15 . . . . 151 B1
Wooburn Green HP10 . . . . .3 E6
May Fields
Sindlesham RG41. . . . . . . 115 A8
Winnersh RG41. . . . . .88 A1
Mayflower Cl 10 RG14 . . . .80 B7
Mayflower Dr GU46 . . . . . . 149 B7
Mayflower Way SL2 . . . . . . .22 B8
Maying The RG2 . . . . 113 B6
Maynard Cl RG18 . . . . 106 C5
Maynard Ct
6 Staines TW18. . . . . .97 A4
Windsor SL4 . . . . .67 A4
Mayors La RG14. . . . . 105 A2
Mayow Cl RG19 . . . . 106 F2
May Pk RG31 . . . . .84 B5
Maypole Rd SL6 . . . . .41 A8
Mays Cl RG6. . . . . .87 B5
Mays Croft RG12. . . . . 118 A5

MAYS GREEN 35 B5
Mays La RG6 . . . . 87 B5
May's La RG7 . . . . 136 A7
Mays Rd RG40 . . . . 116 E6
May Tree Cl SL7 . . . . 1 C6
Maytree Wlk RG4 . . . . 59 E4
Maywood Dr GU15 . . . . . . 152 A7
Meachen Ct **2** RG40 . . . . 116 C6
Mead Ave SL3 . . . . 44 B4
Mead Cl
 Caversham RG4 . . . . 59 D2
 Egham TW20 . . . . 96 B2
 3 Marlow SL7 . . . . 1 F3
 Reading RG31 . . . . 84 B6
 Slough SL3 . . . . 44 B4
Mead Ct TW20 . . . . 96 C2
Meade Ct GU19 . . . . 145 F3
Meadfield Ave SL3 . . . . 44 A3
Meadfield Rd SL3 . . . . 44 B3
Mead Haze SL6 . . . . 20 C2
Meadhurst SL5 . . . . 120 A6
Meadhurst Pk TW16 . . . . . . 98 E2
Meadhurst Rd KT16 . . . . . 124 B1
Mead La
 Chertsey KT16 . . . . 124 C1
 Upper Basildon RG8 . . . . . 55 D6
Meadowbank RG20 . . . . . 129 B7
Meadow Bank **1** SL8 . . . . . 3 B3
Meadowbrook Rd GU18 . . 146 C1
Meadowbrook Cl SL3 . . . . . 69 F6
Meadowbrook Montessori
 Sch RG42 . . . . 91 F4
Meadow Cl
 Blackwater GU17 . . . . 150 D4
 Compton RG20 . . . . 31 E5
 Goring RG8 . . . . 34 C6
 Marlow SL7 . . . . 1 F1
 Moulsford OX10 . . . . 13 F4
 Old Windsor SL4 . . . . 68 B2
 Thatcham RG19 . . . . 106 C3
Meadow Cotts
 Shepperton TW17 . . . . . . 125 B3
 West End GU24 . . . . 153 F7
Meadow Croft RG17 . . . . . . 73 A1
Meadowcroft Rd RG2 . . . . 113 C8
Meadow Ct TW18 . . . . 96 E5
Meadow Gdns TW18 . . . . . 96 D3
Meadow Ho **4** GU17 . . . . 150 E4
Meadow La
 Eton SL4 . . . . 67 C7
 Pangbourne RG8 . . . . 56 D5
Meadowlands RG7 . . . . 81 D4
Meadowlea Cl UB7 . . . . 70 D8
Meadow Rd
 Ashford TW15 . . . . 98 D3
 Earley RG6 . . . . 87 D3
 Henley-on-T RG9 . . . . 15 E1
 Newbury RG14 . . . . 130 F8
 Reading RG1 . . . . 58 D1
 Slough SL3 . . . . 43 E3
 Wentworth GU25 . . . . 121 E4
 Wokingham RG41 . . . . . . 116 A5
Meadows Bsns Pk The
 GU17 . . . . 150 E4
Meadowside RG31 . . . . 57 B1
Meadowside Rd RG8 . . . . . 56 D5
Meadows Sch The HP10 . . . 3 E6
Meadows (Superstores) The
 GU47 . . . . 150 E5
Meadows The HP10 . . . . 3 B8
Meadowsweet Cl RG18 . . 106 E4
Meadow Vale Prim Sch
 RG42 . . . . 117 F8
Meadowview
 Hungerford RG17 . . . . . . 100 D6
 Shepperton TW17 . . . . . . 125 C3
 Stanwell TW19 . . . . 69 F2
Meadow View
 Chertsey KT16 . . . . 124 C1
 Marlow Bottom SL7 . . . . 1 E6
 Winnersh RG41 . . . . 88 D3
Meadow View Cl RG1 . . . . . 58 E1
Meadow View La SL6 . . . . . 64 E8
Meadow Way
 Blackwater GU17 . . . . 150 C5
 Bracknell RG42 . . . . 91 A1
 Caversham RG4 . . . . 59 D2
 Dorney SL6 . . . . 40 F4
 Fifield SL6 . . . . 65 D6
 Old Windsor SL4 . . . . 68 B1
 Theale RG7 . . . . 83 D3
 West End GU24 . . . . 153 F6
 Wokingham RG41 . . . . . . 116 A5
Meadow Wlk
 Bourne End SL8 . . . . 3 A5
 Wokingham RG41 . . . . . . 116 A6
Meads Cl RG20 . . . . 50 D7
Meads The
 Stoke Poges SL2 . . . . 23 A2
 4 Windsor SL4 . . . . 67 A5
Mead The RG17 . . . . 48 B3
Meadway
 Ashford TW15 . . . . 98 A4
 Frimley GU16 . . . . 151 F2
 Staines TW18 . . . . 97 A1
Mead Way SL1 . . . . 41 D8
Meadway Cl TW18 . . . . 97 A1
Meadway Prec RG30 . . . . . 85 A6
Meadway The RG30 . . . . . . 84 F7
Mead Wlk SL3 . . . . 44 B4
Meare Est HP10 . . . . 3 E8
Mearings The RG30 . . . . . 111 F5
Measham Way RG6 . . . . 87 C2
Meashill Way OX11 . . . . 9 F8
Meavy Gdns RG2 . . . . 86 B2

Medallion Pl SL6 . . . . 40 B7
Mede Cl TW19 . . . . 95 D7
Mede Ct TW18 . . . . 96 E5
Medina Cl RG41 . . . . 115 E7
Medlake Rd TW20 . . . . 96 C2
Medlar Dr GU17 . . . . 150 F3
MEDMENHAM 17 A5
Medway Cl
 Thatcham RG18 . . . . 106 B5
 Wokingham RG41 . . . . . . 115 F7
Medway Ct RG30 . . . . 85 D6
Melbourne Ave
 Slough SL1 . . . . 42 C7
 Winnersh RG41 . . . . 88 C1
Melbury Cl KT16 . . . . 124 A2
Meldreth Way
 Earley RG6 . . . . 87 C1
 Shinfield RG6 . . . . 114 D8
Meldrum Cl RG14 . . . . 130 C6
Melford Gn RG4 . . . . 59 E6
Melksham Cl RG6 . . . . 113 E8
Melling Cl RG6 . . . . 87 E3
Mellor Wlk
 1 Reading RG1 . . . . 86 B5
 17 Windsor SL4 . . . . 67 D6
Melody Cl RG41 . . . . 88 C3
Melrose RG12 . . . . 118 B1
Melrose Ave RG6 . . . . 87 A5
Melrose Gdns RG22 . . . . . 114 E2
Melton Ct SL6 . . . . 39 F6
Melville Ave GU16 . . . . . . 151 F1
Membury Bsns Pk RG17 . . 45 E4
Membury Wlk RG12 . . . . . 118 F5
Memorial Ave RG9 . . . . 35 E2
Mendip Cl
 Charvil RG10 . . . . 61 B4
 Harlington UB3 . . . . 71 D7
 Slough SL3 . . . . 44 A1
Mendip Dr RG31 . . . . 84 A6
Mendip Rd RG12 . . . . 118 E4
Menpes Rd RG31 . . . . 57 C4
Mentone Cotts RG10 . . . . . 62 F5
Meon Cl RG26 . . . . 135 A1
Merchants Pl **8** RG1 . . . . 86 A8
Mercia Ho TW15 . . . . 125 C8
Mercian Way SL1 . . . . 41 D5
Mercia Rd SL6 . . . . 39 C4
Mercury Ave RG41 . . . . . . 115 E6
Mercury Ho RG7 . . . . 134 E2
Mercury Pk The HP10 . . . . . 3 E7
Mere Cl SL7 . . . . 1 F2
Mere Rd
 Shepperton TW17 . . . . . . 125 B3
 Slough SL1 . . . . 42 F3
Mereside Pk TW15 . . . . 98 C4
Meridian Ct SL5 . . . . 120 B8
Meridian The RG1 . . . . 86 C8
Merlewood RG12 . . . . 118 D4
Merlin Cl SL3 . . . . 69 B8
Merlin Clove RG42 . . . . 92 B2
Merlin Ct
 Frimley GU16 . . . . 151 D1
 3 Maidenhead SL6 . . . . . 39 B8
Merlin Lo RG30 . . . . 85 D5
Mermaid Cl RG41 . . . . 88 B2
Merrick Ho RG2 . . . . 86 A2
Merrifield Cl RG6 . . . . 114 D8
Merrivale Gdns RG2 . . . . . . 86 B1
Merron Cl GU46 . . . . 149 C5
MERRYHILL GREEN 88 D3
Merryhill Green La RG41 . . 88 D3
Merryhill Rd RG42 . . . . . . 118 B8
Merryman Dr RG45 . . . . . 143 A7
Merryweather Cl RG40 . . 115 F1
Merrywood Pk GU15 . . . . 151 F4
Mersey Way RG18 . . . . 106 B5
Merston Ct RG4 . . . . 59 A4
Merther Vale RG4 . . . . 59 A6
Merton Cl
 Maidenhead SL6 . . . . 39 C3
 Sandhurst GU47 . . . . 143 F2
Merton Ct **10** SL1 . . . . 43 A3
Mertonford RG40 . . . . 116 D5
Merton Rd SL1 . . . . 43 A3
Merton Rd N RG2 . . . . 86 B1
Merton Rd S RG2 . . . . 86 B1
Mervyn Rd TW17 . . . . 125 C2
Merwin Way SL4 . . . . 66 D4
Meryton Ho SL4 . . . . 67 A4
Metcalf Rd TW15 . . . . 98 B3
Meteor Cl RG5 . . . . 88 A7
Metro Ctr The RG41 . . . . . . 89 A2
Mews The
 Ascot SL5 . . . . 120 C4
 Farley Hill RG7 . . . . 140 C7
 Newbury RG14 . . . . 104 E2
 Reading RG1 . . . . 86 E6
 Sonning RG4 . . . . 60 D4
Mey Cl RG31 . . . . 84 B5
Meyrick Dr RG14 . . . . 130 C5
Mezel Hill Cotts SL4 . . . . . 94 C3
Michael Cl SL6 . . . . 39 C5
Michaelmas Cl GU46 . . . . 149 D4
Michaels Chase RG4 . . . . . 59 C3
Micheldever Way RG12 . . 118 F4
Micklands Prim Sch RG4 . . 59 F6
Micklands Rd RG4 . . . . 59 E3
Mickle Hill GU47 . . . . 143 A1
Micro Ctr The RG2 . . . . 86 B2
Midas Ho RG7 . . . . 134 E2
Midcroft SL2 . . . . 22 B1

Middle Cl
 Frimley GU15 . . . . 152 C6
 Newbury RG14 . . . . 130 D7
Middle Farm Cl RG20 . . . . 51 B2
Middlefields RG10 . . . . 61 E6
Middlefields Cl RG10 . . . . . 61 E6
Middle Gn
 Slough SL3 . . . . 43 E6
 Staines TW18 . . . . 97 D1
Middle Gordon Rd GU15 . 151 C5
MIDDLE GREEN 43 E5
Middlegreen Rd SL3 . . . . . 43 D5
Middlegreen Trad Est
 SL3 . . . . 43 D4
Middle Hill TW20 . . . . 95 D3
Middlemoor Rd GU16 . . . 151 E1
Middle Springs RG8 . . . . . . 34 C8
Middleton Ct RG14 . . . . . . 105 E5
Middleton Rd GU15 . . . . . 151 F7
Middletons Cl RG17 . . . . . 100 E7
Middle Wlk SL1 . . . . 21 B2
MIDGHAM 107 E3
MIDGHAM GREEN 108 B4
Midgham Hall RG7 . . . . . . 108 C2
Midsummer Mdw RG4 . . . . 58 F6
Midway Ave
 Chertsey KT16 . . . . 124 A6
 Thorpe TW20 . . . . 123 B6
Midway Cl TW19 . . . . 97 B5
Midwinter Cl RG30 . . . . 84 E8
Milam Cl RG2 . . . . 140 E8
Milbanke Ct RG12 . . . . . . 117 F7
Milbanke Way RG12 . . . . . 117 F7
Mildenhall Cl RG6 . . . . 87 D2
Mildenhall Rd SL1 . . . . 42 E7
Mildridge Farmhouse SL3 69 B7
Mile Elm SL7 . . . . 2 A3
MILE END 25 C6
MILES GREEN 153 F2
Miles Pl GU18 . . . . 152 F7
Milestone Ave RG10 . . . . . . 61 A5
Milestone Cres RG4 . . . . . . 61 A4
Milestone View Ct RG4 . . . 59 E4
Miles Way RG5 . . . . 88 A7
Milford Ct SL1 . . . . 43 A4
Milford Rd RG1 . . . . 86 D6
Military Dr **2** RG10 . . . . . 106 E2
Milkhouse Rd RG20 . . . . . 103 D4
Millars Brook RG41 . . . . . 116 A4
Millars Bsns Ctr RG41 . . . 116 A4
Millbank SL7 . . . . 1 F1
Millbank Cres RG5 . . . . 87 F6
Millboard Rd SL8 . . . . 3 B3
Millbridge Rd GU46 . . . . . 149 B8
Millbrook Way SL3 . . . . 69 E5
Mill Cl
 Bagshot GU19 . . . . 145 D3
 Wokingham RG41 . . . . . . 115 F7
Mill Cotts HP10 . . . . 3 C5
Mill Ct SL3 . . . . 69 C4
Milldown Ave RG8 . . . . 34 C7
Milldown Rd RG8 . . . . 34 C7
MILL END 16 D7
Millennium Ct RG2 . . . . 86 C4
Millennium Mews SL1 . . . . 42 E5
Millennium Way RG12 . . 118 C8
Miller Dr RG41 . . . . 88 A2
Millers Cl
 Goring RG8 . . . . 34 B7
 Staines TW18 . . . . 97 B3
Millers Ct RG4 . . . . 59 D1
Miller's Ct TW20 . . . . 96 D2
Miller's Field RG17 . . . . 48 B3
Millers Gr RG31 . . . . 84 E4
Miller's La SL4 . . . . 68 A1
Millers Thumb RG12 . . . . 118 E2
Milley La RG10 . . . . 62 B8
Milley Rd RG10 . . . . 62 B6
Mill Farm Ave TW16 . . . . . 98 E1
Millfield
 Charlton TW16 . . . . 125 D8
 Thatcham RG18 . . . . 106 B7
Mill Field GU19 . . . . 145 D3
Millgate Ct RG10 . . . . 61 E5
Mill Gn
 Bracknell RG42 . . . . 90 E1
 Caversham RG4 . . . . 59 C1
MILL GREEN 132 F3
Millgreen La RG19 . . . . . . 132 F3
Mill Hall Sch RG19 . . . . . . 131 D8
Millholme Wlk GU15 . . . . 152 C4
Mill House La KT16 . . . . . . 123 B5
Millington Cl RG2 . . . . 86 D3
Millins Cl GU47 . . . . 143 E1
Mill La
 Aldermaston Wharf RG7 . 109 C2
 Ascot SL5 . . . . 121 A7
 Bracknell RG12 . . . . 117 F5
 Colthrop RG19 . . . . 107 B2
 Cookham SL6 . . . . 20 C7
 Earley RG6 . . . . 87 E3
 Henley-on-T RG9 . . . . 35 F8
 Horton SL3 . . . . 69 C2
 Hurley SL6 . . . . 17 F4
 Lambourn RG17 . . . . 25 C2
 Reading, Horncastle RG31 84 E4
 Reading RG1 . . . . 86 B7
 Shiplake RG9 . . . . 36 B2
 Sindlesham RG41 . . . . . . 115 A8
 Taplow SL6 . . . . 40 C8
 Thorpe TW20 . . . . 123 C5
 Tidmarsh RG8 . . . . 56 D2
 Windsor SL4 . . . . 67 A7
 Winnersh RG41 . . . . 87 F1
 Yateley GU46 . . . . 149 D8

Millmead RG41 . . . . 116 A7
Mill Mead TW18 . . . . 96 F4
Millmere GU46 . . . . 149 D7
Mill Pl SL3 . . . . 68 D5
Mill Place Cvn Pk SL3 . . . . 68 E5
Mill Pond Rd GU20 . . . . . 146 B6
Mill Rd
 Burghfield Common RG30 . 84 F2
 Caversham RG4 . . . . 59 C1
 Goring RG8 . . . . 34 C8
 Lower Shiplake RG9 . . . . . 36 B3
 Marlow SL7 . . . . 1 E1
Mill Reef Cl RG19 . . . . 105 F3
Mill Ride SL5 . . . . 119 D8
Millside SL8 . . . . 3 C3
Mills Spur SL4 . . . . 95 B8
Mill St
 Colnbrook SL3 . . . . 69 D7
 Slough SL2 . . . . 42 F5
Millstream Ho RG14 . . . . . 100 D3
Millstream La SL1 . . . . 41 E5
Millstream Way HP10 . . . . . 3 E8
Mill West SL2 . . . . 42 F5
Millworth La RG2 . . . . 113 E4
Milman Cl RG12 . . . . 119 A7
Milman Rd RG2 . . . . 113 C6
Milner Rd SL1 . . . . 41 A8
Milsom Cl RG2 . . . . 113 B5
Milton Cl
 Bracknell RG12 . . . . 118 B3
 Henley-on-T RG9 . . . . 15 D2
 Horton SL3 . . . . 69 A4
Milton Ct RG40 . . . . 116 B7
Milton Dr
 Littleton TW17 . . . . 124 E5
 Wokingham RG40 . . . . . . 116 B7
Milton Gdns
 Stanwell TW19 . . . . 97 F7
 Wokingham RG40 . . . . . . 116 B6
Milton Rd
 Earley RG6 . . . . 87 A7
 Egham TW20 . . . . 95 F3
 Slough SL2 . . . . 22 D1
 Wokingham RG40, RG41 . 116 B6
Milton Way RG10 . . . . 61 F5
Milverton Cl SL6 . . . . 39 E3
Milward Cl RG42 . . . . 91 C8
Milward Gdns RG42 . . . . . 117 C7
Mimosa Dr RG2 . . . . 113 E6
Mina Ave SL3 . . . . 43 D4
Minchin Gn RG42 . . . . 90 C3
Minden Cl RG41 . . . . 115 E6
Minerva Cl TW19 . . . . 70 A2
Minerva Ho RG7 . . . . 134 E2
Minster Ct **4** RG1 . . . . . . 86 B7
Ministry Rd RG19 . . . . 131 A8
Minley Rd GU17 . . . . 149 E1
Minley Rd GU17 . . . . 149 E1
Minniecroft Rd SL1 . . . . . . 21 B2
Minorca Ave GU16 . . . . . . 152 E2
Minorca Rd GU16 . . . . 152 E2
Minoru Pl RG42 . . . . 90 D3
Minstead Cl RG12 . . . . . . 118 F6
Minstead Dr GU46 . . . . . . 149 C5
Minster Ct
 Camberley GU15 . . . . 151 D7
 Camberley, York Town
  GU15 . . . . 150 F4
Minsterley Ave TW17 . . . . 125 E5
Minster St RG1 . . . . 86 B7
Minster Way SL3 . . . . 43 F4
Mint Cl RG6 . . . . 86 F1
Minton Cl RG26 . . . . 134 F1
Minton Rd RG30 . . . . 84 F8
Minton Rise SL6 . . . . 41 B7
Mirador Cres SL2 . . . . 43 B6
Mire La RG10 . . . . 62 D4
Misbourne Ct SL3 . . . . 44 A2
Missenden Cl TW14 . . . . . . 98 F7
Missenden Gdns SL1 . . . . . 41 B7
Mistletoe Rd GU46 . . . . . . 149 D4
Mitcham Cl RG2 . . . . 86 B6
Mitcham Rd GU15 . . . . . . 145 A1
Mitchell Bldgs GU46 . . . . 149 B5
Mitchell Cl
 Pamber Heath RG26 . . . . 135 C2
 Slough SL1 . . . . 42 A4
Mitchell Way RG5 . . . . 88 B7
Mitford Lo RG12 . . . . 113 D8
Mitre Cl TW17 . . . . 125 D3
Mitre Pl RG42 . . . . 91 B2
Mixnams La KT16 . . . . 124 A6
Moat Dr SL2 . . . . 43 C8
Modbury Gdns RG2 . . . . . . 86 C2
Moffats Cl GU47 . . . . 150 A8
Moffy Hill SL6 . . . . 19 E2
Mohawk Way RG5 . . . . 88 B7
Mole Rd RG2 . . . . 114 F6
Moles Cl RG40 . . . . 116 D5
Mollison Cl RG5 . . . . 88 B8
Molly Millar Bridge
 RG41 . . . . 116 B4
Molly Millars Cl RG41 . . . 116 B4
Molly Millar's La RG41 . . 116 A4
Molyneux Rd GU20 . . . . . 146 D4
Molyns Ho RG9 . . . . 15 E3
Molyns Mews SL1 . . . . 41 E5
Monarch Cl TW14 . . . . 98 E8
Monarch Dr RG42 . . . . 91 E2
Monastry The **2** RG30 . . . 85 D6
Monck Ct **12** RG30 . . . . . 71 C7
Mondial Way UB7 . . . . 71 B7
MONEYROW GREEN 65 A7
Monica Gdns RG14 . . . . . 105 C5
Monkey Island Ct SL6 . . . . 65 E8
Monkey Island La SL6 . . . . 40 E2
Monkley Ct **5** RG4 . . . . . . 59 C1

Monksbarn RG2 . . . . 86 D2
Monks Cl SL5 . . . . 120 B3
Monks Dr SL5 . . . . 120 B3
Monksfield Way SL2 . . . . . . 22 A2
Monks Hollow SL7 . . . . 1 E5
Monkshood Ct RG40 . . . . 116 E7
Monks La RG14 . . . . 130 F7
Monks Rd
 Virginia Water GU25 . . . . 122 D5
 Windsor SL4 . . . . 66 D5
Monks Way
 Harmondsworth UB7 . . . . . 70 E8
 Reading RG30 . . . . 85 D5
 Staines TW18 . . . . 97 D1
Monks Wlk SL5 . . . . 120 B3
Monkswood Ct RG14 . . . . 130 E2
Monkswood Ct **7** SL7 . . . . 1 E2
Monktons La RG7 . . . . 137 C5
Monkton La SL6 . . . . 59 A1
Mons Cl RG41 . . . . 115 E6
Monsell Gdns TW18 . . . . . . 96 E3
Mons Wlk TW20 . . . . 96 C3
Montacute Dr RG19 . . . . . 106 F2
Montague Cl
 Camberley GU15 . . . . 151 B5
 Lightwater GU18 . . . . 146 A1
Montague Ho RG1 . . . . 58 E5
Montague Dr RG19 . . . . . . 131 B6
Montague Rd SL1 . . . . 42 F6
Montague St
 Caversham RG4 . . . . 59 C2
 Reading RG1 . . . . 86 D7
Montague Terr RG14 . . . . 131 A8
Montagu Rd SL3 . . . . 68 B6
Montbatten Ct SL3 . . . . 43 B7
Monteagle La
 Yateley GU46 . . . . 149 A6
 Yateley GU46 . . . . 149 B5
Montem La SL1 . . . . 42 B6
Montem Prim Sch SL1 . . . . 42 B4
Montgomery Cl GU47 . . . 150 B8
Montgomery Dr RG7 . . . . 113 B2
Montgomery of Alamein Ct
 RG12 . . . . 118 D8
Montgomery Pl SL2 . . . . . . 43 C7
Montgomery Rd RG14 . . . 130 E8
Montpelier Dr RG4 . . . . 59 D5
Montpellier Cl SL4 . . . . 67 C5
Montreal Terr RG10 . . . . . . 61 E4
Montrose Ave
 Datchet SL3 . . . . 68 C7
 Slough SL1 . . . . 42 B7
Montrose Cl
 Ashford TW15 . . . . 98 C3
 Frimley GU16 . . . . 151 E2
Montrose Dr SL6 . . . . 39 A6
Montrose Rd TW14 . . . . 71 D1
Montrose Way SL3 . . . . 68 D8
Montrose Wlk RG31 . . . . . . 84 E4
Monument Ct RG14 . . . . . 130 D7
Monycrower Dr SL6 . . . . . . 39 E7
Moorbridge Rd SL6 . . . . . . 40 A7
Moor Cl
 Finchampstead RG40 . . . 141 E7
 Sandhurst GU47 . . . . 143 E1
Moor Copse Cl RG6 . . . . . . 87 B3
Moorcroft Ave RG42 . . . . . 90 F1
Moore Cl SL1 . . . . 42 B4
Moore Grove Cres RG8 . . . 95 F1
Moor End SL6 . . . . 40 C1
Moores Gn RG40 . . . . 116 E8
Moores La SL4 . . . . 66 E6
Moore's Pl RG17 . . . . 100 C5
Moorfields Cl TW18 . . . . . 123 E8
Moorfield Terr SL6 . . . . 40 A8
Moor Furlong SL1 . . . . 41 E5
Moorhayes Dr TW18 . . . . 124 C6
Moorhen Dr RG6 . . . . 87 B1
Moorings The
 Old Windsor SL4 . . . . 95 C8
 Windsor SL4 . . . . 67 A7
Moor La
 Bracknell RG12 . . . . 117 C6
 Harmondsworth UB7 . . . . . 70 C8
 Maidenhead SL6 . . . . 19 F1
 Newbury RG14 . . . . 104 E3
 Staines TW19 . . . . 96 D6
Moorland Rd UB7 . . . . 70 C8
Moorlands Dr SL6 . . . . 38 F8
Moorlands Pl GU15 . . . . . 151 B5
Moorlands Prim Sch
 RG30 . . . . 84 F7
Moorlands Rd GU15 . . . . . 151 B4
Moormede Cres TW18 . . . . 96 F4
Moor Park Ho RG12 . . . . . 117 E3
Moor Pl GU20 . . . . 146 B5
Moors Cl RG40 . . . . 141 E8
Moorside HP10 . . . . 3 E8
Moorside Cl
 1 Farnborough GU14 . . . 151 A1
 Maidenhead SL6 . . . . 19 F1
Moors The
 Pangbourne RG8 . . . . 56 D5
 Thatcham RG19 . . . . 106 D2
Moorstown Ct **7** SL1 . . . . 42 E4
Moorth Ct **7** SL1 . . . . 2 D4
Moray Ave GU47 . . . . 150 D7
Moray Dr SL2 . . . . 43 A7
Mordaunt Dr RG45 . . . . . 143 B3
Morden Cl RG12 . . . . 118 F5
Moreau Wlk SL3 . . . . 43 E7
Moreland Ave SL3 . . . . 69 C7
Moreleigh Cl RG2 . . . . 86 C2
Morella Cl GU25 . . . . 122 D5
Morello Dr SL3 . . . . 43 F2

Moretaine Rd TW15 97 D5
Moreton Ct RG1 86 D5
Moreton Way SL1 41 D5
Morgan Ct 2 TW15 98 B3
Morgan Rd RG1 86 C6
Moriston Cl RG30 85 B8
Morlais RG4 59 A5
Morlands Ave RG30 85 A5
Morley Cl
  Slough SL3 43 F4
  Yateley GU46 149 B5
Morley Ct SL5 120 F3
Morley Pl RG17 100 D5
Mornington Ave RG40 141 F8
Mornington Cl RG26 134 E1
Mornington Rd TW15 98 C3
Morpeth Cl RG2 86 C4
Morrell Ct TW18 97 B3
Morrice Cl 3 SL3 44 A2
Morris Ct SL4 66 E6
Morrish Gr RG17 102 B2
Morrison Cl RG8 55 D4
Morriss Ct 10 RG1 86 C7
MORTIMER 137 A5
Mortimer Cl RG2 113 C7
Mortimer Hall RG7 137 C5
Mortimer La
  Mortimer RG7 137 D7
  Silchester RG7 137 D1
Mortimer Rd
  Grazeley RG7 112 D2
  Slough SL3 43 D3
Mortimer St John's CE Sch RG7 137 A5
Mortimer St Mary's CE Jun Sch RG7 137 D5
Mortimer Sta RG7 137 E5
MORTIMER WEST END 136 D4
Morton Dr SL1 21 F8
Morton Pl RG7 83 E4
Mortons La RG7 107 C6
Morval Rd GU17 149 F1
Mosaic Apartments The SL1 42 E4
Moss Cl RG4 59 C3
MOSS END 91 C6
Mossy Vale SL6 19 D1
Mostyn Ho RG42 91 B1
Moulden Way RG7 110 F8
MOULSFORD 13 F4
Moulsford Prep Sch OX10 14 A5
Moulsham Copse La GU46 149 B7
MOULSHAM GREEN 149 B8
Moulsham La GU46 149 B7
Moundsfield Way SL1 41 E4
Mountain Ash SL7 1 D6
Mountbatten Cl
  Newbury RG14 105 C5
  6 Slough SL1 43 A3
Mountbatten Mews GU15 151 D7
Mountbatten Rise GU47 142 F1
Mountbatten Sq 7 SL4 67 C6
Mount Cl
  Farnham Common SL2 22 C8
  Newbury RG14 105 A1
Mount Cl The GU25 122 D3
Mount Felix KT12 125 F2
Mountfield RG8 34 C7
Mount La
  Bracknell RG12 118 C7
  Chaddleworth RG20 49 A8
Mount Lee TW20 95 F3
Mount Pleasant
  Beenham RG7 108 F6
  Bracknell RG12 118 C6
  Reading RG1 86 B6
  Sandhurst GU47 143 A1
  Tadley RG26 135 B1
  Wokingham RG41 116 A6
Mount Pleasant Cl GU18 146 A1
Mount Pleasant Cotts
  7 Bourne End SL8 3 B3
  Englefield Green TW20 95 D2
Mount Pleasant Gr RG1 86 B6
Mount Rd RG18 106 E4
Mountsfield Cl TW19 70 A2
Mounts Hill SL4 93 C3
Mount St RG2 86 B5
MOUNT THE 86 C5
Mount The
  Caversham RG4 58 F3
  Reading RG1 86 D5
  Wentworth GU25 122 D3
Mount View RG9 15 D2
Mount View Ct RG9 15 D2
Mowbray Cres TW20 96 A3
Mowbray Dr RG30 85 A8
Mower Cl RG40 116 F7
Moyleen Rise SL7 1 C1
Mrs Bland's Inf Sch RG7 110 F2
Muckhatch La TW20 123 B7
Mud La
  Finchampstead RG27 140 F1
  Peasemore RG20 50 D6
Mud La Cotts RG27 140 F1
Muirfield Cl RG1 86 D7
Muirfield Ho
  Bracknell RG12 117 E3
  Sunningdale SL5 121 A1
Mulberry Ave
  Stanwell TW19 97 E7
  Windsor SL4 67 F5
Mulberry Bsns Pk RG41 116 A4
Mulberry Cl
  Crowthorne RG45 143 C4
  1 Sandhurst GU47 150 D8
Mulberry Cl *continued*
  Twyford RG10 61 E4
  Woodley RG5 87 E6
Mulberry Ct
  1 Bracknell RG12 118 F4
  2 Newbury RG14 104 F2
  5 Wokingham RG40 116 C6
Mulberry Dr SL3 43 E1
Mulberry Ho RG42 91 B1
Mulberry Trees TW17 125 D2
Mulberry Way RG7 83 E3
Mulberry Wlk SL6 39 C8
Mulfords Hill RG26 135 B1
Mulgrave Rd GU16 151 F2
Mullens Rd TW20 96 C3
Mullens Terr RG4 58 D8
Mullion Ct 10 RG1 85 F7
Mulroy Dr GU15 152 A6
Mumbery Hill RG10 36 E1
Muncaster Cl TW15 98 A4
Muncaster Ho TW18 124 C6
Muncaster Rd TW15 98 B3
Munces Rd SL7 1 D6
Munday Ct RG42 90 E1
Mundaydean La SL7 1 B4
Mundesley Spur SL1 42 E7
Mundesley St RG1 86 B6
Munkle Marsh RG19 107 A3
Munnings Dr GU47 150 E6
Munro Ave RG5 87 F4
Murdoch Cl TW18 97 A3
Murdoch Ct RG40 116 D5
Murdoch Rd RG40 116 D5
Murray Ct SL5 120 C3
Murray Ho RG41 116 A6
Murray Rd RG41 116 A6
Murrellhill La
  Binfield RG42 90 C1
  Bracknell RG42 117 C8
Murrells La GU15 151 B3
Murrin Rd SL6 39 C8
Mushroom Castle RG42 92 B2
Mus of Berkshire Aviation The* RG5 88 B6
Mus of Reading* RG1 86 B8
Mustard La RG4 60 E2
Mustard Mill Rd TW18 96 F4
Muswell Cl RG7 83 E3
Mutton Oaks RG12 117 D8
Myers Way GU16 152 D2
Mylne Sq RG40 116 D6
Mylum Cl RG2 113 C6
MYRKE 42 F2
Myrke The SL3 42 F2
Myrtle Ave TW14 71 E2
Myrtle Cl
  Burghfield Common RG7 111 B3
  Lightwater GU18 153 B8
  Poyle SL3 69 E6
  Purley on T RG31 57 C3
Myrtle Cres SL2 42 F6
Myrtle Dr GU17 150 D5
Myton Wlk RG7 83 E3

N

Nabbs Hill Cl RG31 84 C5
Nairn Cl GU16 151 E2
Nalderhill Rd RG20 103 B6
Napier Cl RG45 143 D5
Napier Ct RG1 86 C8
Napier Dr GU15 152 A8
Napier Lodge TW15 98 D2
Napier Rd
  Ashford TW15 98 D1
  Crowthorne RG45 143 C4
  Maidenhead SL6 39 B6
  Reading RG1 86 C8
Napier Wlk TW15 98 D1
Napper Cl SL5 119 D7
Narromine Dr RG31 84 F4
Naseby RG12 118 B1
Naseby Rise RG14 105 D5
Nash Cl RG6 87 A3
Nashdom SL1 20 F5
Nashdom La SL1 21 A6
Nash Gdns SL5 119 E7
Nash Grove La RG40 115 E1
Nash Pk RG42 90 B2
Nash Rd SL3 44 A2
Natalie Cl TW14 98 D8
Nathan Ct 7 RG1 85 F7
Naylors The RG7 139 D6
Neath Gdns RG30 84 F7
Needham Cl SL4 66 E6
Neil Cl TW15 98 C3
Nell Gwynn Ave TW17 125 D3
Nell Gwynne Ave SL5 120 D5
Nell Gwynne Cl SL5 120 D5
Nelson Cl
  Bracknell RG12 118 E7
  East Bedfont TW14 98 F7
  Slough SL3 43 D2
Nelson Ct 4 KT16 124 A1
Nelson Mews 8 RG1 86 B6
Nelson Rd
  Ashford TW15 97 E3
  Caversham RG4 59 C2
  Harmondsworth TW6 70 F6
  Windsor SL4 66 F4
Nelson's La RG10 89 B6
Nelson Terr 24 RG1 86 B6
Nelson Way GU15 150 F4
Nene Rd TW6, UB7 71 B6
Nene Rd Rdbt TW6 71 B6
Neo Apartments 2 SL1 43 A4
Neptune Cl RG41 115 E6
Neptune Rd TW6 71 C6
Neptune Way SL1 41 E4
Netherton RG12 118 A5
Netley Cl RG4 59 E6
Nettlecombe RG12 118 D3
Nettleton Rd TW6 71 B6
Neuman Cres RG12 118 A3
Neve Ho SL6 39 F8
Nevelle Cl RG42 117 D8
Nevil Ct RG19 106 D2
Neville Cl
  Stoke Poges SL2 22 F6
  Waltham St L RG10 62 F6
Neville Ct SL1 21 C2
Neville Dr RG19 106 E3
Nevis Rd RG31 57 D3
Newall Rd TW6 71 C6
Newalls Rise RG10 36 E2
Newark Rd
  Windlesham GU20 146 B6
  Yateley GU17 149 E2
Newark St RG1 86 B6
New Bath Rd RG10 61 C6
Newberry Cres SL4 66 D5
Newbery Cl RG31 57 D1
Newbery Way SL1 42 D4
Newbold Coll RG42 90 D1
Newbold Rd RG14 104 D5
Newbold Sch RG42 90 D1
Newbolt Cl RG18 106 C5
New Bright St 6 RG1 86 A6
NEWBURY 104 E3
Newbury Bsns Pk RG14 105 C4
Newbury Cl RG10 61 B4
Newbury Coll RG14 131 A7
Newbury Dr SL6 40 B6
Newbury Hill RG18 52 F5
Newbury Ho RG14 130 D6
Newbury La RG20 31 D4
Newbury Racecourse Sta RG14 105 C2
Newbury Rd
  Great Shefford RG17 48 B2
  Harmondsworth TW6 70 F6
  Hermitage RG18 79 B6
  Lambourn RG17 25 C1
Newbury Ret Pk RG14 131 B7
Newbury St
  Kintbury RG17 102 B2
  Lambourn RG17 25 B2
Newbury Sta RG14 105 A2
Newcastle Rd RG2 86 C4
New Christ Church CE Prim Sch RG1 86 B5
Newchurch Rd
  Slough SL2 41 F8
  Tadley RG26 135 A1
New Cl RG9 16 A8
New Cross RG9 35 F2
New Ct SL7 1 D2
Newdale Ct RG20 103 F6
Newell Gn RG42 91 C3
NEWELL GREEN 92 A1
Newell Hall RG42 91 C3
NEW ENGLAND 153 D7
Newfield Gdns SL7 1 F3
Newfield Rd SL7 1 F3
Newfield Way SL7 1 F2
New Forest Ride RG12 118 F4
New Greenham Pk RG19 131 F5
Newhaven Cres TW15 98 D3
Newhaven Spur SL2 22 B1
New Hill RG8 57 C5
New Hope Terr RG1 59 A1
New Horizon Ho RG19 132 A4
New Horton Manor SL3 69 A4
Newhurst Gdns RG42 91 D3
Newlands Ave RG4 59 B3
Newlands Cl GU46 149 D5
Newlands Cotts RG41 114 F7
Newlands Dr
  Maidenhead SL6 39 A7
  Poyle SL3 69 E4
Newlands Girls' Sch SL6 39 A7
Newlands Ho SL6 39 A6
Newlands Prim Sch GU46 149 C5
Newlands Rd GU15 151 B1
New Lane Hill RG30 84 E6
Newlyn Gdns RG2 86 B1
Newmans Pl SL5 121 B2
New Market 12 SL6 39 F7
Newmarket Cl RG6 87 D2
New Mdw SL5 119 D8
New Mile Rd SL5 120 C7
New Mill La RG27 140 E2
New Mill Rd RG40 140 E3
New Par TW15 97 F4
New Park Rd TW15 98 C3
Newport Cl 5 RG14 105 B4
Newport Dr RG42 91 B2
Newport Rd
  Harmondsworth TW6 71 A6
  Newbury RG14 105 B4
  Reading RG1 59 A1
  Slough SL2 21 E1
Newquay Dr RG6 87 B1
New Rd
  Bagshot GU19 145 F3
  Blackwater GU17 150 E4
  Bourne End SL8 3 B4
  Bracknell RG12 118 D7
  Burghfield Common RG7 111 E1
  Cookham Rise SL6 19 E7
  Crowthorne RG45 143 C5
  Datchet SL3 68 D6
  East Bedfont TW14 71 D1
  Egham TW18 96 C4
New Rd *continued*
  Harlington TW6, UB7 71 C7
  Holyport SL6 65 B8
  Hurley SL6 17 F3
  Littleton TW17 125 B6
  Lower Shiplake RG9 36 A3
  Marlow Bottom SL7 1 D6
  Newbury RG14 105 C1
  North Ascot SL5 92 F1
  Reading RG1 86 D5
  Sandhurst GU47 150 A8
  Shiplake RG9 35 B2
  Sindlesham RG41 115 B8
  Slough SL3 44 A3
  Twyford RG10 61 D7
  Twyford, Ruscombe RG10 61 F6
  Windlesham GU19, GU20 146 A4
New Road Hill RG7 108 B3
New Scotland Hill Prim Sch GU47 143 A2
New Sq
  East Bedfont TW14 98 C7
  Slough SL1 42 F4
New St
  Beech Hill RG7 138 B1
  Henley-on-T RG9 15 E2
  Staines TW18 97 A4
Newstead Rise RG2 86 E1
Newton Ave RG4 59 D5
Newton Cl SL3 43 F4
Newton Ct SL4 68 A1
Newton La SL4 68 B1
Newtonside SL4 68 A1
Newton Side Orch SL4 68 A1
Newton's Mews RG17 100 D6
NEWTOWN
  Henley-on-Thames 35 F8
  Newbury 131 B4
NEW TOWN
  Pangbourne 55 D4
  Reading 86 F7
Newtown RG26 135 A1
Newtown Gdns RG9 35 E8
New Town Prim Sch RG1 86 D8
Newtown Rd
  Henley-on-T RG9 35 F8
  Marlow SL7 1 F3
  Newbury RG14, RG19, RG20 131 A7
  Sandhurst GU47 150 B8
New Villas RG20 129 B3
New Way RG7 82 A2
New Wickham La TW20 96 B1
New Wokingham Rd RG45 143 A6
New Zealand Ave KT12 125 F1
Niagara Rd RG9 35 E8
Nicholas Ct 11 RG1 85 F7
Nicholas Gdns SL1 41 E5
Nicholas Rd RG9 35 B8
Nicholas Winton Ct SL6 40 A8
Nicholls SL4 66 C4
Nicholls Wlk SL4 66 C4
Nicholsons Ctr 5 SL6 39 F7
Nicholsons La SL6 39 F7
Nicholson Wlk 2 TW20 96 A3
Nideggan Cl RG19 106 D3
Nightingale Cres RG12 118 D4
Nightingale Ct 9 SL1 43 A3
Nightingale Gdns GU47 150 B8
Nightingale Ho 1 RG1 85 F5
Nightingale La
  Maidenhead SL6 19 D3
  Mortimer RG7 137 D6
Nightingale Pk SL2 21 F5
Nightingale Pl SL6 19 F7
Nightingale Rd RG5 87 D4
Nightingale Shott TW20 95 F2
Nightingales The
  Newbury RG14 131 B8
  Stanwell TW19 97 F7
Nightingale Wlk SL4 67 C4
Night Owls RG19 131 C7
Nimrod Cl RG5 88 B7
Nimrod Ind Est RG1 86 B5
Nimrod Way RG2 86 B5
Nine Acres SL1 41 F5
Nine Elms Cl TW14 98 F7
Nine Mile Ride
  Bracknell RG12, RG40 118 C1
  Crowthorne RG40 142 D7
  Finchampstead RG40 141 D6
Nine Mile Ride Ind RG40 141 D5
Nine Mile Ride Prim Sch RG40 141 F6
Ninth Ave RG31 84 B6
Niplands Cotts HP10 3 D2
Nire Rd RG4 59 E2
Nixey Cl SL1 43 A4
No 4 RG30 85 C6
Noakes Hill RG8 54 B7
Nobel Dr UB3 71 E7
Noble Ct SL2 42 F5
Noble Rd RG9 35 F7
Nobles Way TW20 95 E2
Nodmore RG20 49 B7
Norbury Rd TW13 98 F5
Norcot Rd RG30 84 F8
Norden Cl SL6 39 C4
Norden Mdws SL6 39 C5
Norden Rd SL6 39 C5
Norelands Dr SL1 21 C3
Nores Rd RG2 113 D7
Norfolk Ave SL1 42 C8
Norfolk Chase RG42 91 F1
Norfolk Cl RG41 115 E6
Norfolk Ho RG1 86 D5
Norfolk Park Cotts SL6 39 F8
Norfolk Rd
  Maidenhead SL6 39 F8
  Reading RG30 85 D7
Norland Dr HP10 3 C8
Norlands RG18 106 C5
Norlands La TW18, TW20 123 E7
Norman Ave RG9 15 E1
Norman Ct 4 TW18 97 A4
Normandy Wlk TW20 96 C3
Norman Ho RG9 15 E1
Norman House TW17 125 A2
Normanhurst TW15 98 A3
Norman Keep RG42 118 F8
Norman Pl RG1 59 B1
Norman Rd
  Ashford TW15 98 D2
  Caversham RG4 59 C4
Normanstead RG9 15 D1
Normanstead Rd RG31 84 C8
Normans The SL2 43 B7
Normay Rise RG14 130 C5
Normoor Rd RG7 110 F1
Norreys Ave RG40 116 D7
Norreys Dr SL6 39 D4
Norris Field RG20 49 B8
Norris Gn RG5 61 A1
Norris La RG20 49 B8
Norris Rd
  Reading RG6 87 A6
  Staines TW18 96 F4
Northam Cl RG6 87 E3
Northampton Ave SL1 42 C7
Northampton Cl RG12 118 E6
NORTH ASCOT 119 F8
Northborough Rd SL2 22 B1
Northbourne Cl RG6 87 B2
Northbrook Copse RG12 118 F3
Northbrook Pl RG14 105 A3
Northbrook Rd RG4 59 D6
Northbrook St RG14 105 A3
North Burnham Cl SL1 21 B3
Northbury Ave RG10 61 E5
Northbury La RG10 61 E6
North Cl
  East Bedfont TW14 71 D1
  Medmenham SL7 17 D7
  Windsor SL4 66 F6
Northcott RG12 118 A1
North Cotts SL2 22 C2
Northcourt Ave RG2 86 D4
Northcroft
  Slough SL2 22 B1
  Wooburn Green HP10 3 F6
Northcroft Cl TW20 95 B3
Northcroft Gdns TW20 95 B3
Northcroft La RG14 104 F3
Northcroft Rd TW20 95 B3
Northcroft Terr RG14 104 F3
Northcroft Villas TW20 95 B3
North Ct RG40 141 F4
Northdean 5 SL6 19 F1
Northdene Ct TW20 95 E3
North Dr
  Sulhamstead RG7 110 D7
  Wentworth GU25 121 E4
NORTH END 129 A2
Northend Cl HP10 3 C7
North End La SL5 121 B2
Northern Ave RG14 105 A6
Northern Hts SL8 3 B5
Northern Perimeter Rd TW6 71 E6
Northern Perimeter Road W TW6 70 E6
Northern Rd SL2 22 D1
Northern Way RG2 85 F1
Northern Woods HP10 3 C7
North Farm Cl RG17 25 C3
Northfield GU18 153 B8
Northfield Ave RG9 36 A4
Northfield Ct
  Henley-on-T RG9 15 D3
  Staines TW18 124 B8
Northfield End RG9 15 D3
Northfield Farm Ind Est RG17 48 C6
Northfield Rd
  Eton SL4 41 F2
  Lower Shiplake RG9 36 B4
  Maidenhead SL6 19 F1
  Reading RG1 59 A1
  Staines TW18 124 B8
  Thatcham RG18 106 B4
NORTHFIELDS 61 E7
Northfields
  Chieveley RG20 51 B4
  Lambourn RG17 25 B3
Northfields Terr RG17 25 C3
North Fryerne GU46 149 D8
Northgate Dr GU15 152 A7
North Gn
  Bracknell RG12 118 D8
  3 Maidenhead SL6 19 F1
  Slough SL1 42 E6
North Gr KT16 123 F3
NORTH HEATH 50 D1
Northington Cl RG12 118 F3
North Links Rd HP10 3 B8
North Lodge Dr SL5 119 C7
North Lodge Mews RG30 85 D5
Northmead Rd SL2 41 F8
Northolt Rd
  Harmondsworth TW6 70 E6
  Harmondsworth UB7 70 D6
North Pk SL0 44 D3

178 Nor–Oxf

North Rd
East Bedfont TW14 .... .71 D1
Maidenhead SL6 .... .39 E7
Moulsford OX10.......... .13 F4
Winkfield SL5........... 119 B8
Northrop Rd TW6........ .71 E6
North Row SL3 .... .23 E8
North St
Caversham RG4......... .59 B2
Egham TW20 .... .95 F2
Reading RG1........... .85 F8
Winkfield SL4........... .93 A6
North Standen Rd RG17. 100 A4
North Star La SL6........ .39 C6
NORTH STREET .... .83 D5
North Sydmonton 131 F1
North Terr SL4.......... .67 E7
NORTH TOWN .... .19 F2
North Town Cl 1 SL6 .... .19 F1
North Town Mead 4 SL6.. 19 F1
North Town Moor SL6.... .19 F1
North Town Rd SL6...... .19 F1
Northumberland Ave RG2 .86 C3
Northumberland Cl
Bracknell RG42 .... .91 F1
Stanwell TW19.......... .70 E1
Northumberland Cres
TW14 .... .71 E1
Northumbria Rd SL6 ..... .39 B4
Northview RG17 .... 100 D5
North View RG12........ 117 C6
North View Gdns 2
RG14 .... 105 B4
Northview Hts 2 RG17.. 100 D5
Northway
Newbury RG14.......... 105 B2
Thatcham RG18 .... 106 C5
Wokingham RG41 ...... 115 E7
North Wlk RG7 .... .83 E4
Northwood Dr RG14 .... 105 C4
Northwood Rd TW6 ..... .70 D6
Norton Cl RG14 .... 130 C6
Norton Pk SL5......... 120 C4
Norton Rd
Frimley GU15.......... 152 C4
Reading RG1........... .86 E7
Riseley RG7 .... 139 C3
Wokingham RG40 ...... 116 C5
Woodley RG5.......... .87 F5
Norway Dr SL2 .... .43 B8
Norwich Ave GU15..... 151 E3
Norwich Dr RG5........ .87 C8
Norwich Ho SL6 .... .39 E8
Norwood Cres TW6 .... .71 C6
Norwood Rd RG1 ...... .86 E7
Notley End TW20 ...... .95 C1
Notley Pl RG4 .... .59 B4
Nottrees RG12........ 102 A2
Nottingham Fee OX11... .11 F8
Notton Way RG10...... 113 F8
Nuffield Dr GU47 ...... 143 F1
Nuffield Rd
Arborfield Garrison RG2 ..140 F7
Arborfield Garrison RG2 ..141 A8
Nugee Ct RG45 .... 143 B5
Nugent Cl SL7......... .1 F2
Nuneaton RG12........ 118 E3
Nunhide La RG8, RG31... .83 F6
Nuns Acre RG8........ .34 B7
Nuns Wlk GU25........ 122 D4
NUPTOWN............. .91 F7
Nuptown La
Newell Green SL4 ...... .92 A8
Winkfield RG42 .... .91 F7
Nursery Cl
Hurst RG10 .... .88 E7
Lower Shiplake RG9 .... .36 A4
Nursery Gdns
Purley on T RG8........ .57 B5
Staines TW18.......... .96 F1
Sunbury TW16.......... 125 F7
Nursery La
North Ascot SL5........ 119 E8
Slough SL3............ .43 D5
Nursery Pl SL4 .... .68 B1
Nursery Rd
Burnham SL6 .... .1 B7
Sunbury TW16......... 125 F7
Nursery Way TW19 .... .68 D1
Nursery Wlk SL7....... .1 B1
Nutbean La RG42 ...... 137 F5
Nutbourne Ct TW18 .... .96 F1
Nutfield Ct GU15...... 151 D7
Nuthatch Cl TW19..... .97 F7
Nuthatch Dr RG6 ..... .87 B4
Nuthurst RG12........ 118 E4
Nut La RG10........... .62 E6
Nutley RG12 .... 118 A1
Nutley Cl GU46 .... 149 D5
Nutley La RG10........ .86 F1
Nutter's La RG2....... 140 A8
Nuttingtons RG20...... .49 F6
Nutty La TW17 .... 125 C6

O

Oak Apartments UB3.... .71 D7
Oak Ave
Egham TW20 .... .96 D1
Sandhurst GU47 .... 143 D1
Oak Cott RG10........ .63 A2
Oakdale
Bracknell RG12 .... 118 D3
Windlesham GU20...... 146 D4

Oakdale Cl RG31........ .84 C8
Oakdale Wlk RG5 ...... .88 A8
Oakdene
Burghfield Common RG7 . 111 A2
Sunningdale SL5 .... 120 F3
Oak Dr
Burghfield Common RG7 ..110 F2
Newbury RG14......... 104 F2
Woodley RG5.......... .88 A6
Oaken Copse SL5...... 152 C7
Oak End Way RG7 ..... 109 C4
Oakengates RG12 ..... 118 A1
Oaken Gr
Maidenhead SL6 .... .19 C1
Newbury RG14......... 130 D8
Oakes Ct RG17........ 100 D5
Oakey Dr RG40 .... 116 B5
Oak Farm Cl GU17..... 150 C5
Oakfield RG1.......... .86 D5
Oakfield Ave SL1 ...... .42 B5
Oakfield Ct RG41 ..... 116 A5
Oakfield Fst Sch SL4... .67 B5
Oakfield Rd
Ashford TW15 .... .98 B3
Blackwater GU17....... 150 F3
Bourne End SL8........ .3 A3
Palmer Heath RG25 ... 135 E1
Oakfields GU15 .... 151 B5
Oakfield Works GU47... 150 E7
Oak Gn RG2 .... 113 D8
Oak Grove Cres GU15 ..150 F6
Oakhall Ct TW16....... .98 F3
Oakhall Dr TW16...... .98 F3
Oakham Cl RG31....... .57 D2
Oak Hill SN8.......... .99 C3
Oakhurst SL3.......... .20 B4
Oak La
Englefield Green TW20 ...95 C5
Windsor SL4 .... .67 A6
Oaklands
Curridge RG18......... .78 C3
Reading RG1.......... .86 F6
4 Tadley RG26........ 134 E1
Yateley GU46......... 149 D6
Oaklands Bsns Ctr RG41. 116 A4
Oaklands Cl SL5....... .92 F1
Oaklands Cvn Pk RG41 ..114 F1
Oaklands Dr
North Ascot SL5....... .92 F1
Wokingham RG41 ..... 116 A5
Oaklands Inf & Jun Schs
RG45 .... 143 A6
Oaklands La RG45..... 143 B7
Oaklands Pk RG41..... 116 A4
Oaklea Dr RG27....... 140 E2
Oak Leaf Ct SL5 ...... 119 D8
Oakleigh GU18........ 153 C8
Oakley Cl
Newbury RG20......... 130 A4
West End GU24....... 153 F6
Oak Ridge Cl RG14.... 130 E8
Oakridge Pl SL3 ...... .22 C8
Oakside Way RG2...... 113 E8
Oaks Rd
Lower Shiplake RG9 .... .36 A4
Stanwell TW19......... .70 D1
Oaks The
Blackwater GU17....... 150 A3
Bracknell RG12 ...... 118 D7
Newbury RG14......... 131 A7
Staines TW18.......... .96 F4
Yateley GU46......... 149 D5
Oak Stubbs La SL6..... .40 F4
Oak The OX10 .... .14 C6
Oaktree Ave RG19..... 133 B5
Oak Tree Ave GU47.... .1 D3
Oaktree Cl SL7........ .1 D3
Oak Tree Cl
Tadley RG26.......... 135 B1
Oak Tree Copse RG31 ...57 E3
Oak Tree Dr
Englefield Green TW20 ...95 C5
Slough SL3............ .44 B1
Oak Tree Rd
Marlow SL7 .... .1 D4
Reading RG31......... .57 E2
Thatcham RG19 .... 106 E2
Oaktree Way GU47.... 143 A1
Oak Tree Wlk RG8..... .57 D5
Oakview Gdns SL3..... .43 F2
Oakview RG40........ 116 A4
Oak View RG31........ .84 C8
Oak Way
East Bedfont TW14 .... .98 E7
Woodley RG5.......... .87 D4
Oakway Dr GU16...... 151 D1
Oakwood Cl SL1....... .42 E7
Oakwood Ho RG6...... .87 C4
Oakwood Rd RG45.... 143 A4
Oakwood Rd
Bracknell RG12 ...... 118 E7

Oakwood Rd *continued*
Virginia Water GU25 .... 122 C4
Windlesham GU20...... 146 E4
OARE .... .79 B8
Oareborough RG12..... 118 E4
Oareborough La RG18.. .52 A1
Oast Ct TW18......... .96 F4
Oast House Cl TW19 ... .95 E8
Oatlands Dr
Oatlands Park KT13.... 125 E1
Slough SL3............ .42 D7
OATLANDS PARK 125 E1
Oban Cl SL1........... .42 D4
Oban Gdns RG5....... .87 E4
O'Bee Gdns RG26...... 134 F1
Obelisk Way GU15 .... 151 C6
Oberon Way TW17 .... 124 E6
Observatory The 3 RG30..85 E7
Observer Dr 3 RG19.. 106 E2
Ochre Ct 5 TW13...... .98 F5
Ockwells Rd SL6...... .39 C2
Octavia RG12 .... 118 A1
Octavia Way TW18 .... .97 A2
Oddfellows Rd RG14 ... 104 F2
Odell Cl RG6.......... 114 B8
Odencroft Rd SL2..... .22 A2
Odette Gdns RG26 .... 135 C1
Odiham Ave RG4...... .59 E5
Odiham Rd RG7 ...... 139 D1
Odney La SL6......... .20 B7
Ogden Pk RG12....... 118 E6
Ogmore Cl RG30...... .84 E7
Okingham Cl GU47.... 143 D1
Oldacre GU24......... 153 F7
Oldacres SL4.......... .40 B7
Old Acres La RG10 .... .61 B5
Old Apple Yd The RG41..88 A3
Old Bakehouse Ct RG45..143 B4
Old Bakery Ct SL0 .... .44 F7
Old Bakery The 10 TW20..96 A3
Old Barn Cl RG14...... .59 A6
Old Bath Rd
Charvil RG10 .... .61 B5
Newbury RG14......... 104 F4
Reading RG4 .... .84 C4
Sonning RG4 .... .60 D1
Old Bisley Rd GU16 ... 152 C3
Old Bix Rd RG9 .... .15 A6
Old Bothampstead Rd
RG20 .... .51 D6
Old Bracknell Cl RG12 ..118 B6
Old Bracknell La E RG12 118 B6
Old Bracknell La W
RG12 .... 118 B6
Old Brewery La RG9 ... .15 E2
Oldbury RG12......... 117 F6
Oldbury Rd KT16...... 123 E2
Old Chapel Cotts RG18..53 E1
Old Chapel The RG7 ... 113 A2
Old Charlton Rd TW17 . 125 C4
Old Coach Works RG17 ..25 A2
Old Coalyard The TW20...95 F2
Old College Rd RG42 .. .90 C5
Oldcorne Hollow GU46. 149 A5
Old Court Cl SL6...... .39 B3
Old Dean Rd GU15.... 151 D7
Oldean Ct RG31....... .57 C1
Olde Farm Dr GU17.... 150 B5
Old Elm Dr RG30...... .84 D7
Old Farm Cres RG31 ... .57 C2
Old Farm Dr RG12 .... .91 C1
Old Ferry Dr TW19..... .68 D1
Oldfield Cl RG6....... .87 B7
Old Forest Rd RG41.... .88 F1
Old Fives Ct SL1...... .21 B2
Old Forge Cl SL6...... .40 A3
Old Forge Cres TW17 .. 125 B3
Old Forge End SL7..... .1 C3
Old Forge The
Streatley RG8 .... .34 A6
2 Tadley RG26........ 134 E1
Old Granary The 8
RG17 .... 100 D5
Old Green La GU15.... .29 E8
Old House Cl SL3...... .43 D7
Oldhouse La GU18, GU20. 146 C2
Old Kennels Ct RG30... .85 A5
Old Kiln Ind Est SL6 ... .19 A3
Old Kiln Rd HP10 ..... .3 A8
Old La
Hamstead Marshall
RG20 .... 102 E1
Headley RG19 .... 133 F1
Old Lands Hill RG12 ... 118 D8
Old La The RG14...... .85 F5
Old Library The 10 RG14. 105 A2
Old Marsh La SL6...... .41 D6
Old Mill Ct RG9....... .61 D5
Old Mill La SL6........ .40 D4
Old Mill Pl TW19...... .95 D8
Old Mill The RG8....... .56 D6
Old Monteagle La GU46 .149 B5
Old Moor La HP10..... .3 E8
Old Newtown Rd RG14 .104 F1
Old Nursery Pl TW15... .98 B3
Old Nursery The RG18.. .79 A4
Old Orchard
Iver SL0............... .44 F7
Maidenhead SL6 ...... .39 E5
Old Orch The RG31.... .84 E4
Old Pasture Rd SL6.... .39 D2
Old Papermill Cl HP10 .. .3 E8

Old Pasture Rd GU16,
GU15................ 151 F3
Old Pharmacy Ct RG45 . 143 C4
Old Police Ho The 14
RG14 .... 105 A4
Old Pond Cl GU15 .... 151 C1
Old Portsmouth Rd
GU15................ 152 A5
Old Post Office La 10 SL6 .39 F7
Old Priory La RG42 .... .91 D2
Old Riseley Stores The
RG7 .... 139 C3
Old Row Ct RG40 .... 116 C6
Old Sawmill La RG45... 143 C6
Old Sawmills The RG17.. 127 E6
Old School Ct TW19.... .95 E8
Old School La GU46.... 149 C6
Old School Mews TW20 ..96 D3
Old School The
Hampstead Norreys RG18..52 F5
Wooburn HP10 .... .3 D4
Old School Yd The 4
RG17 .... .25 B2
Old Slade La SL0 ..... .44 F2
Old St
Chieveley, Beedon Common
RG20............... .51 C5
Chieveley RG18 ...... .51 F1
Hermitage RG18 ...... .78 F8
Old Stanmore Rd RG20.. .30 E6
Old Station Bsns Pk RG20 31 E4
Old Station Way HP10... .3 E5
Old Station Yd The RG17..25 B2
Oldstead RG12 .... 118 D4
Old Stocks Ct RG8 .... .54 F5
Old Thornford Rd RG19. 132 E6
Old Vicarage Way HP10 . .3 D4
OLD WARREN 135 E5
Old Watery La HP10 ... .3 E8
Oldway La SL1........ .41 D5
Old Welmore GU46.... 149 E5
Old Whitley Wood La
RG2 .... 113 C6
OLD WINDSOR .... .95 A8
Old Wokingham Rd
RG45 .... 143 C7
Old Woosehill La RG41. 115 F7
Oleander Cl RG45..... 143 A7
Oliver Ct SL1......... .41 E6
Oliver Dr RG31....... .84 C5
Oliver Rd SL1......... .42 B6
Oliver's Paddock SL7 .. .1 D5
Olivia Ct RG41....... 116 B6
Olivia Dr SL3......... .43 F1
Ollerton RG12........ 118 A1
Omega Way RG30..... .84 E7
Omer's Rise RG7...... 110 F3
Om Ho RG30.......... .85 D8
One Pin La SL2....... .22 C8
Onslow Dr SL5........ .93 A1
Onslow Gdns RG4..... .59 C3
Onslow Lodge TW18 .. .96 F1
Onslow Mews KT16 ... 124 A2
Onslow Rd SL5....... 121 B2
Onyx The RG12........ 118 A1
Opal Ct SL3........... .23 C1
Opendale Rd SL1...... .41 E7
Opecks Cl SL2........ .23 B1
Opendale Rd SL1...... .41 B8
Opladen Way RG12.... 118 E4
Oppidan SL6.......... .41 C7
Oracle Ctr The RG1.... .86 B7
Oracle Parkway RG6... .60 A1
Orbit Cl RG42......... .90 E1
Orbit Cl RG40........ 141 E6
Orchard Ave
Ashford TW15 .... .98 C2
Hatton TW14 .... .71 D2
Slough SL1............ .42 A4
Windsor SL4 .... .67 A6
Orchard Bungalow Mobile
Home Pk SL2 .... .21 F5
Orchard Chase RG10... .88 F7
Orchard Cl
Ashford TW15 .... .98 C2
Egham TW20 .... .95 F2
Farnborough GU17 .... 150 F1
Henley-on-T RG9 ...... .15 E1
Maidenhead SL6 ...... .40 A3
Newbury RG14......... 105 C1
Purley on T RG31..... .57 B4
Shinfield RG2......... 113 D7
Shiplake RG9 .... .35 E2
West End GU24....... 153 D6
Wokingham RG40 .... 116 C6
Woodmancott RG7.... 108 C2
Orchard Cotts RG10... .62 F6
Orchard Ct
Bracknell RG12 ...... 118 C7
Camberley GU15...... 151 B2
Harmondsworth UB7... .70 C2
Oatlands Park KT12... 125 F1
Reading RG2 .... .86 C5
Thatcham RG19 ...... 106 E3
Orchard Dene Dr RG7.. 109 C2
Orchard Dr
Sunbury TW17........ 125 E6
Woodley RG5......... .87 D4
Orchardene RG14..... 105 B4
Orchard Est RG10..... .88 F7
Orchard Gate
Farnham Common SL2.. .22 C7
Sandhurst GU47 ...... 143 B1
Orchard Gdns SL6..... .20 B7
Orchard Gn RG17..... .73 A1

Orchard Gr
Caversham RG4........ .59 E4
Flackwell Heath HP10 ... .3 B7
Maidenhead SL6 ...... .39 C7
Orchard Hill GU20 .... 146 D3
Orchard Ho 2 RG8..... .3 A4
Orchard La RG20 ..... .30 E7
Orchard Lodge SL1.... .41 E5
Orchard Mill SL8 ..... .3 B1
Orchard Park Cl RG17.. 100 D4
Orchard Pl RG40...... 116 C6
Orchard The
Hurst RG10 .... .88 F7
Mortimer RG7 .... 137 B5
Old Windsor SL4 ..... .68 B1
Orchards Residential Pk
SL3................. .43 F5
Orchard St RG1....... .86 B6
Orchard The
Flackwell Heath HP10 ... .3 B7
Lightwater GU18 ...... 153 B8
Marlow SL7 .... .1 B1
Theale RG7 .... .83 E4
Virginia Water GU25... 122 E4
Orchard View KT16.... 124 A3
Orchard Village 5 SL6 ..20 D3
ORCHARDVILLE ...... .21 B1
Orchard Way
Ashford TW15 .... .97 F6
Camberley GU15...... 151 B2
Slough SL3............ .43 E5
Orchardwood SL5..... 119 E7
Orchids The OX11..... .10 D7
Oregon Ave RG31..... .57 D3
Oregon Wlk RG40..... 141 E7
Oriel Hill GU15....... 151 D4
Oriental Rd SL5....... 120 D5
Orion RG12 .... 118 A1
Orkney Cl RG31....... .84 E4
Orkney Ct SL6........ .39 B5
Ormathwaites Cnr RG42..91 E1
Ormonde Gdns 5 RG14 .104 F4
Ormonde Rd RG41.... 115 E6
Ormsby St RG1....... .85 E7
Orpheus Ho RG7..... 134 E2
Orpington Cl RG10.... .61 E4
Orts Rd RG30......... .85 B7
Orts Rd
Newbury RG14........ 105 B2
Reading RG1.......... .86 D7
Orville Ct RG5 .... .88 B7
Orwell Cl
Caversham RG4....... .58 F4
Newbury RG14........ .59 B4
Osbert Ho RG4 .... .59 B4
Osborne Cl SL4....... .67 D7
Osborne Ct SL1....... .42 F4
Osborne Dr GU18 .... 153 A8
Osborne La RG42..... .91 C4
Osborne Mews 9 SL4.. .67 C5
Osborne Mews SL4 ... .67 C5
Osborne Rd
Egham TW20 .... .95 F2
Reading RG30 .... .85 B8
Windsor SL4 .... .67 C5
Wokingham RG40 .... 116 C6
Osborne St SL1....... .42 F4
Osier Pl 2 GU25...... .22 B1
Osman's Ct RG42..... .92 B1
Osnaburgh Hill GU15.. 151 B5
Osney Rd SL6......... .39 E6
Osprey Ave RG12..... 117 D5
Osprey Ct 5 RG1..... .86 C7
Osterley Cl RG1...... .86 E6
Osterley Dr RG1...... .86 E6
Osterley Rd SL4...... .59 E6
Ostler Gate SL6...... .19 C1
Ostlers Dr TW15 ..... .98 C3
Oswald Cl RG42...... .91 D2
Othello Gr RG42..... 118 E8
Otter Cl RG45........ 143 A7
Otter Ct RG45........ 143 A7
Our Lady of Peace RC Inf Sch
SL2................. .41 C8
Our Lady of Peace RC Jun
Sch SL1.............. .41 C8
Our Lady of the Rosary RC
Prim Sch TW18....... .97 A2
Ouseley Lodge SL4.... .95 C8
Ouseley Rd TW19..... 123 B5
Overbecks 3 RG14 ... 105 D4
Overbridge Sq RG14 .. 105 E3
Overbury Ave RG41... .88 F1
Overdale Rise GU16... 151 E3
Overdown Rd RG31... .57 D3
Overlanders End RG31..57 E3
Overlord Cl GU15..... 152 A8
Owen Cl 5 SL3....... .43 F1
Owen Rd
Newbury RG14........ 105 B4
Windlesham GU20.... 146 D4
Owlets Gr 4 RG14.... 115 E5
Owl Cl RG45.......... 143 A7
OWLSMOOR
Owlsmoor Prim Sch
GU47................ 143 E1
Owlsmoor Rd GU47... 143 E1
OWNHAM............. .76 C2
Oxenhope RG12...... 118 A5
Oxford Ave
Burnham SL1.......... .21 B3
Harlington TW6....... .71 D6
Slough SL1............ .41 F8
Oxford Cl TW15....... .98 C1
Oxford Ho RG41...... 116 A6

Oxford Rd
Chieveley RG20 . . . . .51 C1
Marlow SL7 . . . . .1 D2
Newbury RG14 . . . . .104 F5
Purley on T RG8, RG30,
RG31 . . . . .57 D4
Reading RG30, RG1 . . . . . . .85 D8
Sandhurst GU47 . . . . .143 E2
Windsor SL4 . . . . .67 C6
Wokingham RG41 . . . . .116 A6
Oxford Rd E SL4 . . . . .67 C6
Oxford Road Com Sch
RG1 . . . . .85 F7
Oxfordshire Pl RG42 . . . . .91 F1
Oxford St
Caversham RG4 . . . . .59 A2
Hungerford RG17 . . . . .100 E7
Lambourn RG17 . . . . .25 B3
Newbury RG14 . . . . .104 F4
Oyster Wharf 13 RG1 . . . . .86 B7

P

Pacific Cl TW14 . . . . .98 F7
Pack and Prime La RG9 . . .15 C2
Packman Dr RG10 . . . . .61 D6
Padbury Cl TW14 . . . . .98 D7
Padbury Oaks UB7 . . . . .70 B6
Paddick Cl RG4 . . . . .60 E3
Paddick Dr
Earley RG6 . . . . .87 D1
Lower Earley RG6 . . . . .114 D8
Paddison Ct 6 RG19 . . . . .106 E2
Paddock Cl
Camberley GU15 . . . . .152 A6
Maidenhead SL6 . . . . .39 A2
Paddock Cotts SL6 . . . . .39 A2
Paddock Ho SL5 . . . . .119 E6
Paddock Hts RG10 . . . . .61 E4
Paddock Rd
Caversham RG4 . . . . .59 D1
Newbury RG14 . . . . .130 F8
Paddocks The HP10 . . . . .3 B8
Paddocks Way KT16 . . . . . .124 B1
Paddock The
Chilton OX11 . . . . .10 D8
Crowthorne RG45 . . . . .143 A6
Datchet SL3 . . . . .68 B6
Maidenhead SL6 . . . . .19 C2
Newbury RG14 . . . . .105 C2
Wentworth GU25 . . . . .122 E3
Winkfield SL4 . . . . .93 B7
Padley Ct 18 RG1 . . . . .86 C7
Padstow Cl SL3 . . . . .43 E3
Padstow Gdns RG2 . . . . .86 B1
Padstow Wlk TW14 . . . . .98 F7
PADWORTH 109 F1
Padworth Coll RG7 . . . . . . .109 E1
Padworth La RG7 . . . . .109 C3
Padworth Rd RG7 . . . . .136 C7
Page Rd TW14 . . . . .71 D1
Page's Croft RG40 . . . . . . .116 D5
Pages Gdns RG8 . . . . .56 D5
Pages Wharf SL6 . . . . .40 C8
Paget Cl
Camberley GU15 . . . . .152 B7
Marlow SL7 . . . . .1 F4
Paget Dr SL6 . . . . .39 A4
Paget Rd SL3 . . . . .43 F2
Pagoda The SL6 . . . . .20 B1
Paice Gn RG40 . . . . .116 D7
Paices Hill RG7 . . . . .135 A5
Painesfield Dr 8 KT15,
KT16 . . . . .124 A1
Pakenham Rd RG12 . . . . . .118 D2
Palace Cl SL1 . . . . .41 F5
Paley St SL6 . . . . .64 B6
PALEY STREET 64 C5
Palgrave Ho RG45 . . . . . . .143 C4
Palmera Ave RG31 . . . . .84 C4
Palmer Cl
Crowthorne RG40 . . . . .143 A8
Peasemore RG20 . . . . .50 D7
Palmer Ct RG40 . . . . .116 C6
Palmer Park Ave RG6 . . . . . .87 A6
Palmer School Rd RG40 . .116 C6
Palmers Cl SL6 . . . . .39 A3
Palmer's Hill RG8 . . . . .54 C5
Palmer's La
Burghfield Common,
Poundgreen RG7 . . . . . .112 A3
Burghfield Common RG7 . .111 A2
Palmerston Ave SL3 . . . . . . .43 B3
Palmerston Cl GU25 . . . . . .122 E4
Palmerstone Rd RG6 . . . . . . .87 B6
Palmer The 23 RG30 . . . . . .85 D6
PAMBER HEATH 135 F1
Pamber Heath Rd RG26 . .135 E1
Pamber Rd RG7 . . . . .136 B1
Pamela Row SL6 . . . . .65 A8
PANGBOURNE 56 D6
Pangbourne Coll RG8 . . . . . .56 A4
Pangbourne Hill RG8 . . . . . .56 C5
Pangbourne Lodge Dr
RG8 . . . . .56 C5
Pangbourne Mews RG8 . . . .56 D6
Pangbourne Pl RG8 . . . . . . .56 D5
Pangbourne Prim Sch
RG8 . . . . .56 E5
Pangbourne Rd RG8 . . . . . . .55 C4
Pangbourne St 2 RG30 . . . .85 B8
Pangbourne Sta RG8 . . . . . .56 C6
Pankhurst Dr RG12 . . . . . . .118 B3
Pannells Ct KT16 . . . . .123 F1
Pan's Gdns GU15 . . . . .151 F4
Pantile Cl RG30 . . . . .84 F6
Pantile Row SL1 . . . . .44 A2

Papist Way OX10 . . . . .14 B8
Papplewick Sch SL5 . . . . . .120 A8
Paprika Cl RG6 . . . . .86 F1
Parade Ct 8 SL8 . . . . .3 A4
Parade The
Ashford TW16 . . . . .98 F1
Bourne End SL8 . . . . .3 A3
Earley RG6 . . . . .87 B3
Egham TW18 . . . . .96 D3
Farnham Common SL2 . . . . .22 C6
Reading RG30 . . . . .85 D5
Tadley RG26 . . . . .135 B1
Wentworth GU25 . . . . .122 D3
Windsor SL4 . . . . .66 D6
Woodley RG5 . . . . .87 E4
Woodley RG5 . . . . .87 F8
Paradise La RG7 . . . . .108 C7
Paradise Mews RG9 . . . . . . .15 D2
Paradise Rd RG9 . . . . .15 D1
Paradise Way RG7 . . . . . . .108 C7
Park Ave
Camberley GU15 . . . . .151 D4
Staines TW18 . . . . .97 A2
Thatcham RG18 . . . . .106 D4
Thorpe Lea TW20 . . . . .96 C1
Upper Halliford TW17 . . . . .125 E6
Wokingham RG40 . . . . .116 B6
Wraysbury TW19 . . . . .68 D3
Park Cl SL4 . . . . .67 D5
Park Close Cotts TW20 . . . . .94 F3
Park End SL4 . . . . .66 E4
Parkcorner La RG2, RG41 .114 F6
Park Cotts
3 Camberley GU15 . . . . . .151 B3
Kintbury RG17 . . . . .101 B3
Park Cres
Reading RG30 . . . . .85 B6
Sunningdale SL5 . . . . .120 F3
Park End Rd SL4 . . . . .105 A4
Parker Ct RG6 . . . . .87 C4
Parker's Cnr RG7 . . . . .83 A3
Parkers Ct GU19 . . . . .145 E3
Parker's La RG42 . . . . .92 B5
Park Farm Ind Est GU15 .151 C1
Parkfield Ho RG45 . . . . .143 C4
Parkfields GU46 . . . . .149 D6
Parkgate SL1 . . . . .21 C1
Park Gr RG30 . . . . .85 B6
Parkham RG42 . . . . .117 D8
Parkhill Cl GU17 . . . . .150 D4
Parkhill Dr RG31 . . . . .57 D2
Parkhill Rd GU17 . . . . .150 D4
Park Ho
Englefield Green TW20 . . . . .95 C2
Maidenhead SL6 . . . . .39 E6
Parkhouse La RG30 . . . . .85 D6
Park House Sch & Sports
Coll RG14 . . . . .130 E6
Parkhurst 20 RG30 . . . . .85 D6
Park La
Arborfield Garrison
RG40 . . . . .141 B5
Beech Hill RG7 . . . . .138 C2
Bracknell RG42 . . . . .90 E1
Burnham SL1 . . . . .21 E7
Camberley GU15 . . . . .151 C5
Charvil RG10 . . . . .61 B3
Horton SL3 . . . . .69 A6
Newbury RG14 . . . . .105 A4
Reading RG31 . . . . .84 C7
Silchester RG7 . . . . .137 C2
Slough SL3 . . . . .43 B3
Stockcross RG20 . . . . .51 C6
Thatcham RG18 . . . . .106 D4
Winkfield SL4 . . . . .93 B7
Parkland Ave SL3 . . . . .43 D2
Parkland Dr RG12 . . . . .118 E8
Parkland Gr TW15 . . . . .98 A4
Parkland Rd TW15 . . . . .98 A4
Park Lane Prim Sch RG31 .84 D8
Park Lane Prim Sch Annexe
RG31 . . . . .84 D8
Park Lawn SL2 . . . . .22 C2
Park Mews TW19 . . . . .97 F8
Park Par SL2 . . . . .22 C2
Park Pl GU17 . . . . .150 F3
Park Rd
Ashford TW15 . . . . .98 B3
Bracknell RG12 . . . . .118 D6
Camberley GU15 . . . . .151 C5
Egham TW20 . . . . .96 A4
Henley-on-T RG9 . . . . .15 E2
Lower Halliford TW17 . . . . .125 A1
Sandhurst GU47 . . . . .150 C8
Stanwell TW19 . . . . .70 C1
Stoke Poges SL2 . . . . .23 B3
Wokingham RG40 . . . . .116 B6
Parkside
Henley-on-T RG9 . . . . .15 C2
Maidenhead SL6 . . . . .19 D1
Parkside Bsns Pk RG5 . . . . . .87 E7
Parkside Cl 11 SL3 . . . . .43 A3
Parkside Pl TW18 . . . . .97 A2
Parkside Rd
Reading RG30 . . . . .85 D6
Sunningdale SL5 . . . . .121 A4
Thatcham RG18 . . . . .106 D5
Parkside Wlk SL1 . . . . .43 A3
Park St
Bagshot GU19 . . . . .145 E3
Camberley GU15 . . . . .151 C5
Hungerford RG17 . . . . .100 D5
Maidenhead SL6 . . . . .39 F7
Newbury RG14 . . . . .105 A4
Poyle SL3 . . . . .69 D6
Slough SL1 . . . . .42 F4

Park St continued
Windsor SL4 . . . . .67 D6
Parkstone Dr GU15 . . . . . . .151 C4
Park Terr RG14 . . . . .105 A3
Park The RG17 . . . . .25 A3
Parkview
Flackwell Heath HP10 . . . . . .3 B7
Maidenhead SL6 . . . . .39 F7
Park View
Ascot SL5 . . . . .120 E8
Bagshot GU19 . . . . .145 D3
Beech Hill RG7 . . . . .138 D5
Burghfield Common RG7 . . .111 A2
Reading RG1 . . . . .86 A5
Parkview Chase SL1 . . . . . . .41 E7
Park View Dr N RG10 . . . . . .61 A5
Park View Dr S RG10 . . . . . .61 A4
Park Wall La RG8 . . . . .34 C1
Parkway
Camberley GU15 . . . . .151 C3
Crowthorne RG45 . . . . .143 A5
Marlow SL7 . . . . .2 A3
Park Way
Hungerford RG17 . . . . .100 E4
Newbury RG14 . . . . .105 A3
Parkway Dr RG4 . . . . .60 E3
Park Wlk RG8 . . . . .57 D5
Parlaunt Park Prim Sch
SL3 . . . . .44 B3
Parlaunt Rd SL3 . . . . .44 B2
Parliament La SL1, SL6 . . . . .20 F5
Parnham Ave GU18 . . . . . . .153 D8
Parry Gn N SL3 . . . . .43 F2
Parry Gn S SL3 . . . . .44 A2
Parsley Cl RG6 . . . . .86 F1
Parsonage Gdns SL7 . . . . . . .1 E1
PARSONAGE GREEN 32 E4
Parsonage La
Farnham Common SL2 . . . . .22 D4
Hungerford RG17 . . . . .100 D6
Lambourn RG17 . . . . .25 A3
Windsor SL4 . . . . .67 A6
Parsonage Pl RG17 . . . . .25 A3
Parsonage Way GU16 . . . . .151 E1
Parsons Cl
Arborfield Garrison RG2 . . .141 A8
Newbury RG14 . . . . .104 E2
Parsons Down Inf Sch
RG19 . . . . .106 B3
Parsons Down Jun Sch
RG19 . . . . .106 A3
Parsons Field GU47 . . . . . . .150 B8
Parsons Rd
Datchet SL3 . . . . .68 F8
Slough SL3 . . . . .43 F1
Parson's Wood La SL2 . . . . .22 D5
Partia Cl RG1 . . . . .86 A6
Part La RG7 . . . . .139 E4
Partridge Ave GU46 . . . . . .149 B6
Partridge Cl
Frimley GU15 . . . . .117 E5
Maidenhead SL6 . . . . .39 F7
Partridge Dr RG31 . . . . .84 C6
Partridge Mead SL6 . . . . . . .19 F2
Pascal Cres RG2 . . . . .113 D7
Paschal Rd GU15 . . . . .151 F8
Passfield Lodge GU18 . . . . .146 B1
Pasture Cl RG6 . . . . .114 B8
Patches Field SL7 . . . . .1 E5
Paterson Cl GU16 . . . . .152 C3
Pates Manor Dr TW14 . . . . .98 D8
Pathway The RG42 . . . . .90 C1
Patricia Cl SL1 . . . . .41 E6
Patrick Gdns RG42 . . . . .91 E1
Patrick Rd RG4 . . . . .59 B2
Patriot Pl RG1 . . . . .86 C7
Patten Ash Dr RG40 . . . . . .116 E7
Patten Ave GU46 . . . . .149 C5
Patterson Cl HP10 . . . . .3 E7
Pattinson Rd RG2 . . . . .113 D6
Pavenham Cl RG6 . . . . .114 B8
Pavilion Gdns TW18 . . . . . . .97 B1
Pavilions End The GU15 . .151 D3
Pavilions The SL4 . . . . .67 B6
Pavy Cl RG19 . . . . .106 F2
Paxton Ave SL1 . . . . .42 C3
Payley Dr RG40 . . . . .116 E8
Paynesdown Rd RG19 . . . . .106 B4
Payton Hos SL6 . . . . .19 F6
Peace La SL6 . . . . .19 F6
Peachey Dr RG19 . . . . .106 F2
Peach St RG40 . . . . .116 C6
Peacock Ave TW14 . . . . .98 D7
Peacock Cotts RG40 . . . . . . .117 C5
Peacock La RG12 . . . . .117 D6
Peacock Rd SL7 . . . . .2 A3
Peacock St SL4 . . . . .67 D6
Pea La RG7 . . . . .107 F7
PEASEMORE 50 B8
Peasemore Hill RG20 . . . . . .50 B8

Pebble Hill RG17 . . . . .128 B6
Peckmoor Dr RG19 . . . . . . .131 C7
Peddlars Gr GU46 . . . . .149 E6
Peel Cl
Caversham RG4 . . . . .59 D2
Windsor SL4 . . . . .67 B4
Woodley RG5 . . . . .88 B8
Peel Ct SL1 . . . . .42 B8
Peel Ctr The RG12 . . . . . . .118 B7
Peel Ho TW20 . . . . .95 F2
Pegasus Cl RG19 . . . . .106 A4
Pegasus Ct
Egham TW20 . . . . .96 B3
2 Lambourn RG17 . . . . . . .25 B2
Reading RG31 . . . . .84 C7
Peggotty Pl GU47 . . . . .143 E2
Peg's Green Cl RG30 . . . . . . .85 B6
Peket Cl TW18 . . . . .123 E8
Pelham Ct
Maidenhead SL6 . . . . .39 E7
Reading RG30 . . . . .85 D6
Pelican Ho RG14 . . . . .104 F3
Pelican La RG14 . . . . .105 A4
Pelican Rd RG26 . . . . .135 E2
Pelling Hill SL4 . . . . .95 B7
Pell St RG1 . . . . .86 B6
Pemberley Lodge SL4 . . . . . .67 A4
Pemberton Gdns RG31 . . . . .84 D4
Pemberton Rd SL2 . . . . .21 E1
Pembroke RG12 . . . . .118 A1
Pembroke Broadway
GU15 . . . . .151 C5
Pembroke Cl
Ascot SL5 . . . . .120 D4
Burghfield Common RG7 . . .111 C3
Pembroke Ho 8 RG4 . . . . . . .59 C1
Pembroke Mews SL5 . . . . . .120 D4
Pembroke Pl RG4 . . . . .59 C3
Pembroke Rd 8 RG14 . . . . .105 A3
Pembury Ct UB3 . . . . .71 D8
Penbere Cl RG26 . . . . .135 E2
Pendals Cl RG18 . . . . .52 F5
Pendeen Ct SL1 . . . . .42 A5
Pendell Ave UB3 . . . . .71 F7
Pendennis Ave RG4 . . . . . . .59 E6
Pendine Pl RG12 . . . . .118 A4
Pendlebury RG12 . . . . .118 A2
Pendragon Ct RG30 . . . . . . .85 D5
Pendragon Way GU15 . . . . .152 D3
Pendred Rd RG2 . . . . .113 D6
Penfurzen La RG42 . . . . .91 D8
Peninsula Pl RG45 . . . . .143 C4
Peninsular Cl
Camberley GU15 . . . . .152 B7
Feltham TW14 . . . . .71 C1
Penling Cl SL6 . . . . .19 E6
Penn Cl RG4 . . . . .59 A6
Penn Ct 11 SL7 . . . . .1 E2
Penneston Cl SL6 . . . . .39 B4
Pennfields RG10 . . . . .61 E6
Penn Ho SL1 . . . . .21 C2
Pennine Cl RG31 . . . . .84 B6
Pennine Rd SL2 . . . . .42 A8
Pennine Way
Harlington UB7 . . . . .71 D7
Maidenhead SL6 . . . . .39 D4
Penn Mdw SL2 . . . . .23 A4
Penn Rd
Datchet SL3 . . . . .68 D6
Newbury RG14 . . . . .104 D5
Slough SL2 . . . . .22 D1
Penn Wood Prim Sch SL2 .22 D1
Penny Hill Cvn Site
GU17 . . . . .149 E2
Penny La TW17 . . . . .125 E2
Pennylets Gn SL2 . . . . .23 A5
Pennypiece RG8 . . . . .34 C7
Pennyroyal Ct RG1 . . . . .86 C6
Penrose Ave RG30 . . . . .85 C6
Penrose Cl RG14 . . . . .105 B4
Penrose Ct RG14 . . . . .105 B4
Penrose Ct TW20 . . . . .95 C2
Pensford Ct RG45 . . . . .143 B7
Penshurst Rd SL6 . . . . .39 D5
Pentangle The 12 RG14 . . .105 A4
Pentland Ave TW17 . . . . . . .125 A4
Pentland Cl RG31 . . . . .57 C1
Pentland Pl 13 RG10 . . . . . . .61 E3
Pentland Pl 13 RG10 . . . . . .106 D2
Pentland Rd SL2 . . . . .42 A8
Penton Ave TW18 . . . . .123 F8
Penton Ct TW19 . . . . .70 E7
Penton Hall TW18 . . . . .124 A8
Penton Hall Dr TW18 . . . . .124 A8
Penton Hook Marina
KT16 . . . . .124 A6
Penton Hook Rd TW18 . . . . .97 A1
Penton Rd TW18 . . . . .96 F1
Pentridge Ho 2 RG12 . . . . .113 C8
Penwood Ct SL6 . . . . .39 B7
Penwood Gdns RG12 . . . . . .117 B3
Penwood La SL7 . . . . .1 C2
Penwood Rd RG20 . . . . .130 C3
Penyston Rd SL6 . . . . .39 C7
Penzance Spur SL2 . . . . .22 B1
Pepler Way SL1 . . . . .21 B2
Peppard La RG9 . . . . .35 E2
Peppard Rd
Caversham, Emmer Green
RG4 . . . . .59 C7
Caversham RG4 . . . . .59 B3
Pepper La RG2 . . . . .86 E3
Pepys Cl SL3 . . . . .69 B8
Perch Cl SL7 . . . . .18 C8
Percheron Cl SL3 . . . . .43 E3
Percy Ave TW15 . . . . .98 A3
Percy Bryant Rd TW16 . . . . .98 E1

Oxf–Pin **179**

Percy Pl SL3 . . . . .68 B6
Peregrine Cl
Bracknell RG12 . . . . .118 B4
Wokingham RG41 . . . . .115 F5
Peregrine Rd TW16 . . . . . . .125 F7
Periam Cl RG9 . . . . .35 C8
Perigee RG2 . . . . .113 E7
Perkins Ct TW15 . . . . .97 F8
Perkins Way RG41 . . . . .116 A5
Perpetual Park Dr RG9 . . . . .35 F8
Perrin Cl TW15 . . . . .97 F3
Perrin Ct TW15 . . . . .98 A4
Perrycroft SL4 . . . . .66 F4
Perryfields Way SL1 . . . . . . .21 B1
Perryhill Dr GU47 . . . . .142 F1
Perry Ho SL1 . . . . .21 B1
Perryman Way SL2 . . . . .21 F2
Perry Oaks RG12 . . . . .118 E7
Perry Way
Bracknell RG12 . . . . .118 E7
Lightwater GU18 . . . . .152 F7
Perseverance Hill RG9 . . . . .35 A5
Perth Ave SL1 . . . . .42 B7
Perth Cl RG5 . . . . .61 A1
Perth Trad Est SL1 . . . . .42 B8
Peterhead Mews SL3 . . . . . .44 A1
Peterhouse Cl GU47 . . . . . .143 F2
Petersfield Ave
Slough SL2 . . . . .43 A5
Staines TW15, TW18 . . . . . .97 C2
Petersfield Rd TW18 . . . . . . .97 C3
Peters La SL6 . . . . .65 B8
Petrel Cl RG41 . . . . .115 E5
Petts La TW17 . . . . .125 A5
Petty Cross SL1 . . . . .41 E7
Petworth Ave RG30 . . . . .84 F3
Petworth Ct
Frimley GU15 . . . . .151 F4
Reading RG1 . . . . .85 E6
Windsor SL4 . . . . .67 A6
Pevensey Ave RG4 . . . . .59 A6
Pevensey Ct RG2 . . . . .86 E1
Pevensey Rd SL2 . . . . .22 A8
Pevsey Vale RG12 . . . . .118 F4
Pheasant Cl RG41 . . . . .88 C2
Pheasant La RG20 . . . . .131 C3
Pheasants Croft SL6 . . . . . . .39 A4
Pheasants Ridge SL7 . . . . . . .1 C7
Pheasant Way RG12 . . . . . .117 D5
Philberds Lodge SL6 . . . . . . .40 B1
Philbye Mews SL1 . . . . .41 F4
Philip Cotts SL8 . . . . .3 C3
Philip Dr HP10 . . . . .3 D7
Philip Rd TW18 . . . . .97 D2
Philip Rd RG4 . . . . .59 C8
Phillip Copse RG12 . . . . . . .118 D2
Phillips Cl RG5 . . . . .61 B1
Phipps Cl SL6 . . . . .39 A2
Phipps Rd SL1 . . . . .41 E8
Phoebe Ct 19 RG1 . . . . .86 A6
Phoenix Cl RG41 . . . . .115 E6
Phoenix Ct
Thatcham TW13 . . . . .98 E4
Maidenhead SL6 . . . . .39 D4
Phoenix Pl
Reading RG1 . . . . .85 F7
5 Staines TW18 . . . . .97 A3
Phoenix Wlk RG14 . . . . . . .130 C6
Phyllis Court Dr RG9 . . . . . .15 E3
Pickering RG12 . . . . .118 A2
Picket Post Cl RG12 . . . . . .118 F6
Picketts La RG8 . . . . .55 E4
Pickford Dr SL3 . . . . .43 F5
Pickfords Gdns SL1 . . . . .42 E5
Pickins Piece SL3 . . . . .69 A5
Pickwell Cl RG6 . . . . .87 C1
Pickwick Gdns GU15 . . . . . .152 B4
Pickwick Terr SL2 . . . . .43 B6
Picton Cl GU15 . . . . .152 B7
Picton Way RG4 . . . . .59 B4
Picture Ho The 1 RG1 . . . . .86 A7
Piercefield RG31 . . . . .84 C4
Pierce's Hill RG31 . . . . .57 C1
Pierce Ct SL6 . . . . .39 C8
Pigeon Gr RG22 . . . . .117 D5
Pigeonhouse La SL5 . . . . . . .92 E4
Pigeons Farm Rd RG19 . . .131 D8
Piggott Sch The RG10 . . . . .61 C7
Piggott's Rd 4 RG4 . . . . . . .59 C1
Pightle The
Newbury RG14 . . . . .111 F3
Peasemore RG20 . . . . .50 D6
Pigott Ct RG40 . . . . .116 D6
Pigott Rd RG40 . . . . .116 D8
Pike Cl SL7 . . . . .18 C8
Pikeshaw Way RG31 . . . . . . .57 C2
Pike St RG14 . . . . .105 B4
Pilgrims Way RG4 . . . . .59 C6
Pilgrims Way The OX11 . . .12 A7
Pimento Dr RG6 . . . . .86 F1
Pimpernel Pl RG18 . . . . . . .106 F4
Pincents Kiln Ind Pk
RG31 . . . . .84 A4
Pincents La RG31 . . . . .84 A4
Pinchington La RG14,
RG19 . . . . .131 B7
Pindar Pl RG14 . . . . .130 D6
Pine Acre SL6 . . . . .120 F2
Pine Ave GU15 . . . . .151 D3
Pine Cl
Maidenhead SL6 . . . . .39 B7
Sandhurst GU15 . . . . .150 E7
Pinecote Dr SL5 . . . . .120 F2

180 Pin–Que

Pinecrest GU17 . . . . .150 E1
Pinecroft SL7 . . . . .1 D4
Pine Croft Rd RG41 . . . .116 A2
Pine Ct RG12 . . . . .118 E5
Pine Dr
  Blackwater GU17 . . . . . . .150 E3
  Mortimer RG7 . . . . .136 F6
  Wokingham RG40 . . . . . . .142 A7
Pinefields Cl RG45 . . . . . .143 B4
Pine Gr
  Twyford RG10 . . . . .61 D5
  Windlesham GU20 . . . . . .146 D4
Pinehill Rd RG45 . . . . . . .143 C3
Pinehill Rise GU47 . . . . . .150 C8
Pinehurst
  Ascot SL5 . . . . .120 D4
  Englefield Green TW20 . . . .95 C1
Pinelands Mobile Home Pk
  RG7 . . . . .135 F4
Pinel Cl GU25 . . . . .122 E5
Pine Mount Rd GU15 . . . .151 D4
Piner Cotts SL4 . . . . .66 E4
Pine Ridge RG14 . . . . . . .105 C5
Pineridge Gdns 10 RG30 . . .85 D6
Pine Ridge Inf Sch GU15 .145 A1
Pine Ridge Rd RG7 . . . . . .111 A3
Pines Prim Sch The
  RG12 . . . . .118 A2
Pines The
  Camberley GU15 . . . . .151 F7
  Slough SL3 . . . . .43 F5
  Twyford RG10 . . . . .61 E2
Pinetree Ct RG4 . . . . .59 A5
Pine Trees Bsns Pk TW18. .96 E3
Pine Way TW20 . . . . .95 B2
Pinewood Ave RG45. . . . .143 C6
Pinewood Cl
  Sandhurst GU47 . . . . .149 F8
  Tadley RG26. . . . . .134 D1
Pinewood Cotts RG45 . . .143 A8
Pinewood Cres RG18. . . . .79 C8
Pinewood Dr
  Caversham RG4. . . . . .58 E5
  Newtown RG20 . . . . .131 A2
  Staines TW18. . . . . .97 A3
Pinewood Gdns GU19 . . .145 C3
Pinewood Mews TW19 . . .70 D1
Pinewood Pk Cvn Site
  RG40 . . . . .143 C8
Pinewood Rd GU25 . . . . .122 A5
Pinfold La RG8, RG18 . . . .54 B5
PINGEWOOD 112 C7
Pingewood Cl RG30. . . . . .85 A2
Pingewood Rd N RG30. . . .85 A1
Pingewood Rd S RG7,
  RG30 . . . . .112 C7
Pinglestone Cl UB7 . . . . . .70 E7
Pink La SL1 . . . . .21 B3
Pinkneys Dr SL6 . . . . .38 F8
Pinkneys Farm SL6 . . . . . .19 B1
PINKNEYS GREEN 19 A2
Pinkneys Rd SL6 . . . . .39 A8
Pinks La RG26 . . . . .134 E1
Pinnacle The RG1. . . . . . . .86 D7
Pipers Cl SL1 . . . . .21 C2
Pipers Ct
  Burnham SL1 . . . . .21 C2
  Thatcham RG19 . . . . .107 A2
Piper's End GU25 . . . . . . .122 D6
Pipers Ind Est RG19. . . . .106 F2
Pipers La RG19 . . . . .106 F1
Pipers Way RG19 . . . . . . .106 F2
Pipistrelle Way RG10. . . . .61 A4
Pipit Cl RG19 . . . . .106 B3
Pippin Gr RG2 . . . . .113 E6
Pippins Ct TW15 . . . . .98 B2
Pippins Sch SL3 . . . . .69 F6
Pippins The SL3 . . . . .43 F5
Pipsons Cl GU46 . . . . .149 D6
Pitch Pl RG42. . . . . .90 D3
Pitcroft Ave RG6. . . . . .87 A6
Pitfield La RG7 . . . . .137 C4
Pitford Rd RG5 . . . . .88 A8
Pitts Cl RG42 . . . . .90 C2
Pitt's La RG6 . . . . .87 B8
Pitts Rd SL1 . . . . .42 C5
Plackett Way SL1 . . . . .41 D5
Plaines Cl SL1 . . . . .41 F5
Planes The KT16 . . . . .124 C2
Plantagenet Pk RG42 . . . .118 F8
Plantation Cl RG18. . . . . . .78 F5
Plantation Rd
  Chilton OX12 . . . . .9 F8
  Tadley RG26. . . . . .134 F2
Plantation Row GU15 . . . .151 B5
Plantinum Apartments 17
  RG1. . . . . .86 B6
Plateau The RG42. . . . . . . .92 A1
Platt Ct RG17. . . . . .100 E3
Platt La RG17. . . . . .45 C6
Players Gn RG5. . . . . .87 E5
PLAY HATCH 60 A5
Playhatch Rd RG4 . . . . . . .60 B5
Play Platt RG7. . . . . .83 D4
Plough La
  Shiplake RG9. . . . . .35 E1
  Stoke Poges SL2 . . . . .23 B4
  Wokingham RG40 . . . . . . .116 F6
Ploughlands RG42. . . . . . .117 F8
Ploughlees La SL1 . . . . . . .42 E6
Plough Rd GU46 . . . . .149 E7
Plover Cl
  Staines TW18. . . . . .96 F5
  Wokingham RG41 . . . . . . .115 F5
Plover La RG27 . . . . .140 E1

Plowden Way RG9 . . . . . . .35 E1
Plummery The 1 RG1 . . . .86 C7
Plumpton Rd 1 RG14. . . .105 C1
Plumtrees RG6 . . . . .87 B2
Pluto Cl SL1. . . . . .41 E4
Pluto Rd OX11. . . . . .9 F8
Plymouth Ave RG5 . . . . . . .87 C5
Plymouth Rd SL1 . . . . .41 E8
Plympton Cl RG6 . . . . .87 E3
Pocket Cl RG42. . . . . .117 D7
Pocket Pl RG6 . . . . .87 B4
Pocketts Yd SL6 . . . . .20 B7
Pococks La SL4. . . . . .42 E1
Poffley Pl RG20. . . . . .107 A3
Pointers Cl RG20 . . . . .51 B2
Point Royal RG12 . . . . . . .118 B4
Points The SL6 . . . . .39 B3
Polar Pk UB7. . . . . .70 F7
Poldark Pl RG2 . . . . .113 B7
Polehampton CE Inf Sch
  RG10 . . . . .61 D5
Polehampton Cl RG10. . . . .61 D4
Polehampton Cl RG10. . . . .61 D4
Polehampton Jun Sch
  RG10 . . . . .61 E6
Pollard Cl SL4 . . . . .68 B2
Pollard Gr GU15 . . . . .152 C4
Pollardrow Ave RG42. . . . .117 F8
Pollards Way RG31. . . . . . .84 D4
Polo Ctr The SL5. . . . . . . .121 C6
Polsted Rd RG31. . . . . .57 D1
Polyanthus Way RG45. . . .143 B8
Polye Pk SL3 . . . . .69 E4
Polygon Bsns Ctr SL3 . . . .69 F5
Pond Cl
  Farnborough (Berks) OX12 . .8 E1
  Newbury RG14. . . . . .130 D7
Pond Croft GU46. . . . . . . .149 E6
Ponderosa Cvn Site TW19 .69 F3
Pond Head La RG6. . . . . . .87 D4
Pond Ho KT16 . . . . .124 B2
Pond La
  Hermitage RG18 . . . . .79 C7
  Mapledurham RG4. . . . . . . .58 A6
Pondmoor Rd RG12. . . . . .118 B4
Pond Rd TW20. . . . . .96 C2
Pondside Cl UB3. . . . . .71 D7
Poole Cl RG30 . . . . .85 A7
Pool End Cl TW17. . . . . . . .125 A4
Pooley Ave TW20 . . . . .96 B3
POOLEY GREEN. 96 C2
Pooley Green Cl TW20 . . . .96 C3
Pooley Green Rd TW20. . . .96 C3
Pool La
  Slough SL1. . . . . .42 E6
  Waltham St L RG10 . . . . . .63 A5
Poolmans Rd SL4. . . . . . . .66 D4
Pope Cl TW14 . . . . .98 F7
Popel's Cotts SL4. . . . . . . .92 D5
Poperinghe Way RG2 . . . .140 D8
Popes Cl SL3 . . . . .69 C7
Popes La SL6 . . . . .19 C7
POPESWOOD. 91 D7
Popeswood Lodge RG42 .117 D8
Popeswood Rd RG42. . . . .117 D8
Popeswood Rdbt RG42. . .117 D8
Popham Cl RG12. . . . . . . .118 F4
Poplar Ave
  Reading RG30 . . . . .84 F5
  Windlesham GU20 . . . . . . .146 B6
Poplar Cl
  Bracknell RG12 . . . . .118 D6
  Brimpton RG19 . . . . .133 A6
  Poyle SL3 . . . . .69 E6
Poplar Gdns RG2 . . . . .86 E1
Poplar La RG2 . . . . .113 D8
Poplar Ho SL3 . . . . .43 F1
Poplar La
  Hurst RG10. . . . . .62 A2
  Winnersh RG41. . . . . .88 D3
Poplar Pl RG14 . . . . .105 A5
Poplar Rd
  Ashford TW15 . . . . .98 C3
  Wooburn Green HP10 . . . . . .3 E7
Poplars The SL5 . . . . .120 A4
Poppy Dr RG18 . . . . .106 F4
Poppyhills Rd GU15. . . . . .151 F8
Poppy Pl RG40. . . . . .116 B6
Poppy Way RG31. . . . . .84 C5
Porchester SL5 . . . . .120 A5
Porchester Rd RG14 . . . . .105 A1
Porchfield Cl RG6. . . . . . . .87 A5
Porlock Cl 5 RG20 . . . . . .106 D2
Porlock Pl RG31. . . . . .84 C4
Port Down RG17. . . . . .100 E5
Porter Cl RG6 . . . . .114 C8
Porter End RG14. . . . . .131 B8
Portesbery Hill Dr GU15 .151 E6
Portesbery Rd GU15 . . . . .151 E6
Portesbery Sch GU15 . . . .151 D6
Portia Gr RG42 . . . . .118 E8
Portland Bsns Ctr SL3 . . . .68 B6
Portland Cl SL2. . . . . .21 D1
Portland Gdns
  Marlow SL7 . . . . .1 D1
  Reading RG30 . . . . .84 D7
Portland Rd TW15 . . . . . . .97 E5
Portlands Mews 1 SL7 . . .1 D1
Portlock Rd SL6 . . . . .39 C7
Portman Cl 5 RG42. . . . . .118 A8
Portman Ctr The RG30. . . .58 D1
Portman Rd RG30 . . . . . . .58 D1
Portman Way RG30. . . . . . .85 D8
Portmeirion Gdns RG30 . .57 F1
Portnall Cotts SL5 . . . . . . .121 C4
Portnall Dr GU25 . . . . . . .121 B4

Portnall Rd GU25 . . . . . . .121 F4
Portnall Rise GU25. . . . . .121 F3
Portrush Cl RG5 . . . . .87 D6
Portsmouth Ct SL1 . . . . . . .42 E6
Portsmouth Rd GU15. . . . .152 A7
Portway
  Riseley RG2 . . . . .139 C2
  Tadley RG26. . . . . .134 E1
Portway Cl RG1. . . . . .85 E6
Post Horn Pl RG31. . . . . . .84 F4
Posting House Mews
  RG14 . . . . .104 E4
Post Office Cotts SL2 . . . .23 A5
Post Office La
  Burghfield RG30 . . . . .111 D5
  Slough SL3. . . . . .43 D7
Post Office Rd RG17 . . . . .127 E5
Potbury Cl SL4 . . . . .93 B2
Potley Hill Prim Sch
  GU46 . . . . .150 A5
Potley Hill Rd GU46. . . . . .149 F5
Pottery La RG17 . . . . .127 C5
Pottery Rd RG30 . . . . .85 C6
Potts Pl 5 SL7 . . . . .1 D2
POUGHLEY 73 F8
Poulcott TW19. . . . . .68 E1
Pound Cotts RG8 . . . . .34 A6
Pound Cres SL7 . . . . .1 C1
Poundfield La SL6 . . . . . . .19 F7
Poundfield Way RG10 . . . .61 F3
POUNDGREEN 112 C3
Pound Green Cotts RG7 . .111 B1
Pound La
  Hurst RG10. . . . . .69 B5
  Little Marlow SL7 . . . . .2 C1
  Marlow SL7 . . . . .1 D1
  Newbury RG20 . . . . .104 D4
  Sonning RG4 . . . . .60 E2
  Thatcham RG18, RG19. . . .106 A3
  Windlesham GU20 . . . . . . .146 C4
Pound Piece RG17 . . . . . .100 C5
Pound Pl RG42 . . . . .90 C3
Pound Rd KT16. . . . . .124 B2
Pound St RG14 . . . . .104 F2
Pound The SL1 . . . . .21 D1
Powis Cl SL6 . . . . .39 B4
Powney Rd SL6. . . . . .39 C7
POYLE 69 E6
Poyle 14 Trad Est SL3 . . . .69 F4
Poyle Gdns RG12 . . . . . . .118 D8
Poyle La SL1. . . . . .21 B3
Poyle New Cotts SL3. . . . . .69 F5
Poyle Rd SL3 . . . . .69 F5
Poyle Tech Ctr The SL3. . . .69 E5
Poynings The SL0. . . . . . . .44 F2
Prancing Horse Cl RG19 .106 E3
Precincts The SL1 . . . . . . .21 C1
Precinct The RG30 . . . . . . .96 A3
Prescott RG12 . . . . .117 F2
Prescott Rd SL3 . . . . .69 E5
Presentation Coll RG30 . . .85 D5
Preston Pl RG14 . . . . .105 D5
Preston Rd
  Littleton TW17 . . . . .125 A4
  Reading RG2 . . . . .86 B5
  Slough SL2. . . . . .43 C6
Prestwick Ct 22 RG1 . . . .86 D7
Prestwood SL2 . . . . .43 B7
Pretoria Rd KT16 . . . . .123 F1
Price Gdns RG42. . . . . .91 B2
Pride Cl RG30. . . . . .85 A6
Prides Crossing SL5 . . . . . .93 A1
Priest Ave RG40 . . . . .116 F5
Priest Hill
  Caversham RG4. . . . . .59 A3
  Englefield Green SL4, TW20 .95 C6
  Farley Hill RG7. . . . . .140 A1
Priest La GU24. . . . . .153 C5
PRIESTWOOD 118 A8
Priestwood Ave RG42. . . .117 F8
Priestwood Court Rd
  RG42 . . . . .118 A8
Priestwood Sq 1 RG42 . .118 A8
Primrose Cl RG8. . . . . .57 C5
Primrose La RG41. . . . . . . .88 C3
Primrose Lea SL7 . . . . .1 D1
Primrose Walk GU46. . . . .149 B6
Primrose Wlk RG12 . . . . . .118 C3
Prince Albert Dr 6 TW16 .98 E1
Prince Albert Dr SL5. . . . .119 D4
Prince Albert's Wlk SL4 . . .119 D4
Prince Andrew Cl SL6. . . . .20 B1
Prince Andrew Rd SL6. . . .20 B1
Prince Andrew Way SL5. . .119 D7
Prince Consort Cotts SL4 .67 D5
Prince Consort Dr
  Old Windsor SL4 . . . . .94 A6
  Windsor SL4 . . . . .67 A1
Prince Dr GU47 . . . . .143 A1
Prince Hold Rd RG19 . . . .106 A3
Prince of Wales Ave
  RG30 . . . . .85 D7
Prince of Wales Wlk
  GU15 . . . . .151 C6
Princes Cl SL4 . . . . .41 F1
Princes Ct
  Bourne End SL8 . . . . .3 C4
  Englefield Green TW20 . . . .95 C3
Prince's La RG20 . . . . .50 D6
Princes Rd
  Ashford TW15 . . . . .97 F3
  Bourne End SL8 . . . . .3 C4
  Egham TW20 . . . . .95 F2
  Feltham TW13 . . . . .98 F5
Princess Ave SL4 . . . . .67 B4

Princess Christians Hospl
  SL4 . . . . .67 C6
Princess Margaret Hospl The
  SL4 . . . . .67 D5
Princess Marina Dr
  Arborfield Garrison RG2 . . .115 A1
  Arborfield Garrison RG2 . . .140 F7
Princess Sq RG12. . . . . . .118 B7
Princess St 9 SL6. . . . . . . .39 F6
Princess St SL1. . . . . .43 B4
Prince's St RG1 . . . . .86 C7
Princess Way GU15 . . . . . .151 C5
Princes Terr SL8 . . . . .3 C3
Princes Way GU19 . . . . . .145 E1
Prince William Ct TW15 . . .97 F3
Prince William Dr RG31. . .57 C1
Prior Croft Cl GU15 . . . . . .152 A4
Prior End GU15. . . . . .152 A5
Prior Heath Inf Sch
  GU15 . . . . .152 A5
Prior Place Cross Roads
  GU15 . . . . .152 B4
Priors Cl SL6 . . . . .39 A3
PURTON 51 D8
Priors Cl
  Maidenhead SL6 . . . . .40 B2
  5 Slough SL3. . . . . .43 A3
Priors Court Cotts
  Chieveley RG18 . . . . .78 D7
  Hermitage RG18 . . . . .78 E7
Priors Court Rd RG18 . . . .78 D8
Priors Court Sch RG18 . . .78 D8
Priors Ct 16 RG1. . . . . .86 B6
Prior's La GU17. . . . . .150 A5
Priors Rd
  Tadley RG26. . . . . .135 A1
  Windsor SL4 . . . . .66 D4
Priors Way SL6 . . . . .40 B2
Priors Way Ind Est SL6. . . .40 B2
Priors Wood RG45 . . . . . . .142 D4
Priory Ave
  Caversham RG4. . . . . .59 A2
  Hungerford RG17 . . . . .100 D4
Priory Cl
  Hungerford RG17 . . . . .100 D4
  Sunningdale SL5 . . . . .121 A2
Priory Ct
  Camberley GU15 . . . . .150 F5
  Caversham RG4. . . . . .59 A2
  Egham TW20 . . . . .96 C2
  Winnersh RG41. . . . . .88 C3
Priory Gdns TW15 . . . . . . .98 D3
Priory Gn TW18. . . . . .97 B3
Priory Hts SL1. . . . . .41 E7
Priory La RG42 . . . . .91 C2
Priory Mews
  8 Chertsey KT16. . . . . . .124 A2
  Staines TW18. . . . . .97 B3
Priory Pl
  6 Hungerford RG17. . . . .100 D4
  Newbury RG19. . . . . .131 B6
Priory Rd
  Burnham SL1 . . . . .41 C8
  Hungerford RG17 . . . . .100 D4
  Newbury RG14. . . . . .105 A1
  Sunningdale SL5 . . . . .121 A2
  Winkfield SL5. . . . . .119 B7
Priory Sch SL1 . . . . .41 D8
Priory The RG41 . . . . .88 C3
Priory Way
  Datchet SL3 . . . . .68 B7
  Harmondsworth UB7. . . . . .70 E8
Priory Wlk RG12 . . . . .118 F5
Priscilla Ho 9 TW16 . . . . .98 F1
Pritchard Cl RG40 . . . . . . .116 F5
Privet Cl RG6. . . . . .87 B1
Proctors Rd RG40. . . . . . .116 F6
Progress Bsns Ctr SL1 . . . .42 D7
Projection D 11 RG1. . . . . .86 A8
Projection W 10 RG1 . . . . .86 A8
Promenade Rd RG4. . . . . .59 A2
Prospect Cotts RG42 . . . .117 D8
Prospect Ct SL2 . . . . .22 C6
Prospect La TW20. . . . . . . .95 A3
Prospect Mews 4 RG1 . . .85 F7
Prospect Park Hospl
  RG30 . . . . .85 B6
Prospect Pl
  Hurley SL6. . . . . .17 F3
  Newbury RG14. . . . . .105 A1
  Staines TW18. . . . . .96 F3
  3 Windsor SL4 . . . . .67 D6
Prospect Rd
  Hungerford RG17 . . . . .100 D5
  Marlow SL7 . . . . .1 D2
  Prospect SG RG30 . . . . . . .85 A5
Prospect St
  Caversham RG4. . . . . .59 A2
  Reading RG1 . . . . .85 F7
Providence Ho UB3. . . . . . .71 D7
Providence La UB3 . . . . . . .71 D7
Providence Pl 14 SL6. . . . .39 F7
Prudential Bldgs 1 SL1. . .42 F4
Prune Hill TW20 . . . . .95 E1
Prunus Cl GU24. . . . . .153 D6
Pryor Cl RG31. . . . . .57 D2
Puccinia Ct TW19 . . . . .97 E2
Pudding Hill RG10 . . . . . . .37 D6
Puddle La RG20 . . . . .28 E1
Pudseys Cl RG6 . . . . .19 B6
Puffers Way RG14. . . . . . .104 E2
Pullar Rd RG2 . . . . .86 B3
Pullmans Pl 6 TW18 . . . . .97 A3
Pullman Pl 2 SL6 . . . . . . .40 A7
Pumpkin Hill SL1. . . . . .21 E6
Pump La
  Ascot SL5 . . . . .120 E8

Pump La continued
  Grazeley RG7 . . . . .112 C2
Pump La N SL7. . . . . .1 F6
Pump La S SL7 . . . . .2 A4
Pundles La SL6 . . . . .63 C6
PUNT HILL. 39 C6
Purbeck Ho 3 RG2 . . . . . .113 C8
Purbrook Ct RG12 . . . . . . .118 E3
Purcell Rd RG45 . . . . .143 B7
Purfield Dr RG10 . . . . .36 E2
Purley CE Inf Sch RG8 . . . .57 C5
Purley Ind Est RG20. . . . . .49 B7
Purley La RG8 . . . . .57 C5
Purley Magna RG8. . . . . . . .57 C4
PURLEY ON THAMES 57 B4
Purley Rise RG8. . . . . .57 A5
Purley Village RG8. . . . . . . .57 C5
Purley Way RG8 . . . . .56 E5
Pursers Ct SL2 . . . . .42 E6
Pursers Farm RG7 . . . . . . .113 B3
Purslane RG40 . . . . .116 D5
Purssell Cl SL6 . . . . .39 A3
PURTON 51 D8
Purton Ct SL2 . . . . .22 C5
Purton La SL2 . . . . .22 C5
Putman Pl RG9 . . . . .15 E1
Pyegrove Chase RG12. . . .118 E2
Pyke Cl RG40 . . . . .116 D6
Pykes Hill RG4 . . . . .58 D4
Pyle Mill RG14 . . . . .105 B1
Pyrcroft La KT16. . . . . .123 F2
Pyrcroft Grange Prim Sch
  KT16. . . . . .123 E2
Pyrcroft Rd KT16 . . . . .123 E2

Q

Quadrant Ct
  Bracknell RG12 . . . . .118 E6
  23 Reading RG1 . . . . .86 B6
Quadrant The SL6 . . . . .40 A6
Quadrivium Point SL1. . . . .42 C5
Qualitas RG12 . . . . .117 F1
Quantock Ave RG4 . . . . . . .59 D5
Quantock Cl
  Charvil RG10 . . . . .61 D4
  Harlington UB3 . . . . .71 D7
  Slough SL3. . . . . .44 A1
Quantocks The RG12 . . . .106 D2
Quarrington Cl RG19. . . . .106 D2
Quarry Bank GU18 . . . . . .153 A8
Quarrydale Dr SL7 . . . . .1 F2
Quarry La
  Lower Shiplake RG9 . . . . . .36 A4
  Yateley GU46. . . . . .149 E5
Quarry Wood Rd SL6, SL7 .19 A8
Quartz Cl RG41 . . . . .115 D7
Quaves Rd SL3 . . . . .43 D3
Quebec Gdns GU17 . . . . .150 D4
Quebec Rd RG19 . . . . .131 C5
Queen Anne Royal Free CE
  Fst Sch The SL4 . . . . .67 D4
Queen Anne's Cl SL4. . . . . .94 B5
Queen Anne's Ct SL4 . . . . .67 C6
Queen Anne's Gate RG4 . .59 C3
Queen Anne's Rd SL4. . . . .67 C3
Queen Anne's Sch RG4. . . .59 B3
Queen Charlotte St 10
  SL4 . . . . .67 D6
Queen Cl RG9 . . . . .15 E1
Queen Elizabeth Rd
  GU15 . . . . .144 D1
Queen Elizabeth's Wlk
  SL4. . . . . .67 E5
Queen Mary Ave GU15 . . .151 A5
Queens Bsns Ctr SL1 . . . . .42 D7
Queen Mary Rd TW17 . . . .125 C7
Queens Acre SL4 . . . . .67 D3
Queens Acre Ho 8 SL4 . . .67 D4
Queensborough Dr RG4 . . .58 E5
Queensbury Pl GU17 . . . .150 C4
Queen's Cl
  North Ascot SL5. . . . . .119 E8
  Old Windsor SL4 . . . . .68 A2
Queen's Cotts
  Reading RG1 . . . . .86 D6
  Wargrave RG10. . . . . .36 D2
Queens Ct
  Goring RG8 . . . . .34 C6
  3 Newbury RG14. . . . . . .105 A1
  Slough SL1. . . . . .42 F6
  5 Slough SL1. . . . . .43 A4
  Slough SL1. . . . . .43 B4
Queen's Ct SL1 . . . . .42 D2
Queen's Dr SL3 . . . . .23 F4
Queens Gate Cotts SL4 . . .67 B3
Queenshill Lodge SL5 . . . .120 B6
Queen's Hill Rise SL5 . . . .120 C6
Queens Keep GU15 . . . . . .151 D5
Queen's La SL6. . . . . .39 F7
Queens Mead RG10 . . . . . .36 D6
Queensmead
  Ashford TW15 . . . . .97 F3
  Datchet SL3 . . . . .68 B6
Queensmere SL1. . . . . .42 F4
Queens Park Gdns 3
  TW13 . . . . .98 F5
Queen's Pine RG12 . . . . . .118 E3
Queen's Pl SL5 . . . . .120 A6
Queens Rd
  Bisley GU24. . . . . .153 F1
  Camberley GU15. . . . . . . .151 A5
  Eton SL4 . . . . .41 F1
  Slough SL1. . . . . .42 F6
  Windsor SL4 . . . . .67 C5
Queen's Rd
  Ascot SL5 . . . . .120 D4
  Caversham RG4. . . . . .59 A2

Que–Riv 181

Queen's Rd *continued*
Datchet SL3 . . . . 68 B7
Egham TW20 . . . . 95 F2
Marlow SL7 . . . . 1 D2
Newbury RG14 . . . . 105 B2
Reading RG1 . . . . 86 C7
Queens Ride RG45 . . . . 143 B7
Queen St
Caversham RG4 . . . . 59 A3
Chertsey KT16 . . . . 124 A1
Henley-on-T RG9 . . . . 15 E1
Maidenhead SL6 . . . . 39 F7
Queen's Terr 5 SL4 . . . . 67 D4
Queensway
Caversham RG4 . . . . 59 D6
Maidenhead SL6 . . . . 19 E2
Queens Way RG17 . . . . 102 C1
Queen's Wharf RG1 . . . . 86 C7
Queens Wlk TW15 . . . . 97 D4
Queens Wlk Mall 3 SL6 . . 39 F7
Queen Victoria Cross Roads
GU15 . . . . 151 A6
Queen Victoria Ho RG40 . 116 D6
Queen Victoria St RG1 . . . 86 B8
Queen Victoria's Wlk SL4 . 67 F6
Quelm Park Rdbt RG42 . . . 91 B2
Quentin Rd RG5 . . . . 87 D6
Quentin Way GU25 . . . . 122 B5
QUICK'S GREEN 54 D5
Quinbrookes SL2 . . . . 43 C7
Quince Cl SL5 . . . . 120 D5
Quincy Rd TW20 . . . . 96 A3
Quinn Ct 4 RG30 . . . . 85 C7
Quintilis RG12 . . . . 117 F1
Quoitings Dr SL7 . . . . 1 C2
Quoitings Gdns SL7 . . . . 1 C2
Quoiting Sq SL7 . . . . 1 D2

R

Racecourse Rd RG14 . . . . 105 B1
Raceview Bsns Ctr RG14 . 105 B2
Rachaels Lake View RG42 . 91 E1
Rackstraw Rd GU47 . . . . 150 D6
Radbourne Rd RG31 . . . . 84 D4
Radcliffe Way RG42 . . . . 117 E8
Radcot Ave SL3 . . . . 44 B3
Radcot Cl
Maidenhead SL6 . . . . 19 E3
Woodley RG5 . . . . 60 E1
Radical Ride RG40 . . . . 141 F7
Radius Pk TW14 . . . . 71 F3
Radley Bottom
Hungerford Newtown
RG17 . . . . 74 B3
Hungerford RG17 . . . . 101 E7
Radley Cl TW14 . . . . 98 F7
Radnor Cl RG9 . . . . 15 E2
Radnor Ho 10 RG1 . . . . 85 E5
Radnor Rd
Bracknell RG12 . . . . 118 F6
Earley RG6 . . . . 87 C3
Radnor Way SL3 . . . . 43 E2
Radstock La RG6 . . . . 87 A2
Radstock Prim Sch RG6 . . . 87 B2
Radstock Rd RG1 . . . . 86 E7
Raeburn Way GU47 . . . . 150 D6
Ragdale RG7 . . . . 111 A3
Raggleswood Cl RG6 . . . . 87 C3
Raghill RG7 . . . . 135 D6
Raglan Ct RG2 . . . . 86 D2
Raglan Gdns RG4 . . . . 59 C4
Ragley Mews RG4 . . . . 59 D6
Ragmans Cl SL7 . . . . 1 D8
Ragstone Rd SL1 . . . . 42 E3
Railside RG7 . . . . 108 F2
Railton Cl RG2 . . . . 113 D7
Railway Cotts RG8 . . . . 34 C6
Railway Rd RG14 . . . . 105 B2
Railway Terr
Egham TW18 . . . . 96 D3
Mortimer RG7 . . . . 137 E5
Slough SL2 . . . . 42 F5
Rainbow Pk RG41 . . . . 88 B2
Rainforest Wlk RG12 . . . . 118 B4
Rainsborough Chase SL6 . . 39 B3
Rainworth Cl RG6 . . . . 114 A8
Raleigh Cl
Slough SL1 . . . . 42 A5
Woodley RG5 . . . . 87 E5
Raleigh Ct TW18 . . . . 97 A4
Raleigh Rd TW13 . . . . 98 F6
Raleigh Way GU16 . . . . 151 F3
Ralphs Ride RG12 . . . . 118 E6
Ralston Ct 25 25 . . . . 67 D6
Ram Alley RG19 . . . . 133 D1
Rambler Cl SL6 . . . . 41 B7
Rambler La SL3 . . . . 43 C3
Ramptons La RG7 . . . . 136 B6
Ramsay Cl GU15 . . . . 152 B8
Ramsay Rd GU20 . . . . 146 E5
Ramsbury Cl RG12 . . . . 117 E3
Ramsbury Cnr RG18 . . . . 106 F8
Ramsbury Dr
Earley RG6 . . . . 87 B4
Hungerford RG17 . . . . 100 E5
Ramsbury Terr RG17 . . . . 100 E5
Ramsey Cl RG6 . . . . 87 E2
Ramsey Ct SL2 . . . . 21 D1
Ramslade Cotts RG12 . . . 118 C6
Ranald Court Cotts SL5 . . . 92 F1
Ranald Ct SL5 . . . . 92 F2
Rances La RG40 . . . . 116 E5
Randall Cl SL3 . . . . 43 F1
Randall Ct SL4 . . . . 68 A1
Randall Mead RG42 . . . . 90 B2
Randell Cl GU17 . . . . 150 E1
Randolph Rd
Reading RG1 . . . . 59 A1
Slough SL3 . . . . 43 E3
Ranelagh CE Sch RG12 . . 118 C6
Ranelagh Cres SL5 . . . . 119 D8
Ranelagh Dr RG12 . . . . 118 C6
Range Rd RG40 . . . . 142 B7
Range Ride GU15 . . . . 150 F7
Range View GU47 . . . . 150 E8
Range Villas TW17 . . . . 124 E2
Range Way TW17 . . . . 125 A2
Rangewood Ave RG30 . . . . 84 F3
Ranikhet Prim Sch RG30 . . 85 A8
Rapley Cl GU15 . . . . 151 F8
Rapley Gn RG12 . . . . 118 C3
Ratby Cl RG6 . . . . 87 C2
Raven Cl GU46 . . . . 149 B6
Ravendale Rd TW16 . . . . 125 F7
Ravenglass Cl RG6 . . . . 87 C3
Ravensbourne Ave TW19 . . 97 E7
Ravensbourne Dr RG5 . . . . 87 E8
Ravenscote Com Jun Sch
GU16 . . . . 152 A3
Ravenscourt
Marlow SL7 . . . . 2 A3
Sunbury TW16 . . . . 125 F8
Ravenscroft Rd RG9 . . . . 15 D2
Ravensdale Mews TW18 . . . 97 B2
Ravensdale Rd SL5 . . . . 120 A4
Ravensfield TW20 . . . . 95 C2
Ravens Field SL3 . . . . 43 D4
Ravenshoe Cl SL8 . . . . 3 A3
Ravenstone Rd GU15 . . . . 152 D5
Ravenswing Pk RG7 . . . . 135 D2
Ravenswood Ave RG45 . . . 142 E5
Ravenswood Dr GU15 . . . 152 A5
Ravenswood Village
Settlement RG45 . . . . 142 E6
Ravensworth Rd
Mortimer RG7 . . . . 136 E5
Slough SL2 . . . . 22 A2
Rawcliffe Ho SL6 . . . . 40 A6
Rawdon Rise GU15 . . . . 152 B5
Rawlinson Rd GU15 . . . . 150 F6
Ray Dr SL6 . . . . 40 B7
Rayfield SL6 . . . . 40 B8
Ray Ho 5 SL8 . . . . 3 A4
Ray Lea Cl SL6 . . . . 40 B8
Ray Lea Rd SL6 . . . . 40 B8
Ray Lodge SL6 . . . . 40 B7
Ray Lodge Mews SL6 . . . . 40 B7
Ray Mdw SL6 . . . . 20 A1
Ray Mead Ct SL6 . . . . 20 C1
Ray Mead Rd SL6 . . . . 40 C8
Ray Mill Rd E SL6 . . . . 20 B1
Ray Mill Rd W SL6 . . . . 40 A8
Raymond Cl SL3 . . . . 69 E6
Raymond Rd
Maidenhead SL6 . . . . 39 D7
Slough SL3 . . . . 44 A3
Rayner Dr RG2 . . . . 140 E8
Rayners Cl SL3 . . . . 69 C7
Ray Park Ave SL6 . . . . 40 B8
Ray Park La SL6 . . . . 40 B7
Ray Park Rd SL6 . . . . 40 B8
Rays Ave SL4 . . . . 66 F7
Ray St SL6 . . . . 40 B7
Raywood Cl UB7 . . . . 71 C7
Reade Ct SL2 . . . . 22 C6
READING 86 B4
Reading Alternative Sch
RG1 . . . . 86 C5
Reading Blue Coat Sch
RG4 . . . . 60 C3
Reading Bridge RG1 . . . . 86 B8
Reading Gate Ret Pk RG2 . 85 F1
Reading Girls Sch RG2 . . . 86 C3
Reading Green Park Station
RG30 . . . . 85 D1
Reading International Bsns
Pk RG2 . . . . 113 A6
Reading Link Ret Pk RG2 . 86 A5
Reading Rd
Aldermaston RG7 . . . . 135 F5
Aldworth RG8 . . . . 33 A2
Arborfield RG2 . . . . 114 C3
Blackwater GU17 . . . . 150 B4
Burghfield Common RG7 . . 111 B2
Finchampstead RG27 . . . . 140 F4
Goring RG8 . . . . 34 E6
Henley-on-T RG9 . . . . 15 E1
Moulsford OX10 . . . . 14 A7
Pangbourne RG8 . . . . 56 D5
Streatley RG8 . . . . 34 A6
Winnersh RG41 . . . . 88 C2
Wokingham RG41 . . . . 115 E8
Woodley RG5 . . . . 87 D8
Yateley GU46 . . . . 149 D6
Reading Ret Pk RG30 . . . . 58 B1
Reading Sch RG1 . . . . 86 D6
Reading Sta RG1 . . . . 86 A8
Reading Stadium
(Speedway) RG2 . . . . 85 F1
Reading West Sta RG30 . . . 85 E7
Recognition Ho 9 SL4 . . . 67 A5
Recreation Cl GU14 . . . . 150 F1
Recreation La RG7 . . . . 113 B2
Recreation Rd
Bourne End SL8 . . . . 3 B3
Burghfield Common RG7 . . 111 A2
Reading RG30 . . . . 84 E8
Wargrave RG10 . . . . 36 E2
Rectory Cl
Bracknell RG12 . . . . 118 C5
Farnham Royal SL2 . . . . 22 C2
Littleton TW17 . . . . 125 A6
Newbury RG14 . . . . 104 F1
Sandhurst GU47 . . . . 149 F8
Rectory Cl *continued*
Windsor SL4 . . . . 67 A6
Wokingham RG40 . . . . 116 C6
Rectory La
Aston Tirrold OX11 . . . . 12 F8
Bracknell RG12 . . . . 118 B5
Letcombe Bassett OX12 . . . . 6 E7
Windlesham GU20 . . . . 146 C4
Rectory Rd
Caversham RG4 . . . . 59 A2
Padworth RG7 . . . . 135 F7
Streatley RG8 . . . . 33 C7
Taplow SL6 . . . . 20 E1
Wokingham RG40 . . . . 116 C6
Rectory Row RG12 . . . . 118 B5
Rectory Terr SL2 . . . . 22 C3
Rectory The RG14 . . . . 104 E2
Redberry Cl RG4 . . . . 59 D5
Red Brick Cotts 13 SL4 . . . 67 D6
Red Cottage Dr RG31 . . . . 84 C4
Red Cottage Mews SL3 . . . 43 C3
Redcrest Gdns GU15 . . . . 151 F5
Red Cross Rd RG8 . . . . 34 C6
Red Ct SL1 . . . . 42 E5
Reddington Dr SL3 . . . . 43 E2
Redditch RG12 . . . . 118 D2
Redesdale Ct RG2 . . . . 86 C3
Redfield Ct RG14 . . . . 105 D4
Redfinch Mews RG18 . . . . 106 E3
Redford Cl TW13 . . . . 98 F6
Redford Rd SL4 . . . . 66 D6
Redgauntlet RG40 . . . . 141 D6
Redgrave Pl SL7 . . . . 1 F3
Redhatch Dr RG6 . . . . 87 A2
RED HILL 129 C5
Red Hill RG9 . . . . 35 A5
Red House Cl RG6 . . . . 114 B8
Red La RG7 . . . . 135 D5
Redlake La RG40 . . . . 116 F2
Redlands Pl RG40 . . . . 115 F2
Redlands Prim Sch RG1 . . . 86 E5
Redlands Rd RG1 . . . . 86 D6
Redlane Ct RG1 . . . . 86 D5
Redlane Hill RG7 . . . . 135 C6
Redlane Rd RG20 . . . . 30 A3
Red Leaf Cl SL3 . . . . 43 F5
Redleaves Ave TW15 . . . . 98 B2
Red Lion Cotts SL2 . . . . 23 B1
Red Lion Way HP10 . . . . 3 E6
Redmayne GU15 . . . . 152 C4
Redpitch Pk HP10 . . . . 3 F6
Red Rd GU18, GU24, GU15 153 C7
Redriff Cl SL6 . . . . 39 D6
Red Roofs SL6 . . . . 40 C7
Red Rose RG42 . . . . 90 C3
Redruth Gdns RG2 . . . . 86 B1
Redshank Ct RG19 . . . . 106 A3
Redshots Cl SL7 . . . . 1 E4
Red Shute Hill RG18 . . . . 79 A4
Red Shute Ind Est RG18 . . . 79 A4
Redvers Rd RG12 . . . . 118 B4
Redwood
Burnham SL1 . . . . 21 B3
Staines TW20 . . . . 123 E7
Redwood Ave RG5 . . . . 88 A6
Redwood Dr
Frimley GU15 . . . . 152 D4
Sunningdale SL5 . . . . 121 B3
Redwood Gdns SL1 . . . . 42 D6
Redwood Mews TW15 . . . . 98 D1
Redwoods The SL4 . . . . 67 D4
Redwood Way RG31 . . . . 57 D3
Reed Cl SL0 . . . . 44 E7
Reed Pl TW17 . . . . 124 F1
Reeds Ave
Lower Earley RG6 . . . . 87 A3
Reading RG6 . . . . 86 F3
Reedsfield Cl TW15 . . . . 98 B5
Reedsfield Rd TW15 . . . . 98 B4
Reed's Hill RG12 . . . . 118 B4
Reed Wlk RG14 . . . . 105 C4
Reeve Rd SL6 . . . . 65 B8
Reeves Way RG41 . . . . 116 A4
Reform Rd SL6 . . . . 40 B7
Regal Ct
Maidenhead SL6 . . . . 40 B2
8 Newbury RG14 . . . . 105 B2
Regatta Ho 8 TW18 . . . . 96 F3
Regency Ho 6 KT16 . . . . 123 F1
Regency Hts RG4 . . . . 58 E4
Regency Pl 7 KT16 . . . . 124 A1
Regent Cl
Earley RG6 . . . . 87 C1
Hungerford RG17 . . . . 100 C5
Regent Ct
Bagshot GU19 . . . . 145 F2
9 Maidenhead SL6 . . . . 39 F7
Reading RG1 . . . . 86 A8
Slough SL1 . . . . 42 E7
Windsor SL4 . . . . 67 D6
Regents Ct
Newbury RG14 . . . . 104 F3
4 Newbury RG14 . . . . 105 B3
Staines TW18 . . . . 97 B2
Regents Ho 3 TW20 . . . . 96 A3
Regents Pl
Maidenhead SL6 . . . . 39 D7
Sandhurst GU47 . . . . 150 C8
Regents Riverside RG1 . . . 59 A1
Regent St RG1 . . . . 86 E7
Regents Wlk SL5 . . . . 120 C2
Regent Way GU16 . . . . 152 A1
Regional Ho SL1 . . . . 43 A4
Regis Cl RG2 . . . . 113 D7
Regis Ct TW14 . . . . 71 D1
Regnum Dr RG14 . . . . 105 B5
Reid Ave SL6 . . . . 39 E5
Rembrandt Cl RG41 . . . . 115 D6
Rembrandt Way RG1 . . . . 85 E5
Remembrance Rd RG14 . . 104 E2
R.E.M.E Mus of Technology*
RG2 . . . . 141 A8
REMENHAM 16 A5
Remenham Church La
RG9 . . . . 16 A4
REMENHAM HILL 16 C2
Remenham La RG9 . . . . 15 F3
Remenham Row RG9 . . . . 15 F2
Remenham Terr RG9 . . . . 16 C2
Renault Rd RG5 . . . . 88 A6
Renfree Way TW17 . . . . 125 A2
Rennie Cl TW15 . . . . 97 D5
Rennie Ct RG14 . . . . 104 F4
Renshaw Ind Est TW18 . . . 96 F4
Repton Cl SL6 . . . . 39 C3
Repton Rd RG6 . . . . 87 C3
Restwold Cl RG30 . . . . 85 C4
Retford Cl RG5 . . . . 60 F1
Retreat The
Englefield Green TW20 . . . . 95 E3
Fifield SL6 . . . . 65 D7
Revel Rd HP10 . . . . 3 D8
Revesby Cl
Maidenhead SL6 . . . . 39 D3
West End GU24 . . . . 153 D6
Rex Ave TW15 . . . . 98 A3
Reynards Cl RG41 . . . . 88 C2
Reynolds Ct RG18 . . . . 106 D3
Reynolds Gn GU47 . . . . 150 D6
Rhema Ct 9 RG1 . . . . 85 F7
Rhigos RG4 . . . . 58 F6
Rhine Cl RG4 . . . . 59 D2
Rhodes Cl
Earley RG6 . . . . 87 E3
Egham TW20 . . . . 96 B3
Rhodes Ct TW20 . . . . 96 C3
Rhododendron Cl SL5 . . . . 92 E1
Rhododendron Cnr
RG40 . . . . 142 B4
Rhododendron Rd GU16 . 152 B1
Rhododendron Ride SL4,
TW20 . . . . 94 F3
Rhododendron Wlk
Brimpton RG19 . . . . 133 B5
North Ascot SL5 . . . . 92 E1
Ribbleton Cl RG6 . . . . 87 E3
Ribstone Rd SL6 . . . . 39 B3
Ricardo Rd SL4 . . . . 68 B1
Richard Ct TW15 . . . . 97 F3
Richard Dodd Pl 16 SL1 . . . 42 F4
Richard Nevill Ct 1 RG4 . 59 C2
Richards Cl UB3 . . . . 71 D8
Richardson Ho TW20 . . . . 95 C5
Richardson's Lawn Cotts
SL4 . . . . 94 B5
Richards Way SL1 . . . . 42 A5
Richborough Cl RG6 . . . . 87 B2
Richfield Ave RG1 . . . . 58 F1
Richfield Pl RG1 . . . . 58 F1
Richings Pl SL0 . . . . 44 E3
Richings Way SL0 . . . . 44 F3
Richmond Ave
Feltham TW14 . . . . 71 E1
Thatcham RG19 . . . . 106 A3
Richmond Cl GU16 . . . . 151 F1
Richmond Cres
Slough SL1 . . . . 43 A5
Staines TW18 . . . . 96 F3
Richmond Dr TW17 . . . . 125 D3
Richmond Ho
Sandhurst GU47 . . . . 150 E7
Sunningdale SL5 . . . . 120 F1
Richmond Rd
Caversham RG4 . . . . 58 E4
Reading RG30 . . . . 85 D8
Sandhurst GU47 . . . . 150 E8
Staines TW18 . . . . 96 F3
Richmond Rise RG41 . . . . 115 E7
Richmond Wood SL5 . . . . 121 B1
Rickman Cl
Arborfield Garrison RG2 . . 114 E1
Bracknell RG12 . . . . 118 C3
Woodley RG5 . . . . 87 D5
Rickman's La SL2 . . . . 22 E6
Riddings La RG19 . . . . 133 C2
Rider's La RG7 . . . . 112 A4
Rideway Cl GU15 . . . . 151 B4
Ridgebank SL1 . . . . 41 F6
Ridge Ct SL4 . . . . 67 C4
Ridge Hall Cl RG4 . . . . 58 E3
Ridgemead Rd TW20 . . . . 95 B5
Ridgemount Cl RG31 . . . . 57 B2
Ridge Mount Rd SL5 . . . . 121 A1
RIDGES THE 142 B3
Ridge The
Cold Ash RG18 . . . . 106 D8
Sunningdale SL5 . . . . 121 A2
Upper Basildon RG8 . . . . 55 F8
Ridgeway
Oatlands Park KT12 . . . . 125 F1
Wargrave RG10 . . . . 36 E2
Ridge Way
Iver SL0 . . . . 44 F6
Virginia Water GU25 . . . . 122 E4
Ridgeway Cl
Hermitage RG18 . . . . 79 B7
Lightwater GU18 . . . . 153 A8
Marlow SL7 . . . . 1 E4
Ridgeway Prim Sch The
RG2 . . . . 86 D1
Ridgeway The
Bracknell RG12 . . . . 118 C6
Caversham RG4 . . . . 59 B3
Letcombe Bassett OX12 . . . . 7 D5
Lightwater GU18 . . . . 146 B1
Marlow SL7 . . . . 1 E4
Ridgeway The *continued*
Woodley RG5 . . . . 87 F5
Ridgeway Trad Est The
SL0 . . . . 44 E6
Ridgewood Ctr (Hospl)
GU16 . . . . 152 C3
Ridgewood Dr GU16 . . . . 152 D3
Riding Court Rd SL3 . . . . 68 D7
Riding Ct SL3 . . . . 68 C8
Ridings The
Caversham RG4 . . . . 59 C8
Frimley GU16 . . . . 152 B3
Iver SL0 . . . . 44 F2
Maidenhead SL6 . . . . 39 A7
Riding Way RG41 . . . . 115 E6
Ridleigh Ct TW15 . . . . 98 A4
Ridlington Cl RG6 . . . . 87 E2
Rigby Lodge SL1 . . . . 42 E7
Righton Cl RG10 . . . . 61 B3
Riley Rd
Marlow SL7 . . . . 1 D2
Reading RG30 . . . . 84 F8
Rimaud Ho 18 RG1 . . . . 86 B6
Ringmead
Bracknell, Great Hollands
RG12 . . . . 117 E4
Bracknell, Hanworth RG12 . 118 B2
Ring The RG12 . . . . 118 C7
Ringwood RG12 . . . . 117 F2
Ringwood Cl SL5 . . . . 120 B5
Ringwood Rd
Blackwater GU17 . . . . 150 C6
Reading RG30 . . . . 58 A1
Ripley Ave TW20 . . . . 95 E2
Ripley Cl SL3 . . . . 43 E2
Ripley Rd RG30 . . . . 58 A1
RIPLEY SPRINGS 95 E2
Ripon Cl GU15 . . . . 152 D3
Ripon Rd GU17 . . . . 149 F1
Ripplesmere RG12 . . . . 118 D5
Ripplesmore Cl GU47 . . . . 150 B8
Ripston Rd TW15 . . . . 98 D3
Risborough Rd SL6 . . . . 39 E8
RISELEY 139 C3
Riseley Bsns Pk RG7 . . . . 139 C3
Riseley Rd SL6 . . . . 39 D7
Rise Rd SL5 . . . . 120 F3
Rise The
Caversham RG4 . . . . 59 B4
Cold Ash RG18 . . . . 106 C7
Crowthorne RG45 . . . . 142 F5
Finchampstead RG40 . . . . 141 A2
Winkfield RG42 . . . . 119 A8
Wokingham RG41 . . . . 116 A7
Rissington Cl RG31 . . . . 57 E3
Riverbank TW18 . . . . 96 F2
Riverbank The SL4 . . . . 67 B7
River Ct
Taplow SL6 . . . . 40 C7
Twyford RG10 . . . . 61 B5
Riverdale Ct RG14 . . . . 105 C3
Riverdene Dr 4 RG41 . . . . 88 A3
Riverfield Rd TW18 . . . . 96 F2
River Gdns
Bray SL6 . . . . 40 D4
Purley on T RG8 . . . . 57 D5
Riverine SL6 . . . . 40 C8
Rivermead Ct SL7 . . . . 18 E8
Rivermead Ind Est RG19 . . 106 F1
Rivermead Prim Sch RG5 . 87 F6
Rivermead Rd
Camberley GU15 . . . . 151 B2
Woodley RG5 . . . . 87 F5
River Mount KT12 . . . . 125 F2
River Park Ave TW18 . . . . 96 D4
Riverpark Dr SL7 . . . . 1 F1
Riverpark Ind Est RG14 . . 105 B3
River Rd
Caversham RG4 . . . . 58 D3
18 Reading RG1 . . . . 86 A6
Staines TW18 . . . . 123 F8
Taplow SL6 . . . . 40 C6
Yateley GU46 . . . . 149 B8
River & Rowing Mus*
RG9 . . . . 15 F1
Riversdale SL8 . . . . 3 B1
Riversdale Cotts SL8 . . . . 3 B1
Riversdale Ct
Bourne End SL8 . . . . 3 B1
Reading RG1 . . . . 86 E8
Riversdell Cl KT16 . . . . 123 F2
Riverside
Bradfield RG7 . . . . 82 C6
Chilton Foliat RG17 . . . . 72 F1
Egham TW20 . . . . 96 A5
Marlow SL7 . . . . 1 E1
Oatlands Park TW17 . . . . 125 E2
Wraysbury TW19 . . . . 95 C8
Riverside Ave GU18 . . . . 153 C8
Riverside Cl TW18 . . . . 123 F8
Riverside Cotts HP10 . . . . 3 E8
Riverside Ct 1 RG4 . . . . 59 A2
Riverside Dr
Egham TW18 . . . . 96 E3
Staines TW18 . . . . 123 F8
Riverside Ho RG1 . . . . 86 A7
Riverside Mus* RG1 . . . . 86 C8
Riverside Pk SL3 . . . . 69 E5
Riverside Pk RG30 . . . . 58 B2
Riverside Pl TW19 . . . . 70 D1
Riverside Rd
Staines TW18 . . . . 96 F1
Stanwell TW19 . . . . 70 E1
Riverside Way GU15 . . . . 151 A3
Riverside Wlk SL4 . . . . 67 D7

River St SL4 . . . . .67 D7
Riverview TW17 . . . . .125 D2
River View
Flackwell Heath HP10 . . . . . . 3 B7
Froxfield SN8 . . . . .99 C5
Riverview Rd RG8 . . . . .56 C5
Riverway
Eton SL4 . . . . .67 C7
Great Shefford RG17 . . . . . . .48 A3
Staines TW18 . . . . .124 B8
River Wlk RG14 . . . . .105 C4
Riverwood Ave SL7 . . . . .2 A1
Riverwoods Dr SL7 . . . . .2 A1
Rixman Cl SL6 . . . . .39 D5
Rixon Cl SL3 . . . . .43 E7
Robert Cort Ind Est RG2 . . .86 B4
Robert Palmer Cotts The
RG4 .60 D3
Robert Piggott CE Inf Sch
RG10 . . . . .36 E1
Robert Piggott CE Jun Sch
RG10 . . . . .36 D1
Robert Sandilands Prim Sch
RG14 . . . . .104 E4
Roberts Cl TW19 . . . . .70 C1
Robertsfield RG19 . . . . .105 F3
Roberts Rd GU15 . . . . .151 A6
Roberts Way TW20 . . . . .95 C1
Robina Ho RG42 . . . . .117 F8
Robin Cl RG7 . . . . .111 B3
Robindale Ave RG6 . . . . .87 D3
Robin Hill Dr GU15 . . . . . . .152 A3
Robin Hill Ho GU46 . . . . . . .149 B5
Robin Hood Cl SL1 . . . . .41 F5
Robinhood La RG40 . . . . .88 C3
Robin Hood Way RG41 . . . . .88 C3
Robin La
Bishops Green RG20 . . . . . .131 F3
Sandhurst GU47 . . . . .143 C1
Robin Par SL2 . . . . .22 C7
Robin's Bow GU15 . . . . .151 B4
Robins Cl RG14 . . . . .130 F7
Robins Grove Cres GU46 .149 B6
Robins Hill RG17 . . . . .127 E6
Robinson Cl OX11 . . . . .12 A8
Robinson Crusoe Pk
RG40 . . . . .141 B6
Robinson Ct
Earley RG6 . . . . .87 A1
Maidenhead SL6 . . . . .39 E4
Robin Way
Reading RG31 . . . . .84 B6
Staines TW18 . . . . .96 F5
Robin Willis Way SL4 . . . . . .68 A1
Robinwood ☒ SL5 . . . . . . .121 B2
Roby Dr RG12 . . . . .118 D2
Rochester Ave
Feltham TW13 . . . . .98 F6
Woodley RG5 . . . . .60 E1
Rochester Rd TW20 . . . . . . .96 D2
Rochfords Gdns SL2 . . . . . . .43 C5
Rochford Way SL6 . . . . .41 A7
Rockall Ct SL3 . . . . .44 B3
Rockbourne Gdns RG30 . . .58 A1
Rockfel Rd RG17 . . . . .25 A2
Rockfield Way ⓪ GU47 . . .150 D8
Rockingham Gate ⓱
RG14 . . . . .104 F2
Rockingham Ho ⓲ RG14 .104 F2
Rockingham Rd RG14 . . . .104 F2
Rockley Ct RG7 . . . . .83 D2
Rockmoor La SP11 . . . . .147 A1
Roddell Ct SL3 . . . . .69 E6
Roddell Pl SL1 . . . . .42 F6
Roden Down Mews RG20 . .31 E5
Rodney Ct ⓱ RG1 . . . . .86 A6
Rodney Way SL3 . . . . .69 E6
Rodway Rd RG30 . . . . .57 F1
Roebuck Est RG42 . . . . .90 C1
Roebuck Gn SL1 . . . . .41 E5
Roebuck Rise RG31 . . . . . . .57 D3
Roebuts Cl RG14 . . . . .130 F8
Rogers La SL2 . . . . .22 F4
Rogers's La RG17 . . . . .47 C6
Rokeby Cl
Bracknell RG12 . . . . .118 D8
Newbury RG14 . . . . .131 A7
Rokeby Dr RG4 . . . . .58 D8
Rokesby Rd SL2 . . . . .21 F2
Rokes Pl GU46 . . . . .149 A6
Roland's Copse RG7 . . . . . .108 C2
Rolls La SL6 . . . . .64 E8
Romana Ct TW18 . . . . .97 A4
Roman Ct ⓲ RG14 . . . . . . .105 B2
Roman Pl SL6 . . . . .39 C6
Roman Ride RG45 . . . . .142 D5
Romans Field RG7 . . . . .136 B1
Romans Gate RG26 . . . . . . .135 F1
Roman Way
Bourne End SL8 . . . . 3 B4
Earley RG6 . . . . .87 D3
Thatcham RG18 . . . . .106 B4
Winkfield RG42 . . . . .118 F8
Romany Cl RG30 . . . . .58 A1
Romany La RG30 . . . . .58 A1
Romeo Hill RG42 . . . . .118 F8
Romney Cl TW15 . . . . .98 C3
Romney Ct ⓱ SL7 . . . . .1 F3
Romney Ho RG12 . . . . .118 E5
Romney Lock Rd SL4 . . . . . .67 D7

Romsey Cl
Blackwater GU17 . . . . .150 C6
Slough SL3 . . . . .43 F3
Romsey Rd RG30 . . . . .58 A1
Rona Ct RG30 . . . . .85 B8
Ronaldsay Spur SL1 . . . . . . .42 E8
Ronita Ct RG1 . . . . .86 F6
Rood Hill RG20 . . . . .76 B4
Rook Cl RG41 . . . . .115 E5
Rookery Ct RG40 . . . . .141 A6
Rookery Cl SL7 . . . . .1 D2
Rookery Rd TW18 . . . . .97 B3
Rookery The RG20 . . . . .50 D7
Rooke's Way RG18 . . . . . . .105 E4
Rook Rd HP10 . . . . .3 D4
Rooksfield RG20 . . . . .132 A2
Rooksmead Rd TW16 . . . . .125 F7
Rooksnest La RG17 . . . . . . .128 A5
Rookswood
Bracknell RG42 . . . . .91 B1
Stockcross RG20 . . . . .103 F6
Rookwood Ave GU47 . . . . .143 E2
Rope Wlk RG19 . . . . .106 C3
Rosa Ave TW15 . . . . .98 A4
Rosary Gdns
Ashford TW15 . . . . .98 B4
Yateley GU46 . . . . .149 D6
Roseacre Cl TW17 . . . . .125 A4
Rosebank Cl SL6 . . . . .19 E7
Rosebay RG40 . . . . .116 E8
Rosebery Rd RG4 . . . . .58 D7
Rose Bsns Est SL7 . . . . .1 D5
Rose Cl RG45 . . . . .143 C8
Rose Cotts
Maidenhead SL6 . . . . .39 C3
Sandhurst GU47 . . . . .143 A1
Rosecroft Way RG2 . . . . . . .113 E5
Rose Ct ⓳ RG40 . . . . .116 C6
Rosedale RG42 . . . . .90 C3
Rosedale Cres RG6 . . . . .87 A8
Rosedale Gdns
Bracknell RG12 . . . . .118 A4
Thatcham RG19 . . . . .106 D2
Rosedene La GU47 . . . . . . .150 D7
Rosefield Rd TW18 . . . . .97 A4
Rose Gdns
Stanwell TW19 . . . . .97 D8
⓼ Wokingham RG40 . . . .116 C6
Rose Hill
Binfield RG42 . . . . .90 C3
Burnham SL1 . . . . .21 A5
Rosehill Ct SL1 . . . . .43 A3
Rosehill Ho RG4 . . . . .59 C7
Rosehill Pk RG4 . . . . .59 C7
Rose Kiln La RG1, RG2 . . . .86 A4
Rose La RG10, RG9 . . . . . . .37 A8
Roselawn Park Cvn Site
RG30 . . . . .111 D5
Roseleigh Cl SL6 . . . . .39 A7
Rose Lodge TW20 . . . . .96 A4
Rosemary Ave RG6 . . . . .86 F1
Rosemary Gdns
Blackwater GU17 . . . . .150 D5
Thatcham RG18 . . . . .106 D4
Rosemary La
Blackwater GU17 . . . . .150 D5
Thorpe TW20 . . . . .123 B6
Rosemary Terr RG14 . . . . . .104 E2
Rosemead KT16 . . . . .124 B2
Rosemead Ave
Feltham TW13 . . . . .98 F6
Purley on T RG31 . . . . .57 B3
Rosemoor Gdns RG14 . . . .105 D4
Rosen Ct RG15 . . . . .106 C3
Rosery The SL8 . . . . .3 A3
Roses La SL4 . . . . .66 D5
Rose St RG40 . . . . .116 C6
Rosevale Dr RG10 . . . . .88 F8
Rose Wlk
Reading RG1 . . . . .86 A7
Slough SL2 . . . . .42 B8
Rosewood RG5 . . . . .87 D4
Rose Wood SL1 . . . . .119 E7
Rosewood Dr TW17 . . . . . .124 F4
Rosewood Way
Farnham Common SL2 . . . .22 C7
West End GU24 . . . . .153 E6
Rosier Cl RG19 . . . . .106 F2
Roslien Gr SL2 . . . . .22 B3
Roslyn Rd RG5 . . . . .87 D6
Rossby RG2 . . . . .113 E7
Rossendale Rd RG4 . . . . . . .59 D3
Rossett Ct RG12 . . . . .118 B5
Ross Ho ⓲ RG30 . . . . .85 D6
Rossington Pl ⓱ RG2 . . . .113 C8
Rossiter Cl SL3 . . . . .43 E2
Rosslea GU20 . . . . .146 A6
Rosslyn Cl TW16 . . . . .98 E2
Ross Rd
Maidenhead SL6 . . . . .39 E4
Reading RG1 . . . . .59 A3
Rosyth Gdns RG14 . . . . . . .131 D8
Rotary Way RG19 . . . . .106 E1
Rothbury Ct RG2 . . . . .86 D3
Rothbury Wlk GU15 . . . . . .152 C4
Rother Cl GU47 . . . . .150 D8
Rotherfield Ave RG41 . . . .116 A7
Rotherfield Cl RG2 . . . . .83 F4
Rotherfield Rd RG4 . . . . . . .59 A3
Rotherfield Way RG4 . . . . . .59 B4
Rothwell Gdns RG5 . . . . . . .61 A1
Rothwell Ho RG45 . . . . . . .143 C4
Rothwell Wlk RG4 . . . . .59 D2
ROTTEN ROW 81 F3
Rotten Row Hill RG7 . . . . . .81 F3
Roughgrove Copse RG42 . .90 B2
Rounce La GU24 . . . . .153 D6
Roundabout La RG41 . . . . .115 D8

Round Cl GU46 . . . . .149 F5
Round End RG14 . . . . .130 D5
Roundfield RG7 . . . . .107 B6
Roundhead Rd RG7 . . . . . . .83 D3
Roundshead Dr RG42 . . . . .91 E1
Roundway
Egham TW20 . . . . .96 C3
Frimley GU15 . . . . .152 C6
Roundway Cl GU15 . . . . . . .152 C6
Routh Ct TW14 . . . . .98 D7
Routh La RG30 . . . . .84 E6
Rowallan Cl RG4 . . . . .59 D6
Rowan Cl RG42 . . . . .118 F4
Rowan Ave TW20 . . . . .96 C3
Rowan Cl
Ashford TW15 . . . . .97 D4
Camberley GU15 . . . . .151 F8
Wokingham RG41 . . . . . . .115 F5
Rowan Ct
Bagshot GU19 . . . . .145 D2
Earley RG6 . . . . .87 B1
Reading RG2 . . . . .113 E7
Rowan Dr
Crowthorne RG45 . . . . . . .143 C6
Newbury RG14 . . . . .105 A5
Rowan Gdns RG45 . . . . .87 F8
Rowan Ho
⓵ Bourne End SL8 . . . . .3 A4
East Bedfont TW14 . . . . . . .71 D1
Rowanhurst Dr SL2 . . . . . . .22 C7
Rowans Cl GU14 . . . . .150 E1
Rowans The TW16 . . . . .98 F3
Rowan Way
Burghfield RG30 . . . . .111 B5
Slough SL2 . . . . .42 B8
Rowanwood RG40 . . . . . . .141 A6
Rowcroft Rd RG2 . . . . .140 F7
Rowdell Dr RG2 . . . . .86 D1
Rowdown RG17 . . . . .24 F5
Rowe Cl RG30 . . . . .85 B8
Rowe La RG4 . . . . .59 E7
Rowland Cl SL4 . . . . .66 D4
Rowland Hill Almshouses ⓳
TW15 . . . . .98 A3
Rowland Rd RG41 . . . . .116 A2
Rowland's Cl RG7 . . . . .136 C5
Rowland Way
Earley RG6 . . . . .86 F2
Littleton TW15 . . . . .98 D1
Rowles Paddock RG20 . . . .10 A2
Rowley Cl RG12 . . . . .118 E6
Rowley La SL3 . . . . .23 D4
Rowley Rd RG2 . . . . .86 B4
Rowlock Gdns RG18 . . . . . . .79 C8
Roxborough Way SL6 . . . . .38 F4
Roxburgh Cl GU15 . . . . . . .152 C4
Roxeth Ct ⓷ TW15 . . . . . . .98 A3
Roxford Ct TW17 . . . . .125 E4
Roxwell Ave SL1 . . . . .41 E5
Royal Ave RG31 . . . . .84 C5
Royal Berkshire Hospl
RG1 .86 D6
Royal Cotts SL6 . . . . .19 C7
Royal Ct ⓷ RG1 . . . . .86 C7
Royal Free Ct ⓲ SL4 . . . . .67 D6
Royal Fst Sch The SL4 . . . . .94 C3
Royal Mans SL6 . . . . .19 C7
London TW20 . . . . .95 D2
Royal Hunt Sch SL5 . . . . . .119 D8
Royal Mans RG9 . . . . .15 E1
Royal Mews SL4 . . . . .67 D6
Royal Military Acad
GU15 . . . . .150 F6
Royal Oak Cl GU46 . . . . . . .149 E6
Royal Oak Dr RG45 . . . . . . .143 B8
Royal Station Ct RG10 . . . . .36 F6
Royal Victoria Gdns SL5 . .120 A4
Roy Cl SL4 . . . . .112 F8
Roy Cl RG18 . . . . .79 F6
Roycroft La RG40 . . . . .141 E8
Roydon Ct TW20 . . . . .96 D2
Royston Cl RG30 . . . . .84 F7
Royston Way SL1 . . . . .41 A8
Rubus Cl GU24 . . . . .153 E6
Ruby Cl
Slough SL1 . . . . .42 A4
Wokingham RG41 . . . . . . .115 C7
Rudd Hall Rise GU15 . . . . .151 E4
Ruddlesway SL4 . . . . .66 E6
Rudland Ct RG19 . . . . .106 D2
Rudsworth Cl SL3 . . . . .69 D7
Rufus Isaacs Rd RG4 . . . . . .59 B2
Rugby Cl GU47 . . . . .143 E1
Ruggles-Brise Rd TW15 . . .97 D3
Rugosa Rd GU24 . . . . .153 E6
Rumsey's La RG17 . . . . .12 A8
Runnemede Rd TW20 . . . . .96 A4
Runnymede* TW20 . . . . . . .95 F5
Runnymede Ct TW20 . . . . . .96 A4
Runnymede Cotts TW19 . .96 D7
Runnymede Ho RG19 . . . . .106 D2
Runnymede Ho ⓯ TW20 . .96 A4
Runnymede Rd GU20 . . . . .146 D4
Runnymede Way TW14 . . . .98 F8
Rupert Cl RG9 . . . . .15 E2
Rupert House Sch RG9 . . . .15 E2
Rupert Rd RG14 . . . . .130 F7
Rupert's La RG9 . . . . .15 E3
Rupert Sq ⓷ RG1 . . . . .86 D7
Rupert St RG1 . . . . .86 D7
Rupert Wlk ⓯ RG1 . . . . . . .86 D7
RUSCOMBE 61 E6
Ruscombe Bsns Pk RG10 . .61 E5
Ruscombe Gdns SL3 . . . . . .68 A7
Ruscombe La RG10 . . . . .61 E6
Ruscombe Pk RG10 . . . . . . .61 E5
Ruscombe Rd RG10 . . . . . . .61 E5
Ruscombe Turn RG10 . . . . .61 F4
Ruscombe Way TW14 . . . . .98 F8

Rushall Cl RG6 . . . . .113 E7
Rusham Park Ave TW20 . . .96 A2
Rusham Rd TW20 . . . . .95 F2
Rusham Terr TW20 . . . . .96 A2
Rushbrook Rd RG5 . . . . .87 C7
Rushburn HP10 . . . . .3 F6
Rushden Dr RG2 . . . . .86 E1
Rushes The
Maidenhead SL6 . . . . .40 C6
Marlow SL7 . . . . .118 D8
Rushey Way
Earley RG6 . . . . .87 C2
Lower Earley RG6 . . . . . . .114 A8
Rushington Ave SL6 . . . . . . .39 F5
Rushmere Cotts RG5 . . . . . .88 A5
Rushmere Pl TW20 . . . . .95 E3
Rushmon Ct KT16 . . . . .123 F2
Rushmoor Gdns RG31 . . . . .84 B4
Rushy Ho RG12 . . . . .118 E5
Ruskin Ave RG4 . . . . .59 D3
Ruskin Ave TW14 . . . . .71 F1
Ruskin Ct RG45 . . . . .142 F4
Ruskin Rd TW18 . . . . .96 F2
Ruskin Way RG41 . . . . .115 D6
Russell Cl RG12 . . . . .118 D2
Russell Ct
Blackwater GU17 . . . . .150 D5
Maidenhead SL6 . . . . .39 F7
Newbury RG14 . . . . .104 E3
Russell Dr TW19 . . . . .70 D1
Russell Gdns RG10 . . . . .88 C8
Russell Ho ⓲ SL8 . . . . .3 A4
Russell Rd
Lower Halliford TW17 . . . .125 C2
Newbury RG14 . . . . .104 E2
Tokers Green RG4 . . . . .58 D7
Russell St
Reading RG1 . . . . .85 F7
Windsor SL4 . . . . .67 D5
Russell Way RG41 . . . . .88 B1
Russet Ave TW17 . . . . .125 E6
Russet Cl TW19 . . . . .69 F1
Russet Glade
Burghfield Common RG7 . .111 B2
Caversham RG4 . . . . .59 C7
Russet Rd SL6 . . . . .39 C3
Russett Gdns RG10 . . . . .61 E6
Russet Way RG20 . . . . .51 C5
Russington Rd TW17 . . . . .125 D2
Russley Gn RG40 . . . . .116 A1
Rustington Cl ⓹ RG6 . . . . .87 B1
Ruston Way SL5 . . . . .119 E7
Rutherford Cl SL4 . . . . .66 F6
Rutherford Wlk RG31 . . . . . .84 A7
Rutherwyk Rd KT16 . . . . . .123 E2
Rutland Ave SL1 . . . . .42 C8
Rutland Gate SL6 . . . . .39 C6
Rutland Pl SL6 . . . . .39 C6
Rutland Rd
Maidenhead SL6 . . . . .39 D6
Reading RG30 . . . . .85 D7
Ruxbury Ct TW15 . . . . .97 E5
Ruxbury Rd KT16 . . . . .123 D3
Ruxley Gdns TW17 . . . . . . .125 C3
Ryan Mount SL4 . . . . .150 A8
Ryans Mount SL7 . . . . .1 C2
Rycroft SL4 . . . . .66 F4
Rydal Ave RG30 . . . . .57 F2
Rydal Cl GU15 . . . . .152 D5
Rydal Dr RG19 . . . . .106 A3
Rydal Pl GU18 . . . . .153 B8
Rydal Way TW20 . . . . .96 B1
Ryde Gdns GU46 . . . . .149 B6
Ryde The TW18 . . . . .124 B8
Rydings SL4 . . . . .66 F4
Rye Cl
Bracknell RG12 . . . . .91 D1
Maidenhead SL6 . . . . .39 C4
Winkfield RG12 . . . . .118 D8
Ryecroft Cl RG14 . . . . .36 E2
Ryecroft Gdns GU17 . . . . .150 E4
Rye Ct ⓱ SL1 . . . . .43 A3
Ryefield Terr SL3 . . . . .69 D7
Rye Gr GU20, GU18 . . . . . .146 F7
Ryehurst La RG42 . . . . .90 F5
RYEISH GREEN 113 C4
Ryeish Green Sch RG7 . . .113 C4
Ryeish La RG7 . . . . .113 C4
Ryemead La RG42 . . . . .92 C5
Ryhill Way RG6 . . . . .113 F8
Ryland Cl TW13 . . . . .98 F4
Rylstone Cl SL6 . . . . .39 C3
Rylstone Rd SL6 . . . . .39 C3
Rymers Cl SL3 . . . . .43 F3
Ryhurst Cl SL3 . . . . .43 D3
Ryvers End SL3 . . . . .43 F3
Ryvers Prim Sch SL3 . . . . . .43 D3
Ryvers Rd SL3 . . . . .43 E3
Ryves Ave GU46 . . . . .149 A5

Sadlers The RG31 . . . . .57 B1
Saffron Cl
Datchet SL3 . . . . .68 B6
Earley RG6 . . . . .87 C4
Newbury RG14 . . . . .104 F3
Saffron Ct TW14 . . . . .98 C8
Saffron Rd RG12 . . . . .118 B5
Sage Cl RG6 . . . . .87 A1
Sagecroft Rd RG18 . . . . . . .106 C5
Sage Ct SL4 . . . . .95 C3
Sage Rd RG31 . . . . .57 C3
Sage Way RG6 . . . . .91 D1
Sailing Club Rd SL8 . . . . .3 A3
Sainsbury Ctr The KT16 . .124 A2
St Adrian's Cl SL6 . . . . .39 B4
St Agnes Mews RG2 . . . . . .86 C2
St Agnes Terr RG17 . . . . . . .25 B2
St Albans Cl ⓲ SL4 . . . . . . .67 D6
St Alban's Sch SL4 . . . . .67 D6
St Andrews RG12 . . . . .117 E3
St Andrew's Ave SL4 . . . . . .66 F5
St Andrews Cl
Bradfield RG7 . . . . .82 C6
Crowthorne RG45 . . . . . . .142 F6
St Andrew's Ct
Old Windsor SL4 . . . . .68 A1
Upper Halliford TW17 . . . .125 D5
Wraysbury TW19 . . . . .68 E1
St Andrews Cotts ⓱ SL4 . .67 A5
St Andrew's Cres SL4 . . . . . .66 F5
St Andrew's Ct
Ascot SL5 . . . . .120 C4
Colnbrook SL3 . . . . .69 D7
⓲ Reading RG1 . . . . .86 D7
⓶ Slough SL1 . . . . .42 E3
St Andrew's Hall (Mus of
English Rural Life)*
RG2 . . . . .86 C6
St Andrew's Rd
Caversham RG4 . . . . .58 F4
Henley-on-T RG9 . . . . .35 D8
St Andrew's Sch RG8 . . . . . .55 C1
St Andrew's Way SL1 . . . . . .41 D6
St Anne's Ave TW19 . . . . . . .97 D8
St Anne's Cl RG9 . . . . .15 D1
St Anne's Rd RG4 . . . . .117 A6
St Annes Glade GU19 . . . .145 D3
St Anne's RC Prim Sch
Caversham RG4 . . . . .59 B2
Chertsey KT16 . . . . .124 A1
St Anne's Rd TW16 . . . . .59 A2
St Ann's Cl KT16 . . . . .123 F3
ST ANN'S HEATH 122 F5
St Ann's Heath Jun Sch
GU25 . . . . .122 E4
St Ann's Hill Rd KT16 . . . .123 D3
St Ann's Rd KT16 . . . . .123 F3
St Anthonys Ct SL3 . . . . . . .118 A8
St Anthony's RC Prim Sch
SL3 .22 C1
St Anthony's Way TW14 . . .71 F3
St Augustine's RC Prim Sch
GU16 . . . . .151 F2
St Barnabas Rd
Caversham RG4 . . . . .59 A6
Earley RG2 . . . . .86 F1
St Bartholomews Rd RG1 .86 F7
St Bartholomew's Sch
RG14 . . . . .104 E1
St Benets Way RG4 . . . . .59 C6
St Bernard's Prep Sch
SL1 .43 B4
St Bernard's RC Gram Sch
SL3 .43 C4
St Bernards Rd SL3 . . . . . . .43 C3
St Birinus Rd RG31 . . . . .84 C5
St Catherine's Cl RG41 . . . .88 B1
St Catherine's Ct
⓶ Staines TW18 . . . . .97 A4
⓷ Windsor SL4 . . . . .67 A5
St Catherines Hill RG7 . . .136 E2
St Catherines Pl ⓱ TW20 .96 A4
St Catherines Rd GU16 . . .151 F1
St Catherines Wood
GU15 . . . . .151 C4
St Cecelia Ct RG2 . . . . .86 C3
St Chad's Rd SL6 . . . . .39 B4
St Christophers Gdns
SL5 .119 D8
St Clements Cl RG6 . . . . .87 C1
St Columba's Cl SL6 . . . . . . .40 A7
St Crispin's Sch RG40 . . . .116 C6
St Cuthbert's Ct TW20 . . . . .95 D2
St Cuthbert's RC Prim Sch
SL4 . . . . .67 A6
St Dominic Savio RC Prim
Sch RG5 . . . . .87 D8
St Donats Pl RG14 . . . . . . .105 A2
St Dunstan's Rd TW13 . . . .98 F4
St Edmund Campion RC Prim
Sch SL6 . . . . .39 B6
St Edward's Rd RG6 . . . . .67 A6
St Edward's Royal Free
Ecumenical Mid Sch
SL4 . . . . .67 A6
St Edward's Sch RG30 . . . . .85 D7
St Elizabeth Cl RG2 . . . . . .113 A7
St Elmo Cl SL2 . . . . .22 C2

S

Sabah Ct TW15 . . . . .98 A4
Sabin Gates RG12 . . . . .118 B6
Sackville St RG1 . . . . .86 B8
Sacred Heart RC Prim Sch
RG9 .15 D1
Saddleback Rd GU15 . . . . .151 E8
Saddlebrook Pk TW16 . . . .98 E1
Saddler Cnr ⓸ GU47 . . . .150 B7
Saddlewood GU15 . . . . .151 B4
Sadlers Ct RG41 . . . . .88 D1
Sadlers End RG41 . . . . .88 C1
Sadlers La RG41 . . . . .115 D8
Sadlers Mews SL6 . . . . .40 B7
Sadlers Rd RG17 . . . . .127 A6

St Elmo Cres SL2 . . . . .22 D1
St Ethelbert's RC Prim Sch
SL2. . . . . .43 A7
St Finian's RC Prim Sch
RG18 . . . . 106 D8
St Francis Cl RG45. . . . . . .142 E4
St Francis RC Prim Sch
SL5 . . . . 120 A3
St Gabriels Ct GU15. . . . . .151 D5
St Gabriel's Sch RG20. . . . .131 B5
St George's Ave RG14 . . . . .104 E2
St George's Cl SL4. . . . . . . .66 E6
St George's Cres SL1 . . . . . .41 D6
St George's Ct GU47 . . . . . .143 E2
St Georges Ind Est GU15 .151 B3
St George's La SL5 . . . . . .120 B5
St Georges Lodge SL6 . . . .20 B7
St George's Rd
  Camberley GU15 . . . . . . .151 D6
  Reading RG30 . . . . .85 C8
St George's Sch
  Ascot SL5. . . . . .120 B6
  Windsor SL4 . . . . .67 D7
St George's Terr
  8 Lambourn RG17 . . . . . . .25 B2
  Reading RG30 . . . . .85 B8
St Giles Cl RG1. . . . . .86 B6
St Giles Ct 1 RG1. . . . . . . .86 B6
St Helens Cres GU47 . . . . .150 B8
St Helier Cl RG41 . . . . .116 B3
St Hilda's Ave TW15. . . . . . .97 E3
St Ives Cl RG7 . . . . .83 D2
St Ives Rd SL6. . . . . .40 A7
St James Cl
  Pangbourne RG8 . . . . .56 C6
  Twyford RG10 . . . . .61 E5
St James Ct TW18 . . . . .97 A4
St James Ctyd 5 SL7 . . . . .1 E2
St James Gate SL5. . . . . . .121 A2
St James Pl SL1 . . . . .41 C7
St James Rd RG40. . . . . . .141 E8
St James Whart 3 RG1 . . .86 C7
St James Wlk SL0 . . . . .44 E4
St John's Beaumont Sch
  SL4. . . . . .95 B6
St John's CE Prim Sch
  RG1 . . . . .86 D7
St Johns Cl RG5 . . . . .87 F8
St Johns Ct TW20. . . . . .96 A3
St Johns Dr SL4 . . . . .67 A5
St John's Gdns 3 RG14. .104 F1
St John's Hill RG1 . . . . .86 C7
St Johns Rd
  Slough SL2. . . . . .43 A6
  Windsor SL4 . . . . .67 A5
St John's Rd
  Caversham RG4. . . . . .59 C2
  Mortimer RG7 . . . . .137 A5
  Newbury RG14. . . . . .105 A1
  North Ascot SL5. . . . . .92 F1
  Reading RG1 . . . . .86 C7
  Sandhurst GU47 . . . . . . .150 C7
  Thatcham RG19 . . . . .105 D3
St Johns St RG45. . . . . . . .143 B4
St John's St RG1 . . . . .86 C7
St Johns Way KT16 . . . . . .124 A1
St John the Evangelist CE Inf
  Sch RG14 . . . . .104 F1
St Joseph's Convent Sch
  RG1 . . . . .86 E5
St Josephs Ct 1 RG41 . . . .105 B4
St Joseph's RC High Sch
  SL2. . . . . .43 A7
St Joseph's RC Prim Sch
  Bracknell RG12 . . . . .118 D7
  Newbury RG14. . . . . .105 B4
St Jude's CE Sch TW20. . . .95 C2
St Jude's Cl TW20 . . . . .95 C3
St Jude's Cotts TW20 . . . . .95 C3
St Jude's Rd TW20. . . . . . . .95 C3
St Katherine's Rd RG9 . . . .35 D7
St Laurence Way SL1 . . . . .43 A3
St Lawrence Sq RG17 . . . .100 C6
St Leger Ct RG4 . . . . .104 E4
St Leonard's Ave SL4 . . . . .67 C5
St Leonards Hill SL4 . . . . . .66 E4
St Leonard's Rd
  Windsor, Clewer Green
    SL4 . . . . .66 D1
  Windsor SL4 . . . . .67 C4
St Leonards Wlk SL0. . . . . .44 F3
St Luke's CE Prim Sch
  SL6. . . . . .39 F5
St Lukes Ct RG4 . . . . .59 B4
St Luke's Rd
  Maidenhead SL6 . . . . .39 F8
  Old Windsor SL4 . . . . .68 A1
St Lukes Way RG4 . . . . .59 B4
St Margaret Clitherow RC
  Prim Sch RG12. . . . . .117 F2
St Margarets Ave TW15 . . .98 B3
St Margaret's Rd SL6 . . . . .39 A7
St Marks Cl RG19 . . . . .106 C3
St Mark's Cl RG7 . . . . .83 B5
St Mark's Cres SL6 . . . . . . .39 B7
St Mark's Hospl SL6 . . . . . .39 C7
St Mark's Pl SL4. . . . . .67 C5
St Mark's Rd
  Bracknell RG42 . . . . .117 C8
  Henley-on-T RG9 . . . . .35 D8
  Maidenhead SL6 . . . . .39 D7
  Windsor SL4 . . . . .67 C5
St Martins Cl 3 RG6. . . . . .87 C1
St Martin's Ct TW15. . . . . . .97 C3
St Martins Prec RG4 . . . . . .59 A2
St Martin's RC Prim Sch
  RG4 . . . . .59 E6

St Mary's All Saints CE Prim
  Sch RG1 . . . . .85 E5
St Mary's Ave
  Purley on T RG8. . . . . .57 D5
  Stanwell TW19. . . . . .97 D8
St Mary's Butts RG1 . . . . . .86 A7
St Mary's CE Prim Sch
  SL1 . . . . .43 A3
St Marys Cl GU47 . . . . . . .150 C8
St Mary's Ct RG1
  Henley-on-T RG9 . . . . .35 A8
  Maidenhead SL6 . . . . .40 A7
  Stanwell TW19. . . . . .97 D8
St Mary's Cres TW19. . . . . .97 D8
St Mary's Ct 6 RG41. . . . .105 A4
St Mary's Dr TW14 . . . . . . .98 C8
St Mary's Farnham Royal CE
  Prim Sch SL2 . . . . .22 C2
St Mary's Gdns GU19. . . . .145 E3
St Mary's Gr RG41 . . . . . . .86 A7
St Mary's Hill SL5 . . . . . . .120 C4
St Marys Ho RG18. . . . . . . .79 C1
St Marys La SL4 . . . . .92 D5
St Mary's Lodge TW19 . . . .97 D8
St Mary's Pl 8 RG14. . . . .105 A4
St Mary's RC Prim Sch
  SL6. . . . . .19 F2
St Mary's Rd
  Ascot SL5. . . . . .120 B3
  Camberley GU15 . . . . . . .151 C6
  Mortimer RG7 . . . . .137 A5
  Newbury RG14. . . . . .105 A4
  Sindlesham RG41. . . . . . .115 B8
  Slough SL3. . . . . .43 E4
  Winnersh RG41 . . . . .88 B1
St Mary's Sch
  Ascot SL5. . . . . .120 B2
  Henley-on-T RG9 . . . . .35 E8
St Mary's Way RG7 . . . . . .111 B3
St Mary's Wlk 16 SL6 . . . .39 F7
St Matthew's Ct 9 TW15 .98 A3
St Michaels CE Prim Sch
  GU47 . . . . .149 F8
St Michael's CE Prim Sch
  SL5 . . . . 120 D4
St Michaels Cl RG17 . . . . . .25 A2
St Michaels Cotts RG40 . .143 C8
St Michaels Ct RG10. . . . . .61 E6
St Michael's Ct SL1 . . . . . . .21 D1
St Michael's Easthampstead
  CE Prim Sch RG12. . . . . .118 A4
St Michaels La RG42 . . . . .110 D5
St Michael's Pl GU15. . . . .151 B5
St Michael's Prim Sch
  SL5 . . . . .85 A7
St Michael's Rd
  Ashford TW15. . . . . .98 A3
  Camberley GU15 . . . . . . .151 B5
St Michael's Rd
  Newbury RG14. . . . . .104 F2
  Reading RG30 . . . . .84 D7
  Sandhurst GU47 . . . . . . .149 F8
St Nazaire Cl TW20 . . . . . . .96 C3
St Nicholas' CE Comb Sch
  SL6. . . . . .20 E1
St Nicholas CE Prim Sch
  Hurst RG10 . . . . .88 F7
  Shepperton TW17 . . . . . .125 B3
St Nicholas Dr TW17 . . . . .125 A2
St Nicholas' Rd RG14 . . . .104 F2
St Nicolas CE Jun Sch
  RG14 . . . . .105 A2
St Olave's Cl TW18. . . . . . . .96 F1
St Patrick's Ave RG10 . . . . .61 A5
St Patricks Cl RG20 . . . . . . .30 E7
St Patrick's Cl SL6 . . . . .39 B4
St Pauls Ave SL2. . . . . .43 A5
St Paul's Comb Sch,
  Wooburn HP10 . . . . .3 D4
St Paul's Ct RG14 . . . . .116 A6
St Paul's Terr TW15 . . . . . . .98 C3
20 Maidenhead SL6. . . . . . .39 F6
  Reading RG1 . . . . .86 A6
St Paul's Gate RG41 . . . . .116 A6
St Paul's Mews RG42 . . . .113 B7
St Paul's Rd
  Staines TW18 . . . . .96 F2
  1 Staines TW18 . . . . .96 F2
St Paul's Rd RG4. . . . . .58 E3
St Peter's Ave RG4. . . . . . . .58 E3
St Peter's CE Comb Sch
  SL1. . . . . .21 B2
St Peter's CE Jun Sch
  GU46 . . . . .149 E6
St Peter's CE Mid Sch SL4 .67 F1
St Peter's CE Prim Sch
  RG6. . . . . .87 B5
St Peters Cl RG19 . . . . . . .132 D2
St Peter's Cl
  Burnham SL1. . . . . .21 B1
  Old Windsor SL4 . . . . .68 A2
  Staines TW18. . . . . .96 F2
St Peter's Gdns GU46 . . . .149 D6
St Peter's Hill RG4 . . . . . . .58 F3
St Peter's Rd GU15 . . . . . . .39 E5
St Peters Rd RG6. . . . . .87 A5
St Peter's Rd
  Maidenhead SL6 . . . . .19 D2
  Reading RG6. . . . . .87 A5
St Peter St SL7 . . . . .1 D2
St Peters Way UB3. . . . . . . .71 D8
St Pinnock Ave TW18 . . . .124 A8
St Pirans SL6. . . . . .19 E1

St Piran's Sch SL6. . . . . . . .18 E1
St Richards Rd RG14. . . . .105 B4
St Ronans Rd RG30 . . . . . . .85 B8
St Saviour's Rd RG1 . . . . . . .85 F5
St Saviour's Terr 11 RG1. . .86 A6
Saint Sebastian's CE Prim Sch
  RG40 . . . . .142 E8
St Sebastian's Cl RG40 . . .142 E7
St Sebastian's Ct RG40. . .142 E7
St Stephens Cl RG4 . . . . . . .59 A2
St Stephens Ct 9 RG1. . . . .86 D7
St Swithins Cl RG20. . . . . . .75 D4
St Swithuns Ct RG10. . . . . .61 D4
St Teresa's RC Prim Sch
  RG40 . . . . .116 D5
St Theresa's Rd TW14 . . . . .71 F3
St Thomas Ct RG18 . . . . . .106 E3
St Thomas Wlk SL3 . . . . . . .69 D7
Salamanca RG45. . . . . .142 E5
Salcombe Dr RG6. . . . . .87 B4
Salcombe Rd
  Ashford TW15. . . . . .97 E5
  Newbury RG14. . . . . .104 E1
  Reading RG2 . . . . .86 D3
Saleby Cl RG6 . . . . .87 E2
Sale Garden Cotts RG40. .116 C5
Salesian Gdns KT16 . . . . .124 A1
Salesian Sch KT16 . . . . . .124 A1
Salford Cl RG2. . . . . .113 C7
Salisbury Ave SL2 . . . . .42 C8
Salisbury Cl RG41. . . . . . . .116 A2
Salisbury Ct SL6 . . . . .39 E5
Salisbury Mews SL2 . . . . . .22 C1
Salisbury Rd
  Blackwater GU17. . . . . . .150 C5
  Harlington TW6 . . . . .71 C1
  Hungerford RG17 . . . . . . .100 C3
  Reading RG30 . . . . .85 B8
Salisbury Row 4 RG17. .100 D5
Salix Gdns RG10 . . . . .61 D6
Salmon Cl RG7 . . . . .113 B2
Salmond Rd RG2 . . . . .113 C6
Salters Cl SL6 . . . . .40 A7
Saltersgate Cl RG6 . . . . . . .87 D2
Salters Rd SL6 . . . . .40 A7
SALT HILL. 42 C5
Salt Hill Ave SL1 . . . . .42 C5
Salt Hill Dr SL1 . . . . .42 C5
Salt Hill Mans SL1 . . . . . . .42 C5
Salt Hill Way SL1 . . . . .42 D5
Saltire Gdns 2 RG42. . . . .118 A8
Salwey Cl RG12 . . . . .118 B3
Samarkand Cl GU15. . . . . .152 B4
Samian Pl RG42 . . . . .90 E1
Sampage Cl RG2 . . . . .87 E4
Sampson Bsns Pk GU15. .151 B3
Sampson Ct TW17 . . . . . . .125 C4
Sampson Pk RG42 . . . . . . .117 D8
Sampsons Gn SL2 . . . . .21 F2
Sanctuary Cl RG30. . . . . . . .84 F8
Sanctuary Rd TW19, TW6. . .71 A1
Sandbrooke Wlk RG2 . . . .111 A3
Sandcroft Rd RG2 . . . . .86 E2
Sanden Cl TW15. . . . . .98 C4
Sanders Cl RG17 . . . . .100 C5
Sandford Ct RG41. . . . . .88 C1
Sandford Down RG12 . . . .118 F4
Sandford Dr RG5 . . . . .60 F1
Sandford La RG5, RG10. . . .88 C6
SANDFORD PARK 88 B2
Sandgate Ave RG30. . . . . . .57 F2
Sandhills Ct GU25 . . . . . . .123 E1
Sandhills Way RG2 . . . . . . .86 F2
Sandhurst Bsns Pk GU47 . .149 C7
SANDHURST 150 C7
Sandhurst La GU17 . . . . . .150 B6
Sandhurst Lodge RG45. . .142 E3
Sandhurst Rd
  Crowthorne RG45 . . . . . .143 B3
  Wokingham RG40 . . . . . . .142 B8
  Yateley GU46. . . . . .149 A6
Sandhurst Royal Military
  Acad Hospl GU15. . . . . . .151 A8
Sandhurst Sch GU47 . . . . .150 E8
Sandhurst Sta GU47 . . . . .150 A7
Sandisplatt Rd SL6. . . . . . .39 A6
Sandleford Cl RG2 . . . . . . .113 C6
Sandleford La RG19 . . . . . .131 B6
Sandleford Lodge Pk
  RG19 . . . . .131 B6
Sandown Ave SL6 . . . . .21 E2
Sandown Cl GU17 . . . . . . .150 D5
Sandown Dr GU16 . . . . . . .151 E2
Sandown Rd SL2. . . . . .41 F8
Sandown Way RG14 . . . . . .105 C1
Sandpipers PR SL6 . . . . .39 A6
Sandpit Hill RG14, RG20. .130 C4
Sandpit La
  Caversham RG4. . . . . .59 F8
  Farley Hill RG7 . . . . .140 B5
Sandringham Ct SL1 . . . . . .42 A5
Sandringham Dr TW15 . . . .97 D4
Sandringham Rd
  Maidenhead SL6 . . . . .19 E2
  Stanwell TW6 . . . . .70 E2
Sandringham Way RG31. . .84 A4
Sands Farm Dr SL1 . . . . . . .21 C1
Sandstone Cl RG41 . . . . . . .88 C1
Sandstone Gr RG18 . . . . . .79 C8
Sandy Cl RG18 . . . . .79 A8
Sandy Dr TW14 . . . . .98 E7
Sandygate Cl SL7. . . . . .1 D3
Sandygate Rd SL7 . . . . .1 D3

Sandy La
  Bracknell RG12 . . . . .118 C8
  Camberley GU15 . . . . . . .151 E6
  Hermitage RG18 . . . . .78 F4
  North Ascot SL5. . . . . . . .119 C8
  Sandhurst GU47 . . . . . . .143 A2
  Sunningdale SL5 . . . . . . .121 A4
  Virginia Water GU25 . . . .122 E5
  Wokingham RG41 . . . . . .115 D4
Sandy Lane Prim Sch
  RG12 . . . . .91 C1
Sandy Mead SL6 . . . . .40 C1
Sandy Ride SL5. . . . . .120 E5
Sandy Way KT12 . . . . .125 F1
SANHAM GREEN 100 D2
Sapphire Cl RG41 . . . . .115 E7
Sapphire Ct RG19 . . . . . . .106 E2
Sarsby Dr TW19. . . . . .96 A6
Sarum RG42 . . . . .117 F1
Sarum Cres RG40 . . . . .116 D7
Sarum Ct 1 RG30 . . . . .85 D6
Sarum Rd RG26. . . . . .135 A1
Sarum Way RG17. . . . . .100 D2
Satis Ho SL3. . . . . .68 C7
Saturn Cl RG41 . . . . .115 E6
Saturn Croft RG42 . . . . .92 B2
Saturn Ho RG7 . . . . .134 E2
Saunders Cl RG10 . . . . .61 E3
Saunders Ct RG8 . . . . .57 B5
Saunton Ave UB3 . . . . .71 F7
Savernake Cl RG30. . . . . . . .84 F7
Savernake Way RG12. . . . .118 F4
Saville Cres TW15. . . . . .98 D2
Saville Gdns GU15 . . . . . . .152 B5
Saville Ho 6 TW20 . . . . . . .96 A3
Savill Gardens The ★
  TW20. . . . . .94 E2
Savill Mews TW20. . . . . . . .95 D2
Savill Way SL7 . . . . .1 F2
Savory Wlk RG42 . . . . .90 C2
Savoy Ct SL6 . . . . .19 F1
Savoy Cl RG42 . . . . .118 C5
Sawmill Cotts SL3 . . . . .23 F2
Sawmill Rd RG18 . . . . .79 A4
Sawpit Rd RG10 . . . . .88 E7
Sawtry Cl RG6 . . . . .87 E2
Sawyers Cl SL6 . . . . .39 A2
Sawyer's Cl SL4 . . . . .66 E7
Sawyers Cres SL6 . . . . .39 A2
Sawyers Ley RG7 . . . . .137 D8
Saxby Cl RG7 . . . . .111 B3
Saxham Lodge RG40 . . . . .116 C5
Saxon Cl SL3 . . . . .43 F4
Saxon Ct
  10 Reading RG1 . . . . .86 D7
  Stanwell TW19. . . . . .70 A2
  Thatcham RG19 . . . . .106 A3
Saxon Dr RG42 . . . . .118 F8
Saxon Gate RG30 . . . . .111 B5
Saxon Gdns SL6. . . . . .20 D1
Saxon Lodge SL1 . . . . .41 F5
Saxon Pl RG8 . . . . .56 D5
Saxon Rd Bsns Cen TW17 .125 A4
Saxon Rd TW15. . . . . .98 D2
Saxons Acre RG20 . . . . .28 D3
Saxon Way
  Harmondsworth UB7. . . . .70 C8
  Old Windsor SL4 . . . . .68 B2
Saxony Way GU46. . . . . . . .149 C4
Saxon Way Trad Est UB7 . .70 D8
Sayers Cl RG14 . . . . .131 B8
Scafell Cl RG31 . . . . .57 B2
Scafell Rd SL2 . . . . .41 F8
Scania Wlk RG42 . . . . .92 B2
Scarborough Rd TW6 . . . . .71 C1
Scarborough Way SL1 . . . . .42 B4
Scarlet Oaks GU15 . . . . . . .151 E3
Scarletts La RG10. . . . . .37 C1
Scholars Cl
  Caversham RG4. . . . . .58 F3
  Great Shefford RG17 . . . . .48 A3
School Cl GU24. . . . . .153 F4
School Dr RG5. . . . . .87 E5
School Gn RG2 . . . . .113 E4
SCHOOLGREEN. 113 F4
School Hill
  Crowthorne RG45 . . . . . .143 D4
  Midgham RG7 . . . . .107 F3
  Sandhurst GU47 . . . . . . .143 A1
  Wargrave RG10 . . . . .36 D1
  West Horsley TW19 . . . . . .70 C1
School La
  Bagshot GU19 . . . . .145 E2
  Boxford RG20 . . . . .76 E4
  Burghfield Common RG7 .110 F2
  Caversham, Emmer Green
    RG4 . . . . .59 B6
  Caversham RG4. . . . . .59 A2
  Cookham Dean SL6 . . . . . .19 B7
  Cookham SL6. . . . . .20 D7
  East Garston RG17 . . . . . .47 D6
  Egham TW20 . . . . .96 A3
  Foxfield SN8. . . . . .99 A1
  Little Marlow SL7 . . . . .2 C5
  Littlewick Green SL6 . . . . .38 B4
  Lower Halstford TW17. . .125 B2
  Medmenham SL7 . . . . .17 B6
  North Ascot SL5. . . . . .93 B6
  Riseley RG7 . . . . .139 A7
  Silchester RG7 . . . . .136 B1
  Stoke Poges SL2 . . . . .23 B5
  Wargrave RG10 . . . . .36 D1
  Windlesham GU20. . . . . .146 D4
  Yateley GU46 . . . . .149 B6

St E–Sew **183**

School of Electronic
  Engineering RG2 . . . . . . .114 C1
School of Military Survey
  RG18 . . . . .78 F7
School Rd
  Arborfield Cross RG2,
    RG41. . . . . .114 F2
  Ascot SL5. . . . . .120 D4
  Ashford TW15 . . . . .98 B2
  Burghfield RG30 . . . . . . .111 C6
  Chieveley RG20 . . . . .77 F8
  Compton RG20. . . . . .31 E4
  Harmondsworth UB7. . . . .70 D8
  Hurst RG10 . . . . .88 F8
  Padworth RG7 . . . . .109 F1
  Reading RG31 . . . . .84 D8
  Riseley RG7 . . . . .139 E3
  Waltham St L RG10 . . . . . .62 F3
  Windlesham GU20. . . . . .146 A5
  Wokingham RG40 . . . . . .116 D6
  Wooburn Green HP10 . . . . .3 E6
School Terr RG1 . . . . .86 E8
Schroder Ct TW20 . . . . .95 B3
Scobell Cl RG2 . . . . .113 D5
Scotland Hill GU47. . . . . . .150 A8
Scotlands Dr SL2 . . . . .22 B6
Scots Cl TW19 . . . . .97 D7
Scots Dr RG41 . . . . .115 E7
Scotswood SL5 . . . . .120 E1
Scottalls La RG18. . . . . .52 F5
Scott Cl
  Caversham RG4. . . . . .59 A5
  Farnham Common SL2. . . .22 C7
  Woodley RG5. . . . . .88 A7
Scott's Ave TW16 . . . . .98 E1
Scotts Mews SL5 . . . . .119 B8
Scott's Way TW16. . . . . .98 E1
Scott Terr RG12. . . . . .118 E8
Scours La RG30. . . . . .58 B1
Scratchface La RG7 . . . . . . .81 E7
Scrivens Mead RG19 . . . . .106 F3
Scutley La GU20 . . . . .146 E3
Scylla Cres TW6, TW14. . . .98 B3
Scylla Rd TW14, TW6. . . . . .71 B1
Seacourt Rd SL3. . . . . .44 B2
Seafield Ct 14 RG1 . . . . . . .85 F7
Seaford Gdns RG5 . . . . .87 E6
Seaford Rd
  Stanwell TW6. . . . . .70 D2
  Wokingham RG40 . . . . . .116 D6
Sealand Rd TW6 . . . . .71 A1
Searing Way RG26 . . . . . . .135 A1
Searles Farm La RG30 . . . .85 B1
Searlwood Ct GU24 . . . . . .153 F5
Seaton Dr TW15 . . . . .97 E6
Seaton Gdns RG2 . . . . .86 C2
Seaton Rd GU15 . . . . .151 B5
Second Ave
  Reading RG31 . . . . .84 B6
  Tadley RG7 . . . . .135 C2
Second Cres SL1 . . . . .42 C8
Seddon Hill RG42 . . . . .91 B2
Sedgefield Rd RG14. . . . . .131 C8
Sedge Gr RG18 . . . . .106 E4
Sedgmoor Cl HP10. . . . . . . .3 A7
Sedgmoor Gdns HP10. . . . .3 A8
Sedgmoor La HP10 . . . . . . .3 A8
Sedgmoor Rd HP10 . . . . . . .3 A8
Seebys Oak GU47 . . . . . . .150 E6
Seer Green Ho SL1 . . . . . . .21 C2
Sefton Cl
  Stoke Poges SL2 . . . . .22 F4
  West End GU24 . . . . .153 F6
Sefton Paddock SL2 . . . . . .23 A5
Sefton Park Cotts SL2 . . . . .23 A4
Sefton Park Sch SL2 . . . . . .23 B5
Segrave Cl RG4. . . . . .60 E2
Segsbury Gr RG12 . . . . . . .118 E5
Selborne RG12 . . . . .118 B6
Selborne Cl GU17. . . . . . . .150 C6
Selborne Ct RG1 . . . . .86 C7
Selborne Gdns RG30. . . . . .58 A1
Selborne Ho 10 SL6 . . . . . . .3 A4
Selby Rd TW15. . . . . .98 C2
Selcourt Cl RG5 . . . . .87 F8
Selim Ct 5 SL1 . . . . .43 A4
Sellafield Way RG6 . . . . . . .87 C2
Selsdon Ave RG5. . . . . .87 F8
Selsey Way RG6 . . . . .114 B8
Selva Ct 6 RG1 . . . . .86 C6
Selwood Cl TW19. . . . . .70 C1
Selwood Gdns TW19 . . . . . .70 C1
Selwyn Cl SL4 . . . . .66 E5
Selwyn Dr GU46 . . . . .149 B6
Selwyn Pl SL1. . . . . .42 A6
Sen Cl RG42 . . . . .91 C2
Send Rd RG4 . . . . .59 C1
Sermed Ct SL2 . . . . .43 C5
Servite Ho SL6 . . . . .40 B8
Setley Way RG12 . . . . .118 F6
Seton Dr RG31. . . . . .84 F5
Setter Combe RG42 . . . . . .91 D2
Settrington Cl 3 RG6. . . . . .87 D1
Sett The GU46 . . . . .149 B5
Sevenoaks Dr RG7 . . . . . . .113 B3
Sevenoaks Rd RG6 . . . . . . .87 B3
Seventh Ave RG31 . . . . .84 B6
Seventh St RG19. . . . . .131 F5
Severalls The SN8 . . . . . . .126 C3
Severn Cl
  Sandhurst GU47 . . . . . . .150 C8
  Thatcham RG18 . . . . .106 B5
Severn Cres SL3 . . . . .69 B8
Severn Way RG30 . . . . .84 F6
Sewell Ave RG41 . . . . .116 A8

Sewell Cl RG18 . . . . 79 B1
Seymour Ave RG2 . . . . .113 E5
Seymour Cl SL6 . . . . 39 B3
Seymour Court La SL7 . . . . 1 B5
Seymour Court Rd SL7 . . . 1 C4
Seymour Ct RG45 . . . . .142 E4
Seymour Dr GU15 . . . . .152 B8
Seymour Ho SL3 . . . . 43 E4
Seymour Park Rd SL7 . . . . . 1 D3
Seymour Plain SL7 . . . . 1 C5
Seymour Rd SL1 . . . . 42 D4
Seymour Way TW16 . . . . . . 98 E1
Shackleton Ct 8 TW19 . . . . 70 E1
Shackleton Rd SL1 . . . . 42 F6
Shackleton Way RG5 . . . . . 88 A7
Shafer Ct RG14 . . . . .105 A1
Shaftesbury Cl RG12 . . . . . 118 D4
Shaftesbury Cres TW18 . . . .97 D1
Shaftesbury Ct
  Maidenhead SL6 . . . . 39 E5
  6 Slough SL1 . . . . 42 E4
  Wokingham RG40 . . . . . .116 D7
Shaftesbury Mount
  GU17 . . . . .150 D3
Shaftesbury Rd
  Bisley GU24 . . . . .153 F3
  Reading RG30 . . . . 85 B8
Shaggy Calf La SL2 . . . . . . 43 A6
Shakespeare Cl RG4 . . . . . . 59 D5
Shakespeare Lodge SL1 . . 41 F5
Shakespeare Rd RG18. . 106 C4
Shakespeare Way RG42 . . 118 E8
Shalbourne Cl RG17 . . . . . .100 B5
Shalbourne Rise GU15 . . . .151 D5
Shamaa Ho 16 SL1 . . . . . . 42 F4
Sharman Row 11 SL3 . . . . . 43 F1
Sharney Ave SL3 . . . . 44 B3
Sharnwood Dr RG31 . . . . . . 84 F5
Sharonelle Ct RG40 . . . . . .116 B6
Sharpthorpe Cl 2 RG6 . . . 87 B1
SHAW 105 C5
Shaw Ct SL4 . . . . .68 A2
Shaw-cum-Donnington CE
  Prim Sch RG14 . . . . .105 A6
SHAW FARM 67 E3
Shaw Farm Rd RG14 . . . . .105 B6
Shaw Gdns 3 SL3 . . . . 43 F1
Shaw Hill RG14 . . . . .105 B5
Shaw Pk RG45 . . . . .143 B3
Shaw Rd
  Newbury RG14. . . . . .105 B4
  Reading RG1 . . . . 85 F5
Shaw The SL6 . . . . 19 E6
Shears Ct TW16. . . . . 98 E1
Sheehy Way SL2 . . . . 43 B6
Sheepcote La
  Holyport SL6 . . . . 64 C4
  Wooburn SL1 . . . . 3 F1
Sheepcote Rd
  Eton SL4 . . . . 42 A1
  Windsor SL4 . . . . 66 E5
Sheepdown RG20 . . . . 30 E7
Sheepdrove Rd RG17 . . . . 25 C3
Sheep Fair Way RG17 . . . . 25 B2
Sheephouse Way RG20 . . . 49 A6
Sheeplands Farm RG10 . . . 61 D8
Sheep Leaze La RG20 . . . . 29 D7
SHEEPRIDGE 2 E7
Sheepridge La SL7, HP10 . . 2 E7
Sheepwalk TW17 . . . . .124 F3
Sheepwash La RG20 . . . . .131 A2
Sheepways La RG4. . . . . . . 58 B8
Sheep Wlk
  Caversham RG4 . . . . 59 B4
  Littleton TW17 . . . . .125 A4
Sheerlands Rd RG42 . . . . .140 F7
Sheet St SL4 . . . . 67 D6
Sheet Street Rd SL4 . . . . . 94 A4
SHEFFIELD BOTTOM. 110 F8
Sheffield Rd
  Harlington TW1, TW6. . . . 71 C2
  Slough SL1. . . . . 42 C7
Sheffield Way TW14, TW6 . 71 D2
Shefford CE Prim Sch
  RG17 . . . . 48 B4
Shefford Cres RG40 . . . . . 116 D8
Shefford Lodge 3 RG14 105 A2
SHEFFORD
  WOODLANDS 74 D7
Sheldon Gdns RG2 . . . . 86 D1
Shelgate Wlk RG5 . . . . 87 C7
Shelley Ave RG12 . . . . .118 E7
Shelley Cl
  Medmenham SL7 . . . . . . 17 D7
  16 Slough SL3 . . . . 43 F1
  Wooburn Green HP10 . . . . 3 E8
  2 Woodley RG5 . . . . 87 E4
Shelley Ct
  Camberley GU15 . . . . . .151 C6
  Reading RG1 . . . . 86 D6
Shelley Dr
  12 Marlow SL7 . . . . 1 F3
  Thatcham RG18 . . . . . . .106 C4
Shelley Wlk GU46. . . . . . . .149 B5
Shellfield Ct TW19 . . . . 70 A2
Shelson Ave TW13 . . . . 98 F4
Shenstone Cl RG42 . . . . . . 90 C3
Shenstone Ct 2 SL4 . . . . . 67 D6
Shenstone Dr SL1 . . . . 21 D1
Shenstone Pk SL5 . . . . . . .120 E5
Shenstone Rd RG2. . . . . . . 86 B4
Shepherds Ave RG6. . . . . . 87 B8

Shepherds Chase GU19 . .145 E2
Shepherds Cl
  Hurley SL6 . . . . 17 F3
  Shepperton TW17 . . . . . .125 B3
Shepherds Ct SL4. . . . . 66 E5
Shepherds Hill
  Bracknell RG12 . . . . .118 C8
  Compton RG20 . . . . 31 E3
  Earley RG6 . . . . 87 C8
Shepherd's Hill RG20 . . . . . 76 E4
Shepherd's House La RG6 87 A8
Shepherds La
  Bracknell RG42 . . . . 91 B1
  Caversham RG4 . . . . 58 D6
  Hurley SL6 . . . . 17 E2
Shepherds Mount RG20 . . . 31 E3
Shepherds Rise RG20 . . . . 31 E4
Shepherds Way RG45 . . . .142 E4
Shepherds Wlk RG6. . . . . . 87 C8
Shepley Dr
  Reading RG30 . . . . 85 C4
  Wentworth SL5 . . . . .121 D3
Shepley End SL5 . . . . .121 D4
Sheppard Ct RG2 . . . . 86 C3
Sheppe Rdbt RG42. . . . . . . 91 E1
SHEPPERTON 125 C4
Shepperton Bsns Park
  TW17 . . . . .125 C4
Shepperton Court Dr
  TW17. . . . . .125 B4
Shepperton Ct TW17 . . . . .125 B3
SHEPPERTON GREEN 125 A5
Shepperton Ho TW17 . . . . 125 C3
Shepperton Rd TW17,
  TW18 . . . . 124 D5
Shepperton Sta TW17 . . . .125 C4
Shepperton Studios
  TW17 . . . . 124 F6
Shepton Ho 12 RG1 . . . . . 86 C7
Sheraton Cl GU17. . . . . . . .150 E4
Sheraton Dr RG31 . . . . 57 B1
Sherborne Cl SL3 . . . . 69 E6
Sherborne Ct SL6. . . . . 39 E6
Sherborne Rd TW14. . . . . . 98 D7
Sherbourne Dr
  Maidenhead SL6 . . . . 39 C3
  Wentworth SL5 . . . . .121 D4
  Windsor SL4 . . . . 94 C4
  Woodley RG5 . . . . 87 F8
Sherbourne Gdns TW17 . .125 E2
Sherbourne Wlk SL2 . . . . . 22 C8
Sherfield Cl RG2. . . . . 86 D4
Sherfield Dr RG2 . . . . 86 D4
Shergold Way SL6 . . . . 19 F6
Sheridan Ave RG4 . . . . 59 A4
Sheridan Cres RG26. . . . . .134 E1
Sheridan Ct
  4 Maidenhead SL6 . . . . 40 B8
  Newbury RG14. . . . . .105 C3
  Slough SL1 . . . . 41 E6
Sheridan Grange SL5 . . . .121 A3
Sheridan Way RG41 . . . . . .115 E5
Sheringham Ct
  5 Maidenhead SL6 . . . . 39 E7
  3 Reading RG1 . . . . 86 C7
Sherman Pl 14 RG1 . . . . . 86 B6
Sherman Rd
  Reading RG1 . . . . 86 B6
  Slough SL1. . . . . 42 E8
Sherrardmead RG14 . . . . .105 B5
Sherring Ct RG42 . . . . 91 C1
Sherwood Cl
  Bracknell RG12 . . . . .119 A7
  Slough SL3. . . . . 43 E3
Sherwood Ct
  Colnbrook SL3 . . . . 69 D7
  Slough SL3 . . . . 43 F1
Sherwood Dr SL6 . . . . 39 A6
Sherwood Gdns RG9 . . . . . 35 C8
Sherwood Ho 8 RG1 . . . . 85 E5
Sherwood Pl RG42 . . . . . . 90 B7
Sherwood Rd RG41 . . . . . . 88 C2
Sherwood Rise RG8 . . . . . . 57 B5
Sherwood St RG30 . . . . . . 85 C8
Shetland Rd TW6 . . . . 71 C1
Shield Rd TW15. . . . . 98 C4
Shifford Cres SL6 . . . . 19 E3
Shildon Cl GU15 . . . . .152 D3
Shilling Cl RG30 . . . . 85 B6
SHINFIELD 113 E4
Shinfield Inf Sch RG21 . . . .113 E4
Shinfield Rd
  Earley RG2 . . . . .113 B8
  Reading RG2 . . . . 86 E1
Shinfield Rise RG2. . . . . . . 86 E1
Shinfield St Mary's CE Jun
  Sch RG2 . . . . .113 F4
SHIPLAKE. 35 F2
Shiplake CE Sch RG9 . . . . 35 E2
Shiplake Coll RG9 . . . . 35 F1
Shiplake Ho
  Bourne End SL8. . . . . 3 B4
  Bracknell RG12 . . . . .118 F5
SHIPLAKE ROW 35 C2
Shiplake Sta RG9 . . . . 36 B4
Shipley Cl RG5 . . . . 61 A1
Shipton Cl RG31 . . . . 84 D5
Shire Cl GU19 . . . . .145 E2
Shire Cotts RG7 . . . . .108 F6
Shire's Head Cl RG30 . . . . 85 D6
Shires The RG41 . . . . .115 D4
Shirley Ave
  Reading RG2 . . . . .113 C7
  Windsor SL4 . . . . 94 B7
Shirley Rd SL6. . . . . 39 C5
Shooter's Hill RG8 . . . . . . 56 B7
Shooters Way RG2 . . . . . . .112 F8

Shop La
  Leckhampstead RG20 . . . . 49 F5
  Newbury RG14. . . . . .104 E6
Shoppenhangers Rd SL6 . 39 C3
Shoppenhanger's Rd SL6 . 39 E4
Shoreham Rd E TW6 . . . . . 70 E2
Shoreham Rd W TW6 . . . . 70 E2
Shoreham Rise SL2 . . . . . . 21 D1
Shorland Oaks RG42 . . . . . 91 C2
Shortfern SL2 . . . . 43 C7
Shortheath La RG7. . . . . . .110 E3
Short La TW15, TW19 . . . . . 97 F7
Shortlands UB3. . . . . 71 D8
Shortlands Hill OX10. . . . . . 13 D4
Short Rd TW19 . . . . 70 E1
Short St
  Caversham RG4 . . . . 59 B2
  Pangbourne RG8 . . . . . . 56 D5
  Reading RG1 . . . . 86 B6
Short The RG8 . . . . 57 D5
Shortwood Ave TW18 . . . . 97 B5
Shortwood Comm TW18 . . 97 B4
Shortwood Inf Sch TW18 . 97 B5
SHOTTESBROOKE PARK . 63 C7
SHREDING GREEN 44 C7
Shrewsbury Rd TW14,
  TW6 . . . . 71 D1
Shrewsbury Terr RG14. . . .104 E1
Shrivenham Cl 3 GU47 . . .150 D8
Shropshire Gdns RG42 . . . 91 F1
Shrubbs Hill La SL5. . . . . .121 C3
Shrubland Dr RG30 . . . . . . 85 A4
Shrublands Dr GU18 . . . . .153 B8
SHRUBS HILL 121 C3
SHURLOCK ROW 63 A1
Shute End RG40, RG41 . . . .116 B6
Shyshack La RG26 . . . . . . .134 F1
Sibley Park Rd RG6 . . . . . . 87 A2
Sibson RG6 . . . . 87 C2
Sidbury Cl SL5. . . . . .121 A4
Sidestrand Rd RG14 . . . . .130 E7
Sidings The TW18 . . . . 97 B3
Sidmouth Ct 8 RG1 . . . . . 86 C7
Sidmouth Grange Cl RG6 . 87 B7
Sidmouth Grange Rd RG6 87 B7
Sidmouth St RG1 . . . . 86 C7
Sidney Harrison Ho RG9 . . 36 B4
Sidney Rd
  Staines TW18. . . . . 97 A4
  Windsor SL4 . . . . 66 C4
Sienna Ct 7 TW13. . . . . . . 98 F5
Signals Ct RG19. . . . . .106 D1
Silbury Cl RG31. . . . . 84 B4
SILCHESTER 136 B5
Silchester CE Prim Sch
  RG7 . . . . .136 B1
Silchester Ct SL6. . . . . 97 E6
Silchester Ho SL6. . . . . 40 B8
Silchester Manor Sch
  SL6. . . . . 40 D7
Silchester Pl RG7 . . . . .113 B5
Silchester Rd
  Reading RG30 . . . . 85 C4
  Tadley RG26. . . . . .135 B3
Silco Dr SL6 . . . . 39 E6
Silk Pl RG40 . . . . 116 D7
Silverbeck Way TW19 . . . . 70 A2
Silver Birches RG41 . . . . . .115 D3
Silver Cl SL6 . . . . 39 A5
Silverdale Ct TW18. . . . . . . 97 B3
Silverdale Rd
  Earley RG6. . . . . 87 C3
  Tadley RG26. . . . . .135 B3
  Wargrave RG10. . . . . 36 E1
Silver Dr GU16 . . . . .152 C3
Silverglades GU46 . . . . . . .149 C4
Silver Hill RG47 . . . . .150 E8
Silver St RG7 . . . . .136 B8
Silver St RG2 . . . . 39 C4
Silverstone Mews SL6. . . . . 39 C4
Silver Street Flats 26 RG1 86 B6
Silverthorne Dr RG4 . . . . . 58 E6
Silvertrees Dr SL6 . . . . 39 A5
Silverwood Dr GU15 . . . . .152 A7
Silverwood Grange SL5 . .122 D7
Silwood Cl SL5 . . . . .120 D7
Silwood Park (Imperial Coll)
  SL5. . . . . .120 F6
Silwood Rd SL5 . . . . .120 F5
Simkins Cl RG42 . . . . 92 B2
Simmonds Cl RG42 . . . . . .117 E8
Simmonds Cres RG6 . . . . . 87 E1
Simmons Malthouse 5
  RG1 . . . . 86 A7
Simmonds St RG1 . . . . 86 A7
Simmons Field RG18 . . . . .106 F4
Simmons Fields RG10. . . . . 61 B3
Simmons Pl TW18 . . . . 96 F3
Simmons Rd RG9 . . . . 15 D3
Simms Farm La RG7. . . . . .136 A2
Simod Ct 3 RG30 . . . . 85 C7
Simons Cl RG31 . . . . 84 C7
Simons La RG41 . . . . .115 D8
Simons Wlk TW20. . . . . 95 F1
Simpson Cl SL6 . . . . 39 C4
Simpsons Way SL1 . . . . . . 42 E5
Sinclair Rd SL4 . . . . 66 D4
Sindle Cl RG41 . . . . 88 B2
Sindlesham Ct RG41 . . . . .115 C7
Sindlesham Farm Cotts 2
  RG41 . . . . 87 E2
Sindlesham Rd RG41 . . . . . 88 B2
Singers Cl RG9. . . . . 35 E8
Singers La RG9 . . . . 15 E1
Sinhurst Rd GU15. . . . . . . .151 A3

SIPSON 71 A8
Sipson Cl UB7 . . . . 71 A8
Sipson La UB3, UB7 . . . . . . 71 B8
Sipson Rd UB7 . . . . 71 A7
Sipson Way UB7 . . . . 71 A7
Sir Henry Peakes Dr SL2 . .22 A6
Sirius Cl RG41 . . . . .115 F6
Siri Cotts SL5. . . . . .120 C5
Sir Robert Mews SL3 . . . . 44 A1
Sir Sydney Camm Ho SL4 .67 B6
Sir William Borlase's Gram
  Sch SL7. . . . . 1 C1
Sir William Perkins's Sch
  KT16. . . . . .123 F1
Six Acre La RG17 . . . . .126 A5
Sixth Ave RG31. . . . . 84 B6
Sixth St RG19. . . . . .131 F5
Skarries View RG4 . . . . 58 D8
Skeffling Cl 4 RG6. . . . . . . 87 E3
Skelmersdale Way RG6. . . 87 E3
Skelton Ct RG30 . . . . 85 D7
Skelton Fields RG42 . . . . . 91 C1
Skerries Ct 5 SL3 . . . . . . 44 A2
Skerritt Way RG8 . . . . 57 D4
Skillman Dr RG19 . . . . . . .106 F3
Skilton Rd RG31 . . . . 57 C3
SKIMPEDHILL 118 B7
Skimpedhill La RG12 . . . . .118 B7
SKINNERS GREEN 130 B7
Skinners Green La RG14 130 B7
Skippons Cl RG14 . . . . . . .130 C6
Sky Bsns Pk TW20 . . . . . .123 C7
Skydmore Path SL2 . . . . . . 21 F2
Skye Cl RG31. . . . . 84 E4
Skylark Way RG2 . . . . .113 E5
Skylings RG14 . . . . .105 A4
Skyport Dr UB7 . . . . 70 D7
Skyway 14 Trad Est SL3 . . 69 F4
Slade Hill Gdns RG20 . . . .129 F2
Slaidburn Gn RG12 . . . . . .118 E2
Slanting Hill RG18 . . . . 79 B4
Sledmere Ct TW14 . . . . 98 F7
Slim Rd GU15. . . . . .151 C7
Sloane Cl RG8 . . . . 34 C6
Slopes The RG4 . . . . 59 D2
SLOUGH 42 D5
Slough Bsns Pk SL1 . . . . . 42 E5
Slough & Eton CE Coll
  SL1 . . . . 42 D3
Slough Gram Sch SL3 . . . . 43 B3
Slough Interchange Ind Est
  SL2. . . . . 43 A5
Slough Mus* SL1. . . . . 42 F5
Slough Rd
  Datchet SL3 . . . . 68 B8
  Eton SL4 . . . . 67 C6
  Slough SL1. . . . . 42 F5
  Slough SL3. . . . . 42 E5
Slough Trad Est SL1 . . . . . 42 E6
Smalley Cl RG41 . . . . .115 C6
Smallholdings TW15 . . . . . 98 B4
Smallmead Rd
  Burghfield Common RG30 85 D1
  Reading RG2. . . . . 86 A1
Smallridge RG41 . . . . .130 C4
Smallwood Dr RG26. . . . . .135 B1
Smeaton Ct 7 RG40 . . . . .116 A8
Smewins Rd RG10, SL6 . . . 63 D5
Smitham Bridge Rd
  RG17 . . . . 100 C5
Smithfield Cl SL6. . . . . 38 F3
Smithfield Rd SL6 . . . . 39 A3
Smith's Hill OX12 . . . . 6 F5
Smiths La SL4 . . . . 66 D4
Smith Sq RG12 . . . . .118 D7
Smithy's Gn GU20. . . . . . .146 D4
Snake La RG20 . . . . .104 A7
Soldiers Rise RG40 . . . . . .141 E7
Snelsmore Common Cntry
  Pk* RG14. . . . . 77 D2
Snipe La RG20 . . . . .131 F2
Snowball Hill
  Maidenhead SL6 . . . . . . 39 A1
  White Waltham SL6 . . . . 64 B8
Snowberry Cl RG41 . . . . . .115 F5
Snowdon Cl SL4. . . . . 66 D3
Snowdon Dr RG31 . . . . 84 A6
Snowdon Rd TW6. . . . . 71 C1
Snowdrop Copse RG18 . . .106 F4
Snowdrop Gr RG41 . . . . . . 88 C3
Snows Paddock GU20 . . . . 147 B8
Snows Ride GU20. . . . . . . .146 B6
Soane End RG4 . . . . 59 A7
Soho Cres RG6 . . . . 114 A8
Soho Mills Ind Est HP10. . . 3 D4
Soke Rd RG7 . . . . .135 C3
Soldiers Rd RG40 . . . . . . .142 D7
Solent Ct 8 RG1. . . . . 86 B6
Somerford Cl RG6 . . . . 40 B8
Somerlea SL6 . . . . 39 E3
Somersby Cres SL6 . . . . . . 39 E3
Somerset Cl
  Hungerford RG17 . . . . . .100 C5
  Wokingham RG41. . . . . . 88 C3
Somerset Gr RG42 . . . . 91 F1
Somerset Hospl SN8 . . . . . 99 B5
Somerset Lodge 3 SL6 . . 39 F6
Somerset Wlk RG31 . . . . . 84 B4
Somerton Gdns RG6. . . . . . 87 C2
Somerton Dr RG19. . . . . . .106 F2
Somerville Cl RG41 . . . . . . 115 C6
Somerville Cres GU46. . . . .149 C6
Somerville Rd SL4 . . . . 42 C1
Somerville Rise RG12 . . . .118 D4

Songbird Cl RG2. . . . . .113 E5
SONNING 60 D4
Sonning CE Prim Sch
  RG4 . . . . 60 D3
Sonninge Cl GU47 . . . . . . .150 D8
Sonning EYE. 60 C5
Sonning Gate RG4. . . . . . . 60 E2
Sonning La RG4 . . . . 60 C2
Sonning Mdws RG4 . . . . . . 60 C1
Sophie Gdns SL3 . . . . 43 D4
Sopwith Cl RG5. . . . . 88 A7
Sorrel Cl
  Burghfield Common RG7 . .111 B3
  Newbury RG14. . . . . .105 D5
  Wokingham RG40 . . . . . .116 E8
Sorrel Dr GU18 . . . . .152 F7
Sospel Ct SL2 . . . . 22 E2
Southampton Cl GU17 . . . .150 C6
Southampton Rd
  Stanwell TW6. . . . . 70 F1
  Stanwell TW19 . . . . 70 F1
SOUTH ASCOT 120 B4
South Ascot Village Prim Sch
  SL5. . . . . .120 A4
South Ave
  Egham TW20 . . . . 96 C2
  Henley-on-T RG9 . . . . . . 35 E8
South Bank RG8 . . . . 14 C3
Southbank Gdns RG17 . . . 25 C2
Southbourne Dr SL8 . . . . . . 3 A3
Southbury La RG10 . . . . . . 61 F5
South Cl
  Burnham SL1 . . . . 41 D6
  Harlington UB3 . . . . 71 D7
  Wokingham RG40 . . . . . .116 D4
SOUTHCOTE 85 C4
Southcote Ave TW13 . . . . . 98 F6
Southcote Dr GU15 . . . . . .152 A5
Southcote Farm La RG30. . 85 D4
Southcote La RG30. . . . . . . 85 C4
Southcote Lodge RG30. . . 85 A3
Southcote Prim Sch RG30 85 B4
Southcote Rd RG30 . . . . . . 85 D6
Southcroft
  Englefield Green TW20. . . 95 B3
  Slough SL2. . . . . 22 B1
Southdown Rd
  Caversham RG4 . . . . 59 B5
  Tadley RG26 . . . . .135 A1
  Thatcham RG19. . . . . . . .105 F4
South Dr
  Reading RG2 . . . . 86 F2
  Sonning RG4 . . . . 60 C1
  Sulhamstead RG7 . . . . . .110 D7
  Wentworth GU25. . . . . . .122 A2
  Wokingham RG40 . . . . . .116 C5
SOUTHEND 28 C1
  Bradfield 82 A2
  Brightwalton 28 C1
Southend Rd RG18 . . . . . .106 D6
Southend Terr RG7. . . . . . . 82 B2
Southern Cotts TW19 . . . . 70 A2
Southern Ct 18 RG1. . . . . . 86 B7
Southerndene Cl RG31 . . . 57 C2
Southern Gate Pk RG2 . . .113 A8
Southern Hill RG1 . . . . 86 D5
Southern Ind Area RG12 . .117 F6
Southern Perimeter Rd
  East Bedfont TW6 . . . . . . 71 B1
  Harlington TW14, TW6. . . 70 F2
  Stanwell TW19, TW6 . . . . 70 D2
Southern Rd GU15 . . . . . . .151 D3
South Farm La GU19 . . . . .146 A2
SOUTH FAWLEY 27 C5
South Field Cl SL4 . . . . . . 41 C3
Southfield Gdns SL1 . . . . . 41 B8
Southfields
  Boxford RG20 . . . . 76 C3
  Chieveley RG20 . . . . 50 B8
Southfields Ave TW15 . . . . 98 B2
South Gate Ave TW13 . . . . 98 D4
South Gate Rd RG17. . . . . 27 A8
Southglade Ho SL6 . . . . . . 39 D2
Southlands RG42 . . . . .113 D8
South Gn SL1. . . . . 42 E6
South Gr RG17 . . . . 73 A2
South Groves RG17 . . . . . . 73 A2
South Hill Rd RG12 . . . . . .118 B3
South Lake Cres RG5 . . . . 87 E5
Southlake Ct RG5 . . . . 87 F5
Southlake Prim Sch RG5 87 E5
Southlands Cl RG40. . . . . .116 D5
Southlands Rd RG40 . . . . .116 D5
Southlea Rd SL3. . . . . 68 B5
South Lynn Cres RG12 . . .118 B4
South Mdw RG45 . . . . .143 D3
South Meadow La SL4 . . . 67 D8
South Oak Way RG2 . . . . .112 F7
South Pl SL7 . . . . 1 D3
South Rd
  Bisley GU24. . . . . .153 F3
  Bracknell RG40, RG12 . . .143 C3
  Crowthorne RG45 . . . . . .143 C3
  Englefield Green TW20. . . 95 C1
  Maidenhead SL6 . . . . . . 39 E6
South Row
  Chilton OX11 . . . . 10 D7
  Fulmer SL3. . . . . 23 A8
Southside KT16 . . . . .124 B3
South St
  Blewbury OX11 . . . . 12 A8
  Caversham RG4 . . . . 59 C2
  Reading RG1 . . . . 86 A6
SOUTH STOKE 14 C4
South Stoke Prim Sch
  RG8 . . . . 14 B4

South Terr SL4. . . . . .67 E6
South View
  Bracknell RG12 . . . . 117 D6
  Cookham Rise SL6. . . . . . . .19 E7
  Hungerford RG17 . . . . . . 100 D5
South View Ave RG4 . . . . . .59 C2
Southview Cl RG10. . . . . . . .61 E6
South View Gdns **3**
  RG14 . . . . 105 B4
South View Pk RG4 . . . . . .59 C2
Southview Rd SL7 . . . . .1 E4
Southville Cl TW14. . . . . . . .98 E7
Southville Cres TW14 . . . . .98 E7
Southville Jun & Inf Schs
  TW14 . . . . .98 F7
Southville Rd TW14 . . . . . . .98 E8
Southwark Cl GU46 . . . . . 149 C6
Southway GU15. . . . . 151 B4
Southwell Park Rd GU15 151 C5
Southwell Ct RG12 . . . . . . 118 E3
Southwold Cl RG12 . . . . . . 117 E1
Southwold Cl RG6 . . . . .87 D1
Southwold Spur SL3 . . . . . .44 C4
Southwood RG40 . . . . 116 D4
Southwood Gdns
  Burghfield Common RG7 . . 111 A3
  Cookham Rise SL6. . . . . . . .19 E5
Southwood Rd
  Cookham Rise SL6. . . . . . . .19 E5
  Yateley GU17. . . . . 149 E1
Sovereign Beeches SL2 . .22 B6
Sovereign Ct **4** SL5 . . . . 121 B2
Sovereign Dr GU15 . . . . . 152 B7
Sovereign Ho SL6 . . . . .97 F4
Sovereign Hts SL3 . . . . . . .69 A8
Sovereign Pk **3** RG31. . .84 D8
Sovereign Way RG31 . . . . .84 C5
Sovoy Ct GU15. . . . . 151 C5
Sowbury Pk RG20. . . . . . . .78 A8
Spackman Cl RG19. . . . . . 106 D2
Spackmans Way SL1 . . . . .42 D3
Spade Oak Farm SL8. . . . . .2 E3
Spade Oak Mdw SL8 . . . . . .2 E4
Spa Meadow Cl RG19 . . . 131 C8
Span Hill RG4 . . . . .60 B7
Sparrowbill RG20 . . . . .28 E2
Sparrow Ct RG41 . . . . 115 E5
Sparvell Way GU15. . . . . . 151 C6
Speedbird Way U87. . . . . . .70 C7
Speedwell Way RG18. . . . 106 F4
SPEEN. 104 C5
Speenhamland Ct **5**
  RG14 . . . . 105 A4
Speenhamland Prim Sch
  RG14 . . . . 104 F4
Speen Hill Cl RG14. . . . . . 104 E4
Speen La RG14 . . . . 104 D4
Speen Lodge Ct RG14 . . . 104 E4
Speen Pl RG14. . . . . 104 E4
Spelthorne Gr TW16 . . . . . .98 F1
Spelthorne Inf Sch TW15 . .98 E2
Spelthorne Jun Sch
  TW15 . . . . .98 D2
Spelthorne La TW15,
  TW17 . . . . 125 C8
Spelthorne Mus* TW18 . .96 F3
Spencer Cl
  Pamber Heath RG26 . . . . . 135 E1
  Wokingham RG41 . . . . 115 D6
Spencer Gdns TW20. . . . . .95 D3
Spencer Rd
  Bracknell RG42 . . . . 117 F8
  Newbury RG14. . . . . 130 D6
  Reading RG2 . . . . 113 B7
  Slough SL3. . . . . .43 F3
Spencers Cl SL6 . . . . .39 D8
Spencers Ct RG7 . . . . 113 A3
Spencers La SL6. . . . . .19 E7
Spencers Rd SL6 . . . . .39 D8
SPENCERS WOOD 113 A1
Spenwood Cl RG7 . . . . . . 113 B2
Sperling Rd SL6 . . . . .19 F1
Spey Rd RG30 . . . . .85 A7
Spinfield La SL7 . . . . .1 B2
Spinfield La W SL7 . . . . . . .1 C1
Spinfield Mount SL7 . . . . . .1 B1
Spinfield Pk SL7. . . . . .1 C1
Spinfield Sch SL7. . . . . .1 B2
Spinis RG12 . . . . 117 F1
Spinner Gn RG12 . . . . 118 B4
Spinners Wlk
  Marlow SL7 . . . . .1 C1
  Windsor SL4 . . . . .67 C6
Spinney SL1 . . . . .42 B5
Spinney Cl RG4 . . . . .59 B7
Spinney Dr TW14 . . . . .98 C8
Spinney La SL4 . . . . .93 B7
Spinney The
  Finchampstead RG40. . . . . 141 F8
  Frimley GU15. . . . . 152 C6
  Reading RG31 . . . . .84 E4
  Sunningdale SL5 . . . . 120 E4
  Yateley GU46 . . . . 149 C7
Spinningwheel La RG42 . .90 C8
Spires Ct KT16. . . . . 124 A3
Spire View RG14 . . . . .70 D1
SPITAL 67 B3
Spitfire Cl SL3. . . . . .44 A2
Spitfire Way RG5 . . . . .88 A7
Spittal St SL7. . . . . .1 D2
Splash The RG42. . . . . .91 B2
Spode Cl RG30 . . . . .84 E8
Spout La TW19 . . . . .70 A3
Spout La N TW19 . . . . .70 B3
Spray La RG20. . . . . .28 C1
Spray Rd SN8, RG17. . . . . 126 E3
Spriggs Cl RG19 . . . . 106 D2

Springate Field SL3. . . . . . .43 E4
Spring Ave TW20. . . . . .95 F2
Spring Cl
  Maidenhead SL6 . . . . .19 F2
  Pangbourne RG8 . . . . .55 D5
Spring Cnr **2** TW13. . . . .98 F5
Spring Cross Ave GU17. . 150 D4
Springdale
  Earley RG6. . . . . .87 B2
  Finchampstead RG40. . . . . 141 E8
Springdale Cotts SL8 . . . . .3 B2
Spring Farm Mews RG8 . .14 C1
Springfield
  Lightwater GU18 . . . . 153 D8
  Slough SL1. . . . . .43 A3
Springfield Cl SL4 . . . . . . .67 B5
Springfield Ct
  Maidenhead SL6 . . . . .40 B7
  Twyford RG10 . . . . .61 E5
Springfield End RG8 . . . . . .34 C8
Springfield Gr TW16. . . . . 125 F8
Springfield La RG14. . . . . 131 B8
Springfield Mews RG4 . . . .59 B4
Springfield Pk
  Maidenhead SL6 . . . . .40 C1
  Twyford RG10 . . . . .61 E4
Springfield Prim Sch
  Reading RG31 . . . . .84 B7
  Sunbury TW16. . . . . 125 F7
Springfield Rd
  Ashford TW15 . . . . .97 F3
  Bracknell RG12 . . . . 117 C8
  Brands Hill SL3 . . . . .69 B7
  Frimley GU15. . . . . 152 B5
  Pamber Heath RG26 . . . . . 135 E1
  Windsor SL4 . . . . .67 B5
Springfields Cl KT16 . . . . 124 A1
Spring Gdns
  Ascot SL5. . . . . 120 B5
  Bourne End SL8. . . . . .3 A4
  Frimley GU15. . . . . 152 A5
  Marlow SL7 . . . . .1 E3
  Newbury RG20. . . . . 130 B3
  Shinfield RG7. . . . . 113 B2
  Theale RG7 . . . . .83 D3
  Wooburn Green HP10 . . . . . .3 E8
Spring Gr
  Reading RG1 . . . . .86 B6
  Sunningdale SL5 . . . . 120 F2
Spring Hill SL6 . . . . .39 E3
Springhill Cl **5** RG12 . . 118 B5
Springhill Rd RG8 . . . . . . .34 C8
Springhurst RG14 . . . . . . 131 B8
Spring La
  Aldermaston RG7 . . . . 135 C6
  Aston Tirrold OX11 . . . . . . .12 E8
  Caversham RG4. . . . . .60 B5
  Cold Ash RG18. . . . . 106 C8
  Cookham Dean SL6 . . . . . . .19 C5
  Farnham Common SL2. . . . . .22 C5
  Mortimer RG7 . . . . 137 A6
  Riseley RG7 . . . . 139 A4
  Slough SL1. . . . . .42 F5
Spring Mdws RG17. . . . . . .48 B4
Springmead Ct GU47. . . . 143 E1
Spring Meadow RG12 . . . 118 D8
Spring Meadows Bsns Ctr
  RG10. . . . . .36 F5
Spring Rd TW13 . . . . .98 F5
Spring Rise TW20. . . . . . . .95 E2
Spring Terr **4** RG1. . . . . .86 B5
Spring Wlk RG10 . . . . .36 D1
Spring Woods
  Sandhurst GU47 . . . . 143 C1
  Virginia Water GU25 . . . . . 122 B5
Sprogsit Ind Est TW19 . . .70 F1
Spruce Ct **1** SL1 . . . . .42 F3
Spruce Dr GU18 . . . . 153 A7
Spruce Rd RG5 . . . . .88 A6
Spurcroft Prim Sch
  RG19 . . . . 106 D2
Spurcroft Rd RG19. . . . . . 106 D2
Spur The
  Slough SL1. . . . . .41 D8
  Wargrave RG10 . . . . .36 E3
Square The
  Bagshot GU19 . . . . 145 E3
  Bracknell RG12 . . . . 118 E5
  Earley RG6. . . . . 114 A8
  Harmondsworth TW6. . . . . . .70 B6
  Lightwater GU18 . . . . 146 C1
  Newtown RG19 . . . . 132 A4
  Pangbourne RG8 . . . . .56 A6
  Shinfield RG7. . . . . 113 B2
  Yattendon RG18 . . . . .53 E1
Squires Bridge Rd KT17. 124 F5
Squire's Bridge Rd
  TW17. . . . . 125 A6
Squires Ct
  Camberley GU15 . . . . 151 C3
  Chertsey KT16. . . . . 124 B1
Squire's Rd TW17 . . . . . . 125 A5
Squires Wlk TW15 . . . . . . .98 D1
Squirrel Cl GU47. . . . . 150 B8
Squirrel Dr SL4 . . . . .93 E7
Squirrel Rise SL7 . . . . .1 D6
Squirrels Drey RG45 . . . . 142 F5
Squirrels Way RG6. . . . . . .87 B2
Squirrel Wlk RG41 . . . . . . 115 F7
Stable Cl RG7 . . . . 111 A3
Stable Cl RG14 . . . . 105 B6
Stables Ct SL7. . . . . .1 B1
Stables The SL5. . . . . 121 B1
Stable View GU46 . . . . . . 149 D7
Staddlestone Cl RG31. . . . .57 C2

Stadium Way RG30. . . . . . .58 B1
Staff College Rd GU15. . . 151 B6
Stafferton Way SL6 . . . . . .40 A6
Stafford Ave SL2. . . . . .22 C1
Stafford Cl
  Burnham SL6 . . . . .41 B7
  Woodley RG5. . . . . .87 F7
Stafford Lake GU21,
  GU24 . . . . 153 F1
Staffordshire Cl RG30. . . . .84 F8
Staffordshire Croft RG42 . .91 F2
Stag Hill RG17 . . . . .73 A2
Stainash Cres TW18. . . . . .97 B3
Stainash Par TW18. . . . . . .97 B3
STAINES 96 E6
Staines By-Pass TW15,
  TW18. . . . . .97 C3
Staines La KT16 . . . . 124 A3
Staines Lane Cl KT16 . . . 123 F4
Staines Prep Sch TW18 . .97 A3
Staines Rd
  Chertsey KT16. . . . . 124 A5
  East Bedfont TW14 . . . . . . .98 D8
  Laleham TW18. . . . . 124 B7
  Wraysbury TW19 . . . . .95 F7
Staines Rd W TW15 . . . . . .98 D1
Staines Sta TW18 . . . . . . .97 A3
Stainford Cl TW15 . . . . . . .98 D3
Stamford Ave GU16 . . . . . 151 F1
Stamford Rd SL6 . . . . .39 C6
Stanbrook Cl RG7. . . . . . . .82 A2
Stanbury Gate RG7 . . . . . 113 A3
Stanfield RG26. . . . . 135 B1
STANFORD DINGLEY. 81 C4
Stanford Dingley Circular
  Wlks* RG18 . . . . .80 E7
STANFORD END 138 F3
Stanham Rd RG30 . . . . . . .84 D8
Stanhope Gate GU15. . . . 118 A5
Stanhope Heath TW19 . . . .70 C1
Stanhope Rd
  Camberley GU15 . . . . 150 F4
  Reading RG2 . . . . .86 D3
  Slough SL1. . . . . .41 D7
Stanhope Way TW19 . . . . .70 C1
Stanlake La RG10 . . . . .61 F4
Stanley Cl SL7 . . . . .1 F3
Stanley Cotts SL2 . . . . .42 F5
Stanley Gn E SL3 . . . . .43 F2
Stanley Gn W SL3. . . . . . . .43 F2
Stanley Gr **1** RG1. . . . . . .85 F7
Stanley Ho SL4 . . . . .68 A2
Stanley Rd
  Ashford TW15 . . . . .97 E3
  Newbury RG14. . . . . 105 B2
  Wokingham RG40 . . . . 116 F6
Stanley Spencer Art Gall*
  SL6. . . . . .20 B7
Stanley St RG1 . . . . .85 F8
Stanley Wlk RG12 . . . . . . 118 C7
STANMORE 120 A5
Stanmore Cl SL5. . . . . 120 A5
Stanmore Gdns RG7 . . . . 136 F5
Stanmore Rd RG20. . . . . . .30 C2
Stanshawe Rd RG1. . . . . . .86 A8
Stansted Rd TW6 . . . . .70 F1
Stanton Cl RG6 . . . . .87 C4
Stanton Way SL3 . . . . .43 E2
Stanway Cotts RG1 . . . . . .86 F6
Stanway Pr KT16. . . . . 123 F2
STANWELL 70 D1
Stanwell Cl TW19 . . . . .70 D1
Stanwell Fields CE Prim Sch
  TW19 . . . . .70 E1
Stanwell Gdns TW19 . . . . .70 D1
STANWELL MOOR 70 A1
Stanwell Moor Rd TW19, TW6,
  U87. . . . . .70 B4
Stanwell New Rd TW18. . .97 B5
STANWELL PLACE. 70 B1
Stanwell Rd
  Ashford TW15 . . . . .97 E3
  East Bedfont TW14, TW19,
  TW6 . . . . .98 B8
  Horton SL3. . . . . .69 C4
Stapleford Rd RG30. . . . . .85 C4
Staplehurst RG12 . . . . . . 117 E2
Stapleton Cl
  Marlow SL7 . . . . .1 E1
  Newbury RG14. . . . . 130 C6
Star Cl
  Knowl Hill RG10. . . . . .37 E4
  Reading RG1 . . . . .86 F8
Starling Cl RG41. . . . . 115 F5
Starlings Dr RG31. . . . . . . .84 B6
Starmead Dr RG40 . . . . . . 116 E5
Star Post Rd GU15 . . . . . . 151 F8
Star Rd RG4 . . . . .59 C2
Starting Gates **3** RG14 . 105 C1
Starting Gate The SL5. . . 120 A4
Startins La SL6 . . . . .19 C8
Starwood Ct SL3. . . . . .43 C3
Statham Ct RG42 . . . . 117 E8
Station App
  Ashford TW15 . . . . .97 F4
  Blackwater GU17. . . . . 150 E4
  17 Maidenhead SL6. . . . . .39 F6
  Marlow SL7 . . . . .1 E1
  Reading RG1 . . . . .86 B8
  Shepperton TW17 . . . . . . 125 C4
  Staines TW18. . . . . .96 F6
  Virginia Water GU25 . . . . . 122 D5
Station Cres TW15 . . . . . . .98 A5
Station Hill
  Ascot SL5. . . . . 120 A5
  Cookham Rise SL6. . . . . . . .19 F7
  Hampstead Norreys RG18. . .52 F6

Station Hill *continued*
  Reading RG1 . . . . .86 A8
Station Ho SL3 . . . . .68 B6
Station Ind Est RG40 . . . . 116 B6
Station Par
  Ashford TW15 . . . . .97 F4
  Cookham Rise SL6. . . . . . . .19 F6
  Sunningdale SL5 . . . . 121 A2
  Virginia Water GU25 . . . . . 122 E4
Station Path TW18 . . . . . . .96 F4
Station Rd
  Ashford TW15 . . . . .97 F4
  Bagshot GU19 . . . . 145 E4
  Bourne End SL8. . . . . .3 A3
  Bracknell RG12 . . . . 118 B7
  Broad Laying RG20 . . . . . . 130 A3
  Chertsey KT16. . . . . 124 A1
  Cookham Rise SL6. . . . . . . .19 F7
  Earley RG6. . . . . .87 C4
  East Garston RG17 . . . . . . .47 C6
  Egham TW20 . . . . .96 A3
  Frimley GU16. . . . . 151 C1
  Goring RG8 . . . . .34 C6
  Great Shefford RG17. . . . . . .48 A3
  Henley-on-T RG9 . . . . .15 E1
  Hungerford RG17 . . . . . . 100 D6
  Kintbury RG17. . . . . 102 B2
  Lambourn RG17 . . . . .25 B2
  Lower Shiplake RG9 . . . . . .36 A4
  Marlow SL7 . . . . .1 E1
  Mortimer RG7 . . . . 137 E5
  Newbury RG14. . . . . 105 A2
  1 Pangbourne RG8 . . . . . .56 C6
  Reading RG1 . . . . .86 B8
  Shepperton TW17 . . . . . . 125 C4
  Slough, Langley SL3. . . . . . .44 A8
  Slough SL1. . . . . .41 E7
  Speen RG14 . . . . 104 C5
  Sunningdale SL5 . . . . 121 A4
  Taplow SL6 . . . . .40 F7
  Thatcham RG19 . . . . 106 E2
  Theale RG7 . . . . .83 E2
  Twyford RG10 . . . . .61 D4
  Wargrave RG10 . . . . .36 C1
  Wokingham RG40 . . . . 116 B6
  Woolhampton RG7. . . . . . . 108 C2
  Wraysbury TW19 . . . . .69 A1
Station Rd N **5** TW20. . . .95 F3
Station Rise SL7 . . . . .1 E2
Station Road Ind Est
  RG19 . . . . 106 F1
Station Terr RG40 . . . . .61 E4
Station Way RG12. . . . . . . 118 C7
Station Yard Ind Est
  RG17 . . . . 100 E5
Staunton Rd SL2 . . . . .42 D8
Staveley Rd TW15. . . . . . . .98 D2
Staverton Cl
  Bracknell RG42 . . . . .91 B1
  Wokingham RG40 . . . . 116 F6
Staverton Rd RG2. . . . . . . .86 D3
Stayne End GU25 . . . . 122 A5
Steam Farm La TW14 . . . . .71 F3
Steeple Cl **2** TW20. . . . . .96 A3
Steeple Point SL5. . . . . . . 120 B6
Steeple Wlk RG6. . . . . 113 F8
Steerforth Copse GU47. . 143 E2
Steggles Cl RG2 . . . . .87 D8
Stepgates KT16. . . . . 124 B2
Stepgates Cl KT16 . . . . . . 124 B2
Stepgates Com Prim Sch
  KT16. . . . . 124 B2
Stephanie Chase Ct
  RG40 . . . . 116 D7
Stephen Cl
  Egham TW20 . . . . .96 C2
  Twyford RG10 . . . . .61 F3
Stephens Cl RG7 . . . . 136 F6
Stephens Firs RG7 . . . . . . 136 F6
Stephenson Cl RG18 . . . . 106 D4
Stephenson Ct
  8 Newbury RG14. . . . . . . 104 F4
  13 Slough SL1. . . . . .42 F4
Stephenson Dr SL4 . . . . . .67 B7
Stephenson Rd RG2. . . . . 141 A7
Stephens Rd RG7 . . . . 136 F6
Sterling Ctr The RG12 . . . 118 D6
Sterling Gdns GU47. . . . . 150 E8
Sterling Ind Est RG14 . . . 105 B2
Sterling Way RG30. . . . . . .58 B1
Stern Ct KT16 . . . . 124 C1
Stevens Ct **4** RG41 . . . . .88 C2
Stevens Hill GU46. . . . . . . 149 E5
Stevenson Dr RG42 . . . . . .90 C3
Stewart Ave
  Littleton TW17. . . . . 125 A7
  Slough SL1. . . . . .42 F8
Stewart Cl SL6 . . . . .39 A8
Stewart Dr SL2 . . . . .22 B8
Stewarts Way SL7 . . . . .1 D7
Stile Rd SL3 . . . . .43 D3
Stilton Cl RG6 . . . . .87 E2
Stilwell Cl GU46 . . . . 149 E5
Stirling Ave TW17. . . . . . . 125 C6
Stirling Cl
  Caversham RG4. . . . . .59 D6
  Frimley GU16. . . . . 151 E2
  Windsor SL4 . . . . .66 D5
Stirling Gr SL6 . . . . .39 B8
Stirling Ho **20** RG1 . . . . . .39 B8
Stirling Pl **4** RG1 . . . . . . .39 B8
Stirling Rd
  Slough SL1. . . . . .42 B8
  Stanwell TW19 . . . . .70 F1
Stirling Way RG18 . . . . . . 106 D4
Stirrup Cl RG14. . . . . 131 B7
STITCHENS GREEN 33 F3
Stockbridge Way GU46. . 149 D4

Stockbury Cl RG6. . . . . . . .87 B1
STOCKCROSS 103 E6
Stockcross CE Sch RG20. 103 E6
Stockdales Rd SL4 . . . . . . .41 F2
Stockton Rd RG2 . . . . .86 C1
Stockwells SL6 . . . . .20 D1
Stockwood Rise GU15. . . 151 F5
Stoke Common Rd SL3. . . .23 B8
Stoke Court Dr SL2 . . . . . .22 F4
Stoke Ct RG2. . . . . .86 B1
Stokeford Cl **5** RG12 . . . 118 F4
Stoke Gdns SL1. . . . . .42 F5
Stoke Gn SL2 . . . . .23 A1
STOKE GREEN 23 B1
Stoke Park Ave SL2 . . . . . .22 C2
STOKE POGES. 22 F3
Stoke Poges La SL1, SL2. .42 F7
Stoke Poges Sch The SL2 .22 F5
Stoke Rd SL2 . . . . .42 F7
Stokesay SL1 . . . . .42 A4
Stokes Farm RG40 . . . . . . 116 F8
Stokes La RG26 . . . . 134 C1
Stokesley Rise HP10 . . . . . .3 E8
Stokes View RG8. . . . . .56 C5
Stoke View SL1 . . . . .42 F5
Stoke Wood SL2 . . . . .22 F8
Stompits Rd SL6. . . . . .65 C8
Stomp Rd SL1 . . . . .41 C8
Stonea Cl RG6 . . . . 114 C8
Stonebridge Field SL4 . . . .42 E1
STONE COPSE 105 E7
Stone Copse RG14 . . . . . . 105 E7
Stone Cres TW14 . . . . .98 F8
Stonecroft Ave SL0 . . . . . .44 E7
Stonefield Pk SL6. . . . . . . .39 C7
Stonegate GU15 . . . . 152 C6
Stoneham Cl RG30. . . . . . .85 A6
Stonehaven Dr RG5. . . . . .88 A6
Stonehill Gate SL5. . . . . . 120 D3
Stonehill Ho GU19 . . . . . . 145 F2
Stonehill Rd GU18 . . . . . . 146 A1
Stonehouse RG8 . . . . .34 E2
Stone House La SL6 . . . . . . .2 C1
Stonehouse Rise GU16 . . 151 F1
Stoneleigh Ct
  Frimley GU16. . . . . 151 F1
  Reading RG7. . . . . .83 D2
Stonemasons Ct **6**
  RG14 . . . . 104 F1
Stone St RG30 . . . . .58 B1
Stone's Wlk RG7 . . . . 111 A3
Stoneyfield RG17 . . . . .48 A7
Stoneyland SL6 . . . . .39 A8
Stoney La
  Farnham Royal SL2 . . . . . . .22 A4
  Newbury RG14, RG18 . . . . 105 D6
  Thatcham RG19 . . . . 106 E3
Stoneyland Ct **6** TW20. . .95 F3
Stoneylands Rd TW20 . . . .95 F3
Stoney Meade SL1 . . . . . . .42 B5
Stoney Meadow SL6 . . . . .19 A8
Stoney Ware SL7 . . . . .18 E8
Stoney Ware Cl SL7 . . . . . .18 D8
Stony La RG17. . . . . .46 D3
Stookes Way GU46 . . . . . . 149 B4
Stork House Dr RG17 . . . . .25 A2
Stornaway Rd SL3 . . . . . . .44 C2
Stour Cl
  Reading RG30 . . . . .85 A8
  Slough SL1. . . . . .42 B3
Stovell Rd SL4 . . . . .67 B7
Stowe Rd SL1 . . . . .41 E6
Stowmarket Cl RG6. . . . . .87 D7
Strachey Cl RG8 . . . . .56 C2
Straight Bit HP10 . . . . .3 B8
Straight La RG17 . . . . .46 F4
Straight Mile The
  Hurst RG10, RG40. . . . . . . .89 D6
  Waltham St L RG10 . . . . . . .62 E1
Straight Rd SL4. . . . . .68 B1
STRAIGHT SOLEY 73 A5
Strande La SL6 . . . . .19 F5
Strande Pk SL6 . . . . .19 F5
Strande View Wlk SL6. . . .19 F5
Strand Way RG6 . . . . .87 C1
Stranraer Gdns SL1 . . . . . .42 E5
Stranraer Way **1** TW6 . . .70 E1
Stratfield Rd SL1. . . . . .42 E5
Stratfield RG12 . . . . 117 E1
STRATFIELD
  MORTIMER 137 D5
Stratfield Rd SL1 . . . . .43 A4
Stratford Cl SL2 . . . . .21 D1
Stratford Dr HP10. . . . . .3 D4
Stratford Gdns SL6 . . . . . .39 C4
Stratford Rd TW6 . . . . .71 C2
Stratford Way RG31 . . . . . .84 C5
Strathcona Cl HP10 . . . . . . .3 C7
Strathcona Way HP10 . . . . .3 C7
Strathearn Ave UB3. . . . . .71 F7
Stratheden Pl **6** RG5 . . . .88 F8
Strathmore Ct **3** GU15. . 151 D5
Strathmore Dr RG10 . . . . .61 A4
Strathy Cl RG30. . . . . .85 B8
Stratton Gdns RG2. . . . . . .86 C1
Stratton Rd TW16. . . . . . . 125 F7
Strawberry Fields RG7 . . 137 B6
Strawberry Hill
  Newbury RG14. . . . . 104 F4
  Newell Green RG42. . . . . . . .91 E2
Streamside SL1 . . . . .41 D7
STREATLEY 34 A7
Streatley CE Sch RG8 . . . .33 F6
Streatley Farm Cotts RG8 .34 A8

Streatley & Goring Bridge
RG8 . . . . .34 B6
Streatley Hill RG8. . . . . . . .33 F6
Streets Heath GU24 . . . . .153 F7
Street The
Aldermaston RG7 . . . . . .135 A7
Englefield RG2 . . . . .83 B5
Mortimer RG7 . . . . .137 D5
Moulsford OX10. . . . . .14 A6
South Stoke RG8 . . . . .14 B3
Swallowfield RG7. . . . . . .139 C6
Tidmarsh RG8 . . . . .56 D2
Waltham St L RG10 . . . . . .63 A6
Stretton Dr RG18 . . . . . . .79 C8
Stretton RG7 . . . . .82 A1
Stretton Cl RG7 . . . . .82 A1
Strode's Coll TW20. . . . . . .95 F3
Strodes College La TW20. .95 F3
Strode's Cres TW18 . . . . . .97 C3
Strode St TW20 . . . . .96 A4
Stroller Cl RG19 . . . . .105 F4
Stroma Cl SL3 . . . . .41 D6
Strongrove Hill RG17. . . .100 C6
Strood La SL5 . . . . .93 C2
Stroud Cl
Pamber Heath RG26 . . . . .135 E1
Windsor SL4 . . . . .66 D4
STROUDE 122 F7
Stroude Rd
Egham TW20 . . . . .96 A1
Virginia Water GU25,
TW20 . . . . .122 E6
Stroud Farm Rd SL6 . . . . .65 B8
STROUD GREEN 105 B1
Stroud La GU17 . . . . .150 A4
Strouds Mdw RG18 . . . . .106 C7
Strouds The RG7 . . . . . . .108 F6
Stroud Way TW15 . . . . . . .98 B2
Stuart Cl
Caversham RG4 . . . . .59 B5
Windsor SL4 . . . . .66 F5
Stuart Ho RG42 . . . . .117 F8
Stuart Rd RG14 . . . . .130 D6
Stuart Way
Staines TW18. . . . . .97 B2
Virginia Water GU25 . . . .122 A5
Styles Cl SL6 . . . . .39 D4
Styles SL5 . . . . .120 F2
Styventon Pl KT16 . . . . . .123 F2
Suck's La RG8 . . . . .54 D3
Suffolk Cl
Bagshot GU19 . . . . .145 E2
Slough SL1 . . . . .41 E7
Wokingham RG41 . . . . . .115 D6
Suffolk Combe RG42 . . . . .91 F1
Suffolk Ct **2** SL6 . . . . . . .39 F8
Suffolk Ho RG1 . . . . .86 D5
Suffolk Rd
Maidenhead SL6 . . . . .39 D4
Reading RG30 . . . . .85 D7
SULHAM 56 E2
Sulham La RG8 . . . .
SULHAMSTEAD
ABBOTS 110 F4
SULHAMSTEAD BANNISTER
UPPER END 110 E5
Sulhamstead Hill RG7. . .110 C6
Sulhamstead Rd
Burghfield RG7, RG30 . . .111 B5
Ufton Nervet RG7 . . . . . .110 D4
Sulhamstead & Ufton Nervet
CE Prim Sch RG7. . . . . .110 D7
Sulham Wlk RG30. . . . . . .85 B4
Sulham Rd GU15 . . . . . . .151 A1
Sullivans Reach KT12 . . .125 F2
Sumburgh Way SL1 . . . . . .42 E8
Summer Ct RG41 . . . . . . .115 A8
Summerfield Cl RG41 . . . .88 F1
Summerfield Rise RG41 . .34 D7
Summer Gdns GU15 . . . .152 C5
Summerhouse La UB7 . . . .70 D8
Summeriscales SL1. . . . . . .42 B5
Summerleaze Rd SL6 . . . . .20 A1
Summer Pl RG12 . . . . . . .118 A7
Summers Rd SL1 . . . . .21 C2
Summit Cl RG40 . . . . . . .141 F7
Summit Ctr UB7 . . . . .70 D7
SUNBURY 125 F6
SUNBURY COMMON 98 E1
Sunbury Cres TW13 . . . . .98 F4
Sunbury Cross Ctr **10**
TW16 . . . . .98 F1
Sunbury Ct SL4 . . . . .67 D8
Sunbury Int Bsns Ctr
TW16. . . . . .125 E8
Sunbury Manor Sch
TW16 . . . . .125 F8
Sunbury Rd
Eton SL4. . . . . .67 D8
Feltham TW13 . . . . .98 F4

Sun Cl SL4 . . . . .67 D8
Sunderland Cl RG5 . . . . . .88 B8
Sunderland Ct **11** TW19 . .70 E1
Sunderland Gdns RG14. . .104 D2
Sunderland Pl RG18 . . . .106 C4
Sunderland Rd SL6 . . . . . .39 B8
Sundew Cl
Lightwater GU18 . . . . . . .153 D8
Wokingham RG40 . . . . . .116 E7
Sundial Cl RG30 . . . . .85 A6
Sundon Cres GU25. . . . . .122 C4
Sundown Rd TW15. . . . . . .98 C3
Sunfield Bsns Pk RG40. . .140 F3
Sun Gdns RG7 . . . . .111 A1
Sun Hill RG7 . . . . .108 F2
Sun La
Maidenhead SL6 . . . . .39 F7
Riseley RG7 . . . . .139 B2
Sunley Cl RG14 . . . . .130 D6
Sunmead Rd TW16. . . . . .125 F6
Sunna Lodge TW16 . . . . . .98 F1
Sunning Ave SL5. . . . . . . .120 E2
SUNNINGDALE 121 B4
Sunningdale Park (Civil
Service Coll) SL5. . . . . .120 F4
Sunningdale Sch SL5 . . . .120 F3
Sunningdale Sta SL5 . . . .121 A2
SUNNINGHILL 120 C4
Sunninghill Cl SL5. . . . . .120 D5
Sunninghill Ct SL5. . . . . .120 D5
Sunninghill Lodge
Ascot SL5. . . . . .120 C7
Ascot, Sunninghill SL5. . . .120 D5
Sunninghill Rd
Ascot SL5. . . . . .120 D5
Windlesham GU20 . . . . . .146 A7
Winkfield SL4, SL5. . . . . . .93 E2
Sunning Ho
Ascot SL5 . . . . .120 C5
Windlesham GU20. . . . . .146 F8
Sunnybank
Ascot SL5. . . . . .120 A5
Marlow SL7 . . . . .1 D4
SUNNYMEADS 69 E4
Sunnymeads Sta TW19. . . .68 E4
Sunnymede Cotts SL6. . . . .20 B1
Sunnyside RG14 . . . . .104 E6
Sun Pas **19** SL4 . . . . .67 D6
Sun Ray Est GU47. . . . . . .150 A8
Sunrise Hill RG20 . . . . . . .36 F7
Sun St RG1 . . . . .86 D7
Superity Cotts RG20 . . . . .31 D6
Surbiton Rd GU15. . . . . . .145 A1
Surley Row RG4 . . . . .59 A5
Surly Hall Wlk SL4. . . . . . .66 F6
Surrey Ave
Camberley GU15 . . . . . . .151 A4
Slough SL2. . . . . .22 C1
Surrey Ct RG42 . . . . .91 F1
Surrey Heath Mus*
GU15 . . . . .151 D6
Surrey Rd RG2. . . . . .86 B4
Surridge Ct GU19 . . . . . .145 E2
Sussex Cl SL1 . . . . .43 B4
Sussex Gdns RG5 . . . . .87 E7
Sussex Ho SL2. . . . . .22 C6
Sussex Keep SL1. . . . . .43 B4
Sussex La RG4 . . . . .113 C1
Sussex Lodge **7** SL6 . . . . . .39 F6
Sussex Pl SL1, SL3 . . . . . . .43 B4
Sutcliffe Ave RG6 . . . . .87 D3
Sutherland Ave TW16 . . .125 F7
Sutherland Chase SL5. . .119 E7
Sutherland Gdns TW16. . .125 F7
Sutherland Gr RG31. . . . . .84 E4
Sutherland Grange SL4 . . .66 D7
Sutherlands RG14. . . . . . .130 E7
Sutherlands Ave RG1 . . . . .86 E5
SUTTON 44 C1
Sutton Ave SL3 . . . . .43 C4
Sutton Cl
Cookham SL6 . . . . .20 B7
Maidenhead SL6 . . . . .39 C5
Sutton Ct RG6 . . . . .87 B7
Sutton La
Brands Hill SL3 . . . . .69 B8
Slough SL3. . . . . .44 C1
Sutton Pl SL3. . . . . .69 B8
Sutton Rd
Camberley GU15 . . . . . . .145 A1
Newbury RG14. . . . . .104 D5
Suttons Bsns Pk RG1 . . . . .86 F8
Suttons Park Ave RG6. . . . .86 E8
Swabey Rd SL3 . . . . .44 A2
Swainstone Rd RG2. . . . . .86 B5
Swaledale RG12 . . . . .118 A4
Swallow Cl
Reading RG31. . . . . .84 C6
Staines TW18. . . . . .96 F4
Yateley GU46. . . . . .149 B6
SWALLOWFIELD 139 C6
Swallowfield TW20. . . . . . .95 B2
Swallowfield Dr RG2 . . . .113 C6
Swallowfield Gdns RG7 . . .83 B8
Swallowfield St RG7 . . . .139 C7
Swallow Ho SL7 . . . . .2 A2
Swallows Croft RG1. . . . . .85 E5
Swallow St SL0 . . . . .44 D8
Swallow Way RG41. . . . . .115 E6
Swanage Gn **6** SL6 . . . . . .40 A7
Swancote Gn RG12 . . . . .118 B4
Swan Ct
3 Blackwater GU17 . . . .150 E4
Newbury RG14. . . . . .104 F3

Swan Dr RG7 . . . . .109 C3
Swandrift TW18. . . . . .96 F1
Swangate RG17. . . . . . . .100 D7
Swan Ho GU47. . . . . .150 B7
Swanholm Gdns RG31. . . .84 F4
Swan La GU17, GU47. . . . .150 B7
Swanmore Cl RG6 . . . . . . .87 E1
Swan Pl **5** RG1. . . . . .86 D7
Swan Rd SL0 . . . . .44 F7
Swanscourt RG10. . . . . . . .61 E3
Swansdown Wlk RG19 . . .106 B3
Swansea Rd
Harlington TW14, TW6. . . .71 D1
Reading RG1. . . . . .59 A1
Swansea Terr RG31 . . . . . .57 D1
Swanston Field RG8 . . . . .56 D7
Swan Terr SL4. . . . . .67 B7
Swan Wlk TW17 . . . . .125 E2
Swedish Hos RG20 . . . . . . .76 B5
Sweeps Ditch Cl TW18 . . .124 A8
Sweeps La TW20 . . . . .95 F3
Sweetbriar RG45. . . . . . . .143 A7
Sweet Briar Dr RG31. . . . . .84 C4
Sweetzer's Piece RG7. . . .136 E6
Swepstone Cl RG6 . . . . . . .87 C2
Swift Cl RG41. . . . . .115 E5
Swift Ho SL7 . . . . .2 A2
Swift La GU19 . . . . .145 F3
Swinbrook Cl RG31 . . . . . .57 D3
Swindon Rd TW6 . . . . .71 C2
Swinley Rd SL5 . . . . .119 C4
Swinnerton Ho RG9. . . . . .15 E3
Swiss Cottage Cl RG31. . . .84 C8
Swiss Ct GU17 . . . . .150 C4
Swiss Farm Park Homes
RG9 . . . . .15 D3
Switchback Cl SL6. . . . . . .19 D2
Switchback Rd N SL6 . . . . .19 E3
Switchback Rd S SL6 . . . . .19 D2
Switchback The SL6 . . . . . .19 D2
Swithin Chase RG42 . . . . .91 E1
Sycamore Cl
8 Bourne End SL8 . . . . . . .3 B3
Burghfield RG30 . . . . . . .111 B4
Frimley GU16. . . . . .151 E1
Maidenhead SL6 . . . . .39 C3
Sandhurst GU47 . . . . .150 B8
Woodley RG5 . . . . .87 C5
Sycamore Ct
Pangbourne RG8 . . . . .56 C6
Windsor SL4 . . . . .67 C4
Sycamore Dr
Frimley GU16. . . . . .151 E1
Marlow Bottom SL7. . . . . . .1 D5
Twyford RG10. . . . . .61 E5
Sycamore Lodge **8** TW16. .98 F1
Sycamore Rd RG2 . . . . . . .86 E2
Sycamore Rise
Bracknell RG12 . . . . .118 D6
Newbury RG14. . . . . .105 C5
Sycamores The SL7. . . . . .150 B5
Sycamore Wlk
Englefield Green TW20 . . .95 B2
Slough SL3. . . . . .43 E7
Sydenham Gdns SL1. . . . .42 C4
Sydenham Ho **4** RG1 . . . . .86 D7
Sydings The RG4 . . . . . . .104 D5
Sydney Cl
Crowthorne RG45 . . . . . .143 C7
Thatcham RG19 . . . . .106 E3
Sydney Gr SL1. . . . . .42 C7
Sydney Loader Pl GU17 . .150 A5
Sydney Lodge RG19. . . . .106 E3
Syke Cluan SL0 . . . . .44 E4
Syke Ings SL0 . . . . .44 F4
Sykes Cotts RG12 . . . . . .118 E2
Sykes Dr TW18. . . . . .97 B3
Sykes Rd SL1 . . . . .42 B7
Sylvan Ridge GU47. . . . . .143 A1
Sylvanus RG12. . . . . .117 F2
Sylvan Wlk RG30. . . . . . . .85 C4
Sylverns Ct RG42 . . . . . . .91 D1
Sylvester Cl
Newbury RG14. . . . . .104 E5
Winnersh RG41. . . . . .88 D3
Sylvester Rd SL6. . . . . .19 E2
Symeon Pl RG4 . . . . .58 F3
Symondson Mews RG42. . .90 C4
Sympson Rd RG4 . . . . .58 F3

T

Tachbrook Rd TW14. . . . . .98 F8
Tadcroft Wlk RG31. . . . . . .84 E3
Tadham Pl RG19 . . . . . . .106 C2
TADLEY 135 B1
Tadley Common Rd
RG26 . . . . .135 C1
Tadmor Cl TW16. . . . . . . .125 F5
Taff Way RG30 . . . . .85 A7
Tag La RG10 . . . . .37 A1
Talavera Cl RG45. . . . . . . .142 F4
Talbot Ave SL3. . . . . .43 F4
Talbot Cl
Caversham RG4. . . . . .59 D2
Newbury RG14. . . . . .104 E5
Talbot Ct
Reading RG1. . . . . .86 A7
Windsor SL4 . . . . .67 B4
Talbot Pl
Bagshot GU19 . . . . .145 E4
Feltham Common SL2. . . . .22 C7
Slough SL3. . . . . .68 C6
Windsor SL4 . . . . .67 E3
Talbot Way RG31 . . . . .84 C6
Talbots Dr SL6. . . . . .39 B6
Talfourd Ave RG6 . . . . . . .87 A5

Talisman Cl RG45. . . . . . .142 D5
Tallis La RG30 . . . . .85 D4
Tall Trees SL3. . . . . .69 E6
Tamar Ct RG30 . . . . .85 D6
Tamar Gdns RG2. . . . . . . .86 C3
Tamarind Ct **3** TW20 . . . . .95 F3
Tamarind Way RG6 . . . . . .86 F1
Tamarisk Ave RG22 . . . . . .21 E1
Tamarisk Ct RG14. . . . . . .106 F4
Tamarisk Rise RG40. . . . .116 C7
Tamarisk Way RG42 . . . . .42 A5
Tamar Way
Slough SL3. . . . . .44 B2
Wokingham RG41 . . . . . .115 E7
Tamesa House TW17 . . . .125 A2
Tamesis Pl RG4. . . . . .59 B1
Tamworth RG12. . . . . . . .118 D2
Tamworth Cl **2** RG6 . . . . . .87 C1
Tangier Cl SL4. . . . . .67 D8
Tangier La SL4. . . . . .67 D8
Tanglewood RG40 . . . . . .142 A7
Tanglewood Ride GU24 . .153 D7
Tangley Dr RG41 . . . . . . .116 B4
Tanglyn Ave TW17 . . . . . .125 B4
Tanhouse La RG41 . . . . . .116 A5
Tank Rd GU15 . . . . .150 F5
Tanner Ct RG14 . . . . .105 A4
Tanners Cl RG7 . . . . .110 F1
Tanners La RG4 . . . . .58 F8
Tanners Row RG41. . . . . .116 A3
Tanners Yd GU19. . . . . . .145 E3
Tape La SL4 . . . . .88 F8
Tapestries Hall SL4 . . . . . .68 A2
Tapestries The SL4. . . . . . .68 A2
TAPLOW 20 D7
Taplow Common Rd SL1 . .21 A3
Taplow Quay SL6 . . . . .40 C7
Taplow Rd SL6. . . . . .41 A7
Taplow Sta SL6. . . . . .40 F7
Tarbat Ct **6** GU47 . . . . . . .150 D8
Tarbay La SL4 . . . . .66 B5
Target Cl TW14 . . . . .71 E1
Target Hill RG42 . . . . .91 D1
Targett Ct RG41. . . . . .88 B2
Tarlton Ct RG30. . . . . .84 F6
Tarmac Way UB7 . . . . .70 B7
Tarnbrook Way RG12. . . .118 E2
Tarn Ho RG41 . . . . .88 A3
Tarn La RG14. . . . . .130 F8
Tarragon Cl
Bracknell RG42 . . . . .91 D1
Earley RG6. . . . . .86 F1
Tarragon Way GU19. . . . .145 E3
Tarrant Ct GU15 . . . . . . .122 E4
Tarrant Gn RG42 . . . . .91 C1
Tarrant's Hill RG17. . . . . .100 D5
TASIS-The American Sch in
England TW20. . . . . . . .123 C6
Tasker Cl UB7 . . . . .71 C7
Tasman Ct TW16 . . . . .98 E1
Tatchbrook Cl SL6 . . . . . . .40 A8
Tattersall Ct RG40. . . . . . .116 C5
Tavistock Cl
Maidenhead SL6 . . . . .39 A8
Staines TW18. . . . . .97 D1
Tavistock Ind Est RG10. . .61 F5
Tavistock Rd RG2 . . . . . . .86 B3
Tawfield RG12. . . . . .117 E2
Tayberry Dr
Marlow SL7 . . . . .17 D6
Slough SL2. . . . . .57 D5
Taylor's Cl SL7 . . . . .1 F2
Taylors Ct RG6 . . . . .87 B8
Taynton Wlk **8** RG6. . . . . .87 C1
Tay Rd RG30. . . . . .85 A7
Tazewell Ct RG1 . . . . .85 F6
Tealgate RG17 . . . . .100 D7
Teal Gr RG12 . . . . .118 E5
Tean Ho RG2 . . . . .86 A2
Tebbit Cl RG12 . . . . .118 D7
Teesdale Rd SL2. . . . . .41 F8
Teikyo Sch (UK) SL3 . . . . .23 D5
Tekels Ave GU15 . . . . . . .151 D4
Tekels Ct GU15 . . . . .151 E4
Tekels Way GU15 . . . . . . .151 F3
Telford Ave RG45. . . . . . .143 C8
Telford Cres RG5. . . . . . . .60 F1
Telford Ct **3** RG40 . . . . . .104 F4
Telford Dr SL1. . . . . .42 A4
Telston Ct SL3 . . . . .3 A5
Tempest Rd TW20. . . . . . . .96 C2
Templar Ct RG42. . . . . . . .150 A8
Templars Lodge RG12. . . .118 D3
Templars Pl **11** SL7 . . . . .1 F2
TEMPLE 18 C5
Templecroft TW15 . . . . . . .98 D2
Templedene Ave TW18 . . .97 C2
Templegate Rd SL6 . . . . . .40 B5
Temple Ho RG19 . . . . .15 E3
Temple La SL7. . . . . .18 D6
Temple Mews RG6. . . . . . .87 F7
Temple Mill Cotts SL7. . . .18 C5
Temple Mill Island SL7. . .18 C5
Temple Park Rdbt RG42. . .90 F2
Temple Pl RG4 . . . . .59 C2
Temple Rd GU15. . . . . . . .151 E4
Templeton Gdns RG2 . . . .86 C1
Templeton Ho RG9. . . . . . .35 F8
TEMPLETON 101 B1
Temple Way
Bracknell RG42 . . . . .90 E1
Farnham Common SL2. . . .22 C7
Templewood Gate SL2 . . . .22 C7
Templewood La SL2 . . . . . .22 B7
Ten Acre La TW20 . . . . . .123 C7
Tenaplas Dr RG8. . . . . .54 F5

Tenby Ave RG4 . . . . .59 D5
Tenby Dr SL5 . . . . .120 D4
Tennyson Cl TW14 . . . . . . .71 F1
Tennyson Rd
Ashford TW15 . . . . .97 E3
Thatcham RG18. . . . . . . .106 C4
Woodley RG5. . . . . .87 E4
Tennyson Way SL2 . . . . . . .21 E1
Tensing Ct TW19 . . . . .97 E7
Tenth Ave RG31. . . . . .84 B6
Teresa Vale RG42 . . . . .91 E2
Tern Cl RG30. . . . . .85 A6
Terrace Rd N RG42. . . . . . .90 C4
Terrace Rd S RG42. . . . . . .90 C4
Terrace The
Ascot SL5. . . . . .120 D4
Bray SL6 . . . . .40 C3
Camberley GU15 . . . . . . .151 A5
Wokingham RG40 . . . . . .116 B6
Terrent Ct SL4. . . . . .67 A5
Terrington Hill SL7 . . . . . . .1 C2
Terry's La SL6 . . . . .19 F8
Tesimond Dr GU46 . . . . . .149 A6
Tessa Rd RG1. . . . . .58 F1
Test Cl RG30. . . . . .85 A8
Testwood Rd SL4 . . . . .66 D6
Tetbury Ct **9** RG1 . . . . . . .85 E7
Teviot Rd RG30 . . . . .85 A8
Thackery Lodge TW4 . . . . .71 D1
Thakerays The RG19 . . . .106 D2
Thamebridge Ct **5** SL6 . . .40 B8
Thames Ave
Chertsey KT16. . . . . .124 A6
Pangbourne RG8 . . . . .56 D6
Reading RG1 . . . . .59 A1
Windsor SL4 . . . . .67 D7
Thames Bank
Goring RG8 . . . . .34 B7
Staines TW18 . . . . .96 F1
Taplow SL6 . . . . .40 F7
Thamesbourne Mews SL8 . .3 A3
Thames Cl
Bourne End SL8 . . . . .3 A4
Chertsey KT16. . . . . .124 C2
Thames Cres SL6 . . . . .20 B2
Thames Ct
Goring RG8 . . . . .34 B6
Reading RG1. . . . . .60 F7
Thames Dr RG10. . . . . .60 F7
Thames Edge Ct **3** TW18 . .96 E4
Thames Ho RG1 . . . . .59 A1
Thamesfield Ct TW17 . . . .125 C2
Thamesfield Ho TW17 . . .125 C2
Thamesfield Mews
TW17. . . . . .125 C2
Thamesgate TW18 . . . . . .124 B8
Thames Mdw RG9 . . . . . . .15 E3
Thameside Prim Sch RG42 .59 B2
Thameside Reach RG8. . . .14 A4
Thames Ind Est SL7. . . . . . .1 F2
Thames Mead TW4. . . . . . .66 C6
Thames Meadow TW17. . .125 E1
Thamesmead Sch TW17. .125 D3
Thames Rd
Goring RG8 . . . . .34 B6
Slough SL3. . . . . .43 F3
Thatcham RG18. . . . . . . .106 B5
Thames Reach
Medmenham SL7. . . . . . . .17 D6
Reading RG8 . . . . .57 D5
Thames Side
Henley-on-T RG9 . . . . .15 E1
Laleham KT16, TW18. . . .124 C4
Reading RG1. . . . . .59 A1
Windsor SL4 . . . . .67 D7
Thames Side Prom RG1. . .59 A2
Thames St
Oatlands Park KT12. . . . .125 F2
Sonning RG4 . . . . .60 D4
Staines TW18. . . . . .96 F3
Windsor SL4 . . . . .67 D7
Thames Terr RG1 . . . . .59 A2
Thames Valley Bsns Pk
RG1 . . . . .60 A1
Thames Valley Nuffield Hospl
The SL3. . . . . .23 C4
Thames Valley Univ SL1. . .42 E5
Thames Valley Univ (Reading
Campus)
Reading RG1. . . . . .86 D7
Reading RG1. . . . . .86 A7
Thanington Way RG6 . . . . .87 B2
THATCHAM 106 E5
Thatcham Nature Discovery
Ctr* RG19 . . . . .106 A2
Thatcham Park CE Prim Sch
RG18. . . . . .106 D4
Thatcham Sta RG19. . . . .106 F6
Thatchers Dr SL6 . . . . .39 A5
Theal Cl GU47 . . . . .150 D8
THEALE 83 D4
Theale CE Prim Sch RG7 . .83 D3
Theale Green Com Sch
RG7 . . . . .83 D3
Theale Lakes Bsns Pk
RG7 . . . . .110 F8
Theale Rd RG30 . . . . .111 C6
Theale Sta RG7. . . . . .83 E2
Theobald Dr RG31. . . . . . .57 D4
Theobalds Way GU16 . . . .152 C3
Thetford Ho **7** RG1. . . . . . .85 E5
Thetford Mews RG4. . . . . .59 C6
Thetford Rd TW15. . . . . . .97 E5
Thibet Rd GU47 . . . . .150 C8
Thicket Gr RG7 . . . . .38 F7
Thicket Rd RG30. . . . . .85 B7
Thickthorne La TW18 . . . .97 C1

Third Ave
Marlow SL7 . . . . 1 F2
Reading RG31 . . . . 84 B6
Tadley RG7. . . . . 135 C2
Third Cres SL1. . . . . 42 C8
Third St E RG19. . . . . . . 132 A5
Thirkleby Cl SL1. . . . . . . 42 C5
Thirlmere Ave
Burnham SL1. . . . . 41 C8
Reading RG30 . . . . 57 F1
Thirlmere Cl TW20 . . . . . 96 B1
Thirlmere Wlk GU15 . . . 152 D4
Thirtover RG18 . . . . 79 B1
Thistledown RG31. . . . . . 57 C1
Thistleton Way RG6. . . . 87 E2
Thomas Askew Ho [1]
RG14 . . . . 104 E1
Thomas Ct SL6 . . . . 39 A2
Thomas Dr RG42. . . . . . . 91 E1
Thomas Knyvett Coll
TW15 . . . . 97 E5
Thomas La RG40 . . . . . . 141 E8
Thomas Merriman Ct
RG14 . . . . 105 A2
Thompkins La SL2 . . . . . 22 A5
Thompson Cl
Hermitage RG18 . . . . . . 78 F6
Slough SL3 . . . . 44 A2
Thompson Dr RG19 . . . . 106 E2
Thompsons Yd [13] RG1 . . 86 B6
Thomson Wlk RG1. . . . . . 84 E4
Thorburn Chase GU47. . 150 E6
Thornaby Pl HP10 . . . . 3 E8
Thornbank Cl TW19 . . . . . 70 A2
Thornbers Way RG10. . . . 61 B5
Thornbridge Rd RG2. . . . 113 B8
Thornbury Cl RG45. . . . . 143 B5
Thornbury Gn RG10. . . . . 61 D5
Thorn Cl RG41. . . . . 115 C3
Thorncroft TW20. . . . . 95 F1
Thorndike SL2. . . . . 42 B8
Thorndown La GU20 . . . 146 D3
Thorn Dr SL3 . . . . 43 E7
Thorne Cl
Crowthorne RG45 . . . . . 143 C4
Henley-on-T RG9 . . . . . . 35 B8
Littleton TW15. . . . . 98 C1
Thorney Cl RG6. . . . . 87 E2
Thorney Ho RG2. . . . . 86 A2
Thorney La N SL0. . . . . . . 44 F6
Thorney La S SL0 . . . . . . 44 F5
Thornfield RG19 . . . . . . 132 D3
Thornfield Gn GU17. . . . 150 F3
Thornford Rd RG19 . . . . 132 E3
Thornhill RG12 . . . . 118 E5
Thornhill Way TW17. . . . 125 A4
Thorningdown OX11 . . . . 10 D8
Thorn La [6] RG1. . . . . 86 B7
Thorn St RG1. . . . . 86 A7
Thornton Mews
Crowthorne RG45 . . . . . 143 C4
Reading RG30 . . . . 85 C8
Thornton Rd RG30. . . . . . 85 C8
Thornycroft Cl [1] RG14. 105 B3
Thorp Cl RG42. . . . . 90 C3
THORPE 123 C6
Thorpe By-Pass TW20. . 123 B6
Thorpe CE Inf Sch TW20 123 B6
Thorpe Cl RG41. . . . . 116 A3
THORPE GREEN 123 A5
Thorpe Ho [4] RG30 . . . . 85 B7
Thorpe Ind Est TW20. . . 123 C7
Thorpe Ind Pk TW20 . . . 123 C8
THORPE LEA 96 B1
Thorpe Lea Prim Sch
TW20 . . . . 96 D2
Thorpe Lea Rd TW20 . . . 96 C2
Thorpe Park TW20 . . . . 123 E5
Thorpe Rd
Chertsey KT16. . . . . 123 D4
Egham TW18, TW20. . . . 96 D3
Thorpeside Cl TW18,
TW20 . . . . 123 E7
Thrale Mews RG30 . . . . . 85 B8
Three Acre Rd RG14 . . . 130 F8
Three Firs Way RG7. . . . 110 F1
Three Gables La RG8 . . . 34 A7
THREE MILE CROSS . . . 113 B4
Three Post La [1] RG17. . 25 B2
Threshfield RG12 . . . . . 118 A4
Thrift La SL6 . . . . 39 D1
Throgmorton Rd GU46. . 149 A5
Thrush Cl RG7. . . . . 111 B3
Thurlby Way SL6. . . . . . . 39 D3
Thurlestone Cl TW17. . . 125 C3
Thurlestone Gdns RG2. . 86 C2
Thurlestone La RG2. . . . . 86 C2
Thurley Bsns Units RG7 112 C1
Thurley Cotts SL3. . . . . . 23 B3
Thurlow Grange [4] RG14 104 F1
Thurnscoe Cl RG6. . . . . . 113 F8
Thurso Cl RG30 . . . . 85 A8
Thurston Rd SL1. . . . . 42 E7
Thyme Cl RG6. . . . . 87 A1
Tichborne Cl GU17. . . . . 150 D5
Tichbourne Cl GU16 . . . 151 F3
Tickenor Dr RG40. . . . . . 141 F7
Tickhill Cl RG6 . . . . 113 F7
Tickleback Row RG42. . . 91 A6
Tides End Ct GU15. . . . . 151 F4
TIDMARSH. 56 C2
Tidmarsh Barn RG8. . . . . 56 C2
Tidmarsh Cl RG8 . . . . 56 C1
Tidmarsh Grange RG8 . . 56 C1
Tidmarsh La RG8 . . . . 56 B2
Tidmarsh St [1] RG30. . . 85 B8

Tidwells Lea RG12 . . . . 118 E8
Tierney Ct [2] SL7. . . . . 1 E1
Tiffany Cl RG41. . . . . . . 115 D6
Tiger Cl RG5 . . . . 88 B7
Tigerseye Cl RG41 . . . . 115 D7
Tiggell Cl RG6. . . . . 87 D4
Tilbury Cl RG4. . . . . 59 C3
Tilbury Wlk SL3 . . . . 44 B3
Tilebarn Cl RG9 . . . . 15 C1
Tile Barn Row RG20. . . . 129 E1
Tilecotes Cl SL7 . . . . 1 D2
TILEHURST 57 E1
Tilehurst La RG42. . . . . . 90 D3
Tilehurst Rd RG1, RG30 . 85 D7
Tilehurst Sta RG31. . . . . 57 E2
Tilling Cl RG31 . . . . 57 B2
Tilly's La TW18 . . . . 96 F4
Tilney Way
Earley RG6. . . . . 113 F8
Lower Earley RG6 . . . . . 114 A8
Tilstone Ave SL4 . . . . 41 E2
Tilstone Cl SL4 . . . . 41 E2
Timberley Pl RG45. . . . . 142 E4
Timbers Wlk SL6. . . . . . . 39 B5
Timber Yd The GU24 . . . 153 D4
Timeline Gn RG12. . . . . . 118 F7
Timson Ct RG14 . . . . 105 B3
Timsway TW18. . . . . 96 F3
Tindal Cl GU46 . . . . 149 D6
Tinkers La SL4. . . . . 66 D5
Tinsway Cl TW20 . . . . 96 B3
Tinsley Cl RG6. . . . . 113 F8
Tintagel Dr [1] GU16 . . . 151 F1
Tintagel Farm Cl RG40 . 142 B8
Tintagel Ho SL1 . . . . 42 C5
Tintagel Rd RG40. . . . . . 142 A8
Tintern Cl SL1 . . . . 42 C3
Tintern Cres RG1. . . . . . . 85 F5
Tinwell Cl RG6 . . . . 87 E2
Tippett Rise RG2 . . . . 86 B5
Tippings La RG5 . . . . 88 A8
Tippits Mead RG42 . . . . 117 D8
Tiptree Cl RG6. . . . . 113 F8
Tiree Ho SL2 . . . . 42 B8
Titan Ho RG7. . . . . 134 C2
TITCOMB. 127 F7
Titcombe Way RG17 . . . 102 A2
Tite Hill TW20 . . . . 95 D3
Tithe Barn Dr SL6 . . . . . . 40 E1
Tithebarn Gr RG31. . . . . 84 F4
Tithe Cl
Maidenhead SL6 . . . . . . 40 C1
Wentworth GU25. . . . . . 122 D3
Tithe Ct
Slough SL3. . . . . 44 A2
Wokingham RG40 . . . . . 116 C7
Tithe La TW19 . . . . 69 A1
Tithe Mdws GU25. . . . . . 122 D3
Titlarks Hill Rd SL5. . . . 121 B1
TITTLE ROW 39 A5
Tiverton Cl RG5. . . . . 60 E1
Tiverton Way GU16. . . . 151 F1
Toad La GU17. . . . . 150 F4
Tobermory Cl SL3. . . . . . 43 E2
Tocker Gdns RG42 . . . . . 91 B2
Tockington Ct GU46. . . . 149 D6
Tockley Rd SL1 . . . . 21 B2
Tofrek Terr RG30. . . . . . . 85 C7
TOKERS GREEN 58 D8
Tokers Green La RG4. . . 58 D7
Tollgate SL6. . . . . 39 A6
Toll Gdns RG12 . . . . 118 F6
Tolpuddle Way RG46. . . 149 F5
Tomlin Cl RG19 . . . . 106 E2
Tomlin Rd SL2 . . . . 21 E1
Tomlins Ave GU16. . . . . 151 F2
Tomlinscote Sch & Sixth
Form Coll GU16 . . . . . 152 A2
Tomlinscote Way GU16. 152 A2
Tomlinson Dr RG40 . . . . 142 A7
Tonkins Dr RG19. . . . . . . 106 E2
Toogood Pl RG42 . . . . . . 91 D3
Topaz Cl
Slough SL1. . . . . 42 B5
Wokingham RG41 . . . . . 115 E7
Topaz Ct [11] TW13 . . . . 98 F5
Top Common RG42 . . . . . 91 D1
Tope Cres RG2. . . . . 140 F7
Tope Rd RG2 . . . . 140 F8
Torcross Gr RG31. . . . . . . 84 B4
Torin Ct TW20. . . . . 95 D4
Torleven Hts RG42 . . . . . 90 D3
Torquay Spur SL2. . . . . . 22 B2
Torridge Rd SL3 . . . . 69 B8
Torrington Rd RG2. . . . . 86 C2
Toseland Way RG6. . . . . . 87 B3
Totale Rise RG42. . . . . . . 91 B2
TOT HILL. 130 E1
Totnes Rd RG2 . . . . 86 C2
Tottenham Wlk GU47 . . 143 C1
Totterdown RG7 . . . . 110 F1
TOUCHEN-END. 64 D5
Toulouse Cl GU15. . . . . . 152 B7
Toutley Cl RG41. . . . . 88 F1
Toutley Rd RG41. . . . . . . 89 A1
Toutley Works RG41. . . . 89 A2
Tower Cl
Caversham RG4. . . . . . . 59 C8
Flackwell Heath HP10 . . . 3 C7
Tower Ct SL4, TW20. . . . . 96 A3
Tower Hill RG20 . . . . 49 A8
Tower Ho
Iver SL0 . . . . 44 F7
Marlow SL7 . . . . 1 B1
[4] Slough SL1 . . . . 42 F4
Towers Dr RG45. . . . . . . 143 B4
Town Farm Prim Sch
TW19 . . . . 97 D8

Town Farm Way TW19. . 97 D8
Town Hall (Mus) KT15 . 124 A2
Town La
Stanwell TW19 . . . . 97 D7
Wooburn HP10 . . . . 3 D4
Townlands Hospl RG9 . . 15 D2
Town Mills [6] RG14 . . . 105 A3
Town Pl [8] RG1. . . . . 86 D7
Town Quay TW18 . . . . . . 124 C6
Townsend Cl RG12 . . . . 118 E4
Townsend Rd
Aldworth RG8 . . . . 32 E3
Ashford TW15. . . . . 97 E3
Streatley RG8 . . . . 34 A8
Townside Pl GU15. . . . . . 151 D6
Town Sq
Bracknell RG12 . . . . 118 C7
Camberley GU15. . . . . . 151 C6
[9] Slough SL1 . . . . 42 F4
Town Tree Rd TW15 . . . . 98 A3
Tozer Wlk SL4 . . . . 66 D4
Tracey Ave [12] SL3 . . . . 43 F1
Tracy Ave SL3 . . . . 43 F1
Trafalgar Cl RG41. . . . . . 115 E6
Trafalgar Ct RG1. . . . . . . 85 D6
Trafalgar Way GU15. . . . 150 F4
Trafford Rd RG1. . . . . 58 E1
Transcend [6] SL4 . . . . . 67 C5
TRAPSHILL 127 F4
TRASH GREEN 111 B7
Travic Rd SL2 . . . . 21 F2
Travis Ct SL2 . . . . 22 B2
Travis La GU47. . . . . 150 C2
Treacher Ct RG10 . . . . . . 61 E5
Treble Ho Terr OX11 . . . . 12 A8
Tredegar Rd RG4 . . . . . . 59 A6
Tree Cl RG30 . . . . 84 F8
Treesmill Dr SL6. . . . . . . 39 C3
Trees Rd SL8 . . . . 3 B3
Treeton Cl RG6 . . . . 113 F8
Treetops RG4. . . . . 58 F2
Tree Tops Ave GU15 . . . . 152 B8
Trefoil Cl RG40 . . . . 116 E7
Trefoil Dro RG18. . . . . . . 106 F4
Treforgan RG4. . . . . 58 F5
Trelawney Ave SL3. . . . . 43 F3
Trelawney Dr RG31. . . . . 57 B1
Trelawney Ind Ct SL3 . . 43 E3
Trelleck Rd RG2. . . . . 86 D2
Tremayne Wlk GU15 . . . 152 C4
Trenchard Rd SL6. . . . . . 65 B8
Trenches La SL0, SL3. . . 44 A6
TRENCH GREEN 58 A8
Trent Cl RG41 . . . . 115 E7
Trent Cres RG18 . . . . 106 B5
Trenthams Cl RG8 . . . . . 57 B5
Trenton Cl RG8 . . . . 67 D7
Trenton Cl GU16 . . . . 152 A1
Trent Rd SL3 . . . . 69 B8
Trent Villas Est SL3 . . . . 68 B6
Tresham Cres RG46. . . . . 149 A6
Tressell The SL6 . . . . 39 D6
Trevelyan RG12 . . . . 117 E2
Trevelyan Ct SL4 . . . . . . 67 B5
Trevelyan Mid Sch SL4 . 67 C3
Trewithick Cl TW14 . . . . 98 F7
Trevor Cl TW19 . . . . 70 A2
Trevor Ho [2] RG30. . . . . 85 B7
Trevose Ho SL2 . . . . 22 B1
Treyarnon Ct RG1. . . . . . 86 E6
Triangle The
Newbury RG14. . . . . 131 B7
Reading RG30 . . . . 84 D8
Trident Ho TW19 . . . . 97 E8
Trident Ind Est SL3 . . . . 69 E4
Trilakes Ctry Pk GU46,
GU47 . . . . 149 E8
Trimble Hall SL5. . . . . . . 120 D2
Trindledown RG42 . . . . . 91 A2
Tringham Cotts GU24 . . 153 F7
Tring Rd RG31. . . . . 57 C2
Trinity Av SL7 . . . . 1 D3
Trinity CE Prim Sch RG9 15 D1
Trinity Cl TW19 . . . . 70 C1
Trinity Cres SL5. . . . . 121 A4
Trinity Ct
Bracknell RG12 . . . . 117 F7
Marlow SL7 . . . . 1 D3
[16] Newbury RG14 . . . 104 F2
Theale RG7 . . . . 83 D3
Trinity Ho SL6 . . . . 19 F6
Trinity Pl
Reading RG1. . . . . 85 F7
Windsor SL4 . . . . 67 C5
Trinity Rd SL7 . . . . 1 D2
Trinity St Stephens CE Fst
Sch SL4. . . . . 67 B6
Trinity Sch RG40. . . . . . . 116 A5
Triumph Cl
Harlington UB7 . . . . 71 C6
Woodley RG5 . . . . 87 F5
Troon Ct
Ascot SL5. . . . . 120 C4
[21] Reading RG1 . . . . . 86 D7
Troston Ct [10] TW19 . . . 70 E1
Trotsford Mdw GU17. . . 150 C4
Trotswood Cl GU15. . . . . 152 C5
Trotsworth Ave GU25 . . 122 D5
Trotsworth Ct GU25 . . . 122 D5
Trotwood Cl GU47. . . . . 143 E2
Troutbeck Cl
Slough SL2 . . . . 43 A6
Twyford RG10 . . . . 61 D6
Troutbeck Wlk GU15. . . 152 D3
Trout Cl
Earley RG6. . . . . 87 A8
Marlow SL7 . . . . 18 C3
Trout Wlk RG14 . . . . 105 C4

Trowe's La
Beech Hill RG7. . . . . . . 138 D4
Swallowfield RG7. . . . . . 139 D5
Trumbull Rd RG40 . . . . . 91 A1
Trumper Way SL1. . . . . . 41 F5
TRUMPS GREEN 122 D3
Trumps Green Ave GU25 122 D3
Trumps Green Cl GU25. 122 E4
Trumps Green Inf Sch
GU25 . . . . 122 D3
Trumpsgreen Rd GU25. 122 D3
Trumps Mill La GU25. . . 122 F4
Truro Cl SL6. . . . . 39 A7
Truss Hill Rd SL5. . . . . . 120 C4
Trust Cnr RG9 . . . . 35 E8
Trusthorpe Cl RG6. . . . . 113 F8
Tubbs Farm Cl RG17 . . . 25 B2
Tubwell Rd SL2. . . . . 23 B4
Tudor Ave RG20. . . . . 51 C4
Tudor Cl
Ashford TW15. . . . . 97 E4
Wokingham RG40 . . . . . 116 F5
Tudor Ct
[2] Egham TW20 . . . . . . 96 A3
[18] Egham TW20 . . . . . 96 A3
Maidenhead SL6 . . . . . . 20 C2
[3] Stanwell TW19 . . . . . 70 E1
Tudor Dr RG42 . . . . 118 C4
Tudor Gdns RG5 . . . . 87 F7
Tudor Ho RG12 . . . . 118 B4
Tudor La SL4 . . . . 95 C8
Tudor Mill HP10 . . . . 3 E8
Tudor Rd
Ashford TW15. . . . . 98 D2
Newbury RG14. . . . . 105 A1
Reading RG1. . . . . 86 A8
Tudor Way SL4 . . . . 66 E6
Tulip Ho RG18 . . . . 106 E3
Tull Way RG18 . . . . 106 E4
Tunnel Link Rd TW6 . . . . 71 A1
Tunnel E TW6 . . . . 71 B6
Tunnel Rd W TW6. . . . . . 71 B6
Tuns Hill Cotts RG6. . . . 87 A5
Tuns La
Henley-on-T RG9 . . . . . . 15 E2
Slough SL1. . . . . 42 C4
Tupsley Rd RG1. . . . . 85 F5
Turbary Gdns RG26. . . . 135 B1
Turf Hill Rd GU15 . . . . . 151 F8
Turing Dr RG12 . . . . 118 A4
Turks Head Ct SL4 . . . . . 67 D7
Turk's La RG7 . . . . 137 A4
Turmeric Cl RG6. . . . . . . 87 A2
Turnberry RG12 . . . . 117 E2
Turnberry Ho SL5. . . . . . 121 A1
Turnberry Rd [18] RG1 . . 86 D7
Turnbridge Cl RG6. . . . . 114 B8
Turner Pl GU47 . . . . 150 D6
Turners Cl RG31 . . . . 84 A5
Turners Ct RG19 . . . . 97 B3
Turners Dr RG19 . . . . . . 106 E2
Turnery The RG19. . . . . . 106 C3
Turnoak Pk SL4. . . . . 66 E3
Turnpike Ind Est RG14 . 105 D5
Turnpike Rd
Bracknell RG42 . . . . 117 D7
Newbury RG14, RG18 . . 105 E4
Turnstone Cl RG41. . . . . 88 B3
Turnstone End GU46 . . . 149 B6
Turnville Cl GU18 . . . . . . 146 A1
Turpin Rd TW14. . . . . 71 F2
Turpins Gn SL6 . . . . 39 A5
Turpins Rise GU20 . . . . . 146 D7
Turtle Twrs RG1. . . . . 86 A7
Turton Way SL1 . . . . 42 D3
Tuscam Way GU15 . . . . 150 F4
Tuscan Cl RG30 . . . . 57 E1
Tuscany Ct [2] SL6 . . . . . 39 E7
Tuscany Villas GU18. . . 146 B1
TUTTS CLUMP 81 F3
Tuxford Mews RG30 . . . . 85 B7
Tweed Cl RG30 . . . . 85 A8
Tweed Rd SL3 . . . . 69 B8
Twelve Trees Ho RG45. . 143 C4
Twinches La SL1 . . . . 42 B5
Twin Oaks RG4 . . . . 59 B6
Twinwoods RG20. . . . . . . 49 A4
Two Mile Dr SL1 . . . . 41 E4
Two Rivers Sh Ctr TW18. 96 E3
Two Rivers Way RG14 . . 105 D3
Two Tree Hill RG9 . . . . . . 35 B8
Twycross Rd RG40 . . . . . 116 E7
TWYFORD. 61 D5
Twyford Bsns Pk RG10 . . 61 D4
Twyford Orchards Cvn Pk
RG10 . . . . 61 F7
Twyford Rd
Binfield RG10, RG42 . . . 90 C7
Waltham St L RG10 . . . . 62 E6
Twyford Sta RG10 . . . . . . 61 E4
Twynersh Ave KT16. . . . 123 F3
Twynham Rd SL6 . . . . 39 B7
Tydehams RG14 . . . . 130 F8
Tyle Pl SL4 . . . . 68 A2
Tyle Rd RG30 . . . . 57 E1
Tylers La RG7 . . . . 80 B1
Tyler's Way RG7 . . . . 84 F8
Tylers Pl RG4 . . . . 84 F8

Tyler Wlk [4] SL3 . . . . . . 43 F1
Tylorstown RG4. . . . . 58 F5
Tymawr RG4. . . . . 58 F5
Tyndale Mews SL1 . . . . . 42 B4
Tyne Way RG18 . . . . 106 B5
Tyrell Gdns SL4. . . . . 66 F4
Tyrrel Ct [20] RG1 . . . . . 86 C7
Tytherton RG12 . . . . 118 C7

U

Uffcott Cl RG6. . . . . 113 F7
Uffington Cl RG31 . . . . . 84 C8
Uffington Dr RG12 . . . . . 118 E5
Ufton Court Yd SL8 . . . . . 3 B4
Ufton Ct SL8 . . . . 3 B4
UFTON GREEN 110 B5
UFTON NERVET 110 D3
Ullswater RG12 . . . . 117 F2
Ullswater Cl
Burnham SL1. . . . . 41 C8
Lightwater GU18 . . . . . . 146 B1
Thatcham RG19 . . . . . . 106 A3
Ullswater Dr RG31. . . . . . 57 D3
Ullswater Rd GU18. . . . . 146 B1
Ulster Cl RG4 . . . . 59 D5
Umberstone GU25 . . . . . 122 D3
Umberville Way SL2 . . . . 21 F2
Underhill OX10 . . . . 14 A4
Underhill Cl SL6. . . . . 39 E6
Underwood RG12 . . . . . . 117 E3
Underwood Cotts RG8 . . 33 F6
Underwood Rd RG30 . . . 57 F1
Underwood Sh Ctr RG30 57 F1
Union Cl GU47. . . . . 143 E2
Union Rd RG7 . . . . 82 D4
Union St RG1. . . . . 86 A8
Unity Cl RG4 . . . . 59 B6
Unity Ct RG4 . . . . 59 B6
Unity Ho RG19 . . . . 132 A4
Univ of Reading
Earley RG6. . . . . 87 B6
Reading RG1. . . . . 86 C6
Reading, Whiteknights RG6 86 F4
Unwin Ave TW14 . . . . 71 D2
Upavon Dr RG1. . . . . 85 F5
Upavon Gdns RG12 . . . . 118 F4
Upcroft SL4 . . . . 67 B4
Upcroft Prim Sch RG30 . 84 F8
Updown Hill GU20 . . . . . 146 D4
Upland Rd GU15. . . . . . . 151 D7
Uplands
Hungerford RG17 . . . . . 100 C5
Marlow Bottom SL7 . . . . 1 D6
Uplands Cl GU47. . . . . . . 150 B8
Uplands Prim Sch GU47. 150 B8
Uplands Rd RG4 . . . . 58 E5
UPPER BASILDON 55 A5
Upper Bray Rd SL6 . . . . . 40 C3
Upper Broadmoor Rd
RG45 . . . . 143 D5
UPPER BUCKLEBURY . . 107 C6
Upper Chobham Rd
GU15 . . . . 152 B4
Upper College Ride
GU15 . . . . 151 E8
Upper Crown St RG1 . . . 86 B6
Upper Culham Farm RG10 36 E8
Upper Eddington RG17. 100 E7
Upper End RG20 . . . . 49 A8
Upper Gordon Rd GU15 151 D5
UPPER GREEN 127 D3
Upper Halliford Rd
TW17. . . . . 125 D5
Upper Halliford Sta
TW17. . . . . 125 E5
UPPER LAMBOURN 24 F6
Upper Lambourn Rd
RG17. . . . . 25 A3
Upper Lees Rd SL2 . . . . . 22 B2
Upper Meadow Rd RG2. 86 D2
Upper Nursery SL5 . . . . 121 A4
Upper Park Rd GU15. . . 151 E6
Upper Raymond Almshouses
[14] RG14 . . . . 104 F2
Upper Red Cross Rd RG8 34 C7
Upper Redlands Rd RG1 86 E5
Upper Star Terr RG41 . . 115 B8
Upper Thames Way SL8 . 3 B3
Upper Ventnor Cotts SL6 19 C8
Upper Verran Rd GU15 . 151 D3
Upper Village Rd SL5 . . . 120 F4
UPPER WARGRAVE 36 F2
Upper Warren Ave RG4 . 58 D3
Upper Wlk GU25 . . . . 122 C5
UPPER
WOOLHAMPTON 108 C4
Uppingham Dr RG5. . . . . 60 F1
Uppingham Gdns RG4. . 59 D6
Upshire Gdns RG12. . . . 118 F5
UPTON 43 A3
Upton Cl
Henley-on-T RG9 . . . . . . 15 E1
Slough SL1. . . . . 42 F3
Upton Court Rd SL3 . . . . 43 B2
Upton Court Sch SL3 . . . 43 A2
Upton Hospl SL1 . . . . 42 F3
Upton House Sch SL4. . . 67 C5
UPTON LEA 43 A5
Upton Lea Par SL3 . . . . . 43 B6
UPTON PARK 42 F3
Upton Pk SL1. . . . . 42 F3

188 Upt–Wav

Upton Rd
Reading RG30 . . . . .85 B7
Slough SL1, SL3. . . . . .43 A3
Urbis Apartments SL4. . . . .66 E5
Urquhart Rd RG19 . . . . . . .106 E2
Usk Rd RG30 . . . . .84 F6
Uxbridge Rd SL1, SL2, SL3. .43 C6

V

Vachel Rd RG1. . . . . .86 A8
Vale Cres RG30 . . . . .57 E1
Vale Gr SL1. . . . . .42 E3
Valentia Rd RG30 . . . . .85 D8
Valentine Cl RG6 . . . . .86 F1
Valentine Cres RG4 . . . . . . .59 C4
Vale Rd
Camberley GU15 . . . . . . .151 A4
Windsor SL4 . . . . .66 F6
Valerie Ct RG1. . . . . .85 E6
Vale View RG10 . . . . .61 B4
Vale View Dr RG7 . . . . .138 D5
Valley Cl
Caversham RG4. . . . . .59 A4
Goring RG8 . . . . .34 C6
Valley Cres RG41. . . . . .116 A8
Valley End SL3. . . . . .23 C1
Valley Gardens* TW20 . .121 E7
Valley Rd
Burghfield Common RG7 . .111 A3
Frimley GU16. . . . . .152 C1
Henley-on-T RG9 . . . . . . .35 B8
Newbury RG14. . . . . .130 C8
Valley Road Sch RG9. . . . . .35 C8
Valley View GU47 . . . . .150 A7
Valley Vineyards* RG10 . .62 A3
Valley Way RG26. . . . . .135 E1
Valon Rd RG2. . . . . .140 F8
Valpy St RG1 . . . . .86 B8
Valroy Cl GU15. . . . . .151 D6
Vanbrugh Ct [1] RG1. . . . . . .86 E7
Vandyke RG12 . . . . .117 E3
Vanguard Ho [5] TW19 . . . . .70 E1
Vanguard Way TW6 . . . . . . .71 E5
Vanlore Way RG31 . . . . .84 C5
Vanners La RG20. . . . . .129 D5
Vansittart Est SL4. . . . . .67 C6
Vansittart Rd
Bisham SL7 . . . . .18 E7
Windsor SL4 . . . . .67 B6
Vantage Ct UB3. . . . . .71 E7
Vantage Rd SL1 . . . . .42 B5
Vanwall Bsns Pk SL6. . . . . .39 C5
Vanwall Rd SL6 . . . . .39 C4
Vastern Rd RG1 . . . . .59 B1
Vaughan Almshouses [1]
TW15 . . . . .98 B3
Vaughan Copse SL4 . . . . . . .42 D2
Vaughan Gdns SL4 . . . . . . .41 F2
Vaughan Way SL2 . . . . .22 E1
Vauxhall Dr RG5 . . . . .88 A6
Vegal Cres TW20 . . . . .95 C3
Veitch Cl TW14 . . . . .98 F8
Venetia Cl RG4 . . . . .59 C7
Venning Rd RG2 . . . . .140 F8
Ventnor Rd RG31 . . . . .57 D1
Venture Ho TW18 . . . . .97 A4
Venus Cl
Slough SL2. . . . . .21 F1
Wokingham RG41. . . . . . .115 F6
Verbena Cl RG41. . . . . .88 A3
Verdon Ct SL2 . . . . .22 B2
Verey Cl RG10 . . . . .61 F3
Verica Gdns RG26. . . . . . . .135 E2
Vermillion Ct [10] TW13 . . . .98 F5
Vermont Rd SL2 . . . . .21 F1
Vermont Woods RG40 . . . . .141 E7
Verney Cl SL7 . . . . .1 D2
Verney Mews RG30 . . . . . . .85 C7
Verney Rd SL3. . . . . .44 A2
Vernon Cl TW19. . . . . .97 E7
Vernon Cres RG2 . . . . .113 B7
Vernon Ct SL5. . . . . .119 D6
Vernon Dr SL5. . . . . .119 E7
Vernon Rd TW13 . . . . .98 F6
Verran Rd GU15 . . . . .151 D3
Vibia Cl TW19. . . . . .97 D8
Viburnum Ct GU24 . . . . . . .153 E6
Vicarage Ave TW20 . . . . . . .96 B3
Vicarage Cl
Cookham SL6. . . . . .20 B7
Finchampstead RG40. . . .141 F6
Vicarage Cres TW20. . . . . . .96 B3
Vicarage Ct
East Bedfont TW14 . . . . . .98 C8
Egham TW20. . . . . .96 B2
Shinfield RG2. . . . . .113 D5
Vicarage Dr SL6. . . . . .40 C4
Vicarage Flats SL4. . . . . . . .67 D8
Vicarage Gdns
Ascot SL5. . . . . .120 A4
White Waltham SL6. . . . . .63 F8
Vicarage La
Cold Ash RG18. . . . . .106 C8
Laleham TW18 . . . . .124 C6
Wraysbury TW19. . . . . . . .95 F7
Yateley GU46. . . . . .149 C7
Vicarage Rd
Ashford TW16. . . . . .98 F2
Bagshot GU19 . . . . .145 E8
Blackwater GU17. . . . . . .150 E4
Egham TW20. . . . . .96 B3
Henley-on-T RG9 . . . . . . .35 E8
Maidenhead SL6. . . . . . . .39 F8

Vicarage Rd *continued*
Reading RG2 . . . . .86 C5
Staines TW18. . . . . .96 E5
Yateley GU46. . . . . .149 C7
Vicarage Way SL3 . . . . .69 D7
Vicarage Wlk SL6. . . . . .40 C4
Vicarage Wood Way RG31 57 B1
Vickers Cl
Shinfield RG2. . . . . .113 F4
Woodley RG5. . . . . .88 B7
Vickers Ct [3] TW19 . . . . . . .70 E1
Vicount Ct [2] TW15. . . . . . . .98 C1
Victor Cl SL6 . . . . .39 B8
Victoria Ave GU15. . . . . . . .151 A5
Victoria Cotts SL6 . . . . .19 C8
Victoria Cres SL0 . . . . .44 F6
Victoria Ct
Bagshot GU19 . . . . .145 E1
Camberley GU15 . . . . . . .151 A5
Henley-on-T RG9 . . . . . . .15 E1
[3] Marlow SL7 . . . . .1 F2
Slough SL1. . . . . .42 E5
Victoria Dr
Blackwater GU17. . . . . . .150 C4
Burnham SL1, SL2. . . . . . .21 F6
Victoria Gdns
Marlow SL7 . . . . .1 E2
Newbury RG14. . . . . .105 A4
Wokingham RG40. . . . . . .116 B8
Victoria Gr [6] RG14. . . . . . . .105 B2
Victoria Ho SL4. . . . . .68 A2
Victoria La UB7. . . . . .71 D8
Victoria Mews RG30 . . . . . .85 C7
Victoria News TW20. . . . . . .95 C2
Victoria Rd
Ascot SL5. . . . . .120 A4
Caversham RG4. . . . . .59 A3
Eton SL4. . . . . .41 F1
Marlow SL7 . . . . .1 E2
Mortimer RG7 . . . . .136 F6
Reading RG31 . . . . .84 D8
Sandhurst GU47 . . . . . . .143 E1
Slough SL2. . . . . .43 B5
Staines TW18. . . . . .96 E5
Wargrave RG10 . . . . .36 E2
Victoria St
Englefield Green TW20 . . .95 C2
Reading RG1 . . . . .86 D7
[10] Slough SL1. . . . . .42 F4
Windsor SL4 . . . . .67 D6
Victoria Way [8] RG1. . . . . . .86 D7
Victoria Wlk RG40 . . . . . . .116 E8
Victor Pl RG7. . . . . .108 C2
Victor Rd
Thatcham RG19 . . . . .106 E3
Windsor SL4 . . . . .67 C4
Victor Way RG5. . . . . .88 A7
Victory Cl
Reading RG30 . . . . .85 A6
Stanwell TW15, TW19. . . . .97 E7
Victory Rd KT16 . . . . .124 A1
Vigo La GU46 . . . . .149 C3
Viking RG22 . . . . .117 E4
Village Cl
Reading RG2 . . . . .113 B6
Wokingham RG41. . . . . . .115 F8
Village Ct SL5 . . . . .120 C4
Village Gate TW17 . . . . . . .125 B4
Village Mews SL5. . . . . . . .120 C5
Village Rd
Dorney SL4 . . . . .41 B3
Thorpe TW20. . . . . .123 C6
Village Sh Ctr The [5] SL3. .42 F4
VILLAGE THE 94 B5
Village The
Finchampstead RG40. . . .141 E3
Old Windsor SL4 . . . . .94 B5
Village Way
Ashford TW15. . . . . .98 A4
Yateley GU46. . . . . .149 D7
Villa Mews [2] RG1 . . . . .86 E7
Villa Pl RG7 . . . . .139 C6
Villiers Ct SL4 . . . . .67 B7
Villiers Mead RG41 . . . . . . .116 A6
Villiers Rd SL2. . . . . .22 D8
Villiers Way RG14. . . . . . . .130 C6
Villiers Wlk RG14. . . . . . . .130 C6
Vincent Cl
Chertsey KT16. . . . . .123 E2
Harmondsworth UB7. . . . .71 A8
Woodley RG5. . . . . .87 F6
Vincent Ct TW17 . . . . .125 E6
Vincent Ho [8] RG1. . . . . . . .85 F8
Vincent Rd
Chertsey KT16. . . . . .123 E2
Thatcham RG18. . . . . . . .106 E4
Vincent Rise RG12 . . . . . . .118 E6
Vine Cl TW19 . . . . .70 A2
Vine Cres RG30 . . . . .85 A4
Vine Ct
Newbury RG14. . . . . .105 B1
Stoke Poges SL2 . . . . .23 A6
Vine Rd SL2 . . . . .22 F6
Vineries Cl UB7. . . . . .71 A8
Vinery The RG10 . . . . .36 D2
Vines The RG41 . . . . .115 C3
Vineyard Dr SL8 . . . . .3 A5
Vinter Ct TW17 . . . . .125 A4
Vintners Ho RG31 . . . . .57 D1
Viola Ave TW19 . . . . .97 E7
Viola Croft RG42. . . . . .118 F8
Violet Gr RG18. . . . . .106 E5
Virginia Ave TW20 . . . . . . .122 C4
Virginia Beeches GU25. . . .122 C6
Virginia Cl TW18. . . . . .124 C6
Virginia Ct
Ashford TW15. . . . . .97 E4
Virginia Water GU25 . . . . .122 D5

Virginia Dr GU25. . . . . . . .122 C5
VIRGINIA WATER 122 C6
Virginia Water* SL5 . . . . .121 E6
Virginia Water Sta GU25 .122 E4
Virginia Way RG30 . . . . . . .85 B5
Viridian Ct [10] TW13 . . . . . . .98 F5
Viscount Ct SL4. . . . . .67 C6
Viscount Ind Est SL3 . . . . . .69 E4
Viscount Rd TW19 . . . . .97 F7
Viscount Way
Hatton TW6 . . . . .71 E3
Woodley RG5. . . . . .88 A7
Vivien Cl SL6 . . . . .19 F6
Vivienne Ho TW18 . . . . . . .97 A3
Voller Dr RG31. . . . . .84 C6
Volunteer Rd RG7. . . . . .83 D2
Vo-Tec Ctr RG14. . . . . .105 E2
Vulcan Cl
Sandhurst GU47 . . . . . . .150 A7
Woodley RG5. . . . . .61 B1
Vulcan Ct GU47 . . . . .150 A7
Vulcan Dr RG12. . . . . .118 D6
Vulcan Ho RG7. . . . . .134 E2
Vulcan Way GU47 . . . . .150 B7

W

Waborne Rd SL8. . . . . .3 B4
Wade Dr SL1 . . . . .42 A5
Wadham GU47. . . . . .143 F1
Wadham Cl TW17 . . . . .125 C2
Wagbullock Rise RG12. . . .118 C3
Waggoners Hollow
GU19 . . . . .145 E2
Wagner Cl SL6. . . . . .38 F3
Wagtail Cl RG10 . . . . .61 E4
Waingel's Copse Sch RG5 .61 A2
Waingels Rd RG5, RG10. . . .61 A2
Wainscot SL5 . . . . .120 F3
Wainwright Cl RG40 . . . . . .117 A6
Wakefield Cres SL2 . . . . . . .22 F6
Wakeford Cl RG26. . . . . . . .135 E1
Wakeford Ct RG26. . . . . . . .135 E1
Wakelins End SL6. . . . . .19 E7
Wakeman Rd SL8 . . . . .3 A3
Wakemans RG8. . . . . .55 D4
Walbury RG12 . . . . .118 E5
Waldeck Ho SL6. . . . . .40 A7
Waldeck Rd SL6. . . . . .40 A7
Waldeck St RG1 . . . . .86 B5
Walden Ave RG2. . . . . .114 C3
Waldens Cl SL8. . . . . .3 A3
Waldorf Hts GU17. . . . . . . .150 D3
Waldron Hill RG12 . . . . . . .118 F6
Waldrons The RG17 . . . . . . .47 C6
Waleys Pl [2] RG4 . . . . .59 C2
Walgrove Gdns SL6 . . . . . . .63 E7
Walker Cl TW14. . . . . .98 F8
Walker Cres SL3 . . . . .43 F1
Walker Ct SL6. . . . . .39 D7
Walker's La RG17 . . . . .25 B3
Walkers Pl RG30. . . . . .85 C7
Walker's Ridge GU15. . . . .151 E5
Walk The
Ashford TW16. . . . . .98 F1
Eton SL4. . . . . .42 A1
Wallace Cl
Marlow SL7 . . . . .1 F4
Upper Halliford TW17 . . . .125 D5
Woodley RG5. . . . . .87 D5
Wallace Gr RG7. . . . . .113 A4
Wallace Wlk SL4. . . . . .42 F1
Wallcroft Cl RG42. . . . . . . .90 E1
Walled Garden The SL7 . .18 A6
Walled Gdn The
Beech Hill RG7 . . . . .138 E5
Wallingford RG10. . . . . . . .36 D2
Waller Ct RG4 . . . . .59 B2
Waller Dr RG14 . . . . .105 E5
Wallingford Cl RG12 . . . . .118 E5
Wallingford Rd
Compton RG20. . . . . .31 E5
South Moreton, OX10 . . . . .14 A1
South Stoke RG8, OX10. . . .14 C5
Streatley RG8 . . . . .34 A7
Wallington Rd GU15 . . . . . .145 A1
Wallingtons Rd RG17. . . . . .101 F1
Wallis Ct SL1 . . . . .43 A4
Wallis Gdns RG41. . . . . . . .131 B8
Wall La RG7 . . . . .136 D2
Wallner Way RG40 . . . . . . .116 C5
Walmer Cl
Crowthorne RG45 . . . . . .143 C5
Reading RG30 . . . . .85 A6
Walmer Rd RG5. . . . . .60 F1
Walnut Cl
Thatcham RG18 . . . . .106 C4
Wokingham RG41. . . . . . .115 F5
Yateley GU46. . . . . .149 D4
Walnut Ct [3] RG40. . . . . . . .116 C6
Walnut Gr HP10 . . . . .3 E8
Walnut Ln SL1. . . . . .42 D3
Walnut Mews RG42. . . . . . .117 F8
Walnut Tree Cl
Englefield Green TW20 . . . .95 B3
Twyford RG10. . . . . .61 F6
Walnut Tree Cotts RG20 . . .75 D8
Walnut Tree Ho RG20 . . . . .34 C6
Walnut Tree Ho TW20 . . . . .95 F3
Walnut Tree Rd TW17 . . . .125 C7
Walnut Way
Brimpton RG7 . . . . .3 B2
Reading RG30 . . . . .84 D8
Walpole Rd
Old Windsor SL4 . . . . .95 B8
Slough SL1. . . . . .41 D7

Walrus Cl RG5 . . . . .88 B7
Walsh Ave RG42 . . . . .91 E1
Walter Inf Sch RG41 . . . . .116 A6
Walter Rd RG41. . . . . .115 F7
Walters Cl RG18 . . . . .106 C8
Waltham Cl
Maidenhead SL6 . . . . .38 F2
Sandhurst GU47 . . . . . . .143 D1
Waltham Ct
Goring RG8 . . . . .34 C8
Wargrave RG10 . . . . .62 B8
Waltham Rd
Maidenhead SL6 . . . . .38 F1
Twyford RG10. . . . . .61 E4
Twyford, Ruscombe RG10 . .62 B5
**WALTHAM ST
LAWRENCE** 62 F6
**Waltham St Lawrence Prim
Sch** RG10 . . . . .62 F3
Walton Ave RG9 . . . . .35 E8
Walton Bridge Rd KT12,
TW17. . . . . .125 E2
Walton Cl RG5. . . . . .87 C7
Walton Dr SL5. . . . . .119 F8
Walton Gdns TW13. . . . . . .98 F4
Walton La
Burnham SL2 . . . . .21 F3
Lower Halliford TW17 . . . .125 D2
Oatlands Park TW17 . . . .125 E1
Walton Lodge KT12. . . . . .125 F1
Walton Manor KT12. . . . . .125 F2
Walton Way RG14. . . . . . . .105 C4
Wandhope Way RG31 . . . . .57 C2
Wansey Gdns RG14 . . . . . .105 D5
Wanstraw Gr RG12. . . . . . .118 A2
Wantage Cl RG12 . . . . .118 E4
Wantage Rd
Great Shefford RG17. . . . . .48 C5
Hungerford RG17 . . . . . . .100 E7
Lambourn RG17 . . . . .25 C5
Reading RG30 . . . . .85 C7
Sandhurst GU47 . . . . . . .150 D8
Streatley RG8 . . . . .33 F8
Wapshott Rd TW18. . . . . . .96 E3
Waram Cl RG17 . . . . .100 E7
Warbler Cl RG31 . . . . .84 B6
Warbler Dr RG6. . . . . .87 B1
Warborough Ave RG31 . . . .84 B6
Warborough Rd OX12 . . . . . .7 A7
Warbreck Dr RG31 . . . . .57 B3
Warbrook La RG27 . . . . . . .141 A1
Ward Cl
Iver SL0. . . . . .44 F7
Wokingham RG40 . . . . . .116 D8
Warde Ave RG31. . . . . .57 D1
Wardle Cl GU19 . . . . .145 E3
Wardour Lodge SL5. . . . . .120 F3
Ward Royal SL4 . . . . .67 C6
Ward Royal Par [1] SL4. . . . .67 C6
Wards Cotts TW7 . . . . .96 C2
Wards Pl TW20 . . . . .123 A6
Wards Stone Pk RG12. . . . .118 E2
Wareham Rd RG12 . . . . . . .118 F4
Warehouse Rd RG19 . . . . . .131 F5
WARFIELD 91 E5
Warfield CE Prim Sch
RG42 . . . . .91 E1
Warfield Rd
Bracknell RG12, RG42. . . . .91 C1
East Bedfont TW14 . . . . . .98 E8
Warfield Rdbt RG42. . . . . . .91 C2
Warfield St RG42 . . . . .91 D3
WARGRAVE 36 D1
Wargrave Hill RG10 . . . . . . .36 D2
Wargrave Rd
Henley-on-T RG9, RG10. . . .36 B8
Twyford RG10. . . . . .61 D5
Wargrave Sta RG10 . . . . . . .36 C1
Wargrove Dr GU47. . . . . . .150 D8
Waring Cl RG6. . . . . .114 C8
Warings The RG7 . . . . .109 A7
Warley Rise RG31 . . . . .57 C3
War Memorial Pl RG9. . . . .35 E7
Warner Cl
Harlington UB3 . . . . .71 D7
Slough SL1. . . . . .41 E5
Warner Ct GU47. . . . . .150 E7
Warners Hill SL6. . . . . .19 C8
Warnford Rd RG30 . . . . . . .84 F7
Warnham Ct RG30 . . . . . . .31 B2
Warnsham Cl [1] RG6. . . . . .87 B1
Warren Cl
Burghfield Common RG7 . .111 A3
Finchampstead RG40. . . .141 F6
Sandhurst GU47 . . . . . . .150 A8
Slough SL3. . . . . .43 E3
Warren Ct
Caversham RG4. . . . . .58 F2
Farnham Common SL2. . . .22 C7
[9] Newbury RG14. . . . . . . .105 B2
Warren Down RG42 . . . . . .117 E8
Warren Farm RG17 . . . . . . .26 B8
Warren Ho RG4 . . . . .58 F2
Warren House Ct RG4. . . . . .58 F2
Warren House Rd RG40 . . .116 D8
Warren La GU46 . . . . .141 E5
Warren Rd
Ashford TW15. . . . . .98 E1
Newbury RG14. . . . . .130 D6
Woodley RG4, RG5. . . . . . .60 D1
WARREN ROW 37 C6
Warren Row RG5. . . . . .119 F7
Warren Row Rd
Knowl Hill RG10. . . . . .37 C6
Warren Row RG10 . . . . .37 F7
Warrenside RG4 . . . . .59 A5

Warren The RG4 . . . . .58 D3
Warrington Ave SL1. . . . . . .42 C7
Warrington Spur SL4 . . . . . .95 B8
Warwick RG12 . . . . .118 E3
Warwick Ave
Slough SL2. . . . . .22 C1
Staines TW18. . . . . .97 C2
Thorpe TW20. . . . . .123 C8
Warwick Cl
Frimley GU15. . . . . .152 B3
Maidenhead SL6 . . . . .39 B4
Warwick Ct [2] SL4. . . . . . . .67 C5
Warwick Dr RG14 . . . . .105 B1
Warwick Ho RG2. . . . . .86 C4
Warwick Rd
Ashford TW15. . . . . .97 E3
Reading RG2 . . . . .86 C4
Warwick Villas TW20 . . . . .123 C8
Wasdale Cl GU47 . . . . .143 D2
Washbury Ho RG14 . . . . . .130 E7
WASH COMMON 130 D5
Wash Hill HP10 . . . . .3 E3
Wash Hill Lea HP10 . . . . . . .3 E4
Wash Hill Mobile Home Pk
HP10 . . . . .3 E3
Washington Ct
Marlow SL7 . . . . .2 A2
Thatcham RG19. . . . . . . .106 A3
Washington Dr
Slough SL1. . . . . .41 D6
Windsor SL4 . . . . .66 F5
Washington Gdns RG40 . . .142 A8
Washington Rd RG4. . . . . . .59 B2
WASH WATER 130 D4
Wasing Cnr RG7 . . . . .134 B6
Wasing La RG7 . . . . .134 B5
Watchetts Dr GU15 . . . . . .151 C2
Watchetts Jun Sch
GU15 . . . . .151 A3
Watchetts Lake Cl GU15. . .151 D3
Watchetts Rd GU15 . . . . . .151 B4
Watchmoor Pk GU15. . . . . .151 B3
Watchmoor Rd GU15. . . . . .151 B4
Watchmoor Trade Ctr
GU15 . . . . .151 A3
Waterbeach Cl SL1 . . . . .42 D7
Waterbeech Rd SL1. . . . . . .42 D7
Waterfall Cl GU25. . . . . . . .122 A6
Waterford Way RG40. . . . . .116 C6
Waterham Rd RG12 . . . . . .118 C4
Waterhouse Mead GU47. . .150 D7
Water La RG19. . . . . .131 C7
Waterloo Cl
Camberley GU15 . . . . . . .152 B7
East Bedfont TW14 . . . . . .98 F7
Moulsford OX10. . . . . .14 A7
Waterloo Cres RG40 . . . . . .116 E4
Waterloo Pl
Crowthorne RG45 . . . . . .143 B4
Reading RG2 . . . . .86 B5
Wokingham RG40 . . . . . .116 F5
Waterloo Rise RG2. . . . . . . .86 B4
Waterman Ct SL1 . . . . .41 E5
Waterman Pl RG1. . . . . .59 A1
Watermans Bsns Pk
TW18 . . . . .96 D4
Waterman's Rd RG9 . . . . . . .35 E8
Watermans Way RG10 . . . . .36 C1
Watermead TW14. . . . . .98 E7
Watermeadows The
RG14 . . . . .105 B4
Watermill Ct RG7 . . . . .108 B4
WATER OAKLEY 65 F8
Water Oakley Cotts SL4 . . . .65 F8
Water Oakley Farm Cotts
SL4. . . . . .65 F7
Water Rd RG30 . . . . .85 B7
Waters Dr TW18 . . . . .96 F4
Watersfield Cl [1] RG6. . . . . .87 B1
Waterside HP10 . . . . .3 E7
Waterside Cotts RG4 . . . . . .60 B4
Waterside Dr
Langley SL3 . . . . .43 F4
Purley on T RG8 . . . . .57 D5
Theale RG7 . . . . .83 B4
Waterside Gdns [4] RG1. . . .86 A7
Waterside Lodge SL6 . . . . . .40 C8
Watersplash La RG42 . . . . . .91 B2
Water Splash La SL5. . . . . .120 E8
Watersplash Rd TW17. . . . .125 A5
Waters Reach SL6 . . . . .20 A1
Water St RG18. . . . . .52 F6
Watery La
Chertsey KT16. . . . . .123 D2
Kintbury RG20 . . . . .128 F5
Wooburn Green HP10 . . . . .3 E8
Watkins Cl RG40. . . . . .141 E7
Watlington St RG1. . . . . . . .86 C7
Watmore La RG41. . . . . .88 D2
Watson Cl
Aldermaston Wharf RG7 . .109 C3
Finchampstead RG40. . . .115 F1
Watt's La OX11 . . . . .12 A8
Wavell Cl RG2 . . . . .86 F1
Wavell Gdns SL2 . . . . .21 F2
Wavell Rd SL6 . . . . .39 B6
Wavendene Ave TW20 . . . . .96 C3
Waverley Ct [8] RG14 . . . . . .117 E4
Waverley Cl GU15 . . . . . . .151 F4
Waverley Dr
Camberley GU15 . . . . . . .151 F5
Virginia Water GU25 . . . . .122 A5

Waverley Rd
Bagshot GU19 . . . . .145 E3
Reading RG30 . . . . .85 C7
Slough SL1 . . . . .42 C8
Waverley Sch RG40 . . . . . . .115 E1
Waverleys The RG18 . . . . . .106 D4
Waverley Way RG40 . . . . . .115 F1
WAWCOTT 102 C5
Wawcott Farm Cotts
RG20 . . . . .102 C4
Waybrook Cres RG1 . . . . . . .86 F6
Wayewood GU5 . . . . .151 E6
Wayland Cl
Bracknell RG12 . . . . .118 F5
Bradfield RG7 . . . . .82 D4
Waylands TW19 . . . . .68 E1
Waylen St RG1 . . . . .85 F7
Ways End GU15 . . . . .151 E4
Waysend Ho GU15 . . . . . . .151 E4
Wayside Cotts GU20 . . . . .146 F6
Wayside Mews SL6 . . . . .39 F8
Wealden Way RG30 . . . . . . .84 F8
Weald Rise RG30 . . . . .57 F2
Weardale Cl RG2 . . . . .86 D4
Weatherane Cotts
RG17 . . . . .100 C5
Weather Way RG12 . . . . . .118 C2
Weaver Moss GU47 . . . . . .150 B7
Weavers Cl
27 Reading RG1 . . . . .86 D7
Wokingham RG40 . . . . . . .116 C6
Weavers La RG17 . . . . .127 C6
Weavers Way RG10 . . . . . . .61 D4
Weavers Wlk **2** RG14 . . .105 A3
Webb Cl
Bagshot GU19 . . . . .145 E1
Bracknell RG42 . . . . .90 E1
Slough SL3 . . . . .43 D2
Webb Ct RG40 . . . . .116 E8
Webbs Acre RG19 . . . . . . .106 F2
Webb's Cl RG1 . . . . .85 F6
Webbs La RG7 . . . . .109 B7
Webster Cl SL6 . . . . .39 A5
Wedderburn Cl RG41 . . . . . .88 D2
Wedgewood Way RG30 . . . .57 F1
Weedon Cl OX10 . . . . .14 A8
Weekes Dr SL1 . . . . .42 B4
Weighbridge Row RG1 . . . . .58 F1
Weint The SL3 . . . . .69 C7
Weir Cl RG31 . . . . .84 F4
Weir Pl TW18 . . . . .123 E8
Weir Pool Ct RG10 . . . . .61 C4
Weir Rd KT16 . . . . .124 B2
Weirside Ct **1** RG1 . . . . . . .86 D7
Welbeck RG12 . . . . .117 E4
Welbeck Rd SL6 . . . . .39 D5
Welby Cl SL6 . . . . .39 A4
Welby Cres RG41 . . . . .88 E1
Weldale St RG1 . . . . .85 F8
Welden SL2 . . . . .43 C7
WELFORD 76 A7
Welford Park Gdns*
RG20 . . . . .75 F7
Welford Pk RG20 . . . . .75 E7
Welford Rd
Wickham RG20 . . . . .75 D4
Woodley RG5 . . . . .88 A8
Welford & Wickham CE Prim
Sch RG20 . . . . .75 D4
Welland Cl
Brands Hill SL3 . . . . .69 B8
Reading RG31 . . . . .57 C1
Wellbank SL6 . . . . .20 E1
Wellburn Cl GU47 . . . . .150 B7
Well Cl GU15 . . . . .151 B4
Wellcroft Rd SL1 . . . . .42 B5
WELL END 2 F5
Well End Cotts SL8 . . . . .2 F5
Weller Dr
Arborfield Garrison
RG40 . . . . .141 A6
Camberley GU15 . . . . .151 C3
Weller's La RG42 . . . . .91 C7
Wellesley Ave SL0 . . . . .44 F4
Wellesley Cl GU19 . . . . . . .145 C3
Wellesley Ct
Crowthorne RG45 . . . . .142 F4
Iver SL0 . . . . .44 F4
Wellesley Dr RG45 . . . . . . .142 E5
Wellesley Ho SL4 . . . . .67 B6
Wellesley Path SL1 . . . . .43 A4
Wellesley Rd SL1 . . . . .43 A4
Welley Ave TW19 . . . . .68 E3
Welley Rd TW19 . . . . .68 E3
Wellfield Cl RG31 . . . . .84 C7
Wellhill Rd OX12 . . . . .27 C6
WELLHOUSE 79 E6
Wellhouse La RG18 . . . . . . .79 E6
Well House La RG27 . . . . . .140 B3
Wellhouse Rd SL6 . . . . .19 E2
Wellington Ave
Reading RG2 . . . . .86 D4
Virginia Water GU25 . . . . . .122 B4
Wellington Bsns Pk
RG45 . . . . .142 E4
Wellington Cl
4 Maidenhead SL6 . . . . . . .39 B8
Newbury RG14 . . . . .105 C5
Oatlands Park KT12 . . . . . .125 F1
Sandhurst GU47 . . . . .150 C8
Wellington Coll RG45 . . . . .143 A3
Wellington Cotts
Ball Hill RG20 . . . . .129 B2
Knowl Hill RG10 . . . . .37 C6
Wellington Cres RG26 . . . .134 D1
Wellington Ct
Ashford TW15 . . . . .97 E3
Camberley GU15 . . . . .151 C5

Wellington Ct continued
Shinfield RG7 . . . . .113 A3
Stanwell TW19 . . . . .97 E8
Wellington Ctry Pk*
RG7 . . . . .139 D1
Wellington Dr RG12 . . . . .118 E4
Wellington Gdns RG7 . . . . .82 A1
Wellingtonia Ave RG45,
RG40 . . . . .142 C3
Wellingtonia Ho **20** RG30 .85 D6
Wellingtonia Rdbt RG45 . .142 E4
Wellingtonias RG42 . . . . . . .92 A1
Wellington Ind Est RG7 . . .113 A1
Wellington Lodge SL4 . . . . .93 B6
Wellington Rd
Ashford TW15 . . . . .97 E3
Crowthorne RG45 . . . . .143 C4
Hatton TW14 . . . . .71 C2
Maidenhead SL6 . . . . .39 D7
Sandhurst GU47 . . . . .150 C8
Wokingham RG40 . . . . .116 B5
Wellington St SL1 . . . . .43 A4
Wellington Terr GU47 . . . . .150 D8
Well Mdw RG14 . . . . .105 B5
Wells Cl SL4 . . . . .42 E1
Wells La SL5 . . . . .120 B5
Wellswood SL5 . . . . .120 B6
Welsh La RG7, RG42 . . . . .139 A2
Welshman's Rd RG7 . . . . .136 A5
Welwick Cl RG6 . . . . .87 E2
Welwyn Ave TW14 . . . . .71 F1
Wendan Rd RG14 . . . . .130 F8
Wendover Ct RG18 . . . . .96 C3
Wendover Dr GU16 . . . . . . .152 C3
Wendover Pl TW18 . . . . .96 D3
Wendover Rd
Bourne End SL8 . . . . .3 A5
Burnham SL1 . . . . .41 B8
Egham TW18 . . . . .96 D3
Wendover Way RG30 . . . . . .84 D7
Wenlock Edge RG10 . . . . . . .61 B4
Wenlock Way RG19 . . . . . .106 D2
Wensley Cl RG10 . . . . .61 D5
Wensleydale Dr GU15 . . . .152 D5
Wensley Rd RG1 . . . . .85 E5
WENTWORTH 121 F3
Wentworth Ave
North Ascot SL5 . . . . .119 C7
Reading RG2 . . . . .113 D8
Slough SL2 . . . . .22 A2
Wentworth Cl
Ashford TW15 . . . . .98 B4
Crowthorne RG45 . . . . .142 F6
Yateley GU46 . . . . .149 D5
Wentworth Cres SL6 . . . . . .39 C6
Wentworth Ct RG41 . . . . . .105 B1
Wentworth Dr GU25 . . . . . .121 F5
Wentworth Golf Club
GU25 . . . . .122 A4
Wentworth Ind Ct **1** SL2 . .22 A2
Wentworth Lodge RG14 . . .104 E2
Wentworth Pl GU15 . . . . . .151 A4
Wentworth Way SL5 . . . . . .119 C7
Wescott Inf Sch RG40 . . . .116 D6
Wescott Rd RG40 . . . . .116 D6
Wesley Dr TW20 . . . . .96 A2
Wesley Pl SL4 . . . . .93 B6
Wessex Cl RG17 . . . . .100 C5
Wessex Ct
4 Stanwell TW19 . . . . .70 E1
Tadley RG26 . . . . .135 B1
24 Windsor SL4 . . . . .67 D6
Wessex Gdns RG10 . . . . .61 E3
Wessex Prim Sch SL6 . . . . . .39 B4
Wessex Rd
Bourne End SL8 . . . . .3 B2
Harmondsworth TW6, TW8 .70 E4
Wessex Road Ind Est SL8 . . . .3 B2
Wessex Way SL6 . . . . .39 B4
Wessons Hill SL6 . . . . .19 C7
Westacott Bsns Ctr SL6 . . . .38 E7
Westacott Way SL6 . . . . .38 D4
WEST BEDFONT 97 F8
West Berkshire Com Hospl
RG18 . . . . .105 E4
West Berkshire Mus*
RG14 . . . . .105 A3
Westborough Ct SL6 . . . . . . .39 C6
Westborough Rd SL6 . . . . . . .39 C6
Westbourne Rd
Feltham TW13 . . . . .98 F5
Sandhurst GU47 . . . . .150 E7
Staines TW18 . . . . .97 B1
Westbourne Terr
1 Newbury RG14 . . . . . . .105 A4
Reading RG30 . . . . .85 C7
WESTBROOK 76 D5
Westbrook SL6 . . . . .40 E1
Westbrook Cl RG17 . . . . . . .100 C5
Westbrook Ct **1** RG41 . . . . .88 B2
Westbrook Gdns RG12 . . . .118 D8
Westbrook Gn OX11 . . . . . . .11 F8
Westbrook Rd
Reading RG30 . . . . .58 C1
2 Staines TW18 . . . . .96 F3
Westbrook St OX11 . . . . .11 F8
Westbury Cl
Crowthorne RG45 . . . . .143 B6
Thatcham TW17 . . . . .125 B3
Westbury La RG8 . . . . .57 A6
West Cl
Ashford TW15 . . . . .97 E4
Medmenham SL7 . . . . .17 D7
Westcoign Ho SL6 . . . . .40 B8
Westcombe Cl RG12 . . . . . .118 E2
Westcote Rd RG30 . . . . .85 D6
Westcotts Gn RG42 . . . . . . .91 D1
West Cres SL4 . . . . .66 F6

Westcroft SL2 . . . . .22 B1
West Ct
Bray SL6 . . . . .40 C4
Sonning RG4 . . . . .60 E2
West Dean SL6 . . . . .39 F8
Westdene Cres RG4 . . . . . .58 E4
West Dr
Reading RG31 . . . . .84 E5
Sonning RG4 . . . . .60 D1
Wentworth GU25, SL5 . . . .121 E2
WEST END . . . .
Bisley 153 F6
Bracknell 91 B3
Waltham St Lawrence 62 E3
West End Ct SL2 . . . . .22 F4
Westende RG40 . . . . .116 D6
Westende Jun Sch RG40 .116 D6
West End La RG14 . . . . . . .105 B5
West End La
Harlington UB7 . . . . .71 C7
Newell Green RG42 . . . . .91 B3
Stoke Poges SL2 . . . . .22 E4
West End Rd RG7 . . . . . . .136 F5
Westerdale RG19 . . . . .106 D2
Westerdale Dr GU16 . . . . .152 B3
Westerham Wlk **7** RG1 . .86 B5
Western Ave
Chertsey KT16 . . . . .124 A6
Henley-on-T RG9 . . . . .35 E8
Newbury RG14 . . . . .104 E4
Thorpe TW20 . . . . .123 B6
Woodley RG5 . . . . .60 E1
Western Cl
Chertsey KT16 . . . . .124 A6
Henley-on-T RG9 . . . . .35 E8
Western Ctr The RG12 . . .117 F7
Western Dr
Shepperton TW17 . . . . . . .125 D3
Wooburn Green HP10 . . . . . .3 E5
Western Elms Ave RG30 . . .85 E7
Western End RG14 . . . . . .104 E2
Western House Prim Sch
SL1 . . . . .41 F4
Western Ind Area RG12 . .117 F7
Western Oaks RG31 . . . . . . .57 E2
Western Perimeter Rd TW19,
TW6, UB7 . . . . .70 B4
Western Perimeter Rd Rdbt
TW19 . . . . .70 C2
Western Rd
Bracknell RG12 . . . . .117 F7
Henley-on-T RG9 . . . . .35 E8
Reading RG1 . . . . .85 E6
Westfield Bglws SL7 . . . . . .16 F6
Westfield Cotts SL7 . . . . . . .16 F6
Westfield Cres
Lower Shiplake RG9 . . . . . . .36 B3
Reading RG18 . . . . .106 B4
Westfield Rd
Camberley GU15 . . . . .151 B2
Caversham RG4 . . . . .59 B2
Cholsey OX10 . . . . .13 C6
Maidenhead SL6 . . . . .39 B7
Slough SL2 . . . . .22 B1
Thatcham RG18 . . . . .106 B5
Winnersh RG41 . . . . .88 B2
WEST FIELDS 104 E2
Westfields
Compton RG20 . . . . .31 D4
Kintbury RG20 . . . . .128 A3
Westfield Sch SL8 . . . . .3 B4
Westfields Inf Sch GU46 . .149 B5
Westfields Jun Sch
GU46 . . . . .149 B5
Westfield Way RG14 . . . . .104 E2
Yateley GU46 . . . . .149 D8
West Fryerne
Reading RG30 . . . . .85 D6
Yateley GU46 . . . . .149 E8
Westgate Cres SL1 . . . . .41 F6
Westgate Ct
Newbury RG14 . . . . .104 E1
Reading RG30 . . . . .85 C8
Westgate Rd RG14 . . . . . . .104 E2
Westgate Ret Pk SL1 . . . . . .42 A6
Westgate Sch The SL1 . . . . .42 A5
West Gn GU46 . . . . .149 B7
West Green Ct RG1 . . . . .85 F5
Westhatch Cnr RG42 . . . . . .90 F3
Westhatch La RG42 . . . . . . .91 C5
West Hill RG1 . . . . .86 B6
Westhorpe Park Cvn Site
SL7 . . . . .2 B3
Westhorpe Rd SL7 . . . . .1 F3
WEST ILSLEY 10 B1
West Ilsley Ho RG20 . . . . . .10 A1
West La RG9 . . . . .15 D2
Westland RG18 . . . . .106 B4
Westland Cl TW19 . . . . .70 E1
Westlands Ave
Earley RG2 . . . . .86 E1
Slough SL1 . . . . .41 C7
Westlands Cl SL1 . . . . .41 C7
Westlands Rd RG14 . . . . . .131 A8
West Lawn RG41 . . . . .115 A7
Westleigh Ho RG31 . . . . . . .84 B7
Westley Mill
Binfield RG42 . . . . .90 E8
Holyport RG42 . . . . .63 F1
Westlyn Rd RG26 . . . . .134 E2
Westmacott Dr TW14 . . . . .98 F7
Westmead SL4 . . . . .67 B4
West Mead SL6 . . . . .19 F2
Westmead Dr RG14 . . . . . .131 A8
West Mills RG14 . . . . .104 F3
West Mills Yd RG14 . . . . . .104 F3
Westminster Way RG6 . . . . .87 C1
Westmorland RG41 . . . . . .115 D6

Westmorland Dr
Bracknell RG42 . . . . .91 F1
Frimley GU15 . . . . .152 B3
Westmorland Rd SL6 . . . . . .39 D6
WESTON 75 D8
Westondirt Dr RG4 . . . . . . .58 E3
Weston Gr GU19 . . . . .145 F2
Weston Rd SL1 . . . . .41 F8
Weston's RG20 . . . . .51 D8
West Point SL1 . . . . .41 D5
West Ramp TW6 . . . . .71 A6
West Rd
Bracknell RG40 . . . . .117 D2
Camberley GU15 . . . . .151 D5
East Bedfont TW14 . . . . .98 D8
Maidenhead SL6 . . . . .39 E7
West Ridge SL8 . . . . .3 B4
West Rise RG4 . . . . .58 E4
WESTRIDGE GREEN 33 B4
Westside GU20 . . . . .153 E6
West Sq SL0 . . . . .44 F7
West St
Henley-on-T RG9 . . . . .15 D2
Maidenhead SL6 . . . . .39 F7
Newbury RG14 . . . . .1 D1
Newbury RG14 . . . . .104 F3
Reading RG1 . . . . .86 A7
West Surrey Estates
TW15 . . . . .125 C8
West View
East Bedfont TW14 . . . . .98 C8
Peasemore RG20 . . . . .50 C7
West View Cotts RG18 . . . . .52 F6
West View Ctr RG17 . . . . .100 D6
Westview Dr RG10 . . . . .61 E6
Westward Rd RG41 . . . . . .115 F7
Westwates Cl RG12 . . . . . .118 D8
West Way
Goring RG8 . . . . .34 C8
Shepperton TW17 . . . . . . .125 D3
Westwood Farm Inf Sch
RG31 . . . . .57 C3
Westwood Farm Jun Sch
RG31 . . . . .57 C3
Westwood Glen RG31 . . . . .57 C1
Westwood Gn SL6 . . . . .19 F6
WEST WOODHAY 128 C3
Westwood Rd
Marlow SL7 . . . . .1 C1
Newbury RG14 . . . . .105 B1
Reading RG31 . . . . .57 D1
Windlesham GU20 . . . . . . .146 E6
Westwood Row RG31 . . . . .57 C2
Wetherby Cl RG4 . . . . .59 C6
Wetherby Ho GU15 . . . . . .151 D7
Wethered Pk SL7 . . . . .1 D1
Wethered Rd
Marlow SL7 . . . . .1 D2
Slough SL1 . . . . .41 B8
Wetton Pl TW20 . . . . .95 F3
Wexford Ct SL6 . . . . .40 B7
Wexham Court Prim Sch
SL2 . . . . .43 C7
Wexham Park Hospl SL2 . .23 C1
Wexham Park La SL3 . . . . . .23 C1
Wexham Rd SL2 . . . . .23 D6
Wexham Rd SL1, SL2 . . . . . .43 B6
Wexham Sch SL3 . . . . .43 C8
Wexham St SL3 . . . . .23 B3
WEXHAM STREET 23 C4
Wexham Woods SL3 . . . . . .43 C8
Wey Ave KT16 . . . . .124 A6
Weybridge Mead GU46 . . .149 E7
Wey Cl GU15 . . . . .151 B5
Weycrofts RG42 . . . . .90 F1
Weymead Cl KT16 . . . . . . .124 C1
Whale Ave RG2 . . . . .86 A2
Whaley Rd RG40 . . . . .116 D8
Wharf Bsns Ctr SL8 . . . . .3 A3
Wharfedale Rd RG41 . . . . . .88 A3
Wharfe La RG9 . . . . .15 E2
Wharf La SL8 . . . . .3 A3
Wharf Rd
Newbury RG14 . . . . .105 A3
Wraysbury TW19 . . . . .95 D8
Wharfside RG7 . . . . .109 C3
Wharf St RG14 . . . . .105 A3
Wharf The
Newbury RG14 . . . . .105 A3
Pangbourne RG8 . . . . .56 C6
Whatley Gn RG12 . . . . . . .118 B3
Whatmore Cl TW19 . . . . . . .70 A1
Wheatash Rd KT15 . . . . . . .124 B1
Wheatbutts The SL4 . . . . . . .41 F2
Wheatfield Cl SL6 . . . . .39 A4
Wheatfields Rd RG2 . . . . . .113 E5
Wheat Ho TW19 . . . . .97 E7
Wheatlands Cl RG31 . . . . . . .84 E4
Wheatlands La RG14 . . . . .130 B6
Wheatley RG12 . . . . .117 E4
Wheatley Cl RG42 . . . . .86 E1
Wheatlands La RG14 . . . . .115 A7
Wheatsheaf La
Newbury RG14 . . . . .105 A4
Staines TW18 . . . . .96 F1
Wheatsheaf Par SL4 . . . . . .68 A2
Wheatstone Cl SL3 . . . . .43 A3
Wheble Dr RG5 . . . . .87 D8
Wheeler Cl
Burghfield Common RG7 . . .111 B3
Wokingham RG41 . . . . .115 F5
Wheeler Ct RG31 . . . . .57 E1
Wheelers Green Way
RG19 . . . . .106 F2
Wheelton Cl RG6 . . . . .87 C1
Wheelwrights Pl SL3 . . . . . .69 C7
Whins Cl GU15 . . . . .151 B4

Whins Dr GU15 . . . . .151 B4
Whinshill Ct SL5 . . . . .121 A1
Whistler Gr GU47 . . . . .150 D6
Whistlers La RG7 . . . . .136 B1
Whistley Cl RG12 . . . . .118 E6
Whistley Court Farm
RG10 . . . . .61 E1
WHISTLEY GREEN 61 E1
Whitaker Cl RG18 . . . . . . .106 B4
Whitamore Row RG9 . . . . . .35 E8
Whitby Cl RG6 . . . . .59 D6
Whitby Dr **1** RG1 . . . . .86 C5
Whitby Gn RG4 . . . . .59 D6
Whitby Rd SL1 . . . . .42 C6
Whitchurch Cl SL6 . . . . .19 E3
WHITCHURCH-ON-
THAMES 56 C7
Whitchurch Prim Sch
RG8 . . . . .56 E7
Whitchurch Rd RG8 . . . . . . .56 D6
Whiteacres Dr SL6 . . . . .40 C1
Whitebeam Cl RG41 . . . . . .115 D3
White Bridge Cl TW14 . . . . .71 F1
Whitebrook Pk SL6 . . . . .20 C4
White City RG45 . . . . .143 D5
White Cl
Hermitage RG18 . . . . .78 F6
Slough SL1 . . . . .42 D5
Whitefields Cotts RG14 . . .104 F7
Whiteford Rd SL2 . . . . .42 E8
White Gates RG20 . . . . .75 D5
Whitegates La RG6 . . . . .87 A7
WHITEGROVE 91 E2
Whitegrove Prim Sch
RG42 . . . . .91 F1
Whitegrove Rdbt RG42 . . . .91 D2
Whitehall SL6 . . . . .20 B1
Whitehall Dr RG2 . . . . .140 E8
Whitehall Farm La GU25 .122 E6
Whitehall La
Egham TW20 . . . . .95 F1
Wraysbury TW19 . . . . .69 A1
Whitehart Cl RG7 . . . . .83 E4
White Hart Ho **2** GU17 . .150 E4
White Hart Ind Est **1**
GU17 . . . . .150 E4
White Hart Rd
2 Maidenhead SL6 . . . . . . .39 F7
Slough SL1 . . . . .42 D3
White Hart Row **3** KT16 .124 A2
Whitehaven SL1 . . . . .42 F6
White Hermitage SL4 . . . . . .68 C2
White Hill
Ashampstead RG8 . . . . .54 D6
Remenham Hill RG9 . . . . . . .16 A2
Shiplake RG9 . . . . .35 A5
Windlesham GU20 . . . . . . .146 B6
Wooburn Moor HP9 . . . . .3 F8
Whitehill Cl
Camberley GU15 . . . . .151 D7
Marlow SL7 . . . . .1 C6
Whitehill Pl GU25 . . . . .122 E4
Whitehills Gn RG8 . . . . .34 C6
White Horse La RG40 . . . . .141 A6
White Horse Rd SL4 . . . . . . .66 D5
Whitehouse Farm RG26 . .135 D2
White House Gdns GU46 .149 C7
WHITEHOUSE GREEN 110 F6
White House La RG7 . . . . .138 F8
White House Prep Sch
RG40 . . . . .116 A3
White House Rd OX10 . . . . .14 F8
Whitehouse Way SL3 . . . . . .43 D3
WHITEKNIGHTS 86 F5
Whiteknights Prim Sch
RG6 . . . . .86 F1
Whiteknights Rd RG6 . . . . .86 F5
Whitelands Dr SL5 . . . . . . .119 D8
Whitelands Park Prim Sch
RG18 . . . . .106 C5
Whitelands Rd RG18 . . . . .106 D4
Whiteley SL4 . . . . .66 F7
White Lilies Island SL4 . . . . .67 B7
White Lion Way GU46 . . . .149 D7
Whitelock Ho RG9 . . . . .15 E3
Whitelocks Piece RG17 . . . .73 A2
White Lodge Cl
Marlow Bottom SL7 . . . . .1 C6
Purley on T RG31 . . . . .57 B3
Whitemoor La
Lower Basildon RG8 . . . . . . .34 C1
Upper Basildon RG8 . . . . . . .54 E5
White Paddock SL6 . . . . .39 A2
Whiteside La HP10 . . . . .3 E7
White Rd
Chilton OX11 . . . . .10 D8
Sandhurst GU15 . . . . .150 F6
White Rock SL6 . . . . .20 B1
White's Hill RG7 . . . . .110 D5
White Shoot OX11 . . . . .12 A5
White Lodge Cl . . . .
Whites La
Beenham RG7 . . . . .109 B7
Datchet SL3 . . . . .68 B8
Whitestone Cl RG6 . . . . .87 B2
Whitewalls Cl RG20 . . . . . . .31 E5
WHITE WALTHAM 63 E7
White Waltham CE Sch
SL6 . . . . .63 D7
Whiteways TW14 . . . . .97 B1
Whitewell Cl RG2 . . . . .114 C2
WHITLEY 86 C1
Whitley Cl TW19 . . . . .70 E1
Whitley Park Bsns Pk
RG2 . . . . .86 B2

Whitley Park La RG2 . . . . . .86 D4
Whitley Rd SL4 . . . . .149 D4
Whitley St RG2 . . . . .86 B5
WHITLEY WOOD 113 C7
Whitley Wood La RG2 . . . .113 C7
Whitley Wood Rd RG2 . .113 C7
Whitmoor Rd GU19 . . . . . . .145 F2
Whitmoor Ct GU47 . . . . . .143 D1
Whitmore La SL5 . . . . .121 A5
Whitstone Gdns RG2 . . . . . .86 C1
Whittaker Rd SL2 . . . . .21 E1
Whittenham Cl SL2 . . . . . . .43 A5
Whittle Cl
  Finchampstead RG40. . . . . .141 E7
  Sandhurst GU47 . . . . .143 A1
Whittle Parkway SL1 . . . . .41 D7
Whitton Cl ⑦ RG6 . . . . . . .87 D1
WHITTONDITCH 72 A5
Whittonditch Works SN8. .72 A5
Whitton Rd RG12 . . . . .118 F6
Whitworth Rd RG2 . . . . . . .141 A7
Whurley Way SL6 . . . . .19 E2
Whybrow Ct RG18 . . . . . . .106 D3
Whynstones Rd SL5 . . . . . .120 A4
Whyteladyes La SL6 . . . . . . .19 E6
Wickens Cnr RG7 . . . . .109 A6
Wickets The
  Ashford TW15 . . . . .97 E4
  Maidenhead SL6 . . . . .39 C7
Wickford Way RG6 . . . . . .113 F8
WICKHAM 75 C4
WICKHAM HEATH 103 B8
Wickham La TW20 . . . . .96 A1
Wickham Rd
  Camberley GU15 . . . . .151 E8
  Earley RG6 . . . . .87 E1
  Stockcross RG20 . . . . .103 E6
Wickham Vale RG12 . . . . . .117 E3
WICK HILL
  Bracknell 118 C8
  Finchampstead 142 A6
Wick Hill Ho RG12 . . . . . . .118 C8
Wick Hill La RG40 . . . . .142 A5
Wickhurst Cotts SL6 . . . . .38 B5
Wick La TW20 . . . . .94 F3
Wick Rd TW20 . . . . .95 B1
Wicks Gn RG42 . . . . .90 B3
Wicks La RG10. . . . . .62 E2
Widbrook Rd SL6 . . . . .20 B3
Widecroft Rd SL0 . . . . .44 E7
Widmere La SL7 . . . . .1 A6
Wield Ct RG6 . . . . .87 E1
Wiggett Gr RG42 . . . . .90 C2
Wiggington Ho SL4 . . . . . . .67 D7
Wigmore La
  Reading RG30 . . . . .58 B1
  Reading RG30 . . . . .58 C1
  Theale RG7 . . . . .83 C1
Wigmore Rd RG26 . . . . . . .134 F1
Wilberforce Mews ⑮ SL6 .39 F7
Wilberforce Way RG12 . .118 E4
Wilbury Lodge SL5. . . . . . .120 F3
Wilcox Gdns TW17 . . . . . . .124 F6
Wild Briar RG40 . . . . .141 F7
Wild Cl RG6 . . . . .114 C8
Wildcroft Dr RG40 . . . . . . .116 A1
Wilder Ave RG6 . . . . .56 E5
Wilderness Ct RG6. . . . . . . .87 A3
Wilderness Rd
  Earley RG6. . . . . .87 A4
  Frimley GU16. . . . . .151 E2
Wilders Cl
  Bracknell RG42 . . . . .91 A1
  Frimley GU16. . . . . .151 E3
Wilde Theatre RG12 . . . . .118 C2
Wildgreen N ⑪ SL3. . . . . . .44 A2
Wildgreen S ⑫ SL3. . . . . . .44 A2
Wildoaks SL5 . . . . .97 B3
WILDRIDINGS 118 A5
Wildridings Prim Sch
  RG12. . . . . .118 A5
Wildridings Rd RG12 . . . . .118 A5
Wildridings Sq RG12 . . . . .118 A5
Wildwood Dr RG26 . . . . . .134 D1
Wildwood Gdns GU46 . . .149 C4
Wilford Rd SL3 . . . . .43 F2
Wilfred Way RG19 . . . . . . .107 A3
Wilfrids Wood Cl HP10 . . . .3 B6
Willant Cl SL6 . . . . .38 F2
Willats Cl KT16 . . . . .124 A3
William Byrd Sch UB7. . . .71 C8
William Cl RG19 . . . . .106 D2
William Ellis Cl SL4 . . . . . . .68 A1
William Hartley Yd SL3. . .23 B1
Williams Ct RG17 . . . . .100 D5
William Sim Wood RG42 .92 B2
Williamson Cl RG41. . . . . . .88 B3
William St
  Reading RG1 . . . . .85 F8
  Slough SL1. . . . . .42 F5
  Windsor SL4 . . . . .67 D6
Willington Cl GU15 . . . . . .151 B6
Willink Sch The RG7 . . . . .110 F2
Willis Cl RG18 . . . . .79 B3
Willowers SL2 . . . . .42 A7
Willoughby Rd
  Bracknell RG12 . . . . .117 F6
  Slough SL3. . . . . .44 A3
Willow Bank SL7 . . . . .1 D7
Willow Bank Inf Sch RG5. .60 F1
Willow Bank Jun Sch RG5 60 F1
Willowbrook SL4 . . . . .42 D2
Willowbrook Ct ⑪ TW20 .96 A3
Willowbrook Rd TW19. . . .97 E6

Willow Cl
  Burghfield RG30 . . . . .111 B5
  Colnbrook SL3 . . . . .69 C7
  Flackwell Heath HP10 . . . . . .3 C6
  Maidenhead SL6 . . . . .19 D1
  Newbury RG14. . . . . .104 F1
Willow Cotts OX10 . . . . . . .13 F5
Willow Court La OX10. . . .13 F5
Willow Ct
  ② Ashford TW16 . . . . .98 E1
  Frimley GU16. . . . . .151 D1
  Wokingham RG41 . . . . .116 B6
Willowdale RG40. . . . . .141 F8
Willow Dr
  Bracknell RG12 . . . . .118 C8
  Maidenhead SL6 . . . . .40 B2
  Twyford RG10 . . . . .61 D6
Willowford GU46. . . . . .149 D6
Willow Gdns
  Purley on T RG31. . . . . .57 B2
  Reading RG2 . . . . .86 E1
Willow Gn GU24 . . . . .153 F6
Willowherb Cl RG40. . . . . .116 E7
Willow Ho RG14 . . . . .130 E8
Willow La
  Blackwater GU17. . . . . .150 D4
  Wargrave RG10. . . . . .36 C4
Willow Lodge ⑦ TW16. . . .98 F1
Willowmead TW18 . . . . . . .124 B8
Willowmead Cl
  ⑩ Marlow SL7 . . . . .1 F3
  Newbury RG14. . . . . .1 F3
Willowmead Gdns SL7 . . . .1 F3
Willow Mead Rd ⑧ SL7. . . .1 F3
Willowmead Sq ⑨ SL7. . . .1 F3
Willow Par SL3 . . . . .44 A3
Willow Pk SL2 . . . . .23 A5
Willow Pl SL4 . . . . .67 C8
Willow Rd
  Bishops Green RG20 . . . . . .131 F2
  Poyle SL3 . . . . .69 E5
Willows Ct ② RG6 . . . . .58 C6
Willows End GU47 . . . . . . .150 B8
Willowside RG5. . . . . .60 F1
Willows Prim Sch The
  RG14 . . . . .131 B8
Willows Rd SL3 . . . . .3 B4
Willows Riverside Pk The
  SL4. .66 C7
Willow St ⑧ RG1 . . . . .86 A6
Willows The
  ⑩ Bourne End SL8 . . . . .3 B3
  ⑪ Bracknell RG12. . . . . . . .118 F5
  Brimpton RG7 . . . . .133 F6
  Caversham RG4. . . . . .59 A2
  Lightwater GU18 . . . . .146 C1
  Windsor SL4 . . . . .66 D7
Willow Tree Glade RG31. .84 C4
Willow Way GU47. . . . . . . .142 F1
Willow Wlk
  Chertsey KT16. . . . . .124 B2
  Englefield Green TW20 . . . . .95 C3
Willow Wood Cl SL1 . . . . . .21 B3
Willson Rd TW20. . . . . .95 B3
Wilmington Cl RG5 . . . . . . .87 F8
Wilmot Cl RG42. . . . . .90 C2
Wilmot Rd SL1 . . . . .21 B2
Wilmot Way GU15 . . . . . . .151 F3
Wilmot Wlk RG14 . . . . . . .130 C6
Wilsford Cl RG6 . . . . .113 E7
Wilson Ave RG9 . . . . .35 E8
Wilson Cl RG20. . . . . .31 E4
Wilson Ct RG42 . . . . .88 B1
Wilson Prim Sch RG30 . . .85 C7
Wilson Rd RG30 . . . . .85 C7
Wilson Valkenburg Ct
  RG14 . . . . .104 E4
Wilstrode Ave RG42. . . . . . .90 F1
Wilton Cl UB7 . . . . .70 D8
Wilton Cres SL4 . . . . .66 D4
Wilton Rd
  Camberley GU15 . . . . .151 B3
  Reading RG30 . . . . .85 D8
Wiltshire Ave
  Crowthorne RG45 . . . . .143 B5
  Slough SL2. . . . . .22 C1
Wiltshire Cl RG17 . . . . . . .100 C5
Wiltshire Dr RG40. . . . . . . .116 D7
Wiltshire Gr RG42. . . . . .91 F2
Wiltshire Lodge ② SL6 . . .39 F6
Wiltshire Rd
  Marlow SL7 . . . . .1 F4
  Marlow SL7 . . . . .2 A4
  Wokingham RG40 . . . . .116 C7
Wiltshire Wlk RG31. . . . . . .84 B6
Wilwood Rd RG42. . . . . . . .117 E8
Wilwyne Cl RG4 . . . . .59 C4
Wimbledon Cl GU15 . . . . .144 F1
Wimbledon Rd GU15 . . . .144 F1
Wimblington Dr RG6. . . . .114 C8
Wimborne Gdns RG30. . . .58 A1
Wimbushes RG40. . . . . . . .141 D6
Winbury Cl SL6. . . . . .39 E7
Winbury Sch SL6 . . . . .40 B4
Wincanton Rd RG2. . . . . . .113 C6
Winchbottom La SL7, HP10 .2 B6
Winch Cl RG42. . . . . .90 C3
Winchcombe Rd
  Newbury RG14. . . . . .105 A2
  Twyford RG10 . . . . .61 E4
Winchcombe Sch The
  RG14 . . . . .105 A4
Winchendon Pl RG4. . . . . . .59 B6
Winchester Cl SL3. . . . . . . .69 E6
Winchester Ho ⑤ RG14 . 105 A2
Winchester Rd
  Harlington UB3. . . . . .71 E7

Winchester Rd continued
  Reading RG2 . . . . .86 B4
Winchester Way GU17 . .150 C6
Winchgrove Rd RG42. . . . . .91 A1
Winchstone Cl TW17 . . . .124 F5
Winch Terr SL4 . . . . .66 D5
Wincroft Rd RG4. . . . . .58 E5
Windermere Cl
  East Bedfont TW14 . . . . .98 F7
  Stanwell TW19 . . . . .97 D6
  Thorpe Lea TW20 . . . . .96 B1
  Winnersh RG41. . . . . .88 C3
Windermere Rd
  Lightwater GU18 . . . . .146 B1
  Reading RG2 . . . . .86 D3
Windermere Way
  Slough SL1. . . . . .41 C7
  Thatcham RG19 . . . . .106 A3
Windermere Wlk GU15. .152 D5
WINDING WOOD 74 F2
Winding Wood Dr GU15. .152 B3
Windlebrook Gn ⑧
  RG42 . . . . .118 A8
Windlesham Ct SL5 . . . . . . .42 F3
Windlesham Cl GU20 . . . .146 D4
WINDLESHAM 146 C4
Windlesham Ct GU20 . . . .146 C6
Windlesham Rd
  Bracknell RG42 . . . . .117 F8
  West End GU24 . . . . .153 F7
Windlesham Village Inf Sch
  GU20 . . . . .146 B6
Windmill Ave RG41 . . . . . .113 D6
Windmill Bsns Village
  TW16. . . . . .125 E8
Windmill Cl
  Charlton TW16. . . . . .98 E1
  Slough SL3. . . . . .43 E4
  Wokingham RG41 . . . . .115 E8
Windmill Cnr RG7 . . . . . . .137 A6
Windmill Ct
  Earley RG6. . . . . .87 C4
  Mortimer RG7 . . . . .137 A6
Windmill Field GU20 . . . .146 D4
Windmill Ho TW16 . . . . . .125 E8
Windmill La RG7. . . . . .108 A5
Windmill Lodge TW16. . . .125 E8
Windmill Rd
  Bracknell RG42 . . . . .118 A8
  Charlton TW16. . . . . .98 E1
  Cookham Rise SL6. . . . . .19 E6
  Fulmer SL3 . . . . .23 D7
  Mortimer RG7 . . . . .137 A6
  Slough SL1. . . . . .42 D5
Windmill Rd W TW16. . . . .125 E8
Windmill Shott TW20. . . . . .95 F2
Windmill Terr TW17 . . . . .125 E8
Windrush Ave SL3 . . . . .44 B3
Windrush Ct ③ RG30. . . . .85 B7
Windrush Ho SL8 . . . . .3 A4
Windrush Hts GU47 . . . . . .150 B8
Windrush Way
  Maidenhead SL6 . . . . .39 F8
  Reading RG30 . . . . .84 E8
WINDSOR 67 E6
Windsor Boys' Sch The
  SL4. .67 B6
Windsor Castle* SL4 . . . . . .67 C7
Windsor Castle* SL4 . . . . . .67 C7
Windsor Ct
  Camberley GU15 . . . . .151 C3
  Newbury RG14. . . . . .105 B2
  ⑪ Reading RG1 . . . . .85 E7
Windsor Dr TW15 . . . . .97 D4
Windsor & Eton Central Sta
  SL4. .67 D6
Windsor & Eton Riverside Sta
  SL4. .67 D7
Windsor Forest Ct SL5 . . .119 D8
Windsor Girls' Sch SL4. . . .67 A4
Windsor Great Pk* SL4 . . .94 D4
Windsor Hall SL4 . . . . .67 F4
Windsor Hill HP10 . . . . .3 F5
Windsor Ho
  ⑫ Egham TW20 . . . . .96 A3
  Henley-on-T RG9 . . . . .35 E8
Windsor La SL1 . . . . .21 C1
Windsor Park Rd UB3. . . . .71 F7
Windsor Pl KT16. . . . . .124 A3
Windsor Rd
  Datchet SL3. . . . . .68 A7
  Englefield Green SL4, TW19,
    TW20 . . . . .95 A8
  Fulmer SL2. . . . . .23 A8
  Maidenhead SL6 . . . . .40 C1
  North Ascot SL5. . . . . .120 A8
  Oakley Green SL4 . . . . .66 A7
  Slough SL1. . . . . .42 E4
  Wraysbury TW19 . . . . .68 E1
Windsor Ride
  Bracknell RG12 . . . . .118 C1
  Bracknell SL5. . . . . .119 D8
  Sandhurst GU15 . . . . .151 A8
  Wokingham RG40 . . . . .132 D8
Windsor Rise RG14 . . . . . .131 C8
Windsor Royal Sta ⑧ SL4 .67 D6
Windsor Sq ② RG1. . . . . . . .86 B6
Windsor St KT16. . . . . .124 A3
Windsor Way RG31. . . . . . . .84 B4
Winfield Dr RG19 . . . . .131 C7
Wingate Rd RG14 . . . . .87 E6
Wing Cl SL7 . . . . .1 C1
Winglield Gdns GU15 . . . .152 C6
Wingrove Rd RG30 . . . . . . .85 C6
WINKFIELD 92 D5
Winkfield Cl RG41 . . . . . . .116 B3
Winkfield La SL4 . . . . .92 D7

Winkfield Manor SL5 . . . . .92 D2
Winkfield Rd
  Ascot, Brookside SL5. . . . . . .93 A1
  Ascot SL5. . . . . .120 B7
  Windsor SL4 . . . . .66 E2
WINKFIELD ROW 92 B2
Winkfield Row RG42 . . . . . .92 B3
Winkfield St Mary's CE Prim
  Sch RG42. . . . . .92 B3
Winkfield St SL4. . . . . .92 C6
Winkworth La RG7, RG26 135 C2
WINNERSH 88 D3
Winnersh Gate RG41. . . . . .88 D2
Winnersh Gr RG41 . . . . .88 C1
Winnersh Prim Sch RG41 .88 D3
Winnersh Sta RG41 . . . . . . .88 C2
Winnersh Triangle Ind Est
  RG41 . . . . .88 B3
Winnersh Triangle Sta
  RG41. . . . . .88 A3
Winscombe RG12 . . . . .117 E4
Winser Dr RG30 . . . . .85 D5
Winsford Par ④ SL1 . . . . . . .42 F3
Winslet Pl RG30 . . . . .58 B1
Winston Cl RG2 . . . . .113 B7
Winston Ct SL6 . . . . .39 B8
Winston Way
  Purley on T RG8. . . . . .57 B5
  Thatcham RG19 . . . . .105 F4
WINTERBOURNE 77 C5
Winterbourne Ct RG12 . .118 D7
Winterbourne Rd RG20. . . .76 E4
Winter Cl ⑪ SL7. . . . . .1 E2
Winter Hill SL6 . . . . .2 C1
Winter Hill Rd SL6 . . . . .19 A4
Winterton Dr RG14. . . . . . .104 D5
Winton Cres GU46 . . . . . . .149 D5
Winton Rd RG2 . . . . .113 D8
Wintoun Path SL2 . . . . .21 E1
Wintringham Way RG8 . . . .57 D5
Winvale SL1. . . . . .42 E3
Winwood
  Slough SL2. . . . . .43 C7
  Windsor SL4 . . . . .66 F3
Wisdom Ct ⑭ RG30. . . . . . .85 D6
Wise's Firs RG7. . . . . .110 D3
Wishmoor Cl GU15. . . . . . .151 E8
Wishmoor Rd GU15 . . . . . .151 E8
Wispington Cl RG6. . . . . . . .87 D2
Wistaria La GU46. . . . . .149 C5
Wisteria Cl RG41 . . . . .115 F5
Wiston Terr RG1 . . . . .86 B8
Witcham Cl SL4 . . . . .114 D8
Withey Cl SL4. . . . . .66 E6
Witheygate Ave TW18 . . . .97 B2
Withybed La RG17 . . . . . . .101 E3
Withybed Way RG18 . . . . .106 B5
Withy Cl
  Lightwater GU18 . . . . .146 C1
  Reading RG31 . . . . .84 C5
Withycroft SL3. . . . . .43 E7
Withys The SL6 . . . . .19 B1
Wittenham Ave RG31. . . . . .84 B8
Wittenham Rd RG12 . . . . .118 F8
Wittington Cotts SL7. . . . . .17 D6
Woburn Cl
  Caversham RG4. . . . . .58 E4
  Frimley GU16. . . . . .152 A1
  ⑪ Reading RG6 . . . . .84 B5
Wofford Way RG19. . . . . . .132 A5
Wokefield Row RG7. . . . . .137 D8
WOKINGHAM 116 B5
Wokingham Hospl RG41. .116 A6
Wokingham Rd
  Bracknell RG42 . . . . .117 F8
  Earley RG6. . . . . .87 C4
  Reading RG10 . . . . .88 F8
  Sandhurst RG45, GU47 . . . .142 E2
  Wokingham Sta RG40 . . . .116 B6
Wolf La SL4 . . . . .66 E4
Wolseley St RG1. . . . . .86 A6
Wolsey Ct ② TW16 . . . . . . .98 F1
Wolsey Rd
  Ashford, Felthamhill TW16 . .98 F1
  Ashford TW15 . . . . .97 E4
  Caversham RG4. . . . . .59 B2
WOOBURN 3 D4
Wooburn Grange HP10 . . . .3 D3
WOOBURN GREEN 3 E7
Wooburn Manor Pk HP10 . .3 E5
Wooburn Mead HP10 . . . . . .3 E4
Wooburn Mews HP10 . . . . . .3 E5
WOOBURN MOOR 3 D4
Wooburn Town HP10 . . . . . .3 D4
Woodberry Gdns RG18. . .106 A5
Woodbine Cl
  Earley RG6. . . . . .87 C4
  Sandhurst GU47 . . . . .150 C7
Woodbine Cotts TW20. . . .95 F2
Woodbine La RG20. . . . . . .130 F1
Woodbridge Bsns Pk
  GU15 . . . . .151 D7
Woodbridge Manor
  GU15 . . . . .151 D7
Woodbridge Rd
  Blackwater GU17. . . . . .150 D4
  Reading RG31 . . . . .84 B6
Woodbury Cl SL8 . . . . .3 B4
Woodbury Ct RG42 . . . . . . .90 B3
Woodby Dr SL5. . . . . .120 F2
Wood Cl SL4 . . . . .67 C2

Woodcock Ct RG7 . . . . . . .113 A4
Woodcote SL6. . . . . .39 D6
Woodcote House Sch
  GU20 . . . . .146 B5
Woodcote Pl SL5 . . . . .119 F8
Woodcote Rd
  Caversham RG4. . . . . .58 E4
  South Stoke RG8 . . . . .14 E4
Woodcote Way SL6. . . . . . .58 D5
Woodcott Ho RG26. . . . . . .135 A1
Woodend RG15 . . . . .152 A7
Wood End RG45. . . . . .142 F4
Wood End RG41 SL5 . . . . .119 E8
Woodend Dr SL5. . . . . .120 B4
Woodenhill RG12 . . . . .117 E1
Woodern Hill Prim Sch
  RG12 . . . . .117 E2
Woodfield Cl RG20 . . . . . . .130 B4
Woodfield Cotts RG8. . . . .34 A6
Woodfield Dr SL6 . . . . .39 A6
Woodfield Way RG2 . . . . . .83 E4
Woodford Cl RG4 . . . . .58 E4
Woodford Gn RG12 . . . . . .118 F5
WOODFORD PARK. 87 E8
Woodford Way SL2 . . . . . . .22 A2
Wood Gn RG2 . . . . .113 D8
Wood Green Cl RG30. . . . . .85 E7
Wood Hall SL5. . . . . .146 E8
Woodhall La SL5. . . . . .146 E8
Woodhaw TW20 . . . . .96 B4
Woodhouse La RG19 . . . . .133 E2
Woodhouse St RG42 . . . . . .90 E1
Woodhurst La RG41. . . . . .115 E8
Woodhurst Rd SL6. . . . . . . .20 B1
Woodhurst South SL6. . . . .20 C1
Woodies Cl RG42 . . . . .90 C1
Wood La
  Arborfield RG41. . . . . .114 F3
  Beech Hill RG7. . . . . .138 E5
  Binfield RG42. . . . . .90 D1
  Iver SL0. . . . . .44 C8
  Slough SL1. . . . . .42 A4
Woodland Ave
  Slough SL1. . . . . .42 D6
  Windsor SL4 . . . . .66 F3
Woodland Cl SL7 . . . . .1 E4
Woodland Cres RG42. . . . . .91 C1
Woodland Dr RG30. . . . . . . .84 D7
Woodland Grange SL0 . . . .44 E3
Woodlands GU46 . . . . .149 D4
Woodlands Ave
  Burghfield Common RG7 . .111 A3
  Wokingham RG41 . . . . .115 E8
  Woodley RG5 . . . . .87 C2
Woodlands Cl
  Ascot SL5. . . . . .119 F3
  Curridge RG18 . . . . .78 D5
  Farnborough GU17 . . . . . . .150 E1
Woodlands Ct
  Sandhurst GU47 . . . . .143 F1
  Woodley RG5 . . . . .87 D8
Woodlands Farm SL6 . . . . .19 C6
Woodlands Gr RG4. . . . . . . .58 E4
Woodlands La GU20. . . . . .146 E3
Woodlands Park Ave
  SL6. .39 A1
Woodlands Park Rd SL6. . .39 A2
Woodlands Rd
  Camberley GU15 . . . . .151 B5
  Shiplake RG9 . . . . .35 E4
  Tadley RG26. . . . . .134 F1
  Virginia Water GU25 . . . . . .122 C5
Woodlands Rd E GU25 . . .122 C5
Woodlands Rd W GU25. .122 C5
Woodlands Ride SL5. . . . . .120 E3
WOODLANDS ST MARY . . .46 E2
Woodlands The RG11 . . . .115 D4
Woodlands Wlk GU17. . . .150 E1
Woodlark Glade GU15. . . .151 D7
Woodlee Cl GU25 . . . . .122 C4
Woodleigh Mans SL5 . . . .120 E4
WOODLEY 87 D7
Woodley CE Prim Sch
  RG5 .88 B8
Woodley Gn RG5 . . . . .87 F8
WOODLEY GREEN. 88 A8
Woodley Park Est RG5 . . .87 D8
Woodman's La RG7 . . . . . .110 F3
Woodman's La RG7 . . . . . .110 F3
Woodmere RG12 . . . . .87 B2
Woodmere Cl RG6 . . . . .87 B2
Woodmill Ct SL5 . . . . .119 D6
Woodmoor End SL6. . . . . . .20 B7
Woodpecker Cl RG10 . . . . .61 E3
Woodpecker Wlk RG41. . .115 F5
Wood Rd
  Camberley GU15 . . . . .151 B5
  Littleton TW17. . . . . .125 A5
Wood Ridge RG14 . . . . . . .130 E4
Woodridge Cl RG12 . . . . . .118 C6
Woodridge Ho
  Bracknell RG12 . . . . .118 C2
  Newbury RG14. . . . . .130 F2
Woodrow Dr RG40 . . . . . . .116 E6
Woodsend Cl RG6 . . . . . . .113 E8
Woodshore Cl GU25. . . . . .122 B3
WOODSIDE. 93 C4

Woodside
Blackwater GU17........ 150 C3
Cold Ash RG18........... 79 C1
Flackwell Heath HP10 ......3 C6
Newbury RG14........... 130 D7
Sandhurst GU15 .... 150 F7
Woodside Ave HP10........3 C7
Woodside Bsns Pk RG2 ..113 B7
Woodside Cl
Finchampstead RG40..... 141 E8
Mortimer RG7 .... 137 A6
Upper Bucklebury RG7 ... 107 C5
Woodside Dr RG18.......79 B6
Woodside La SL4 .... 93 C3
Woodside Rd SL4 .... 93 B2
Woodside Way
Reading RG2 .... 113 D7
Virginia Water GU25 .... 122 B6
WOODSPEEN 104 B7
Woods Rd RG4 .... 59 E4
Woodstock ◼ RG40...... 116 C6
Woodstock Ave SL3......43 D2
Woodstock Cl SL6 .... 19 F1
Woodstock St RG1....... 86 E7
Woodthorne Cl RG31.....57 B4
Woodthorpe Rd TW15.... 97 D4
Woodview Rd RG8 .... 56 D5
Woodville Cl GU17...... 150 B5
Woodville Ct ◪ RG1..... 86 A6
Woodward Cl RG41 ...... 88 D1
Woodway GU15........ 151 B5
Woodwaye RG5.......... 87 D7
Woodway Rd OX11....... 12 A7
Woodyer Cl RG5 .... 87 E5
Woolacombe Dr RG6.....86 F2
Wooldridge Cl TW14 ... 98 C7
Woolf Dr RG40........... 116 C7
Woolf Memorial Cotts
RG40 .... 116 C7
Woolford Cl RG42........ 90 E8
WOOLHAMPTON 108 D2
Woolhampton CE Prim Sch
RG7 .... 108 D4
Woolhampton Hill RG7.. 108 C3
Woolhampton Way
RG12 .... 118 D4
Woolley Firs SL6........ 118 D4
WOOLLEY GREEN 38 D5
Woolton Lodge Gdns
RG20 .... 129 F2
WOOSE HILL 115 F6
Woosehill RG41........ 115 G6
Woosehill Ct RG41..... 115 F7
Woosehill La RG41..... 115 F6
Wootton Cl RG31........ 84 C8

Wootton Dr HP10 ....3 E8
Wootton Rd RG9..........35 C8
Wootton Way SL6.........39 C6
Worcester Cl
Maidenhead SL6 ....39 D3
Reading RG30 ....85 A5
Worcester Ct
◪ Ashford TW15 ....98 B3
◪ Camberley GU15 ....151 B3
◪ Staines TW18............97 A3
Worcester Dr TW15 ....98 B3
Worcester Gdns SL1 .....42 D4
Worcestershire Lea RG42 .91 F1
Wordsworth RG12 ....117 F4
Wordsworth Ave GU46 ...149 B4
Wordsworth Ct RG4......59 C7
Wordsworth Rd
Slough SL2................21 D1
Thatcham RG18 ....106 C4
World Bsns Ctr TW6 ......71 C6
WORLD'S END 51 D6
Worlds End Hill RG12 ...118 F3
Wormersley Rd RG19 ... 131 D7
Worple Ave TW18 ....97 B2
Worple Rd TW18.........97 B1
Worple The TW19 ....68 F1
Worrall Way RG6 ....113 F8
Worsley Pl RG7..........83 E4
Worster Rd SL6..........19 E6
Worton Dr RG2 ....113 A8
Worton Grange Ind Est
RG2 .... 113 A8
Wrabness Way TW18 ....124 B8
WRAYSBURY 68 E1
Wraysbury Gdns TW18 ...96 E4
Wraysbury Prim Sch
TW19 ....68 E1
Wraysbury Rd TW18,
TW19 ....96 C5
Wraysbury Sta TW19 ......69 A1
Wren Cl
Egham TW20 ....96 A3
Slough SL3...............44 A3
Wrenfield Dr RG4........58 F5
Wrens Ave TW15.........98 C4
Wrensfield SL7 ....1 C2
Wrenswood Cl RG2 .....113 B7
Wright SL4 ....66 C4
Wright Cl RG5...........88 A7
Wright Gdns TW17 ..... 125 A4
Wright Sq SL4...........66 C4

Wright Way SL4 ....66 C4
Wroxeter Ct RG2..........86 E1
Wroxham RG12 ....117 F4
Wroxham Rd RG5.........87 D8
Wulwyn Ct RG45.........142 F5
Wyatt Cres RG6...........87 D1
Wyatt Ct GU47.......... 150 D7
Wyatt Rd
Staines TW18............97 A3
Windsor SL4 ....66 D4
Wychcotes RG4...........58 F3
Wychelm Rd
Lightwater GU18 .... 153 C8
Shinfield RG2........... 113 E5
Wychwood GU15........ 151 D7
Wychwood Ave RG12 ...118 F5
Wychwood Cl RG6........86 F2
Wychwood Cres RG6.....86 F2
Wychwood Pl GU15 ....152 B8
Wycombe La HP10........3 E7
Wycombe Rd
Marlow Bottom SL7........1 E6
Marlow SL7 ....1 E4
Wye Cl
Ashford TW15 ....98 B4
Reading RG30 ....84 F6
Wye Ct SL8...............3 A3
Wye Rd HP10 ....3 D8
Wye Valley Sch The SL8 ...3 B4
Wykeham Cl UB7 ....71 A8
Wykeham Rd RG6.........87 A6
Wylam RG12.............117 F4
Wylands Rd SL3..........44 A2
Wyld Court Hill RG18 ....53 B5
Wyldewood SL5 .... 120 D3
Wymers Cl SL1 ....21 B3
Wymers Wood Rd SL1 ...21 A3
Wyncote Cl RG2...........86 F1
Wyndale Cl RG9 ....15 E1
Wyndham Cl GU46 ...... 149 D7
Wyndham Cres
Burnham SL1...............21 B3
Woodley RG5..............60 D1
Wyndham Rd RG14 ......105 D5
Wynford Cl RG30 ....85 C4
Wynnstay Gdns SL7........1 E5
Wynsham Way GU20 ...146 B6
Wyre Ct RG31............57 C3
Wyresdale RG12 .... 118 F2
Wythe Cl RG18............79 C8
Wythegate TW18 ....96 F1
Wythemede RG42........90 B2
Wyvern Cl RG12 .... 118 A5
Wyvern Ct TW15 ....97 E5

Y

Yale Cl GU47.............143 F2
Yardley RG12 ....117 F4
Yard Mead TW20........96 A5
Yarmouth Rd SL1 ....42 C6
Yarnold Cl RG40 ....116 F7
Yarnton Cl RG4 ....59 C6
Yarrow Cl RG18........ 106 D5
Yateley Common Ctry Pk *
GU17, GU46............. 149 F3
YATELEY GREEN........ 149 C7
Yateley Industries GU46. 149 D7
Yateley Inf Sch GU46.... 149 D6
Yateley Manor Sch
GU46 .... 149 D6
Yateley Rd GU47........ 149 F8
Yateley Sch GU46 .... 149 C5
Yates Copse RG14...... 105 E5
YATTENDON 53 F1
Yattendon CE Prim Sch
RG18 ....53 E2
Yattendon Ct RG18.......53 F2
Yattendon La RG8, RG18 ..54 D2
Yattendon Rd RG18 ......79 C7
Yaverland Dr GU19...... 145 D2
Yelverton Rd RG2.........86 C3
Ye Meads SL6............40 F5
Ye Meads Cotts SL6......40 F5
Yeoman Dr TW15 ....97 E7
Yeoman Pl RG5...........87 C7
Yeomanry Cl ◼ RG19 ...106 E2
Yeomans La RG20....... 131 A1
Yeomans Way GU15.....151 E5
Yeosfield RG7 ....139 C3
Yeovil Ct GU19..........145 D2
Yeoveney Cl TW19 ....96 D6
Yeovil Ent Ctr SL1 ....41 F8
Yeovil Rd
Sandhurst GU47..........143 E1
Slough SL1...............41 E8
Yew Cl
Newell Green RG42.......92 A1
Wokingham RG41........115 F5
Yew Cnr RG12 ....118 C6
Yew Gate RG14 ....104 F6
Yewhurst Cl RG10.........61 D6
Yew La RG1 ....85 F5
Yew The TW15............98 B4
Yew Tree Cl SL6..........39 E8
Yew Tree Ct RG8 ....34 C6
Yew Tree Mews RG20.....31 E4
Yew Tree Rd SL1..........43 A3
Yew Tree Rise RG31......84 C5

Yewtrees TW20 .... 123 C6
Yew Trees TW17.........124 F5
Yew Tree Stables RG20 ...31 E4
Yew Tree Wlk GU16 ..... 151 F1
Yield Hall La ◼ RG1 ......86 B7
Yield Hall Pl RG1 ....86 B7
Yockley Cl GU15 .... 152 D3
Yoreham Cl RG6 ....87 E1
York Ave
Slough SL1................42 D7
Windsor SL4 ....67 B5
York Cl RG14 ....105 B2
York Ho
Bracknell RG42 ....117 F8
Reading RG31 ....84 B4
York Pl GU15 ....151 D7
York Rd
Binfield RG42.............90 D3
Camberley GU15 .... 151 D7
Henley-on-T RG9 ....15 D2
Hungerford RG17 .... 100 D4
Maidenhead SL6 ....40 A7
Marlow SL7 ....1 D2
Newbury RG14........... 105 B2
Reading RG1 ....59 A1
Windsor SL4 ....67 B5
Yorkshire Pl RG42........91 F2
York Terrace La GU15 ... 151 A5
YORK TOWN............ 151 A5
York Town Ind Est GU15.. 151 A4
Yorktown Rd
Sandhurst GU47......... 150 C7
Sandhurst GU47......... 150 E7
York Way GU47.......... 150 B8
Youlden Cl GU15 .... 152 A5
Youlden Dr GU15 .... 152 B6
Young Cres RG19 .... 131 D8
Young's Ind Est RG7 ....134 F4

Z

Zealand Ave UB7 ....70 E7
Zenith Ave RG2.........113 D7
Zenith Ct GU47.........143 E1
Zephyr Ho RG7..........134 E2
Zetland Ct SL6...........40 B8
Zinnia Cl RG41..........115 D7
Zinzan St RG1...........85 F7
Zodiac Ho RG7..........134 E2

PHILIP'S MAPS
the Gold Standard for drivers

◆ **Philip's street atlases cover every county in England, Wales, Northern Ireland and much of Scotland**

◆ Every named street is shown, including alleys, lanes and walkways

◆ Thousands of additional features marked: stations, public buildings, car parks, places of interest

◆ Route-planning maps to get you close to your destination

◆ Postcodes on the maps and in the index

◆ Widely used by the emergency services, transport companies and local authorities

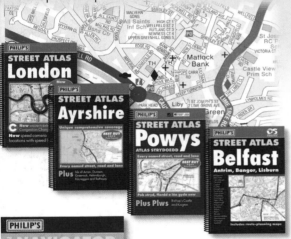

For national mapping, choose
Philip's Navigator Britain
the most detailed road atlas available of England, Wales and Scotland. Hailed by Auto Express as 'the ultimate road atlas', the atlas shows every road and lane in Britain.

'The ultimate in UK mapping'
The Sunday Times

Street atlases currently available

England
Bedfordshire and Luton
Berkshire
Birmingham and West Midlands
Bristol and Bath
Buckinghamshire and Milton Keynes
Cambridgeshire and Peterborough
Cheshire
Cornwall
Cumbria
Derbyshire
Devon
Dorset
County Durham and Teesside
Essex
North Essex
South Essex
Gloucestershire and Bristol
Hampshire
North Hampshire
South Hampshire
Herefordshire Monmouthshire
Hertfordshire
Isle of Wight
Kent
East Kent
West Kent
Lancashire
Leicestershire and Rutland
Lincolnshire
Liverpool and Merseyside
London
Greater Manchester
Norfolk
Northamptonshire
Northumberland
Nottinghamshire
Oxfordshire
Shropshire
Somerset
Staffordshire
Suffolk

Surrey
East Sussex
West Sussex
Tyne and Wear
Warwickshire and Coventry
Wiltshire and Swindon
Worcestershire
East Yorkshire
Northern Lincolnshire
North Yorkshire
South Yorkshire
West Yorkshire

Wales
Anglesey, Conwy and Gwynedd
Cardiff, Swansea and The Valleys
Carmarthenshire, Pembrokeshire and Swansea
Ceredigion and South Gwynedd
Denbighshire, Flintshire, Wrexham
Herefordshire Monmouthshire
Powys

Scotland
Aberdeenshire
Ayrshire
Dumfries and Galloway
Edinburgh and East Central Scotland
Fife and Tayside
Glasgow and West Central Scotland
Inverness and Moray
Lanarkshire
Scottish Borders

Northern Ireland
County Antrim and County Londonderry
County Armagh and County Down
Belfast
County Tyrone and County Fermanagh

How to order
Philip's maps and atlases are available from bookshops, motorway services and petrol stations. You can order direct from the publisher by phoning **0207 531 8473** or online at **www.philips-maps.co.uk**
For bulk orders only, e-mail philips@philips-maps.co.uk